Dealing with pensions

The practical impact of the Pensions Act 2004 on mergers, acquisitions, restructurings and insolvency

Robin Ellison

Grant Jones

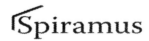
Spiramus

Published in June 2006 by

ʕSpiramus

Spiramus Press Ltd
The Boathouse Office
57a Gainsford Street
London SE1 2NB
Telephone +44 20 7357 0861
www.spiramus.com

ISBN 1 904905 06 4

Printed and bound in Great Britain by Biddles, King's Lynn, England

Cover design: David Shaw and associates

SQUIRE SANDERS | LEGAL COUNSEL WORLDWIDE

Preface

The changes introduced primarily by the Pensions Act 2004 in relation to the protection of defined benefit pension schemes have now been seen to have had an impact on day-to-day commercial and corporate activity which was not widely foreseen at the time.

Anyone thinking of buying or selling a business or company, or involved with any corporate reconstruction, is now aware that where there is a defined benefit pension scheme anywhere in the equation then deep and often unproductive discussion is required as well as extensive expenditure on professional fees.

While the intention of the legislation was clearly benign, the effect has been mixed. Many of the changes have been developed on the presumption that defined benefit obligations were guaranteed by employers, a presumption that was not in the mind of plan sponsors at the time they were established. In addition much of the drive from the regulator has emerged from the statutory objective (s.5) of attempting to limit claims against the newly established Pension Protection Fund.

Combined with complex and sometimes impenetrable rules, and tensions in public policy, the effect on daily corporate transactions has been profound. This book is an early attempt to find a practical pathway through the thicket of regulation; it is based on early practical experience, but there is no doubt that practice will change perhaps radically in the next few years, and the regulations and guidance notes issued by the regulators are also likely to have a short life span. Nonetheless it was thought to be useful to gather together in one place both the underlying documents necessary to form a view on practice, such experience as was available, and a guide to the way in which these issues might be approached for corporate lawyers and others for whom pensions may not be the primary interest.

As the book goes to press we are all too aware of its imperfections – infelicities of style, sometimes difficult concepts not explained as well as they might be, views which perhaps are braver than should be evinced from the evidence – but the raw material on which the writing has been based is not the most straightforward either. Many of the problems emerge as a result of parliament trying to make rules based on imperfectly articulated policy, and there are few signs of that articulation improving in the near future. In the meantime any ideas, comments, corrections and suggestions will be warmly welcomed and incorporated in any future edition.

Finally, while the authors have written the chapters separately, we remain rather hesitantly responsible for each other's work, subject to the usual caveats.

Robin Ellison and Grant Jones

May 2006

Acknowledgements

We would like to thank Stephen Nelson and Carmelo Lam of Squire, Sanders & Dempsey and Samantha Bewick of KPMG LLP for their comments on the text, and Neil Chesterton of the MacDonald Partnership plc and Pensionassist Limited for the FSD flowchart at appendix 4.1.

We are also grateful to staff at the Pensions Regulator for their comments on the text. Our chapter 4 relies on existing clearance guidance from the Regulator which is in the process of being reviewed.

Contents

CONTENTS

Abbreviations used in this book

Term   **Explanation**

APB   *Auditing Practices Board* The APB is a part of the Financial Reporting Council. Its role is to establish auditing standards which set out the basic principles and essential procedures with which external auditors in the United Kingdom and the Republic of Ireland are required to comply.

ARD   A European Directive, the *Acquired Rights Directive*, on which TUPE regulations are based

AVC   *Additional Voluntary Contributions* allow members to 'top-up' employer-based (usually DB) pensions schemes.

CVA   A *Company Voluntary Arrangement* under the Insolvency Act 1986, whereby 75% of the unsecured creditors agree to an insolvency plan under the auspices of a Supervisor, who is a Licensed Insolvency Practitioner.

CVL   a *creditor's voluntary liquidation* is one of the two forms of insolvent liquidation under IA 1986; the other being a compulsory liquidation. A CVL is a non-Court procedure unlike a compulsory liquidation. In a CVL the shareholders/directors initiate the process whereas in a compulsory liquidation a creditor's petition initiates the procedure.

DB   A *defined benefit (or final salary) scheme* is an arrangement where the benefits payable to the members are determined by the scheme rules. In many cases there will be a compulsory employee contribution (and typically this would be of the order of 5% of salary) but over and above this all costs of meeting the quoted benefits are the responsibility of the employer. DB schemes should be contrasted with DC schemes. In a DB scheme the benefits (not the contributions) are fixed.

DC   *Defined contribution* arrangements are also known as money purchase schemes. Under defined contribution schemes contributions are paid into the fund by the employer and the employee and these are invested with the proceeds from the contributions and investments being used to buy a pension, called an annuity, at retirement.

Eb   *Related employer balances* ("Eb") means any amount which has been taken into account in the calculation of the value of the resources of the employer which, were it also to appear in the calculation of the value of the resources of a business associate, would result in the value of the resources of the business associate and the employer together being overstated or understated by that amount.

EVD The best way of differentiating between defined benefit and defined contribution schemes is in determining where the risks lie.

FSD A *financial support direction* ('FSD') allows the Pensions Regulator to direct that associated and connected persons put in place arrangements to support the pensions liabilities of an employer who is insufficiently resourced or is a "service company" as defined in the legislation.

FV *Fair value* In a defined benefit schemes it is the employer that underwrites the vast majority of costs so that if investment returns are poor or costs increase the employer needs to either make adjustments to the scheme (often very unpopular with the workforce), or to increase levels of contribution.

FVD *Fair value difference* ("FVD") means the difference between the fair value of an asset or liability at the calculation date and the amount at which that asset or liability is recorded in the accounts.

GAAP *Generally Agreed Accounting Principles (UK)* In a defined contribution scheme the contributions are paid at a fixed level and therefore it is the scheme member who is shouldering these risks. If they fail to take action by increasing contribution rates when investment returns are poor or costs increase, then their retirement benefits will be lower than they had planned for.

GMP The *Guaranteed Minimum Pension* is the pension that the scheme has to pay as a minimum in order to be allowed to contract out of the State Earnings Related pension (SERPS).

IAS *International Accounting Standards* are accounting standards issued by the International Accounting Standards Committee.

ICAEW *Institute of Chartered Accountants of England and Wales*

IP *Insolvency Practitioner*.

MFR The *Minimum Funding Requirement* was brought in by the Pensions Act 1995 and is now replaced by the Pensions Act 2004 SFO requirement. The MFR created a minimum regular funding obligation on DB schemes.

MVL A *Members Voluntary Liquidation*, whereby a solvent company is liquidated under the Insolvency Act 1986 & a Licensed Insolvency Practitioner is appointed as the Liquidator

P *Relevant pension scheme related balances* ("P") means any assets or liabilities included within the accounts of the entity which relate to the scheme in relation to which section 43 applies, including any assets or liabilities relating to the scheme's deficit or surplus net of any related deferred tax asset or liability together with any other creditor or prepayment balances related to the scheme in question as calculated in accordance with the generally accepted accounting practice used for the accounts.

PPF   The *Pension Protection Fund* was established to pay compensation to members of eligible defined benefit pension schemes, when there is a qualifying insolvency event in relation to the employer and where there are insufficient assets in the pension scheme to cover Pension Protection Fund levels of compensation.

Se   *Subordinated liabilities* ("Se") means any liabilities included within the accounts of the employer which in the event of the entity being wound up would rank for payment after the unsecured creditors whether as a matter of general law or contract or otherwise.

SFO   A new Scheme Specific *Statutory Funding Objective* (SFO) must be put in place by September 2005. The intention of this is to ensure that there are sufficient assets to cover past and future liabilities. A Statement of Funding Principles must then be prepared as to how the SFO will be met, highlighting the methods and assumptions to be used, together with details of the period over which any shortfall is to be met.

SFP   A *Statement of Funding Principles* ('SFP') must then be prepared as to how the SFO will be met, highlighting the methods and assumptions to be used, together with details of the period over which any shortfall is to be met.

UITF   *Urgent Issues Task Force* The main role of the UITF is to assist the Accounting Standards Board in resolving unsatisfactory or conflicting interpretations about a requirement of an accounting standard or the Companies Act.

Legislation and regulations

In this book, where no Act is specified references are to the Pensions Act 2004.

CA 1985   Companies Act 1985

IA 1986   Insolvency Act 1986

FA 2005 etc. Finance Act 2005 etc.

PA 2004 etc. Pensions Act 2004 etc.

TUPE   Provisions relating to employment rights on the transfer of an undertaking are contained in the Transfer of Undertakings (Protection of Employment) Regulations 2006 (SI 246), often abbreviated to TUPE.

Tables of authorities

Cases

Statutes

1   Introduction

1.1   Background

The buying and selling of businesses, and their restructuring, is a central part of economic activity in the UK, as is the proper disposal of insolvent enterprises. The efficient execution of such activity is an essential element in the development of commerce and national wealth.

But the last few years have seen material impediments to commercial operations because of heavy regulation. The excess of regulation generally is being addressed by a number of government departments (cf. www.brc.gov.uk; and www.cabinetoffice.gov.uk/regulation) – but a major element of the regulatory overload, the regulation of company sponsored pension schemes, has not come under current consideration. Meanwhile, anecdotal evidence suggests that pensions issues are now one of the leading considerations for both the buyer and the seller and their financiers, when companies are bought or sold. This book examines the practical impact of pension issues in commercial transactions including insolvency and suggests some solutions to some of the impediments.

Pensions issues have been particularly affected by the length and complexity of legislation in the last few years. Some of it has been related to tax but most of it has been related to consumer protection. The knock-on effect of much of this legislation for employers, and their bankers and advisers, however, has been material and has created significant problems in practice.

The changes were not, of course, designed either to improve corporate activity or make it more difficult, but were intended to respond to the perceived lack of protection of pension scheme members, especially where employers who sponsored defined benefit schemes were taken-over or restructured. There is no doubt that individual members of pension schemes were uncomfortable with some aspects of their membership, particularly where their schemes were defined benefit arrangements. They were concerned in particular about security and about their future ability to take benefits – and a few of them were right to be concerned.

The reasons for the perceived lack of stability of defined benefit pension schemes were widely recognised: reductions in their capital reserves following falls in the value of underlying assets; changes in annuity rates and longevity expectations; changes in accountancy rules; and increases in taxation on pension schemes. But whilst falling fund values and increasing longevity expectations did not help, the main reason for the instability of funds after seventy years of satisfactory (though not entirely flawless) and improving operations was the impact of counter-productive, though understandable, legislation and regulation. When a pension scheme failed (by which was meant it 'did not deliver the total entirety of what members expected') the political process required increased regulation. Much of this regulation eventually emerged as counter-productive in its effect.

There were two main stages in this legislative process:

- Following the collapse of the Mirror Group of Newspapers on the death of Robert Maxwell (the Maxwell Affair) at the beginning of the 1990s and the report of the inspectors appointed by the DTI, the Pensions Act 1995 required pension funds to offer certain guarantees to scheme members (guaranteed minimum funding, indexation of benefits) which increased the cost of providing pensions for most employers and applied often destructive priority rules. Awarding for example more than 100% of a fund in deficit to retired members, with a balance of what was left to people coming up to retirement.
- Following a series of failures in the early 21st century, when it became apparent that PA 1995 did not operate to guarantee DB benefits to scheme members, the Pensions Act 2004 (PA 2004) was introduced to shore up employee expectations, which again increased the cost of providing pensions for most employers.

By April 2005, PA 2004 imposed a number of new requirements on DB schemes; they included:

- The introduction of a new Pensions Regulator (the Regulator), with a dual responsibility to both consumers (scheme members) and to the Pension Protection Fund (PPF)(see below) – obligations which in many cases involve a conflict of objective
- The introduction of a Pension Protection Fund intended by levying taxes on the remaining solvent pension funds to support and guarantee (within limits) the pension benefits of scheme members.
- The introduction of extensive rules to limit the number of claims against the PPF – including in particular a regime of control by the Regulator to ensure the avoidance of 'moral hazard' – i.e. activity by companies, their shareholders and bankers to take steps to avoid liability under pension schemes by ensuring they are passed over to the PPF.

It is this last, the so-called moral hazard rules, which some regard as a material blockage in the normal activity of companies in buying, selling and restructuring companies to ensure efficiency in a worldwide competitive market. Such activities now carry with them a most extraordinary danger – the exposure to personal liability of company directors, advisers and bankers and funders which cannot be protected by the usual process of limited liability.

1.1.1 The kinds of pension promise

These rules invariably affect the management of defined benefit schemes (sometimes known also as final-salary or salary-related schemes) whose arrangements offer a benefit to an employee in exchange for his or her service of employment with the employer. In the simple form, the promise might be of say one-sixtieth of salary for each year of service (with a maximum of 40 such years) offering a maximum of say 40 such sixtieths, i.e. 40/60s (= 2/3rds).

For the individual member in most cases the existence of sufficient assets in the pension scheme is a secondary issue. Indeed in the public sector (Civil Service, police, fire, teachers) there is no need for investments at all. Such schemes are unfunded – and the promise by the employer is one backed by central or local government. There is, therefore, a perception that the individual has no need of any protection against the employer failing or going out of business once the date of retirement has been reached.

But in the private sector, the existence of investments or some other security backing the 'promise' by the employer is a great comfort. If the employer ceases trade or becomes insolvent, at least there is something available to help support the individual who may have given many years of dedicated service and otherwise would have nothing to show for it in retirement.

Until 1997 because of the absence of any statutory need to have assets supporting a pension expectation not only was there no guarantee that the pensions would be paid – but there was an unwritten (and often non-understood) proviso that the pensions were an expectation and not a guarantee. Even with asset backing in a pension fund it is all but impossible for the employer to give a guarantee because there are too many unpredictable factors. No one can really predict what will happen to the stock market (or even bonds) over the next 30 years, and there are not enough government bonds or other "stable" debt instruments to go around even if they were attractive. Other unpredictable factors include: salary rates, inflation and longevity. Most of all, few can predict with any certainty what the longevity of the employer will be.

This will come as little comfort to an employee – but in practice over the last 80 years since funded schemes have been allowed by the tax structure, relatively few people have lost any significant amount of their pensions. It is paradoxically only since legislation (mostly since the Maxwell Affair in the early 1990s) that pension scheme expectations have been badly hit and it may be that the regulation and legislation that has been introduced had concealed within it the law of unintended consequences.

Defined contribution schemes (sometimes known as money-purchase schemes) do, of course, have to maintain an asset pool – the contributions of employers and employees have to be invested as best they can, with a creative tension between security and return, to produce the largest amount possible for members at retirement. The members have limited expectations; there is no expectation of an income related to salary perhaps at retirement and members are aware that the benefit they will eventually enjoy depends on a variety of circumstances that will apply at retirement – what annuity rates are, what the fund will amount to, what has been the impact of inflation and other factors. They have been given no expectations by their employers as to the level of benefits; it is something they may have to work out for themselves. Accordingly, the management of such arrangements in corporate transactions is relatively straightforward.

1.1.2   Corporate transactions

Although few new defined benefit schemes are established these days, not so much because of their costs but because of their over-regulation, many companies and businesses maintain legacy schemes. The regulatory framework makes it is hard and sometimes all but impossible to either close them or move them off balance sheet, although efforts are being made to find ways to do this.

In the meantime, anyone looking to buy a company with a related defined benefit scheme, or looking to restructure their existing corporate arrangements needs to take account of the presence of such schemes.

Taking on a company with a defined benefit scheme poses challenges because liabilities can increase under such schemes due to no fault of the shareholders – changes in taxation, actuarial assumptions or interest rates can have a material impact on the liabilities of such schemes. And these liabilities have now to be underwritten by the employer. Fluctuations in the value of the scheme may also have to appear on the employer's balance sheet.

Accordingly, companies thinking either of acquisitions or trying to restructure need to have close regard to the contingent liabilities of any legacy defined benefit arrangements. Closing a scheme may seem a superficially attractive way of limiting liability – but may inadvertently trigger a requirement to meet any deficit within a short time frame, rather than over ten years or more. In addition, the amount of the deficit can be artificially increased, perhaps by as much as 100%, as a consequence of the trigger.

Not only are corporations caught by the rules – but also their funders and other associates. In extreme cases pensions liabilities can pierce the corporate veil, so that holding companies and others can be caught – and in the ultimate limited liability protection does not apply to the directors of companies involved – or their financiers.

The pension issue is now therefore, even more than governance, environmental or health and safety issues, a critical element in corporate decision-making in mergers and acquisitions.

1.1.3   Insolvency

In modern legal systems insolvency has operated on the jubilee principle, wiping away debts sometimes to allow a business to survive and move on. In order to avoid issues of moral hazard, that a company deliberately may become insolvent in order to dispose of its pension liabilities and be reborn to compete another day, the pension rules require insolvency practitioners (or even company directors who participate in voluntary liquidations) to meet certain criteria. The concept, as in the US, of entering Chapter 11, clearing pension liabilities, and then trading as the same entity without the pension overheads is possible in the UK only with the consent of the authorities. The rules on insolvency are now complex and are set out in some detail elsewhere in this work.

1.2 Pensions Act 2004 ("PA 2004")

PA 2004, the product of several green and white papers and an independent report by Alan Pickering (a former Chairman of the National Association of Pension Funds) (see e.g. *A Simpler Way to Better Pensions*, an independent report by Alan Pickering, The Stationery Office, July 2002; Department for Work and Pensions, *Simplicity, Security and Choice, Working and Saving for Retirement*, The Stationery Office, Cm 5677, December 2002) was intended originally to simplify the pensions structure to make it more attractive for employers to establish and run pension funds, and for employees to join them. Because of press comment, and some well-publicised pension scheme failures in the interim, the direction of the legislation changed radically. The drafting of PA 2004 developed into something of an embarrassment, with inadequate time to debate the drafts, many government clauses being introduced at the last minute, and the eventual passing of a badly-drafted and illogical piece of legislation. This simplifying measure now consists of 325 sections and 13 Schedules, and around 125 sets of regulations, few of them written in plain English. It is inevitable that the deep flaws in the legislation will necessitate further reforming legislation at some time in the future.

The direction of the Act (Bill) changed during its introduction from a simplification measure to one of attempting to guarantee the previously non-guaranteed defined benefits of pension scheme members. In the end PA 2004 introduced several major changes; including:

The Pensions Regulator
A new Pensions Regulator (the Regulator) to replace the previous one (OPRA – the Occupational Pensions Regulatory Authority), intended to operate via a risk-based approach to scheme regulation, and with slightly wider objectives, including close interaction with the Pension Protection Fund. The Regulator has a statutory duty to produce Codes of Practice, to try to avoid the need for prescription.

Funding and solvency
The previous regime of a 'minimum funding requirement' had barely survived ten years; by September 2005 it was removed in favour of an EU Directive-driven 'scheme specific funding principles'. This is detailed in actuarial guidance which, if applied rigorously, may deal a serious blow to the survival of any remaining defined benefit arrangements.

Member representation

Simpler procedures for determining member representation within schemes by member-nominated trustees; the Act also gives power for a future administration to raise the requirements from one-third representation to one-half.

Trustee expertise

Material requirements placed on scheme trustees to acquire 'knowledge and understanding' of pensions law, trust law and investments.

Employment

Pensions are now specifically included within the Transfer of Undertakings (Protection of Employment) Regulations 2006 (TUPE) on business transfers. The new rules may make stakeholder pensions more attractive for some employers, and there are new rules intended to simplify the resolution of disputes, and enhance benefits on winding-up, as well as extend the consultation process on changing scheme arrangements.

Some of these reforms are dealt with in more detail below.

1.2.1 Pensions Regulator ("The Regulator")

The functions of the previous regulator (Occupational Pensions Regulatory Authority – OPRA) were transferred in 2005 to the Pensions Regulator, which is intended to target its resources where members' benefits are at greatest risk. The Regulator's board involves a chairman appointed by the Secretary of State, a chief executive and a minimum of five other government-appointed members. A non-executive committee consisting of the chairman and other non-executive members monitors the activities of the Regulator. A Pensions Regulator Tribunal (with at least seven members) reviews contested decisions of the Regulator. The Regulator has been granted powers to allow it to protect the interests of scheme members and to minimise the number of claims against the Pension Protection Fund (PPF). These powers include:

- Provision of information, education and assistance to those involved in the administration of work-based pension schemes.
- Registration of pension schemes (involving the dismantling of the previous pension schemes register).
- Collection of information relevant to the Board of the PPF.
- Collection of information more generally with a power to require individuals to provide any information or documentation relevant to the Regulator's functions and to enter and inspect premises.
- Issuing of improvement notices requiring individuals to take (or refrain from taking) certain actions.
- Issuing of third party notices to any person who has not, themselves, contravened pensions legislation but whose behaviour nevertheless causes a breach of the pensions legislation.

- Issuing freezing orders in relation to the winding-up of pension schemes.
- Recovery of unpaid contributions.

These provisions are supplemented by at least a dozen Codes of Practice with quasi legal effect issued by the Regulator.

1.2.2   Pension Protection Fund ("PPF")

The PPF came into operation in April 2005, and covers 'eligible schemes' (i.e. defined benefit schemes that did not wind-up before April 2005). The PPF is run by a board consisting of a chairman, chief executive and at least five other members. An eligible scheme becomes involved with the PPF if its sponsoring employer becomes insolvent or the trustees of the scheme (or the Regulator) apply to issue a notice to the PPF because they are concerned that the employer cannot continue as a going concern.

Once involved with the PPF, a scheme undergoes an 'assessment period', following which the PPF assumes responsibility for the scheme if it is in serious financial difficulties. During the assessment period, no benefits may accrue and no contributions may be made. Benefits paid out of the scheme during the assessment period are paid at a reduced level.

The trustees continue to operate the scheme, but their powers are limited and the PPF has power to intervene. At the end of the assessment period the PPF, if it thinks fit, assumes responsibility for the scheme where no 'scheme rescue' has occurred (e.g. by a company within the same group as the sponsoring employer, or perhaps, although rare, a purchasing company) and there are insufficient assets to meet the scheme's 'protected liabilities' (normally the level of compensation which the PPF would pay out if it assumes responsibility for the scheme).

If the PPF assumes responsibility for the scheme it issues a 'transfer notice', as a result of which the scheme's assets and liabilities automatically transfer to the PPF. The scheme is treated as if it had been wound up, and the PPF, out of the scheme's assets plus its own resources, discharges the scheme's protected liabilities.

Not all members are treated equally; members above the scheme's normal pension age and those who have retired early due to ill-health receive preferential treatment. Members above normal pension age receive 100% of their benefits (with the exception of limited increases on their pensions in payment); other members receive 90% of their benefits. In addition, the annual 'compensation cap' (currently £25,000) applies to all benefits. The compensation can be reduced if there is too great a call on the PPF.

The PPF raises funds both by acquiring the assets of the schemes it takes control of, and by levies imposed on eligible schemes. An 'initial levy' applies for the first year of operation; after April 2006 there are 'pension protection levies', both 'scheme-based' and 'risk-based'.

1.2.3   Financial assistance scheme ("FAS")

For scheme members not protected by the PPF (usually because their scheme became insolvent before 6 April 2005) the FAS applies. There is a database of potentially eligible schemes, which establishes the scale and nature of the scheme failure. There is a limited fund available (£400M over 20 years); schemes which began to wind up before 6 April 2005 are not eligible for the FAS; the FAS is unlikely to be applicable to pension schemes that had not already started to wind-up before that date and claims must have been submitted by 28 February 2006[1]. Regulatory guidance is available to trustees of pension schemes which are currently in the process of being wound up and are not eligible for the PPF which suggests that trustees in this situation should continue to progress the winding-up actively, although they should ideally postpone securing members' benefits with an insurance company until any compensation for members from the FAS can be calculated.

Members are not excluded from compensation if benefits are secured with an insurance company before compensation can be calculated. In practice, the FAS and the possibility of compensation from it is considered by trustees of pension schemes which are currently in the process of being wound up. For schemes that have already been wound up, the absence of trustees or professional advisers to notify the FAS of the potential eligibility of the scheme's former members may prove to be an issue.

1.2.4   Disputes

Internal dispute resolution

Under PA 2004 s.273 the internal dispute resolution (IDR) process will not be required to be in two stages. As the trustees or managers of a scheme have responsibility to make IDR decisions, they are able to set up bespoke IDR procedures that suit their scheme and membership. However, the DWP have not yet commenced this section, ans so the existing IDR framework remains in place.

Pensions Ombudsman

The jurisdiction of the Pensions Ombudsman now includes those persons or organisations responsible for carrying out a single act of administration for a pension scheme. The backlog of complaints to be dealt with by the Pensions Ombudsman is intended to be reduced by the appointment of deputies.

Review and reconsideration of decisions of the PPF

The PPF exercises statutory functions under the 2004 Act; the exercise or non-exercise of certain designated functions of the Board is subject to a two-stage review and reconsideration process at the request of an affected party. Once this process is exhausted, the matter can be taken to the PPF Ombudsman.

---

[1] see www.dwp.gov.uk/lifeevent/penret/penreform/fas

PPF Ombudsman

The PPF Ombudsman has the power to determine matters arising from PPF decisions and re-submit them to the PPF with directions. Any order of the PPF Ombudsman is enforceable as an order of the court, with appeals to the Court of Appeal (or the Court of Session in Scotland) available on points of law only.

Admissibility

PA 2004 imposes obligations to provide information to the Regulator, which will generally be admissible where the normal common law rules of evidence are complied with. Trustees will be provided with limited protection by these provisions. However, they will not be protected in relation to the offences under PA 2004 relating to providing false information or refusing to provide information to the Regulator or the Board of the PPF.

Legal privilege

Documents do not have to be disclosed under any requirement to supply information under PA 2004 if they are subject to legal advice privilege or litigation privilege. It will be useful for trustees to be able to rely on a particular statutory provision in these circumstances rather than having to fall back on the protections that are available at common law.

1.2.5   Amending schemes

Many employers and/or trustees seek to amend the terms of pension schemes from time to time, to meet changes in circumstances. In practice, the introduction of the Pensions Act 1995 s.67 made it difficult to make such changes, and created severe practical difficulties for employers, trustees, pension lawyers and actuaries alike. The intention of the 1995 legislation was to re-phrase the established trust law principle that trustees should generally not reduce members' benefits and their expectations. The wording of the section, however, posed material difficulties, and in particular impeded scheme and corporate restructuring actions.

The Pickering Report in 2003 suggested that PA 1995 s.67 be simplified to allow changes to be more easily made. In fact the replacement s.67 is around ten times the length of the original, and is deeply prescriptive. The replacement provisions protect 'subsisting rights', rights which have accrued to or in respect of a member to future benefits or any other entitlements. This reflects the former legislation. The new section, however, imposes structural changes, and certain amendments are constrained by the need to obtain member consent (i.e. 'protected modifications') where trustees must undertake certain process, including notification. Changes which would or might adversely affect subsisting rights are called 'detrimental modifications' and may be made either using the same consent requirements as for protected modifications or new 'actuarial equivalence requirements'. These requirements allow amendments where the overall actuarial value of subsisting rights is at least maintained, and where the trustees have issued prescribed notices to members.

1.2.6 Vesting

A scheme member who leaves the scheme after three months' service has the option of taking a cash equivalent transfer value to another pension arrangement as an alternative to taking a refund of his contributions. The provisions impose additional administration on schemes, although certain costs may be deducted from the transfer payments.

1.2.7 Indexation

For defined benefit schemes, pensions in payment pre-commencement day (6 April 2005) must be increased annually by the lesser of the RPI and 5%. On or after the commencement date they must be increased annually by the lesser of the RPI and 2.5%. For defined contribution schemes, the requirement to provide statutory increases in respect of pensions coming into payment after the commencement date has been removed.

1.2.8 Deferment of state pension

Those who defer their state pensions are offered a choice of taking the increments in the form of a taxable lump sum or extra income when their state pension is paid. The former five-year limit on how long a person is permitted to defer payment of a state pension was removed.

1.2.9 Member-nominated trustees or directors (MNTs/MNDs)

The employer is no longer able to put in place alternative opt-out arrangements. At least one-third of trustee body (eventually one-half) must be member-nominated.

1.2.10 Surplus repayments

The requirement to dispose of excessive surplus is now removed. Surpluses in a scheme are now measured on a buy-out basis. And in relation to those schemes that are prevented by their rules from making a surplus repayment, the trustees have five years to decide if they wish to have a power to make payments to the employer.

1.2.11 Revaluation

Schemes are allowed to revalue all benefits by reference to RPI; this must cover the total preserved benefit (including GMP). The option may confer administrative benefits by removing some complexity but, against that, there may be increases in the cost of funding on a full RPI basis.

1.2.12 Investment

The investment provisions in PA 2004 are relatively modest and are driven predominantly by the requirements and provisions of the European Pensions Directive.

1.2.13 Decision-making

The European Pensions Directive imposes certain funding standards and liberalises investment constraints. The Directive limits investments for example in derivatives so that they may only be used for the reduction of investment risk or for the purposes of efficient portfolio management, rather than as an investment per se. These rules apply insurance company constraints to pension funds in a manner generally regarded as inappropriate. Self-investment is liberalised under the Directive to 10% of the fund assets in the sponsoring group, although the pre-existing control of 5% which applies to the sponsoring employer continues.

1.2.14 Insolvency and winding-up (Pensions Act 1995 ss.75, 75A)

There are two types of s.75 debts:
- those which arise in some circumstances if the scheme goes into winding-up, and
- those where a 'relevant event' occurs in relation to the employer.

PA 1995 s .75A gives the power to make regulations modifying PA 1995 s.75 as it applies to multi employer schemes. Regulations provide that the debt on withdrawal will normally be on the full buy-out basis but an alternative basis can be used.

1.2.15 Moral hazard

The Regulator has been provided with a range of sanctions available to counter instances of financial engineering designed to relieve employers of pension costs at the expense of the PPF.

There are two forms of moral hazard provisions in PA 2004; contribution notices where there is an avoidance of an employer debt and financial support directions issued to secure financial support for a scheme.

Contribution notices may be issued by the Regulator to require the person to whom they are issued to pay an amount to a pension scheme where the Regulator detects actions intended to avoid meeting a debt owed to a pension scheme. The persons to whom contribution notices are issued must be connected or associated persons as defined in insolvency legislation. These provisions will apply to any acts or failures to act occurring on or after 27 April 2004.

Financial support directions may be issued by the Regulator who is then required to take into account what benefit is received by any employer who has been an employer in relation to a scheme (or to a connected or associated party). It is not possible to issue these to individuals unless they are the relevant employer (i.e. a sole trader) or a partner in a partnership.

Parties are vulnerable in transactions or compromises which reduce (or might reduce) the debt on the employer under the pension scheme. Consequently the Regulator operates a clearance procedure so companies can get prior clearance that transactions etc. will not result in a contribution notice or financial support direction. Insolvency practitioners (together with other prescribed persons) are not liable to contribution notices or financial support directions.

1.2.16 Preferential liabilities (Pensions Act 1995 s.73)

A new statutory priority order under the PA 1995 s.73 was introduced by the Pensions Act 2004. It applies to all schemes other than money purchase schemes and prescribed schemes. The current priority order is:

- Pre-6 April 1997 insured benefits.
- Pensions not exceeding the corresponding PPF liability.
- Non-money purchase benefits derived from AVCs.
- Any other benefits.

The policy intention is that the priority order mirrors the PPF, so that there is no explicit distinction between pensioners and non-pensioners. The position of AVCs in the order has generated concerns.

1.2.17 Regulator's powers

The Regulator has power to make a restoration order if assets of a scheme are transferred out of the scheme at an undervalue. This is an order that restores the position to what it would have been if the transaction had not been entered into. If the order includes the payment of an amount of money, that amount becomes a debt due upon which the person to whom it is owed is able to sue.

1.2.18 Freezing orders

Before a freezing order can be issued, the Regulator must:

- Investigate a scheme with a view to it being wound-up to protect the members.
- Feel that there is a likely risk to members' interests or scheme assets.
- Feel it is necessary to protect those interests.

A freezing order expires after three months, though it can be renewed, but cannot exceed six months.

1.2.19 Implications for insolvency practitioners

It is the Regulator's function (rather than as previously the insolvency practitioner), when a scheme sponsor becomes insolvent, to appoint an independent trustee. An insolvency practitioner must provide information relating to an employer's insolvency to the Board of the PPF, the Regulator and the scheme trustees.

1.2.20 Funding and actuarial

Schemes need to prepare a statement of funding principles, based on the Statutory Funding Objective (SFO) which is designed not only to mitigate some of the imperfections of the previous funding standards (MFR – minimum funding requirement) but also to bring the UK into line with the requirements of the European Pensions Directive.

Trustees or managers take actuarial advice to meet the SFO by choosing from a range of calculation bases, normally agreed with the sponsoring employer. In the absence of any agreement the dispute can be referred to the Regulator who may impose directions on how calculations are to be undertaken.

Actuarial valuations are required every three years, supplemented by annual actuarial reports. Actuarial valuations disclosing a failure to meet the SFO trigger a requirement for the scheme to prepare a recovery plan. The plan must be agreed with the sponsoring employer and submitted to the Regulator.

A schedule of contributions is required, again normally agreed with the employer. Where not agreed, the scheme trustees have power to modify future accrual of benefits with employer consent.

An employer who fails or delays contributions triggers an obligation on the scheme trustees to inform the Regulator. Breach of these extensive requirements may engender civil penalties and directions by the Regulator.

1.2.21 Trustees' standard of care

The Myners Review, instigated by the Government in 2000, acted as a catalyst of change in trustee duties and the standard of care expected of trustees (see *Myners Report: Institutional Investment in the UK: a Review*, HM Treasury, 6 March 2001). PA 2004 implements the Myners' original recommendations in an expanded form, by introducing new statutory obligations on individual and corporate trustees to be 'conversant with' and have 'knowledge and understanding' of certain matters. The new obligations can be interpreted as going beyond the standards of care which currently apply, as they incorporate specific standards which supplement the current mix of statutory and best practice standards.

There are two standards of care introduced by PA 2004. In relation to scheme specific matters, such as the trust deed, statement of investment principles, statement of funding principles, and any other document recording policy on the administration of the scheme, the trustee in question must be 'conversant with' those specific documents. In addition, trustees must have knowledge and understanding of other general matters of relevance, including the law relating to pensions and trusts, and the principles of scheme funding and investment. The Regulator issues guidance under a Code of Practice as to the degree of knowledge, training, experience or qualifications necessary to fulfil these requirements, although the yardstick by which the requirements will be measured is whether or not the trustee possesses the requisite knowledge and understanding in order to exercise his functions properly as a trustee.

Practical points include:
• The need for and desirability of tailored and effective trustee training, both to improve knowledge, and to enable the trustees to be risk averse.

- Possible difficulties in attracting people who are not pensions specialists to act as trustees, coupled with a growth in independent trusteeship, in order to improve standards and reduce the likelihood of claims.
- The need for transparency, independence and proper governance in relation to trustee decisions, so that the trustees can demonstrate compliance with the standard of care requirements, if required.

1.2.22 Employment

Financial planning

There were new powers and obligations aimed at encouraging individuals to be more active in planning their retirement finances (*PA 2004 ss.234-238*). In particular, as from 6 April 2005, employers were allowed to promote their pension schemes to their employees without needing to be authorised by the Financial Services Authority (*Financial Services and Markets Act 2000* as amended).

Pension protection on transfers of employment

TUPE Regulations now extend in a limited fashion to pension benefits provided in occupational pension schemes (*PA 2004 ss.257- 258*). To benefit from protection, transferring employees must have been active members of the transferor's occupational pension scheme at the date of transfer or eligible (or in a waiting period for eligibility) to join the scheme at the date of transfer. Where a person qualifies for protection, the transferee must provide either membership of a defined benefit or defined contribution occupational pension scheme, stakeholder or other personal pension scheme to which the transferee makes 'relevant' contributions. Employers are required to match employee contributions to a maximum of 6%.

Consultation by employers

There are now pensions-specific consultation obligations imposed upon the sponsoring employers of occupational pension schemes and on employers who operate direct payment arrangements for employees who are members of personal pension schemes (*PA 2004 ss.259, 260, 261*). The obligation to consult falls upon the employer where it or the trustees or managers of the scheme are proposing to make a prescribed decision in relation to that scheme. Only decisions likely to mean 'major and significant' changes trigger the consultation obligation.

Maternity, adoption and parental leave

Pension rights during paid maternity leave have long been safeguarded; in particular employer contributions should for many years have been made as if the employee was working normally, while member contributions are based on the actual salary received (*PA 2004 s.265; Social Security Act 1989, Schedule 5, para 5A and 5B*). The new provisions bring paid paternity leave and paid adoption leave into line with the former legislation on paid maternity leave. It is uncertain whether the provisions apply to money purchase schemes but the general view seems to be that the wording in the new paragraphs can be interpreted so that the provisions do apply.

1.3   Finance Act 2004 ("FA 2004")

FA 2004 was intended similarly to simplify the pensions system, but on the fiscal side. So far as merger, acquisition, reconstruction and insolvency issues are concerned, they should have little impact – except that for tax efficiency purposes it is now normally not sensible to provide pension benefits through a registered pension scheme. Pension schemes are no longer approved by HMRC but simply registered, and subject to draconian penalties if they fail to meet certain specified criteria. Implications for corporate transactions include an increasing tendency to provide pension arrangements for higher-paid individuals through 'SUBURBS' – unfunded but secured retirement benefit schemes – and there continue to remain grandfathered higher registered benefits as part of the legacy. Due diligence will normally reveal that these not always properly documented extra-mural arrangements. In addition HMRC has caused some concern by not always permitting tax relief on contributions required or encouraged by the Regulator in the year of payment which they consider to be in excess of the annual requirements.

1.4   European Pensions Directive

Following almost a decade of discussion the future for implementation of pan-European pensions move forward to reality. In 2003 the Council adopted the Directive on the activities of institutions for occupational retirement provision, which Member States needed to introduce into their national legislation by 23 September 2005. The Directive is a major step towards the creation of an internal market in Europe for occupational pensions, under a prudential framework designed to protect the rights of future generations of European pensioners.

For many corporations the opportunities offered by the EPD are enticing; it is easier to establish defined benefit arrangements with cash caps (i.e. benefits along DB lines but without the need to disclose any deficits in the balance sheet, or to make them up in any limiting time frame), and there are no pension protection fund levies to pay or Pensions Regulator rules to follow. Regulatory arbitrage (e.g. by deregistering schemes in the UK and registering them in another jurisdiction of the EU) has not so far been an issue in UK pension fund design but is bound to play an increasing part.

1.5   Scheme funding: deficiencies and surpluses

The real reason for the need for a book such as this has been the change in approach in recent years to the funding of defined benefit pension arrangements. Complex but unsophisticated legislation has converted best endeavours into guarantees underwritten by the employer which were never intended by the employer to be issued in that form.

In previous times the consulting actuary would calculate from time to time how much both employers and employees would need to put into the scheme to meet the expected benefits. This would be revised periodically as external circumstances changed. Schemes were rarely in perfect balance, because however skilled the actuary, events always transpired rather differently than expected. In addition, liabilities could be calculated in many different ways. Accordingly, during different time periods, schemes could emerge in surplus (as happened in the 1980s) or in deficit (as is happening now) or at various levels in between. In the immediate past employers had the luxury of being able to take a contribution holiday if the scheme was in surplus, or of paying off deficits over 20, 30 or more years.

The rules now make this rather difficult. Chapter 2, therefore, considers the different ways in which funding can be carried out and how surpluses and deficits can be dealt with.

1.6 Outline of this book

This book is intended to offer a guide to company directors and their advisers who are thinking of buying or selling or reconstructing the corporate arrangements of their business, and to insolvency practitioners and others interested in insolvency. This follows changes to law and practice in response to the coming into force of the Pensions Act 2004 which has transformed the obligations of companies associated with defined benefit pension schemes. This book, therefore, looks first at the practical effects of the new regulatory policy in relation to the funding of defined benefit arrangements, and it then goes on to provide an outline of conventional merger and acquisition (and restructuring) practice in as far as it affects pensions arrangements. There is a chapter on the, so far only lightly used, practice of obtaining clearances to transactions by the pensions regulator, including the pros and cons of making an application. There is also a chapter dedicated to the impact of pensions legislation on insolvent businesses. Finally, we look in detail at the legislation covering employer liabilities.

Appendices set out the legislation, regulatory materials, some relevant case law and some general information. Future editions will take account of the growing experience as it develops, and readers are invited to comment, criticise, make improvements and add experience (robin@pensionslaw.net; gjones@ssd.com).

2 The issues of funding

2.1 Introduction

The major concern for any company intending to purchase a business which has a DB pension scheme involved is whether there are adequate assets to meet the scheme's liabilities. This simple concern, however, poses significant problems in practice.

A primary issue is whether the scheme's liabilities are properly stated. There are many ways of calculating pension liabilities and much depends on the assumptions made in those calculations. For example a pension scheme will need more money if the method of calculation assumes that future returns on investments will be modest or that longevity of the staff will be greater than expected. The actuarial assumptions used in such calculations can vary widely and in many cases are merely educated guesses as to future returns, interests rates etc. To calculate or at least estimate the scheme's liabilities, actuaries consider funding methods, i.e. the appropriate way in which to ensure there are adequate funds in the scheme to meet the liabilities.

Funding methods can be calculated in several ways, and each calculation basis is likely to result in a different outcome. For example:

Projected unit credit funding

This is a method under which the contributions required in a year are calculated as the present value of future benefits estimated to have accrued in the year. Under this method, the contribution required in a year comprises two parts; the normal cost and an amount to cover any unfunded accrued liabilities. The normal cost is the present value of all future benefits accrued in the year; the unfunded accrued liability component allows for the financial effect of actual past experience being different to the actuarial assumptions. US financial accounting standards prefer the use of this method. It uses a form of accrued benefit funding which takes into account only the benefits which have accrued to date and not any future benefits which might accrue as a result of membership or service periods. Using accrued benefit funding an annual contribution rate is set in line with the present value of benefits arising in the next year. The liability is the value of benefits for service completed prior to the valuation date calculated taking into account all the different circumstances in which benefits could be paid and, in the case of active members, allowing for pay projected from the valuation date to the assumed date of retirement, date of leaving service or date of death as appropriate.

Projected benefits funding

An alternative approach is to take into account all the benefits which may be paid under a fund for current or even some future members. A level of contributions is set so that it covers both the benefits which have already accrued and benefits associated with membership in the future.

Current Unit Method
The liability is the value of benefits for service completed prior to the valuation date calculated taking into account all the different circumstances in which benefits could be paid, but without making any allowance for future salary growth for active members. Although pay is not projected, allowance is made for increases in the benefits between the relevant date and the assumed date of retirement, date of leaving service or date of death as appropriate, for example due to increases applied to preserved pensions as required by legislation or by scheme rules.

Partly Projected Unit Method
The liability is calculated as for the Current Unit Method except that, for active members, pay is projected throughout a 'control period', which could end before all active members reach retirement age.

Defined Accrued Benefit Method
The liability is calculated on the assumption that the scheme will be discontinued on the valuation date. In some cases a control period is used, in which case it is assumed the scheme will be discontinued as at the end of the control period, in which case pay for active members is projected to that date.

Accordingly different actuarial approaches will deliver different contribution rates – and hence different liabilities. In addition there are several different ways of calculating defined benefit liabilities. Some of the more widely discussed methods include:

Buy-out liabilities (full buy-out basis, s.75 buy-out) basis
This assumes that no further benefits will be earned by members of the scheme, but existing benefits earned will be secured by buying deferred annuities with an insurance company. Deferred annuities are expensive for many reasons, including inadequate capacity in the market (there are not many providers), high reserves required by the FSA, and inappropriate investments required by the FSA – as well as the fact that providers are invariably profit-making bodies with a need to secure a return on their own capital. Pension schemes were normally established on the basis that they would not be required to buy deferred annuities – they were not funded on that basis, and employers would not have established them if they had been. In a way workplace pensions were established to avoid the high costs of insured arrangements.

FRS17 liabilities
These assume the adoption of a liability basis nowadays used in company accounts. FRS 17 refers to the Financial Reporting Standard No. 17 which applies in the UK. It requires the market value of the assets to be compared with the value of the

liabilities using the yields on corporate bonds (which are expected to be higher than for example government bonds, and there less money is required). It is based on the view that while for pension schemes with investments in equities, the value of the fund rises and falls with the market, the value of the liabilities moves in line with bond yields – and the two can be different. For example in 1999 UK equities increased in value by around a quarter – at the same time that bond yields rose by about ½%, equivalent to around 15% reduction in liabilities. A year later the market dropped by 6% and bonds reduced by 1/4% equivalent to increasing liabilities by around 7%. FRS17 requires all surpluses and deficits to be shown as an asset or liability on the company balance sheet, and as can be seen that can mean high volatility. FRS17 is an auditing standard set by the Accounting Standards Board that prescribes the use of a AA rated bond discount rate for calculating pension liabilities - for some companies FRS17 will have been replaced by IAS19, which uses similar principles.

Other bases will have correspondingly lower (or higher) liability conclusions. In recent years regulations have required sponsor companies to estimate liabilities using FRS17 basis, an arrangement which may require a higher level of funding compared with conventional arrangements. And regulators and the press and some risk-averse commentators are more comfortable with the use of buy-out liabilities. It is the move in recent years to toughen funding requirements which has proved to be a major factor contributing to the decline of willingness of sponsors to continue supporting DB arrangements.

Now there are detailed requirements for the funding of DB schemes. The scheme funding requirements replace the Minimum Funding Requirement (MFR) introduced by the Pensions Act 1995. The MFR was the first formal statutory funding regime to be applied to occupational schemes in the UK. It was intended to set a standard benchmark against which scheme security could be measured. However, it became unpopular with employers because of its inflexibility and some public opinion considered it did not provide adequate security for scheme members.

In 2002, the Government promised to replace the MFR with a less prescriptive approach that could take into account the particular circumstances of the scheme and the sponsoring employer. Eventually this was subsumed into the scheme funding regime mandated by the Pensions Act 2004 (which amalgamated the original legislative intentions with requirements imposed by the European Pensions Directive in 2003).

The European Pensions Directive was intended initially to liberalise pension scheme regulation across the European Union. It established a common basis of supervision for occupational pension schemes throughout the Union. The unintended consequence has led to the UK adopting a less flexible funding regime than was originally intended.

2.2 Pensions Act 2004

PA 2004 imposed new and broadly tougher funding rules on defined benefit arrangements from the end of 2005. The rules were intended to comply both with EU requirements and reduce the likelihood of claims on the PPF where DB pension arrangements failed. Pension schemes had already (by a government announcement in June 2003) been required to be fully funded on a buy-out basis if they were closed by employers; and the European Pensions Directive could be interpreted as requiring certain pension schemes at least to be 'fully funded' at all times. As a consequence PA 2004 (and consequent regulations) in particular now requires schemes:

- to conform with the new rules three years after last valuation;
- to take more account of the balance of power in scheme rules; and
- to remove the previous 'minimum funding requirement' (MFR) underpin from any transfer values

PA 2004 replaces the previous scheme funding provisions with a requirement for each scheme to have a statutory funding objective, and to have 'sufficient and appropriate assets' to meet its 'technical provisions' (a phrase adopted from EU legislation which has been read as meaning an estimate of the assets needed today to meet the payment of future benefits as they fall due, and allowing for future investment returns). Schemes are required to adopt a statement of funding principles which exposes the trustees' policy in relation to funding. The provisions (PA 2004, the regulations and a code of practice from the Pensions Regulator ('the Code')) came into effect from 30 December 2005, but affect all valuations carried out with an effective date on or after 22 September 2005. The main elements of the regime include:

- The requirement for a statement of funding principles, covering the statutory funding objective and where there is a deficit the recovery period over which the objective must be met together with other items (such as the policy on reducing transfer values);
- The requirement for an actuarial valuation (carried out at least every three years) including the calculation of technical provisions. The trustees must set prudent assumptions for this calculation; and
- The requirement for an adoption of a schedule of contributions agreed between the employer and trustees covering the contributions for the following five years (or the recovery period if longer).

These must be prepared within 15 months of the effective date of the valuation (although where the last actuarial valuation fell due between 22 September and 29 December 2005 inclusive this is extended to 18 months).

Before the preparation of these documents, trustees are required to take advice from their actuary and invariably obtain the agreement of the employer. The regulations closely reflect the existing balance of power in scheme rules so that in the rare cases where a scheme gives the trustees the sole power to set contributions and there is no third party power to suspend or reduce them, then the employer's agreement is not needed. Nonetheless, even in such cases the trustees must consult the employer. Where the rules provide for the actuary to set the rate, then the employer's agreement is required but the actuary's recommendations must be taken into account.

In addition, unless valuations are carried out yearly, annual funding reports must usually be completed. These must use an effective date no later than one year from that of the last actuarial valuation or report and must be obtained within one year of that date.

The regulations amend existing legislation in preparation for the phasing out of the Minimum Funding Requirement (MFR). The MFR (or reduced MFR) underpin to transfer values no longer applies, and amended disclosure regulations require an annual summary of a funding statement to be delivered to scheme members, based on the information in the annual valuation or report.

2.2.1 Transitional

There are of course transitional arrangements. These broadly apply to any valuations with an effective date on or after 22 September 2005, which are completed after 29 December 2005. Where the effective date of the valuation falls before 22 September 2005, the former regime can apply.

Where the scheme is currently subject to the MFR the effective date of the first valuation under the new requirements must normally be no later than three years after the last MFR valuation. Valuations following MFR recertification failures are carried out under the new regime if the valuation date is on or after 22 September (but not completed before 30 December). In these cases trustees have 18 months from the recertification failure to complete the valuation.

The requirement for annual valuations or funding reports applies only after the first scheme specific valuation. However, in most cases, schemes must have produced their first annual summary funding statement for members by 21 September 2006.

2.3 Pensions Regulator requirements

2.3.1 Code of practice

The details of the requirements are set out in the Code issued by the Pensions Regulator, together with some additional guidance issued by the same office. The Code proposes that trustees establish an action plan for the valuation process, but there are no specific time constraints. In particular the Code suggests that:

- although trustees must take advice from their actuary regarding the various elements of the funding process, it is ultimately their responsibility to set the statement of funding principles and the method and assumptions for calculating the technical provisions. In particular trustees need to choose the assumptions with some degree of prudence if they wish to be confident about the adequacy of those provisions. The trustees can take some account of higher expected returns on equities relative to bonds if this is appropriate and if the employer appreciates the effect that underperformance may have on the contribution rate;
- the employer needs to understand the implications of the funding method and assumptions, and may wish to take advice from the scheme actuary or a separate actuary;
- in order to decide on the assumptions used for calculating the technical provisions and the recovery period, the trustees must form an independent assessment of the employer's financial position. They should ask the employer to provide all relevant information, and may use external sources to check the employer's ability to fund the scheme. Some trustees may have conflicts of duty or interest in this area, but are reminded that they must only consider their trustee duties;
- trustees need to negotiate with the employer if necessary, or use mediation if agreement is not possible otherwise;
- any recovery plan to remedy any deficit should ensure that the shortfall is eliminated as quickly as the employer can reasonably afford. This will take account of matters such as company cash commitments and contingent funding.

The new regime requires trustees to consult and, in most cases, reach agreement with the sponsoring employer on all the significant steps in the valuation process. This includes setting the method and assumptions for calculating the assets needed by the scheme to meet benefits as they fall due (the 'technical provisions'), the period over which any shortfall in the assets against the technical provisions is to be met and the content of the schedule of contributions. The Regulator regards the responsibility for achieving a satisfactory conclusion to the valuation process to be that of the trustees; it looks to see due process, including the establishment of an action plan (to set out the process and dispute management arrangements). Employers and trustees need inevitably to work closely together, and the sponsor may need to provide confidential information on short and long term business plans, and management accounts.

Improved scheme funding is intended to reduce claims on the PPF. In practice the assumptions used for scheme funding valuations are invariably stronger than those used previously and the period over which any shortfalls are corrected are shorter. If the Regulator suspects that the desired outcome is improbable, but it may intervene. It is for the trustees to ensure that the valuation process is completed; this may not always be easy to achieve. The Regulator suggests that an action plan might be created by the trustees to help monitor funding progress. Employers will in almost all cases reach agreement with trustees over the scheme funding process. If they fail, then the ultimate sanction is that the Regulator will intervene. Where it does, it is likely to impose harsher funding requirements.

With limited exceptions the statutory funding regime applies to all defined benefit schemes with effective valuation dates on or after 22 September 2005. Normally trustees have 15 months from the effective date of the valuation to complete the valuation process. Shorter periods apply where the Regulator gives directions that a valuation be carried out because the trustees have been unable to complete the funding process themselves. 'Completion' means that within 15 months after the effective date the trustees must have final versions of the statement of funding principles, the schedule of contributions and recovery plan and have received certificates of the technical provisions and the schedule of contributions from their actuary.

Schemes exempt from the statutory funding objective include:
- Schemes established under an enactment and guaranteed by a public authority;
- Pay as you go schemes;
- Schemes established in the UK but only with overseas non-EU members;
- Schemes that are not tax registered (from 6 April 2006) and have fewer than 100 members;
- SSASs (small self-administered schemes, i.e. schemes with fewer than 12 members where all members are trustees and either decisions taken by the trustees have to be made unanimously) or there is an independent trustee appointed by the Regulator;
- Death benefit only schemes, where benefits are insured;
- Schemes in an assessment period with the Pension Protection Fund; and
- Schemes being wound up, provided that the actuary provides an estimate of the solvency of the scheme at least annually.

2.3.2 Agreement with employer

There is a statutory requirement for trustees to consult with employers in relation to the proper funding of the scheme. The employer's consent can be unnecessary where the scheme's governing documents grant the trustees the right to set contributions regardless of consent (or, perhaps, subject to the advice of their actuary) but even in these cases it is conventional to consult. Sometimes (rarely) the actuary alone has the right to set the rate of contributions in which case neither consent nor consultation applies.

The Code nonetheless encourages a free exchange of information amongst all parties whatever the method of rate-setting. There may need to be a process established to formalise the information gathering, and to manage confidentiality and conflicts, and the proper role of advisers e.g. when it might be appropriate to have separate advisers for parties where there is a conflict of interests.

2.3.3 Timing

The scheme funding regime applies to the first valuation with an effective date on or after 22 September 2005. For most schemes this is three years after the effective date of their previous valuation. Any valuations carried out outside the normal cycle need to comply with the new requirements. There is no need for an actuarial report until after the first valuation under the scheme funding regime.

2.3.4 Summary funding statements

Schemes need to issue annual funding statements to scheme members, the first statement being no later than 22 September 2006; it can be based on the MFR valuation if there is no more recent one.

2.3.5 The statement of funding principles

The scheme funding regime is based around a single funding target, called the statutory funding objective. The 'statutory funding objective' is that the scheme must have sufficient assets to meet 'technical provisions' a phrase taken from the European Pensions Directive and which had no exact equivalent in English law or practice. It is thought that the phrase was taken over to offer deliberate ambiguity, in other words to allow schemes to adopt whatever actuarial assumptions they thought appropriate. Schemes, which statutorily need a statement of funding principles, may use that statement to state what actuarial assumptions they will adopt in determining the pace and level of funding. The statement must include:

- the trustees' approach towards the method and assumptions to be used in the calculation of the 'technical provisions'; and
- the way in which any gap between the assets and the technical provisions will be filled.

Since investment strategy must also be taken into account, the Regulator suggests that schemes should consider merging the statement of investment principles into the statement of funding objectives to save paper and reduce inconsistencies. There are slightly different rules about consultation with employers for investments and funding, although in practice few will be concerned about such issues.

2.3.6 Content of statement of funding principles

A statement of funding principles must include:

The trustees' policy for securing that the statutory funding objective is met.
- A record of any decisions made by the trustees as to:
  - o the methods and assumptions to be used to calculate the scheme's technical provisions; and
  - o the period and manner in which any failure to meet the statutory funding objective is to be remedied.

- Additional funding objectives adopted by the trustees.
- Whether, and in what circumstances, any other person than the employer can contribute to the scheme.
- Whether the trustees have the power to make payments from the scheme funds to the employer and the circumstances in which they can be exercised.
- Whether the trustees have any discretionary powers to provide or increase benefits and the extent to which they are taken into account in drawing up the funding objective.
- The trustees' policy towards reducing cash equivalent payments due to shortfalls in the scheme's assets.
- How frequently the trustees will obtain an actuarial valuation and the circumstances in which they will consider obtaining more frequent valuations.

2.3.7 Calculation of 'technical provisions'

'Technical provisions' are defined in an act of circularity as 'the amount required to make provision for the scheme's liabilities'; the Regulator in its code indicates that these are merely the assets needed to make provision for benefits already accrued. Schemes will use such actuarial methods as are appropriate having regard to the history and needs and future of the scheme. While the technical provisions should represent a 'prudent' estimate of the provision needed to meet benefit payments, the Regulator emphasises that there is no regulatory attempt to eliminate all risk from the calculation. Actuaries might be asked at some time in the future to justify any particular method adopted, and working papers might have to include a sensitivity analysis of various funding methods to various risks.

2.3.8 Recovery plan

When the value of a scheme's assets is less than its technical provisions, a scheme must produce a 'recovery plan' that sets out how the shortfall will be met. The statement of funding principles in any event will have set out the general approach trustees will follow in case there is a shortfall. The Regulator for its own purposes seeks that shortfalls be eliminated as soon as the employer can reasonably afford to, but there will be cases when it is appropriate to defer shortfall payments, for example:

- if the employer's spending commitments are such that immediate payment could be difficult; or
- if the employer and trustees agree to acceptable alternative means of funding, including some forms of contingent security. The Code lists examples of contingent securities it might find acceptable.

The paradox is that the Regulator anticipates schemes with strong sponsor covenants to fund the shortfall within a short period while weaker employers are usually given a longer period. At the same time the calculation of the technical provisions will vary in each case and trustees with a strong employer may be able to justify lower technical provisions than those with a weak employer. This is because strong employers are assumed to be able to bear the risk that the experience anticipated by a basis that allows for investment in equities, for example, will not be borne out in practice. Thus, it is possible that in both cases the recovery plan could record the same size of payment, albeit made over different periods. Recovery plans will need to be adjusted from time to time, for example following a new valuation or change in the employer's circumstances. The Regulator will be uncomfortable with a revision of a plan that includes any new deficits that have arisen in the meantime which may extend the time for making up a deficit.

2.3.9 Contingent securities

Funding of pension liabilities is not necessarily limited to cash and equities or bonds. It can also include other support for funding. Certain contingent assets are regarded by the Regulator as to be considered as assets of a fund; these include:

- a guarantee (called by the Regulator a letter of credit) issued by a third party triggered by insolvency of the sponsor;
- a guarantee from another company within the same group triggered by the insolvency of the employer;
- secured assets (called by the Regulator securitised assets) available on the event of the sponsor's insolvency; and
- an escrow account being an account into which the sponsor pays which is available to the scheme in the event of the sponsor's insolvency, but which could be recovered by the sponsor in the event it becomes unnecessary (perhaps because the investments do well).

The PPF will also take contingent securities into account in the calculation of the risk related levy, provided trustees can certify that the securities satisfy certain conditions (see PPF website). While the PPF requirements do not relate to scheme funding, in practice trustees considering whether contingent securities can be used to assist scheme funding also consider whether the proposed assets would be recognised by the PPF.

If there is a deficit the scheme needs to prepare a 'recovery plan' with a programme to deal with the deficit. Matters to be taken into account when drawing up a recovery plan include:

- whether and if the employer can afford to pay enhanced contributions, including taking regard of the sponsor's business plans and expenditure commitments, and the impact of regulation in regulated industries;
- the effect the recovery plan would have on the employer's viability and the ability of the trustees to pursue any debt if the scheme wound up;
- the scheme's membership profile, including impending membership movements that could have a material effect on scheme security;

- the worth of any contingent securities provided by the sponsor, and taking account of the fact that despite the European Pensions Directive 2003 and PA 1995 which all but outlaws self-investment, any opportunities for self-investment;
- contingency plans if the assumptions underlying the recovery plan are not borne out by experience; and
- the cost of the risk-based element of the PPF levy and how this is paid for by the employer.

2.3.10 Schedule of contributions

The need to agree a schedule of contributions which sets out the rates of contribution being paid to the scheme and the payment dates is carried over from the previous requirements when MFR applied. It is required to cover a period of five years, or the term of any recovery plan if this is longer. The purpose of the schedule is to serve:

- as an auditing tool, enabling trustees to monitor that contributions are being paid to the scheme as expected; and
- to confirm that the contributions being paid are consistent with the statement of funding principles.

The schedule is accompanied by a certificate from the scheme actuary stating that the rates of contribution being paid are sufficient to ensure that the statutory funding objective will be met by the end of the schedule period or, for schemes with no shortfalls, that it will continue to be met throughout the period the schedule is in force. The actuary must also certify that the schedule is consistent with the statement of funding principles.

2.3.11 Changing the benefits: modifying future accrual

If there is insufficient funding available then the scheme may have to consider reducing the benefits, at least in respect of future accrual for active members. The Regulator may insist on this if there is no other way of meeting any deficit, which may cause complex industrial relations issues for the employer in dealing with the active workforce whose goodwill may be necessary to be able to trade out of a problem. Modifying accrual involves the trustees in becoming involved in changing the employment terms for staff which is not a conventional role of trustees. Where unions and other representative groups are represented on the board of trustees, this may pose complex difficulties. But if the employer is in financial difficulties the Regulator consider, it is the duty of trustees to consider cutting current accrual. Where the trustees insist on this step (and so far there is no recorded example available) employers are required to undertake the normal consultation process with affected employees when making material amendments to the scheme. Given that the consultation process can take at least two months, not to mention the time taken to reach the decision to consult, and that consultation must be meaningful, trustees may be hard pressed to meet the statutory fifteen month time frame to complete the various schedules and plans required.

2.3.12 Actuarial input

The actuarial valuation must include a certificate of the 'technical provisions' and an estimate by the actuary of the scheme's solvency. The estimate is calculated on a buy-out (*PA 1995 s.75*) basis, however unrealistic this may be in practice. The actuarial professional guidance note requires the actuary to produce a commentary on the valuation. A simple actuarial valuation is required annually although full actuarial valuations are only required every three years. The actuarial report must set out how the scheme's technical provisions have changed since the previous actuarial valuation was prepared. It must give information on how the assets and the likely future benefit payments have changed since the previous valuation, carried out at least once a year. There is no need for detailed calculations and the report can be discursive rather than financial. Schemes with fewer than 100 members must have a fresh valuation once membership rises above 100.

Actuarial advice is now subject to peer review, which does not mean there is a need for a second opinion. Although the actuary's responsibility is to the trustees, it is possible for him or her to give advice to the employer also. There needs to be a process of managing any emerging conflicts this may engender. The Code suggests that the customer agreement should provide that trustees may ask the actuary to resign from the company appointment if a conflict of interest arises. The actuary may prefer to resign the trustee appointment, provided:

- this has been discussed and agreed with the trustees;
- the trustees understand the reasons for the actuary's position and agree that it is justifiable; and
- part of the agreement ensures that a suitable alternative adviser is available to the trustees should conflict arise; then it could be possible to make a different arrangement.

2.3.13 Providing information to the Regulator

Following a valuation which discloses a material deficit, a scheme must send copies of any new or revised recovery plans and any new or revised schedule of contributions, to the Regulator, within a 'reasonable time' (broadly ten working days after receiving the certified schedule from the actuary). When a recovery plan is submitted, it must be accompanied by a summary of the results from the valuation, including the value of the assets and the technical provisions, information on the method and assumptions used to calculate the technical provisions and an estimate of the cost of buying out the benefits with an insurer.

If the scheme funding negotiations break down, the fact of the lack of progress must be reported to the Regulator; examples include where:

- the actuary cannot certify the schedule or the technical provisions;

- the trustees cannot reach agreement with the employer; or
- the employer does not pay contributions due under the schedule (if material).

Where the scheme funding process has not been completed within the designated time the Regulator may issue a direction to the trustees to enable them to complete the valuation. A report to members might also be necessary.

2.3.14 Providing information to members

Once an actuarial valuation or actuarial report under the statutory funding regime has been completed and agreed, a summary statement must be sent to members, preferably within three months of it being agreed. The Regulator places a great deal of reliance on the document but it is only one of several documents that members receive. Nonetheless, it does (or should) explore the level of security available under the scheme, perhaps in slightly clearer terms than the previous actuarial reports. The summary in particular needs to state:
- the percentage level of cover if there were an immediate wind-up, and
- a summary of any recovery plan.

There is pressure from the Regulator to express all this in plain terms but given the problems that have arisen in the past in government and others being held to account for simple explanations that do not contain the usual caveats, this may not be easy.

2.3.15 Special cases

Many schemes relate to employees of a particular company. But there are special requirements where schemes cover employees of a group (multi-employer schemes) or where schemes have agreed to share costs (balance of costs schemes) between employers and employees.

Multi-employer schemes
Multi-employer schemes which are organised so as to have separate sections for funding purposes are treated as separate schemes by the Regulator.

Balance of cost schemes
Where scheme rules indicate that contributions are such that the employees (members) pay a fixed contribution rate, and the employer pays on top whatever is appropriate, the scheme has power to share the cost of any recovery plan between the employer and members, in line with scheme rules, unless the employer agrees to pay a greater proportion of the cost.

Cross border schemes
Cross border schemes are permitted under HMRC and EU regulations. This allows tax relief to be available on contributions to schemes outside the jurisdiction (provided they are in the EU or EEA). They are regulated by the state in which they are registered, rather than the state where the member makes the contributions. Such schemes need to inform local regulators of their existence, but

are likely as experience develops to offer major planning opportunities to contain the excesses of regulation. It is almost certain that over the next few years multi-national employers will consolidate their schemes using one jurisdiction (unlikely to be the UK). The UK imposes curious scheme funding differences, suggesting that cross-border schemes need to be funded to greater levels than UK-member-only schemes, which seems improbable. The Regulator believes this is adirect interpretation of the underlying EU harmonisation Directive. Where the transaction is a cross-border one or employees are employed by one entity but work in different jurisdictions it is usually advisable to ensure that the scheme is a non-UK one, to avoid the UK restrictions on certain kinds of defined benefit schemes. The UK probably uniquely prohibits such schemes from incorporating a funding cap (i.e. limiting the DB promise to that available with such funds as are in the scheme at the time of wind-up). The Netherlands, for example, actively encourages the establishment of such schemes, which are outside the funding requirements. For cross border schemes established in the UK, the compliance requirements include:

- scheme funding valuations at least annually;
- valuations to be completed within 12 months; and
- the actuarial liabilities must be 'fully funded at all times'. The UK interprets this as meaning that any deficit must be dealt with within two years of the effective date of the valuation.

Since the period for meeting any deficit statutorily prescribed, there is no requirement for any recovery plan; the period covered by a schedule of contributions is restricted to two years. There are transitional arrangements for pre-existing schemes (i.e. before 6 April 2006 for tax purposes, and 23 September 2005 for regulatory purposes) mostly Anglo-Irish schemes that were already operating as cross border schemes. The Regulator will grant approval provided:

- the first statutory funding valuation was completed by 22 September 2006; and
- any deficit is cleared by 22 September 2008.

2.3.16 Intervention by the Regulator

The Regulator may intervene where schemes do not meet its funding requirements. The process and criteria for intervention include the following aspects:

- valuations and recovery plans submitted to the Regulator being filtered to identify potential risks to members and to the PPF.
- filters expressed in terms of triggers that will prompt further review. The triggers are based on the strength of the funding target, the period over which the deficit is being corrected and employer covenant information.
- a review by the Regulator does not mean that the trustees' approach has been deemed unacceptable, just that further justification may be sought.
- normally the trigger point is likely to be determined by the proportion of buy-out funding targeted. The Regulator believes that, for most schemes, 100% funding

on a basis that would be compliant with FRS17 or PPF levy liability bases produces a target in the range 70%-80% of buyout funding, and this appears to be its point of reference. If the Regulator believes that buy-out has become relatively stronger than FRS17, it can reconsider the percentages used as the trigger. Where employer covenant is weak or the scheme more mature, the trigger would be at the higher end of the range. Assumptions for FRS17 (or IAS19) are set by the employer and the Regulator regards it as inappropriate to adopt them as part of its statement of funding principles without going through due process for testing its own assumptions. The Regulator is looking for trustees to seek buy-out targets, but this seems ambitious in most cases.

- Recovery plans of longer than 10 years are also likely to trigger scrutiny, although the Regulator paradoxically might use a shorter period for trustees of schemes with more financially stable employers.

The Regulator intends to use an alternative trigger of 110% of the MFR for schemes that have not yet adopted the new funding regime. Schemes with lower funding levels are to be asked if they have taken appropriate actions to improve funding in advance of their next valuation (e.g. by considering bringing forward the first scheme funding valuation) which lends an unexpected element of aggression to the tone of the supervisory regime.

When carrying out any review, the Regulator will look at a range of factors, including trustee compliance with knowledge and understanding regulations, the strength of employer covenants and the work that has been carried out to challenge decisions and assumptions of the employer. This is broadly an unwelcome requirement from the Regulator and later practice may cause the Regulator to ease its stance on the adverse relationships it is currently engendering between trustees and sponsors.

Not unnaturally, the Regulator has made clear that it is expecting the general level of scheme funding to improve dramatically over the next few years, perhaps even to the levels prevailing at the end of the 1990s (without government regulation). It has encouraged this already through the clearance procedure it operates for companies involved in corporate restructuring, where in some cases commitment to fund schemes to FRS17 levels has been necessary to gain the Regulator's approval. The Regulator expects employers of 65% of schemes to be able to meet FRS17 deficits within 10 years. This is clearly the direction the Regulator expects trustees to move their schemes in. This objective is now reinforced by the Regulator's statement on its approach to the regulations even more than the specific provisions of the regulations or Code. The Code permits a weaker funding target than the equivalent of FRS17, since it allows technical provisions to be calculated including an allowance for equity outperformance relative to the return from lower risk investments, provided that trustees consider this to be justifiable. The implication is that this could be justified whilst a company remains financially strong, but it would then be the trustees' responsibility to monitor the employer's covenant closely to identify any weakening that could leave the employer unable to meet the consequent higher funding target required.

It is notoriously difficult to identify when the slide from strong to weak begins. Trustees who want to take advantage of this relaxation must be prepared to justify to the Regulator how they reached this view. The Code is relatively silent on how the trustees' investment strategy should help determine the content of the statement of funding principles, apart from noting that it should be taken into account. However, investment strategy should be key to determining the statutory funding objective for the scheme, as well as to the approach taken to the recovery plan.

2.4   The impact of funding issues on corporate finance

The scale of liabilities relating to company pension schemes has increased substantially over recent years and have become much more visible in corporate finance. In particular, pension scheme deficits now appear in company accounts and it has become common for pension scheme liabilities to be discussed in the press and in analysts' reports. Funders and bankers are now placing pensions issues (especially funding issues) at the forefront of their discussions when considering the acquisition or restructuring of companies. Indeed, some companies have been reported as using pension liabilities as a form of poison pill to fend off hostile takeovers.

It is, however, important to put these issues into in context. Deficits can be halved in a year by a modest movement in the stockmarket; asset-liability conventions, that certain liabilities should be matched by appropriate fixed interest assets, are now less fashionable following unprecedented (and probably unrealistic) low bond rates. Companies are beginning painfully and slowly not only to reassess the costs of pension arrangements but also the benefits for there are erratic reports of some companies beginning to discuss the feasibility of re-introducing some form of salary-related pension benefits.

Nonetheless, finance directors need to consider whether the volatility of the assets within a pension fund (which need annually to be reflected in the company balance sheet) is manageable in conjunction with the operations of the business. It is this volatility, and the need to make payments to meet deficits which may never actually crystallise, which causes so many difficulties for finance directors.

Scheme deficits, especially if they are significant items, can often be manageable within the normal trading of the enterprise, but can also be used either to encourage restructuring or to defend against hostile take-overs. In particular, leveraged buy-outs, funded by private equity, have become much less attractive than before, because of the attitude of the Regulator to a consequent material reduction in the calibre of the employer's covenant, i.e. its ability to meet over time the deficit in the pension scheme.

Several high-profile deals have been reported to have aborted because of the level of the scheme's deficit, and the requirements of the Regulator and trustees for a new buyer to inject substantial sums into the scheme if it looks as though the strength of the employer's covenant is affected by the relevant transaction. Such threats however can be curtailed by potential purchasers where it would be counter-productive to wind up the scheme, or a demand for the full s.75 buy-out could well destroy the ability of the scheme to continue and for benefits to accrue for the existing work-force. The decision by trustees to call for the wind-up of a scheme is a final option but not one that is easily exercised. In most cases even if the deal goes ahead and the trustees are unhappy with it, they are unlikely to press for the wind-up of the scheme and it is improbable, in practice, that the Regulator will serve a contribution notice without a great deal of further investigation. Many of the sanctions may eventually turn out to be paper tigers; in the meantime, there is no doubt that the tigers have had a material impact on corporate transactions.

The ability of companies either to be outside the jurisdiction (i.e. not within the EU) and, therefore, outside the control of the Regulator to recover under a financial support direction, or to re-register in another jurisdiction and avoid the application of the Regulator has so far not been exercised. But there is no doubt that such options are being reviewed continually and will at some time in the future be used.

2.4.1 Liabilities of group companies

Pension liabilities usually fall on the employing company. PA 2004 gives the Regulator the right to demand contributions from any other group company or any company which holds at least one-third of its share capital (including non-UK companies) in the following circumstances:

- if that party has acted to reduce the liability of any group company to the pension scheme at any time since 27 April 2004; or
- the Regulator believes that the company with the pension scheme does not have sufficient assets to service the pension scheme liabilities.

This cross-company or intra-group liability is giving pause for thought to many finance directors who had previously sought to buffer each group company against liabilities incurred by another. So far there is little reported experience in the way these requirements are being operated by the Regulator.

2.4.2 Accounting

Under FRS17, all company accounts prepared up to an accounting date on or after 1 January 2005 must show in the balance sheet any pension scheme deficit or surplus. In each case the calculation must be done on an FRS17 basis. Variations to the scheme defecit or surplus on a year-on-year basis will be reflected in the profit and loss account and the statement of recognised gains and losses.

ISSUES OF FUNDING

Listed companies also have to comply with IAS19, the international accounting standard for pensions. This differs from FRS17 in allowing companies to spread certain losses over the working life of the employees who are members of the scheme. However, IAS19 has been varied to allow the immediate statement of all losses in the balance sheet to comply and conform with FRS17.

The effect of FRS17 and IAS19 is that pension scheme liabilities are clearly disclosed to the public by way of company accounts and also have substantial effects on financial ratios, such as earnings per share and gearing levels. Because FRS17 gives the value of pension scheme liabilities on a set of market led assumptions, the level of FRS17 is frequently volatile and may not be representative of the company's true liability to the pension scheme. Some suggest that it may be helpful as part of calculating the real liabilities of a company to calculate ratios both with and without the FRS17 element to give a clearer indication of the status of a company.

3 Pensions issues in mergers and acquisitions

3.1 Introduction

The pensions issues when buying and selling a company can be complex, all the more so when a defined benefit scheme is involved. At one time, although pensions were always material, the importance of the issue was invariably secondary to more imminent commercial matters. But now that defined benefits plans have been converted into crystallised financial obligations (never intended at the time the scheme was introduced and sponsored by the employer) pensions have achieved a higher profile than before. This section gives some general guidance on the terms of sale and purchase agreements in relation to pensions issues.

Pension 'schemes' (in British English) or 'plans' (in American English) cover not only registered plans (i.e. registered with the HMRC) but also non-registered plans, and in particular unregistered plans and pension obligations sometimes inadvertently hidden in contracts of employment of service agreements.

Pensions emerge as an issue not only on the simple purchase of a company or business from a vendor, but also where joint ventures are entered into, and where there are takeover bids. And nowadays pensions are an issue not only for the buyer, but also for the seller – and increasingly the funder, whether a banker or venture capitalist. Transactions are further complicated not only by the new compliance requirements of The Pensions Regulator, but by the privity problem – that pension trustees, an essential player in the transaction, are invariably not a party to the transaction. Finally, decision-taking is made more difficult because of the fact that conflicts of interest that arise where a company director is also a trustee of the pension scheme are now much more difficult to manage.

3.1.1 Purchaser's and funder's objectives

The objectives of a transaction in relation to pensions are usually relatively straightforward for a purchaser or banker: is there enough in the pension scheme kitty to pay the pension obligations to date incurred by the vendor in relation to the employees? In defined contribution systems, the issues are usually much simpler – have the contributions been paid, and are the assets still there?

In relation to defined benefit plans, not only are there concerns about past liabilities, but nowadays there are concerns about future liabilities. There might be a (moral or commercial) obligation to continue what might be generous pension arrangements which the purchaser would not normally support. A requirement by a purchaser to cut such arrangements following acquisition might provoke industrial relations concerns. Current employees of a purchaser might look askance at welcoming a new group of employees who join them with pension arrangements better than the incumbents enjoy. So a purchaser needs to estimate not only the cost of both past and future liabilities, but also the knock-on effect of the changed aspirations of the existing workforce.

If there are insufficient funds in the pension plans, then the cost of making up any deficits, a common enough condition theses days, needs to be built into the purchase price – and consideration given as to the speed and manner of reducing such deficits over future years. And there may be hidden future costs; these can include for example the (unquantified and possibly unquantifiable at point of purchase) costs of equalising benefits between male and female employees if there is a suggestion that such benefits have not been equalised in the past in accordance with the legislation and case law (notably *Barber v Guardian Royal Exchange Assurance Group [1991] 1 QB 344*).

Where the vendor's scheme is a group scheme (i.e. covers the employees of a group of employers) the employees will cease to be members of that scheme on transfer, and become members of another scheme. A buyer needs to ensure that the transfer arrangements are adequate – and since usually such transfer payments are subject to the approval of trustees, the group scheme trustees need to be involved – or at least the purchaser needs a warranty from the vendor himself that sufficient funds will be forthcoming if the trustees do not deliver. The trustees may not deliver, especially where the plan is in deficit, and they are not party to the transaction. In many cases the employees may need to be retained in the vendor's scheme for a short while, while fresh pension arrangements are established, and arrangements need to be agreed to ensure the vendor and his trustees are protected against claims in such a case, and that contribution rates are reasonable.

3.1.2   Vendor's objectives

A vendor (so far as pensions are concerned) has usually only one objective – to ensure that his company carries no future obligations in relation to employees who are now leaving his employment. Where the plan carries a deficit, he may continue to be liable to make good any such deficit despite any sale (see e.g. *PA 1993 s.144*). And there is a small though material concern to ensure that a purchaser maintains pension benefits at the same level to ensure that there is no possible claim against the vendor for loss of pension rights under the employment contracts of employees.

Today surpluses are much rarer than before; but they do exist, and a vendor who has been responsible over many years for building up such a surplus may be reluctant in current circumstances to see it pass out of his hands without due reward. Nor will he wish to see too great a transfer payment made on too generous assumptions, if only to ensure that remaining members in his scheme are not prejudiced.

3.1.3 Trustees

Trustees, who are rarely party to the transaction, however, play a part in agreeing or consenting to any transfer – or seeking where there is a deficit an accelerated payment toward such deficits if they conceive the covenant of the new employer to be less strong. They may or may not agree to pay the transfer payment agreed between the purchaser and the vendor. The agreement normally contains a 'shortfall' clause so that any inadequacy in the payment made by the trustees when it comes to be paid is made good by the vendor (perhaps out of the sale price).

3.1.4 Advisers

It is common in all but the smallest of transactions to employ both lawyers and actuaries to handle much of the detailed negotiation, and to ensure that the hidden surprises are few. In practice most of the pensions element of a transaction is relegated to a schedule, and the assumptions which both sides will use when calculating pension liabilities are provided in a letter agreed by the actuaries on each side. Also in practice it is common for larger pension funds to have their own actuary rather than the trustee's actuary.

3.2 Nature of transaction and financing

The nature and importance of pensions issues vary considerably depending on (1) the nature of the transaction, which might include the sale of a company, the sale of a business, joint venture, sale on insolvency – and, following the Pensions Act 2004, (2) the nature of the financing.

In some cases there are very few pensions issues: this can happen where neither the buyer nor the seller has a formal pension plan, either defined benefit (DB) or defined contribution (DC) (and where there is simply a mere technical legal obligation to establish a stakeholder). In practice such a transaction poses limited pensions issues. A stakeholder system, for example, does not necessarily involve any financial obligations, although there will invariably be a regulatory obligation.

Where the sale involves an employer with a stand-alone pension plan, then the formalities are relatively simple – a document establishing a change of principal employer is executed. But there remain strategic issues: who owns the surplus in the fund, or is responsible for the deficit? Have all the compliance formalities been complied with? Are there hidden contingent liabilities for former employees, for example because of equal treatment requirements for part-time employees? Is there a need for a clearance certificate from the Regulator?

Where the sale involves the sale of a business, the employees change status, they cease to be employees of the seller and become employees of the purchaser. As a consequence they leave the old pension scheme, and therefore become leavers, and enjoy rights to a deferred pension or a transfer payment to another scheme. This would mean that in a DB arrangement, employees would not necessarily enjoy 'years' of service' benefits and there may be pressure on a purchaser to increase benefits, resulting in an unexpected cost. Tactics such as making all the employees redundant before the transaction so as to avoid pensions and TUPE obligations are invariably ineffective.

Where there is a sale from a group of companies, and an employer resigns as a participating employer of a group scheme, it may trigger a demand for the payment of a deficit in relation to the employees being transferred; the way in which this deficit is dealt with is now a complex issue.

3.2.1 Defined benefit, defined contribution and non-trusteed schemes

As mentioned, there are many different kinds of pension scheme – defined benefit schemes have now been converted by legislation into guaranteed defined benefit arrangements so that employers must ensure that they are adequately funded to meet the members' expectations. Defined contribution schemes, known also as money-purchase arrangements, make few promises other than simply agreeing to accept a fixed contributions from employers and employees, and investing the funds as best they can. Both are managed and controlled by trustees.

For many reasons, not least the increasing liabilities that are being imposed on trustees, many employers these days are moving to non-trusteed, or contract-based, arrangements, often established by insurance companies or asset managers. These are often individually-based arrangements, and while their provisions may be reflected in the contracts of employment, so far as the parties of a transaction are concerned they are usually of only minor importance.

3.2.2 Documentation

The purchaser needs full information about pension liabilities, both those included in any registered schemes and those offered elsewhere (perhaps in contracts of employment or service agreements).

The documents will include:
- The trust deed and rules which establish the benefit expectations of members, transfer obligations, impact of surpluses and deficits, equal treatment obligations, liabilities of trustees and ability to amend the terms of the scheme (subject to legislation).
- The sponsor's accounts and scheme accounts which indicate the state of funding of the scheme, the contributions made, value of assets of the fund, and actuarial assumptions adopted. A purchaser's actuary will be able to indicate whether the way in which the liabilities of the fund have been calculated are along the lines the buyer might accept – or not.
- Actuarial valuations, essential where DB schemes are involved (as are statement of funding objectives) which give additional information about the health or otherwise of the scheme. In many cases they can be over three months old, and therefore not of immediate relevance, with a need for a later update. In addition

there will be a contribution schedule and statement of funding objectives which will give an indication of the rate of funding of the scheme.

- Member documents include announcements and handbooks for members; while these are of secondary importance from a contractual point of view, they provide a quick view of the kind of scheme that is involved, and the expectations of the members. In addition there may be particular promises set out in side letters and service agreements not evidenced in the main scheme documents.
- Deeds covering unregistered schemes being schemes which are not registered with HMRC but which are often established by deed (such as FURBS – funded unapproved/unregistered retirement benefit schemes and UURBS, the same but unfunded) for higher earners when the earnings cap applied before April 2006. Similar arrangements to overcome the £1.5M lifetime cap which now applies will exist in due course, perhaps as lifetime employment contracts.
- Investment documents (where appropriate) indicating whether the scheme is insured (where there might be penal surrender terms on any transfer) or self-administered, details of investment management agreements with fund managers, details of any self-investment or borrowings (now strictly controlled) including property assets let to an employer, and any unusual investments such as alternatives (hedge funds or private equity) where valuations are less easy. Small self-administered schemes (SSAS) are common in smaller companies and they often have investments closely connected with the employer; these will need special consideration. It is important not to devote time to the control of SSASs which are not intended to be regulated or controlled in the same manner as larger schemes. Vendors will need to take particular care to retain control of the schemes even as they relinquish control of the company, especially where there may be an element of surplus within them.
- Membership data is in larger cases requested by the purchaser's actuary to confirm the extent of liabilities; it is important not to contravene the requirements of the data protection legislation. Such data is invariably corrupt, albeit slightly, so that warranties given by the vendor should be limited.
- Other contracts, including engagement arrangements with advisers, such as actuaries or consultants, and quasi-contractual issues such as appointment and removal of trustees where appropriate.

3.3 Sale and purchase agreement

Different documents will be appropriate depending on whether they are issued by the purchaser's or vendor's lawyers, and whether the sale is one of shares or of the business. From a pensions point of view, as from employment, it is no longer so easy by using the business sale route to avoid pension obligations. In addition management buy-outs will be aware of the pension obligations (and may indeed wish to continue them). Proportionality is also critical; pensions are not always critical in a deal, especially if the UK element of a large international transaction is relatively minor. Nor will matters always be critical where the target company is not the principal employer of the pension scheme and is to cease to participate in it on completion.

Now that pension schemes can be registered outside the UK, it may be that overseas legal advice is required. Under EU law, pension arrangements may have a restricted meaning; in the UK "relevant benefits" mean any pension (including an annuity), lump sum, gratuity or other like benefit given or to be given on retirement or on death, or by virtue of a pension sharing order or provision, or in anticipation of retirement, or, in connection with past service, after retirement or death, or to be given on or in anticipation of or in connection with any change in the nature of the service of the employee in question. "Employee" includes (a) any officer of the company, any director of the company and any other person taking part in the management of the affairs of the company, and (b) a person who is to be or has been an employee; and the terms "service" and "retirement" are to be construed accordingly. The wording reflects the definition in *ICTA 1988 s.612(1)* (repealed from 6 April 2006 under Finance Act 2004 but still relevant). There are current issues as to whether benefits which are to be afforded solely by reason of the disablement by accident of a person occurring during his service or of his death by accident so occurring and for no other reason are covered.

3.3.1 Warranties

To limit liabilities, the purchaser will seek a number of warranties in the sale and purchase agreement, including:

1. That the vendor is not a party to any agreement or arrangement other than the pension scheme for the provision of any relevant benefits for any person. In practice there are often pension obligations contained in side letters or in special schemes for the higher-paid, such as FURBS or UURBS.

2. That the vendor has no obligation to contribute to any personal pension scheme (as defined in *Pension Schemes Act 1993 s.1*); or make available to any person a stakeholder pension scheme (as defined in *Welfare Reform and Pensions Act 1999 s.1*). Group personal pensions arrangements are now increasingly popular, because of reduced compliance requirements, and as an alternative to occupational defined contribution schemes.

3. That full documentation has been delivered to the buyer, including the trust deeds, rules and any other documents governing the pension scheme; full details of both the benefits and entitlements, and the contributions; copies of all explanatory booklets and announcements issued to members of the pension scheme (but not individual benefit statements); documents issued to members governing the current procedure for appointing member-nominated trustees or trustee directors or opting out of such a procedure; the current statement of investment principles; documents under which any actuary, auditor or other professional adviser is appointed; the current internal dispute resolution

procedure; actuarial certificates for the purposes of *PA 1995 s.67* or *Pension Schemes Act 1993 s.37*; the latest three trustees' reports and accounts (including the relevant actuarial certificates); the current schedule of contributions as required by PA 1995 (defined benefit schemes only); the current schedule of payments as required by PA 1995 (defined contribution schemes only); and a list of employees who are members of the pension scheme with enough information to be able to calculate the benefits due, and a list of employees who may be eligible to join the pension.

4. Also important is for the purchaser to be aware of details of discretionary practices (for example, in relation to early retirement terms and pension increases); and any discretion exercised under the pension scheme to augment benefits, admit to membership any individual who would not otherwise have been eligible for admission to membership, transfer any member's benefits, if the transfer payment has not yet been made (wholly or partly), provide a benefit which would not otherwise be provided, or pay a contribution which would not otherwise have been paid. A purchaser will also seek to gain confirmation that no power to augment benefits or provide additional or different benefits has been exercised under the pension scheme and no undertaking or assurance was given to any person as to the continuance introduction increase or improvement of any relevant benefits (whether or not there is any legal obligation to do so).

5. In order to enable the actuaries and other to calculate possible liabilities the purchaser will need details of all employees participating in the pension scheme including terms of participation, and in particular whether there are any arrangements outstanding in relation to the making of any bulk transfer payment from or to the pension scheme.

Technical assurances are invariably sought as to:
- Confirmation that the vendor was properly admitted as a sponsor of the pension scheme and complied with its obligations.
- Whether amounts due to the pension scheme by the vendor and members have been paid.
- Whether the vendor can terminate liability to contribute to the pension scheme without notice, without the consent of any person and without further payment.
- Whether death in service benefits are fully insured, and insurance premiums have been paid.
- Whether actuarial, consultancy, legal and other fees have been paid.

6. The purchaser will need to know who the current trustees are, together with details of any member-nominated trustees (and when and how they were appointed).

7. The purchaser will need to know about any litigation or complaints (whether internal or external).

8. The purchaser will need to know that the scheme is registered under *FA 2004 s.150(2)*.

9. The purchaser will need to know whether the scheme is contracted-out, and if so that it has a proper contracted-out certificate.

10. It is important that the pension scheme, the trustees and the various sponsors have been compliant (with their own provisions and those of legislation). There are often issues with part-time employees who may have been illegally excluded from membership

11. Purchasers need to know whether there are ex-gratia benefits, unenforceable but troublesome if discontinued.

12. Employers frequently indemnify the scheme for administrative and other expenses; purchasers need to get a feel of the level of such expenses and whether they can be incurred without consent. In addition the purchaser should be told of any employer guarantees or indemnities.

13. There is usually a declaration as to whether the scheme is closed to new members and whether any steps have been taken to wind-up the scheme (which might trigger large payments from the employer).

14. A TUPE assurance is often requested (i.e. that since 1 May 1982 no employee has had his contract of employment transferred in from another employer in circumstances where the Transfer of Undertakings (Protection of Employment) Regulations (TUPE) applied to the transfer. Similarly assurance can be sought that no transfer value has been paid into the scheme from another arrangement under which the benefit contravened the equal treatment provisions of the Treaty of Rome.

15. Purchasers are keen to establish that there is no prospect of financial support directions or contribution notices nor that any sponsor has entered into a withdrawal arrangement (*Occupational Pension Schemes (Employer Debt) Regulations 2005 reg.2*). The usual warranties in connection with insolvency are also invariably sought (in particular that actions have been taken to avoid a pensions debt).

16. It is conventional to explore whether actuarial advice has been taken on funding gain and confirmation that contributions have been properly paid. It is helpful if copies of the last two actuarial valuation reports and all actuarial advice on funding matters made within the last three years are made available.

17. Assurances are given on the quality of the data supplied The data delivered to the actuary preparing the latest actuarial valuation reports relating to the pension scheme referred to in paragraph 16 above was accurate and complete in all material respects. Such reports give a true and fair view of the liabilities under the pension scheme at the effective dates of such valuations on the basis of the methods and assumptions set out therein. There has been no material adverse change in the financial position of the pension scheme since the effective dates of the valuations.

18. The critical element, over and above any compliance and technical issues is the question of whether the assets are sufficient to meet the liabilities on a basis which satisfies both the needs of the regulator and the requirements of the purchaser. The funding requirements will need to take account of not only the current accrued rights but also discretionary benefits normally given, and equalisation costs, and costs which arise from future increases in salary. There is nowadays sometimes a request that there should be sufficient funds to meet any s.75 (wind-up) costs, but such an assurance is rarely given.

19. The pension scheme accounts and trustees reports can help to give a better picture of the strength of the scheme; as can the statement of investment principles. Most purchasers look to see recent copies of any other documents available and need some comfort that there are no employer-related investments or that assets are being used for stock-lending where there may be a risk of non-recovery.

20. More relevantly, purchasers and vendors now are keen to see some warranties in relation to possible clearance by the Regulator. The purchaser may seek a warranty that the information the vendor provides in contemplation of an application (or decision not to apply for clearance) by the vendor to the Regulator for clearance *PA 2004 ss.42 or 46* are accurate.

21. Similarly it is fashionable now to seek assurances that the vendor is not conflicted in relation to investments or professional or administrative services provided to the fund.

22. Life assurance (and permanent health insurance) is frequently organised outside the pension fund; the purchaser needs to inspect the policy, and be satisfied that there are no claims under the policy, that it is in force, and that the insurer is not going to repudiate liability. There are implications (see page 46) in relation to the application of TUPE (or not) in relation to non-pension benefits offered by the scheme.

23. It is conventional to give an assurance that there have been no reports made to the Regulator about the operation of the scheme.

24. Where there is a possibility of the vendor having taken over employees from the public sector, a purchaser will need to explore what kinds of special pension guarantees have been given; these can prove expensive and difficult to manage

25. Family-managed companies often have what used to be known as 'small-self administered pension schemes' (SSASs) which at one time had special compliance requirements including the need for the appointment of HMRC approved trustees. Most of those requirements no longer apply, but there may be legacy obligations (e.g. to pay for trustees) and any surpluses will need to be dealt with separately.

The purpose of the warranties is both to protect the purchaser (given that liability is conventionally based on caveat emptor) and to encourage the vendor to disclose as much material as possible so that the purchaser is left under no misapprehension as to the extent of liabilities. In practice, disclosure may be more important than warranties. It may be preferable for a purchaser to abort a deal where disclosures indicate a potential problem than for detailed warranties to be agreed in the absence of extensive disclosures. Disclosures provide a purchaser with a good indication of potential financial and other exposures; warranties may be less beneficial, especially since it is inefficient to rely on the need for litigation to enforce warranties, which in any event may be worthless if the warrantor is not in funds.

Also in practice some of the concerns may be dealt with elsewhere in a sale and purchase agreement (perhaps, in relation to pensions, with the employment warranties). Any due diligence report and engagement letter from the lawyers will invariably indicate that the purchaser client should rely on actuarial, accountancy or consultancy advice especially in relation to funding adequacies.

It is generally recognised that warranties can be distinguished from indemnities in several ways; a warranty is a statement by the warrantor as to a particular state of affairs, a breach of which will only give rise to a successful claim in damages if the purchaser for example can show that the warranty was breached and that the effect of the breach is to reduce the value of his purchase. A purchaser therefore needs to demonstrate both a breach and a quantifiable loss. An indemnity by contrast is a promise to reimburse the purchaser where a particular liability arises; the purpose of an indemnity is to provide a guaranteed remedy on an indemnity basis in circumstances where a breach of warranty does not necessarily give rise to a claim in damages, or to provide a specific remedy which might not otherwise be available. For example, if the vendor warrants that the scheme is compliant with relevant legislation and the purchaser later discovers a breach, the value of the purchase may not have been adversely affected but the scheme may incur expense to ensure compliance. An indemnity from the vendor to the purchaser would enable recovery of those costs.

Warranties are also generally distinguished from undertakings. A warranty is a statement of fact, the truth of which is guaranteed by the warrantor; an undertaking is a promise by a party to take certain action, which is only worth considering where the party giving the undertaking is in fact able to take the action undertaken when required.

Practical constraints on claims under the pension warranties include de minimis provisions and, usually, an overall cap. Potential pension scheme liabilities alone can often exceed such caps. There are also invariably limitation periods for the pension warranties. Claims under a simple contract or claims in respect of breach of trust must be brought within six years of the date on which the cause of action accrues (*Limitation Act 1980*). A right of action is not deemed to have accrued to any beneficiary entitled to a future interest until the interest falls into possession, so claims may be brought by beneficiaries (especially dependants) in respect of actions that occurred some time before such breach of trust. An express or implied agreement to exclude the provisions of the Limitation Act may be valid where supported by consideration. A clause which provides, for example, a seven year limitation period for claims under the pension warranties may exclude the Limitation Act by implication; in practice an express exclusion is usually sought if appropriate. It is good practice for a purchaser to seek to extend the period for pension warranties (as with tax warranties) beyond the period given for warranties generally (say six years instead of three years).

Since there is often a time gap between exchange and completion, it may be appropriate to ensure that the warranties are given as at completion; and where (rarely these days) there is to be an interim participation period, some of the warranties are taken as starting as at the end of the participation period.

Weasel phrases such as "as far as the vendor is aware" intended by a vendor to weaken the strength of warranties (or "use reasonable/best endeavours", "as far as the vendor/guarantor is aware", "reasonable", "significant", "substantive", "relevant" or "material") may nonetheless indicate a duty for the vendor to use reasonable endeavours to investigate before giving any warranty; and contractual provisions that, in the case of a breach of warranty, the purchaser has the option to recover normal damages or to recover on an indemnity basis, whichever is more favourable. There is little consistency in practice in putting the warranties on an indemnity basis; and indemnities may be agreed for specific identified risks. Much depends on the relative bargaining strength of the parties.

There is a material distinction, however, made between "reasonable endeavours" and "best endeavours". A best endeavours obligation is not "the next best thing to an absolute obligation or a guarantee" (*Midland Land Reclamation Ltd and Leicestershire County Council v Warren Energy Limited, 1997, unreported*); the concept of reasonableness is an intrinsic part of "best endeavours". An obligation to use best endeavours imposes a duty to do what can reasonably be done in the circumstances: "the standard of reasonableness is that of a reasonable and prudent board of directors, acting properly in the interest of their company." (*Terrell v Mabie Todd & Coy Ltd [1952] 69 RPC 234*). Accordingly a party which has given a best endeavours undertaking must:

- take action which, having regard to costs and degree of difficulty, is commercially practicable. However, performance of such an undertaking would not require the company to take action which could lead to its financial ruin, or which would undermine its commercial standing or goodwill;

- incur such expenditure which is reasonable in taking such action; and
- act in the interests of the company.

3.4   Pensions and TUPE

3.4.1   Introduction

Special considerations now apply to the issue of the protection of employees' pension rights when their employer is sold above their heads. The issue of employee protection was initially considered by lawmakers too difficult to resolve. The original Acquired Rights Directive 1977 (ARD), as implemented by TUPE, introduced into the UK the idea that on the transfer of an undertaking, or part of an undertaking, the transferor employer's rights, obligations and liabilities arising under the contracts of employment of the transferring employees pass to the transferee employer.

But, under the ARD, pension rights were excluded from protection; these excluded rights were defined as 'employees' rights to old-age, invalidity or survivors' benefits under supplementary company or inter-company pension schemes outside the statutory social security schemes in Member States' (ARD Article 3(3)). In the UK the exemption was reflected in the terms of Transfer of Undertaking Regulations 1981 Regulation 7(1) (TUPE 1981) which provided that TUPE did not apply:
'(a) to so much of a contract of employment or collective agreement as relates to an occupational pension scheme...; or
(b) to any rights, powers, duties or liabilities under or in connection with any such contract or subsisting by virtue of any such agreement and relating to such a scheme or otherwise arising in connection with that person's employment and relating to such a scheme.'

The exclusion was limited; it did not cover 'any provisions of an occupational pension scheme which do not relate to benefits for old age, invalidity or survivors shall be treated as not being part of the scheme.' (cf. *TUPE 2006 Regulation 10(2)*). This exclusion of an exclusion was eventually the subject of court decisions.

3.4.2   The pensions exclusion

By and large the pensions exclusion operated to make transferee employers free from any requirement to provide any pensions arrangements at all to transferring employees. In practice many employers recognised the industrial relations consequences of a failure to provide, but at the same time it made it easier for purchasers of business to provide if they wished uniform pension arrangements for both existing and acquired workforces. Any ill-will that could be engendered by having colleagues working side-by-side but on different pension arrangements because of their employment history (i.e. which particular acquisition they had come across with) could therefore be ameliorated. But any provision was purely discretionary at the option of the new employer.

The exclusion appeared to relate only to workplace pensions. It did not appear to cover personal pensions established under the contract of employment – or even group personal pensions. The position of stakeholder pensions is anomalous, because they are treated in the social security legislation as occupational schemes – though (at one time before the distinction was removed) as personal pensions for tax purposes, but the consensus is that they did not come under the exclusion provisions. Accordingly contract-based pension obligations, such as personal pension arrangements, even though intermediated by the employer, seemed to pass under TUPE from a transferor employer to a transferee employer. A transferee employer is therefore obliged to continue to contribute to a transferring employees' personal pension schemes at the same rate at which the transferor employer was making contributions immediately prior to the date of the TUPE transfer. The formerly separate treatment of workplace and personal pensions under the fiscal legislation was consolidated under FA 2004 as from April 2006, but this does not affect the social security or employment treatment, under which the distinction continues (*Pension Schemes Act 1993 s.1*, as amended by *PA 2004 s.239*).

There were political objections to the TUPE pensions exclusion (mostly by unions), but its legal validity was upheld by the courts. In *Warrener v Walden Engineering Co Ltd (1992) PBLR 1* for example the query was whether following a TUPE transfer, a transferee employer could refuse to provide replacement pension arrangements for transferring employees, even though the transferring employees had been members of the transferor employer's occupational pension scheme at the time the business was sold.

Initially the Industrial Tribunal held that, although the ARD 'could not protect rights of membership of a particular pension scheme', the occupational pension scheme in question was not a 'supplementary pension scheme" for the purposes of Article 3(3) (because as a contracted-out scheme, it stood in place of, rather than 'supplemental' to the state pension scheme) – and therefore did not fall within the scope of the pensions exclusion under the ARD. On appeal the Employment Appeal Tribunal overturned the decision (*Walden Engineering Co Ltd v Warrener (1993) PBLR*) and held that even a contracted-out occupational pension scheme (i.e. one which also provides state benefits) is a supplementary scheme for the purposes of ARD and TUPE and therefore capable of falling within the exclusion provisions of both pieces of legislation.

Warrener was later approved in *Adams & Others v Lancashire County Council and BET Catering Services Ltd ([1996] PBLR; [1997] PBLR)*. Eleven (part-time) dinner ladies had their employments transferred from Lancashire County Council to BET Catering Services. Whilst they had worked directly for the Council, the dinner ladies had built up rights under the Local Government Pension Scheme. Following the transfer the dinner ladies were not offered membership of the scheme of the new employer and sued. The High Court and later the Court of Appeal held that an employee's occupational pension rights broadly did not transfer under TUPE from a transferor employer to a transferee employer regardless of the transfer of his or her employment.

3.4.3 Limited effect of the exclusion

Later cases explored whether certain rights offered by a pension scheme, but (1) which may not be pension rights subject to the exclusion, and therefore (2) capable of passing under TUPE (notwithstanding Warrener and Adams) were in fact protected. In *Beckmann v Dynamco Whicholoe Macfarlane (2002 PBLR)* Mrs Beckmann was employed by the National Health Service and a member of the NHS Scheme and her employment was transferred to Dynamco in 1995. In 1997 she was made redundant, and a dispute arose as to whether she was entitled to certain benefits payable as a result of redundancy, which were provided under her former employer's pension scheme (the NHS pension scheme). The question was whether the relevant benefits (being an early retirement pension and certain lump sum benefits) were 'old age benefits' and therefore capable of falling within the scope of the pensions exclusion of TUPE 1981. The ECJ concluded that the exception contained in Article 3(3) of ARD was to be interpreted strictly and that exception applied only to the types of benefits specifically listed in the exclusion – and in particular not redundancy benefits.

The Beckmann decision, and the later ruling in *Martin v South Bank University (2003 PLR 199)* contributed to considerable uncertainty. In Martin nursing lecturers had been employed by the NHS and were members of the NHS pension scheme. In 1994 the college in which they lectured became part of South Bank University and they ceased to be eligible to be members of the NHS pension scheme. They became instead members of the (less generous) teachers' scheme.

In 1997 the lecturers accepted early retirement, but the University considered that they were entitled to the less generous early retirement benefits provided under the teachers' superannuation scheme. Eventually the ECJ held that early retirement provisions which applied on dismissal were not excluded by TUPE 1981. The TUPE pensions exclusion was therefore limited and some (pensions-like) rights did pass on a transfer. As a consequence some employers and pension schemes have reviewed the terms and benefits offered. Pension schemes meanwhile continue to distinguish between the position of a deferred pensioner seeking early retirement from the early retirement of an active member.

Trying to establish just what are the obligations capable of being transferred therefore can be difficult, and the parties may either simply take such risks as there are, or rely on vendor's warranties. In the meantime, TUPE 2006 Regulation 10(3) provides that a TUPE employee is not entitled to bring a claim against his former (transferor) employer for breach of contract or constructive unfair dismissal under the Employment Rights Act 1996 s.95(1)(c) arising out of a loss or reduction in his rights under an occupational pension scheme in consequence of the TUPE transfer, except where the alleged breach of contract or dismissal occurred before 6 April 2005. Accordingly liability rests with the transferee employer, rather than the transferor employer.

The TUPE pensions exclusion does not prevent the transfer of responsibility for discrimination claims from passing from a transferor employer to a transferee employer on a TUPE transfer. This might be relevant where there are possible claims for breach of equal pensions treatment, (e.g. where there are different retirement ages) (see e.g. *Barber v GRE* and *Coloroll*) particularly acute where a company employed part-timers.

Public sector deals
Public sector transfers do not enjoy exemption from pensions issues, and there are special rules protecting such employees issued by the Treasury and the Government Actuary's Department. To protect past service rights, a new employer's replacement pension scheme must be prepared to accept a bulk transfer of accrued pension rights, and appropriate transfer credits provided (see also Cabinet Office's "Statement of Practice on Staff Transfers in the Public Sector").

3.4.4   TUPE and the Pensions Act 2004
The Pensions Act 2004 adds limited pensions protection for transferring employees who are members of occupational pension schemes and who are subject to a TUPE transfer (*PA 2004 ss.257, 258; The Transfer of Undertakings (Protection of Employment) Regulations 2006 SI 2006 No 246 (TEPPR)*). The legislation follows lengthy consultation over many years. PA 2004 s.257(I) indicates the circumstances which must exist before the new pension protection requirements apply and in particular:
(a) there must be a transfer of undertaking (or part of an undertaking) capable of constituting a TUPE transfer;
(b) as a consequence of the TUPE transfer, the (transferring) employees must cease to be employed by the transferor employer and instead become employed by the transferee employer; and
(c) immediately before the TUPE transfer occurs, the transferor employer must have participated in an occupational pension scheme, and the transferring employees must either have been:
   (i) active members of the scheme (and if the scheme provides money purchase benefits, the transferor employer must either be required to make employer contributions on behalf of those of the transferring employees who are active members of the scheme, or have previously made one or more such contributions even if not legally obliged to do so); or

(ii) eligible to have become active members (and, if the scheme provides money purchase benefits, the transferor employer must have been obliged to make employer contributions in respect of any transferring employee had that employee in fact been an active member of the scheme); or

(iii) be in a "membership waiting period" which (had they been able to complete but for the fact of the TUPE transfer) would upon its conclusion enabled them to either become active members of the scheme or otherwise be eligible to become active members (and, again, if the scheme provides money purchase benefits, the transferor employer must have been obliged to make employer contributions in respect of any transferring employee had that employee in fact been an active member of the scheme).

'Eligibility' in *PA 2004 s.257* could mean either (1) where employees have an unfettered right to accrue to the pension scheme (which they may or may not choose to exercise), or (2) where employee access requires the consent of, for example, the employer (see e.g. David Pollard, *Pensions and TUPE*, (2005) (June) 34 (2) *Industrial Law Journal*).

Where the transferee employer is required to provide a minimum level of replacement pension provision, the transferor employer may resolve his outstanding obligations in one of several ways *(PA 2004 ss.258 (2) and (3)* and Regulations). The transferor employer can ensure that as from the date of the transfer:

(a) the transferring employees are, or are able to be, active members of the employer's occupational pension scheme; or

(b) the transferee employer either makes relevant contributions to an appropriate stakeholder pension scheme.

If the transferee employer provides an occupational pension scheme for the transferring employees, certain technical conditions apply. There are further conditions that the transferor employer must satisfy. Where there is a money purchase scheme, the transferee employer must make relevant contributions on behalf of those transferring employees who elect to become active members of the scheme *(PA 2004 s.258(2)(b))*. Where the scheme is not a money purchase scheme, the transferee employer must ensure that the pension scheme satisfies a minimum standard *(Pension Schemes Act 1993 s.12A*; the Pension Protection Regulations; *PA 2004 s.258(2)(c))*.

The Pension Protection Regulations provide that the transferee employer's pension scheme satisfies the prescribed conditions if it provides either (reg. 2):

(a) for members to be entitled to benefits the value of which equals or exceeds 6% of pensionable pay for each year of employment (rather than each year of pensionable service) together with the total amount of any contributions made by the members, and, where members are required to make contributions to the scheme, for them to contribute at a rate which does not exceed 6% of their pensionable pay; or

(b) for the transferee employer to make relevant contributions to the scheme on behalf of each employee (and it should be noted that the reference is not to each transferring employee) who is an active member of the pension scheme.

A member's "pensionable pay" is that part of the remuneration payable to a member of a pension scheme by reference to which the amount of contributions and benefits are determined under the rules of the scheme (reg. 2(2)). Some schemes provide different definitions of pensionable pay for the purposes of calculating contribution rates and determining pension benefits (as in the case for some pension schemes); in these cases the transferee employer complies if it treats the members' pensionable pay as being the greater of the pay as defined for the purposes of calculating contribution rates and the pay as defined for benefit calculation purposes.

The transferee employer's contributions are "relevant contributions" for the purposes of the legislation if (reg. 3(1)):

(a) the contributions are made in respect of each period for which the employee is paid remuneration, provided that the employee also contributes to the pension scheme in respect of that period; and

(b) the amount contributed by the transferee employer in respect of each such period is of an amount which is at least equal to the amount contributed by the employee, provided that if the employee's contribution in respect of the relevant period equals or exceeds 6% of the employee's remuneration, the transferee employee is only obliged to contribute at a rate which is at least equal to 6% of the employee's remuneration.

Only gross basic pay (ignoring any pension contributions other than minimum payments within the meaning of the Pensions Schemes Act 1993 in relation to contracted-out pension schemes) is taken into account; no account is taken of bonuses, commission, payments, overtime or payments of a similar nature. The transferring employee(s) and the transferee employer may agree to disapply the pension protection requirements, and agree to an alternative pension arrangement of their own choosing (*PA 2004 s.258(6)*).

3.4.5 Summary
Even under the new TUPE provisions, pensions exclusion continues, and can prevent the transfer of legal obligations in respect of occupational pension schemes from a transferor employer to a transferee employer. Public sector transfers have no exclusion arrangements at all. Beckmann/Martin-type rights are capable of passing from one employer to another upon a TUPE transfer. Meanwhile,

uncertainty remains about the extent to which rights in pension schemes are regarded as not pension rights and therefore not capable of exclusion. Finally, PA 2004 requires transferee employers in the private sector to provide minimum replacement pension arrangements.

3.5 Consultation with employees

Where there is any material change to pension arrangements, as invariably occurs on a merger or reconstruction, employers are required to consult with employees (*The Information and Consultation of Employees Regulations 2004 SI 2004 No. 3426; The Occupational Pension Schemes (Consultation by Employers) (Modification for Multi-employer Schemes) Regulations 2006 SI 2006 No.16; The Occupational and Personal Pension Schemes (Consultation by Employers and Miscellaneous Amendment) Regulations 2006 SI 2006 No. 349*). If a stakeholder pension arrangement is intended to be established, an employer is required to consult with the relevant employees and any organisations representing them (*Welfare Reform and Pensions Act 1999 s.(2)*).

Consultation generally

In principle employers and employees can always agree contractually to consultation on pension matters. The default consultation requirements (not the specific pensions consultation regulations) (reg. 20) require employers to:

(a) provide information on recent and probable development of the employer's activities and economic situation;

(b) provide information on, and consult about, probable development of employment and relevant measures; and

(c) provide information on, and consult about, decisions likely to lead to substantial changes in work organisation or contractual relations.

Some observers have suggested that pensions fall within (c) (see e.g. DTI, Guidance, January 2006); this seems improbable since the category does not cover changes in pay or benefits that have a monetary value, and the EU Information and Consultation Directive 2002/14/EC (on which the regulations are based) are promoted under EU Treaty Article 137 which does not cover pay; under EU law it is clear that pay includes pensions.

Recognised trade unions

An independent trade union may demand that an employer recognises it with respect to a specified group of workers with respect to negotiations on pay, hours and holiday (*Trade Union and Labour Relations (Consolidation) Act 1992 s.70 and schedule 1; Employment Relations Act 1999 s.1 and schedule 1*). In UNIFI and the *Union Bank of Nigeria plc [2001] IRLR 712, CAC* it was held that pay may include certain aspects of pensions (for example contributions to defined contribution pension schemes and benefits payable under defined benefit schemes).

Contracting Out

Employers are required to consult trade unions and employees in relation to the issue, variation or surrender of a contracting out certificate (*Pension Schemes Act 1993 s.11; Occupational Pension Schemes (Contracting-Out) Regulations 1996 SI 1996 No 1172*).

TUPE

As mentioned the TUPE reg. 10 requires an employer to:

"inform appropriate representatives of the affected employees, long enough before a relevant transfer to enable consultation with the appropriate representatives, on various matters in relation to the transfer; and

consult with appropriate representatives of any affected employees in relation to whom the employer envisages taking measures".

The provisions have now been overtaken by the dedicated pensions regulations mentioned above; even so the duty to consult only arises when the employer envisages taking "measures" (an undefined term) in relation to the affected employee. TUPE does not give any assistance as to what is meant by "measures". There is no formal timetable for consultation under TUPE, although failure to inform and consult may result in a "protective award" issued by an employment tribunal, subject to a maximum of 13 weeks pay per employee.

TULRCA

The Trade Union and Labour Relations (Consolidation) Act 1992 sets out consultation requirements in relation to certain redundancy exercises. Where an employer proposes to make 20 or more redundancies to take effect within a period of 90 days, these redundancies must be the subject of consultation with the trade union or elected representative. Consultation must begin in "good time" and in any event:

(a) where the employer is proposing to dismiss 100 or more employees, at least 90 days; or

(b) otherwise at least 30 days.

before the first of the dismissals take effect.

The consultation process must include consultation about ways of avoiding redundancies, reducing the number of employees to be made redundant and mitigating the consequences of the redundancies.

In *GMB v Man Truck & Bus UK Limited (2000) IRLR 636* it was held that where sufficient employees are dismissed and re-engaged on new terms this triggers the consultation requirements of TULCRA s.188. Where the decision to dismiss has already been taken prior to the consultation, the consultation may well be viewed as a sham (*Middlesbrough Borough Council v TGWU [2002] IRLR 332*). There are suggestions that the UK implementation of the requirements does not meet the terms of the EU Directive (*Jung v Kuhnel (Case ECJ 188/03 ECJ)*) where the ECJ held that a period of notice and consultation cannot take place concurrently and that consultation would not be proper if notice to terminate employment had already been given, compared TULCRA s.188 and the Collective Redundancies Directive (*Directive 98/59/EC*). The Directive for example indicates consultation is required where collective redundancies are "contemplated". TULCRA s.188 requires consultation where dismissals are "proposed". Public sector employers are able to rely on the direct enforceability of the Directive.

3.5.1 Duty of mutual trust and confidence

A duty of mutual trust and confidence applies to the way in which employers deal with pension arrangements. It seems probable that this duty requires employees to be consulted on changes to pension schemes.

3.5.2 Pensions Act 1995 s.67

There are complex restrictions on the amendments of scheme provisions. PA 1995 s.67 as amended by PA 2004 s.262 provides that a power to amend the rules cannot be exercised so as to affect any accrued right or pension credit right unless certain consent or actuarial certification requirements are met. The consent and actuarial certification requirements require the trustees to:

- give the member information in writing adequate to explain the nature of the modification and its effects on him;
- notify the member in writing that he may make representations to the trustees about the modification;
- give the member a reasonable opportunity to make such representations; and
- notify him in writing that the consent requirements apply in his case in respect of the modification (or the certification requirements as appropriate).

3.5.3 Other requirements

In special circumstances, there may be additional requirements for consultation. These could include:

- Some schemes have rules which require a form of democratic governance, with consultation required of members before material changes are made.
- There may be collective agreements entered into with a workforce or with appropriate trade unions.
- There are requirements to consult on member nominated trustee arrangements under the regulations relating to the appointment of member-nominated trustees.

4 Clearance

4.1 Background

4.1.1 The moral hazard issue

Now that defined benefit pension funds enjoy the benefit of a protection fund in case of failure, there is always the possibility of employers and trustees engineering the structure of their companies to take undue advantage of the protection. They could do this for example by restructuring a plan sponsor as an uncapitalised shell company, and then allowing the scheme to wind-up in deficit. This would impose unacceptable costs on the protection fund (funded by the contributions of solvent schemes and employers) and controls were therefore imposed to limit such claims.

These 'moral hazard' controls, set out in the Pensions Act 2004 impose unlimited contingent personal liabilities on company directors and even their advisers and bankers – liabilities which may breach any veil of incorporation.

The unlimited extent of these potential liabilities (which could be imposed using draconian powers of the Regulator) which far outweighed in many if not most cases the personal wealth of individuals, have led to considerable pressure from industry to change the original draft legislation. The reform introduced a system of 'clearance', so that the Regulator could confirm as a deal was being completed, that there would, in that particular case, be no possibility of personal liability.

In practice it is not yet clear whether the clearance procedure is working to give the protections sought; the reason for this is that the Regulator finds it difficult to grant absolute clearances, and reserves the right to reopen matters if there is a future deficit and corporate failure of the sponsor. A 'provisional' or limited clearance may reduce the risk on directors, trustees and others, but the contingent liabilities remain and can be invoked if the Regulator subsequently finds information it was not properly informed of but which could have led it to refuse clearance had it been aware of it the time. The fact that, even if there is no successful claim in future years, the Regulator could open or reopen an expensive investigation in the event of a future corporate failure is a material risk, and for most individuals such risk is too high to carry; the fact that the Regulator itself is reluctant to assume risk highlights the issue.

Nonetheless, clearances are available, and in some cases may be helpful for the parties to obtain. The procedures of obtaining clearance are set out below; they can involve some complexity and expense, which may be some of the reasons that they are infrequently sought.

In practice, it is not yet clear whether clearance procedures are having a detrimental impact on legitimate (i.e. non evasive) corporate activity; the evidence seems mixed. Nonetheless, the potential piercing of the corporate veil raises financial reporting, tax and distributable profits issues. Some of these issues were identified by a multi-disciplinary ICAEW Moral Hazards Working Party, comprising insolvency practitioners, corporate restructuring specialists, M&A lawyers, actuaries, financial reporting specialists, pensions auditors, and representatives from the APB and SRAP (Special Reports of Accountants Panel), which had been established by the ICAEW to identify and deal with such issues. Issues still outstanding include:

- Financial reporting – whether financial support directions should be recorded as provisions, and how they sit with the requirements of IAS 19 that allows groups to have a policy to spread liabilities around the group or opt to record the whole amount in the employer's accounts;
- Tax – whether group companies issued with financial support directions requiring them to pay contributions into another group scheme be given tax relief if the employer would have received relief; and
- Distributable profit implications – whether payments to fellow subsidiaries are considered to be distributions, the payment might be illegal if the paying company does not have sufficient distributable profits.

Initial recommendations made to the Regulator included that financial support directions should be worded to allow the most sensible financial reporting, tax and distributable profits treatment, and approaches might need to be made to HMRC and UITF to ascertain tax and accounting treatments in individual circumstances.

4.2   Whether to apply for clearance

Two of the main statutory objectives of the Regulator are both the protection of members' benefits and the reduction of risks to the newly-created Pension Protection Fund (PPF); it regards the greatest threat to defined benefit schemes in both these respects is that of underfunding; other observers might regard the major threat to be that of employer insolvency or withdrawal of support. Nonetheless the Regulator is understandably keen to see the funding of defined benefit schemes promoted to a high level to reduce risks to the PPF, even though this may eventually result in schemes being overfunded or at the expense of the proper use of capital.

In the Regulator's opinion, a particular risk to members' benefits arises when an employer sponsoring a defined benefit pension scheme carries out certain types of corporate transactions. Some transactions (such as highly leveraged private equity buy-outs, or the purchase of a solvent employer by a less solvent purchaser) can affect the strength of employer support to the scheme – and hence its viability. The Regulator worries that these kinds of transactions can put members' benefits at risk, and result in an unnecessary or inflated call on the PPF. The PPF is of course funded by competing and more solvent elements of industry who do not take kindly to subsidising their less efficient competitors.

The Regulator is therefore armed with anti-avoidance powers which are intended to ensure that work-based pension schemes are strongly financed. Where it considers that there has been a deliberate attempt to avoid pension liabilities, the Regulator can take a number of steps, including:

- issue a contribution notice, not only to the employer, but to anyone involved in the attempted avoidance, requiring payment of any amount (up to the full buy-out debt).
- Where the sponsoring employer is an insufficiently resourced company within a group for example, following corporate restructuring, issue a financial support direction requiring financial arrangements to be put in place to support the employer's pension liabilities.

Where used these powers can be material; they were introduced into the legislation without consultation because of a certain paranoia at the time that companies would seek to avoid their responsibilities if given time to do so. Nonetheless, following something of an uproar within industry trade bodies, a clearance procedure was introduced, designed to give protection against future contribution or financial support notices by the Regulator. The intention was that those considering transactions involving companies with defined benefit pension schemes could gain certainty, through a clearance statement, that their intended actions would not be found retrospectively to have fallen foul of the legislation.

There is no requirement to apply for clearance; but having regard to the number of corporate transactions completed every day in the UK the number of applications for clearance is surprisingly low. While a clearance statement from the Regulator provides some comfort, particularly in transactions involving the rescue of core solvent businesses, the procedure for obtaining one can also be time-consuming and expensive. And in any event the obtaining of such a certificate does not give perfect indemnity against future claims. In practice most parties after due consideration (perhaps because the scheme is adequately funded, or because they do not wish to run the risk of being refused clearance) avoid seeking a certificate.

The power for a Regulator to issue clearance certificates is not unknown amongst regulators; it applies with HMRC, or with the Financial Services Authority for example. But the Regulator in this case constrains its risk by adding the caveat that any certificate is subject to the parties having made due disclosure of all relevant facts – leaving it free to reopen the case if there is a corporate failure at some time in the future where a defined benefit scheme finds itself short of funds or making a claim against the PPF.

4.3   The Regulator's methodology

The Pensions Regulator is the regulatory body for work-based pension schemes in the UK; it replaced the former Occupational Pensions Regulatory Authority which was dissolved as not being fit for purpose. The former regulator had been abolished and replaced because of criticism by several government agencies that it had been excessively pedantic, bureaucratic and interested in form rather than substance. Accordingly PA 2004 gave the Pensions Regulator a set of specific objectives. These include:

- to protect the benefits of members of work-based pension schemes;
- to reduce the risk of situations arising that may lead to claims for compensation from the PPF; and
- to promote good administration of work-based pension schemes.

The first two objectives can on occasion prove mutually incompatible; in some cases the interests of members conflict with the need to limit claims on the PPF, and these conflicting objectives pose practical dilemmas to the Regulator. It appears in practice that it places the interests of the PPF above those of day-to-day commercial activities.

In order to meet these objectives, however, its policy (though not necessarily practice) is to adopt a risk-based approach and to concentrate its resources on schemes where it identifies the greatest risk to the security of members' benefits. It also adopts an approach not universally (or even widely) accepted by independent observers, that under the legislation a defined benefit pension scheme is made a material unsecured creditor of the sponsor. The Regulator in practice seems to have extended even this view to a view that a DB pension scheme in deficit should be regarded as one of the company's bankers responsibilities, something which many observers consider inappropriate. The analogy certainly seems an awkward one [see Ian Greenstreet, *Should trustees be more like bankers?*, paper to the Association of Pension Lawyers, 17 July 2004, (www.apl.org.uk)].

4.3.1 The Regulator's powers

The Pensions Regulator has stated that its principal approach to meeting its objectives is to prevent problems from developing in the first place. Where possible, the Regulator indicates, it will provide support and advice to trustees, administrators, employers and others where potential problems are identified, and aim for transparency (both by communication and by action) from all the relevant parties.

However, the Pensions Act 2004 provides it with a range of powers – as well as those inherit under former legislation – to enable it to meet its ostensible objectives. It has declared that it would use its powers 'flexibly, reasonably, proportionately and appropriately', with the aim of achieving a sustainable balance between the rights and obligations of the pension scheme as a creditor and the commercial objectives of the employer. There are serious concerns about whether these aspirations are in fact being achieved or indeed are even achievable.

4.3.2 Background - general

Until 1997 there was no statutory requirement (deeds and rules apart) prescribing the amount of funding of defined benefit pension arrangements. In practice, this caused few problems; a combination of trust law, employer paternalism and common sense operated to ensure that schemes most of the time maintained sufficient assets to meet most obligations. A combination of circumstances (inflation, tighter preservation rules) over time converted the 'best endeavours' promise into semi-guaranteed obligations to meet pension expectations. In 1997 the Pensions Act 1995 set a 'minimum funding requirement'. On 11 June 2003, solvent and insolvent companies were required at all times to at least meet the MFR when they closed schemes. Later these requirements were extended to those explored in the earlier chapters.

The Pensions Act 2004, the introduction of the PPF and regulations regarding the deficit on wind-up (*The Occupational Pension Schemes (Winding Up and Deficiency on Winding Up etc) (Amendment) Regulations 2004* and *The Occupational Pension Schemes (Winding Up, Deficiency on Winding Up and Transfer Values)(Amendment) Regulations 2005 (SI 2005/72)*) increased employer liabilities so that the debt owed to the pension scheme when it winds up, regardless of whether the employer is solvent or insolvent, is calculated on a full buy-out basis. This is the most expensive basis, representing the cost of buying equivalent benefits from an insurer; the cost is higher because of the insurer's need to make solvency reserves and profits as well as making prudent assumptions about future mortality experience. It also far and away exceeds the employer's expected obligations when establishing the scheme; it was one of the reasons the scheme was in the first place established as a workplace arrangement rather than an insured arrangement.

The Regulator has been given specific powers to deal with two particular situations. The powers maybe less in order to protect scheme members' benefits, and more to ensure that employers do not avoid their pension liabilities or do not stand behind them in a meaningful way, thus increasing the levy paid to the PPF by responsible employers. The two main situations are:

- *Contribution notices (PA 2004 ss.38-42)* – where there is an act or failure to avoid pension liabilities.
- *Financial support directions (PA 2004 ss.43-51)* – when the employer in relation to the scheme is a service company or insufficiently resourced.

These are not the only powers; the Regulator is also awarded a range of other instruments and tools to achieve its objectives, e.g. to appoint an independent trustee (*PA 1995 s.7*) or to require additional funding on a different basis to that adopted by the parties.

The contribution notice and financial support direction powers were brought into the Pensions Bill in April 2004 without consultation, to avoid giving notice to those who might try to avoid their pension liabilities; certain amendments were later made – in particular the introduction of a statutory clearance procedure. It was justified not only as a way of allowing business to proceed – but also as a method of rescuing insolvent businesses and the jobs that go with them. Accordingly clearance is intended to protect jobs, particularly where clearance is needed to prevent the employer becoming insolvent, and continuation of appropriate deal activity involving employers with defined benefit schemes. An application for a clearance statement is not required by the law, but in practice is essential in all but a very few cases.

4.3.3   Internal process

The Regulator maintains a multi-disciplinary team, involving pensions experts, lawyers, actuaries, financial and business experts, many on secondment. The objective is to maintain a pragmatic and non-bureaucratic approach with access to current practice.

Every application for clearance is allocated its own case team, consisting of one member of each discipline; the team liaises with the applicants and trustees, either in person or by phone. Any concerns about the application are discussed at length to allow applicants to satisfy the Regulator that a clearance statement can be issued, or to amend the application. Issues can also be dealt with by email (clearance@thepensionsregulator.gov.uk). Queries can include technical questions from advisers, and 'no-names' enquiries which may develop into formal clearance applications. The main issue for the Regulator is whether a proposed transaction is likely to have a financially detrimental effect on the scheme's ability to meet its liabilities; if this is not the case, clearance is not appropriate and no further action is required. The Regulator seeks early contact to improve risk control, and in particular looks to see the employer's engagement with trustees. This can be evidenced by treating the pension scheme as a creditor, and providing it (unlike most creditors) with information about current finances and future plans. It also looks to see that trustees have access to appropriate (including financial and commercial) advice.

4.4   Clearance procedure

The Regulator has adopted a policy of dealing with applications for clearance in a 'flexible, responsive and proportionate manner'; there is also a user-group to enable it to receive feed-back on its operations. It also accepts that it is impractical and probably impossible to devise rules, regulations and codes of practice in sufficient detail to cover all circumstances and events which may arise. It operates guiding principles to cover both its own behaviour and that of parties applying for clearance.

Its guiding principles in particular focus on identifying events which may have a detrimental affect on an underfunded pension scheme which might increase the possible future risk of a claim on the PPF. Its principles (and guidance) are expected to change from time to time; any guidance changes do not have retrospective effect on any clearances already issued.

4.4.1 Guiding principles

General

The Regulator regards a pension scheme in deficit as 'any other material unsecured creditor of the sponsor company and that it should be treated in the same way'. In fact it treats the employer more as a bank than as a trade creditor. Such a view fits imperfectly with the special position of pension funds and employers, and challenges to this rather idiosyncratic view may be expected in the course of time. Ordinary creditors can decide to do or not to do business with the debtor; ordinary creditors can agree to change the terms of business; ordinary creditors can decide not to pursue claims; ordinary creditors have very different time horizons; and ordinary creditors operate as volunteers.

Nonetheless, the Regulator considers the pension scheme to be a 'key company stakeholder'. It expects (unlike ordinary creditors) trustees to be given access to both information and decision makers – and key financial and other confidential information about the company; they are permitted in exchange to enter into confidentiality arrangements, so that the trustees are prohibited from disclosing such confidential information elsewhere. This may mean that certain trustees whom the employer would not normally trust with information and might for example be in a relationship with a competitor, must be provided with key information. The Regulator suggests that trustees who find themselves in a situation of conflict of duty should seek independent advice.

It is, however, in the process for applications for clearance that the major dilemmas emerge. The Regulator requires such applications to contain 'concise, relevant and accurate' information to enable the Regulator to reach a properly informed decision, to include all events having a materially detrimental effect on the ability of pension scheme to meet its liabilities. The brevity enables decisions to be made quickly. But that leaves the Regulator, if a failure later occurs, free to complain later that it was not in possession of all the information needed to make a full clearance, and to withdraw it retrospectively. Accordingly it is advisable to ensure that the parties applying for clearance provide all conceivable information to avoid a later challenge that the clearance was made in the absence of full information.

4.5 The Regulator's objectives

In deciding whether to issue a clearance notice, a series of principles have been issued; because of their subjective nature they offer little comfort to parties wishing to engage in corporate restructuring. If there is later found to be a breach, the protection conventionally offered by the corporate veil, indeed the protection originally invented to allow capitalism to flourish, is removed. And it is not clear where the burden of proof lies, and what the level is. The principles include:

- a preferred outcome of a properly funded defined benefit pension scheme with a solvent employer;
- regulation in a risk-based manner;
- maintaining a balance between reducing the risk to members' benefits and not intervening unnecessarily in the conduct of employers;
- consistency in the exercise of anti-avoidance powers and the operation of clearance.

Professional advisers are required to ensure that directors, trustees and any other parties involved in an event which may affect the pension scheme creditor are aware of their obligations under the principles.

4.5.1 Specified events

The Regulator's power to issue a contribution notice is triggered by an act or failure to act; the power to issue a financial support direction arises because of the circumstances of the employer. In practice, clearance is sought to protect the applicant against being subject to both any future contribution notice and a financial support direction. To limit the number of applications for clearance, the Regulator encourages clearance to be sought only in relation to events which are financially detrimental to the pension creditor – called 'specified events'. A specified event is an event affecting a scheme sponsor which is financially detrimental to the ability of a defined benefit scheme to meet its pension liabilities. Indeed the Regulator may refuse to issue clearance for non-specified events, which can make life unpredictable for the parties involved in such non-specified events, for which clearance apparently will not be given, even if later there might be a call for contributions from a scheme sponsor or an individual. The Regulator is able to add further notifiable events *(PA 2004 s.69(2)(b)*; [Notifiable Event Regs] which may cover changes in priority and returns of capital. The definition of 'employer' in respect of notifiable events is extended to connected and associated parties.

4.6 Schemes in deficit

Clearance is neither available for, nor needs to be sought for, schemes which are not in deficit. Any transaction or event only ranks as being financially detrimental to the scheme's ability to meet its liabilities where the scheme is in deficit. Deficit can be defined by reference to several methodologies. For example, deficit can be calculated on a wind-up basis (which schemes were never intended, when designed, to meet) or on a continuing basis (which they were). There are also other mechanisms: statutory funding objective, the former Revenue method for calculating surpluses, the former minimum funding requirement and many others.

The Regulator has chosen to use an accounting system, widely criticised, known as FRS17 (the current UK GAAP accounting standard for retirement benefits, the primary objective of which was intended 'to ensure that the financial statements reflect at fair value the assets and liabilities arising from the employees' retirement benefits obligation and any related funding'). The use of FRS17 as a trigger is intended by the Regulator to give clarity to the market as to when a director or connected or associated party could be exposed to a contribution notice.

Exceptions

FRS17 is only available as an appropriate measure of deficit where there is no doubt that the employer will continue as a going concern; where there is doubt (according to the Regulator) the appropriate measure is a s.75 buy-out deficit. Where trustees have already fixed a funding standard higher than FRS17, it is the higher level that should be used to determine if there is a deficit.

Companies with different valuations

Where companies have adopted a different accounting standard, such as IAS 19, the deficit should be measured as any shortfall between the Defined Benefit Obligation and the Fair Value of any Plan Assets, as defined under IAS 19, and shown in the notes to the financial statements. Where neither accounting methods are in operation, the full s.75 (buy-out) level must be used and the presumption is that every case is classified as a 'Type A' (see below) unless the applicant can demonstrate to the contrary.

In summary therefore:

- To be financially detrimental there must be a deficit.
- The relevant basis to determine the deficit for clearance purposes is FRS 17 or IAS 19 unless:
  - The trustees have fixed a higher funding level; or
  - There is no FRS17 valuation; or
  - There is a question over the continuation of the employer as a going concern.

4.6.1 Classification of events

In order to assess whether a particular event has a financially detrimental effect on the pension fund, it is necessary to consider first where the pension fund ranks in the allocation of proceeds in the event of the insolvency of the employer, and then the impact of that event on the potential allocation. The pension fund in deficit is regarded by the Regulator as an unsecured creditor. The priority of an unsecured creditor, with regard to the assets of a company in the event of insolvency normally ranks below other creditors (including HMRC) such as creditors with fixed charges, preferential creditors, creditors with floating charges but above subordinated creditors and shareholders. The Regulator divides all events affecting a company into three categories:

- *Type A events* being events that affect the scheme sponsor; these include all events which are financially detrimental to the ability of a defined benefit scheme to meet its pension liabilities (known as 'specified events'. The Regulator advises that clearance is sought where these events take place);

- *Type B events*, being events that do not affect the scheme sponsor; these include all events which are neither Type A – "Specified Events" or Type C events below. Clearance is not necessary; and

- *Type C events*, that might affect the scheme sponsor; these are events which indicate a possible deterioration in the strength of the employers' covenant, which may be outside the control of the directors or the company. The Regulator refuses to give clearance for these events.

Events include all transactions, acts and failures to act and, in some cases, circumstances which affect a company; The Regulator seeks to protect itself by insisting on notification of an event that might amount to a breach of the intentions of the anti-avoidance legislation. Events which involve a breach of law are not eligible for clearance and must be reported to the Regulator.

In recent years, following a well known decision in *Bradstock Group Pension Scheme [2002] 69 PBLR* (see A3.1) many trustees who felt their chances of recovering full payment were slim attempted to reach a compromise with their sponsor, and indeed acted as responsible creditors should. Often they acted following a court application. Such compromises are now strongly frowned upon, and any attempt to compromise the debt due to the pension scheme is regarded as a notifiable event and a Type A event for which clearance is required.

4.6.2   Type A specified events

All Type A events are specified events. It is only in respect of specified events that have a material detrimental affect on the pension creditor that clearance should be sought. All Type A events are manifested through one or more of the following three effects on the pension creditor; these events are said by the Regulator to be somewhat modelled on HMRC systems for tax clearance; but they extend to much greater activities, including borrowings:

- *Priority* – a change in the level of security given to creditors with the consequence that the pension creditor is likely to receive a reduced dividend in the event of insolvency. Examples include granting a fixed charge or floating charge.

- *Return of capital* – a reduction in the overall assets of the company which could be used to fund a pension deficit. Examples include dividends, share buy back, dividend strip, distribution in specie, demergers.

- *Control structure* – a change or partial change in the control group structure of an employer, which reduces the overall employer covenant, and could affect the ability of an employer to meet a potential s.75 debt and lead to the Regulator imposing a financial support direction. Examples include change of principal employer, change in control group structure of the DB scheme.

4.6.3   Priority

The Regulator assesses whether a priority change (for example when a plan sponsor issues a debenture) affects the pension fund's rights and therefore should be classified as a Type A event using certain tests, including:

- whether a plan sponsor has a pension deficit, and if so
- whether a plan sponsor grants a fixed or floating charge over assets that do not specifically relate to new money, and if so
- whether the granting of fixed or floating charge materially affects security because it applies to:
  - more than 25 percent of the total assets of the group, or
  - more than 25 percent of the total assets of the employer.

If it does, the Regulator regards it as a Type A event which it requires notice of and for which an application for clearance should be considered. In practice such applications seem to have been rare.

4.6.4   Return of capital

The Regulator regards a return of capital as including any reduction in the assets of a company resulting from a return to shareholders, which leads to an overall reduction in the level of shareholders' funds – and hence security to the pension fund. Events which could result in a reduction in the level of shareholders' funds include dividend payments, share buy backs and distributions in specie.   The Regulator considers any return of value to shareholders who are otherwise lower in the overall priority listing than the pension fund to be a concern. There are a large number of events within the UK which fall within the definition of a return of capital. The Regulator looks at such transactions in a 'risk-based and proportionate' way, limiting its interest to activities which affect the funding of the pension fund. In relation to the payment of dividends (which could affect the pension fund's security) for example the Regulator seeks a balance between identifying significant returns of capital and hindering reasonable dividend payments. Tests to determine if a return of capital is a Type A Event include:

- whether an employer within the group has a pension deficit on a relevant basis, and if so
- whether the employer has negative profit and loss reserves after reflecting the deficit, and if so
- whether a plan sponsor is making a return of capital to an entity outside the group or outside the EU or to an entity not subject to a financial support direction, and if so
- whether the cumulative annual return of capital is large or unusual. Large or unusual means;

- more than two times the average of the last three years' return of capital; and/or
- less than two times dividend cover (i.e. the ratio of retained after tax profit for the period divided by the total return of capital for the same period).

If so, The Regulator considers the transaction to be a Type A event which ideally requires notices of, and for which clearance should be considered.

4.6.5 Change in control structure

The Regulator is concerned with changes in the control structure of plan sponsors; the main changes of interest are those which affect the strength of the employer covenant and its ability to meet a potential full-buy-out liability. For example, a decision by a holding company to relinquish control of a sponsor subsidiary is regarded as a notifiable event (*PA 2004 s.69.; The Pensions Regulator (Notifiable Events) Regulations 2005 SI 2005 No 900 Reg. 2(2)(f)*). Other examples include the sale of some or all of the shares of the employer, a change in parent company, or ultimate holding company of the employer; or change in connected or associated parties who could be subject to a financial support direction.

The Regulator even if uncomfortable with the changes may be persuaded that it is ultimately beneficial to the pension fund or necessary to ensure the survival of the plan sponsor or associated and connected companies. It uses existing market practice in looking at financial ratios or banking covenants, and in particular compares the credit rating before and after the change of control event (if available).

4.6.6 Type B events

A Type B event is an event affecting a plan sponsor which is not financially detrimental to the ability of a defined benefit scheme to meet its pension liabilities. Type B events are commercial transactions undertaken at arms' length and include (provided there is no element of Type A involved):
- Mergers and acquisitions, including
  - sale and purchase of assets
  - sale and purchase of non-employer subsidiary
  - management buy-in and buy-out
  - Privatisation and joint venture
- Fundraisings, including:
  - flotation and private placement
  - venture capital fund raising
  - rights issue and preference share issue
  - unsecured debt
- Other contractual negotiations, for example operating or finance lease negotiations.

The Regulator does not question the way in which directors make commercial decisions about how to use their assets, apart from where their actions involve a Type A event.

4.6.7   Type C events

Type C events are events which indicate a deterioration in the employers' covenant, and which may be inside or outside the control of the employer or its directors. Type C events include all Type A events, as being any event which is financially detrimental to the ability of a defined benefit scheme to meet its pension liabilities and which may also point towards a deterioration in the employer's covenant. 'Notifiable events' are a subset of Type C events and include the events which must be notified to the Regulator (*PA 2004 s.69*). The purpose of notifiable events is to provide an early warning of potential insolvency or underfunding to the Regulator, giving the opportunity to intervene before a call on the PPF is made. Not all Type C events are notifiable or specified events – for example the loss of a major customer. However, they are events the Regulator may choose to monitor for schemes it considers most at risk.

4.6.8   Parties to clearance

The Regulator may serve contribution notices or financial support directions not only on a plan sponsor, but also on connected and associated persons. Any and all of these might therefore seek clearance – first having squared the trustees if possible. It is not for the Regulator to act on behalf of schemes every time a specified event occurs; but it is prepared to act where the parties struggle to come to an agreement.

4.6.9   Trustees duty to negotiate on funding

In many ways the Regulator is determined to delegate decision making to trustees, rather than become involved itself. Since scheme trustees are already responsible for safeguarding members' interests, with powers and duties set out in statute, trust law and the scheme's trust deed and rules, one might wonder what additional precautions are needed by a regulator. In some cases trustees' bargaining position in relation to an employer is uneven, and the Regulator feels that the mere existence of a regulator can strengthen their hand. In particular not all trustees have the power to set contributions or precipitate the wind-up of a scheme, although they could always have asked a regulator to wind-up a scheme on their behalf (*PA 1995 s.11(1)(c)*).

The Regulator requires trustees to treat any deficit as a bank-type loan to the sponsor, on the grounds that

• it is usually large in relation to other unsecured creditors;
• it is material – especially where there is a large number of active members; and

DEALING WITH PENSIONS   67

- they have the power to threaten the sponsor, particularly because of trustees' ability to call in the Regulator, and seek the exercise of the Regulator's powers to issue contribution notices or financial support directions.

The Regulator also requires trustees to monitor the sponsor's financial position, strength of its commitment to the funding of the scheme and corporate activity. The trustees will almost certainly need to ensure such commercially sensitive information was kept confidential (perhaps also signing a confidentiality agreement). In practice this can raise issues, especially where trustees are also union representatives. It is helpful sometimes where conflict of interest issues arise, (as invariably they do) which are otherwise unmanageable, to explore whether the appointment of an independent trustee might be helpful (even one appointed by the Regulator, although this should normally be avoided, as it appoints on a rota basis, rather than as appropriate).

In cases where there is a material issue (a Type A event) the Regulator suggests that those trustees with significant issues in the negotiations should absent themselves from discussions. This is a purist suggestion; similar conflicts of interest for example in Parliament or in local authority decision-making is dealt with by making a minuted declaration of interest – whilst preserving the skills, experience and abilities within the committee or board. It is rare in practice that the conflicts are so great that absence should be required and in fact most discussions and decisions benefit from the fact that individuals have several ways of looking at issues, and the value that chief executives and financial directors can bring to the board of trustees is invariably invaluable. The danger of partisanship is usually outweighed by the danger of uninformed decision-making. The Regulator indicates that the absence of financial skills can be countervailed by the hiring of external financial expertise. In any event, skills in understanding the strength or otherwise of the sponsor's covenant is useful, and helpful in devising constructive solutions to any deficit problems.

4.6.10 Directors, connected and associated parties

Directors have a range of duties to stakeholders in the company, including an obligation to act in good faith with the trustees. The Regulator is deeply concerned that directors understand the nature of the company liability to the fund, especially following the requirement to fund a scheme to buy-out levels when a scheme is wound-up (which is why in practice so few schemes are wound-up) (see e.g. *The Occupational Pension Schemes (Winding Up and Deficiency on Winding Up etc) (Amendment) Regulations 2004* as from June 2003). This level of debt is not the level of debt that appears on the balance sheet under the accounting rules.

The Regulator urges sponsors to inform trustees of information (including any independent reports) on their financial position and future plans and any Type A event that may occur – and to pay any trustees' expenses in obtaining independent reports, although there is a general recognition that costs should be proportionate. Sponsors should also try to open negotiations with trustees at an early stage – and if necessary open negotiations with the Regulator.

4.6.11   The Regulator's solutions

The Regulator is determined to see pension funds better funded than they have been in the recent past – and possibly up to levels last seen in the mid-1990s. The remedies they are looking for, perhaps as part of an arrangement between sponsor and trustees when the sponsor needs the trustees' agreement to a deal or restructuring, include:

- revised contribution schedule with higher contributions and a shorter period to make up the deficit.
- one-off cash payments (or other assets or security)
- a guarantee of contributions where there is doubt over the employer's ability to continue such payments, perhaps covering the following three to five years' contributions.
- establishment of escrow accounts (as reportedly happened in the Marconi case, where as part of the sale of a major part of the company the sponsor agreed to set aside several hundred million pounds from the proceeds of sale in a separate account which could be called upon to meet any future deficit)
- improving the priority by which any deficit would be met over and above the security, for example, required by a bank or a venture capitalist. In practice such arrangements are rare for obvious reasons, and it has been reported that such requests have meant that refinancing or restructurings have not been able to be completed as a consequence.

The Regulator is insisting that trustees are armed with corporate information about the employer's covenant so that they should examine on a continuing basis such information as:

- monthly management accounts, key performance data and access to selected executives
- banking and financing covenants relating to the sponsor's ability to pay and retention of assets

It even suggests that trustees might seek negative pledges to restrict the activities of the company which may be seen to prejudice the strength of the employer's covenant. Such requirements are an uneasy obligation which offers the danger of trustees second-guessing the risk taking and commercial activities of a sponsor.

4.6.12   The Regulator's dispensations

Because the Regulator is deeply concerned to limit claims on the PPF, and because it has an obligation to secure employment, it is prepared to allow trustees to undertake transactions which conventionally are unacceptable. These include:

- Taking a stake in the employer, by way of share or otherwise; this may actually increase the risk of failure and increased liability on the PPF. Banks sometimes do this, by exchanging their loan rights in exchange for shares (debt for equity swap), but it has so far been broadly improper for pension fund trustees to do this, especially where shares may not be tradeable easily; and
- Increasing contributions in proportion to an increase in profit, perhaps until the FRS17 debt is met.

4.6.13 The Regulator's practice

Applications for clearance should be in accordance with the Regulator published guidance (see Appendix A1.1), made as soon as possible and with as much information as possible. The Regulator makes considerable caveats in its offer of clearance, making it clear that any clearance offered will be later ineffective if it is found to have been based on inadequate or insufficient information. This is a particular risk for all parties, and the extent of the risk is as yet too soon to determine. It will only be where there has been a failure that any clearances will be inspected, and possible withdrawal considered. The Regulator will later explore the true intent of the parties (for example if the transaction was intended to help maintain employment, but there were actually other motives). Few transactions in practice have single motives. The level of information sought is that which a non-executive directors of a quoted company would normally expect in order to enable them to make informed decisions. All parties seeking clearance need to make separate applications.

4.7 The Regulator's powers

The legal powers available to the Regulator are material, even draconian. They include the powers to serve:

- a contribution notice
- a financial support direction

4.7.1 Contribution notice

The Regulator can issue a contribution notice, requiring an amount up to the PA 1995 s.75 ('buy-out debt') to be paid to the scheme trustees or the PPF (during an assessment period within the meaning of section 132 of the PA 2004) if it considers there has been an act or failure to act, one of the main purposes of which was:

- to prevent the recovery of the whole or part of the debt which was or might become due from the employer to the scheme under the PA 1995 s.75; or
- otherwise than in good faith, to prevent a debt under section 75 becoming due, compromise or otherwise settle such a debt, or reduce the amount of such a debt.

There is no obligation to serve such a notice, and there seems to be discretion to allow the Regulator to permit such reconstruction if despite that intention there is a bona fide purpose (for example to allow the sponsor to be free to pursue its commercial objectives and the fund is adequately funded, perhaps to FRS17 levels).

As part of considering whether it is reasonable to issue a contribution notice the Regulator must consider, among other things "all the purposes of the act or failure to act (including whether a purpose of the act or failure was to prevent or limit loss of employment)." *(PA 2004 s.38(7))*

A contribution notice can be served only on a person who is party to the act or failure to act and who is either the employer or a person connected or associated with the employer; this includes parties who knowingly assist in the act or failure to act. A contribution notice may be served on more than one person. A person includes individuals, companies, limited liability partnerships and partnerships. The Regulator can only serve a notice if it thinks it reasonable to make the person pay the amount in the notice. What is 'reasonable' has so far not been tested, but according to the Regulator includes:

- the degree of involvement of the person in the act or failure to act (for example, was the individual aware of or sanction the transaction?)
- whether the person was senior or junior in the transaction
- whether the person was connected with the transaction (a trustee or an employer)
- whether the act or failure to act was a notifiable event in respect of which the person committed a breach of duty to notify to the Regulator
- what was the purpose of the act or failure to act, including whether the purpose was to prevent or limit loss of employment; and
- what were the financial circumstances of the person (for example, where paying the deficit would trigger an insolvency)

4.7.2 Financial support direction

The Regulator can serve a financial support direction on the employer and persons connected and associated with the employer, requiring financial arrangements be put in place to support an employer's pension liabilities when the employer is a service company (i.e. employs the members, who work for other companies in the group, but has no material assets of its own) or is insufficiently resourced within the relevant time. A financial support direction cannot be served on an individual (with some exceptions, e.g. where the employer is a sole trader). The Regulator can only serve a direction on a person if it considers it is reasonable to impose the requirements on that person. Once the Regulator has issued a direction, it must approve the arrangements in a Notice. The support may be for the whole or part of the employer's pension liabilities. Normally a notice will not be issued until six months after the funds should have been paid *(The Pensions Regulator (Financial Support Directions etc) Regulations 2005 SI 2005 No 2188 reg 4; cf also The Pensions Regulator (Contribution Notices and Restoration Orders) Regulations 2005 SI 2005 No 931 and The Pensions Regulator (Notifiable Events) Regulations 2005 SI 2005 No 900).* The amounts are either contributions due *(PA 2004 s.227)*, or the wind-up debt *(PA 1995 s.75)*. A sponsor is 'insufficiently resourced' if its net asset value is less than 50% of the s.75 debt AND the value of the net assets together with connected parties is more than 50% *(The Pensions Regulator (Financial Support Directions etc) Regulations 2005 SI 2005 No 2188 reg. 6).*

Whether to issue a financial support direction can pose severe dilemmas for the Regulator and at the time of writing no such directions have been reported; issuing a direction which brings down the sponsor may do more harm than good. When deciding whether it is reasonable to do so the Regulator will consider *inter alia:*

- the relationship the person has (had) with the sponsor (e.g. whether it is a parent or former parent company);
- any benefits such as dividends or tax credits received as a consequence of the relationship;
- any connection with the scheme (e.g. whether a trustee or sponsor);
- the ability to pay; and
- any other factors it thinks fit.

4.7.3 Financial support arrangements

The Regulator must set out what it seeks in its notice; these factors include whether it applies joint and several liability for the whole or part of the employer's pension liabilities in relation to the scheme. A financial support direction requires:

- financial support for the scheme to be established within a period specified;
- the financial support continues while the scheme continues; and
- the Regulator is informed in writing of prescribed events affecting the financial support as soon as reasonably practicable.

If there is a failure to comply with a financial support direction the Regulator may, if it considers it reasonable, issue a contribution notice to one or more persons who were issued with the direction requiring them to pay the whole or part of the sum specified in the notice. When deciding whether it is reasonable the Regulator considers:

- whether the person has taken reasonable steps to comply with the financial support direction;
- the relationship the person has or had with the employer;
- the benefits the person has received directly or indirectly from the employer;
- the relationship the person has or has had with the parties to any arrangements put in place;
- any connection or involvement the person has or had with the scheme; a person is connected with a company if he is a director or shadow director of the company or an associate of such a director or shadow director; or he is an associate of the company (see *IA 1986 s.24 and s.435*). A person is an associate of an individual if that person is the individual's husband or wife, or is a relative, or the husband or wife of a relative, of the individual or of the individual's husband or wife. A person is an associate of any person with whom he is in partnership, and of the husband or wife or a relative of any individual with whom he is in partnership; and a Scottish firm is an associate of any person who is a member of

the firm. A person is an associate of any person whom he employs or by whom he is employed. Any director or other officer of a company is to be treated as employed by that company;

- the financial circumstances of the person;
- other factors.

The sum due under a contribution notice becomes a debt due to the trustees or managers of the scheme. The Regulator has the power to enforce that debt unless the scheme is in an assessment period (*PA 2004 s.132*) when the PPF carries out enforcement. Enforcing the statutory debt is carried out through the county court or high court. Trustees are not associated purely because of their capacity as trustee of a pension scheme.

4.8   Anti-avoidance issues for lenders and corporates

There are a number of unresolved issues in particular for the funders of plan sponsors.

4.8.1   Accounts

Dividends can only be paid if there are sufficient distributable reserves. Once pension deficits are brought on balance sheet under FRS17, a company's ability to pay dividends is affected. This may also lead to breaches of covenant under loan agreements. It is not clear as to what extent must potential liabilities under moral hazard contribution notices be taken into account in FRS17 accounts. Nor is it clear as to what extent all associated and connected companies need to be individually audited in order to prepare pension scheme and group accounts.

4.8.2   Contribution notices against banks

Few banks take an equity stake in a debtor customer. Where they do, such an equity stake may take the form of non-voting preference shares, partly to ensure that the bank does not become connected with the borrowing company. Some funders accept 'equity kickers' under which there is a right to be issued with shares (usually voting shares) at some time in the future. This may be less attractive if it materially increases the likelihood that the lender as shareholder becomes exposed to the risk of contributing towards the borrower's pension deficit. A shareholder is deemed to have control of a company if he is entitled to exercise, or control the exercise of, one third or more the voting power at any general meeting of the company or of another company which has control of it (including where two or more persons together satisfy this condition) (*IA 1986 s.435(10(b))*).

Where the lender has no equity stake, the main concern for the lender is the insolvency risk of the borrower and the likelihood of default on covenants under loan agreements. In practice lenders are beginning to explore with pension scheme trustees their attitudes and carry out increased due diligence.

4.8.3   Directors' duties

After April 2005, full buy-out debts on the cessation of participation of an employer in a multi-employer scheme is avoided if financial support is put in place by other group companies or the parent. Since directors of such other companies are supposed to act in the best interests of their shareholders, they are faced with a dilemma since it might be hard to demonstrate the benefit to their company of financing another group company's pension scheme liabilities. The isolation of liabilities is often the very reason for separate corporate entities; it may be that catastrophic consequences of support may be a defence. Directors who fail to carry out thorough pensions due diligence risk becoming liable for unlawful trading if a significant pensions liability has been disregarded.

4.8.4   Consolidation of group under holding company

Because of the Regulator's requirements, corporate groups continually experience difficulties in selling-off subsidiary companies participating in a multi-employer final salary pension scheme. The sale of the subsidiary (whether as part of a sale or business sale) entails its cessation of participation in the multi-employer scheme, triggering a debt on the employer. Before 5 April 2005, no debt arose as long as the funding position of the scheme at the time was 100% on the MFR basis. Now a s.75 buy-out debt is triggered, unless financial support is put in place.

The debt on the employer on cessation of participation is greater than many employers appreciate since the proportion of the scheme's whole buy-out debt is shared among current employers according to their shares of the scheme's liabilities. This means a subsidiary can have a disproportionately large share of deficit if other companies have previously withdrawn and the subsidiary now has the majority of liabilities compared to other actively participating group companies. Employers' leaving debt may include a large amount attributable to orphan liabilities (i.e. in respect of non-active members whose former employer no longer participates in the scheme).

One way of making business sales easier was to transfer the businesses of all subsidiaries to the (already participating) parent company before 6 April 2005. Business sales and transfers of employees would then not trigger the cessation of participation of any company (since the relevant companies would have ceased to participate before 6 April 2005).

The Regulator's views are not known on such a practice (i.e. whether it constitutes avoidance of the debt on the employer, potentially triggering liability under a contribution notice). It is, however, arguable that the action was not to avoid an employer debt (since the act of consolidation would trigger such debts, albeit of nil value if the scheme was funded to 100% of the MFR), and the consolidation had actually improved the position of members (by ensuring they were directly employed by the parent company, rather than a subsidiary that may be a service company or otherwise hold few assets). In practice, there were however few such reconstructions because of other unknown consequences in relation to tax and employment.

4.8.5 Setting contributions

The Regulator has power to set contributions in default of agreement between trustee and sponsor. The Regulator is under considerable pressure to require employers to pay as much as possible without provoking employer insolvency or otherwise substantially damaging the employer's ability to do business. It is at the time of writing unclear as to how the new scheme specific funding requirement fits in with schemes' contribution rules (especially rules giving trustees full power to set contributions), and in particular whether such rules override, or whether trustees are obliged to negotiate with the employers.

4.8.6 Control of investment powers

Sponsors are concerned about the trustees' unfettered ability to set investment policy (subject only to the duty to consult) – particularly because of the volatility of pension liabilities and the effect on FRS17 accounts. Decisions in *T&N [No 1], [2004] 75 PBLR, [2004] EWHC 1680 (Ch); T&N (No 2) [2004] 78 PBLR, [2004] EWHC 2361 (Ch); T&N (No 3) [2005] 30 PBLR, [2004] EWHC 2448 (Ch)* indicate that trustees cannot be forced to accept employer proposals; as yet it is unclear what redrafting of the scheme documents could take place to give sponsors a greater say. Sponsors might for example incentivise trustees to adopt a certain policy (e.g. by offering to increase contributions by a certain percentage or by agreeing certain guarantees) but conditionally on trustees continuing to pursue a certain investment policy. The trustees would not need to enter any binding agreement and would retain their discretion. However, if they changed their policy against the employers' wishes, the employers could withdraw their incentive payments. Employers may put pressure on trustees (especially employer-nominated trustees) to enter morally binding agreements.

4.8.7 Trustees' positions under CVAs

The position of trustees under CVAs is as yet unsettled. Where the s.75 debt forms the largest liability, trustees may well be the largest creditors, in which case, trustees will have a blocking vote in respect of CVAs and, in particular, rights of appeal if they feel they have been treated less fairly than other creditors. Insolvency practitioners meanwhile are under a duty to treat all unsecured creditors fairly. T&N indicates the wide extent of trustees' powers; in particular, the powers granted to trustees under statute and trust law cannot be overridden by the terms of a CVA.

4.8.8 Company/trustee agreements reflecting loan agreements

Since the Regulator is intent on comparing the powers of trustees of schemes in deficit with the position of bank creditors, trustees may wish to adopt banking techniques. In practice they may wish to check the employer's strength of covenant annually; and they may wish to put in place covenant agreements similar to banking documents. These agreements might compel the employer to reveal certain details about its financial strength and future development. Certain triggering events would amount to a breach of covenant (triggering, for example, an increase in the contribution rate). The triggering events could match those already provided in the relevant loan agreements to banks, which would give the trustees a basis for claiming they were reasonable. Employers may wish to regain the initiative by proposing such agreements to trustees before trustees themselves first propose them.

4.8.9   Conflicts of interest

Professional advisers see an obvious opportunity in relation to the new conflicts not only providing separate advice to the sponsors and trustees, but also to lenders and funders. Some professional firms indicate that they are able to manage the conflicts using Chinese walls; most law firms, however, have stricter rules than accountants and actuaries. Confidentiality issues arising in trustee boards may be mitigated by limiting the disclosure of advice to summary advice only to certain board members; such limited disclosure needs to be agreed before the relevant advisory work is commissioned.

Where conflicts arise (e.g. in the negotiation of covenant agreements or generally in relation to all funding issues), trustee boards could in practice delegate relevant powers to such individuals who lack a conflict, possibly any independent trustee or any pensioner trustee. The Pensions Minister at the time of the introduction of the legislation, Baroness Hollis, announced that the appointment of independent trustees fall outside the member-nominated trustee requirements so that while trustee boards eventually are required to ensure that one-half of their number are member-nominated, an additional independent trustee (with the balance of power) can be appointed. The number and role of independent trustees is likely to increase.

4.9   Anti-avoidance and clearance

The Regulator's anti-avoidance powers are potentially applicable to events which have a detrimental impact on an underfunded scheme's ability to meet its liabilities, so it is in these situations that clearance should be considered. Because the Regulator cannot identify every such situation, it has identified principles to guide those potentially affected, and the types of event that can have a financially detrimental effect. Examples include transactions (such as granting a fixed or floating charge) which have the effect of changing the level of security given to creditors so that the pension scheme receives a reduced dividend in the event of insolvency. Similarly, clearance is regarded as advisable for a transaction involving a large or unusual return of capital, such as a share buyback, which reduces the overall assets potentially available to fund a pension deficit. A third type of event which affects the employer's ability to meet a debt to the scheme is a material change in control structure, particularly one which downgrades the employer's credit rating (although curiously moving a scheme off balance sheet might improve the rating).

In deciding whether to apply for clearance, the funding level of the scheme and the strength of the employer should be taken into account. This is because where there is doubt that the employer is a going concern, the Regulator for the moment considers the full buy-out (*PA 1995 s.75*) cost should be used to establish the deficit. Where a scheme specific valuation has not yet been carried out, FRS 17 provides a pragmatic and readily available measure.

When considering clearance applications the Regulator usually has to be satisfied that it would not be reasonable in the circumstances to issue a contribution notice or financial support direction. It, therefore, looks particularly for evidence of mitigation of risks to the pension scheme. If the employer covenant is likely to be weakened by the transaction, for example, the Regulator would expect to see measures such as accelerated repayment of the deficit, security over assets, or parent company guarantees in support of the scheme.

The prime responsibility for safeguarding members' interests lies with trustees; the Regulator expects them to 'negotiate assertively' with the employer on behalf of the scheme, with evidence, for example, that trustees have taken independent advice if appropriate, and have considered ways in which the impact of the proposed transaction can be minimised and the security of the scheme improved.

In addition to dealing with enquiries and engaging in preliminary clearance discussions, the Regulator receives around 15 to 30 formal clearance applications a month. By March 2006 (i.e. in the first year), over 100 clearance statements had been issued, while clearance was refused in two cases. The total value of schemes involved in transactions for which clearance was granted was around £17bn, with aggregate FRS 17 deficits of around 3.4bn, or about 3% of total UK FRS 17 deficits.

The Regulator expects to deal with an application for clearance within three weeks, although more time may be required in more complicated cases such as leveraged deals, or corporate restructuring which severely weakens the employer covenant. Once a final deal has been agreed, a final clearance application can be available within 48 hours.

The Regulator has approved a range of solutions to deal with scheme deficits; a proposal to raise additional secured debt in order to buy out a number of shareholders (which would have weakened the position of the pension scheme (which was in deficit) as an unsecured creditor, and where the scheme's trustees were also shareholders and therefore conflicted, an independent trustee was appointed, who commissioned an independent financial report. Eventually the sponsor dealt with the deficit by a combination of a capital injection and additional annual contributions, funds being placed in an escrow account so that matching annual payments could be made to shareholders.

The Regulator disclosed another example where the employer could not commit to dealing with a deficit in the short term, and following financial restructuring and disposal of non-core business, the employer was better placed to confront increasing debt and deteriorating profits. Unsecured debt (which the banks were about to call) was replaced with borrowing facilities, a proportion of which was secured. It was also agreed that, although the banks would have priority for the secured debt, equal security would be given to the banks and the pension scheme once the secured debt had been repaid and net debt fell below a specified level for three consecutive months.

Clearance has been refused in an arm's-length management buy-in, where the relatively robust position of the pension scheme (which had previously ranked pari passu with creditors) was diluted by a deal financed by a bank debt secured by fixed and floating charges. The Regulator took account of a report from the trustees' financial advisers who were unable to recommend acceptance of the proposed transaction, and that the trustees were affected by a conflict of interest which had not been resolved. Ultimately, the lack of mitigation (for example, through a reduced period for eliminating the deficit, or the provision of good security) meant that the Regulator was not totally satisfied that it would be unreasonable to issue a contribution notice or financial support direction.

Similarly, in a complex restructuring and sale transaction in which a number of sponsors and schemes were involved, the schemes were not offered immediate cash payments toward the reduction of deficits; the only security offered to trustees was dependent on the future success of the restructured group. At the same time, an exceptional dividend was to be paid to some shareholders, and a certain amount of secured debt was to be paid down.

Purchasers of businesses with a substantial pension deficits are concerned as to how to protect their other businesses from the possibility that the Regulator issues them with a financial support direction. The Regulator is required by the legislation to be satisfied that it is reasonable to issue a direction on each particular company. When deciding what is reasonable, the Regulator considers whether the person has (or has had) control of the employer; and in particular looks at the control structure within the corporate group. The Regulator also considers whether benefits have been received directly or indirectly. This includes not only cash, assets and loans, but also associations, names, knowledge, tax advantages, rent and common ownership benefits such as a division into an operating company and a property company to make assets safe. The funding of the scheme, the schedule of contributions, the length of the person's connection with the scheme and the terms of scheme membership are also considered. It is possible for acquirers who are not content to rely on the 'reasonableness' test to apply for ongoing clearance in respect of financial support directions. This usually involves an agreed funding plan for the scheme to an appropriate level, as well as an agreed business plan including details of the employer's resources and benefits to be taken.

4.10 Future developments

The Regulator is dedicated to (some might say obsessed with) the reduction of deficits in defined benefit schemes. As the new scheme specific funding regime comes into play, and the former MFR disappears as a funding base, the Regulator expects trustees and employers to work together to start reducing deficits. The new requirements mean that funding strategies, deficits and recovery plans will become more transparent, and this will provide a clearer context for negotiations and decisions over planned corporate transactions.

The introduction of the risk-based PPF levy is expected to add pressure to sponsor-employers to deal with their deficits as quickly as practicably possible in order to minimise levy payments. Accordingly, in time, the Regulator expects the need for clearance to diminish as schemes become better funded.

The Regulator also reports that deficits are already being factored into corporate transactions, reducing the need for the Regulator's involvement. It expects that shareholder expectations will shift once its approach to the nature of pension scheme liabilities is better understood by the market.

Where a corporate transaction poses a potential threat to a scheme, the Regulator's policy is to respond in a flexible and proportionate manner. Whether once there have been a number of high profile failures that policy can continue, and whether the high level policy is reflected in day-to-day regulation, is as yet unclear. Its documents suggest it is aware that there is a balance to be struck between reducing risks to schemes and not intervening unnecessarily in the conduct of employers; and that there are conflicting and proper needs of investors and sponsoring employers - who may well be struggling to keep their businesses afloat - as well as those of trustees and members, and its intention is to work with all parties towards achieving the goal of a properly funded scheme supported by a solvent employer.

5 Insolvency, Solvency and Reconstruction

5.1 Introduction

Given that the major concern of the Pensions Act 2004 (PA 2004) is the preservation of members' funds, and that members' funds are at greatest risk from insolvency, it is not surprising that the Act focuses so much on insolvency. This chapter presupposes some knowledge of insolvency. The PPF has published an excellent guide for insolvency practitioners ("The IP Guide") which is reproduced as Appendix A1.6. The IP Guide should be regarded as an overview, especially of the practice issues, while this chapter serves more as a critique of PA 2004, paying special attention to potential IP pitfalls. For those without any knowledge of insolvency, an introduction can be obtained from http://www.rzorg.uk. A more detailed online freeware publication (co-authored by Grant Jones) is the "A-Z of Rescue of Insolvency" obtainable at

http//www.tmp.co.uk/software/index.html

The structure of this chapter is broadly to consider PA 2004 and the issues that it raises, and thereafter to consider separately relevant regulations promulgated under PA 2004, some of which are still in the course of being drafted or finalised at the time of writing.

5.2 "Insolvency event", "insolvency date", "insolvency practitioner duties" and 'what happens upon insolvency': "the assessment period"

5.2.1 Background

The duties of insolvency practitioners (IPs) are set out primarily in PA 2004 Chapter 2 and are limited, as is much of PA 2004, to 'occupational schemes'. An insolvency practitioner appointed over an employer has, as a general rule, a duty to notify the PPF, the Regulator, or trustees of the scheme *(s.120(2))* upon the later of his appointment or when he becomes 'aware' of the scheme *(s.120(3))*. Notification must be in a form to be prescribed by regulations *(s.120(4)* & IP Guide).

Chapter 2 of PA 2004 prescribes three insolvency terms ('insolvency event', 'insolvency date' and 'insolvency practitioner' *(s.121(1)))* which affect the application of the legislation; the definitions of these terms are used elsewhere within PA 2004:

An 'insolvency event' *(s.121(2-5))* applies to individuals, companies, partnerships and other groupings 'as to be prescribed', such as unusual structures like credit unions, etc. These are not covered by the Insolvency Act (IA 1986), so regulations under PA 2004 will extend IA 1986's ambit in this regard. IA 1986 is generally limited to companies formed under the Companies Act (CA 1985), individuals, and (only latterly by regulation) to partnerships. IA 1986 does not cover every UK insolvency procedure. Two are of special interest: for companies, 'schemes of arrangement' under CA 1985 and, for individuals, 'deeds of arrangement' under the Deed of Arrangements Act 1914. It can thus be seen that the ambit of IA 1986 as it relates to an "insolvency event" under PA 2004, has had to be greatly extended by regulation.

An 'insolvency event' is any appointment under IA 1986, save for a 'solvent or Members' Voluntary Liquidation' ('MVL'). It should be remembered that IA 1986 is slightly misnamed in that it also covers 'solvent liquidations': hence the necessity of excluding MVLs from the definition of insolvency event. IPs considering taking an MVL appointment over an employer with an occupational pension scheme should be cautious. PA 2004 and supporting regulations now mean that the calculation of the pension scheme liability in an MVL will usually be on the 'cessation basis', i.e. the estimated section 75 debt and the calculation method that results in the highest claim. Consequently, it may be difficult to declare that the company is solvent; hence an MVL may not be possible.

'Insolvency date', in relation to an insolvency event, means the date on which the event occurs *(s.121(8))*.

Only licensed IPs can be appointed under IA 1986. It is an imprisonable offence for a non-licensed individual to act as an IP *(IA 1986 s.389(1))*, except in the case of each of the following: the Official Receiver ('OR'), a 'receiver and manager' *(IA 1986 s.29(1))*, and a director nominee under IA 1986 Schedule A1 (see also *IA 1986 s.389A & B*). Insolvency appointments outside IA 1986 (subject to extending regulation) are therefore not within the definition of an 'insolvency event'.

'Insolvency practitioner' is anyone who can ordinarily accept Insolvency Act appointments *(s.121(9))* under IA 1986 s.388. The government has considered 'loosening the monopoly of pessimism' which some have accused the IA 1986 licensing system of creating, whereby only licensed IPs can take IA 1986 appointments. Consequently, non-licensed IPs will be able to come within the PA 2004 definition *(s.121(9)(b))* in due course.

As has been noted above, some appointments which may be termed 'quasi-insolvency practitioner' appointments, either (a) fall within IA 1986 but do not require the appointment of a licensed IP; or (b) fall outside IA 1986 and therefore do not require the appointment of a licensed insolvency practitioner. On the whole, regulations have addressed the problem of the quasi-insolvency practitioner appointments, but three quasi-insolvency practitioner appointments remain which present difficulties. These will all cause difficulties because they have the characteristics of an insolvency but are excluded from the PA 2004 provisions and have not been accounted for in regulations. Exclusions occur because they are excluded from s.388 of IA 1986. They are:

(a) receivers or managers such as those appointed under the Law of Property Act 1925 ("LPA receivers") over an asset or class of assets of a company but not over the company itself. These are mentioned in IA 1986, but not within the s.388 definition. It appears that this omission stems from the draftsman considering only those appointments for which a licence is required (a licence is not required to act as a 'receiver or manager'). In practice, the omission may not be particularly burdensome because a 'receiver or manager' is often appointed in conjunction with an IP covered by PA 2004; indeed, often it is the same individual.

(b) Court-appointed receivers appointed by the Court to protect and safeguard assets are invariably overlooked by legislative draftsmen. A Court-appointed receiver could fall outside an appointment of the type provided for in PA 2004.

(c) The self-explanatory analogous foreign appointment over a UK or non-UK company with a relevant [occupational] pension scheme is, as far as the EU is concerned, specifically excluded from IA 1986 s.388 by s.388(6), and non-EU appointments are ignored altogether. The lack of consideration for foreign insolvency procedures is surprising given that the appointment of a foreign quasi-insolvency practitioner can have the same effect on a UK company as a properly appointed IP, and that PA 2004 makes much of foreign connections (see e.g. PA 2004 Part 7).

If a foreign company has UK occupational scheme members, but there is no UK insolvency (as defined by PA 2004), what are the trustees to do? The first outcome is that the foreign insolvency is an EU insolvency and that "secondary proceedings" are opened (under *Council Regulation (EC) No 1346/2000*) in the UK. If no secondary proceedings are opened and/or the foreign company is not based in the EU, then the trustee may wish to petition to liquidate the company under IA 1986 s.221, as an "unregistered company". The courts have found sufficient nexus between the liquidation of a company and assisting its former employees to claim statutory redundancy payments (*re Eloc Electro-Optieck and Comunicatie BV [1982] Ch. 43*) so it should be assumed that a s.221 petition could be made on the same basis.

In all three cases the onus is on the trustees of the scheme to apply under *PA 2004 s.129* for the PPF to assume responsibility. If an IP had been appointed, the onus would be on the IP. The notification period commences with the date of appointment, i.e. the self-explanatory date of the 'insolvency event' (*s.121(8)*) and ends with the date of the IP becoming 'aware' of the scheme.

5.2.2 Distinction between 'insolvency event' and 'qualifying insolvency event'

"Except as provided by subsections (2) to (5) [the definition of an 'insolvency event' for individuals, companies, partnerships and 'as to be prescribed' respectively] for the purposes of this Part [Part 2] an event is not to be regarded as an insolvency event in relation to a person" *(PA 2004 s.121(6))*. Section 121(6) emphasises that only IA 1986 appointments (as defined by IA 1986 s.388, as amended by regulation) are regarded as 'insolvency events' for this part of the Pensions Act. The rationale for the distinction is unclear given that PA 2004 does not refer elsewhere to an 'insolvency event' (as opposed to 'qualifying insolvency event') outside IA 1986 s.388.

5.2.3 Date of notification

PA 2004 requires the IP to inform the Board, the Regulator and the trustees, or managers of the scheme on becoming 'aware' of the scheme *(s.120(2))*. Given the inevitable circumstances surrounding an appointment, this may be ambitious, and difficult to achieve in practice. Circumstances making it difficult to be 'aware' include the general confusion of the post-appointment period (known to IPs as the 'hiatus period') and confusion as to the nature of the scheme, i.e. is it an occupational scheme proper, subject to notification? An IP can be 'aware' of a scheme, but not confident in his 'awareness'. During the hiatus period, following insolvency, a company's managers may seek to give assurances on a number of matters relating to the company, including its pension arrangements, but some of these may not be accurate and the IP understandably may not be sufficiently comfortable with such assurances. It is recommended that the IP immediately includes a reference to the company's pension schemes, with supporting detailed questions in the standard post-appointment director questionnaire. A standard letter addressed to the trustees of any pension scheme should be included in the series of first-day letters, issued by IPs upon their appointment.

5.2.4 Distinction between private and public insolvency practitioners

One of the many public versus private IP imbalances is that public officials (notably the Official Receiver), whilst performing the same function as a private IP, are not usually regulated by the same regime. For example, in most cases the Official Receiver is not subject to the same exacting licensing regime as a private IP, and is exempt from the general provisions of s.388 *(see IA 1986 s.388(5)*, but the Official Receiver is bound by the PA 2004 provisions *(PA 2004 s.121(11)(b))*. Indeed he faces the same consequences for failure to carry out his function, albeit at the tax payers', rather than his personal, expense.

5.2.5 The assessment period

The assessment period, i.e. assessment by the PPF for eligibility to the PPF, commences with either the 'qualifying insolvency event' *(s.132(2)(a))* or with a s.129(1) or s.129(5)(a) application by the trustee and manager for the PPF to assume responsibility.

5.3 Insolvency Practitioner duties: the appointment of an 'independent person', formerly the 'independent trustee'

5.3.1 The Pensions Act

The insolvency practitioner at one time had a duty (dropped under *PA 2004 s.36*) to appoint an 'independent trustee' in certain circumstances (*PA 1995 ss.22-25*). PA 2004 s.36 shifts the duty of the IP from that of 'appointment of an independent trustee' to that of merely 'notification of insolvency practitioner appointment'. A similar obligation is placed on the Official Receiver *(s.36(2))*. Notice must be given to: the Regulator, the PPF and the trustees of the scheme of their beginning or ceasing to act.

'Insolvency practitioner' now includes (*PA 1995 s.22* as amended by *PA 2004 s.36(2)*) cases where an interim receiver of the employer's property is appointed at any time during an assessment period (i.e. assessment by the PPF for eligibility to the PPF) and at any time when the scheme is authorised to continue as a closed scheme *(see PA 2004 s.153)*. The term 'interim receiver' applies to personal insolvency i.e. bankruptcy and is therefore unlikely to be of practical importance.

Until the changes contained in PA 1995 s.23(1) the IP or Official Receiver was required to appoint an independent trustee where one was not already in place; now the Regulator 'may' by order appoint an 'independent person'. It is unclear whether the word 'may' indicates that the Regulator 'may sub-contract this service elsewhere' or 'may not act at all'; the latter is the preferred view. The change of term from 'independent trustee' to 'independent person' may not be material, although it may indicate a lowering of expectations and duties on the person appointed.

The definition of 'independent' remains fundamentally unaltered: "no interest in assets of the employer" *(PA 1995 s.23(3)(a)*, as amended); "neither connected with, nor an associate of [see *IA 1986 ss.249 and 435*] (i) the employer; (ii)... the [insolvency practitioner] or (iii) the Official Receiver and (c) he satisfies any requirements" *(PA 1995 s.23(3)(b)*, as amended). In relation to '(c)' ('he satisfies any requirements') the Authority, "must... compile and maintain a register of persons who satisfy the prescribed condition for the regulations". If any 'independent person' subsequently loses his independence (for example where an IP becomes a liquidator following the appointment of an administrative receiver) "he must as soon as reasonably practical" inform the Regulator *(PA 1995 s.25(4)(a))*. There is now a penalty for failure; previously there was no sanction and the requirement was merely to inform the IP.

In relation to the independent person's (formerly trustee's) fees, there has been a material (and possibly unfortunate) change in legislative policy. Until the change, "a trustee [Independent Trustee]... is entitled to be paid out of the scheme's resources his reasonable fees for acting in that capacity reasonably incurred by him in doing so, and to be so paid in priority to all other claims falling to be met out of the scheme's resources" *(PA 1995 s.25(6))*. There had been some public criticism that there was no system of 'taxation of costs' for the independent trustee (in the same way as there was for the IP and lawyers involved in the insolvency).

PA 2004 fails to address this criticism and may even compound the problems (but see below for how this is dealt with in the Independent Trustee Regulations). The revised section provides: "an order under section 23(1) [by the Regulator to appoint an independent trustee] may provide for any fees and expenses of the trustee appointed under the order to be paid - (a) by the employer, (b) [by the] scheme, or (c) partly by the employer and [the scheme]" *(PA 1995 s.25(6))*. The use of the word 'may' rather than 'shall' is unhelpful. The lawmakers might have expected that there would be a body of independent persons willing to act on an unpaid basis but the size of such a cohort is likely to be small if not miniscule; this is especially so where the potential liabilities are so great. The change from 'reasonable fees and expenses' to 'any fees and expenses' seems odd. There may be some informal control to be exercised by the Regulator (by obtaining registry membership) but it seems less protective than before. The 'natural brake on excessive independent trustee fees', especially of late, is the existence of pensions fund deficiencies, since any fees taken have a direct impact on members' benefits, and such members are likely to have a view even if they have little power.

5.3.2 The regulations

The Occupational Pension Schemes (Independent Trustee) Regulations 2005 ("Independent Trustee Regulations") primarily provide for the Regulator to "compile and maintain a register of" independent trustees and is therefore of particular interest to those seeking a position on the register of 'independent trustees'. The fact that these regulations are termed 'Independent Trustee', rather than the 'Independent Persons' regulations, may mean that the statutory change from 'independent trustee' to 'independent person' is of little significance.

Only one of the "conditions for registration" on the register of independent trustees warrants comment, namely the condition that "the Regulator is satisfied that... the applicant has adequate indemnity insurance cover" *(regulation 3(b)(iv))*. The existence of cover presupposes the possibility of claim. The legal relationship between a trustee and a beneficiary (i.e. pension scheme member) is based on trust law and consequently the ability of a member to sue for negligence is difficult. Given that the Regulator appoints and upon insolvency the employer liability is transferred to the PPF, would any negligence action be brought by the Regulator or the PPF, and if so under what provision? The terms of the insurance cover should be considered given the PA 2004 s.256 'no indemnification for fines or penalties' requirement. This is to the extent that standard insurance law does not already preclude indemnification for fines or penalties. Can (and indeed should) any independent trustee limit their liability and if so how? The obvious choice is via a letter of engagement.

Given that the Independent Trustee Regulations focus on the independent trustee register, it is unsurprising that they fail satisfactorily to address the criticisms levied at the independent trustee sections of PA 2004. These criticisms do not centre around the maintenance of the register of independent trustees but, rather, around the costs of the independent trustee.

The Regulator now has the discretion over whether or not to appoint an independent trustee, and it is uncertain how it will perform this role in practice. For example, how long it will take to decide whether or not to appoint. Whatever the practice, the readiness of the existing pension trustees to make decisions in the interim, more especially in the post-formal insolvency hiatus period, is likely to be hindered. This is unfortunate given the higher profile required of trustees following PA 2004. The Independent Trustee Regulations should have provided for some form of cut-off period whereby the Regulator would not appoint (or there would at least be a presumption against appointing) after the cut-off period, i.e. 'three business days after notification'. Given the Regulator's discretion over whether or not to appoint, many employers may appoint their own independent trustee in the pre-formal insolvency hiatus period, especially as the Regulator's power to appoint will remain, notwithstanding any employer appointment. Employers and non-independent trustees should, however, consider that if an existing independent person is in place, the Regulator may well decide not to appoint; consequently the independent trustee can make all the necessary decisions in the insolvency hiatus period. Ideally, the regulations should have provided for a presumption against the Regulator's appointment if an independent trustee was in place; more especially an independent trustee that was on the Regulator's register of independent trustees.

The defect in PA 2004 mentioned above, regarding the challenge to independent trustee fees, is answered in part in the Independent Trustee Regulations. Anyone seeking a position on the register of independent persons should be wary of at least one of the "conditions for registration". An "applicant agrees to have his fees and costs scrutinised by an independent adjudicator and to be bound by that adjudicator's final adjudication as to his fees and costs" (*Independent Trustee Regulations, regulation 3(e)(i)*). No information is provided as to the costs of the independent adjudicator. If there is no cost to the complainant in losing in a fee objection then, unfortunately, the independent trustee is placed in an invidious position. Any pension scheme member or his representative will object because 'he has nothing to lose'. However, the situation will be made worse if the costs of defending the fees in front of the independent adjudicator cannot themselves be claimed. Without some fail-safe device, the position of the independent trustee in justifying his fees will become untenable. Further, no information is provided as to how the adjudicator should reach his decision, i.e. 'reasonable costs reasonably incurred'. This lack of uncertainty is both unfair to the independent trustee and the consumer of his services. The Regulator needs to give some guidance here. Most importantly, no mechanism is provided as to the methodology of objection to the independent person's fees.

However, regulation 13 (supported by regulation 8) is of some assistance. The independent trustee must, upon pain of penalty, provide information to scheme members and relevant trade unions, but surprisingly not to an IP *(regulation 13(3))*."The information specified [includes]…the scale of fees that will be chargeable by the appointed trustee and payable by the scheme [and]…details of each of the amounts charged to the scheme by the appointed trustee in the past 12 months" *(regulation 13(2))*. If, as is often the case, the trustees are 'non-independent' (i.e. say the Finance Director of the company) then it is probable that fees will not have been charged. Consequently the charging of fees will seem more onerous to the members and relevant trade unions; thus there will be therefore be a downward pressure on fees.

If the independent trustee's fees rank as an expense of the insolvency (see below), whether directly or indirectly, then the IP should also have a right to object, via the independent adjudicator, to the independent trustee's fees. Indeed, even if the independent trustee's fees do not rank as an expense of the insolvency, but increase the liability of the pension scheme in the insolvency, then the IP should have some right of objection, over and above simply admitting the pension claim or not. Further, the IP should receive the information noted in regulation 13(2).

The Independent Trustee Regulations conspicuously fail to answer directly the most pressing of questions, 'are the fees and expenses of the independent trustee an expense of the insolvency and if so where do they rank in the priority of expenses'? However, regulation 13(2) (noted above) may assist. The independent trustee is to provide specified information, including, "the scale of his fees that will be chargeable…and *payable by the scheme*" (emphasis supplied). If the fees of the independent trustee are payable by the scheme then they may not rank as an expense of the insolvency.

The rest of the Independent Trustee Regulations are the expected tidying-up exercise. "Regulations 10, 11 and 12 make certain modifications to sections 22 to 26 of the 1995 Act, in respect of the application of those sections [to multi-employer schemes], cases where the employer is a partnership, and schemes which have no members who are employees" (from the Explanatory Note to the Independent Trustee Regulations). The purpose of all three of these regulations is consistent with the subordinated PA 2004 legislation, i.e. extending the term 'employer' to cover multi-employer and cessation of employment scenarios, and extending the legislation to cover partnerships which sit uneasily between corporate law on the one hand and sole traders on the other.

Regulation 10(1) states: "…in relation to a trust scheme which is a multi-employer scheme…sections 22 to 26 of the [1995]… Act (provisions relating to independent trustees) are modified so that references to the employer…are to be treated as if they were references to each employer".

Regulation 11(1) states: "sections 22 to 26 of the 1995 Act are modified [in]…any case where …[an insolvent] partnership is the employer or one of the employers…and… the courts of England and Wales have jurisdiction to wind up the insolvent partnership… [then] section 22(1) shall be modified so as to apply in relation to the scheme - (a) if a person begins to act as an IP in relation to the insolvent partnership; or (b) if the official receiver becomes the liquidator or provisional liquidator of the insolvent partnership… [so that] those provisions to a company included references to the insolvent partnership".

Regulation 12 extends the meaning of 'employer'. "For the purposes of sections 22 to 26 of the 1995 Act and these Regulations references to the employer shall include a person who would have been an employer…but for the fact that, immediately before an insolvency practitioner or the official receiver began to act…[so] that person no longer employed any persons…to which the scheme in question relates".

5.4   Insolvency Practitioner's duties: "scheme rescue"

5.4.1   Background

The IP and the PPF are required to explore the question of the scheme's viability following an 'insolvency event' *(PA 2004 Chapter 2, ss.122-125)*, and in particular to explore whether the scheme can be rescued without a claim on the PPF. Even though the duty emerges *(s.122(1))* where an 'insolvency event' has occurred, it may still be advisable for a 'receiver or manager' whose appointment does not necessarily give rise to an "insolvency event" to consider his position under s.122.

5.4.2   Notices

An IP is obliged to issue one of two notices:

(i)   a 'scheme failure notice' (i.e. a notice that a scheme rescue is not possible) *(s.122(2)(a))*; or

(ii)   a 'withdrawal notice' (i.e. that a scheme rescue has occurred) *(s.122(2)(b))*.

The obligation to notify continues notwithstanding the termination of the IP appointment *(s.122(4))*. The notice may be in a prescribed form *(s.122(8))*. Like the appointment notice, the 'rescue notice' must be sent to the PPF, the Regulator and the trustees and managers of the scheme *(s.122(6))*. Unlike the appointment notice, however, the 'rescue notice' can sensibly be issued, 'as soon as reasonably practical', rather than the opaque 'once the IP is 'aware' of the situation'.

5.4.3   Definition of a scheme rescue and the Pensions Act 2004

While an IP must give notice of a scheme rescue, the requirements as to what constitutes a scheme rescue were unclear until the regulations under s.122(5) were published. The Pension Protection Fund (Entry Rules) Regulations 2005, regulation 9 defines a scheme rescue as: "another person or other persons has or have assumed responsibility for meeting the employer's pension liabilities under the scheme". This is a very high hurdle and is unlikely to be met very often.

5.4.4   Scheme Rescue and the PPF approval

The PPF reviews (i.e. 'makes a determination' of – see *s.123(4))* the IP's decision and will, or will not, approve the 's.122 notice'. If it approves the notice, it will issue, in a prescribed format, a 'determination notice'. The review is governed by *s.123(3)* and is twofold:

first, whether the IP was required to issue a notice, whether it was an 'insolvency event' covering an occupational scheme *(s.123(3)(a))*; and

secondly, the PPF must consider whether the 's.122 notice' complies with (as yet to be published) regulations as to the required form and information *(s.122(8) & s.123(3)(b), (s.123(3)(b)).*

The PPF's 'determination notice' is then provided to the Regulator, the scheme trustees and managers, and any IP and/or the company employer.

Even where the PPF issues a 'determination notice', it is not binding on the PPF where it is subject to appeal *(PA 2004 Chapter 6)* or is referred to the PPF Ombudsman. Once the relevant time periods have passed, a 'binding notice' is issued to the Regulator, the trustee and managers, IPs/former IPs and/or the company *(s.125)*.

5.4.5   The PPF fails to approve a s.122 notice or the insolvency practitioner fails to issue a s.122 notice

Where the PPF fails to approve s.122 notice, the PPF steps into the role of the IP; the IP's obligations become the PPF's obligations *(s.124)*. Two issues emerge in practice: (1) the circumstances in which the PPF would not approve the IP's s.122 notice; and (2) the time-frame for issuing a s.122 notice.

In practice, the PPF will no doubt be reluctant to reject any IP s.122 notice, and although there appears to be no formal requirement, natural justice would appear to require the PPF to give reasons for such rejection. With the current drive towards proportionality, it seems unlikely that the notice would be rejected for failure to meet the required form.

Although, in theory, the PPF can only either reject or accept the notice, it seems probable that the PPF will liaise with the IP to remedy any formal or technical errors. In any event the Regulator can issue an 'improvement notice' (i.e. remedy any formal or technical errors) to try to avoid any bureaucratic impediments.

In other cases, the s.122 notice may be rejected by the PPF on the grounds that in its opinion a scheme rescue 'could have been achieved'. Hindsight reviews of an effectively commercial decision taken by an IP perhaps several years previously will no doubt have to be dealt with sensitively. Given the consequences of a 'scheme failure notice' (the fund picking up the tab for the deficiency), there may be a natural desire to question (or simply not to approve) a s.122 notice in order to save PPF funds.

5.4.6 Timing

One major concern is the appropriate timeframe for issuing a s.122 notice. In practice, CVAs can take several years to complete and even upon completion, an IP, or former IP, may not be able to determine with satisfaction whether a 'scheme rescue' has or more properly could occur.

5.4.7 Members' views

Scheme members understandably will be concerned that, in order to achieve a corporate turnaround (and hence a scheme rescue), the inevitable delay prejudices their position. There will, in practice, be pressure to seek immediate PPF compensation, to liquidate the company forthwith and avoid any form of rescue. The PPF may not continue indefinitely, or even offer lower benefits, and members may prefer to see an end to uncertainty. An IP may be subject to criticism for delaying, in an attempt to explore whether a CVA or other corporate turnaround mechanism is eventually successful. The delay would be in the issue of a s.122 notice (s.124(1)(a)). In practice there will be inappropriate pressure exerted on an IP to proceed to liquidation, which it is a professional duty to resist.

5.4.8 Fees

If an IP attempts a turnaround, since he must eventually fulfil the s.122 notice obligations, he will be at risk of losing his fees as a former IP to the company. The IP regulatory body is concerned to ensure that the fees at the close of the appointment will equal the fees to date, i.e. there is no mechanism for post-closure fees. It may be appropriate for an IP, as a disbursement, to take out insurance against the eventuality of post-appointment fees and disbursements or post-termination pension compliance. However, at present, no such product seems to be available.

5.4.9 Practice

The PPF and the Regulator will need, in due course, to ensure that IPs are not over-regulated so that corporate recoveries where possible can continue. In time it will become clearer whether the Regulator's inclinations to limit members' concerns will affect the policy drive towards corporate recovery.

5.5 Pension scheme debts provable in an insolvency

5.5.1 Background

DB scheme debts in an insolvency are likely to be one of the more difficult claims to prove i.e. as to quantum. In practice, IPs are likely to offer every courtesy to trustees and the Regulator in attempting to recover debts. At the same time the trustee and manager and/or the PPF, in quantifying their claims, will be aware that the IPs (and their regulators) and/or other creditors will question any apparent delay in exercising statutory duties in debt admittance. IPs will need to ensure that there is immediate quantification of creditor claims (see e.g. Insolvency Rules 1986 rule 11.2 for liquidators).

Given the complexities involved, it is slightly surprising that no special provision has been made for the submission and proving of pension deficits within the Insolvency Rules 1986, particularly when the opportunity was not only available following recent revisions to the Insolvency Act, but also following the coming into force of the Enterprise Act, at a time when the Pensions Act was being envisaged. It might be that when fresh legislation is introduced, pensions will be treated rather as banks currently are: *cf.* the position of the Deposit Protection Fund in a bank collapse in Insolvency Rules rule 4.72(7) and the special rules for government departments. The legislation makes it clear however that the PPF is treated as a non-governmental organization rather than a department of state *(PA 2004 Schedule 1)*.

Finally, it should be remembered that IA 1986 Schedule 6, category 4 makes "contributions to Occupational Pension Schemes etc." preferential creditors in an insolvency. The extent of the preferential liability is contained within Schedule 4 of the Pension Schemes Act 1993.

5.5.2 Special issues under the Insolvency Rules 1986

All the special issues addressed in the Insolvency Rules can (and therefore should) apply to a pension scheme (and arguably also a PPF) liability claim:

1. A scheme deficiency is invariably a contingent claim (i.e. it is not a liquidated claim) and is governed therefore (in a liquidation) by Insolvency Rules 1986 Rule 4.86, which states: "The liquidator shall estimate the value of any debt which, by reason of its being subject to any contingency or for any other reason, does not bear a certain value; and he may revise any estimate previously made, if he thinks fit by reference to any change of circumstances or to information becoming available to him".

2. The scheme, to the extent it holds assets, is 'secured': accordingly, only the deficiency is provable. The claim is governed by (in a liquidation) Insolvency Rules 1986 Rule 4.88 which lays down the procedures for valuing the 'secured deficiency', namely: "(1) If a secured creditor realises his security, he may prove for the balance of his debt, after deducting the amount realised. (2) If a

secured creditor voluntarily surrenders his security for the general benefit of creditors, he may prove for his whole debt, as if it were unsecured".

3. In some cases there may be the possibility of a set-off: for instance via shared costs, such as the pension scheme "piggy-backing" payroll services. Therefore, the value of any claim by the scheme against the company is governed (in a liquidation) by Insolvency Rules 1986 Rule 4.90 ("the set-off rules") which states: "An account shall be taken of what is due from each party to the other in respect of the mutual dealings, and the sums due from one party shall be set off against the sums from the other".

4. The debt due from the scheme to the member may be periodic in nature. Thus, the Insolvency Rules rule 4.92 (the periodic payment rule) may therefore apply which states: "In the case of rent and other payments of a periodical nature, the creditor may prove for any amounts due and unpaid up to the date when the company went into liquidation".

5. The liability to pay under a pension (not the pension scheme deficit itself) may be a 'debt payable at a future time': regardless of any contingency. Thus the claim is under Insolvency Rules 1986 Rule 4.94 which demands "discounting" for such debts.

Given that there is no special provision for PPF and/or pension scheme liabilities in either the Insolvency Act or the Insolvency Rules, then these rules should apply. These rules may, however, conflict with actuarial practice.

5.5.3 Case law

In addition to the Insolvency Rules, case law has addressed the issue of debts which do not represent an immediately payable sum and/or are payable over a period of time. One of the most famous decisions is: *Re Park Air Services plc; Christopher Moran Holdings Ltd v Bairstow and another [1999] 1 All ER 673* ("Park Air"). Park Air went into solvent liquidation, i.e. an MVL. A major creditor was the landlord for the remainder of the lease. The calculation of outstanding lease payments in a liquidation has many similarities to a pension scheme liability. Liabilities under a pension scheme are like lease payments; periodic and relating to the future. Additionally there are various contingencies to consider. In the case of a lease the contingency is the likelihood of a possible new tenant; in the case of a pension scheme, the contingency is longevity expectations.

Relevant extracts from the Park Air judgment are noted below: -

"Any award of damages involves arriving at a single monetary figure which in present terms quantifies that loss. Where the loss will be suffered over a period in the future, the computation will have to make allowance for any advancement that has occurred…To fail to take into account the element of advancement leads to an over-compensation of the claimant…Rule 11.13 is concerned with the proof of debts payable at a future time. It provides as follows:

1. Where a creditor has proved for a debt of which payment is not due at the date of the declaration of dividend, he is entitled to receive the dividend equally with other creditors, but subject as follows. [To what extent is a pension scheme liability not due at the date of the declaration of the dividend, especially when the liability is not a section 75 liability?].

2. For the purpose of dividend (and for no other purpose), the amount of the creditor's admitted proof (or, if a distribution has previously been made to him, the amount remaining outstanding in respect of his admitted proof) shall be reduced by [a percentage] calculated as follows: I x M/12 where I is 5 per cent. and M is the number of months (expressed, if need be, as, or as including, fractions of months) between the declaration of dividend and the date when payment of the creditor's debt would otherwise be due. [To what extent does this discount rate not apply to a section 75 calculation and should it?]...

By *Rule 4.94*, a creditor whose debt is not due at the date when the company went into liquidation is entitled to prove for the nominal, i.e. undiscounted, amount of the debt; but this is subject to adjustment of the dividend when payment is made before the time it would have become due.

Rule 11.13(2) adjusts the dividend payable in respect of the proof by requiring it to be discounted at the rate of 5% pa over the period of acceleration.

Rule 11.13(3) is a very curious provision, newly introduced in 1986, when interest during the winding-up was for the first time made payable on debts proved in the winding-up...There is a critical distinction between contracts which have been fully performed by the creditor and contracts which remain executory on his part. [To what extent does this logic apply to a pension scheme creditor?] The creditor who has lent money which has not been repaid or supplied goods or services which have not been paid for sues or proves in respect of a debt. If the debt is not yet due at the date on which a dividend is declared, the dividend is subject to adjustment under rule 11.13. The creditor who has contracted for payment for goods or services still to be supplied by him, however, is not and may never become entitled to payment. He cannot sue or prove in respect of a debt....It would be wrong for me to leave rule 11.13 without drawing attention to the respects in which its drafting appears to be seriously defective. For more than a hundred years provision has been made for future debts to be discounted at the rate of 5% pa in order to arrive at their present value. The process of discounting involves applying the discount to the reducing amount of the debt, thus arriving at a sum which, invested at compound interest, would equal the nominal value of the debt at the date when it fell due. Rule 11.13(2), however, applies the discounting formula to the full (i.e. unreducing) amount of the admitted proof. Such a process would reduce the proof to zero after 20 years, and at no stage yields an amount which, invested at 5% compound interest, would equal the nominal value of the debt at the date fixed for payment…The first issue concerns the rate of discount. The best evidence of the appropriate discount rate is the yield on gilt-edged securities for an equivalent term. The judge found that this was 8·435% pa…The 5% rate is a purely nominal rate which has remained constant for more than a hundred years during periods of high and low interest rates alike, and its application would not yield a correct assessment of the amount of the respondent's loss…I would allow the appeal and restore the order of the judge but varied so as to reflect a discount rate of 8·435% pa ['the Park Air discount rate']."

5.5.4 The Trust Deed and 'the debt on employer rule'

It should not be forgotten that the trust deed itself can dictate the liability. The trust deed should make reference to the insolvency of the employer and state upon insolvency, what is the liability? Ordinarily the liability should be the section 75 liability. For the IP, the question is, 'is the trust-imposed liability acceptable, i.e. is it contrary to public policy and/or not a genuine estimate of the likely loss in the event of an insolvency? If the trust deed imposes a section 75 liability then it should be acceptable.

5.5.5 The application of the Insolvency Rules

In making any claim on behalf of the scheme, it is necessary to consider who is acting for the scheme – is it the trustees and managers and/or the PPF? As a general rule the IP should always try to give notice at all times (especially as to intended dividends (*Insolvency Rules 1986 rule 11.2*)) to both the trustees and managers, and the PPF.

The control of the submission of the claim is governed by the assessment period provisions (*ss.132, 137*); during the s.132 assessment period, in relation to an eligible scheme, the PPF acts as the creditor. The s.132 assessment period begins with the 'qualifying insolvency event' (as defined in s.132(2), and ends because either:

(a) a scheme rescue is possible, or no scheme rescue is possible but there are sufficient assets to meet protected liabilities, in which case the trustees and managers now represent the scheme; or

(b) the PPF refuses to assume responsibility, because it is an ineligible scheme or because it was 'a new scheme seeking to replace an existing scheme, whose purpose was to receive compensation' (*s.147*) in which case the trustees and managers now represent the scheme; or

(c) the scheme has been transferred to the PPF (*s.160*) in which case the PPF will continue to represent the scheme.

Where the IP is confused as to who is representing the scheme, and the trustees and managers wrongly represent the scheme, the PPF may validate any act of the trustees and managers (*s.136*).

Performing the calculation is also uncertain. At first glance the 'liabilities of the scheme are transferred to the PPF' and hence the contingent claim of the PPF in the insolvency should be based upon the deficiency *(s.161(2)(a))*. But once a liability is transferred, or the extent of the liability changes, several issues emerge:

First, the PPF may modify a term of an insurance contract perhaps thereby 'reducing' the deficiency *(s.161(7))*. But if the PPF takes a proactive step to 'mitigate' (but not to increase) its loss (as all creditors should legitimately do) then the mitigated loss may accordingly be the value of the claim.

Secondly, a complicated compensation package may be offered to or put in place for former members. The actuarial calculation involved (which is beyond the scope of this book) involves both contingent and periodic payments; these payments may (and probably will) differ from those used in the original employer's scheme (s.162; Schedule 7). Inevitably the aggregate compensation package provided to former members of the employer's scheme, given the PPF cap on compensation, will be less than they would have received if the former scheme was solvent and continuing. At its simplest the compensation cap is 90%. Whilst the scheme liabilities are transferred to the PPF *(s.161(2)(a))*, the nature of those liabilities change once the assessment period has ended and the PPF assumes the responsibility of providing the compensation. In short the PPF will owe the members less than the company owed, i.e. it will only owe 90% of what was owed. It is not immediately clear whether the PPF's claim in the employer insolvency should be (based on this simplistic logic alone) 100% or 90%, of that owed to members. If the claim of the PPF in the insolvency is 90% (the current upper limit for compensation), what would happen to the remaining 10%? Do the trustees still have a claim for 10%? Surely not, given that the liabilities of the scheme are transferred to the PPF. If the liabilities are transferred then the trustees can have no claim. But from the members perspective they have lost, in this example, 10%. Could the members apply individually as creditors in the insolvency? If they could, then the claim would have to be based upon tort, given there was no direct nexus between the member and the insolvent company. If the member has no claim and the PPF claim is limited to (say) 90%, then the remaining creditors have an unfair boost.

At first sight, the logic of the position is that the Regulator and PPF seem to have created a 'stealth tax on insolvency'. But is that true? The Board only acts as the "creditor of the employer" during the assessment period *(s.137(2))*. If the Board does not assume responsibility at the end of the assessment period, then responsibility reverts to the trustee. Under s.132(2)(b)(iii) an assessment period would end because there had been "no scheme rescue but [there were] sufficient assets to meet protected liabilities." If the PPF ceases to be involved (see *s.150*) then there can be no 'stealth tax on insolvency'. However, if the PPF assumes responsibility, then the position remains: the PPF is claiming more in insolvency than its concomitant liability which itself arises because of the insolvency. In reality, this 'stealth tax' is more apparent than real. The PPF will only assume responsibility if the dividends fall below the protected liabilities. Thus, even if the PPF claim is inflated (i.e. above the cap) the opportunity to 'stealth tax' will be low because the dividends from the insolvency will be low. Nevertheless, is it morally tenable? The statutory basis of PPF funding is by way of levy. This backdoor taxation is unparliamentary: it would seem the only form of hypothecated taxation assumed in PA 2004 and supporting legislation were the levies. The PPF claim in the insolvency may well be the section 75 debt, whereas its liability will be the capped compensation.

Thirdly, the PPF and/or Secretary of State can alter, at will, the statute-based arithmetical bases for a calculation (see in part PA 2004 Schedule 7 clauses 29 and 30). It seems improbable that the legislation intended to allow the PPF to prove for the full amount, without taking into account its own statutory power to alter the value of the claim.

Ignoring section 75 and winding up (see below) but given the above, the contingent nature of any pension fund deficit claim will change depending upon whether the assessment period is continuing or has elapsed; this will be especially so following upon a transfer notice (*PA 2004 s.160*). Indeed the contingent scenarios (either: (a) calculation of the original employee liability via the scheme deficiency; or (b) calculation of the PPF liability via the Schedule 7 compensation) are contingent upon the other. Thus (a) the calculation of the PPF liability under the Schedule 7 compensation requires (b) the calculation of the original employee liability through the scheme deficiency. If the IP (frequently, although not exclusively a liquidator) was minded to value the scheme deficiency (ignoring section 75 and winding up, see below) as to the basis of the creditor claim, he would perhaps have to discount that contingent claim calculation further, on the contingency that in any event, the PPF 'may' suffer a lesser loss under the Schedule 7 calculation. Certainly, the Liquidator can "revise any estimate... [as to a contingent debt] if he thinks fit by reference to any change of circumstances [the section 160 transfer?] on the information becoming available to him. He shall inform the creditor as to his estimate and any revision of it" (*Insolvency Rules 1986 4.86(1)*). Importantly "where the value of a debt is estimated under this rule, or by the court under section 168 (3) or (5), the amount provable in the winding-up in the case of that debt is that of the estimate for the time being" (*Insolvency Rules 1986 4.86(2)*).

5.5.6 The position of the Regulator and the PPF under the Pensions Act 2004

The position is twofold, 'pre-scheme winding up' and 'post-scheme winding up'. The position of the Regulator and PPF post winding up is best explained with a quote from the *Guidance on Clearance Statements* provided by the Regulator:

Before 11th June, 2003, solvent and insolvent companies could legally walk away from their pension creditor by reference to the scheme's Minimum Funding Requirement. Not only was this amount often not demanding, but the circumstances in which it was relevant to Directors carrying out their day-to-day duties was not often clear or obvious.

The Pensions Act 2004, the introduction of the Pension Protection Fund and new regulations regarding the deficit on wind-up [The *Occupational Pension Schemes (Winding Up and Deficiency on Winding Up etc) (Amendment) Regulations 2004* and the *Occupational Pension Schemes (Winding Up, Deficiency on Winding Up and Transfer Values) (Amendment) Regulations 2005]* has changed that. Now the debt owed to the pension scheme when it winds up, regardless of the employer's status as solvent or insolvent, is calculated on a full buyout basis - that is the amount estimated by the actuary that is needed to secure the pensions promise with an insurance company [i.e. the section 75 debt]. This has made the cost of pension obligations much clearer, and introduced a steep learning curve for Directors, Trustees, financial stakeholders and advisers (paragraphs 6 & 7).

The pre-scheme winding up position is similar to the position noted above under the Insolvency Act. One difference is perhaps section 17 ('Power of the Regulator to recover unpaid contributions'):

Where any employer contribution payable towards an occupational or personal pension scheme is not paid on or before its due date, the Regulator may, on behalf of the trustees or managers of the scheme, exercise such powers as the trustees or managers have to recover that contribution (*s.17(1)*).

It should be assumed that an insolvency will be accompanied by a failure to abide by a recovery plan. However, this outstanding debt will also be subsumed within the general deficiency claim (however calculated) in the insolvency. Its effect in an insolvency is therefore of limited value.

5.5.7 The interaction between the Insolvency Act and the Pensions Act 2004

Two questions need to be asked: (i) when, if ever, does the PA 2004 (and its supporting legislation) apply to the exclusion of the IA 1986 (and its supporting legislation); and (ii) vice-versa?

The Pensions Act does not specifically override Insolvency Rules. Consequently, the Insolvency Rules still apply. The question is the extent of the application. At its most basic, the Insolvency Rules should apply in a relatively simple way to reduce the section 75 debt through consideration of Contribution Notices, Financial

Support Directions, security guarantees, etc. The value of these can be merely deducted from the section 75 debt. The IP could go one stage further, and argue that the statute-imposed debt merely bound the employer and the trustee, but not necessarily the IP. Consequently, the IP had to look at 'the real underlying loss to the scheme' following the insolvency.

However, despite the section 75 estimate being a genuine estimate of loss, unfortunate incompatibilities may develop between pension scheme and other creditors. As noted above, *Park Air* imposed a discount rate of 8·435% ('the Park Air discount rate'). What if the section 75 calculation imposed a different discount rate from that of Park Air, which resulted in a disproportionately unfair result to non-pension scheme creditors? The situation of an insolvent entity, with large leasing and section 75 liabilities is foreseeable; this problem is therefore real.

There appears to be three options available:
(i)   'do nothing' and accept the disproportionately unfair result to non-pension scheme creditors;
(ii)   'alter the section 75 calculation by applying a Park Air discount to the calculations'; or
(iii)   'apply a section 75 discount rate to Park Air-type creditors'.

It may be cost-ineffective 'to take the PPF on and dispute the section 75 calculation'. Inevitably, altering the section 75 discount rate will also take on the PPF and proving that a statutory rate should not apply is a difficult hurdle to overcome. Like statute, the Park Air decision is binding, although Park Air may allow more room for manoeuvre, i.e. the section 75 discount rate could be applied to non-pension scheme discounted creditors. There is, also, the third constituency to consider: creditors who do not have any discount rate applied. They may object to Park Air creditors who have their calculations uplifted.

5.5.8   Winding up

It should be remembered that the section 75 debt is a consequence of a scheme winding up. Section 22 ('Powers in relation to winding up of occupational pension schemes') governs the situation by amending section 11 of PA 1995. Thus the "Authority may, during an assessment period…in relation to an occupational pension scheme, by order direct the scheme to be wound up if they are satisfied that it is necessary to do so in order - (a) to ensure that the scheme's protected liabilities do not exceed its assets, or (b) if those liabilities do exceed its assets, to keep the excess to a minimum". Protected liabilities are "(a) the cost of securing benefits for…members of the scheme which correspond to the compensation…if the Board assumed responsibility for the scheme…(b) liabilities of the scheme which are not liabilities to, or in respect of, its members, and (c) the estimated cost of winding up the scheme" *(s.131)*. "References to the assets of the scheme are references to those assets excluding any assets representing the value of any rights in respect of money purchase benefits (within the meaning of that Act) under the scheme" *(s.22)*. But this power "does not have effect to authorise the Authority to make an order ...if their doing so would be unlawful as a result of section 6(1) of the Human Rights Act 1998 (unlawful for public authority to act in contravention of a Convention right)" *(s.22)*.

Given the inevitably large difference between a cessation (i.e. section 75) calculation and a non-cessation calculation, the IP is obliged to question any decision by the Regulator to instigate a winding up. So, the IP needs to know the appeal procedures and, in that regard, note the specific reference to the Human Rights Act.

5.5.9 Submission of claims timing and valuation problems

Section 22 may cause timing problems. It is understandable that the Regulator may not be able to carry out its duty immediately under PA 2004 s.22. It may be some time before it can be ascertained whether it is satisfied that a winding-up is appropriate "to ensure that the schemes protected liabilities do not exceed its assets, or ...if those liabilities do exceed its assets, to keep the excess to a minimum". In the interim, the IP may have to declare dividends. Those dividends must necessarily be based on a claim. The question is, 'is the claim, in this interim period, a section 75 debt or not'? If it is obvious to the IP that there will be no scheme rescue (indeed he has issued a notice to that effect) and that the dividend will be insufficient to meet the protected liabilities then, despite there being no formal winding-up or trust deed statement as to a debt upon insolvency, the IP may wish to accept a section 75 claim in the insolvency. Outside these parameters, it will be understandable for an IP to question a 'pre-scheme winding up section 75 claim' in an insolvency.

The PPF is obliged to obtain valuations. These valuations will form the basis of any claim, including a section 75 claim. Timing and valuation problems may arise. The PPF obligations arise because of:
s.127 ('Duty to assume responsibility for schemes following insolvency event');
s.128 ('Duty to assume responsibility for schemes following application or notification');
s.143 ('Board's obligation to obtain valuation of assets and protected liabilities');
s.144 ('Approval of valuation'); and
s.145 ('Binding valuations').

Under section 127: "(2) The Board must assume responsibility for the scheme...if - (a) the value of the assets of the scheme at the relevant time was less than the amount of the protected liabilities at that time...(b) after the relevant time the Board issues a scheme failure notice under s.130(2) in relation to the scheme and that notice becomes binding, and (c) a withdrawal event has not occurred".

Under section 128: "(1)Where the trustees...of an eligible scheme become aware that...the employer in relation to the scheme is unlikely to continue as a going concern...they must make an application to the Board for it to assume responsibility for the scheme under s.128".

Under section 143: "(1) This section applies in a case within...section 127 or 128. (2)...the Board must, as soon as reasonably practicable, obtain an actuarial valuation [i.e. the assets and the protected liabilities] of the scheme".

Under section 144: "(1) This section applies where the Board obtains a valuation in respect of a scheme under s.143. (2) Where the Board is satisfied that the valuation has been prepared in accordance with that section, it must - (a) approve the valuation, and (b) give a copy of the valuation to...any IP in relation to the employer...Where the Board is not so satisfied, it must obtain another valuation under that section".

Under section 145: "(1)...a valuation obtained under s.143 is not binding until - (a) it is approved under s.144, (b) the period within which the approval may be reviewed...has expired, and (c) if the approval is so reviewed - (i) the review and any reconsideration, (ii) any reference to the PPF Ombudsman in respect of the approval, and (iii) any appeal against his determination or directions, has been finally disposed of. (2) For the purposes of determining whether or not the condition...that scheme assets are less than protected liabilities...is satisfied...a binding valuation is conclusive. This subsection is subject to s.172(3) and (4) (treatment of fraud compensation payments). (3) Where a valuation becomes binding under this section the Board must as soon as reasonably practicable give a notice to that effect together with a copy of the binding valuation to...any insolvency practitioner in relation to the employer".

Once binding, the valuation is conclusive, especially as to 'whether or not the condition in *s.127(2)(a)* or, as the case may be, *s.128(2)(a)* (the condition that scheme assets are less than 'protected liabilities') is satisfied in relation to a scheme *(s.145(2)'*. This is save to the extent that fraud compensation has been made under *s.172(3) and (4)*, which themselves can become assets of the scheme. There may be considerable potential difficulties with timing. The PPF will take some time in fulfilling its statutory duties under *ss.127(2)(a)* and *128(2)(a)* ('the difference between the assets and the protected liabilities quantified'): whereas the IP is under similar duties to expedite the insolvency by having creditors' claims finalised. Section 145 makes the valuation binding on the PPF only, *not* on the IP. The IP can alter the creditor claim as circumstances change, such as the existence of the valuation. Nevertheless, it is quite possible that the IP will have legitimately demanded the submission of final creditor claims before the valuation is finalized; this is especially before the *s.145(1)(c)* ('disposal of any review') condition is satisfied. There will therefore be a perverse situation: a difference between the claim as admitted by the IP and a different claim (by valuation) by which the PPF is bound. Whilst elsewhere we have asked the IP to be sympathetic, as far as possible, to the position of the PPF, such a difference will be untenable for the IP and the non-scheme creditors represented by the IP. A better solution would be a statutory alteration allowing for expedited procedures, especially of the review process, notwithstanding the requirements of the Human Rights Act 1998. This is all the more so given the difficulty caused by any possible incremental delay due to the *s.172(3) and (4)* ('fraud compensation payment') exemptions.

5.5.10 Winding up and timing

Timing may well be an issue because the Regulator may not be prepared to wind up the scheme in the time which the IP requires in order to facilitate dividends. The IP may well therefore require a claim to be made on a non-section 75 basis.

The following Insolvency Rules (using liquidation as an example) provide for a potential timing clash:

Rule 4.82(2) (Rejection): "If the liquidator rejects a proof in whole or in part, he shall prepare a written statement of his reasons for doing so, and send it forthwith to the creditor." The rejection would be on the grounds that: (a) a section 75 calculation was not acceptable, because winding-up had not occurred; or (b) the section 75 calculation was either incorrect or used (say) inappropriate discount rates.

Rule 4.83(1) (Application by creditor): "If a creditor is dissatisfied with the liquidator's decision [i.e. the rejection of the PPF's section 75 pre-scheme winding up claim]…he may apply to the court for the decision to be reversed or varied."

Rule 4.82(2) (timing): "The application must be made within 21 days of his receiving the statement." During this 21 day period it may be possible to instigate a winding up.

Rule 4.83(6) [Costs re application]: "The official receiver is not personally liable for costs incurred by any person in respect of an application under this Rule; and the liquidator (if other than the Official Receiver) is not so liable unless the court makes an order to that effect." This latter rule may well wrongly discourage IPs from questioning the PPF's claim.

Despite the existence of rule 4.83 (6), a liquidator should not be discouraged from rejecting the section 75 claim. All things being equal, if the PPF submits a section 75 claim, yet the scheme has not yet begun to be formally wound up, the Court could find in favour of the Liquidator and/or not require personal liability for costs.

5.5.11 What is the section 75 debt?

A section 75 debt is defined by *PA 1995 s.75* as: "(1) If, in…an occupational pension scheme which is not a money purchase scheme, the value at the applicable time of the assets of the scheme is less than the amount at that time of the liabilities of the scheme, an amount equal to the difference shall be treated as a debt due from the employer to the trustees or managers of the scheme...(2) If in...an occupational pension scheme which is not a money purchase scheme - (a) a relevant insolvency event occurs in relation to the employer...[then] the debt in question shall be taken, for the purposes of the law relating to winding up...to arise immediately before that time (4)...a relevant insolvency event occurs...where the employer is a company, when it goes into liquidation... (6) In calculating the value of any liabilities for those purposes, a provision of the scheme which limits the amount of its liabilities by reference to the amount of its assets is to be disregarded... (10) Regulations may modify [and have much modified] this section as it applies in prescribed circumstances."

Subsection (4) relates only to an insolvent liquidation; it makes no reference to a solvent liquidation. Thus, only an insolvent liquidation (i.e. excluding an MVL) results in an automatic section 75 debt.

One of the modifying regulations is the Occupational Pension Schemes (Employer Debt) Regulations 2005 (the "Employer Debt Regulations", see below). Regulation 5 ('Calculation of the value of scheme liabilities and assets: defined benefit schemes') of the Employer Debt Regulations states: "(1) The liabilities and assets of a scheme which are to be taken into account for the purposes of section 75...and their amount or value must be determined, calculated and verified by the actuary as at the applicable time - (a) in the case of liabilities in respect of pensions or other benefits, on the assumption that the liabilities will be discharged by the purchase of annuities of the kind described in section 74(3)(c) of the 1995 Act (discharge of liabilities: annuity purchase);...(2) ...the actuary must estimate the cost of purchasing the annuities. (3) The liabilities of a scheme...include all expenses (except the cost of the annuities referred to in paragraph (1)(a)) which, in the opinion of the trustees...of the scheme, are likely to be incurred in connection with the winding up of the scheme...(5) The value of the assets and the amount of the liabilities of a scheme which are to be taken into account for the purposes of section 75...must be certified by the actuary..."

Under PA 2004 an automatic winding up (hence a section 75 debt) may occur regardless of the insolvency process involved, i.e. a liquidation or not. Under s.161 ('Effect of Board assuming responsibility for a scheme'): "(1) Where a transfer notice is given to the trustees...the Board assumes responsibility for the scheme...(2) The effect of the Board assuming responsibility for a scheme is that...the scheme is to be treated as having been wound up immediately after that time".

5.5.12 The special position of public body partially guaranteed schemes

According to the Pension Protection Fund (Partially Guaranteed Schemes)(Modification) Regulations 2005 (the "Partially Guaranteed Regulations") a "partially guaranteed scheme" means: " an eligible scheme [in respect of] which a relevant public authority has –

(a) given a guarantee in relation to (i) any part of the scheme; (ii) any benefits payable under the scheme rules; or (iii) any members of the scheme; or

(b) made any other arrangements for the purposes of securing that the assets of the scheme are sufficient to meet any part of its liabilities" *(regulation 1)*.

Whereas the "unsecured part" means: "any part of a partially guaranteed scheme - (a) in respect of which no guarantee has been given by a relevant public authority; and (b) which relates to benefits payable under the scheme in respect of which…no such guarantee has been given", the Regulations modify the Act in respect of partially guaranteed schemes. The modifications operate so that the Board only takes into account the assets and liabilities of the unsecured part of a partially guaranteed scheme and can only assume responsibility for that part" (from the *Explanatory Notes to the Partially Guaranteed Regulations*).

For all intents and purposes, a partially guaranteed scheme is treated as two schemes: the 'unsecured part' and the 'guaranteed part'. The 'unsecured part' is treated in a normal PA 2004 fashion. As far as the guaranteed part is concerned, the Regulator and the PPF are little concerned. As far as the IP is concerned, he would be dealing with two claims: that of the PPF in respect of the 'unsecured part' and that of the relevant public body in respect of the 'guaranteed part'. As to the 'guaranteed part', the IP should treat this guarantee as he would treat any other guarantee, i.e. subrogation would apply.

5.5.13 The special position of hybrid schemes

According to PA 2004 s.307(4) ('modification of this Act in relation to certain categories of schemes'), "hybrid scheme" means: "an occupational pension scheme - (a) which is not a money purchase scheme, but (b) where some of the benefits that may be provided are (i) money purchase benefits attributable to voluntary contributions of the members, or (ii) other money purchase benefits". The governing rules are the Pension Protection Fund (Hybrid Schemes) (Modification) Regulations 2005 (the "Hybrid Schemes Regulations").

"These Regulations modify…the Act…in relation to hybrid schemes…. Regulation 2 prescribes the circumstances…to which the prohibition in section 135(4) ['the existence of the assessment period'] on transferring, or making transfer payments in respect of, any member's rights and discharging any liability to… a member, does not apply. Regulation 3(1) modifies section 134 of the Act to provide for the Board to give directions to a relevant person (defined in section 134(3) of the Act) regarding the exercise of his powers during an assessment period (see section 132 of the Act) in respect of discharging liabilities of the scheme which relate to money purchase benefits. Regulation 3(2) and (3) modifies Schedule 7 ['the pension compensation provisions'] so that compensation is not payable…in relation to benefits or contributions that relate to money purchase benefits. Regulation 3(2) and (4) allows the Board to repay a person's contributions to the scheme in respect of a pension or a lump sum (which are not money purchase benefits) in certain cases" (from the *Explanatory Notes to the Hybrid Schemes Regulations*).

A hybrid scheme is treated similarly to a partially guaranteed scheme, i.e. the two separate elements are treated separately. Therefore the IP will be dealing with two separate claims, namely the occupational scheme element ("the pensions compensation provisions") and the money-purchase scheme element. However, unlike a partially guaranteed scheme, the authorities retain some control over the money purchase element. An example is regulation 3(1) which states: "The Board may give a relevant person directions regarding the exercise during that period of his powers in respect of discharging the liabilities of the scheme to, or in respect of, a member of the scheme in respect of money purchase benefits".

5.5.14 The special position of multi-employer schemes

Multi-employer and/or segregated schemes need separate consideration and, at first sight, appear highly problematic. As the name suggests multi-employer schemes involve many employers and such schemes may be segregated or non-segregated, or indeed partially segregated. A segregated multi-employer scheme has separate 'sections' (i.e. it is 'sectionalised') and the assets and liabilities of an individual employer's scheme are held separately from other employers involved in the scheme. Essentially, a multi-employer segregated (or sectionalised) scheme merely shares overheads. The assets and liabilities do not mix. Consequently a multi-employer segregated scheme differs little from an ordinary employer's scheme. For the IP, conceptually (if not procedurally) there is little difference between a multi-employer segregated scheme and an ordinary employer's scheme. The opposite is the case with a non-segregated scheme: assets and liabilities mix. In some segregated schemes there is an element of cross-subsidisation, i.e. the scheme has elements of being segregated and of being non-segregated.

The statutory instruments created under PA 2004 contain many references to multi-employer schemes. One of the main statutory instruments, for the purposes of multi-employer schemes and insolvency is the Occupational Pension Schemes (Winding Up) (Modification for Multi-Employer Schemes and Miscellaneous Amendments) Regulations 2005 ("the Multi-Employer Winding Up Regulations"). Another is the Occupational Pension Schemes (Employer Debt) Regulations 2005 (the "Employer Debt Regulations", see above).

5.5.14.1 *Definitions of Multi-Employer Schemes*

The legislative definition of multi-employer varies. A PA 2004 definition of multi-employer is found in s.272 (13). "In this section "multi-employer scheme" means a trust scheme which applies to earners in employments under different employers".

INSOVENCY, SOLVENCY AND RECONSTRUCTION

In the Multi-Employer Winding Up Regulations paragraph 1 of regulation 2: "multi-employer scheme" means an "occupational pension scheme - (a) in relation to which there are two or more employers; and (b) the rules of which do not provide for the partial winding up of the scheme if one of the employers ceases to participate in the scheme" (regulation 2(2)).

Regulation 2 of Employer Debt Regulations, states: "multi-employer scheme" means "a scheme in relation to which there is more than one employer (including, except in regulation 8, any section of a scheme treated under that regulation as a scheme if there is more than one employer in relation to that section)".

Regulation 8 (Multi-employer schemes: sectionalised schemes'), referred to in Regulation 2, states: "(1) In its application to a multi-employer scheme - (a) which is divided into two or more sections; and (b) the provisions of which are such that the sections meet conditions A and B...(2) Condition A is that contributions payable to the scheme by an employer, or by a member in employment under that employer, are allocated to that employer's section (or, if more than one section applies to that employer, to the section which is appropriate in respect of the employment in question). (3) Condition B is that a specified part or proportion of the assets of the scheme is attributable to each section and cannot be used for the purposes of any other section".

As can be seen these definitions are not generic, but specific to certain sections or regulations. The fact that the definitions vary is indicative of the difficulties that can arise with multi-employer situations.

Great importance should be attached in all cases to what the trust deed says, but even more so with multi-employer deeds. The separate (unless sectionalised) obligations of the various employers in the trust deed may include the 'last standing rule', i.e. the last standing or last one to fall victim to insolvency will often bear the total liability in a non-segregated or 'non-sectionalised' scheme. This is merely a reflection of the 'joint and several liability' of multi-employer non-segregated schemes. Ordinarily (and regardless of section 75), an insolvency would bring about a winding up of a scheme. In a multi-employer segregated scheme, it could bring about a 'partial winding up', i.e. a winding up of that segregated part of the scheme. The legislation provides for the possibility of such a partial winding up. An example is in the Explanatory Notes to the Multi-Employer Winding Up Regulations: "These Regulations modify the position under the Pensions Act 1995 ...[for an] occupational pension scheme that has more than one employer or has had more than one employer at any time since 6 April 2005 and whose rules do not provide for the partial winding up of the scheme if it is being wound up" As a rule of thumb, if a scheme is segregated (or sectionalised), it should provide for a "partial winding-up", and the IP can view the segregated element as a single scheme and act accordingly. However, it is recommended then whenever multi-

DEALING WITH PENSIONS

employer schemes are involved, the IP should take advice. From an IP's perspective, problems will most commonly arise with totally non-segregated (i.e. an element of cross-subsidisation) multi-employer schemes.

5.5.14.2 Multi-Employer Winding Up Regulations

The *Explanatory Notes to the Multi-Employer Winding Up Regulations* state:

"Regulation 2 provides for cases where an insolvency event has occurred in relation to one of the persons who is an employer...and the trustees...of the scheme have determined in the last three months that it is probable that the scheme will enter an assessment period in the next 12 months (that is, a period when the Board of the...[PPF] ("the Board") determines whether to assume responsibility...). In such cases the normal obligation of the trustees...under section 73A of the 1995 Act to reduce the benefits that they pay out ...during the winding up period so that members do not receive more than they should according to the priority rules in section 73 of the 1995 Act is modified. The modification enables the trustees...to pay in full the level of benefits that would be payable if the Board were to assume responsibility...Regulation 2 also modifies section 73A of the 1995 Act so that if the trustees cease to expect the scheme to enter an assessment period in the next 12 months, they may recover any overpayments made as a result of exercising the power to pay greater amounts. Where sections 73 to 74 of the 1995 Act apply as if a part of a scheme were a scheme, regulation 2 applies in the same way."

"Regulation 3 [means that] the order of priority to be given to scheme liabilities being paid out during the winding up period of an occupational pension scheme under section 73(4) of the 1995 Act is the same whether or not during the winding up period there is an assessment period."

"Regulation 4 amends...the MFR Regulations so that assets representing the value of any rights in respect of money purchase benefits under an occupational pension scheme are excluded from minimum funding valuations...This is consequential [to] the exclusion ...of a scheme's money purchase liabilities from the liabilities..., because it is those liabilities that are valued for the purposes of those valuations and the valuation would be misleading if the corresponding assets were not also excluded."

Regulations 2-4 (of the Multi-Employer Winding Up Regulations) will therefore affect the liability of the scheme in the insolvency.

In short, regulation 2 allows for different rules to apply to different sections in the pre-insolvency period, thereby altering the eventual claim in the final insolvency. Regulation 4 provides for money-purchase schemes and, thus, the eventual insolvency claim will exclude the same.

5.5.14.3   Employer Debt Regulations

Given the importance of Regulation 6 ('Multi-employer schemes: general') to the calculation of a debt with a non-sectionalised multi-employer scheme, the Explanatory Note is reproduced below, almost in full:

"Regulations 6 to 8 deal with how section 75 of the 1995 Act [the deficiency on winding up calculation] and these Regulations apply to multi-employer schemes. Regulation 6 provides that a debt only arises under section 75(2) while a multi-employer scheme is being wound up if a deficit in the scheme assets occurs before a relevant event has occurred in relation to all the employers, and all the employers are then responsible for a share of the debt. But whether a debt arises under section 75(4) is judged by reference to each of the employers separately and debts under that section are also taken to arise as respects an employer if he ceases to have any employees in pensionable service to which the scheme applies. The debt on each employer under section 75(4) is his share of the deficit in the assets. Regulation 7 modifies the rules in regulation 5 where a debt arises because of an employer in a multi-employer scheme ceasing to have any employees in pensionable service. The provisions about buying annuities and including winding up costs are disapplied. Regulation 8 provides that section 75 and these Regulations apply as if sections of multi-employer schemes were separate schemes ...Regulation 12 modifies how regulation 10 applies where the money purchase scheme is a multi-employer scheme, apportioning the deficit among the employers in a similar way to regulation 6...Regulation 14 provides that sectionalised schemes covering United Kingdom and foreign employment are to be treated as separate schemes...Regulation 16 enables trustees to modify schemes by resolution for the purpose of apportioning debts under section 75 of the 1995 Act amongst employers in different proportions from those that would otherwise apply" (from the *Explanatory Note to the Employer Debt Regulations*).

Regulation 6 itself is reproduced below:

"(1)   In its application to a multi-employer scheme, section 75 of the 1995 Act has effect in relation to *each employer* [emphasis supplied] as if-
(a) the reference in section 75(2)(a) to a time which falls before any relevant [insolvency] event in relation to the employer which occurs while the scheme is being wound up were a reference to a time which falls before relevant events have occurred in relation to *all the employers* [emphasis supplied];
(b) the reference in section 75(2) to an amount equal to the difference [i.e. the liability] being treated as a debt due from the employer were a reference to an amount equal to that employer's share of the difference being treated as a debt due from *that* [emphasis supplied]employer;
(c) the references in section 75(3)(a)(i) and (b) to no relevant event of the kind there mentioned occurring in relation to the employer were references to no

event of that kind occurring in relation to *all* [emphasis supplied] the employers;

(d) the reference in section 75(4)(a) to a relevant event ("the current event") occurring in relation to the employer were a reference to a relevant event or an employment-cessation event [i.e. insolvency] occurring only in relation to *that* [emphasis supplied] employer;

(e) the reference in section 75(4) to an amount equal to the difference being treated as a debt due from the employer were -

    (i) in a case where the difference is ascertained immediately before a relevant event occurs in relation to the employer, *a reference to an amount equal to the employer's share of the difference being treated as a debt due from the employer* [emphasis supplied]; and

    (ii) in a case where the difference is ascertained immediately before an employment cessation event occurs in relation to the employer, a reference to an amount equal to the sum of the cessation expenses attributable to the employer and the employer's share of the difference being treated as a debt due from the employer; and....

(2) For the purposes of paragraph (1), an employer's share of the difference is -

    (a) such proportion of the total difference as, in the opinion of the actuary after consultation with the trustees or managers, the amount of the scheme's liabilities attributable to employment with that employer bears to the total amount of the scheme's liabilities attributable to employment with the employers; or

    (b) if the scheme provides for the total amount of that debt to be otherwise apportioned amongst the employers, the amount due from that employer under that provision.

(3) For the purposes of paragraph (2)--

    (a) the total amount of the scheme's liabilities which are attributable to employment with the employers; and

    (b) the amount of the liabilities attributable to employment with any one employer,

are such amounts as are determined, calculated and verified by the actuary in accordance with the guidance given in GN 19; and a determination under this paragraph must be certified by the actuary as being in accordance with that guidance.

(4) For the purposes of these Regulations an employment-cessation event occurs in relation to an employer if he ceases to be an employer [i.e. upon insolvency] employing persons in the description of employment to which the scheme relates at a time when at least one other person continues to employ such persons.

(5)   For the purposes of paragraph (1), the cessation expenses attributable to an employer are all expenses which, in the opinion of the trustees or managers of the scheme, are likely to be incurred in connection with the employment-cessation event occurring in relation to the employer."

The power of the actuaries and of the trustees/managers is striking, when compared to the lack of direct involvement of the employer in agreeing "the total amount of liabilities attributable" to an employer. It should also be remembered that the provisions of the trust deed continue: "if the scheme provides for the total amount of that debt to be otherwise apportioned amongst the employers, the amount due from that employer [is that under that provision]" (regulation 2 (b)).

The thrust of the legislation is clear: to sectionalise as far as is practicable, multi-employer schemes. The IP must question this procedural part of his creditor liability validation exercise, i.e. he must question the trustees and actuary so as to ensure correct 'sectionalisation' has occurred. However, the IP's powers appear limited, save for reverting to his traditional powers under the Insolvency Rules.

5.6   What happens if the PPF does not assume responsibility?

If in the event the PPF does not assume responsibility, and there remains a deficiency, the costs appear to fall on the remaining creditors. Such a situation may arise in a number of scenarios (see *s.149(2)*) particularly where:

(a)   "the scheme was not, or was not an eligible scheme throughout the relevant period" *(s.146)*

Provided the due process of appeal has occurred then, under PA 2004, the only compensation possibly remaining is under the financial assistance provisions *(s.286)*. If the scheme was not eligible, it is unlikely to have been a DB scheme; the scheme is likely therefore to be either a money-purchase or industry-wide scheme and the employer insolvent. The IP needs to deal with the issue of claim quantification. However, unless the financial assistance provisions of s.286 are invoked, without the added difficulties of analysing the claim in terms of what actual compensation was paid by the Regulator, the creditor claim on the scheme will not be affected by the transfer of scheme liabilities to the PPF nor by analysing whether the claim should be fixed at either the compensation cap or liability at transfer. A further factor (considered elsewhere) to review is, 'has the scheme been wound up and is section 75 therefore invoked'?

(b)   "a new scheme was created to replace an existing scheme and "one of the main purposes of establishing the new scheme...was to enable... members to receive compensation...where [otherwise]... regulations under s.146 would have operated to prevent such [compensation]" *(s.147)*

The IP needs to quantify any potential claim, but such quantification is not easy to complete because of the financial assistance provisions *(s.286)* which confuse the issue, and make it unclear just how much compensation has been or is to be paid. The illegitimate creation and transfer of the scheme may have increased the schemes' deficiencies and this may of itself create claim quantification difficulties. Accordingly, it is not clear whether any schemes in deficit have claims against the trustees and/or the employing company for any increased liability. Despite the absence of PPF assumption of responsibility, would the creation and transfer lead to 'moral hazard' claims against trustees or those connected /associated with the schemes? If so how would this affect claim quantification? Finally, it is unclear whether once a scheme has been absorbed (despite being subsequently dropped) by the PPF, its rights against the employer could continue. A further factor (considered elsewhere) to review is, 'has the scheme been wound up and is section 75 therefore invoked'?

(c) "a scheme rescue notice has become binding *(s.122(2)(b)* or *s.130(3))* but there are otherwise insufficient assets"

The issue here is relatively simple: the deficiency (however calculated) will be the amount claimed in the insolvency.

(d) "no insolvency event has occurred or is likely to occur" *(s.149(2)(d))*

The language of the legislation may lead to confusion, and some of the sections indicate there may be a conflict of intention (see in particular *s.148, s.149(2)(d)* and *s.122(4))*. An insolvency event conventionally occurs when an IP is appointed; PA 2004 provisions make it somewhat uncertain when, in its own terms, there is an insolvency event. The first area of uncertainty lies in the way in which PA 2004 s.148 is drafted; the section imposes two hurdles to determine when an insolvency event for its purposes has occurred.

The powers and duties of the trustee and managers will vary, according to the scenarios, during the assessment period.

The first hurdle is in s.148(1)(a) which requires a notice under s.122(4) (inability to confirm status of scheme) to be issued and become binding, that is "if a person who *was* [emphasis supplied] acting as an . . . [insolvency practitioner] in relation to the employer and immediately before... has *not* [emphasis supplied] been able to confirm in relation to the scheme (a) that a scheme rescue is not possible or (b) that a scheme rescue has occurred, he must issue a notice to that effect" *(s.122(4))*.

Accordingly, where a former IP (one whose appointment has been terminated) cannot say whether a scheme rescue is not possible, the first limb of s.148(1)) applies -'the don't know notice' *(s.148(1)(a))*. In addition, the former IP may also have issued a notice that he 'has not been able to confirm... that a scheme rescue has occurred'. In practice, an IP will almost invariably know whether a scheme rescue has occurred or not; that is, unless his appointment is followed by a CVA.

The second limb *(s.148(1)(b))* provides: 'a withdrawal event has not occurred in relation to the scheme in respect of a withdrawal notice which has been issued during the period:

(i)   beginning with the occurrence of the last insolvency event in relation to the employer, and

(ii)   ending immediately 'before the notice under section 122(4) becomes binding.'

The IPs' and the trustees' duties are amended by the requirements imposed during the assessment period. The assessment period is the 'cooling down period' that follows an insolvency event or an application by the trustee for the PPF to assume responsibility, during which time the status quo is generally sought to be preserved by the eligible scheme.

5.7   TUPE Solvent reconstruction

5.7.1   Sale of business (i.e. assets not shares) by an insolvency practitioner or others and TUPE

On the sale of a business (rather than an asset sale) there is invariably a transfer of the undertaking covered by the Transfer of Undertaking (Protection of Employment) Regulations 1981 (as amended) ('TUPE'). With some exceptions the purchaser acquires employment rights and liabilities; in particular liabilities owed by the insolvent employer to the employees transfer automatically to the purchaser.

Occupational pensions rights have for many years been one of those exceptions and have conventionally been excluded from protection *(TUPE reg. 7)*. From 6 April 2005 pensions became (partially) protected *(PA 2004 ss.257 and 258)* and some pension rights are now transferred.

Where there is an employment transfer *(s.257(1)(b))* and at the time 'immediately before the employee ceases to become employed by the transferee... there is an occupational pension scheme ('the scheme') [in place]', with the former employer or an associated employee (as defined by IA 1986 s.435, PA 2004 s.257(8)) then regardless of whether the employee is an active member or not of that scheme, certain 'rights' are transferred. Where s.257 applies then s.258 offers the former employee a 'form of protection' by requiring that the 'employer secures that... the employee is, or is eligible to be an active member of an occupational pension scheme of the transferee' *(s.258(2)(a))*.

If the scheme was a money purchase scheme, the transferee should make 'relevant contributions to the scheme' *(s.258(2)(b))*. If the scheme was not a money-purchase scheme, then the transferee should satisfy 'the statutory standard referred to in 12A of Pension Scheme Act 1993' *(s.258(2)(c))* or as regulations (not yet published) so demand.

5.8 Solvent reconstruction

A transfer of employment within a solvent reconstruction may give rise to a section 75 debt because the trust deed dictates that a section 75 debt arises. This nightmare scenario is rumoured to have occurred several times of late, when professional firms (accountants and lawyers) have converted from traditional unlimited liability partnerships to limited liability partnerships (LLPs). The LLP conversion exercise has therefore increased the overall personal liability of the partners, the opposite of their intention.

5.9 CVAs and creditor approval

5.9.1 Background

A CVA is a company voluntary arrangement. It is not intended in this book to deal with insolvency procedures in detail. Essentially, a CVA is a deal between an insolvent company and its creditors.

5.9.2 CVAs and the PPF

During an assessment period, 'the rights and powers of the trustees or managers of the scheme in relation to any debt (including a contingent debt) due to them by the employer... are [only] exercisable by the PPF' *(s.137(2))*. The assessment period *(s.132(2))* begins with insolvency and ends with:

(a) a scheme rescue or refusal of the PPF to be involved *(s.149(2))*;

(b) a transfer of the scheme to the PPF by way of the pension contribution provisions *(s.160)*; or

(c) when there is no scheme rescue but there are sufficient assets to meet protected liabilities.

In short it is likely that: (i) the assessment period will last for the period of the IP appointment; and (ii) the pension fund deficit will be one of the largest creditors in the insolvency. IPs and the PPF (or at least the Independent Trustee/Person appointed by the PPF *(PA 1995 s.23)*) must therefore work together.

The Pension Bill (a draft version of PA 2004) contained several sections (especially the draft s.125(4) 'the CVA section', see the House of Lords Bill 7353/3) that effectively precluded a CVA. The CVA section stated that the PPF was not bound by a CVA without its specific consent and was, quite sensibly, dropped. Presumably therefore (although it is open to doubt as to whether a trustee can agree to a compromise under common law, see the 'Bradstock compromise') the PPF and/or the scheme is bound by any CVA and thus the section 75 Pensions Act debt is compromised.

5.9.3 Debt/equity swaps

Many CVAs involve debt/equity swaps. These may pose issues under PA 2004, given the general bar on a pension scheme holding more than 5% (now 10% in groups) of the shares of the employer. In practice the problem may disappear once the fund is acquired by the PPF ('the property, rights and liabilities of the scheme are transferred to the PPF without further assurance' *(s.161(2)(a))* since the 5% limit on self-investment may not apply: the PPF is not investing in its employing company as such. Indeed, there may be a material advantage in folding the fund into the PPF, since one of the biggest difficulties (the 5% limit) in saving a company, by way of a CVA-backed debt/equity swap, becomes achievable. Where, because of the deficit (however defined) the pensions scheme (or the PPF following upon assumption) is a substantial creditor (i.e. more than 5%), then a debt/equity swap (more especially through a CVA) seems effectively precluded. It was previously possible to minimise this difficulty by creating an immediate market for the shares (i.e. other creditors purchasing the schemes shares as part of the CVA process so as to come within the 5% limit), although this was not easy, given the insolvency of the company. However, it now appears that following PA 2004, the PPF simply becomes a shareholder in the former company. The PPF has indicated that if it is involved in a debt equity swap, then its upper shareholding limit is 33%. It is assumed that this limit is set because the PPF does not wish to be classed as a 'connected or associated party' for the purposes of the 'moral hazard provisions'. There would be a certain irony if the PPF itself fell victim to a FSD. At the time of writing, the PPF has agreed to a CVA which effectively involved a debt/equity swap – Pittards Ltd.

5.9.4 The Occupational Pension Schemes (Winding up etc) Regulations (the "Winding Up Regulations")

The Winding Up Regulations apply to a section 75 debt compromised by a CVA.

Regulation 10 modifies sections 73 to 74 of the 1995 Act where liabilities of a scheme are discharged (via a CVA compromise) during an assessment period by virtue of regulations under section 135(4) of PA 2004. An assessment period is defined in section 132 of that Act as the period beginning with an insolvency event occurring in relation to a scheme's employer and ending with either the Board of the PPF assuming responsibility for the scheme or ceasing to be involved with it. Regulation 10 ensures that sections 73 to 73B of the 1995 Act do not apply to such discharged liabilities, but that they are treated as fully discharged under section 74 of the 1995 Act.

5.10 Personal liability of IPs

5.10.1 Background

There was criticism of PA 2004 at the time of its passage through Parliament on the grounds that it adversely affected both the 'turnaround culture' (supported by the DTI) and the exposure to personal liability of IPs. In the event, the Department for Work and Pensions (DWP) accepted that IPs should be excluded from liability to meet debts under contribution notices demanding third parties' contributions to a pension scheme deficiency. Contribution notices can apply only if the "the

Regulator is of the opinion that the person…is not acting [i.e. it is a carve-out clause] in accordance with his functions as an [insolvency practitioner]" *(s.38(3)(c))*.

5.10.2 The proper functions of an IP

This raises the issue of the proper functions of an IP and to what extent these functions overlap with those of a non-insolvency practitioner.

For example, the right of the Regulator to issue a contribution notice requires an 'act or failure' which "prevented the recovery of the whole or any part of the [scheme] debt" *(s.38(5)(1))*. It might be argued that the very act of commencing an insolvency process is in itself 'an act' leading to a contribution notice, to the extent that the insolvency has not already 'prevented the recovery of the whole or any part of the [scheme] debt' *(s.38(5)(1))*. The legislation raises questions about who, if anybody, is protected by the IP carve-out clause at the formal commencement of the insolvency procedures and whether special procedures should be adopted to maximise the use of this clause. These issues are dealt with below.

The statutory carve-out is narrow; it is restricted to IPs. The Turnaround Management Association ("TMA") consists of individuals who work closely with distressed companies. The Regulator has advised the TMA on an informal basis that action will not be taken against its members. Such an assurance, whilst welcome, is of little concrete support. TMA members and similar professionals should accordingly review their insurance policies. It must be assumed that similar considerations apply to the Society of Turnaround Practitioners (STP).

5.10.3 CVA/Administration order

Apart from where the small company moratorium procedure applies (see IA 1986 schedule 1A, which is in any event unlikely to involve eligible pension schemes), it is the directors of the company who conventionally propose a CVA (unless the company is already in liquidation or administration) *(IA 1986 s.1(1))*. Directors are not protected by the IP carve-out clause, unlike liquidators or administrators. Directors are therefore advised to consider either a liquidation, or more properly an Administration Order application as a precursor to the CVA. The directors' proposal "is one which provides for some person ('the nominee') to act" *(IA 1986 s.1(2))*. The nominee will be an IP within s.38(11)(a) of IA 1986 and therefore within the IP carve-out clause. It is improbable, although not beyond logic, that the directorial act of commencing the Administration Order is itself an 'act'. Consequently, a 'belt and braces' approach could be a creditor-driven (if one can be found) Administration Order *(IA 1986 s.9(1))* application. Whilst a creditor petition could again feasibly and logically be an 'act', it would be absurd if action was even considered against a third-party debtor trying to recover its debt.

The IP will, however, have advised the directors, prior to becoming the nominee and, unfortunately, this pre-appointment advisory role (nor any other informal role) does not appear to fall within the IP carve-out exemption. The proto-nominee should therefore carefully consider how to protect his position. The IP should always advise the directors to have regard to the clearance provisions contained within PA 2004 *s.42*. The standard letter of engagement should therefore advise the directors always to seek clearance from the Regulator and/or liaise with the trustees. Beyond this, there is little that the proto-nominee can do. This is unfortunate because a corporate turnaround process (as opposed to a liquidation) is potentially ripe for the Regulator 'moral hazard' attack. Whilst there is a general carve-out for good faith, it is unclear what good faith means in this context. Certainly, if the pension fund deficit is pressing, 'one of the main purposes' *(s.38(5))* of the insolvency process may be to avoid the pressing deficit; to prove good faith in such a set of circumstances may be difficult.

5.10.4 Liquidation and/or administrative receivership

Both liquidation and administrative receivership crystallise the creditor priority position, in which an unsecured pension scheme liability falls below a secured (usually bank) position. The question arises whether the process of crystallising that creditor priority position (in which invariably the unsecured pension scheme liability suffers) is an 'an act preventing scheme debt recovery'. In theory, the protective provisions concerning CVAs/administration orders apply. However, where for example a bank (or other secured creditor) forces liquidation, or more usually an administrative receivership, in order to crystallise the creditor priority position, there is an argument that that act is inevitably an act 'preventing recovery of a pension fund deficit'. Whilst the Regulator may wish to impose duties of good faith (i.e. duties to it, the public and the pension fund members), it is hard to criticise a creditor simply for trying to better its position, e.g. by limiting the recovery of the pension fund deficit. There are concerns that an IP, especially an IP de facto instructed by a secured creditor, usually a bank, is vulnerable in the pre-appointment phase.

5.11 Clearance Provisions and Insolvency

5.11.1 Turnarounds such as Administration/CVAs

There are several difficult areas for the IP in a CVA with or without an administration order. The first chronological difficulty is the position of the 'proto-insolvency practitioner' stage, i.e. that of advising the stakeholders of the insolvency outcome, not least because at this early stage, there would be nothing to clear. The IP cannot clear the fact that he is acting in accordance with his function as an IP because he is not yet an IP within the carve-out clause under s.38(3)(c). The best the IP can do, at this stage, is to ensure that the trustees and managers notify the Regulator, in accordance with the notifiable events regime of the inevitable notifiable event such as a breach of covenant. The director of the company should also notify the Regulator as appropriate. Once the advice has been finalised (i.e. the nature of the nominee proposal in a CVA) then there is a valid twofold practical, if not legal, argument for clearance: this is subject to the proviso of speed. First, there is a positive duty upon the nominee to consider whether the administration (especially if it involves a CVA) will get creditor support; the PPF will be probably a major creditor. The clearance procedure can (although in practice it may not) provide a platform whereby a major (albeit a contingent) creditor can be consulted about the proposal and support garnered. Secondly, the finalised proposal is a solid plan of action that can be 'cleared'; it is not amorphous advice.

The situation is slightly different in an Administration, without a CVA. "An application to the court for an Administration Order shall be by petition, presented either by the company, or the directors, or by a creditor or creditors (including any contingent or prospective creditor or creditors [therefore it includes the trustees or managers, or even the PPF] or by the clerk of the Magistrates' Court" *(IA 1986 s.9(1))*. In short, none of those able to apply are covered by the IP carve-out clause in s.38(3)(c). The same concerns as have been voiced above concerning CVAs therefore apply, including the position of the advising proto-Administrator.

There is an odd position from the perspective of PA 2004 if a CVA is approved either with or without a concomitant Administration Order. The Supervisor is in place and is acting as an IP and therefore within the carve-out, but the real action is with the directors who now run the company. The Directors 'report' to the Supervisor to ensure that they are running the company in accordance with the CVA, but they will have no IP protection. Further, the monies built up through the CVA are (if the CVA has been 'correctly' drafted) trust monies, held on trust for the creditors of the company (see Sealy and Milman, *Annotated Guide to the Insolvency Legislation*, at page 35). As such, they are certainly freely available for contribution notices. Further, if the contribution claim was not even a contingent creditor at the date of the CVA, it is arguable, although perhaps doubtful, that the trust monies are available pro-rata to the extent of the contribution notice.

5.11.2 Insolvency: liquidation
The situation of a liquidation, which is not preceded by an Administration Order or CVA, is again similar to the Administration Order Petition. In a CVL the company (that is the directors) call a meeting of members and of creditors, who agree the appointment of a Liquidator (subject to the creditors' meeting having the final decision) *(IA 1986 s.98)*. All those involved, the directors, the company, the shareholders and creditors, agree a process which can be (especially if the Liquidator is given instructions) an 'act or omission' within the contribution notice regime, yet they do not fall within the IP carve-out clause.

In a compulsory liquidation, a creditor petition for the winding up of the company again falls outside the carve-out clause, yet the immediately-appointed Official Receiver (possibly acting as Receiver and Manager) falls within it.

5.11.3 The PPF and the provision of information

The Pension Protection Fund (Provision of Information) Regulations 2005 ("PPF Information Regulations") do as they suggest. "Regulation 3 makes provision as to the information to be provided by the Board to IPs in relation to insolvent employers who sponsored an occupational pension scheme, trustees or managers of such schemes where an insolvency event has occurred in relation to the sponsoring employer, such employers and the members and beneficiaries of such schemes" (from the *Explanatory Notes to the PPF Information Regulations*).

Under regulation 3(2): "Where the Board receives a notice under section 120(2) (duty to notify insolvency events in respect of employers) from an IP that an insolvency event has occurred in relation to an employer, and
(a) the scheme to which the notice relates is an eligible scheme; or
(b) in the case of a multi-employer scheme which is a segregated scheme, the section to which the notice relates is an eligible section,
[then the Board]…shall, within the period of 28 days beginning with its receipt of that notice, provide that IP, the Regulator, and the trustees or managers of that scheme or section with [certain]…information".

The information noted in regulation 3(3) is: "(a) where the insolvency event is not a qualifying insolvency event, that the insolvency event is not such an insolvency event; or (b) where the insolvency event is a qualifying insolvency event, that the insolvency event is such an insolvency event and the date on which the assessment period began".

6 Liabilities: Fund Compensation, Protection and Maintenance

6.1 Introduction

Fund protection and maintenance are based on new PA 2004 powers, notably the 'moral hazard' provisions, and are the joint responsibility of the trustees and managers, and of the Regulator. The self-explanatory fund compensation is primarily the function of the PPF and ordinarily commences at the start of the assessment period. As such, it centres around 'entity insolvency' and therefore reference should be made to the insolvency chapter of this book.

COMPENSATION

6.2 The assessment period

6.2.1 Start of assessment period

The assessment period commences either with the 'qualifying insolvency event' (*s.132(2)(a)*) or with a s.129(1) or s.129(5)(a) application by the trustee and manager for the PPF to assume responsibility.

6.2.2 End of assessment period

The assessment period ends upon the earlier of the PPF ceasing to be involved by way of:

(a) the issue of a transfer notice; or

(b) there being no scheme rescue, but sufficient assets to meet protected liabilities (*s.154(2)*).

The PPF can cease to be involved by finding that:

(a) the scheme is not, or was not an eligible scheme throughout the relevant period (*s.146*);

(b) a new scheme was created illegitimately to obtain compensation (*s.147*);

(c) a scheme rescue notice has become binding but there is still a scheme deficiency, or

(d) that "no insolvency event has occurred or is likely to occur" (*s.149(2)(d)*). The assessment period may be resuscitated under s.159 in the case of a pension fund winding-up (*s.132(5)*).

6.2.3 Trustees' powers during assessment period

During the assessment period, the trustees' and managers' powers are limited, namely:

(a) the admission of new members and the payment of contributions are curtailed (*s.133*);

(b) their powers of investment and management may be subject to PPF direction (*s.134*)

(c) there are restrictions on the winding up of the scheme and discharge of liabilities *(s.135)*;

(d) only the PPF can compromise or otherwise deal with the scheme debt *(s.137)*.

If s.135 is breached "the PPF may validate an action...[but] only if satisfied that to do so is consistent with the objectives of ensuring that the scheme's protected liabilities do not exceed its assets or if they do exceed its assets, then the excess is kept to a minimum". There are no other specific validation clauses.

6.2.4 Liability for breach

Trustees, who without reasonable cause violate ss.133, 134 or 137 are liable to a penalty under PA 1995 s.10. During the assessment period the trustees and managers should only pay scheme benefits up to the limit that would be paid as if the PPF had assumed responsibility *(s.138)*. If the trustees and managers are even unable to pay compensation limit amounts, then the PPF may lend money *(s.137)*. The trustees and managers are required to consider any application for an award of benefit on the grounds of ill-health (early retirement) during the assessment period *(s.140-141)*.

6.3 Pension protection - eligible schemes

In order to obtain protection, an occupational pension scheme must be:

(i) a non-money purchase scheme;

(ii) that is not being wound up before the appointed date *(s.126 (2)*, (but see also *s.286)*; and

(iii) is not otherwise prescribed.

The PPF has a duty to 'to assume responsibility' in each of the following two circumstances:

(i) 'an insolvency event' *(s.127)*; and

(ii) 'an application or notification' by the trustees *(s.128)*.

In each case there must be:

(i) a 'scheme failure notice' (that has not been withdrawn by a withdrawal notice) *(s.127(2)(b))* which has been issued by either the IP or the trustee and managers; and

(ii) the scheme assets must be less than protected liabilities. This imposed a positive duty on an IP to apply to assume responsibility by issuing a scheme failure notice *(s.122(2)(a))*.

Likewise, where either the trustees and managers or the Regulator "become aware that - (a) the employer in relation to the scheme is unlikely to continue as a going concern and (b) [as yet unpublished] prescribed requirements are met" *(s.128(1)* or *s.128(4))*, they must also apply. The PPF must refuse responsibility, however, if it is satisfied that a new scheme has been established *(s.147(1)(a))* by the same employer *(s.147(1)(b))* with transfers having been made from the old to the new scheme *(s.147(1)(c))* and "the main purpose or one of the main purposes of the arrangements was to receive compensation" *(s.147(1)(d))*.

6.4 What happens if the PPF assumes responsibility?

Once the PPF assumes responsibility, the effect under s.161 is dramatically fourfold:

1. "all the property, rights and liabilities of the scheme are transferred to the PPF without further assurance with effect from that time the trustees or managers receive notice" *(s.161(2)(a))*. This is subject to the employment contract of the trustees and managers not being transferred *(schedule 6, para 2)* and to there not being any "liabilities in respect of any existing or future courses of action against the trustees and managers of the scheme if … the trustees and managers would have been personally liable to meet the claim and would *not* [emphasis supplied] have been indemnified from the assets of the scheme" *(schedule 6C, clause 5(2))*.

2. "the trustees or managers of the scheme are discharged from the pension obligations from that time".

3. "the PPF is [henceforth] responsible for securing that compensation is (and has been) paid in accordance with the pension compensation provisions".

4. "the scheme is to be treated as having been wound up immediately" *(s.161(2))*. The responsibility of the PPF continues until and if discharged under s.169 (2) either by: (i) the taking out, entry into or transfer of a policy of insurance annuity *(s.169(2)(a - c)* or (ii) as prescribed, the provision of cash.

PROTECTION

6.5 The Regulator's powers

Apart from the 'moral hazard' provisions, the Regulator's powers include

(a) improvement notices;

(b) third party notices;

(c) injunctions and interdicts;

(d) restitution;

(e) contribution recovery; and

(f) pension liberation.

Improvement and third party notices are similar and can be considered together.

6.5.1 Improvement notice (Pensions Act 2004 s.13)

An improvement notice is a notice from the Regulator to a party that the Regulator is of the opinion (not necessarily, it is emphasised 'reasonable opinion') that the party 'is or has and is likely to do so again, [in] breach [of] pension legislation, including the Pensions Act' *(s.13(1))*. The improvement notice is a statement identifying the breaches *(s.13(2)(a))* and the evidence of those breaches *(s.13(2)(b))*, and of the steps needed to rectify the position *(s.13(2)(c))*.

The improvement notice may give rise to a double jeopardy: a breach of both the improvement notice and a contravention of the underlying pensions legislation giving rise to the improvement notice *(s.13(6),(8) and (9))*. If the underlying contravention, "consists of a failure to take action within a time limit... the contravention continues until such time as action is taken" *(s.13(6))*. There is a separate penalty for a failure to "take all reasonable steps to secure compliance" with the improvement notice, on the trustees and managers of an occupational, or 'a personal pension scheme' *(s.13(8))*. This is significant because PA 2004 usually applies only to occupational schemes. Section 13(9) seems to extend the *s.13(8)* 'double jeopardy' to persons other than trustees or managers whom the Regulator thinks should be involved.

6.5.2 Third party notices (s.14)

As section 13 improvement notices apply to the pensions legislation 'contravener', so section 14 replicates section 13, and applies it to third parties. Under section 14, the underlying contravention, "is or was wholly or partly as a result of a failure of... 'the third party' to do anything" *(s.14(1)(b))*. Significantly, the third party failure need not, "itself [be] a contravention of the pensions legislation". Thus a civil liability is created for a pensions legislation breach that of itself does not otherwise exist.

The Regulator 'may' issue a third party notice, not 'shall'; the power is permissive, but not constrained by any reasonableness requirement. The third party may simply be conducting its own legitimate business. Indeed the third party may be acting in accordance with an existing duty in 'failing to do anything': no matter, the sweeping power overrides this existing duty *(s.14(7))*. The only third party defence to the imposition of a penalty is that the third party acted reasonably. Given the very broad range of the new PA obligations, it would seem likely that section 14 is ripe for abuse.

6.5.3 Pension liberation

The pension liberation rules *(s.18-21)* apply to both occupational and personal pension schemes. 'Liberated pension money' is, broadly, money which is misused, rather than simply liberated. Money is regarded as being liberated from a pension scheme if the members' accrued rights have been legitimately transferred from the scheme, on the 'basis that a third party ('the liberator') was to secure that the amount was used in an authorised way, and the liberator has not secured, and is not likely to secure, that the money will be used in unauthorised way' *(s.18(2))*.

6.5.4 The relationship of s.18 rights with other powers of the Regulator to recover contributions

The pensions liberation regime applies to both occupational and personal pension schemes. This is unlike the other 'contribution recovery powers' or 'restorative powers', especially the 'moral hazard provisions' of s.52 ('transactions at an undervalue') and s.58 ('transaction to defraud creditors').

The 'event' giving rise to the pension liberation order is not a transaction (within s.52 and s.58) nor a misuse nor misappropriation (within s.16) of the pension fund assets. The assets have left the fund, they have been 'liberated'; the event is rather that the funds have not found a satisfactory home post-liberation. To what extent is this a distinction without a difference? All the restorative remedies require funds to leave the pension scheme; all the restorative remedies predicate 'liberation of a sort'. If X takes illegitimately from the fund for the benefit of X, then X has no doubt committed a 'transaction at an undervalue, a 'transaction to defraud creditors' and a 'misuse' or 'misappropriation', regardless of whether 'the trustees or managers of the scheme transferred the amount out of the scheme on the basis that a third party ('the liberator') would secure that the amount was used in an authorised way'. There is consequently and almost invariably a transaction at an undervalue (s.52), a misappropriation (s.16) and possibly a transaction to defraud (s.58) in any 'liberation'. Section 18 may therefore be superfluous.

Like section 16 (restitution) and section 58 (transaction to defraud creditors), but unlike section 52 (transaction at undervalue), section 18 requires a Court order: "The Court, on the application of the Regulator, may make such order as the Court thinks just and convenient" (s.19(4)). However, the Regulator has the power, without court involvement, to grant injunctive relief by restraining/extension orders (s.20) and restitution through repatriation orders (s.121) over money held by a deposit taker (as defined by s.18(1)(b)).

Unlike section 53 (transaction at an undervalue) with its two year limit, the pensions liberation sections do not contain a time limit. Theoretically the pension liberation remedies are available in perpetuity.

What relief is available? As to temporary injunctive relief, the only comparative is section 15 (in support of section 16 restitutionary relief). The equivalent restraining/extension order is made by the Regulator against a deposit; the reliefs are therefore, unlike section 15, non-Court driven and limited to deposit takers. Specifically, "'The Regulator may make a restitution order [restraining movement on an account] in relation to an account with a deposit taker if:
(a) it is satisfied that the account contains money which has been liberated from a pension scheme, and
(b) it is satisfied that the account is held by [or operated in accordance with the liberator's instructions] and the order is made pending... making ... repatriation orders" (s.20(1)).

A restitution order lasts for six months unless extended by an extension order (s.20 (4)(b) and (5)).

The restorative pensions liberation provisions are twofold:

(i) Regulator-granted repatriation order *(s.21)* and

(ii) the Court-granted restitution order *(s.19)*.

Both provisions contain similarities with other restorative PA 2004 orders, but the similarities may be limited because of the specific nature of 'liberated pensions'. The interests of third parties is a case in point. Section 19 dictates that no order may be made, "where a person acquires the beneficial interest in recoverable property [that directly or indirectly represents the liberated pensions] in good faith, for value and without notice that the property is, or (as the case maybe) represents [recoverable property]". This is the widest of the third party safeguards as, unlike other PA restorative orders, it contains the tripartite test of:

(i)   good faith;

(ii) value; and

(iii) notice.

The traditionally worded safeguard is not present within section 21 (repatriation orders). At first sight this may not present a problem. A repatriation order can only be made against a restrained account *(s.21(1) and (2))* and a restrained account not only contains liberated pensions money, but is controlled by the liberator *(s.20(1))*. Consequently some, if not all the accounts, come within the tripartite safeguard.

If some of the money in the account is not liberated money, the Regulator must limit the extent of the order to the liberated amounts *(s.21(1)(2)(a))* and/or divide that amount amongst the various liberated members *(s.21(3))*. Unlike other PA 2004 restorative orders, both liberated pensions orders are narrowly defined. Both orders require that the sums be paid, "(i) towards a pension scheme, (ii) towards an annuity or insurance policy [both to benefit the members] or (iii) to the liberated member" *(s.21(2)(a) and s.19(4))*. Perversely, only the Court (and not the Regulator) is required to consider whether it is 'just and convenient' to make an order *(s.19(4))*.

6.6   Fund protection and fraud compensation

Fraud compensation can only be paid where two conditions are met:

First, "the value of the assets of the scheme has been reduced...[and] the PPF considers that there are reasonable grounds for believing that the reduction was attributable to an act or omission constituting a prescribed offence" *(s.182(1)(b))*. There seems to be a general drafting policy of not including the word 'reasonable' when the decision advances the cause of the PPF, but not of the trustees, etc.

Secondly, "the application is made within the authorised period" *(s.182(1)(e))*, generally within 12 months of "the time when the [scheme auditors, actuaries or trustees and managers] knew or ought reasonably to have known that a reduction of value....had occurred" *(s.182(6)(b))*. However, this second condition is subject to the proviso "that the PPF has not assumed responsibility for the scheme under section 160" *(s.182(7))*.

Fraud compensation application methods can be by the issue of a binding scheme failure notice:

(a) by the IP, following upon an insolvency *(s.182(2))*; or

(b) following a s.129 application by the trustees or managers *(s.182(3))*; or

(c) by the trustees in the case of a non-eligible scheme, where the employer is unlikely to continue as a going concern *(s.182(4))*.

"Where an application for fraud compensation... is made, the trustees and managers must obtain any recoveries of value, to the extent that they may do so without disproportionate costs and within a reasonable time" *(s.184(1))*. Further, "no fraud compensation may be made until ... the PPF ... after consulting the trustees and managers of the scheme ... [considers] further recoveries of value are unlikely to be obtained without disproportionate costs or within a reasonable time" *(s.184(2))*.

"It is for the PPF to determine [not subject to a reasonableness proviso] whether anything received by the trustees and managers of the scheme is to be treated as payment received for a fraud" *(s.184(4))*. Any aggregate payment must not exceed the net loss to the scheme of the fraud *(s.185(3))*. Once the PPF has assumed responsibility *(s.187(1))* for the scheme and it considers that it is unlikely that there will be further recoveries without disproportionate cost *(s.187(4))*, the PPF may *(not must)* transfer funds from the Fraud Compensation Fund to the PPF *(s.187(2))*. Pending such a transfer the PPF may make interim payments to the scheme trustees or managers *(s.186)*.

LEVIES

6.7 Introduction

The PPF is financed by levies; a form of insurance premium.

There are four types of levies through which the PPF finances its [pension protection] funds:

(a) the initial levy *(s.174)*;

(b) the pension protection levy *(s.175)* (or 'the insolvency levy');

(c) the fraud compensation levy *(s.189)* and

(d) the administration levy *(s.117)*.

This section will concentrate on the insolvency levy because, in terms of both amount and controversy, it is by far the most important.

Much of the detail of the levies will be contained in regulations and, at the time of writing, these regulations have not been published. However, a PPF Levy Consultation Document has been published and gives an insight as to how the insolvency levy will be raised (available from the PPF website http://www.pensionprotectionfund.org.uk/rbl_dec_05v4.pdf).

6.8 Pension protection or insolvency levy (s.175)

"For each financial year [to 31st March] ... the PPF *must impose both* [emphasis supplied] ... (a) a risk based ... [on] *all* [emphasis supplied] eligible schemes; and (b) a scheme based levy in respect of eligible schemes' *(s.175(1))*. The risk based levy focuses on the solvency of the scheme, whilst the scheme based levy focuses on the size of the scheme.

In assessing the risk based levy to be levied on all schemes, the PPF considers:
(a) the scheme's deficiency *(s.175(2)(a)(1))*;
(b) the likelihood of employer insolvency *(s.175(2)(a)(ii))*; and
(c) if appropriate, the comparative riskiness of the scheme's investments or other as yet unpublished factors *(s.175(2)(a)(iii)* and *175(3))*.

In assessing the scheme-based levy, the PPF considers:
(a) the amount of the scheme's liabilities *(s.175(b)(1)*; and
(b) if appropriate, the total amount of pensionable earnings, together with the number of members, or other as yet unprescribed factors *(s.175(2)(b)* and *175(4))*.

The PPF's decision-making process is multifactorial.

First, the "PPF must, before the beginning of each financial year, determine in respect of that year: (a) the factors and timing [by] which the ... levies are to be assessed *(s.175(5)(a)(b))*; and (b) the rate (including a nil rate, *s.175(7)*) and payment date of the levies ((c) and (d))."

Secondly, the PPF "*must* [emphasis supplied] consult such persons as it considers [without a reference to reasonableness] appropriate in the prescribed manner before making [*s.175(5)*] a determination... if: (i) it is the first section 175 levy *(s.176(1)(a))*; (ii) the proposed levy factors and levy rates differ from last year *(s.176(1)(b)*; or (iii) no consultation has occurred for the last two financial years".

Thirdly, subject to transitional arrangements, before determining the levies, the PPF must estimate "the amount which will be raised by the levies it proposes to impose" *(s.177(1))* which must "not exceed the ceiling for the financial year" *(s.177(2))* and which must "be in a form which the PPF estimates will result in at least 80 per cent (this is subject to change) of the amount raised being raised by the risk based levy" *(s.177(3))*.

The levy ceiling is set by the Secretary of State, subject to approval by the Treasury, and is based upon the level of UK earnings *(s.178)*. The levies are debts *(s.181(6))* on the employer and may be recovered by the PPF or the Regulator *(s.181(7))*.

6.9 The PPF Levy Consultation Document and the insolvency levy

According to the PPF Levy Consultation Document, 'the scheme-based element must take account of the level of a scheme's liabilities relating to members'. Further, 'if the PPF considers it appropriate, it may also take account of the number of members within the scheme, the total amount of pensionable earnings of active members within a scheme and/or any other scheme factor as set out in regulations. Additionally, 'the risk-based element must take account of the funding level of the scheme and, in some cases, the risk of the sponsoring employer(s) becoming insolvent'. Finally, 'if the PPF considers it appropriate, it may also take account of a scheme's assets allocation and/or any other risk factor as set out in regulations.'

Both the scheme-based and risk-based levy elements are to be based upon the level of a scheme's PPF liabilities using 'a section 179 basis', as at 31 December 2005. The risk-based levy element, however, will also utilise the risk of insolvency in relation to the sponsoring employer(s) as at the same date.

The PPF Levy Consultation Document does not propose an immediate change to the PA 2004 regarding the proposed split between risk and scheme-based elements. The proposal is "that for the Financial Year commencing 1st February 2006, 80% of the pension protection levy is risk-based and the remaining 20% is scheme-based."

Dun and Bradstreet are to be used for the purposes of calculating the risk based levy element. They propose to categorise employers into 100 insolvency risk bands.

6.10 The employer's responsibility for scheme funding and the statutory funding objective (Part 3 (sections 221 – 233))

PA 2004, which applies new funding requirements to defined benefit schemes, may significantly affect the balance sheet of sponsors of every occupational pension scheme (money purchase and certain other schemes are unaffected (s.221)). It requires every scheme to be subject to a 'statutory funding objective'. The statutory funding objective is that the scheme must have sufficient and appropriate assets to cover its 'technical provisions' (s.222(1)) which are the amounts required, on a [prescribed] actuarial calculation, to make provision for the scheme liabilities" (s.222(2)). "The trustees or managers must prepare and from time to time review, and if necessary revise, a written statement of ... their policy for securing that the statutory funding objective is met" (s.223(1)(a)). This includes the "method and assumptions to be used in calculating the technical provision" (s.223(2)(a)) and "the period and manner in which any failure to meet the statutory funding objective is to be remedied" (s.223(2)). Failure of the trustees and managers to obtain regular actuarial reports will result in a penalty.

The actuarial report must state "that in the opinion of the actuary the calculation is made in accordance with regulations under section 222" (s.225(2)) or "if the actuary cannot [so report] he must report [failure to do so results in a penalty] the matter ... to the Regulator" (s.225(3)). "If having obtained an actuarial valuation... it appears to the trustees and managers... that the statutory funding objective was not met... they must prepare or review their existing recovery plan" (s.226(1)). "A recovery plan must set out - (a) the steps to be taken to meet the statutory funding objective, and (b) the period within which that statutory objective is to be achieved" *(s.226(2))*. The steps and period should include "a schedule of contributions payable towards the scheme by the employer" *(s.227)* and certification by the actuary as "being consistent with the statement of funding principles" *(s.227(6))*.

"If the trustees and managers have reasonable cause to believe that … the failure [to abide by the plan is] likely to be of material significance … they must give notice … to the Regulator" *(s.228(2))*. Not only is "the amount unpaid … to be treated as… a debt" *(s.228(3))* the failure to pay can result in a civil liability on the employer *(s.229(4)*. The recovery plan, including the schedule of contributions to be agreed between employer and trustees or managers *(s.229)* must be agreed between employer and trustee. A failure to agree is to be reported to the Regulator *(s.229(5))*.

6.11 Liabilities for mishandling affairs under the Pensions Act

6.11.1 The public sector (Schedule 1 Part 6/Schedule 5 Part 5)

PA 2004 creates several exposures to civil and criminal liabilities, most of which, save for some notable exceptions (including the Official Receiver) fall on private sector individuals. The Regulator and staff are exposed, but the degree of immunity seems very high.

There is no sovereign immunity; neither the Regulator *(Schedule 1 Part 6 para 29(1)(b))* nor the PPF *(Schedule 5, Part 5 para 24(1)(b))* enjoy any status, privilege or immunity of the Crown. Nonetheless, "neither …[the Regulator nor the PPF], nor a person who is a member of…[the Regulator or the PPF], a member of its committees, or a member of its staff is to be liable in damages for anything done or omitted in the exercise of the purported exercise of the functions of…[the Regulator or the PPF], unless it were shown that the act or omission was in bad faith or so as to prevent an award of damages made in respect of an act or omission that was unlawful as a result of s.6(1) Magistrates' Courts Act 1998" . Where an official becomes liable in damages and the Magistrates' Court Act 1998 s.6(1) applies, it is expected that he would be indemnified by his employer. An indemnity to a private trustee is normally not permitted under PA 2004.

6.11.2 The private sector (s.256)

No amount can be paid out of assets of an occupational or personal pension scheme for the purposes of reimbursing any trustee or manager of the scheme for a Pensions Act penalty *(s.256(1)*. Nor can the scheme provide for an equivalent insurance policy *(s.256(2))*, and if reimbursement occurs that itself is an offence *(s.256(5))*. There is no such prohibition in relation to PPF funds; by implication therefore indemnification seems available for members of the Board of the PPF, although hardly necessary given the general bar against liability.

6.12 Transfer of property, rights and liabilities to the PPF (Schedule 6)

6.12.1 Background

Where a scheme is adopted by the PPF on the insolvency of the employer, the property, rights and liabilities of an occupational pension scheme are transferred to the PPF in accordance with s.161 *(Schedule 6 para 1)*. Property, rights and liabilities, subject to provisos, are defined as:

(a) property, rights and liabilities that would not otherwise be capable of being transferred or assigned;

(b) property situated anywhere in the United Kingdom or elsewhere; and

(c) rights and liabilities under the law of any part of the United Kingdom or of any country or territory outside the United Kingdom. *(Schedule 6 para 2)*.

6.12.2 The provisos

"Where...any rights or liabilities under a contract of employment between the trustees or managers of the scheme and an individual would be transferred to the PPF...[then Schedule 6 para 2(c)] operates to terminate the contract of employment on the day preceding the day on which the transfer notice is received by the trustees or managers of the scheme" *(Schedule 6 para 2(c))*. Both rights and liabilities of employment contracts are terminated. This produces a finality and has a superficial fairness in that both rights and liabilities are eradicated simultaneously. However, there is an argument that if legitimate rights and liabilities exist, they should then be actioned, rather than eradicated. Employment contracts will, on the whole, give the employee, not the employer (in this case the scheme) the balance of rights; but it is the employer (the scheme) and not the employee, that gains from this eradication of rights and liabilities, which appears surprising. If the employment contract is illegitimate (such as a transaction at an undervalue) there is a plethora of remedies available. If the employment contract is (as, it must be presumed, it usually is) legitimate, then the rights of the members of the scheme have been elevated beyond the rights of other creditors of the scheme. Of itself this is illegitimate but moreover, scheme members will enjoy a guaranteed compensation (from the PPF) which other scheme creditors (i.e. employees) will not. It is true to say that all employees of insolvent entities currently enjoy some form of guaranteed compensation (through the National Insurance Fund) but it is certainly not of the order of that guaranteed by the PPF.

A further issue is whether former scheme employees enjoy any rights to statutory compensation, that their colleagues in the insolvent company will enjoy (by virtue of the Insolvency Services Redundancy Payment offices and the Employment Rights Act 1996). The answer is a probable no, for two reasons. First, it is unlikely that the employer (the scheme) has become insolvent in the traditional sense of the word. Second, whilst the employment has ceased, it is unlikely that there was a redundancy.

6.12.3 Continuation of legal proceedings

Any legal proceedings or applications to any authority pending immediately before the transfer by or against any of the trustees or managers of the scheme in their capacity as trustees or managers are continued by or against the PPF *(Schedule 6 para 3(1))*.

6.12.4 Trustee personal liabilities

Personal liability of former trustees and managers continues; the liabilities transferred do not include any liabilities in respect of an existing or future cause of action against the trustees or managers of the scheme if, disregarding the transfer, the trustees or managers would have been personally liable to meet the claim and would not have been indemnified from the assets of the scheme *(Schedule 6 para 3(2))*.

The reference to 'the liabilities transferred' indicates that 'relevant assets' are not transferred. The provisions in para 3(2) for continued personal liability of former trustees and managers differ from the general provision in para 2 for transfer of property, rights and liabilities in that it only refers to liabilities, rather than assets and liabilities. Given that, for example, in any contract of employment, liabilities fall within 'causes of action', para 3(2) covers ground already covered by the para 2 employment contracts exclusions. The intention appears to be to cover claims of negligence or similar torts. Paradoxically, a cause of action against the trustees and managers would not, in the accounts of the scheme ordinarily be a liability; rather the claim for negligence would be an asset. Consequently, it is hard to see how a liability for negligence could emerge.

There are thus, it would appear, internal contradictions within para 3(2).

It is perhaps surprising that para 3(2) ends with the words, 'and [the trustees and managers] would *not* (emphasis added) have been indemnified from the assets of the scheme'. If there is a scheme indemnity, there is a scheme liability which can be excluded. However, if the liability is merely personal to the trustees and managers, it will not in any event get transferred by s.161 as it is merely personal and would not have been indemnified.

Given this apparent inconsistency it is hard to gauge how the courts might apply para 3(2) without adopting a 'purposive analysis'. If the intention was to exclude indemnification of the trustees and managers by the scheme, there would have been simpler ways of doing so. Where legal proceedings are justifiable against a trustee or manager, but not the scheme, it seems improbable that the members were intended to suffer by way of indemnification, especially where they are already suffering. The same applies to all the other employees who will have to pay enhanced premiums to cover the trustees' and managers' culpability.

6.12.5 Scheme indemnities to trustees

Indemnities (from the scheme to trustees) are, if appropriately drafted, fair and reasonable; but trustees would not normally give personal warranties in respect of the scheme's funds. The possible removal of such indemnities seems unreasonably harsh, and probably unintended. In practice, regardless of whether the courts adopt a purposive definition or not, the safest course of action for trustees and managers for the future will be to rely less on indemnification by the scheme, but more (at the fund's expense) on an insurance policy to cover personal liability. Such a policy is not excluded (nor it seems was it intended to be excluded) by the para 3(2) carve-out; instead the liability to pay outstanding premiums would be transferred under s.161. It should be remembered, however, that the insurance policy should not cover indemnification of civil penalties.

Surely, in the event of scheme insolvency and trustee indemnification, the real question is to address the mischief: 'was the indemnity value for money?' Blanket carve-outs (especially if badly drafted) will only increase the nervousness of trustees and managers about taking the more risky appointments: thus, in this respect (as with other parts of PA 2004), the legislation could have the opposite effect of its intentions. It should be remembered that an illegitimate scheme indemnity to a trustee would already be subject to attack prior to the section 161 transfer. An illegitimate indemnity providing for indemnification in the case of negligence would no doubt be a 'misuse or misappropriation' under the s.16 restitution remedy. Alternatively such an indemnity would be a 'transaction at undervalue' within s.52. It would be sensible, however, for all trustees to have a 'legitimate indemnity' in place and that only 'illegitimate indemnities' are attacked. If the object was to attack all indemnities, then the para 3(2) approach of excluding liabilities, but not assets, has some superficial fairness. It may, however, become unfair in its consequences. Invariably 'causes of action' relating to schemes will be both multi-party and possess cross claims and/or set-offs. Adopting a purposive analysis (of excluding indemnification) will mean that such causes of action will become further complicated, and assets themselves may be lost; the net position, liability or assets will not be known until completion of the action.

Again the problem would be solved by dropping para 3(2) and relying on the restitution *(s.16)* and transaction at an undervalue *(s.52)* remedies. Why are the trustees and managers excluded? If indemnification is wrong, it is wrong per se and should apply in all cases. Why does the exclusion only apply to being 'indemnified from the assets'? If an insurance policy is not taken out as a trustee protection measure, but rather indemnification is provided by the employer, not only will the trustees and managers suffer, but the trustees and managers and the PPF may also be affected because the assets transferred under section 161 will include debts from the employer of the scheme. These debts will be subject to 'equities', counter-claims, set-off, including any claims incurred on behalf of the scheme by the company i.e. the indemnification. There would appear to be no difficulty under para 3(2) in the company employer indemnifying the trustee and manager and seeking (and getting) a guarantee (rather than an indemnification) of that indemnity from the scheme. The guarantee would then be subject to set-off (not least because of the set-off rules in 2.85 and 4.90 of the Insolvency Rules 1986) and therefore set off against debts already (or to be) transferred under section 161. It would not necessarily even be a liability. A set-off is a 'shield not a sword'. It reduces an asset, but does not necessarily create a liability, and therefore would not fall within the para 3(2) requirements of 'liabilities transferred' (even if a purposive definition is adopted).

Given that there is no PA 2004 definition of indemnification for the schedule, it can only be concluded that indemnification does not include a 'guarantee'; this is so even if a purposive interpretation is adopted. The concepts of indemnity and guarantee, although often confused, are radically different, but nevertheless achieve much the same aim.

6.13 The obligation of the PPF during the 'assessment period'

Following an application to assume responsibility for a scheme, either as a result of an insolvency event *(s.127(1))* or an application from the trustees and managers *(s.128(1)(a))* (a 'section 129 application') or having received a notice from the PPF *(s.128(1)(b))* ('a section 129 notification') "the PPF is obliged to obtain a valuation of the assets and protected liabilities of the scheme and where it is satisfied [that 'the value of the assets of the scheme at the relevant time was less than the amount of the protected liabilities'] …, the PPF must, as soon as reasonably practicable, obtain an actuarial valuation" *(s.143(2))*. The actuarial valuation calculation is subject to as yet unpublished regulations and is beyond the scope of this book. However, section 143 gives legal guidance, both as to the protected liabilities, but especially as to the assets.

The legal guidance is supplemented by [yet to be published] regulations. Obviously the core of the scheme assets is the PA 1995 section 75 deficiency *(s.143(5)(a))*. However, 'assets' also include:
(a) contribution notices *(ss.38, 47 and 55), (s.143(5)(b))*;
(b) financial support directions *(s.43), (s.143(5) (c))*; and
(c) transactions at under value and restoration orders *(s.52), (s.143(5)(c))*.

Given that invariably the employer company (and its associates/connected companies) will be insolvent and may well have (through the IP) counter-claims, the 'actuarial calculation' of those 'assets' (the PA 2004 statutory debts) will be difficult; not least because these assets will be contingent, until finally determined i.e. no further appeal. Recognising this, section 143(9) states, "Nothing … requires the actuarial valuation to be obtained during any period when the PPF considers [not reasonably considers] that an event may occur which [such as consideration of sections 38, 47, 55, 43 and 52] may affect the value of the assets."

There seems to be some confusion in the drafting of section 143 over the difference between assets and liabilities. Section 143(3) states: "regulations may provide that any of the following [the PA 1995 s.75 deficiency, as well as the PA 2004 statutory debts of sections 38, 47, 55, 43 and 52] are to be regarded as assets or *protected liabilities* [our emphasis added] of the scheme". Yet, given the statutory definition of protected liabilities, let alone the general understanding of what constitutes a 'liability', it is hard to imagine that the PA 1995 s.75 deficiency or the statutory debts of section 38, 47, 55, 43 and 52, could legitimately be classed as 'protected or indeed any other kind of liabilities'.

The valuation needs to be in the prescribed form, containing prescribed information, but most importantly prepared and signed by a qualified actuary *(s.11(a))*. "When the PPF is satisfied [not reasonably] that the valuation has been prepared [as described] it must... approve the valuation" *(s.144(2)(a))* or "where the PPF is not so satisfied it must obtain another valuation" *(s.144(3))*. The valuation is not binding until: "(a) it is approved ... (b) the period within which the approval may be reviewed by Chapter 6 [by an appeal] has expired and the approval is so reviewed... [and it] has finally been disposed of *(s.145(1))* after which the PPF must serve notice on (a) the Regulator (b) the trustees and managers (c) any insolvency practitioner" *(s.145(3))*.

The constituent elements of the valuation of protected liabilities are: "(a) the cost of securing benefits for and in respect of members of the scheme which correspond to the compensation which would be payable... in accordance with the pension compensation provision (see *s.162*) if the PPF assumed responsibility for the scheme ... (b) liabilities of the scheme which are liabilities to, or in respect of, its members, and (c) the estimated cost of winding up scheme *(s.131)*".

An insolvency event is the appointment of a subsequent IP, "if the PPF determines...that no insolvency event has occurred or is likely to occur as mentioned...it must issue...a withdrawal notice" *(s.148(3))* leading to, after the period set aside for review under chapter 6, the PPF ceasing to be involved with the scheme.

6.14 The obligation of the PPF following a 'scheme rescue'
So what happens if a scheme rescue has occurred under section 122(2)(b) or section 130(3) (the PPF reports a 'scheme rescue')? Does the PPF truly cease to be involved as stated in section 149 (the IP reports a 'scheme rescue') i.e. 'circumstances in which the PPF ceases to be involved with an eligible scheme'? This will depend upon the extent of the scheme rescue. There are three options:
(a)   an application for reconsideration *(s.151)*;

(b) 'closed schemes' *(s.153)*; or

(c) scheme winding up.

Once binding, the valuation is conclusive, especially as to 'whether or not the condition in s.127(2)(a) or, as the case may be, s.128(2)(a) (the condition that scheme assets are less than 'protected liabilities') is satisfied in relation to a scheme *(s.145(2))*; save to the extent that fraud compensation has been paid under s.172(3) and (4), which itself can become an asset of the scheme. Elsewhere we have noted that there will be considerable potential difficulties with timing. The PPF will take some time in fulfilling its statutory duties under the ss.127(2)(a)/s.128(2)(a) ('the difference between the assets and the protected liabilities quantified') whereas the IP is under similar duties to expedite the insolvency by having creditors' claims finalised. Section 145 makes the valuation binding on the PPF only, not on the IP. The IP can alter the creditor claim as circumstances, such as the existence of the valuation change, but it is quite possible that the IP will have legitimately demanded the submission of final creditor claims before the valuation is finalised; this is especially likely to happen before the s.145(1)(c) (disposal of any review) condition is satisfied. We could therefore have a perverse situation: a difference between the claim as admitted by the IP and a different claim (by valuation) by which the PPF is bound. Whilst elsewhere we have asked the IP to be sympathetic, as far as possible, to the position of the PPF, such a difference will be untenable for the IP and the non-scheme creditors represented by the IP. A better solution would be to amend the legislation to allow for expedited procedures, especially of the review process, notwithstanding the requirements of the Human Rights Act 1998. The incremental delay arising from the s.172(3) and (4) (fraud compensation payment) exemption underlines the case for change.

6.15 Application for reconsideration

At this point the PPF has refused responsibility solely because the conditions in section 127(2)(a) and section 128(2)(a) have not been satisfied, i.e. ' the value of the scheme assets was less than the protected liabilities'. However, if a different financial test is satisfied, the PPF may nevertheless assume responsibility. The PPF "must assume responsibility for the scheme ... if it is satisfied that the value of the assets of the scheme at the reconsideration time is less than the aggregate of: (a) the amounts quoted in the protected benefits quotation accompanying the application, (b) the amount at that time of the liabilities of the scheme which are not liabilities to, or in respect of members of the scheme, and (c) the estimated costs of the winding up of the scheme at that time"*(s.152(2))*. There appears to be no equivalent to section 143(3) which allows for the Regulator to regard statutory debts created under sections 38, 43, 47, 52 and 55 as assets, when performing the section 152(2) calculation. This seems perverse. Statutory debts are assets in the ordinary sense of the word and hence, there would appear to be no reason not to include them as assets in the 'reconsideration calculation'. However, given the absence of section

143(3) and its supporting regulations in sections 151 and 152 which deal with reconsideration, the real difficulty is how to calculate the value of those assets. The protected benefits quotation means "a quotation for one or more annuities from companies willing to accept payment in respect of the members from the trustees or managers of the scheme, which would provide in respect of each member of the scheme from the reconsideration time - (a) benefits for all in respect of the member corresponding to the compensation which would be payable to all in respect of the member in accordance with the pension compensation provisions if the [PPF] assumed responsibility of the scheme by virtue of this section, or (b) benefits in accordance with the member's entitlement or accrued rights... under the scheme rules (other than his entitlement or rights in respect of money-purchase benefits), which benefits can, in the case of that member, be secured at the lower cost" (s.151(8)).

The regulations made under section 143(3) and (4) as to the valuation of assets, more especially statutory debts under sections 38, 47, 53, 43 and 52 are applicable to the reconsideration sections of section 154 and 152. Other regulations determine how the protected benefits quotation will be calculated.

It is not the purpose of this book to consider both the actuarial calculations involved and the reconsideration calculation (particularly the protected benefits quotation) and how they differ actuarially from sections 127(2)(a) and 128(2)(a) calculations in detail. However, the salient differences and the mischief involved can be considered. Both protected liabilities and the protected benefits quotation are based upon the equivalent of what a member would obtain if the PPF assumed responsibility and the compensation provisions applied. The difference is that the protected benefits quotation is market based, i.e. are there 'companies willing to accept payment in respect of the members...which would provide...each member...benefits corresponding to the compensation'? The regulations make it clear that for the purposes of sections 127(2)(a) and 128(2)(a) it is assumed that the assets will cover, for example, an annuity. If they do not, then the situation must be reconsidered.

The reconsideration application process is similar to the section 127 or section 129 application or notification process, except perhaps by being more involved. Each application form is prescribed, as is the supporting information, including audited scheme accounts, which must be made within a prescribed period and the PPF has the right to obtain its own valuation/quotation. The duty on the trustees and managers is permissive: "a trustee or manager may [not must] make an application to the PPF" (s.151(1)). There is a noticeable lack of any threat of civil penalties in the reconsideration sections of PA 2004 in contrast to other sections. Following an application, subject to review processes similar to those to which the original application is subject, the PPF must assume responsibility for the scheme if it is satisfied that the assets are less than the protected benefits, etc (s.152(2)).

Surprisingly (or not given the time that will have elapsed since the PPF became involved) if the PPF makes a 'determination' to assume responsibility, it need only notify the trustees and managers and not the Regulator, nor any IP *(s.152(3))*.

How does a reconsidered assumption of responsibility affect the IP (if he is still around) with regard to the creditor claim? There is now further evidence in respect of the claim if the IP has not already finalised it. The quotes (i.e. the protected benefits quotation from an insurance company) can provide a basic calculation from which the claim can be quantified.

6.16 Closed Scheme Application (s.153)

A closed scheme application has the same starting point as the earlier reconsideration application, namely that section 151(2) or (3) applies: "that is, a scheme rescue is not possible for an eligible scheme, but the scheme has sufficient assets to meet protected liabilities" *(s.153(1))*. The difference between a closed scheme application under section 153 and a reconsideration application under section 151 is the extent of the scheme deficiency: it is the difference between the section 151 'protected benefits quotation' and the section 153 'full buyout quotation'. Thus, "If the trustees or managers...are unable to obtain a full buyout quotation, they must [*not* may] within the authorised period apply to...the [PPF] for authorisation to continue as a closed scheme" *(s.153(2))*. Further "they must take all reasonable steps to obtain a full buyout quotation" *(s.153(3))*.

A 'full buyout quotation' means: "a quotation for one or more annuities from one or more insurers (being companies willing to accept payment in respect of the members from the trustees or managers of the scheme) which would provide in respect of each member of the scheme, from a relevant date, benefits in accordance with the member's entitlement or accrued rights, including pension credit rights, under the scheme rules (other than his entitlements or rights in respect of money purchase benefits)" *(s.153(7))*. In short, it means an annuity where the members would receive their agreed non-money-purchase-benefits, i.e. the scheme is not insolvent. Where the PPF "receives...[such] an application... if it is satisfied that the trustees or managers ... are unable to obtain a full buyout quotation, it must authorise the scheme to continue as a closed scheme" *(s.153(5))*. "Where the PPF determines an application in respect of a scheme under this section, it must issue a determination notice and give a copy of that notice to (a) the trustees or managers and (b) ...[the Regulator, but surprisingly not any IP in office]' *(s.153(6))*. Perhaps because a closed scheme determination will not result in the PPF assuming responsibility, the PA 2004 Chapter 6 determination review provisions do not apply. Hence the determination, save for Ombudsman's involvement, appears to be final. Section 153 reverts to the PA 2004 form by again threatening the trustees and managers with civil penalties for breach.

What is the overlap between a 'closed scheme application' and a "reconsideration application"? Section 153 does not state that the two are mutually exclusive. The section 151 application is permissive, whereas the section 153 application is mandatory. Certainly if the trustees and managers are unable to obtain a section 153 full buyout quotation, then in all probability they will not be able to obtain a 'protected benefits quotation'. Depending upon the timing, a closed scheme application may well become a reconsidered scheme application. If the scheme is closed, there would appear to be little further impact on the IP save that, with no additional information, the calculation of the scheme claim (to the extent that the IP is still accepting claims after this period of time), may be more precise.

6.17 Pension Protection Fund (Entry Rules) Regulations 2005

Considering one of the main aims of PA 2004 is to provide compensation, it is not surprising that the Pension Protection Fund (Entry Rules) Regulations 2005 ("the PPF Entry Regulations") run to 50 pages with 25 separate regulations. Nor is it really surprising that the PPF Entry Regulations have already been subject to amendment by the Pension Protection Fund (Entry Rules) Amendment Regulations 2005 ("the PPF Entry Regulations Amendments"). The PPF Entry Regulations make provision relating to various requirements under Part 2 of PA 2004.

The extracts from the *Explanatory Notes to the PPF Regulations*, set out below, explain the effects of Regulations:

"Regulation 1 provides for...interpretation and includes an extension of the meaning of "employer" for the purposes."

The extension of the meaning of "employer" is familiar throughout all of PA 2004 subordinate legislation and refers primarily to alterations to take account of multi-employer schemes, references to which feature heavily in the PPF Entry Regulations.

"Regulation 2 sets out those schemes which are not "eligible schemes"...and which are not able to receive [PPF] compensation."

All occupational pension schemes are eligible schemes unless they fall within the exceptions of regulation 2 (1) (a) – (p) inclusive. As a general rule of thumb, all standard tax approved UK private enterprise schemes are eligible. Of particular note, however, are the small scheme exemptions. Regulation 2(1)(m) excepts a "scheme with fewer than twelve members where all the members are directors of a company which is the sole trustee of the scheme and either

(i) the rules of the scheme provide that all decisions are made only by members of the scheme by unanimous agreement; or

(ii) one of the directors of the company is independent in relation to the scheme for the purposes of section 23 of the 1995 Act and is registered in the register maintained by the Authority in accordance with regulations made under subsection (4) of that section".

Why directors should suffer more than employees when they often also personally guarantee the business's obligations is not explained.

A "scheme with fewer than two members" is also exempted (exception (k)): again it appears without justification.

Importantly, even a standard tax approved UK private enterprise scheme will become ineligible: "where, at any time, the trustees or managers...enter into a legally enforceable agreement . . . the effect of which is to reduce the amount of [the] section 75 [debt]"(regulation 2 (2)). However, the regulation 2(2) exception is subject to three sensible non-multi-employer exceptions.

The first exception (regulation 3(a)) requires that: "before the beginning of an assessment period - the value of the scheme's assets would be sufficient to secure benefits...which correspond to the...compensation which would be payable...if the Board were to assume responsibility". Further, it requires that an "actuary has provided the Board with a written estimate of the current value of the assets and the protected liabilities of the scheme together with a statement about the effect which the agreement would have on the value of the scheme's assets as recorded in that estimate", which the Board has (subject to review by the PPF Ombudsman, etc) validated. In short, given the actuarial assurance that protected liabilities are covered, then following the agreement, the PPF will not be called to provide compensation. Given that the agreement occurs "before the beginning of an assessment period", this compromise (i.e. legally enforceable agreement) occurs outside IA 1986. This exception however does not answer the query as to whether the scheme itself can enter into a legally enforceable agreement which compromises the section 75 debt.

The second exception (regulation 3(b)) requires that: "before the beginning of an assessment period, the trustees or managers of the scheme enter into a legally enforceable agreement . . ., as part of an arrangement under section 425 of CA 1985 (power of company to compromise with creditors or members), the effect of which is to reduce the amount of the debt due to the scheme . . . under [section 75] of the 1995 Act". Section 425 is a procedure similar to the IA 1986 CVA procedure whereby a compromise may be forced upon creditors. A section 425 debt compromise is often referred to as a 'scheme of arrangement'. Given that a section 425 compromise is outside the IA 1986, its commencement does not trigger an assessment period. The effect of the regulation 3(b) exception is the same as the regulation 3(a) exception, except that, perhaps surprisingly, there is no requirement under the regulation 3(b) exception ('the section 425 exception') for an actuarial report! It should be remembered that the actuarial report under the regulation 3(a) exception must be validated by the Board and state that the protected liabilities are covered. Save for insurance companies, section 425 is little-used in corporate reconstruction, it being too cumbersome a procedure. However, provided that the scheme itself can enter into a legally enforceable agreement which compromises the section 75 debt, regulation 3(b)) may give a reason to use section 425 outside insurance company reconstructions.

The third exception (regulation 3(c)) requires that: "after the beginning of an assessment period...the Board...has entered into a legally enforceable agreement...the effect of which is to reduce the amount of the [section 75] debt". Simply put, the employer has entered an insolvency process (i.e. the assessment period has begun) which has resulted in a CVA (i.e. a legally enforceable agreement reducing the section 75 debt). The term "entered into a legally enforceable agreement" is perhaps misleading. Providing that 75% of the creditors agree, the CVA may well be forced upon the Board.

"Regulation 3 provides that where, after the beginning of an assessment period in relation to an eligible scheme, the scheme ceases to be an eligible scheme in prescribed circumstances, the scheme shall...be treated as remaining an eligible scheme."

As noted elsewhere, regulation 4 "makes provision in respect of the period in which an IP is required to notify the Board of the occurrence of an insolvency event in relation to the employer in relation to an eligible scheme. If an insolvency event is a "qualifying insolvency event"...the start of an assessment period will be triggered in relation to an eligible scheme and the scheme will become subject to the various requirements in Part 2 of the Act". Sensibly, the notification, in addition to requiring basic information, also allows the IP to state "whether the notice issued contains any commercially sensitive information" *(regulation 4(2)(j))*.

"Regulation 5 provides for certain events in relation to certain types of bodies (such as building societies, friendly societies and limited liability partnerships) to be classified as insolvency events for the purposes of Part 2 of the Act".

IA 1986 and its supporting legislation do not cover all types of corporate structure. Consequently provision has to be made for such structures.

"Regulation 6 sets out the circumstances in which insolvency proceedings in relation to the employer in relation to an eligible scheme are stayed or come to an end. Where these circumstances exist, the insolvency practitioner will be required to issue a notice to the effect that he is not able to confirm whether a scheme rescue has occurred or is not possible. This may lead to the Board ceasing to be involved with a scheme".

In short, for some reason, the IP's proposed office terminates prior to its planned completion. As regards corporate insolvency, the list is in regulation 6(1)(a)(i) - (v) inclusive:

(i) a nominee proposed CVA fails, when the nominee is not a liquidator or administrator;

(ii) a director-proposed moratorium under Schedule A1 of the Insolvency Act fails to produce a CVA;

(iii) the appointment of an administrator ceases to have effect and there is no replacement IP;

(iv) an administrative receiver vacates office under section 45 of IA 1986; and

(v) all proceedings in the winding up of a company are stayed altogether or an order for the winding up of the company is rescinded or discharged, without any order being made against a company.

Similar provisions are made for individuals and partnerships. All the provisions under regulation 6 fall within IA 1986, save for regulation 6(2) which deals with a void deed under the Deed of Arrangements Act 1914, which deals with personal insolvency, i.e. the bankruptcy of an individual. It is, therefore, unlikely to be of relevance to DB schemes, as individuals are unlikely to be employers with such schemes. It is surprising that no similar extension was made in the corporate sphere, i.e. as regards section 425 of the Companies Act 1986, but this may be because the likelihood of a corporate deal becoming subsequently void is improbable.

> "Regulation 7 makes provision in respect of applications and notifications to the Board under section 129 of the Act for it to assume responsibility for an eligible scheme in circumstances where the employer in relation to the scheme is unlikely to continue as a going concern and meets prescribed requirements."

Public bodies, charities not formed under the Companies Act and registered trade unions do not fall under IA 1986. Consequently no PA 2004 'insolvency event' can exist. Regulation 7 allows these entities to fall under PA 2004 if they are 'unlikely to continue as a going concern'. Regulation 7A (inserted by the PPF Entry Regulations Amendments) makes similar provision for multi-employer schemes.

> "Regulation 8 sets out the time limit for making applications to the Board under section 129 of the Act. Regulation 8 also makes provision in respect of the form and content of such applications and about the form and content of notifications to the Board which the Pensions Regulator is required to make in circumstances where it becomes aware that an employer in relation to an eligible scheme is unlikely to continue as a going concern and meets prescribed requirements."

Where no "insolvency event" can occur (because the employer does not fall within IA 1986, e.g. it is a trade union) then the 'trustees or managers of the scheme', instead of an IP, must notify the PPF. The timeframe is similar to that of an IP, i.e. it is "the period of 28 days beginning with the date on which the trustees or managers of an eligible scheme become aware that the employer in relation to the scheme is unlikely to continue as a going concern" (regulation 8 (1)). Interestingly, there are similar obligations on the Board and the Regulator. Regulation 8A (inserted by the PPF Entry Regulations Amendments) makes similar provision for multi-employer schemes.

> "Regulations 9 and 10 set out the circumstances which must exist before an insolvency practitioner in relation to an employer in relation to an eligible scheme or the Board is able to determine whether or not a scheme rescue has occurred or is not possible in relation to the scheme. They also make provision regarding the form and content of the notices which must be issued by the insolvency practitioner or the Board in order to confirm the status of a scheme. Regulations 11 and 12 modify the application of regulations 9 and 10 so as to make similar provision in respect of multi-employer schemes."

Regulation 9 is the "confirmation of scheme status by insolvency practitioner" and it goes to the heart of both the PPF involvement and the IP's PA 2004 responsibilities. The "scheme status" is whether a "scheme rescue" is or is not possible.

The matters an IP must confirm under regulation 9 depend upon whether a scheme rescue is possible or not. For instance, in relation to corporates and a scheme rescue, the IP: "must be able to confirm…(i) the company has been rescued as a going concern and the employer - (aa) retains responsibility for meeting the pension liabilities under the scheme, and (bb) has not entered into an agreement [to reduce the amount of the section 75 debt, i.e. a CVA]…; or (ii) another person or other persons has or have assumed responsibility for meeting the employer's pension liabilities under the scheme" (regulation 9 (1) (a)). Whereas if there is no scheme rescue, the IP must confirm: "(i) that [the] employer has entered into an agreement [to reduce the amount of the section 75 debt, i.e. a CVA]; or (ii) that [the] employer is not continuing as a going concern and - (aa) no other person or other persons has or have assumed responsibility for meeting the employer's pension liabilities under the scheme, and (bb) the insolvency practitioner is of the opinion that the employer's pension liabilities under the scheme will not be assumed by another person" *(regulation 9(2)(a))*. Similar provisions apply to individuals and partnerships.

The method of confirmation is by way of a notice containing the information prescribed by regulation 9(3), much of which is perfunctory, but several aspects require comment. The regulation emphasises that a former IP is still under an obligation and that the IP's judgment is potentially open to question as the notice must confirm: "(h) if a scheme rescue is not possible, a statement from the insolvency practitioner or former insolvency practitioner as to why, in his opinion, that is not possible; (i) if…the former IP has not been able to confirm in relation to the scheme that a scheme rescue is not possible, a statement from that IP as to why, in his opinion, that is the case; (j) a statement that the notice issued will not become binding until it has been approved by the Board". Regulation 9(3)(k) goes on to state: "whether, in the opinion of the IP or former IP, the notice issued contains any commercially sensitive information". The equivalent subsection for the original IP notice *(regulation 4(2)(i))* does not call for the opinion of the IP: the statement that the notice contains "commercially sensitive information" appears to be taken for granted. The original IP notice *(regulation 4(2)(i))* is less likely to contain "commercially sensitive information" as a sale by the IP of the insolvent business is less likely to have occurred during the notification period. This is not the case with the scheme rescue notice *(regulation 9(3))*. IPs and their advisers should take into account the requirements to notify in their negotiations and sales contracts with purchasers.

Regulation 10 governs the 'confirmation of the scheme status by the Board' as required by section 130(5)(a) and (b) PA 2004 ("employer's business has been rescued as a going concern" and either (i) "that employer has entered into an agreement [to reduce the amount of the section 75 debt, i.e. a CVA]...; or (ii) that employer is not continuing as a going concern". The Board's duty to notify the Regulator, the trustees and managers and the employer is not onerous. The notification statement generally mirrors the statement received from the IP, save for two exceptions, which further illustrate that the IP's judgment may be called into account. The notice should state *(regulation 10(4))*: "(i) whether the issue of the notice by the Board is a reviewable matter and, if so, the time limit for applying for a review of or appeal against the issue of the notice; [and] (j) the date on which the notice issued will become binding."

As noted above, regulations 11 and 12 modify the application of regulations 9 and 10 so as to make similar provision in respect of multi-employer schemes.

> "Regulation 13 makes provision regarding the form and content of binding notices confirming the status of a scheme. A notice is not binding until the period in respect of which it is possible for the issue of the notice to be reviewed under Chapter 6 of Part 2 of the Act has expired or, if an application for a review has been made, until the review or any subsequent appeal has been conclusively resolved."

Regulation 13(1) states: "Where the Board determines to approve or not to approve a notice issued by an IP or former IP...the determination notice which the Board must issue...shall contain" [mostly non-noteworthy information save for] "(g) a statement of whether or not the Board has determined to approve the notice issued by the insolvency practitioner or former insolvency practitioner". In short, the Board reserves the right to approve the statement from the IP.

> "Regulation 14 makes provision in respect of the types of payments that may be made to a scheme during an assessment period."

For the IP carrying on the trade of the entity during the assessment period, regulation 14 is not particularly helpful both in aim and in clarity. It states: "(1) During an assessment period...the prescribed circumstances in which further contributions *may* [emphasis added] be paid to the scheme by an employer...are where those contributions relate to - (a) all or any part of that employer's liability for any [section 75] debt...; and (b) the value of an asset of the scheme arising from a debt or obligation [arising from the] Board's obligation to obtain valuation of assets and protected liabilities". The question regulation 14 should address for the trading IP is, 'What costs do I have to incur by way of contributions to the pension scheme during the trading period'? Regulation 14 seems to leave open the choice to the IP of whether to contribute or not during the trading period. First, contributions "may" (not "must") be made. Second, the contribution under limb (a) may be "all or any part", so if contribution is made, the amount is not specified. If it all had to be paid by the trading IP, it would be a most onerous obligation. The position of a trading IP under regulation 14 should be clarified. The worst-case scenario for a trading IP is that, after the event, he is found not to have accounted for the cost of trading (the cost being an obligation to make good the pension deficit).

"Regulation 15 makes provision in respect of the "relevant person" in relation to an eligible scheme to whom the Board may issue directions under section 134 of the Act."

Regulation 15 states: "The "relevant person"...is any individual who is appointed by the trustees or managers of the scheme as the scheme administrator responsible for the discharge of [certain]...functions". Those functions are "(a) the investment of the scheme's assets, (b) the incurring of expenditure, (c) the instigation or conduct of legal proceedings" and "with a view to ensuring that the scheme's protected liabilities do not exceed its assets or, if they do exceed its assets, that the excess is kept to a minimum, the Board may give a relevant person in relation to the scheme directions regarding the exercise" of those functions (s.134(2)).

"Regulation 16 provides for the circumstances in which a transfer payment may be made during an assessment period in respect of a member's rights under an eligible scheme. It also provides for the other circumstances in which the trustees or managers of a scheme may take steps to discharge a member's rights under an eligible scheme during an assessment period."

"Regulation 17 makes provision in respect of the circumstances where a member of an eligible scheme may postpone the receipt of his entitlement to a pension or lump sum payment under the scheme during an assessment period."

"Regulation 18 makes provision in respect of the rate of interest [it being base rate] which is payable by the trustees or managers of an eligible scheme to which the Board has made a loan to pay scheme benefits under section 139 of the Act. It also makes provision in respect of how the rate of interest payable is to be calculated."

Base rate means "the rate for the time being quoted by the reference banks", and 'reference banks' means "the four largest" UK banks.

"Regulation 19 makes provision in respect of the form and content [both of which are perfunctory and contain nothing of note] of withdrawal notices issued by the Board under section 148 of the Act."

"Regulation 20 makes provision in respect of the accrual of benefits under a scheme in respect of an assessment period in relation to an eligible scheme when that assessment period comes to an end."

If a "scheme rescue" has occurred, then provided contributions have been paid during the assessment period "benefits [generally] are to accrue under the scheme rules to or in respect of any member of the scheme in respect of any period of service in employment during that assessment" *(regulation 20(1))* .

"Regulations 21 and 22 make provision in respect of the period in relation to which the Board is to determine whether or not to refuse to assume responsibility for a scheme under sections 146 and 147 of the Act. Regulation 23 makes provision in respect of the form and content of withdrawal notices issued by the Board under sections 146 and 147 of the Act."

Section 146 ('schemes which become eligible schemes') states: "(1) Regulations may provide that where the Board is satisfied that an eligible scheme was not such a scheme throughout such period as may be prescribed, the Board must refuse to assume responsibility". Whereas regulation 21 states: "(1) The prescribed period [referred to in section 146(1) ...] (schemes which become eligible schemes) throughout which the Board must be satisfied that an occupational pension scheme is not an eligible scheme shall - (a) in the case of a scheme which was established at least three years before the date on which an assessment period began in relation to the scheme, be the period of three years preceding the date on which that assessment period began; and (b) in the case of a scheme which was established less than three years before the date on which an assessment period began in relation to a scheme, be the period beginning with the date on which the scheme was established and [ending with] the date on which that assessment period began.

Section 147 ('new schemes created to replace existing schemes') states: "(1) The Board must refuse to assume responsibility for a scheme ("the new scheme")... where it is satisfied that - (a) the new scheme was established during such period as may be prescribed...and (d) the main purpose or one of the main purposes of establishing the new scheme...was to enable those members to receive compensation". Whereas regulation 22 (1) states: "(1) The prescribed period referred to in section 147(1)(a) of the Act…during which the Board must be satisfied that a new occupational pension scheme was established shall be the period of three years preceding the date on which an assessment period began in relation to the scheme".

As noted above, 'regulation 23 makes provision in respect of the form and content of withdrawal notices issued by the Board under sections 146 and 147 of the Act'. Much of the required content *(regulation 23(1))* is perfunctory save for: "(f) the period in relation to which the Board is satisfied that the scheme in respect of which the notice is issued is not an eligible scheme; (g) a statement of reasons for the Board's decision to refuse to assume responsibility for the scheme in respect of which the notice is issued; (h) whether the issue of the notice by the Board is a reviewable matter and, if so, the time limits for applying for a review of or appeal against the issue of that notice;…; and (k) whether the notice issued contains restricted information and, if so, the nature of any restrictions."

"Regulation 24 makes provision in respect of the [non-noteworthy] form and content of applications for reconsideration made under section 151 of the Act. It also makes provision in respect of the time limits for making such applications and the documents which are to accompany the application."

"Regulation 25 and the Schedule make provision in respect of the [non-noteworthy] prescribed form and content of the audited scheme accounts and report from the auditor which is to accompany an application for reconsideration."

6.18 The Pension Protection Fund (Provision of Information) Regulations 2005

The Pension Protection Fund (Provision of Information) Regulations 2005 ("The PPF Information Regulations") do as they suggest.

"Regulation 3 makes provision as to the information to be provided by the Board to insolvency practitioners in relation to insolvent employers who sponsored an occupational pension scheme, trustees or managers of such schemes where an insolvency event has occurred in relation to the sponsoring employer, such employers and the members and beneficiaries of such schemes" (from the *Explanatory Notes to the PPF Information Regulations*).

Under regulation 3(2): "Where the Board receives a notice under section 120(2) (duty to notify insolvency events in respect of employers) from an insolvency practitioner that an insolvency event has occurred in relation to an employer, and (a) the scheme to which the notice relates is an eligible scheme; or (b) in the case of a multi-employer scheme which is a segregated scheme, the section to which the notice relates is an eligible section, [then the Board…shall, within the period of 28 days beginning with its receipt of that notice, provide that insolvency practitioner, the Regulator, and the trustees or managers of that scheme or section with [certain]…information". The information noted in regulation 3(3) is: "(a) where the insolvency event is not a qualifying insolvency event, that the insolvency event is not such an insolvency event; or (b) where the insolvency event is a qualifying insolvency event, that the insolvency event is such an insolvency event and the date on which the assessment period began."

6.19 Fund maintenance: Financial Support Directions

6.19.1 Financial Support Directions – Section 43: Background

This is the most controversial PA 2004 'reform': it cuts through the internationally accepted notions of limited liability and consequently does not augur well for new capital investment in 'UK plc'. Its overall effect is imprecise and may be incapable of being satisfactorily curtailed.

The restorative remedies in PA 2004 stem from principles of equity and are in accordance with long-standing UK and international legal practice. The areas now considered differ from the restorative remedies where assets have been misappropriated in that the aim of these sections is not to restore the status quo, but to adopt a proactive approach to scheme funding by placing assets in the scheme. The self-explanatory term 'financial support directions' require funding from others with regard to third parties. In contrast to the concept of limited liability, this part of PA 2004 elevates persons, associated or connected with the company, for unspecified reasons, beyond other creditor classes. It is not clear why there is no financial support directions regime for 'trade creditors' of the insolvent employer, as well such a provision for 'pension creditors'.

PA 2004 draws heavily on IA 1986 and there are already measures available within IA 1986 for those who abuse limited liability. Those remedies (notably 'fraudulent and wrongful trading', let alone 'transactions to defraud creditors' and other restorative remedies copied within PA 2004) could be applied to the pension fund deficiencies, as they are reactive and available to all. In the same way as with the transaction at an undervalue provisions, PA 2004 could have 'tweaked' these remedies to create a level playing-field between pension and other creditors to suit pension deficits. However, the Government chose to create a radical new remedy, which goes against the generally accepted international norm of limited liability, which has led to the acceptance of risk and consequently the provision of capital accumulation.

6.19.2 What is a Financial Support Direction?

Section 43(1) excludes money purchase 'and other yet to be prescribed schemes' from the provisions of financial support directions. The Regulator "may issue a 'financial support direction'… if the Regulator is of the opinion [not reasonable opinion] that the employer… is (a) a service company, or (b) is insufficiently resourced" *(s.43(2))*. A 'financial support direction' "requires… (a) that financial support… is put into place [by a third party]… (b) remains in place and (c) that the

Regulator is notified of prescribed events... [re] the financial support as soon as reasonably practical". Subject to further regulation *(s.45(2)(c) and (d))* the definition of such financial support in section 45 is simple: a full or partial intra-group, joint and several guarantee of the employers' scheme liability *(s.45(2)(a) and (b))*. Section 45 draws a distinction between the meaning of financial support with regard to a 'group service company' or a 'group insufficiently resourced company'; both types of company are subject to extensive and it is suspected difficult to implement definitions.

A 'service company' is defined as a 'group company whose accounts are prepared under section 226 of the Companies Act', such that turnover is 'solely or principally derived from intra-group charges for employees' *(s.44(2))*. Not every company (as defined by *CA 1985 s.735(1)*) prepares accounts under section 226 of the Companies Act. Further, when such accounts are prepared they are invariably well out-of-date; audited accounts are necessarily a snapshot of the past. In any event, the audited accounts may not show from where the turnover emanates. Finally, what does 'principally derived from' intra-group charges mean? Nothing within the section 44(2) definition of 'service company' addresses the mischief to be eradicated: that of being 'insufficiently resourced'. It is therefore theoretically possible (but note the 'reasonableness requirement' in section 43(7)) to have a 'sufficiently resourced service company', being subject to a 'financial support direction'.

The definition of an 'insufficiently resourced' company is twofold. First, "the value of the resources of the employer is less than the prescribed percentage of the estimated section 75 [employer] debt" *(s.44(3)(a))*. The percentage has been prescribed at 50%. This debt includes contingent section 75 debts *(s.51(1)(2))* but excludes current debts *(s.44(6))*. Second, 'that a connected or associated person (as defined by IA 1986 usually, but not necessarily, a group company) with assets sufficient to make good the section 75 deficiency *(s.44(3))* exists.'

The definition of 'insufficiently resourced' differs from the 'service company' definition, but the two definitions overlap and are not mutually exclusive. Accordingly the 'insufficiently resourced' definition possibly makes the 'service definition' redundant and in any event is more sensible. First 'insufficient resource' is the mischief to be attacked, not the mere existence of a 'service company'. Second, the definition requires a 'third-party with sufficient resources': why have a financial support direction if there is no one to support? Certainly the Regulator could, it appears, challenge a 'service company' as an 'insufficiently resourced' company. Arguably therefore the PA 2004 reference to a 'service company' could be dropped, since the only 'service company' that is of interest is an 'insufficiently resourced service company' with a relevant sufficiently resourced third party.

6.19.3 Connected, associated and control

The Financial Support Direction and Contribution Notice provisions of PA 2004 make much reference to entities or individuals that are 'connected, associated or otherwise have control' of employers that have 'occupational eligible pension schemes'. These concepts (connected, associated and control) are borrowed directly from IA 1986 s.249.

A person is 'connected with a company' if: (a) he is a director or shadow director (i.e. acts like a director) of the company or an associate of such a director or shadow director; or (b) he is an associate of the company.

A 'person is an associate of an individual' if that person is the individual's husband, wife or civil partner, or is a relative, or the husband, wife or civil partner of a relative, of the individuals or the individual's husband, wife or civil partner. A person is an associate of any person with whom he is in partnership, and of the husband, wife or civil partner or a relative of any individual with whom he is in partnership. A person is an associate of any person whom he employs or by whom he is employed. However, employees are not generally treated as associates, if they are associates merely by being an employee. A company is 'an associate of another company' if: (a) the same person has control of both companies, or a person has control of one company and persons who are his associates, or he and persons who are his associates, have control of the other company, or: (b) if a group of two or more persons has control of each company, and the groups either consist of the same persons or could be regarded as consisting of the same persons by treating (in one or more cases) a member of the group as replaced by a person of whom he is an associate. Further, a 'company is an associate of another person' if that person has control of it or if that person and persons who are its associates together have control of it.

A 'person is taken as having control of a company' if: (a) the directors of the company or of another company which has control of it (or any of them) are accustomed to act in accordance with his directions or instructions, or; (b) he is entitled to exercise, or control the exercise of, one third or more of the voting power at any general meeting of the company or of another company which has control of it. Additionally, where two or more persons together satisfy either of conditions (a) - (b), they are taken to have control of the company. As can be seen, this is an extensive definition. Despite that, the Regulator wishes to extend the ambit of this definition, even though extensions have already occurred in respect of the definition of employer, to include 'former employers'.

6.19.4 Insufficiently resourced

We must assume that the third party is a group company. However, given the meaning of 'connected and associated' third parties, the definition of a third party is theoretically much wider than the group company references found in section

44(2)(b) and defined in section 51(1). What then is the section 75 debt for the purposes of 'insufficiently resourced' to which the prescribed percentage applies *(s.44(3)(a))*? For the purposes of a 'financial support direction', the connected/associated definition is slightly altered *(s.43(6)(b and c))* to exclude those who are connected/associated by reason of employment. An associated individual (not a connected nor indeed a 'non-individual') is excluded if the association is "by reason *only* [emphasis added] of employment". A similar exclusion (with regard to reversing the burden of proof) can be found in IA 1986 s.239(c) in the context of 'preferences', which is a restorative creditor remedy. Although unlikely to be of practical significance, the exclusion is for connected (not associated) employees. PA 2004 s.43(6)(c) excludes 'non-individuals' from being 'connected'. The provisions are not particularly clear. If the draftsman was concerned at employees incurring personal liabilities then it is perhaps surprising that he did not address the issue directly when considering whether it is 'reasonable' to impose a liability at all *(s.47(4))*.

6.19.5 What should a Financial Support Direction/Contribution Notice contain?

There is no 'reasonableness requirement' in determining whether an employer is a 'service company' or 'insufficiently resourced'. Section 43(2) merely requires the Regulator to be 'of the opinion'. However, the Regulator can only issue a financial support direction if it is reasonable to do so *(s.43(5)(b))*. In deciding whether it is reasonable, the Regulator should have regard to those factors noted in section 43(7) (a - e).

Factor (a) is "the relationship which the person has or has had with the employer"; this includes the section 435 Insolvency Act definition of associate. Remember that the Regulator cannot issue a financial support direction unless the recipient is 'connected' or 'associated' *(s.43(5)(a)* and *s.43(6)(b)* respectively) refer to section 435 ('the definition section' of IA 1986 through section 51(3)(d)). To that extent is factor (a) circuitous as to what constitutes 'associated entities'? The drafting emphasises the importance of IA 1986 s.435(10), that is 'whether the person has or had control of the employer'. What of 'connected parties'? Thus 'control' is implicit and further reference to it is circuitous. The Regulator cannot issue a financial support direction unless there is an associated or a connected person *(s.43(5)(a)* and *s.43(6)(c))*, and the combined effect of the wide definitions of these terms and the guidance is that factor (a) itself provides little practical guidance as to whether the 'financial support direction' is reasonable.

Factor (b) is "the relationship which the person has or has had with the employer ...including, where the employer is a company...whether the person has or has had control of the employer". Factor (b) fairly considers the benefits that a third party received, directly or indirectly from the employer. Factors (a) and (b) specifically refer to the financial support directions issued to a third party, not to the employer, unlike factors (c) and (d) which could refer to both the employer and third parties.

Factor (c) ('any connection or involvement which the person has or has had with the scheme') is so wide-ranging that it is of limited benefit in analysing the potential outcomes. The word 'any' implies that even the most minor connection or involvement equals potential liability. The words 'to the extent of any direct connection or involvement with' would have been clearer.

The reference to the 'scheme' as opposed to the employer is problematical. A connection or involvement with the employer must be assumed to amount to connection or involvement with the scheme, at least indirectly. It is not clear whether such indirect involvement falls within factor (c) and, if so, to what extent.

The word 'connection' is of dubious value in this context. Given that a third party has to be legally connected (see *IA 1986 s.249*) (to the extent not legally associated by *IA 1986 s.435*) what is the difference between being 'connected' and having a 'connection'; more especially since it is 'any connection', not, 'to the extent connected'.

Factor (d) ('financial circumstances') appears sensible, but does not assist greatly in practical terms. For a 'financial support direction' to apply to an 'insufficiently resourced company 'there must be a group company 'sufficiently resourced' to meet the deficiency *(s.44(3)(b))*. Does not the existence of a 'sufficiently resourced' group company and 'insufficiently resourced employer', cover 'financial circumstances'? It would appear so.

Factor (e) refers to 'such other matters as may be prescribed'.

Section 43(8) states what an FSD notice should contain: "A financial support direction must identify all the persons to whom the direction is issued". However, it is hoped that the Regulator would set out its requirements in detail under factors (a) - (e) in the notice.

6.20 The Pensions Regulator (Financial Support Direction, etc) Regulations 2005 ("the FSD Regulations")

The FSD Regulations clarify PA 2004, especially section 43, by dictating when a Financial Support Direction ("FSD") can be made.

Extracts from the *Explanatory Note to the FSD Regulations* are set out in this section, with commentary.

"[The FSD Regulations] also, in relation to all the anti-avoidance provisions (that is, contribution notices, financial support directions and restoration orders), extend the meaning of employer to include former employers in specified circumstances and modify those provisions of the…[PA 2004] in their application to multi-employer schemes."

"As [the FSD Regulations] are made before the expiry of the period of six months beginning with the coming into force of the sections of the [PA 2004] by virtue of which they are made, the requirement for the Secretary of State to consult [in drafting and implementing the regulations] such persons as he considers appropriate does not apply."

The FSD Regulations proceed on the basis that statutory accounts (i.e. accounts prepared under *CA 1985 s.226*) do not show the value of the resources of an 'entity available at any time'. The FSD Regulations therefore require an adjustment to statutory accounts or the "individual accounts" as described in the FSD Regulations.

"Regulation 2 defines the meanings of terms used in the regulations"

These terms predominantly relate to adjustments to "individual accounts" to show "entity value" –

(a) "the fair value difference" (abbreviated in the FSD Regulations to "FVD") is the difference between "individual accounts" and the "amount for which an asset could be exchanged, or liability settled, between knowledgeable willing parties at arm's length";

(b) "related employer balances" (abbreviated in the FSD Regulations to "Eb") are 'items appearing in individual accounts of two or more entities that would lead to resources being overstated or understated by that amount';

(c) "relevant pension scheme related balances" (abbreviated in the FSD regulations to "P") whether in credit or deficit should be self-explanatory; and

(d) "subordinated liabilities" (abbreviated in the FSD Regulations to "Se") i.e. subordinated in the accounts of the employer and/or "subordinated employer funding" i.e. liabilities of the "business associate" of the employer, treated as subordinated.

The FSD Regulations draw a distinction between an 'entity' which is a corporate entity and an individual or natural person. Thus the: "entity value difference ("EVD") means the difference between the entity value at the calculation date ["the date specified by the Regulator"] and the aggregate of that entity's net assets as set out in the FSD reference accounts and any identified FVDs".

It is sensible to require accounts adjustments, for the reasons stated above, and because statutory accounts do not necessarily take into account group balances. There is some ambiguity over the definition of fair value ("FV") and whether the FSD Regulations require FV calculations to be based on individual assets or liabilities, as opposed to looking at the FV of the total. Although in most cases where a company disposes of its assets as a going concern, the total (value) of the company should be greater than the sum of its parts, there could be a difference as to goodwill. Goodwill is an intangible asset which may not appear in the statutory accounts, has value, and this would support the view that assets need to be valued individually. This, however, is not stated explicitly in the Regulations.

LIABILITIES

The FV is to be calculated on the basis of "knowledgeable willing parties in an arm's-length transaction". "Arm's length" is often difficult in practice to define. Whereas "willing" seems to introduce a motivational desire to 'exchange' (i.e. to decrease the value of the asset in the books of the hypothetical vendor or to increase the amount of the offer by the hypothetical purchaser) or to settle (i.e. to decrease the value of the debt in the books of the debtor or to encourage the creditor to settle).

"Knowledge" will inevitably include questions of both conjecture ('will this patent application be granted'?) and commercial secrecy. The existence of an FSD based upon commercial secrecy presents obvious difficulties and should be avoided.

A possibly circular argument arises in the FV of the pension liability, which is, according to regulation 2 of the FSD Regulations, the 'amount by which the liability could be settled, between knowledgeable willing parties at arm's length'. If this definition is applied to the pension liability, the amount of that liability is the 'estimated section 75 debt', i.e. the cost of settling by securing annuities from a 'knowledgeable willing party' such as an insurance company. Further there is nothing in the "relevant pension scheme related balances" FSD Regulations definition that precludes this conclusion. The FSD Regulations provide for calculations to adjust "individual accounts" for FVD, to see whether the entity's resources exceed 50% of the estimated section 75 debt (see below). If one of the FVDs is the section 75 debt itself, the exercise is open to manipulation. Commonsense may prevail over literalism.

The FSD Regulations rightly focused on 'assets and liabilities', and not cash flow. An 'FSD arrangement', unlike a contribution notice, provides for "joint and several" liability, not immediate cash. There is a slight departure from this when considering an FSD against an individual. FSD Regulation 11(3) requires a report on an individual to include "a list detailing any income and usual outgoings".

The accounts used as a basis for an FSD (prior to adjustment for "fair value", etc.) are the "FSD reference accounts". These will usually be the most recent statutory accounts save for two exceptions. The first exception is "where the Regulator and the entity agree, subsequent accounts [may be] prepared on a basis consistent with the most recent individual accounts taking into account any changes required in order to comply with generally accepted accounting practice ["GAAP"] (FSD Regulation 2). The second exception is "in the case of an entity not subject to section 226 CA 1985 [i.e. a foreign company, or 'non- section 226 entity' then]... that entity's most recent set of approved accounts [may be used] or if the Regulator and the entity agree, subsequent accounts prepared on a basis with the most recent approved accounts, taking into account any changes required in order to comply with [GAAP]".

For both exceptions there appears to be no reasonableness requirement on either the entity or the Regulator to agree subsequent accounts. Presumably GAAP refers to UK GAAP and not to, for instance, US GAAP. Nevertheless it would be open for any foreign entity to argue for instance, US GAAP should apply; this is especially if consistency is required. Elsewhere the FSD Regulations make reference to international accounting standards ("IAS") and thus 'international GAAP'. The reference to GAAP is in any event surely nugatory. Certainly in the case of a 'section 226 entity' (i.e. required to prepare accounts under section 226 of the Companies Act) and probably in the case of a 'non-section 226 entity' (i.e. not required to prepare accounts under CA 1985 s.226 and therefore probably a foreign company) the subsequent accounts, in order to be prepared on a consistent basis, would take account of GAAP: taking account of GAAP would include changes to GAAP.

"Regulation 3 prescribes those schemes to which the provisions on financial support directions do not apply."

Perversely the FSD Regulations merely cross-refer to "regulation 3 of the Pensions Regulator (Contribution Notices and Restoration Orders) Regulations 2005". As a general rule, under regulation 3, the FSD Regulations will apply to a corporate defined benefit scheme.

"Regulation 4 prescribes those events [prescribed for the purposes of section 43(3)(c) as contents of an FSD] the occurrence of which must be notified to the Regulator."

The events are:

"(a) any event specified in...regulation 2(2) of the Pensions Regulator (Notifiable Events) Regulations 2005 (employer-related notifiable events) which occurs in respect of any party named in arrangements approved in a notice issued under section 45(1) (meaning of "financial support");

(b) any insolvency event...in relation to any person named in a financial support direction;

(c) any failure to abide by, or any alteration to, an arrangement falling within section 45(2) (meaning of "financial support"--arrangements) and approved by the Regulator in a notice issued under section 45(1)." (*regulation 4*).

As a general rule, under regulation 4, if it is likely to be notifiable, then it should be notified.

"Regulation 5 prescribes the period [being 12 months] which is the "relevant time" for the purposes of the provisions on financial support directions, being the period during which, for example, the employer or an associated or connected person must meet the conditions set out in the test as to whether or not the employer is insufficiently resourced"

"Regulation 6 prescribes the percentage [being 50%] of the estimated section 75 debt which relates to the test as to whether or not the employer is insufficiently resourced."

This is a high hurdle to reach. The section 75 debt is invariably by far the largest measure of pension scheme liability, even at 50%.

"Regulation 7 sets out what constitutes the resources of persons to whom that test applies."

In the case of a corporate, "The resources of an entity shall constitute all those aspects of the entity that would be taken into account when arriving at the entity value" *(regulation 7(1))*: when ""entity" means an employer or a business associate" and ""entity value" means the fair value of the entity" *(regulation 2)*. In the case of an individual, the "resources of a person to whom regulation 11 applies shall constitute all that person's property" *(regulation 7(2))* [when] "property" has the same meaning as in section 53(7) (restoration orders meaning of "property") *(regulation 2)* .

"Regulation 8 prescribes how the value of such a person's resources is to be determined."

The calculations under the FSD Regulations are complex and require a 'building block' approach, looking at each relevant regulation within the FSD Regulations. Regulation 8 is the starting point for valuing the resources of an employer or of a "business associate", namely an entity or individual, connected or associated with the employer, against whom an FSD may be made.

Regulation 8(2) states: "the value of the resources [as defined by regulation 7] of the employer [not a business associate] should be the greater of zero or its [adjusted] entity value". To recap: the "resources of an entity shall constitute all those aspects of the entity that would be taken into account when arriving at the entity value"; whereas, "[the] "entity value" means the fair value of the entity" and "[the] "fair value" means the amount for which an asset could be exchanged…between knowledgeable, willing parties in an arm's length transaction". The regulation 8(2) adjustments are: "its entity value excluding relevant pension scheme related balances [or "P"] and any subordinated liabilities [or "Se"] together with any related fair value differences [or "FVD"]". A question which arises is, if the adjusted entity value of an employer is negative, then is it fair to adjust upwards to nil?

Regulation 8(3) defines the value of a business associate's resources in the same way as for regulation 8(2), save for, as noted above, the reference to 'the greater of zero or its [adjusted] entity value'. The regulation 8(2) adjustments are the same as the regulation 8(1) adjustments.

The Regulation 8 calculation of the 'value of resources' differs, depending upon whether the entity is an 'employer' or a 'business associate'. Both sets of calculations use the section 75 debt as the starting point. The section 75 debt is sometimes referred to as the 'buyout' or 'cessation basis' debt. The reference to the section 75 debt in PA 2004 s.43(1)(b) has been adjusted by the FSD Regulations. As noted above, regulation 6 states that the prescribed limit of the section 75 debt for the purposes of a FSD calculation is 50%. The section 75 pension scheme liability computation leads to by far the largest liability, i.e. it is usually much larger than the FRS 17 or SFO computations.

For employers, the base calculation is the section 44(3)(a) PA 2004 calculation, namely: "is the value of the resources [as defined by the FSD Regulations] of the employer... less than the... prescribed percentage [i.e. 50%] of the estimated section 75 debt?". Regulation 9(2) states that if the value of the employer's resources "is greater than 50 per cent of the... section 75 debt... then the employer may seek the agreement of the Regulator that the employer *be deemed* [emphasis added] to be not insufficiently resourced... and if the Regulator so agrees no further calculation in relation to either the employer or the business associate need be undertaken". Why should the Regulator not "so agree"? PA 2004 s.44(3)(a) is clear. If the value of the resources of the employer exceeds the prescribed 50% of the estimated section 75 debt, then under PA 2004 s.44(3)(a), the employer is sufficiently resourced and no FSD can be issued. The FSD Regulations appears to give the Regulator enhanced permissiveness in this regard.

An FSD can only be made if there is a business associate and "the value of... that person's resources is not less than [i.e. is more than]... the difference between - (i) the resources of the employer ... and (ii) [50 per cent] of the... section 75 debt". It will be noted that PA 2004 s.44(3)(d)does not account for the plural, i.e. it does not say that 'there is a person or persons whose resources exceed the employer's pension scheme deficiency, if the pension scheme deficiency is valued at 50 per cent of the section 75 debt'. This seems very odd given that an FSD could otherwise apply to "all the members [i.e. more than one] of a group" *(PA 2004 s.45(2))*. Thus it would appear that if the group, excluding the employer, satisfied the test of having sufficient resources to cover 50 per cent of the section 75 debt, but no single member did, then no FSD can be made. Regulation 3 seems to confirm this lack of plurality, by only referring to the singular. Further, in neither the interpretation section of the FSD Regulations *(regulation 2)*, nor the specific FSD interpretation section of PA 2004 *(s.51)* nor the general interpretation section of PA 2004 *(s.318)* does the singular equate to the plural, i.e. there is no statement saying that 'any reference to the single incorporates, where relevant, reference to the plural', or such like phrase.

FSD calculation

"Regulation 9 prescribes the calculation to be undertaken to determine the value of the resources of a business to which the test applies."

There are three stages to an FSD calculation in the FSD Regulations: stage one being regulation 9(4) for an 'employer' and regulation 9(5) for a 'business associate'; stage two *(regulation 9(6))* for both an 'employer' and a 'business associate'; and stage 3 *(regulation 9(7))* for both 'employer' and 'business associate'.

6.20.1   Stage one calculation for the employer

"NA [or net assets, as noted that in the "individual accounts"] + P ([that is the "relevant pension scheme related balances"] assuming P is a liability; if P is an asset then deduct P) + Se [or "subordinated liabilities"]." *(regulation 9(4))*

6.20.2   Stage one calculation for the business associate

NA [or net assets, as noted that in the "individual accounts"] + P ([that is the "relevant pension scheme related balances"] assuming P is a liability; if P is an asset then deduct P) - Eb ([or "related employer balances"] assuming Eb is an asset; if Eb is a liability then add Eb)." *(regulation 9(5))*

6.20.3   Stage two calculation for both employer and business associate

"Stage two of the calculation [for both an employer and a business associate] is to add to the amount resulting from the applicable stage one any identified FVD [or "fair value differences"], calculated in relation to any asset (or assets) or liability (or liabilities) selected by the relevant entity." *(regulation 9(6))*

Two items are worthy of note for the stage two calculation. First, the calculation language presupposes, but does not mathematically exclude the possibility, that the FVD will produce an uplift, i.e. that the value of the assets and/or the liabilities after accounting for the FVD will be greater than that noted in the accounts (namely, it is positive). This is because, unlike stage one, there is no reference to a 'deduction'. However, mathematically, if the FVD were a reduction in value, it is a negative and adding a negative will always produce a deduction. Second, the reference to "selected by the relevant entity", seems to presuppose a volunteerism on behalf of the entity, i.e. the entity is not obliged to account for the FVD. This voluntariness is inconsistent with the general prescriptiveness of PA 2004 and FSD Regulations.

6.20.4   Stage three: calculate the Entity Value Difference (EVD)

"Stage three of the calculation is to calculate the EVD ["entity value difference"] and add that to the amount that resulted from the stage two calculation" *(regulation 9(7))* when the EVD (as defined by regulation 9(2)) is "the difference between the entity value at the calculation date and the aggregate of that entity's net assets as set out in … [its] accounts and any FVD".

"Regulation 10 prescribes what will constitute the verification of the value of the resources."

More especially, regulation 10 looks to the "investigation of value of resources - business". The calculation submitted to the Regulator must generally be accompanied by statutory declaration of the board or its equivalent for a company not formed under CA 1985. The statutory declaration should state that "in the Board's opinion [the calculations] fairly reflect the value of the resources of that entity... in accordance with regulation 9 [of the FSD regulations]".The "statutory declaration shall be accompanied by evidence of such underlying assumptions and calculations as the Board considers necessary" *(regulation 9(5))*. The "statutory declaration should be accompanied by a report from a reporting accountant, or where approved by the Regulator, another appropriately qualified person, that in his opinion the calculations [etc, are] consistent with...regulation 9 [of the FSD regulations]"*(regulation 10(5))*.

The reporting accountant will probably be the entity's auditor *(regulation 10(8))* but it is hoped that the Regulator will approve others. The existing auditor may well face a dilemma in reporting on accounts on which he has already reported, but now has to make FVD adjustments.

"Regulation 11 sets out the calculation and the verification of the resources of an individual associated with the employer in a capacity other than a business associate, to whom the test applies."

Regulation 11 looks to the "value of resources - individuals - calculation and verification", and as it refers to individuals, it is assumed that audited accounts have not been prepared and therefore a "declaration of resources" *(regulation 11(3))* possibly supported by an "independent valuations" are required *(regulation 11(5))*.

"Regulation 12 allows the Regulator to deem the value of the resources of a person, in circumstances where that person has failed to co-operate [i.e. "to provide...any required information or documentation within a reasonable time"] with the Regulator."

A "relevant person" means a person the value of whose resources the Regulator is seeking to have verified in accordance with regulation 10 [i.e. an entity, being the employer or business associate] or 11 [i.e. "an individual associated with the employer in a capacity other than a business associate"]".

"Regulations 13 and 14 prescribe requirements and arrangements in respect of arrangements to be put in place in compliance with a financial support direction."

"For the purposes of section 43 of PA 2004 (financial support directions), "financial support" for a scheme means one or more of the arrangements falling within [PA

2004 s.45(2)]...the details of which are approved in a notice issued by the Regulator" *(s.45(1))*.

Regulations 13 and 14 add to the original PA 2004 s.45(2) definition of "arrangements", so that "arrangements" falling within this subsection now refer to "arrangements" whereby:

"(a) ...all the members of the group are jointly and severally liable for the whole or part of the employer's pension liabilities [this subsection remains unaltered by the FSD Regulations],

[or] (b)...the holding company of the group is liable for the whole or part of the employer's pension liabilities...[and by regulation 13] the party or parties to the arrangement consent to the jurisdiction of the courts of England and Wales, and... where there is more than one party to the arrangement, those parties enter into a legally enforceable agreement,

[or] (c) ...additional financial resources are provided to the scheme...[and by regulation 13] the party or parties to the arrangement consent to the jurisdiction of the courts of England and Wales, and...where there is more than one party to the arrangement, those parties enter into a legally enforceable agreement,

[or] (d)...[by regulation 14]...the party or parties to the arrangement consent to the jurisdiction of the courts of England and Wales, and...where there is more than one party to the arrangement, those parties enter into a legally enforceable agreement...".

Regulations 13 and 14 have an eminently sensible aim, namely that of ensuring that any financial support arrangement is legally enforceable in England and Wales as against any foreign party. However, concerns can be raised as to the drafting.

The first concern is, what PA 2004 s.45(2)(d) (now amended by regulation 14) means. The pre-amended PA 2004 s.45(2) envisaged three types of arrangement to enhance the creditor position of the pension scheme liability, namely the provision of:

(i)   'joint and several liability' *(s.45(2)(a) and (b)*;

(ii) 'additional financial resources' *(s.45(2)(c))*; and

(iii) "such other arrangements as may be prescribed" *(s.45(2)(d))*.

Regulation 14 amends PA 2004 s.45(2)(d) but does not specifically provide for the provision of an arrangement to enhance the creditor position of the pension scheme liability. Rather, regulation 14 does what regulation 13 already sensibly does; ensuring the enforceability in England and Wales of any arrangement as against any foreign party. Regulation 14 does not identify a particular sort of arrangement, such as 'joint and several liability' or 'additional financial resources'. All it does is to repeat the regulation 13 requirement of consent to enforcement through the courts of England and Wales. If regulation 14 and the amended PA

2004 s.45(2)(d) have any meaning, then that meaning must be exceptionally wide-ranging. The amended PA 2004 s.45(2)(d) must allow for any arrangement (regardless of whether it is particularly prescribed by the FSD Regulations or any other regulations) provided the parties consent to enforcement via the courts of England and Wales.

The second concern is, why there was no FSD Regulations amendment to PA 2004 s. 45(2)(a). As it now stands, an arrangement can be made whereby "all the members of the group are jointly and severally liable for the whole or part of the employer's pension liabilities", but the parties need not consent to a legally enforceable contract submittable to the courts of England and Wales. It may be possible that in a group, the holding company could consent on behalf of all its members.

The third concern is that, whilst the arrangement has to be submittable to the courts of England and Wales, there is no requirement that the legally enforceable agreement itself be made under English law. But, given that it is rare for the laws of a country where a company is incorporated to preclude the company from being subject to the law of another country, it is unlikely to cause a difficulty in practice. It may well be that the Regulator is acting reasonably in not agreeing to any arrangement made under non-English law.

> "Regulation 15 extends the meaning of "employer" in relation to the anti-avoidance provisions of the Act to include former employers in certain circumstances."

> "Regulation 16 modifies the sections of the Act relating to the anti-avoidance provisions to apply to multi-employer schemes."

The meaning of "employer" is extended by regulations 15 and 16 of the FSD Regulations which amend the anti-avoidance provisions in PA 2004 where the term "employer" occurs, namely in sections 38-56. In regulation 15, "employers" may include former employers in certain circumstances, depending upon whether the scheme is, or is not a multi-employer and/or non-segregated scheme. In single employer schemes, "employer" now includes a former employer "at which time the scheme or section [i.e. in multi-employer schemes] ceased to have any active members". In non-segregated schemes, all former employers are included, unless a number of conditions, centring around the recoverability of the section 75 debt, are satisfied.

Regulation 16 will be worrying for any employer in a multi-employer scheme because PA 2004 is now modified, "so that references to the employer are to be treated as references to any [scheme] employer" and "so that it applies as if it were a reference to the section 75 debt due from any specified [scheme] employer". Unlike regulation 15, regulation 16 makes no reference to segregated multi-employer schemes and could theoretically therefore apply to segregated schemes.

6.21 Contribution Notices

6.21.1 Background

Contribution notices occur where there is an alleged avoidance of employer debt.

6.21.2 The Act

Sections 38 - 42 consider the position of pension liability manipulation, i.e. the avoidance of the section 75 (deficiencies in scheme assets) employer debts in defined benefit occupational schemes. The solution to the possibility of manipulation is to ensure that any such scheme is properly regulated, and that employers are required to give an account of their position (see *Financial Reporting Standard 17*). Instead, in the author's view, PA 2004 provides a 'sledge hammer', in the form of a 'contribution notice' issued by the Regulator, to crack a rather arcane nut. A number of conditions must be met before a notice can be issued:

1. the Regulator "is of the opinion that the person was a party to an act or a deliberate failure to act" *(s.38(3)(a))*;
2. "the person was...(i) the [scheme] employer...or (iii) ...connected with, or an associate of, the employer" *(s.38(3)(b))*;
3. the Regulator "is of the opinion that... the act or failure", did not involve an IP *(s.38(3)(c)*;
4. that the Regulator "is of the opinion that it is reasonable to impose [a] liability" *(s.38(3)(d))*; but
5. the Regulator "may not issue a contribution notice in such circumstances as may be prescribed" *(s.38(4))*.

An 'act or failure' under section 38(3)(a) is mainly defined in section 38(5) as a two-limbed test revolving around PA 1995 s.75.

It is not the intention of this book to consider the actuarial intricacies of 'a section 75 Pensions Act 1995 debt', but to take it as read that the section 75 conditions apply. The two-limbed test is disjunctive: one limb possibly requiring good faith on behalf of the perpetrator *(s.38(5)(ii))*, whereas the other does not so require. It is important therefore, although it maybe difficult, to differentiate between the two limbs.

The two limbs are where the 'act or failure' was "(i) to prevent the recovery of the whole or any part of the debt which was, or might become due [under section 75 of the Pensions Act 1995] or (ii) otherwise than in good faith, to prevent such a debt becoming due, to compromise or otherwise settle such a debt, or to reduce the amount of a debt which would otherwise become due" *(s.38(5))*.

6.22 Transactions at an undervalue: Sections 52 to 58

6.22.1 Introduction
The provisions of PA 2004 dealing with transactions at an undervalue are contained in sections 52-58. Section 52 only applies to DB schemes and provides for restoration orders where there has been a transaction at an undervalue. Section 53 prescribes the nature and extent of a restoration order under section 52 and again parallels can be seen in the equivalent provision of IA 1986 s.241.

6.22.2 Section 52
It is to be expected that judicial guidance on this section will over time be drawn from the long-standing IA 1986 s.238 which is the equivalent to PA 2004 s.52. A comparative analysis should be adopted.

Section 52(2) provides for major differences between the PA 2004 and IA 1986 s.238(2). Whereas section 238(2) requires an application to Court, section 52(2) states, 'the Regulator may make a restoration order'. Section 238 therefore has the major judicial safeguard: the absence of such a safeguard within section 52(2) gives cause for concern.

Section 52(2)(a) is the equivalent of, but has a wider ambit than, section 238(1). Section 52(2)(a) requires a 'relevant event' (see section 52(4)) which is, as far as corporate insolvency is concerned, any corporate insolvency. Section 238(1) is limited to either a liquidation or administration. Consequently section 52(2)(a) includes an Administrative Receivership and/or a standalone CVA (i.e. without an Administration Order).

Section 52(2) has the same effect as its equivalent in section 240. Section 52(2)(b)(ii) states: that a Restoration Order following a transaction at an undervalue maybe made only if the transaction is not more than two years before the occurrence of the relevant event in relation to the employer. Both section 52(2)(b)(ii) and section 240(2) provide for a two-year period: that is, the transaction occurred within two years of the appointment of an IP. But unlike section 52(2)(b)(ii), section 240(2) requires that at the relevant time the company was insolvent. There is no such similar requirement under PA 2004. A rationale for this difference may be the trust nature of a scheme. Regardless of section 52, trustees probably could not enter into any legitimate transaction that was a 'transaction at an undervalue', unlike company directors. Alternatively, it could be said that this combined with the lack of requirement for a Court Order is worrying.

Section 52(3) is directly equivalent to section 242(3) in language; both provide for orders for 'restoring the position to what it would have been' if the transaction had not been entered into. There is a subtle difference in wording between section 52(3) and section 238(3). Both allow the Court or the Regulator to make an order if 'it thinks fit'. However, the Court 'shall' make an order, whereas the Regulator 'may' make an order.

Section 52(4) defines a 'relevant event' as an insolvency event in relation to the employer, on application to or notification from the PPF under section 129, which occurs on or after at the 'appointed day'.

Section 52(5) defines 'appointed day' and provides that the meaning of insolvency event under section 121 applies when deciding if and when such an event has occurred in relation to the employer.

Section 52(6) is directly equivalent in language to section 238(4). In both sections, a 'transaction at an undervalue' may include an absolute gift (see subsection (a) in both sections) or some form of dealing between the parties *(re Taylor Sinclair (Capital) Ltd [2001] 2 BCLC 176)*. In a gift, the absence of consideration is obviously significant, but in both section 52(6) and section 238, if the transaction is not a gift, the difference in consideration must be 'significant' (see subsection (b) in both sections).

As far as section 238(4)(b) of IA 1986 is concerned, the decision in *re MC Bacon Ltd [1990] BCC 78* established that a transaction at an undervalue required a diminution in the value of the estate of the transferor. Thus the creation of a security over the company's assets was not a transaction at an undervalue. Similarly, in *re Lewis's of Leicester Ltd [1995] BCC 514*, a retailer, creating a trust of monies received from concessionaires in anticipation of ceasing operations, was not a diminution in the assets of the estate.

In *Philips v Brewin Dolphin Bell Lawrie Ltd [2001] 1 WLR 143*, the House of Lords reversed a Court of Appeal decision involving a complex series of linked transactions. The Court of Appeal considered that the term 'transaction' should be limited and should exclude related contracts. The House of Lords held that it was necessary to look at the 'arrangement as a whole'. The logic was taken further in *re Thoars (deceased) [2002] EWHC 2416 (Ch)*, where post-transaction events could be taken into account in assessing the value of the property for consideration.

Section 52(7) defines an 'appropriate person' as a person of a prescribed description who is entitled to exercise powers in relation to the scheme.

Section 52(8) defines 'assets' and 'transaction', within sections 52 and 53. 'Assets', includes 'future assets', so that the Regulator can make a restoration order as to future assets under section 52(3). The benefits of this extended definition (to include 'future assets') are possibly twofold.

First, and to the extent that it is necessary it may deal with the development of case law in *re MC Bacon Ltd [1990] BCC 78* and *re Minstral Finance Ltd [2001] BCC 27*. As mentioned above, these cases were applicable to the section 52 equivalent in IA 1986 s.238 and stated that in order for there to be a transaction at an undervalue, that there had to be a diminution in the value of the estate. A future asset is difficult to define and certainly difficult to value. It must be something more than a current asset whose valuation is determined by a future event. Rather, it may well be an asset, which is not yet currently an asset, but for some reason will become an asset. Therefore, there is an argument that if a 'future asset' is the subject of a 'transaction', it not being a current asset, there is no diminution in the estate. Consequently the logic in *re M C Bacon Ltd* and *re Minstral Finance Ltd* would apply were it not for this separate proviso within section 52.

Secondly, it is expected to circumvent any legal difficulties stemming from: (a) the trust nature of the scheme ('future assets may be purely equitable in nature and therefore cannot be something which an equitable instrument such as a trust could ordinarily bring into account'); (b) the legal nature of a debt between an employer and the scheme ('is the PA 1995 s.75 debt a future asset?') and; (c) the length of time over which a pension scheme operates.

Interestingly, and perhaps unfortunately, the definition of asset within section 52(8) does not include a 'contingent asset'. Rarely is a 'future asset' not a 'contingent asset', i.e. the future realisation or recovery of the asset is dependent upon some sort of a contingency, in the sense that the recovery or realisation is not a guaranteed certainty. Given that PA 2004 has elsewhere drawn a distinction between a 'future asset' and a 'contingent asset', it has to be legitimately assumed that the draftsman was making a specific point here.

The failure to refer to 'contingency' could lead to a criticism that the Regulator was overstepping its authority. This could be the case if an order was made as to a 'future asset' that was itself further subject to a contingency, i.e. it was a 'contingent asset'.

A 'transaction' as defined by section 52(8) further includes an 'agreement and arrangement'. This sensibly deals with the judicial development in *Philips v Brewin Dolphin Bell Lawrie Ltd [2001] 1 WLR 143* in which it was held that the term 'transaction' within section 238(4)(b) of IA 1986 includes an 'arrangement'. IA 1986 s.238(4)(b) only refers to a 'transaction' and not an 'agreement and arrangement', which is wider, at first sight, than the term 'transaction'.

Section 52(9) sensibly states that, even if section 52 is activated, other remedies are not precluded, even if the transaction is at an undervalue.

6.22.3 Section 53

Section 53(1) notes that section 53 considers further the restoration order.

Section 53(2) has an equivalent in section 241(1) in that the extent of the "possible orders" is listed. Section 52(2) states that a restoration order of the Regulator, 'may' in particular include those listed in section 52(a)-(d); whereas section 241(1) states that the power to apply for an order, is "without prejudice to the generality of section 283(3)". The Court, unlike the Regulator, has an inherent and well-honed power to make orders and the permissive guidance of section 241(1) is appropriate.

Section 53(2)(a)-(d) draws a distinction between 'assets', 'property' and 'benefits'.

'Assets' and 'property' are specifically defined in section 52(8) and section 53(7) respectively. 'Property', unlike 'assets', is widely defined in section 53(7) to include: "(a) money, goods, remedies in action, land and every description of property wherever situated, and (b) obligations and every description of interest, whether present or future or vested or contingent, arising out of, or incidental to, property".

It must be assumed that 'assets' are included within the definition of 'property' given the reference to 'every description of property' *(s.53(7)(a))*. On the other hand section 53(7)(b) draws an apparently important distinction between 'assets' and 'property'. As noted above, assets do not specifically include 'contingent', only 'future' assets in the section 52(8) definition. Section 53(7)(b) specifically includes 'contingent' as well as 'future' property.

Section 53(2)(a) allows for a restoration order re 'assets of the scheme (whether money or other property) which were transferred as part of the transaction to be transferred back'. Semantically this is problematical. If the assets 'were transferred as part of the transaction', then unless the transaction was void *ab initio*, 'the assets of the scheme' are no longer 'assets of the scheme'. Rather they are 'former assets of the scheme'; they have been transferred as part of the transaction. At best the assets of the scheme are contingent assets being contingent upon the restoration order. However, given the wide definition of "assets" which, as noted above, is included in the definitions of "property" it can be assumed that any such assets would be covered.

Section 53(2)(b) allows for a restoration order for: "any property to be transferred [back] if it represents in any person's hands - (i) any of the assets of the scheme which were transferred … or (ii) property derived from any such assets [which] are transferred [to be transferred back]".

Section 53(2)(c) allows for a restoration order to order a transfer of property from the scheme to a third party.

Section 53(2)(d) allows for a restoration order to require benefits (not exceeding the value of the benefits received) to be paid back.

Section 53(3)-(4) constrains the power of the Regulator and is the equivalent of IA 1986 s.241(2) as to assets or benefits which have been acquired in good faith and for value which are not therefore available for a restoration order.

In section 53(5) the burden of proof is ordinarily on the Regulator to prove (to himself, given the absence of a requirement for a Court?) that there was an absence of 'good faith' and 'value'. However, this is not the case with the exceptions noted in the two limbs of section 55(5); which again present some difficulties.

The first limb *(s.53(5)(a))* is obvious: 'a trustee or manager or appropriate person' (regulations to be drafted to define an 'appropriate person') involved in the transaction at an undervalue has the burden reversed. Interestingly, the burden is only partially reversed: section 53(5) continues, 'then, unless the contrary is shown it is to be presumed for the purposes of section 53(3) and (4) that the [acquisition] was received otherwise than in good faith'. No mention is made of 'and for value'. Yet, it would seem that it is 'value' which is primarily of importance to members. However, 'value' will be difficult to measure and its inclusion (certainly as to subsection 4) may present difficulties when applied to the fees of 'a trustee or manager or appropriate person'.

The second limb *(s.53(5)(b)(i)-(iii))* focuses not on the transaction, but on the 'time of the acquisition or receipt'.

Section 53(5)(b)(i) states: 'at the time of the acquisition or receipt – (i) he has notice of the fact that the transaction was a transaction at an undervalue'. This seems anomalous in that there was notice that the transaction was at undervalue 'at the time of receipt', not at the 'time of the transaction'. If a pension scheme and 'A' enter into a transaction which unknown to 'A' at that time was a 'transaction at undervalue', why does the subsequent receipt (and subsequent notice that the transaction was at an undervalue) later become tainted? It is to be remembered that the transaction, at the time of the transaction itself, was not necessarily improper. Is 'A' to lose out to the scheme members by not being able to enforce his rights, merely because of a post-transaction notice which did not necessarily indicate culpability on his behalf? Presumably there is little that 'A' could do 'at the time of the acquisition or receipt' to unwind the transaction; this is especially so if he has already provided some (admittedly proven at a later time not to be full) benefit to the pension scheme.

Section 53(3)(b)(ii) is less problematical and states: "(b) at the time of the acquisition or receipt - ...(ii) [he was] a trustee or manager, or the employer in relation to the scheme". It is perhaps to be expected that a trustee should endure this higher burden, it being in keeping with the role of a trustee. In this regard, it is similar to section 55 (a) quoted above. It is fair that such persons are automatically put on notice of the possibility of a transaction at an undervalue; a scheme after all is a trust. The inclusion of the term 'employer' makes the failure to include the term 'employer' in section 53(5)(a) all the more odd ('Where a person has acquired an interest in property from a person or has received a benefit as a result of the transaction and – (a) he is one of the trustees or managers or appropriate persons who entered into the transaction as mentioned in subsection (6) of section 52').

Surely, an employer who entered into the transaction should be included in subsection 5(a).

Finally, section 53(5)(b)(iii) refers to parties "connected with, or an associate of any of the persons mentioned in subsection 5(a) or 5(b)(ii)": these terms being defined by IA 1986 s.249 and s.435 respectively. 'Connected' is either a director/shadow director (a *de facto* as opposed to a *de jure* director) of the company *(IA 1986 s.435)* or 'an associate of such a director' or an 'associate of the company'. The definition of 'associate' found in of IA 1986 s.435 is wide-ranging, referring to: (a) relatives by blood, marriage, civil partnership or reputed marriage; (b) group companies; (c) employees; (d) trustees; (e) directors; and (f) partnerships. The general rule is, if it feels associated with, it probably is associated with. Interestingly, section 435(5) specifically mentions, by exclusion, "any relationship of the association formed merely by the trust deed beneficiary relationship formed by a pension scheme trust". Given the wide-ranging definition of "associate", the lack of inclusion of the employer in subsection 5(a) may well be rectified in the case of 'non-independent' trustees as they will invariably be employees, or directors of the employer company, or of a company associated with the employer company.

6.22.4 Section 54

The fundamental difference between PA 2004 and IA 1986 'transaction at an undervalue' provisions is, as noted above, that the latter involves a Court Order. So, it is initially difficult to see how the Regulator enforces a section 52 restoration order.

The problem is partially addressed in section 54. In order to enforce any order it is a clear requirement laid down in section 54(2) that time limits must be stated. If the obligation is monetary, the restoration order becomes a debt and is thereby enforceable. The Regulator has power to enforce that debt, unless the scheme is an assessment period, when the PPF will enforce it. In the words of the Regulator (*Dealing with Pensions: Regulatory Guidance,* paragraph 145) "Enforcing a statutory debt is a straightforward procedure using the Civil Courts".

6.22.5 Sections 55 and 56

The situation where the obligation is not monetary and there has been a failure to comply is addressed in section 55. The Regulator converts the non-monetary obligation to a monetary obligation and the obligation is thereby directly enforceable. Strictly, the new monetary obligation is enforced by a contribution notice. Section 56 ensures that any section 55 contribution notice is clearly spelt out. More especially, section 56(2) states that the "notice must - (a) contain a statement of the matters which it is asserted constitute the failure to comply with the restoration order...in respect of which the notice is issued, and (b) specify the sum which the person is stated to be under a liability to pay". The existence of the section 56(2)(a) requirement sits uneasily with the apparent lack of a requirement to "contain a statement" found in the similar FSD provision of section 43(8).

6.23 Transaction to defraud creditors – Section 58

6.23.1 Introduction

The 'transaction at undervalue' provisions (s.52 *et seq*) of PA 2004 borrow heavily from IA 1986, but the 'transaction to defraud creditors' provisions in section 58 go further. Section 58 directly adopts the 'transaction to defraud creditor' provision of IA 1986 s.423, i.e. application can only be directly made under IA 1986, not under PA 2004. The PA 2004 merely "piggy-backs" IA 1986.

6.23.2 Insolvency Act 1986 Section 423 ("Section 423"): an initial explanation

Section 423(1) and (2) state the two requirements of 423, namely that it is necessary to show that the debtor entered:

(a) into a transaction with another person at an undervalue *(IA 1986 s.423(1))*; and
(b) the transaction was for the purpose of putting assets beyond the reach of a person who is making, or may at some time make, a claim, or otherwise prejudicing the interests of such a person in relation to the claim *(IA 1986 s.423(2))*.

The definition is similar to that in section 238(4) ('the transaction at an undervalue' 'provision) of IA 1986, and consequently 52-56 of PA 2004.

As to what constitutes a 'transaction' see *National Westminster Bank v Jones [2002] BPIR 361* in which a transaction transferring land by way of a rack rent lease was deemed to be a 'transaction'.

The term 'transaction' covers the surrounding circumstances and in this regard, the Court will probably look to 'transaction at undervalue' cases. Thus in *Agricultural Mortgage Corporation plc v Woodward [1994] BCC 6888* the Court of Appeal held that a grant of a fair market agricultural tenancy, by a farmer to his wife to defeat the mortgagee's right to enforce, was a 'transaction' (i.e. a 'transaction at an undervalue') and should be set aside. In *Midland Bank v Wyatt [1996] BPIR 2888* a sham family trust established to protect assets in the event of business failure was avoided under section 423. Additional guidance can be sought from: *Schuppan [1997] BPIR 271; Trowbridge v Trowbridge [2003] BPIR 258; Menzies v National Bank of Kuwait SAK [1994] BCC 119; Pinewood Joinery v Starelm Properties Ltd [1994] BCC 569; Re Brabon [2000] BPIR 537 Re Taylor Sinclair (Capital) Ltd [2002 BPIR 203; Ashe Mumford [2001] BPIR 1*.

The wide-ranging remedies available to the Court are stated in section 423(2) ("restoring the position to what it would have been if the transaction had not been entered into, and... protecting the interest of persons who are victims of the transaction"). The particulars of the remedies are noted in section 425.

6.23.3 Section 423(3)

Section 423(3) states: "an order shall only be made... [if] it was entered into... for the purpose - (a) of putting assets beyond the reach... or (b) of otherwise prejudicing the interests of such a person..." Thus the transaction must have been intended to have a detrimental effect.

In *Arbuthnot Leasing International Ltd v Havelet Leasing Ltd (No.2) [1990] BCC 636,* Scott J held that a debtor acting on legal advice could still have the purpose of 'putting assets beyond the reach'. Further, if there is a prima facie breach of section 423 the court may lift the veil of legal professional privilege to ascertain motives: *Barclays Bank v Eustace [1995] 1 WLR 1238; [1995] BCC 978.*

There has been some confusion as to whether the motivation (that of 'putting assets beyond the reach' or 'prejudicing') needs to be the 'dominant' or merely a 'substantial' purpose. In *Chohan v Saggar [1992] BCC 306* the court held that it had to be a 'dominant purpose'; that is in contradiction to the finding of the courts in respect of IA 1986 s.238 ('transaction at an undervalue') and consequently the equivalent PA 2004 s.52. The dominant purpose test was approved by Lightman J in *Banca Carige v Banco Nacional de Cuba [2001] BPIR 407.* In *Royscot Spa Leasing Ltd v Lovett [1995] BCC 502* the Court of Appeal accepted a substantial purpose analysis, but emphasised the distinction between the purpose and result of the transaction. The 'substantial' motive view is now the prevalent view see: *Hashmi v IRC [2002] EWCA Civ 981;Kubiangha v Ekpenyong [2002] EWHC 1567 (Ch); [2002] 2 BCLC 597.* What is not relevant, however, is the mental state of the recipient when determining the purpose of the debtor: *Moon v Franklin [1997] BPIR 196.*

6.23.4 Section 423(4) and (5)

These provisions define 'Court' and 'victim' (see *ss.423(2)(b), 424(1)(a)-(c), and 424(2)*). 'Victim' has been widely defined. In *Moon v Franklin [1997] BPIR 196* the victims were persons who were suing the debtor for professional negligence. See also *Pinewood Joinery v Starelm Properties Ltd* (above) and *Jyske Bank (Gibraltar) v Spjeldnaes (No.2) [1999] BPIR1.*

Section 423 can be invoked by a plaintiff in any part of the High Court provided the claim does not form part of proceedings being conducted in the Bankruptcy Court or the Companies Court: *TSB Bank plc v Katz [1997] BPIR 147.* On extra territoriality, see *Jyske Bank (Gibraltar) v Spjeldnaes (No.2) [1999] BPIR1* (above). In *Banca Carige v Banco Nacional de Cuba [2001] BPIR 407,* Lightman J stressed that leave is required in order to serve a section 423 claim abroad.

6.23.5 Section 424

This section prescribes who can make a section 423 application, namely an IP and/or the victim of the transaction, but if an IP is already involved, the victim must obtain the leave of the court to take action. Leave can be granted retrospectively; see *Dora v Simper [2000] 2 BCLC 561.* If the person entering into a ransaction was a company, then the transaction may be challenged under this provision by the Liquidator or Administrator. Unusually, a Supervisor of a CVA or IVA can also bring proceedings. Supervisors cannot bring proceedings under the other IA 1986 anti-avoidance provisions, such as the 'transaction at an undervalue' rules. A creditor of an insolvent company (and consequently a member of an insolvent pension scheme?) can be a victim: see *Re Ayala Holdings Ltd [1993] BCLC 3256*.

6.23.6 Section 425(1)

Section 425(1) illustrates the potentially wide range of section 423 Court Orders, including: declaratory relief *(Moon v Franklin [1996] BPIR 196)*; interim relief *(Aiglon Ltd v Gau Shan Co. Ltd [1993] 1 Lloyds Report 164)*; and extra-territorial effect *(Jyske Bank (Gibraltar) v Spjeldnaes (No.2) [1999] BPIR1)*. Note the limitation imposed on any relief by the Proceeds of Crime Act 2002 s.419.

6.23.7 Section 425 (2) and (3)

Although third party rights may be affected, there is protection for 'bona fide purchasers, for value and without notice', as defined by section 425(3). For example, the relief in *Arbuthnot Leasing International Ltd v Havelet Leasing Ltd (No.2) [1990] BCC 636* took the form of an order that the assets wrongly transferred should be held on trust for the transferor, but without prejudice to the claims of those who had become creditors of the transferee since the date of the transfer. In *Chohan v Saggar [1994] BCC 134*, the Court of Appeal held that whilst the Order should reinstate the status quo, sometimes the need to guard third parties may preclude a complete restoration. Incomplete transaction reversal may be a solution to the difficulty of protecting the competing interests of wronged creditors and bona fide third parties.

6.24 The similarities between section 423 and section 52

A wronged pension scheme member has a number of weapons at his disposal, including these two very similar proceedings. Why would one be chosen over the other?

6.24.1 The similarities

First, the section 423 'transaction to defraud creditors' definition is for all purposes the same as both: (i) the transaction at undervalue provisions contained in both PA 2004 s.52(6) and IA 1986 s.238(4). This is because all require either, 'a gift or a transfer of significantly less [than the] value' in money or money's worth, of the consideration provided.

Secondly, no order under a section 423 application shall prejudice 'an acquisition that is in good faith, for value and significantly (in that it is directly referred to, but consider the anomalous section 53(5)(b)(i) in section 423) without notice'. It will be recalled that section 53(5)(b)(i) states: " Where a person has acquired an interest in property from a person or has received a benefit as a result of the transaction and…(b) at the time of the…receipt - (i) he has notice of the fact that the transaction was a transaction at an undervalue…then…it is to be presumed…that the interest was acquired or the benefit was received otherwise than in good faith"

A Pensions Act 'transaction at undervalue restoration order' is similarly curtailed (in the sense of 'good faith', 'for value' and "without notice), but not so significantly. Save perhaps for the anomalous section 53(5)(b)(i), there is no requirement 'for notice' within the 'transaction at an undervalue' provision of PA 2004. Thus all PA 2004 requires for a 'transaction at undervalue restoration order' is both 'good faith' and 'value'. On this ground, the wronged member should consider 'transaction at an undervalue' (s.52) as his prime weapon.

Thirdly, the purpose of both a PA 2004 restitution order and that of IA 1986 transaction to defraud creditors order are the same. The purposive language of PA 2004 s.52(3) states that the restitution order is for 'restoring the position to what it would have been if the transaction had not been entered into' and is identical to the purposive section in IA 1986 s.423(2).

However, section 423 goes further. Section 423(2)(b) of IA 1986 states that, not only must a 'transaction to defraud creditors' order restore the position, it must also 'protect the interest of persons who are victims of the transaction'. Section 423 is a victim-led remedy. The monies obtained via section 423 can go straight to the victim. Thus in the case of a corporate failure, specific creditors of the failed corporate (not just the general body of creditors) can obtain the benefit of section 423 without sharing pari passu with other creditors. Likewise, in a pension scheme failure specific members of the scheme may be able to make a specific claim directly, as opposed to all scheme members claiming directly. However, save for a segregated multi-employer scheme, it is hard to see in practice how any one member would suffer more than any other. Nevertheless, on this ground alone, the wronged member should consider a 'transaction to defraud creditors' (IA 1986 s.423) action as his prime weapon.

6.24.2 The differences

First, the most obvious difference is the time limits. There are no time limits to a 'transaction to defraud creditors' application whereas a Pensions Act 'transaction at an undervalue restoration order' is limited to two years from the transaction (s.52(2)(b)(ii)). However, this 'advantage' is more apparent than actual. The Courts understandably are reluctant to reopen transactions going back many years – see *The Law Society v Southall (2001) EWCA 2001*. Obviously if the transaction is outside the two year period, the wronged member can only consider Section 423.

Secondly, a 'transaction to defraud creditors' application is to Court: it is a classic judicial remedy whereas a Pensions Act 'transaction at an undervalue restoration order' is a regulatory decision which leads to a Court-enforceable debt.

Direct court application (i.e. not by way of a regulatory decision) has its merits, to both the 'victim' and 'the defendant'. The Regulator has wide-ranging powers to issue orders, judicial in nature, but outside the court structure. Accordingly, 'the defendant' may legitimately prefer the protection of the Court, which by its very nature is judicial.

At first sight 'regulatory action' (through section 52) may be quicker, but this is not necessarily so. Assuming the same speed of consideration of the merits and demerits of the case, ultimately the Court will always be quicker when it comes to enforcing non-monetary (i.e. debt-like) orders. If a non-monetary restoration order is disobeyed, it leads to a monetary order equivalent (i.e. a debt) which is then enforced as a debt. This is because, correctly, the Regulator does not enjoy the extensive and inherent powers of a Court.

In the case of non-monetary restoration orders, 'the victim' may prefer direct and initial court involvement as: (a) invariably, internationally, a court order will be easier to enforce than a 'mere regulatory decision'; and (b) whilst the ambit of the type and nature of restoration orders is wide (s.53(2)) it can never be as wide as the inherent powers of the court. The unfettered nature of a 'transaction to defraud creditors' order is helpfully assisted by statutory guidance as to the type of order (s.45(1)(a)-(f)).

Thirdly, there is a subtle difference between PA 2004 'transaction at undervalue provisions' and 'section 423' as to the burden of proof in proving motivation. As mentioned above, PA 2004 'transaction at undervalue restoration orders' can only be made if there is either an absence of good faith and/or value and/or notice, and in the case of 'connected or associated parties', the burden of proof may be reversed.

Section 423 makes no reference to 'associates' or 'connected parties': the burden therefore can never be reversed. Further, the section 423 test is different, making no reference to 'good faith, or value or notice', terms common in civil proceedings. Rather, the transaction to defraud creditors has motivational requirements that smack of criminal proceedings, which belies the history of section 423. Such a provision has been in English law since 1571!

6.25 Who represents the wronged member under Section 423?

All section 58 allows the Regulator to do is to apply to the Court as representing the victim(s), and only then if the scheme is an occupational scheme (s.58(2)(a)) which is 'actually insolvent under either section 58(3) and (4)'.

Even if the Regulator can apply, if the employer is formally insolvent, i.e. there is an IP in place (s.58(5)), then the Regulator can only apply with the permission of the Court. Presumably this section 58(5) bar is intended to mirror the logic of IA 1986 section 424(1)(a) and (b) which requires Court permission if an IP is in place in respect of a company. However, the logic is flawed. An IP acts for the creditors of the insolvent entity, i.e. in the case of a pension scheme, the IP acts on behalf of the employer company, not on behalf of the scheme. Consequently, it is sensible for the Court to consider, in the case of direct victims (i.e. direct creditors of an insolvent company) whether anything is advanced by direct 'victim 'involvement; the IP is acting on behalf of all creditors of the company and so direct creditor involvement would only complicate matters further. It is a basic element of pension law that scheme assets are held in trust. In a corporate failure, the scheme assets are not freely available to the company's creditors. The IP does not represent the scheme members/creditors; to do so would be a conflict of interest.

APPENDICES

A1 Regulatory Guidance

A1.1: Clearance statements: guidance from the Pensions Regulator

Introduction

1. The Pensions Regulator (the Regulator) is the new regulatory body for work-based pension schemes in the UK. We open for business on 6 April 2005, replacing the previous regulator OPRA (the Occupational Pensions Regulatory Authority).

2. The Pensions Act 2004 gives the Pensions Regulator a set of specific objectives:
   - to protect the benefits of members of work-based pension schemes;
   - to reduce the risk of situations arising that may lead to claims for compensation from the Pension Protection Fund; and
   - to promote good administration of work-based pension schemes.

3. In order to meet these objectives we will adopt a risk-based approach and concentrate our resources on schemes where we identify the greatest risk to the security of members' benefits. We will also promote high standards of scheme administration, and work to ensure that those involved in running pension schemes have the necessary skills and knowledge that reflect their position as a material unsecured creditor of the employer.

Our powers

4. The Pensions Regulator's principal approach to meeting its objectives will be to prevent problems from developing. Where possible, we will provide support and advice to trustees, administrators, employers and others where potential problems are identified. We will aim for transparency both in communication and in action as to what we expect from all the relevant players and expect that to be reciprocated.

5. The Pensions Act 2004 provides us with a far-reaching range of powers – as well as those we inherit from OPRA – to enable us to meet our objectives. We will use our powers flexibly, reasonably, proportionately and appropriately, with the aim of achieving a sustainable balance between the rights and obligations of the pension scheme as a creditor and the commercial objectives of the employer.

Background

6. Before 11 June 2003, solvent and insolvent companies were only required to fund their scheme to the Minimum Funding Requirement level on winding up. This level did not provide an adequate level of protection for scheme members, and directors often misunderstood its significance.

7. The situation has changed with the Pensions Act 2004, the introduction of the Pension Protection Fund (PPF) and new regulations regarding the deficit on winding up (*The Occupational Pension Schemes (Winding Up and Deficiency on Winding Up etc) (Amendment) Regulations 2004 and The Occupational Pension Schemes (Winding Up, Deficiency on Winding Up and Transfer Values)(Amendment) Regulations 2005 (SI 2005/72)*). Now the debt owed to the pension scheme when it winds up, regardless of the employer's status

as solvent or insolvent, is calculated on a full buy-out basis - that is, the amount estimated by the actuary that is needed to secure the pensions promised with an insurance company. This has made the cost of pension obligations more transparent but has introduced a steep learning curve for directors, trustees, financial stakeholders and their advisers.

8. In order to protect scheme members' benefits, and to ensure that employers do not avoid their pension liabilities or fail to support them in a meaningful way, thereby increasing the levy paid to the PPF by responsible employers, the Pensions Regulator has been given specific powers to deal with two particular situations:

    Contribution Notices – where there is an act or failure to avoid pension liabilities (*ss.38* 42).

    Financial Support Directions (*s.43-51*) – when the employer in relation to the scheme is a service company or insufficiently resourced.

9. These powers are only part of the Pensions Regulator's approach to ensuring that schemes are properly funded, administered and supported. We will consider an employer's level of on-going support to the scheme and the need to correct any deficits outside such situations. Where such situations occur the Regulator may choose to use powers other than a contribution notice or financial support direction referred to above, for example by appointing an independent trustee (*PA 1995 s.7*) or using one of its powers in relation to scheme funding.

10. The Contribution Notice and Financial Support Direction powers were introduced to the Pensions Bill by the Government in April 2004 without consultation, to avoid giving notice to those who might try to avoid their personal liabilities.

11. The Government then consulted on the powers and a number of amendments were made to the powers in the House of Lords as a result.

12. The main change, at the request of industry, was the introduction of a statutory clearance procedure. This was introduced to give greater certainty to those who were considering transactions involving companies with defined benefit schemes. The intention is that those concerned could gain assurance via a clearance statement that the action they intended would not be found later to fall foul of the legislation.

13. In particular, transactions that involved rescue of core solvent businesses (and the jobs that historically would have been saved) could be jeopardised by this uncertainty. Clearance was therefore introduced with the underlying aims being:
    *   the protection of jobs, particularly where Clearance is needed to prevent the employer becoming insolvent, and
    *   the continuation of appropriate deal activity involving employers with defined benefit schemes.

14. Clearance applications are optional but do not provide certainty to those who may be liable to the imposition of a contribution notice or financial support direction.

Clearance

15. In order to ensure the Regulator is able deal with applications for clearance in a flexible, responsive and proportionate manner, we have consulted widely on our approach and have taken into account the experience of other regulators who have similar powers.

16. We would like to take this opportunity to thank all those with whom we have consulted. It is our intention to establish a panel of key stakeholders who have been consulted to ensure the system continues to work and evolve efficiently and effectively.

17. We will seek to continually improve our performance and guidance in this area – learning from our, and your, experience.

Our approach

18. We accept that it is impractical and probably impossible to devise rules, regulations and codes of practice in sufficient detail to cover all circumstances and events which may arise.

19. We have therefore drawn upon the example of the City Code of Takeovers and Mergers, and developed guiding principles that will govern both our behaviour and that of parties applying for clearance.

20. We believe that this is an approach which will be helpful to all parties in eliminating uncertainty and establishing the conduct that should help to enable pension schemes and employers to thrive.

21. In setting our guiding principles and drafting guidance for clearance, we have sought to identify events which may have a detrimental effect on an underfunded pension scheme. We have also, where possible, tried to use existing market tools and solutions.

22. We will build on this guidance and seek to improve and add to it. However, any changes made to guidance will not affect clearance statements already issued.

23. We encourage those with queries to phone us on 0870 6063636 or email us at **clearance@thepensionsregulator.gov.uk** for assistance.

Guiding principles

General

- A pension scheme in deficit should be treated in the same way as any other material unsecured creditor

- The pension scheme is a key company stakeholder. Trustees should be given access to information and decision makers; in return they should accept confidentiality responsibilities.

- Conflicted trustees should recognise their position and act appropriately. We encourage the use of independent advice in such circumstances.

- Applications for clearance should contain concise, relevant and accurate information to enable the Regulator to reach a properly informed decision.

- All parties to clearance should act in accordance with issued guidance.

- The Regulator will wish to know about all events having a materially detrimental effect on the ability of the pension scheme to meet its liabilities.

The Pensions Regulator
- The Regulator's preferred outcome is a properly funded Defined Benefit pension scheme with a solvent employer.
- The Regulator will deploy its resources in a risk-based manner.
- The Regulator will seek to strike the right balance between reducing the risk to members' benefits and not intervening unnecessarily in the conduct of employers
- The Regulator will be consistent in its exercise of anti-avoidance powers and the operation of Clearance

24. Parties who may become liable to a contribution notice or financial support direction should be aware that the spirit of these principles, as well as the precise wording of the guidance, should be observed – in particular in circumstances not explicitly covered by guidance.

25. Professional advisers should ensure that directors, trustees and any other parties involved in an event which may affect the pension scheme creditor are aware of their obligations under these principles.

Events affecting the pension creditor

26. The Regulator's power to issue a Contribution Notice is triggered by an act or failure to act, whereas the power to issue a Financial Support Direction arises because of the circumstances of the employer.

27. Although we recognise that in many cases clearance will be sought in respect of both a Contribution Notice and a Financial Support Direction, we have chosen to talk of an 'event' occurring in order to simplify matters.

28. It is clear that there are many events which may affect the pension creditor. However, in order to be risk-based and proportionate, the Regulator expects clearance to be sought only in relation to events which are financially detrimental to the pension creditor – we call these 'specified events'.

Specified events
A specified event is an event affecting an entity which is financially detrimental to the ability of a Defined Benefit scheme to meet its pension liabilities.

29. We are working with the Department for Work and pensions with the intention of adding further notifiable events to the regulations made under *section 69(2)(b)*. This will have the effect of making the majority of specified events also notifiable. In the same regulations the Government intends to exercise the powers in section 318(4)(b) of the Act to extend the definition of "employer" to connected and associated parties in respect of these notifiable events.

Financially detrimental

30. For an event to be measurably financially detrimental to the scheme's ability to meet its liabilities, the scheme must be in deficit. But how do we and the employer assess whether there is a deficit? The basis used to measure the deficit has been an issue of considerable debate and consultation. We have considered a number of different

measures of funding and the fact that many schemes are today underfunded on a section 75 basis.

31. In our view, there is a distinction between the Regulator's duty to protect all pension benefits (which ultimately points to the section 75 basis of measuring deficits) and the choice of a sensible trigger for operating a risk-based approach to clearance.

32. The statutory funding objective – individual to each scheme and agreed by employer and trustees – might in due course become the right calculation, but until available we will not be able to assess its suitability as a trigger for clearance.

33. We believe using FRS17 would apply a higher test than protected liabilities (on average) and therefore moves towards a full funding level. FRS 17 has the additional advantage of being audited and within a company's balance sheet.

34. We therefore consider that, for the purposes of clearance applications, FRS 17 is currently the best way to measure the pension scheme deficit as a pragmatic, prescribed and readily available solution.

35. This choice of a trigger for clearance does not mean that we encourage employers and trustees to fund only to this level. The use of FRS 17 as a trigger is designed to give clarity to the market as to what levels at which an employer or connected or associated party could be exposed to a contribution notice.

Exceptions

36. FRS17 should only be available as an appropriate measure of deficit where there is no doubt that the employer will continue as a going concern. If there is doubt the appropriate measure is a section 75 buy-out deficit.

37. Where trustees have at the time of the event fixed a funding standard higher than the FRS17 level, that is the level that should be used to determine if there is a deficit.

Companies with different valuations

IAS 19

38. Where companies adopt IAS 19, the deficit should be measured as any shortfall between the defined benefit obligation and the fair value of any plan assets, as defined under IAS 19, and shown in the notes to the financial statements.

No FRS 17 or IAS 19

39. If there is no relevant FRS 17 calculation, the full s.75 (buy-out) level must be used. This includes groups where the FRS 17 deficit cannot be allocated on a company by company basis.

Relevant basis

To be financially detrimental there must be a deficit. The relevant basis to determine the deficit for Clearance purposes will be FRS 17 or IAS 19 unless:

• The trustees have fixed a higher funding level; or
• There is no FRS17 valuation; or
• There is a question over the continuation of the employer as a going concern.

Classification of events

40. In order to assess whether a particular event has a financially detrimental effect on the pension creditor, it is necessary to consider where the pension creditor sits in the allocation of proceeds in the event of the insolvency of the employer, and then consider the impact of that event on the potential allocation.

41. The pension fund in deficit is usually an unsecured creditor. The priority of an unsecured creditor, with regard to the assets of a company in the event of insolvency, and when compared with other creditors is broadly summarised below:
    i.   creditors with fixed charges;
    ii.   preferential creditors;
    iii. creditors with floating charges;
    iv.   (including the pensions creditor);
    v.   subordinated creditors;
    vi.   equity.

42. When looking at events which occur it is therefore helpful to classify them according to how they affect unsecured creditors and hence the pension creditor.

43. All events affecting a company can be classified into three distinct categories:

    - *Type A events*, that do affect the pension creditor. Specified events which are financially detrimental to the ability of a defined benefit scheme to meet its pension liabilities and for which it may be appropriate to seek Clearance.

    - *Type B events*, that do not affect the pension creditor. All events which are not specified events. Clearance is not necessary for these events.

    - *Type C events*, that might affect the pension creditor. All events which point towards a deterioration in the employers' covenant, and which may be outside the control of the directors or the company. Clearance is not available for these events if they do not also fall within type A.

44. Events include all transactions, acts and failures to act and, in some cases, circumstances which affect a company.

45. It is important for the Regulator, trustees, employers and their advisers to understand the impact of an event on the pension creditor. Focussing on the underlying consequence of an event on the pension creditor will enable the applicants for clearance and the Regulator to determine when the event could be exposed to contribution notices and financial support directions.

46. It is in respect of those events where the pension creditor is materially affected that it is appropriate to seek Clearance.

Breaches of the law

47. Events which involve a breach of law will not be given clearance and are required to be reported to the Regulator. Guidance is given in the Pensions Regulator's code of practice on reporting breaches.

Compromises

48. Any attempt to compromise the debt due to the pension scheme is a notifiable event irrespective of the level of the deficit before or after the compromise, and a Type A event for which clearance should be sought.

Type A Specified Events
It is only in respect of specified events that have a material detrimental affect on the pension creditor that clearance should be sought.

---

49. Type A events generally have one or more of the following three effects on the pension creditor:

Change in Priority – a change in the level of security given to creditors with the consequence that the pension creditor might receive a reduced dividend in the event of insolvency. For example:

- the granting or extending of a fixed charge or floating charge.

Return of capital – a reduction in the overall assets of the company which could be used to fund a pension deficit. For example:

- dividends, share buy-backs, dividend strips, distribution in specie, demergers

Change in Control structure – a change or partial change in the control group structure of an employer, which reduces the overall employer covenant, and could affect the ability of an employer to meet a potential section 75 debt and lead to the Regulator imposing a financial support direction. For example:

- change of employer or participating employer
- change of parties connected or associated with the employer

Change in priority

50. The principal types of security which can be granted to creditors are fixed and floating charges. The effect of granting a charge to an unsecured creditor is to allow it a better call on the assets covered by the charge in the event of insolvency.

51. A fixed charge is a charge over assets of the company which are ascertained and defined, or capable of being ascertained and defined.

52. Fixed charges can be secured upon or include charges over:

- land and buildings;
- fixed plant (i.e. fixed to the fabric of the building such as a central heating system); or
- intellectual property rights such as patents.

53. A floating charge by comparison has three characteristics:

- a charge over a class of assets present and future;
- changing from time to time in the ordinary course of business; and
- the company remaining free to carry on business in the usual way in relation to those assets.

54. Generally, to be valid, all fixed and floating charges must be registered with Companies House within 21 days of creation.

55. So how will we determine whether a change in priority will impact the pension creditor and therefore be classified as a type A event?

Test to determine if a change in priority is a Type A event:
- Does an entity within the group has a pension deficit on the relevant basis? If yes
- Is an entity within the group of companies is granting a fixed or floating charge over assets that does not specifically relate to new money? If yes
- Is the granting of fixed or floating charge materially affecting
  - more than 25 percent of the total assets of the group, or
  - more than 25 percent of the total assets of the employer?

If yes,
- It is a Type A event which the Regulator requires notice of and for which an application for clearance should be considered.

Return of capital

56. A return of capital includes any reduction in the assets of a company resulting from a return to shareholders, which leads to an overall reduction in the level of shareholders' funds.

57. Events which could result in a reduction in the level of shareholders' funds include:
- dividend payments,
- share buy-backs, and
- distributions in specie.

58. In each of the examples there is a return of value to shareholders who are otherwise lower in the overall priority listing than the pension creditor and therefore there is a loss of value to the employer which could not be recovered in the event of insolvency.

59. There are many events within the UK which fall within the definition of a return of capital. In order to be risk-based and proportionate, we propose:
- to use existing Companies Act legislation and concepts, where possible, to assess the return of capital; and
- to focus on those events which would be considered material in relation to the pension creditor.

60. In setting a materiality threshold for dividends, the Regulator seeks to strike a balance between identifying significant returns of capital and hindering reasonable dividend payments.

Tests to determine if a return of capital is a Type A Event include:
- Does an employer within the group have a pension deficit on a relevant basis? If yes
- Is an entity within the group of companies making a return of capital to an entity who is outside the group or outside the EU or to an entity who would not be subject to an FSD? If yes
- Is the cumulative annual return of capital large or unusual? Large or unusual means:
  - more than two times the average of the last three years' return of capital; or
  - reducing dividend cover to less than 1.25 times (i.e. the ratio of retained after tax profit for the period divided by the total return of capital for the same period).
- If yes, it is a Type A event which we would like to be notified of and for which an application for clearance should be considered.

Change in control structure

61. A change in the control structure is a change or partial change in the control group structure of an employer which reduces the overall employer covenant and could affect the ability of an employer to meet a potential s.75 debt. A decision by a controlling company to relinquish control of the employer company is a notifiable event under section 69 of the Pensions Act 2004.

62. Examples include:
   - change in parent company, or ultimate holding company of the employer; or
   - change in connected or associated parties who could be subject to a Financial Support Direction.

63. Some changes in control group structure will prove to be beneficial to the pension fund or may be necessary to ensure the survival of the employer or associated and connected companies.

64. Measuring the effect of a change in the Control Structure is difficult: however, some guidance can be found in existing market practice, in particular by looking at commonly applied financial ratios or banking covenants. The most obvious starting point is to compare the credit rating before and after the change of control event (if available).

65. We have looked at adapting existing ratios and covenants to target specifically the headroom around pension contributions and the level of the pension creditor in relation to group assets and will look further at this area with a view to publishing additional guidance.

Test to determine if a Control Structure change is a Type A Event
- Does the employer within the group have a pension deficit on a relevant basis, if yes
- Is there a full or partial change in the control structure including:
  - Change in connected or associated parties who could be subject to an FSD, or
  - Change in one of the parent companies of the employer.
- If yes, is the change in the control structure material – for example has the change negatively affected the employers credit rating?
- If yes, it is a type A event which may require notification and for which an application for clearance should be considered.

Type B events

66. A Type B event is an event affecting an entity which is not financially detrimental to the ability of a defined benefit scheme to meet its pension liabilities.

67. Type B events are commercial transactions undertaken at arms' length and include:

   Mergers and acquisitions, including:
   - sale and purchase of assets
   - sale and purchase of non-employer subsidiary
   - management buy-in and buy-out
   - privatisation and joint venture

   Fundraisings, including:
   - flotation and private placement

- venture capital fund raising
- rights issue and preference share issue
- unsecured debt

Other contractual negotiations, for example operating or finance lease negotiations.

68. The above events are classed as Type B events **providing** they do not contain a Type A event within them.

69. Commercial transactions undertaken at arm's length, that do not involve a type A event, will not lead to the Regulator issuing a contribution notice or financial support direction.

Type C events

70. Type C events comprise events which point towards a deterioration in the employers' covenant, and which may be inside or outside the control of the employer or its directors.

71. Type C events will include all Type A events, as any event which is financially detrimental to the ability of a defined benefit scheme to meet its pension liabilities will also point towards a deterioration in the employer's covenant. Events which pass a type A test may still fall into type C.

72. Notifiable events are a subset of Type C events and include the events which must be notified to the Regulator under section 69 of the Act.

73. The purpose of notifiable events is to provide an early warning of potential insolvency or underfunding to the Regulator, giving the opportunity to intervene before a call on the Pension Protection Fund is made.

74. Not all Type C events are Notifiable or specified events – for example the loss of a major customer. However they are events the Regulator may choose to monitor for schemes it considers most at risk.

Parties to Clearance

75. As well as the employer, connected and associated persons may be served a contribution notice or financial support direction. It is these parties, or persons who may become those parties, who will be seeking Clearance. Where possible, we expect applicants for clearance to have spoken to the relevant trustees.

76. It would, in our view, be inappropriate for the Regulator to be negotiating on behalf of every pension scheme every time a specified event occurs – not least because of the resources that would be needed. Our preference is to be a referee rather than a player. We recognise that this is an aspiration and that we will need to drive best practice.

The Pension Regulator's role

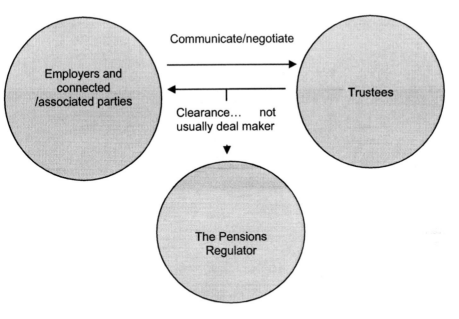

Trustees

Background

77. The scheme trustees have the prime responsibility for safeguarding members' interests. Their powers and duties are set out in statute, trust law and the scheme's trust deed and rules. They need to be familiar with those powers and duties and act in accordance with them.

78. Although some trustees have had the power to set contributions or wind up the scheme, many have not. This has meant that many trustees have felt themselves to be in a weak negotiating position when discussing scheme funding with the employer.

79. Trustees were able to report breaches of the law to OPRA under section 48(1) of the Pensions Act 1995. They were also able to ask OPRA to exercise its powers, for example to wind-up the scheme if it is in the interests of the generality of members[2].

80. In Update 10 OPRA sought to raise the awareness of trustees regarding the implications of the Pensions Act 2004 and the new powers of the Pensions Regulator.

Next steps

81. The pension scheme, if in deficit, is an unsecured creditor of the employer. Usually, because of the size of the deficit, it is a material unsecured creditor and although not identical to a large unsecured bank loan, it does have many similarities in the form of:
   - its size relative to other unsecured creditors;

---

[2] s11(1)(c) Pensions Act 1995

- its importance – particularly in cases where there is a large number of active members; and
- its ability to exert leverage over the company, particularly because of trustees' ability to whistleblow to the Regulator, with the Regulator's powers to issue contribution notices or financial support directions.[3]

82. The trustees should therefore learn from the way a bank with a large unsecured loan would look to negotiate with a company.

83. In order to negotiate, and to protect scheme members' interests, trustees need to understand the sponsoring employer's financial position and the strength of its commitment to the funding of the scheme. They should monitor corporate activity and seek the employer's agreement to be given information at an early stage subject to the usual restrictions such as those on handling price-sensitive information.

84. If the trustees are concerned, they should raise their concerns with the sponsoring employer and, where appropriate, other companies in the group.

85. Trustees can also contact the Pensions Regulator who will be able to help and advise them.

Confidentiality

86. Trustees must understand that information they receive in their position as trustees is confidential. This is particularly important when it comes to sensitive information – involving either scheme members or the employer. Trustees cannot expect to be given "inside information" from the employer if they pass it on.

87. One way of ensuring that all parties understand the importance of confidentiality is to enter into a confidentiality agreement. This should ideally be done every time a new trustee joins the board, rather than waiting until there is an important issue which the employer is reluctant to discuss because of confidentiality issues.

Conflicts of interest

88. Many trustee boards have members who may have a conflict of interest – for example trustees who are directors of the employer or union representatives. Trustees must remember that at all times they must act in the interests of scheme members and other beneficiaries.

89. Trustees and employers should plan in advance their approach for when a conflict of interest arises. They may for example set triggers which would result in an independent trustee being appointed.[4]

90. The issue of conflict becomes more important when the trustees are negotiating with the employer when a Type A event is likely. Trustees should plan in advance what they are going to do in these situations. The Regulator expects a trustee who could be involved in both sides of the negotiation (for example a Finance Director or Chief

---

[3] When the Scheme Specific Funding regime comes into force trustees and the Regulator will have additional powers in respect of funding.

[4] Trustees, employers and scheme members can apply to the Regulator for a trustee to be appointed (PA 1995 s.7)

Executive) to ensure that the trustees have the appropriate information on a timely basis and to draw his fellow trustees' attention to the potential conflict and to absent himself from trustee meetings when the issue is discussed and to play no part in decision making.

91. Trustees may need to commission an investigating accountant or insolvency specialist with industry knowledge to assess the financial circumstances of the employer or group of companies before negotiating, particularly if the conflicted trustee is the trustee board's main source of financial knowledge.

Negotiations

92. As noted above, in order to negotiate properly, trustees must understand the employer's financial situation and its commitment to the pension scheme. They must also understand the position of the scheme and its funding.

93. Most importantly, they need to understand the impact of the Type A event on the scheme and what they can ask for in negotiations.

94. We have identified areas which can mitigate the effect of a Type A event on the pension creditor and should be considered during negotiations.

Directors, connected and associated parties

95. Directors have a fiduciary duty to act in the best interests of the shareholders, the company and the creditors. In practice, treatment of pension creditor has sometimes been different to that of other material unsecured creditors.

96. In particular, because of the many ways of calculating the pension scheme deficit, there has been a general lack of appreciation of the true liability. Since June 2003 [5], the debt due to a pension scheme when it is wound up is the full section 75 buy-out debt. We also note that the introduction of FRS 17 and IAS 19 reporting standards, which will appear on balance sheets, should assist in this area.

97. Employers with a pension scheme should recognise that it is in their best interest to have properly informed and knowledgeable trustees. They should provide the trustees with information on their financial position and future plans and any Type A event that may occur. Increased dialogue and understanding will help both parties.

98. If a Type A event is due to occur, responsible employers will wish to share independent reports on the transaction with the trustees. The Regulator expects that in a Type A event that is material to the pension creditor, the employer will pay for the trustees to obtain an independent report if there is not one available.

99. Parties to a Type A event should enter into discussions with Trustees at an early point and consider what can be done to minimize any impact on the pension creditor.

100. The Regulator wishes to work with employers, potential employers and other parties connected or potentially connected to the employer as well as trustees, to ensure we achieve our aim of a well funded scheme and a solvent employer.

---

[5] The Occupational Pension Schemes (Winding Up and Deficiency on Winding Up etc) (Amendment) Regulations 2004

Ways in which the pension scheme security may be improved

101. **A new contribution schedule** could be drawn up, with higher contributions and a shorter period to make up the deficit.

102. **Additional cash or other assets** could be requested to make up a shortfall in a scheme funding or in return for supporting an event taking place.

103. **Insurance of contributions** could be requested where there is doubt over the employer's ability to make contributions. This could cover the next three to five years' contributions.

104. **Escrow accounts / deposit up front** may be appropriate and is used, for example, commercially to cover interest costs on bond offerings over a number of years, or a deposit of new tenant to the landlord.

105. **An improvement in priority** can be achieved by granting a fixed or floating charge to the pension creditor. For example, an event which trustees may be asked to consider could be the purchase of a company with a pension deficit by a private equity fund. These transactions will often be leveraged with the bank providing debt to buy the company secured on the assets of the company. In these circumstances, a charge which ranks alongside, or in priority to, the bank should be considered, along with associated covenants and reporting obligations[6].

106. **Information is something which a bank may require as part** of an arrangement agreed with a company and should be requested in addition to one of the items discussed above. Information can take the form of:
    - monitoring information, including monthly management accounts, key performance data and access to selected executives
    - covenants which the company is required to comply with as a condition of an agreed compromise. Covenants may for example help to ensure that the company has enough cash flow to meet contribution levels, and that it does not dispose of key assets.
    - Advance notice of any type A events

107. **Negative pledges** could be used to restrict the activities of the company which may be seen to prejudice the pension creditor.

Cases which will result in a call on the Pension Protection Fund

108. When a Type A event is going to lead to the scheme being assessed by the PPF we wish to ensure maximum return without risking employment. In severe situations, creditors are often forced to negotiate for equity in the rescued ongoing business in order to maximise their chance to have their debt repaid. Pension creditors should be no exception. We have therefore considered areas that are not normally acceptable to pension schemes.

109. Equity return is something which pension funds have traditionally avoided due to the legal restrictions around a pension scheme owning more than a certain percentage of

---

[6] Taking security over assets is one of the more common techniques used by the PBGC when negotiating with companies in the US

shares in an employer. Options for an equity return include taking (individually or in combination):

- **straight equity** in the form of ordinary shares. Traditionally the level of equity to be taken by a creditor would be calculated as part of a debt for equity swap calculation. Where other creditors (such as banks) are also accepting a compromise, any debt being carried forward should be ranked alongside the FRS17 deficit and dealt with equitably.
- **increased contributions related to a prescribed share of profits**. This can be a prescribed percentage over a number of years which applies until the pension deficit is paid off in full. The advantage of this over straight equity is that it can be difficult to realise value from a minority shareholding in a company
- **priority on equity return**, which will give a prescribed percentage return to the pension scheme on a future disposal of the new company to a third party.

Applications for Clearance

10. Any party seeking Clearance should comply with the Regulator's published guidance.

11. Any party who believes they may need to make an application for Clearance should involve the Regulator as early as possible in the process to ensure the Regulator is able to consider the Request in appropriate time scales.

12. Any application for Clearance should be accompanied by full and accurate disclosure.

Applying for Clearance

13. Clearance will only be effective in relation to the information provided to the Regulator. The clearance will cease to be valid if the circumstances described in the application are materially different from the real circumstances: for example, if an application is made on the grounds it would not be reasonable to impose a contribution notice because the main purpose of the act is to protect employment, but later the Regulator found out that this was not in fact one of the main purposes of the act. For example, if a material fact was known or should have been known to the applicant and was not declared in the application for clearance.

14. As a general principle, we would expect the information provided to the Regulator to be similar to the amount of information and level of detail provided to non-executive directors of a quoted company which allow them to make informed decisions.

15. The Regulator has the option to ask for further information, if necessary, in particular from independent advisers and experts, the cost of which may be passed onto the Applicant.

16. All parties seeking Clearance must make a separate application, although multiple applications may be supported by the same information.

17. A template for all Clearance Applications can be found on the website in a PDF and Microsoft Word format. This should be used to ensure that all relevant information is included and to avoid unnecessary delays in the clearance process.

18. Queries about the clearance procedure are encouraged and can be made by email to **clearance@the pensionsregulator.gov.uk** or by calling 0870 6063636.

119. Completed applications may be sent electronically to **clearance@the pensionsregulator.gov.uk** or posted to:

> Clearance Department
> The Pensions Regulator
> Napier House
> Trafalgar Place
> Brighton BN1 4DW

and marked "To be opened by the Addressee Only"

Powers

Contribution notices

120. The Regulator can issue a contribution notice, requiring an amount up to the full amount due under section 75 of the Pensions Act 1995 ("the buy-out debt") to be paid to the scheme trustees or the Pension Protection Fund if the Regulator's opinion is that the main purpose or one of the main purposes of an act (or failure to act) was:

- to prevent the recovery of the whole or part of the debt which was or might become due from the employer to the scheme under section 75 of the Pensions Act 1995; or
- otherwise than in good faith, to prevent a debt under section 75 becoming due, compromise or otherwise settle such a debt, or reduce the amount of such a debt.

121. A contribution notice can only be issued to a person who is party to the act or failure and who is either the employer or a person connected or associated with the employer. This will include parties who knowingly assist in the act or failure. A contribution notice may be issued to one or more persons.

122. A 'person' includes:

- individuals, and
- companies, limited liability partnerships and partnerships.

123. The Regulator can only issue a notice if it considers it is reasonable to make the person pay the amount in the notice.

Reasonable to issue a contribution notice

124. When deciding whether it is reasonable the Regulator must consider:

- The degree of involvement of that person in the act or failure. For example, was this a business deal the person sanctioned? Did the person know about this act?
- The relationship the person has with the employer. For example, is the person a director or senior executive of the employer? Is the person a company that is the parent company of the employer?
- Any connection or involvement the person has or had with the scheme. For example, was the person a trustee of the scheme or an employer in relation to it?
- Was the act or failure a notifiable event that the person had a duty to notify to the Regulator but failed to do so?
- The purpose of the act or failure, including whether the purpose was to prevent or limit loss of employment.
- The financial circumstances of the person. For example, if the person is a company would the sum required make it insolvent?

125. The Regulator may consider other factors relating to the act or failure to act, for example the status of the scheme.

Financial Support Directions

126. The Regulator can issue a Financial Support Direction to the employer and persons connected and associated with the employer requiring financial arrangements be put in place to support an employer's pension liabilities when the employer is a service company or insufficiently resourced within the relevant time.

127. However, a Financial Support Direction cannot be issued to an individual save in certain circumstances, for example where the employer is a sole trader.

128. The Regulator can only issue a Direction to a person if it considers it is reasonable to impose the requirements on that person.

129. Once the Regulator has issued such a Direction, it must approve the arrangements in a Notice. The support may be for the whole or part of the employer's pension liabilities.

Relevant time

130. For the purpose of financial support directions, regulations will prescribe the relevant time. This is likely to be a period of 9 months, ending with the decision by the Regulator to issue a direction.

Pension liabilities

131. Pension liabilities are:
   * Contributions due under the schedule of contributions (s.227); and
   * The amount which is or may become due under Pensions Act 1995 s.75.

Service company

132. An employer ("E") is a "service company" if
   * E is a company within the meaning given by section 735(1) of CA 1985 (c. 6),
   * E is a member of a group of companies, and
   * E's turnover, as shown in the latest available accounts for E prepared in accordance with section 226 of that Act, is solely or principally derived from amounts charged for the provision of the services of employees of E to other members of that group.

Insufficiently resourced

133. An employer is insufficiently resourced if
   * The value of its resources are less that 50% of the estimated debt due under section 75 of the Pensions Act 1995, and
   * The value of resources of a connected or associated person when added to the employers would be 50% or more of that debt.

Value of resources

134. Regulations will prescribe how to calculate, verify and determine the value of a person's resources. It is likely to be the fair value of the company on a market value basis. However, if the associated or connected person can show that it has sufficient resources to meet at least 50% of the section 75 debt when added to the employer's resources by other means such as published accounts, fair value accounts or interim / management accounts and the directors are confidant that these show a true and fair value, a market value valuation may not be required.

A1: REGULATORY GUIDANCE

Reasonable to issue a financial support direction

135. When deciding whether it is reasonable the Regulator must consider

- The relationship the person has or has had with the employer (for example, is the person a company that is the parent company of the employer?)
- The benefits the person has received directly or indirectly from the employer (for example, has the person received assets or dividends from the company, or tax advantages?)
- Any connection or involvement the person has or had with the scheme (for example, was the person a trustee of the scheme or an employer in relation to it?)
- The financial circumstances of the person

136. The Regulator may consider other factors, for example the status of the scheme.

Financial support arrangements

137. The arrangements which must be out in place and approved in a Notice issued by the Regulator are:

- an arrangement whereby, at any time when the employer is a member of a group of companies, all the members of the group are jointly and severally liable for the whole or part of the employer's pension liabilities in relation to the scheme; or
- an arrangement whereby, at any time when the employer is a member of a group of companies, a company (within the meaning given in section 736 of CA 1985) which meets prescribed requirements and is the holding company of the group is liable for the whole or part of the employer's pension liabilities in relation to the scheme.

Regulations may prescribe other arrangements.

Failure to put arrangements in place

138. A financial support direction will require the person(s) it is issued to secure that:

- financial support for the scheme is put in place within the period specified in the direction;
- thereafter that financial support or other financial support remains in place while the scheme is in existence, and
- the Regulator is notified in writing of prescribed events in respect of the financial support as soon as reasonably practicable after the event occurs.
- A financial support direction is therefore not complied with if any of the above are breached.

Non-Compliance Contribution Notice

139. Once there is a failure to comply with a Financial Support Direction the Regulator may, if it considers it reasonable, issue a contribution notice to one or more persons who were issued with the direction requiring them to pay the whole or part of the sum specified in the notice.

Reasonable to issue a non-compliance contribution notice

140. When deciding whether it is reasonable the Regulator must consider

- Whether the person has taken reasonable steps to comply with the Financial Support Direction.
- The relationship the person has or had with the employer
- The benefits the person has received directly or indirectly from the employer.

- The relationship the person has or has had with the parties to any arrangements put in place
- Any connection or involvement the person has or had with the scheme
- The financial circumstances of the person.

141. The Regulator may consider other factors, for example the status of the scheme.

Prescribed events
142. These will be similar to events that must be notified under section 69 of the Pensions Act 2004

Enforcing Contribution Notices
143. The sum due under a contribution notice becomes a debt due to the trustees or managers of the scheme. The Regulator has the power to enforce that debt unless the scheme is in an assessment period[7], when the Board of the Pension Protection Fund will enforce it.

144. Enforcing a statutory debt is a straightforward procedure using the Civil Courts.

Connected and associated
145. The Pensions Act 2004 uses the same definition of 'connected and associated' as the Insolvency Act 1986.

Connected
146. A person is connected with a company if
- he is a director or shadow director of the company or an associate of such a director or shadow director; or
- he is an associate of the company.[8]

Associated Individuals
147. A person is an associate of an individual if that person is the individual's husband or wife, or is a relative, or the husband or wife of a relative, of the individual or of the individual's husband or wife.

148. A person is an associate of any person with whom he is in partnership, and of the husband or wife or a relative of any individual with whom he is in partnership; and a Scottish firm is an associate of any person who is a member of the firm.

149. A person is an associate of any person whom he employs or by whom he is employed. Any director or other officer of a company is to be treated as employed by that company.

Associated Companies
150. For the purposes of association "Company" includes any body corporate whether incorporated in Great Britain or elsewhere.

151. A company is an associate of another company—

Section 132 Pensions Act 2004
Section 249 of the Insolvency Act 1986

- if the same person has control of both, or a person has control of one and persons who are his associates, or he and persons who are his associates, have control of the other, or
- if a group of two or more persons has control of each company, and the groups either consist of the same persons or could be regarded as consisting of the same persons by treating (in one or more cases) a member of either group as replaced by a person of whom he is an associate.

152. A company is an associate of another person if that person has control of it or if that person and persons who are his associates together have control of it.

Control

153. A person is to be taken as having control of a company if:

- the directors of the company or of another company which has control of it (or any of them) are accustomed to act in accordance with his directions or instructions, or
- he is entitled to exercise, or control the exercise of, one third or more of the voting power at any general meeting of the company or of another company which has control of it;

where two or more persons together satisfy either of the above conditions, they are to be taken as having control of the company.

Trustees

154. Trustees are not associated purely because of their capacity as trustee of a pension scheme.

Other Regulators with similar powers

	PBGC (Pension Benefit Guarantee Corporation	HMRC	Takeover Panel
Guidance and Principles	PBGC provides guidance to the market via its website ,which details the rules and regulations Rule driven, with technical updates on website Simple customer service pledge issued	HMRC lists types of transaction needing Clearance on the website No limits published, advisors historically know the rules Feedback on the process published on website Codes of practice detailing how the Inland Revenue will serve its customers published	Takeover Panel uses "Blue Book" guiding principles to drive the decision making process Practice statements published on the website clarify technical issues
Clearance and Volume	No Clearance process 300-400 reportable events a year for smaller entities, in contrast, larger entities are not required to notify as constantly reviewed by specific team	Statutory obligation to provide Clearance within 30 days, Only 2% of all 8,000 transactions rejected, i.e. no Clearance given	Provide Clearance for takeover, but also try to minimise the length of time a bid can "hang over" a target Always call on day receive application 100 - 300 cases a year
Frequency of Utilisation of Powers	Very rarely, currently only one case taken to prosecution Instead uses the good citizen approach to help drive the market in the right direction.	On occasion, where Clearance not provided Anti-avoidance legislation more effective through public pressure rather than prosecution.	If spirit of guidance not adhered to, the Takeover Panel will not allow transaction to go ahead

Funding bases

	Advantages	Disadvantages
S75	The Regulator's powers are set in relation to recovery of S75 debt which measures members' benefits	The most prudent basis (inevitably resulting in large deficits) that does not reflect the concept of going concern, applicable to many companies

	on termination.	applying for Clearance
	50% of S75 debt is intended to be used in the "insufficiently resourced" test	No legal responsibility to fund to this level.
		S75 funding levels will not be available automatically for all schemes until 2006 valuations are completed (this could in practical terms translate end of 2007)
		Will not in all circumstances be available to directors and other external parties that may wish to apply for Clearance (e.g. hostile bidders).
PPF buy-out basis	Addresses one of the Regulator's objectives (protection of PPF benefits)	Does not fully protect members benefits
	Is used for the purposes of setting the risk based levy	Due to PPF transitional period rules may not be available to all schemes until 2009
	Will be available to the directors and the Regulator (through scheme return forms).	Differs scheme by scheme due to benefit caps.
		Will not be known to all parties
MFR (Minimum Funding Requirement)	Readily available to trustees	Widely perceived as too weak a basis; it has been discredited by the market
		Currently in the process of being replaced by SSF.
		Would be contrary to the underlying purpose and principles of the Act.
SSF (Scheme Specific Funding)	Going forward may prove to be the most relevant option as it requires trustees and directors to negotiate on the appropriate contribution levels and should in theory reflect financial covenant of the employer.	SSF will not be in place until September 2005 at the earliest. In practice, this may mean that details of funding levels for all schemes may not be available until 2009.
		By definition, basis not consistent and comparable across the schemes
		It is still unclear how the standard of funding will evolve as much is left to the concept of prudence and consultation will take place over the summer.

FRS 17/ IAS 19	Part of GAAP (Generally Accepted Accounting Principles), audited and available in financial statements.	Does not relate to the buy-out cost of benefits (inappropriate treatment of pensioners and deferreds)
	Broadly consistent measure across all corporates (subject to sensible mortality assumptions)	May not be available for individual entities within multi-employer schemes.
	Easily accessible to directors and external parties that may wish to apply for Clearance	Permits use of a range of mortality assumptions that are not discloseable but may have a significant impact on the calculated level of liabilities (IAS 19 may require disclosure of mortality assumptions)
	Used by Companies Act as a measure that affects distributable reserves and hence dividends	
	Reflects the going concern concept, applicable to corporates seeking Clearance	IAS 19 allows spreading of deficits and the number entering balance sheet may be quite different to the level of scheme underfunding (although the appropriate figure will still be found in disclosure notes)
	Readily understood and accepted.	FRS 17 does not require disclosure of mortality basis and therefore gives rise to potential manipulation.

A1.2: Application for Clearance

Part 1: Application details

The Pensions
Regulator ☼

1	Name of applicant:	
2	Address of applicant:	
3	Applicant's relationship to the scheme:	
4	If this form is being completed by someone other than the applicant, please give details including address:	
5	What is the event giving rise to the request for clearance?	
6	What effect does this event have on the pension scheme? NB: *Where the event has no impact on the scheme there is generally no need to apply for clearance, and any application will be treated as low priority.*	
7	For which of the following would you like the regulator to issue a statement? In the Pensions Regulator's opinion … ☐ the applicant would not be, for the purposes of subsection (3)(a) of section 38 of Pensions Act 2004, a party to an act or a deliberate failure to act falling within subsection (5)(a) of that section. ☐ it would not be reasonable to impose any liability on the applicant under a contribution notice issued under s 38. ☐ it would not be reasonable to impose the requirements of a financial support direction, in relation to the scheme, on the applicant.	
8	On what basis do you believe these statements to be true? In particular, if you do not believe it would be reasonable for the Pensions Regulator to impose liability, please detail why not:	

9	What are the timescales for carrying out this event including any critical deadlines?	
10	What discussions have been held between the employer and the trustees in relation to the event or situation and its impact on the pension scheme? *If there has been no contact please confirm permission for the Pensions Regulator to approach trustees or if refused, reasons for that refusal.*	
11	Please provide names and contact details of any parties holding security over the employer, and consent to enable the Pensions Regulator to approach them:	
12	Please provide names and contact details of any key advisers with whom the applicant believes it would be useful for the Pensions Regulator to discuss the application:	
13	I confirm that the contents of this application and the information provided with it are true to the best of my knowledge and belief. Signed by (applicant): Dated:	
14	I am being represented by the person detailed in section 4 above. I confirm I am content for them to represent me. Signed by (applicant): Dated:	
15	Address for correspondence:	

16	Please provide us with the following documents:

Where the information asked for is not relevant or available please tell us why.

a) ☐ Family tree showing the group structure to which any employer relating to the pension scheme belongs including company registration numbers

b) ☐ Proposed board minute regarding the event / situation described in the application

c) ☐ Relevant correspondence with key stakeholders regarding the event / situation

d) ☐ Any resolutions required in relation to the event / situation

e) ☐ Any other relevant board minutes

f) ☐ Executive summaries of any independent reviews or reports relating to the event or the employer's viability

Where relevant:

g) ☐ Table showing comparison of position of all creditors pre- and post-event

h) ☐ Statutory accounts

i) ☐ Financial forecasts / management accounts

j) ☐ Details of debt that ranks above the pension scheme

k) ☐ Up-to-date valuation of significant assets

Please provide any other documents relating to the application.

NB: Please ensure that documents are relevant. Receiving a large amount of irrelevant information means that it will take us longer to make a decision on clearance.

Part 2: Scheme information

Scheme name:			
PSR number:			
Type of scheme:	☐ DB ☐ DC ☐ Hybrid	Scheme status:	☐ Open ☐ Paid-up ☐ Frozen ☐ Winding-up
Principal employer:			
All participating employers: *Please include any employers who have ceased to participate since 27 April 2004.*			
Number of members:	Total		
	Pensioners		
	Deferred		
	Active		
Where there are no active members, how many deferred members are employed by employers related to the scheme?			
Size of fund:		Date of valuation:	
Deficit:	On s75 buy-out		
	FRS17		
	On-going		
	PPF		
Payments specified on schedule of		When is the schedule of	

contributions:		contributions due to be re-negotiated?	

Please provide name and contact details of all scheme trustees:

Do trustees have any conflicts of interest and how are these dealt with?

What is the trustee's view of the application?

Please provide:

☐ any independent reports that the trustees have commissioned in respect of the event or situation described in this application

☐ a copy of the winding-up power from the scheme deed and rules

☐ a copy of the power to set contributions from the scheme deed and rules

All documents and correspondence should be clearly labelled and addressed as follows:
Clearance Department
The Pensions Regulator
Napier House
Trafalgar Place
Brighton
BN1 4DW

To be opened by the Addressee Only

Alternatively you can email this document to
clearance@thepensionsregulator.gov.uk
Please note that sending information by email is not secure and is done so at your own risk.

A1.3: The Notifiable Events Framework

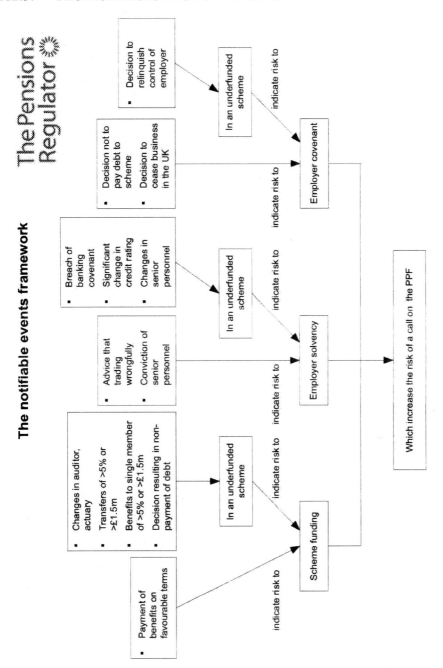

A1.4: The Pensions Regulator Code of Practice 02 – Notifiable Events

Introduction

1. This code of practice is issued by the Pensions Regulator, the body that regulates work-based pension arrangements (occupational pension schemes, stakeholder pension schemes and certain aspects of personal pension schemes which have direct payment arrangements, whereby the employer pays contributions on behalf of the employee).

2. The Pensions Regulator's objectives are to protect the benefits of pension scheme members, to reduce the risk of calls on the Pension Protection Fund, and to promote the good administration of work-based pension schemes.

3. The Pensions Regulator has a number of regulatory tools, including issuing codes of practice, to enable it to meet its statutory objectives.

4. Codes of practice provide practical guidelines on the requirements of pensions legislation and set out the standards of conduct and practice expected of those who must meet these requirements. The intention is that the standards set out in codes are consistent with how a well-run pension scheme would choose to meet its legal requirements.

The status of codes of practice

5. Codes of practice are not statements of the law and there is no penalty for failing to comply with them. It is not necessary for all the provisions of a code of practice to be followed in every circumstance. Any alternative approach to that appearing in the code of practice will nevertheless need to meet the underlying legal requirements, and a penalty may be imposed if these requirements are not met. When determining whether the legal requirements have been met, a court or tribunal must take any relevant codes of practice into account.

Other relevant codes

Users of this code are also likely to find relevant the code of practice on reporting breaches of the law and the codes on late payments, and funding defined benefit schemes

The Code of Practice

Notifiable events

What is the notifiable events duty?

. The duty to notify requires written notice to the Pensions Regulator of events:

   i.   in respect of pension schemes (scheme-related events); and

   ii.   in respect of employers, in relation to their pension schemes (employer-related events).

. The duty to notify falls on trustees, individually as well as collectively[9], in respect of the former and employers in respect of the latter[10].

. Notification is only required in respect of schemes which are eligible for entry to the Pension Protection Fund, and their related employers. In practice, the duty falls on pension schemes which are neither wholly defined contribution nor ineligible for the Pension Protection Fund by virtue of being in the public sector or other reasons[11].

Purpose of notifiable events

. The purpose of notifiable events is to reduce the risk of the circumstances which may lead to compensation being payable from the Pension Protection Fund. Calls on the Pension Protection Fund will arise when, broadly speaking, an employer becomes insolvent and its scheme is underfunded. Notifiable events will provide an early warning of possible insolvency or underfunding giving the Pensions Regulator the opportunity to assist, or to intervene, before a call is made. A consequence of intervention will also be in many cases to improve the protection of scheme members' benefits.

Legislative framework

. The Pensions Act 2004 places a duty on the trustees of schemes, and employers, to notify the Pensions Regulator when certain events occur[12].

. Regulations made under section 69 of the Pensions Act 2004 set out which events have to be notified[13].

. Directions, issued by the Pensions Regulator, give exceptions to the duty to notify[14]. In summary, you need to notify fewer events if the scheme of which you are trustee or

---

Throughout this code any reference to trustees should be read as referring likewise to managers of non-trust based schemes which are eligible for entry to the Pension Protection Fund. In the case of corporate trustees it is the company which has the duty to notify.

[10] The Department for Work and Pensions has the power, which it has not exercised, to make regulations to require other groups to notify, for example advisers to schemes or employers connected or associated with the employer in relation to the scheme.

[11] See section 126(1)(a) and (b) of the Pensions Act 2004 and regulations made under that section.

[12] See section 69 of the Pensions Act 2004.

[13] See The Pensions Regulator (Notifiable Events) Regulations 2005 (Statutory Instrument 2005/900). There may be additional regulations in future made under section 69. A description of the events is in separate guidance issued by the Pensions Regulator.

employer is funded above the Pension Protection Fund buy out level[15], and is adhering to its schedule of contributions. The events which are not referred to in the directions have to be notified by all trustees or employers irrespective of the funding level of the scheme.

Notification arrangements

8. The Pensions Regulator appreciates that trustees in particular might prefer to agree a collective approach to notification. If, however, a consensus cannot be reached, or not all the trustees are aware of the event, the Pensions Regulator will expect an individual trustee or group of trustees to notify.

9. With respect to employer-related events, when the employer is a company the individuals who give effect to the legal personality of the company will be responsible for notification in the same way as they are for other legal obligations which fall on companies[16]. Employers may wish to channel notifications through one individual such as the company secretary.

10. Confidentiality The Pensions Regulator acknowledges that some information which is notified may be confidential. Nevertheless the duty on employers and trustees to notify overrides any other duty of confidentiality[17], and any such duty is not breached by notifying. There are also restrictions on the extent to which the Pensions Regulator can in turn pass on confidential information10[18] .

Public disclosure

11. The Pensions Regulator does not require public disclosure of events notified to it. In the event that notification is made public by others, because for example an employer considers it necessary in order to comply with other legal requirements, the Pensions Regulator would draw attention to the following.

---

[14] The directions are in separate guidance issued by the Pensions Regulator.

[15] When the directions use the term 'Pension Protection Fund buy out level' this refers to the level of scheme funding (at the last formal actuarial valuation) which would be required to provide scheme members with the amount of compensation to be offered by the Pension Protection Fund. For these purposes this level should be calculated for each scheme on the same basis as will be used for assessing the size of the Pension Protection Fund's risk-based levy. This basis will be set out in regulations to be issued by DWP and guidance to be issued by the Board of the Pension Protection Fund.

[16] Likewise, if the employer is not a company but is, for example, a partnership it is the individuals who give effect to the employer's legal personality who will be responsible for notification.

[17] The requirement to notify does not however arise in certain circumstances. Communications (oral and written) between a professional legal adviser and his or her client, or a person representing that client, whilst obtaining legal advice, do not have to be disclosed (see section 311 of the Pensions Act 2004). Where appropriate a legal adviser will be able to provide further information on this.

[18] See sections 82-87 of the Pensions Act 2004.

12. First, that notifiable events are only one of a number of requirements to provide information to the Pensions Regulator; others include to complete a scheme return. The provision of information to the Pensions Regulator should be regarded as a normal part of an employer's interaction with the Regulator.

13. Second, that the duty to notify is triggered automatically when an event occurs; not all the events, for example a change in credit rating, are under the direct control of an employer.

14. Third, and in contrast to certain other duties to report to the Pensions Regulator such as breaches of the law or failure to adhere to a schedule of contributions, the requirement to notify is not triggered by any wrongdoing by an employer (with the exception of a conviction of a director or partner of the employer for an offence involving dishonesty).

15. Fourth, that taken in isolation a notifiable event gives no indication of the financial position of an employer or of its pension scheme.

Timing of notification

16. An event must be notified in writing to the Pensions Regulator as soon as reasonably practicable. It is important that events are notified quickly in order to act as an effective early warning of calls on the Pension Protection Fund. What is reasonably practicable depends on the circumstances. In all cases however it implies urgency. For example, where a trustee is made aware of a notifiable event on a Sunday, the Regulator should be notified on Monday.

17. The requirement to notify as soon as reasonably practicable is likely to mean that procedures for notification will be necessary outside the usual framework for considering pensions issues such as trustees' quarterly meetings. Procedures should also be put in place to require those such as administrators working on behalf of trustees and employers to alert trustees and employers quickly to notifiable events.

18. The events are intended to be relatively straightforward to identify; it should not be necessary to seek professional or expert advice on whether an event has occurred. There is no expectation that the decision to notify should require a special meeting of the trustees.

19. The events are worded to make clear when they should be notified. In some cases the duty to notify arises before the actual event has taken place. For example, when an employer decides not to pay in full a debt it owes to the scheme, the notifiable event is when the decision is taken by the employer's decision-making body, such as its board of directors, rather than implementation of the payment itself.

20. In other cases events may not be able to be notified until after they have taken place, for example a change in credit rating.

How to notify

21. All notifications must be in writing. Notifiers should where practicable use the standard form available on the Pensions Regulator's website at **www.thepensionsregulator.gov.uk.** Reports can be sent by post or electronically, including by email or by fax. Contact details and other information about the Pensions Regulator is on the Pension Regulator's website.

22. The minimum information that should be included in a notification is the:
    - description of the notifiable event;
    - date of the event;
    - name of the pension scheme;
    - name of the employer; and
    - name, position and contact details of the notifier.

23. The information that would in addition be useful is the:
    - address of the pension scheme;
    - name and address of the main trustee contact;
    - pension scheme registration number;
    - name and address of the main employer contact;
    - employer's current trading status; and
    - name of any controlling company or group to which the employer belongs.

24. The Pensions Regulator's preference is to be notified quickly than for there to be delay incurred in confirming exactly whether an event has occurred; whether the exceptions apply; or in obtaining all the information which would be useful.

Follow up by the Pensions Regulator

25. Where contact details are provided, the Pensions Regulator will aim to acknowledge notifications within five working days of receipt.

26. Notifiable events will be one source of information for the Pensions Regulator. Follow-up will depend on the event and on other information known about the scheme, the trustees and the employer.

Failure to notify

Trustees

27. Trustees must take all reasonable steps to comply with the notifiable events duty. This is interpreted as whether, in the event of failure to notify when a scheme-related notifiable event has occurred, an objective person would consider that a trustee nevertheless took all the steps it would be reasonable to expect them to take in order to comply.

Employers

28. Employers must comply with the duty to notify unless they have a reasonable excuse for not doing so. This is interpreted as whether, when an employer-related notifiable event has occurred, an objective person would consider that there was nonetheless a reasonable basis for the failure by the employer to notify.

29. In practice this means that trustees and employers should:
    i. be aware of the notifiable events including those which all
       trustees and employers must notify;
    ii. know whether the scheme of which they are trustee or employer is required to notify all the events, i.e. is not within the exceptions; and
    iii. have a procedure which enables identification and notification to occur.

30. In the event of failure to notify, the Pensions Regulator will seek an explanation. Following this, it will have a range of actions it can take including requiring training or other assistance. Where appropriate, however, civil penalties can be imposed.

31. Failure to notify of itself will not lead to any transaction being unwound by the Pensions Regulator. However a court or tribunal may consider failure to notify if it considers it relevant; the Pensions Regulator will have regard to failure to notify any relevant event when deciding whether it is reasonable to issue a contribution notice[19].

32. If another party (such as a scheme actuary or an independent financial adviser), who is subject to the duty to report breaches of the law to the Pensions Regulator, becomes aware of a failure by trustees or an employer to notify, that party should report the failure as a breach of pensions legislation likely to be of material significance to the Pensions Regulator[20].

---

[19] See section 38 of the Pensions Act 2004.

[20] See section 70 of the Pensions Act 2004 and the code of practice on reporting breaches of the law.

Annex

GB legislative reference	NI legislative reference
Section 38 of the Pensions Act 2004 (Contribution notices where avoidance of employer debt)	Article 34 of The Pensions (Northern Ireland) Order 2005 (Statutory Instrument 2005/255 (N.I. 1)) (Contribution notices where avoidance of employer debt)
Section 69 of the Pensions Act 2004 (Duty to notify the Regulator of certain events)	Article 64 of The Pensions (Northern Ireland) Order 2005 (Statutory Instrument 2005/255 (N.I. 1)) (Duty to notify the Regulator of certain events)
Section 70 of the Pensions Act 2004 (Duty to report breaches of the law)	Article 65 of The Pensions (Northern Ireland) Order 2005 (Statutory Instrument 2005/255 (N.I. 1)) (Duty to report breaches of the law)
Sections 82-87 of the Pensions Act 2004 (Disclosure of information)	Articles 77-82 of The Pensions (Northern Ireland) Order 2005 (Statutory Instrument 2005/255 (N.I. 1)) (Disclosure of information)
Section 126 of the Pensions Act 2004 (Eligible schemes)	Article 110 of The Pensions (Northern Ireland) Order 2005 (Statutory Instrument 2005/255 (N.I. 1)) (Eligible schemes)
Section 311 of the Pensions Act 2004 (Protected items)	Article 283 of The Pensions (Northern Ireland) Order 2005 (Statutory Instrument 2005/255 (N.I. 1)) (Protected items)
The Pensions Regulator (Notifiable Events) Regulations 2005 (Statutory Instrument 2005/900)	The Pensions Regulator (Notifiable Events) Regulations (Northern Ireland) 2005 (Statutory Rule 2005 No. 172)

A1.5: Directions issued by the Pensions Regulator under section 69(1)[1] of the Pensions Act 2004
Version 1 – Dated 6 April 2005[2]

Introduction

1. Trustees, managers and employers of eligible schemes[3] are under an obligation[4] to notify the Pensions Regulator of certain events prescribed in The Pensions Regulator (Notifiable Events) Regulations 2005 SI 900[5] ('the Regulations'), except where the Regulator otherwise directs.

2. These directions set out those exceptions under which the trustees, managers and employers are released from their obligation to report certain notifiable events where certain conditions are satisfied at the time that the event occurs.

Direction 1

3. Trustees and managers are not required to notify the Regulator of the events prescribed in sub-paragraphs (b) (two or more changes in key scheme posts), (c) (inward and outward transfer payments of more than five per cent of scheme assets or £1.5 million) and (e) (granting of benefits which cost more than five per cent of scheme assets or £1.5 million) of paragraph 2(1) of the Regulations, provided that both conditions A and B in paragraph 7 below are satisfied.

Direction 2

4. Trustees and managers are not required to notify the Regulator of the event prescribed in sub-paragraph (a) of paragraph 2(1) of the Regulations (a decision by trustees or managers which results in a debt not being paid in full), provided that each of the conditions A, B and C in paragraph 7 below is satisfied.

Direction 3

5. Employers are not required to notify the Regulator of the events prescribed in sub-paragraphs (d) (breach of an employer banking covenant), (f) (decision by a controlling company to relinquish control) and (g) (two or more changes in key employer posts) of paragraph 2(2) of the Regulations, provided that both conditions A and B in paragraph 7 below are satisfied.

Direction 4

6. Employers are not required to notify the Regulator of the event prescribed in sub-paragraph (e) of paragraph 2(2) (a change in the employer's credit rating or the employer ceasing to have a credit rating) of the Regulations provided that each of the conditions A, B and D in paragraph 7 below is satisfied.

Conditions

7. **Condition A** The value of the scheme's assets is equal to or greater than the value of the scheme's liabilities calculated on the relevant basis described in paragraph 8 below.

   Condition B The trustees or managers have not incurred a duty to make a report in the previous twelve months in accordance with:

   i. section 228(2) of the Pensions Act 2004[6] and regulations made thereunder (reasonable cause to believe that failure by the employer to make a payment to the scheme in accordance with the most recently agreed schedule of contributions is likely to be of material significance); or

    ii.   section 59(1) of the Pensions Act 1995[7] and regulations made thereunder (a failure by the employer to pay contributions due under the schedule of contributions on or before the due date).

Condition C The decision by the trustees or managers (to compromise a debt) is in respect of a debt where the full amount is less than 0.5 per cent of the scheme's assets calculated on the relevant basis described in paragraph 8 below.

Condition D The change in credit rating is other than from investment to sub-investment grade where the credit rating is provided by a recognised credit rating agency[8].

Relevant Basis

8.   The relevant basis is that on which the scheme's assets and liabilities are calculated in the most recent actuarial valuation carried out in accordance with:

    i.   section 179 of the Pensions Act 2004[9] (valuations to determine scheme underfunding for the purposes of risk-based pension protection levies) and regulations made thereunder ('section 179 valuation'); or

    ii.   section 56 of the Pensions Act 1995[10] (minimum funding requirement) and regulations made thereunder, where no section 179 valuation has been carried out.

Notes

[1]Also issued under corresponding power under article 64 of the Pensions (Northern Ireland) Order 2005 No. 255 (N.I.1)

[2]The directions will be reviewed and updated from time to time and trustees, managers and employers should ensure that they are relying on the current version which can be found at www.thepensionsregulator.gov.uk.

[3] Eligible Scheme has the meaning given by section 126 of the Pensions Act 2004 and article 110 of the Pensions (Northern Ireland) Order 2005

[4]Section 69(1) of the Pensions Act 2004; Article 64 of the Pensions (Northern Ireland) Order 2005

[5]Corresponding regulations will be made in relation to Northern Ireland

[6]NI corresponding reference article 207(2) of the Pensions (Northern Ireland) Order 2005

[7]NI corresponding reference article 59(1) of the Pensions (Northern Ireland) Order 1995 No. 3213

[8]For the purposes of these directions Standard and Poor's, Moody's and Fitch are recognised credit rating agencies.

[9]NI corresponding reference article 162 of the Pensions (Northern Ireland) Order 2005

[10]NI corresponding reference article 56 Pensions (Northern Ireland) Order 1995

A1.6: Guidance from the PPF for insolvency practitioners and official receivers

Part 1 – Overview

1.1   This guidance aims to provide assistance on the process for beginning an 'assessment period' in relation to a pension scheme and the key elements of an assessment period so far as they relate to insolvency practitioners and official receivers.

1.2   Unless stated otherwise any references to the Act, sections, schedules and regulations relate to those under the Pensions Act 2004.

1.3   This guidance is for information purposes, it is not a definitive statement of law.

1.4   **'An Introductory Guide to the Pension Protection Fund'** can be found within the publications section of our website:

     www.pensionprotectionfund.org.uk

1.5   A number of parties may be involved in the assessment process and they may include:

- an insolvency practitioner or official receiver;
- existing and independent trustees;
- The Pensions Regulator; and
- The Pension Protection Fund.

1.6   The Pension Protection Fund assessment teams will work closely with insolvency practitioners and official receivers during the assessment process to provide guidance and aid the assessment of the pension scheme in accordance with the Act.

1.7   An assessment period is the period during which a pension scheme is assessed to determine whether the Pension Protection Fund should assume responsibility for the pension scheme. During this period the pension scheme continues to be administered by its trustees – subject to various restrictions and controls. The role of creditor of the employer (on behalf of the pension scheme) will be assumed by the Pension Protection Fund. It will be the trustees' role to continue to communicate with members and make pension payments where due, taking into account Pension Protection Fund rules.

1.8   A key role of the Pension Protection Fund during the assessment period is that of acting as creditor of the employer in relation to the money due to the pension scheme by the employer. The rights and powers of the trustees to represent the pension scheme as a creditor cease during this period. If an assessment period ends and the Pension Protection Fund does not assume responsibility for the pension scheme then, if the trustees are still appointed to the pension scheme, the role of creditor will pass back to the trustees.

1.9   The Pension Protection Fund will only assume responsibility for a pension scheme where a qualifying insolvency event has occurred in relation to an eligible pension scheme, **and:**

- a pension scheme has not been rescued, for example where the insolvent employer is in liquidation, its employees made redundant and its assets sold off piecemeal; **and**

- the valuation of the pension scheme shows that the assets of the pension scheme are below the Pension Protection Fund level of protected liabilities.

1.10   Where these conditions are not met the Pension Protection Fund will cease to be involved with the pension scheme once the relevant processes and procedures have been completed.

1.11   Where these conditions are met, the Pension Protection Fund will assume responsibility for the pension scheme and compensation will then become payable to its members.

1.12   An assessment period is likely to last a minimum of one year, although it may vary significantly depending on the complexity of the financial situation of both the employer and the pension scheme and the possibility of a pension scheme rescue.

1.13   The diagram below sets out the key stages for an insolvency practitioner or official receiver during the initial stages of the assessment period.

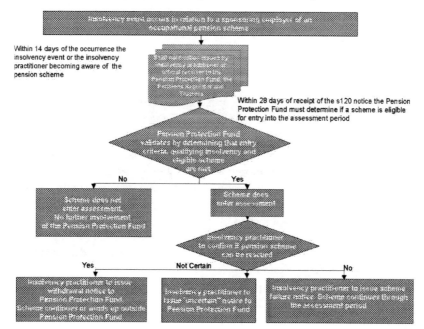

Part 2 – Actions for insolvency professionals – Notification of an insolvency event

Sections 120, 121, 126, 127 & 129 Regulations 2, 3, 4 & 5 of the Pension Protection Fund (Entry Rules) Regulations 2005

2.1   If an employer, with an *occupational pension scheme,* suffers an insolvency event, for example a company enters administration or an individual goes bankrupt, the Pension Protection Fund should be informed. A list of the insolvency events is set out in *Appendix 1.*

2.2   The Pension Protection Fund should be notified by using the **section 120** notice pro-forma. This document is available on the Pension Protection Fund website. Alternatively the requisite information can be provided in some other written form. If you do not intend to use the notice pro-forma you will find a list of the information that should be included in the notice at *Appendix 2.*

2.3   This notice should be sent to the Pension Protection Fund, the Pensions Regulator and the trustees of the pension scheme within 14 days of the insolvency event or, if later, the date the insolvency practitioner or official receiver became aware of the existence of the occupational pension scheme. If more than one insolvency event occurs in relation to an employer a notice is required in respect of each event. If the employer sponsors more than one occupational pension scheme a notice will be required in relation to each and every one of the occupational pension schemes involved.

2.4   The Pension Protection Fund needs to be satisfied on two points before it can validate the notice and before it can confirm an assessment period has begun. They are that:
- an insolvency event is a qualifying insolvency event (a list of the events is set out in *Appendix 1* although you will also find that information in *sections 120, 121 & 127* and Regulations 4 & 5 of the Pension Protection Fund (Entry Rules) Regulations 2005); **and**
- the insolvency event must be in relation to a sponsoring employer of an eligible pension scheme (the criteria are set out in *section 126* and Regulation 2 of the Pension Protection Fund (Entry Rules) Regulations 2005). However, insolvency practitioners and official receivers are **not** required to determine whether or not the occupational pension scheme is eligible.

2.5   Where these two points are satisfied, the Pension Protection Fund will issue a validation notification and will confirm that an assessment period has begun. The start of the assessment period will be the date on which the insolvency event occurred. This date is known as 'the assessment date'. The assessment date is a key date in the assessment process and is the date from which any requirements or restrictions, placed upon the pension scheme by the Act, apply. This includes the application of the Pension Protection Fund rules to any payment of pensions or benefits.

2.6   The situation may be different for pension schemes where there is more than one participating employer and how the situation differs depends on the structure of the pension scheme. A high level diagram showing the impact of the different structures of multi-employer pension schemes is at *Appendix 3* and more information can be found in the Pension Protection Fund (Entry Rules) Regulations 2005. The insolvency practitioner or official receiver must notify the Pension Protection Fund of each insolvency event in relation to each employer participating in the pension scheme.

2.7   Once the insolvency practitioner or official receiver informs the Pension Protection Fund of the insolvency event the Pension Protection Fund will carry out the necessary validation to satisfy itself that the relevant criteria have been met.

2.8   The Pension Protection Fund can also assess certain eligible occupational pension schemes where the employer *cannot* enter formal insolvency proceedings, for example some public bodies and unincorporated charities, in circumstances where that employer is unlikely to be able to continue as a going concern.

2.9   In these circumstances, as no insolvency event is available to the employer it will be for either trustees of the pension scheme or the Pensions Regulator to inform the Pension Protection Fund and request that the Pension Protection Fund assumes responsibility for the pension scheme. The assessment period will begin on the date of receipt by the Pension Protection Fund of the notification or application. Further information can be found in *sections 128 & 129* and Regulations 7 & 8 of the Pension Protection Fund (Entry Rules) Regulations 2005.

2.10   It should be noted that this is not an alternative entry route for pension schemes. It is only for those pension schemes whose sponsoring employer cannot have a normal insolvency event.

Part 3 – Actions for insolvency professionals – Pension scheme failure, withdrawal or uncertain notice

Sections 122, 123 & 148 Regulations 6, 9 & 11 of the Pension Protection Fund (Entry Rules) Regulations 2005

3.1   Once it becomes clear that:
  - financial support for the occupational pension scheme will continue ('a scheme rescue'), for example, because the company is rescued and the business continues with the pension scheme in place; **or**
  - financial support for the pension scheme will not continue ('no scheme rescue'), for example, because the business has been closed down, or entered liquidation and the employees have been discharged; **or**
  - the appointment of the insolvency practitioner comes to an end before a view can be formed on whether support for the pension scheme will continue or not, for example, because the court brings the insolvency proceedings to an abrupt end on rescission of a winding up order on the grounds that it ought not to have been made;
  - the insolvency practitioner or official receiver should inform the Pension Protection Fund, preferably by using the relevant pro-formas available on the website, or alternatively by sending us the requisite information in writing as soon as reasonably practical. If you do not intend to use the notice pro-formas

you will find a list of the information that should be included in the notice at *Appendices 4 and 5*.

3.2   The situation may be different for pension schemes where there is more than one participating employer – and how the situation differs depends on the structure of the pension scheme. A high level diagram that shows the impact of the different structures of multi-employer pension schemes is at *Appendix 3* and more information on when, and if, to issue a notice under *section 122* can be found in Regulation 11 of the Pension Protection Fund (Entry Rules) Regulations 2005.

3.3   The notices should be issued to the Pension Protection Fund, the Pensions Regulator and trustee of the pension scheme. Once the notices are received, the Pension Protection Fund will determine whether the notice can be approved.

3.4   If a pension scheme rescue is confirmed, and after the relevant procedures have been completed and rights of review exhausted, the Pension Protection Fund withdraws from the pension scheme and the assessment period ends.

3.5   If a pension scheme rescue is not possible, and after the relevant procedures have been completed and rights of review exhausted, the pension scheme continues to the next stage of the assessment period.

3.6   Where the insolvency practitioner or official receiver is unable to confirm whether or not a pension scheme rescue is possible and a notice is issued to that effect, and that notice becomes binding, the Pension Protection Fund must consider whether another insolvency event is likely to occur in the next six months:
   • if this is unlikely, the Pension Protection Fund will issue a withdrawal notice terminating the assessment period; and
   • if the Pension Protection Fund reaches such a decision and six months has passed without another insolvency event, the Pension Protection Fund is then required to issue a withdrawal notice, terminating the assessment period; or
   • if an insolvency event is likely to occur, and because the pension scheme is still in an assessment period, the process for determining the pension scheme status re-starts when the Pension Protection Fund is notified of a further insolvency event.

Part 4 – Pension scheme creditor rights

Section 137

4.1   When an assessment period begins, the Pension Protection Fund will assume all the creditor rights of the pension scheme trustees (whether contingent or not) in relation to the insolvency of the employer. All documents, such as notice of creditors' meetings, etc should be sent to the Pension Protection Fund so it can be properly informed and exercise the creditor rights of the pension scheme in the insolvency. Contact details are shown at *Part 6*.

4.2   It also means that, during the assessment period, the Pension Protection Fund (rather than the pension scheme trustees) should receive any sums recovered from the employer, for example a dividend in relation to the pension scheme. The Pension Protection Fund will then pay that amount to the trustees of the pension scheme.

4.3   In the event that the Pension Protection Fund assumes responsibility for a pension scheme, the trustees will cease to have any responsibility for the pension scheme and all rights will pass to the Pension Protection Fund.

4.4   In the event that it is determined that the pension scheme should withdraw from the assessment period the Pension Protection Fund relinquishes its rights in relation to the creditor responsibility for the pension scheme. In this event, the trustees will resume all rights and responsibilities to act for the pension scheme as creditor and the Pension Protection Fund will have no further part to play in relation to the scheme.

Part 5 – Employees and pensioners

5.1   During an assessment period any pension scheme enquiries from employees or existing pensioners should be directed to the trustees of the pension scheme rather than the Pension Protection Fund. This is because the trustees remain responsible for administering the scheme (subject to statutory restrictions) until the end of an assessment period or where it has been determined whether or not the Pension Protection Fund will assume responsibility for it.

5.2   In dealing with enquiries from employees or pensioners on the Pension Protection Fund more generally, and for a basic understanding of the compensation that may be payable, you may find it helpful to refer them to our website and the leaflet 'An Introductory Guide to the Pension Protection Fund'.

5.3   This leaflet can be accessed on our website:

www.pensionprotectionfund.org.uk

Hard copies are available for distribution, if required.

Part 6 - Further information

6.1   Further useful and more detailed information, for example the Guidance for Trustees, can be found on the Pension Protection Fund website:

www.pensionprotectionfund.org.uk

6.2   The contact address for the Pension Protection Fund is:

The Pension Protection Fund
Knollys House
17 Addiscombe Road
Croydon
Surrey
CR0 6SR

Tel: 0845 600 2541

Appendix 1
Insolvency events
Insolvency events' in relation to a company

Section 121(3) & Regulation 5 of the Pension Protection Fund (Entry Rules) Regulations 2005

An insolvency event occurs in relation to a company where:

a the nominee under Part 1 of the Insolvency Act 1986 either:

    i (who is not the liquidator or administrator) submits a report to the court stating his opinion that meetings of the company and its creditors should be summoned to consider the proposal; **or**

    ii (who is an administrator or liquidator) summons a meeting of the company and

b the directors of the company file (or in Scotland, lodge) with the court documents and statements which begin a moratorium where the directors propose a voluntary arrangement;

c an administrative receiver is appointed in relation to the company;

d the company enters administration;

e a resolution is passed for creditors' voluntary liquidation or an administrator issues a notice which converts the administration to creditors voluntary liquidation;

f a creditors' meeting is held which converts a members' voluntary liquidation into a creditors' voluntary liquidation;

g a winding up order is made or an administration is converted to winding up by court order.

Note: paragraph 84 of schedule B1 to the Insolvency Act 1986 is not an 'insolvency event'.

'Insolvency events' in relation to a partnership

Section 121(4) & Regulation 5 of the Pension Protection Fund (Entry Rules) Regulations 2005

An insolvency event occurs in relation to a partnership where:

a an order for the winding up of the partnership is made or an administration is converted

    to a winding up by court order;

b sequestration is awarded on the estate of the partnership under section 12 of the

    Bankruptcy (Scotland) Act 1985 or the partnership grants a trust deed for its creditors;

c the nominee under Part 1 of the Insolvency Act 1986 either:

    i *(who is not the liquidator or administrator)* submits a report to the court stating his opinion that meetings of the partnership and its creditors should be summoned to consider the proposals; **or**

    ii *(who is an administrator, liquidator or trustee)* summons a meeting of the company and its creditors to consider the proposal;

d the members of the partnership file with the court documents and statements which

    begin a moratorium where the members propose a voluntary arrangement;

e an administration order is made in relation to the partnership.

Note: In the above, **e** will be amended by secondary legislation when the Insolvent Partnerships Order 1994 is amended to apply to partnerships the administration regime introduced by the Enterprise Act 2002.

'Insolvency events' in relation to an individual

Section 121(2) & Regulation 5 of the Pension Protection Fund (Entry Rules) Regulations 2005

An insolvency event occurs in relation to an individual where:

a   he is adjudged bankrupt or sequestration of their estate has been awarded;

b   a nominee submits a report to the court pursuant to section 256(1) or 256A(3) of the Insolvency Act 1986 stating his opinion that a meeting of the creditors should be called to consider the proposals;

c   a deed of arrangement made by or in respect of the affairs of the individual is registered in accordance with the Deeds of Arrangement Act 1914;

d   he executes a trust deed for his creditors or enters into a composition or contract;

e   he has died and:
   i an insolvency administration order is made, **or**
   ii a judicial factor appointed under section 11A of the Judicial Factors (Scotland) Act 1889 is required by that section to divide the individual's estate amongst their creditors.

Additional insolvency events

Section 121(5) & Regulation 5 of the Pension Protection Fund (Entry Rules) Regulations 2005

An insolvency event occurs:

a   in relation to a company, where an administration order is made by the court in respect of the company by virtue of any enactment which applies Part 2 of the Insolvency Act 1986 Act (administration orders) (with or without modification);

b   in relation to a relevant body, where:
   i any of the events referred to in section 121(3) of the Act (see company insolvency events above) occurs in relation to that body by virtue of the application (with or without modification) of any provision of the Insolvency Act 1986 Act by or under any other enactment; **or**
   ii an administration order is made by the court in respect of the relevant body by virtue of any enactment which applies Part 2 of the Insolvency Act 1986 Act (with or without modification);

c   in relation to a building society, where there is dissolution by consent of the members under section 87 of the Building Societies Act 1986;

d   in relation to a friendly society, where there is dissolution by consent of the members under section 20 of the Friendly Societies Act 1992; **and**

e   in relation to an industrial and provident society, where there is dissolution by consent of the members under section 58 of the Industrial and Provident Societies Act 1965.

'administration order' means an order whereby the management of the company or relevant body, as the case may be, is placed in the hands of a person appointed by the court;

'relevant body' means:
• a credit union;
• a limited liability partnership;
• a building society;
• a person who has permission to act under Part IV of the FSMA;

- the society of Lloyd's and Lloyd's members;
- a friendly society; **or**
- a society which is registered as an industrial and provident society.

A reference to Part 2 of the Insolvency Act 1986 Act, insofar as it relates to a company or society listed in section 249(1) of the Enterprise Act 2002 (special administration arrangements), has effect as if it referred to Part 2 of the 1986 Act as it had effect immediately before 15 September 2003.)

Appendix 2

Information to be supplied by the insolvency practitioner on the occurrence of an 'insolvency event'

Regulation 4(2) of the Pension Protection Fund (Entry Rules) Regulations 2005

A notice issued by an insolvency practitioner under section 120(2) shall be in writing and shall contain the following information:

a   the name or type of the notice issued;

b   the date on which the notice is issued;

c   the name, address and pension scheme registration number of the scheme in respect of which the notice is issued;

d   the name of the employer in relation to the scheme in respect of which the notice is issued;

e   the nature of the insolvency event which has occurred and the date of the occurrence of that event;

f   the name of the insolvency practitioner acting in relation to the employer in relation to the scheme;

g   the date on which the insolvency practitioner was appointed to act or consented to act in relation to the employer in relation to the scheme or, in any case where the insolvency practitioner is the official receiver, the date on which the official receiver began to act in relation to that employer;

h   the address for communications at which the insolvency practitioner may be contacted by the Board in connection with the issue of the notice; **and**

i   whether the notice issued contains any commercially sensitive information.

Section 120 Insolvency Event Notice

We recommend you use this form – downloaded from our website – to notify the Pension Protection Fund that an insolvency event has occurred. This is because it contains all the information you are required to provide. Our website address is:

www.pensionprotectionfund.org.uk

Section 120 Insolvency Event Notice

Pension Protection Fund

This notice should be issued in accordance with section 120 of the Pensions Act 2004.

This notice is to be used by an insolvency practitioner or official receiver to inform the necessary parties that a sponsoring employer of an occupational pension scheme has suffered an insolvency event

as defined by Section 121 of the Pensions Act 2004 and paragraph 5 of the Pension Protection Fund (Entry Rules) Regulations 2005.

Please use mark ink and **CAPITAL LETTERS** throughout. Where tick boxes appear, tick all that apply.

Name of Insolvency Practitioner or official receiver

Insolvency Practitioner number (if applicable)

Firm name (where applicable)

Address of Insolvency Practitioner or official receiver

Postcode

Telephone   Fax

Email

Date I took office (paragraph 4(2)(g) of the Regulations)

I hereby give notice as required under the Pensions Act 2004 that the following employer:

Employer name

Address of employer

Postcode

Telephone   Fax

Email

Contact name

has suffered the following insolvency event

This insolvency event occurred on   as evidenced by the relevant document, for example the court order or resolution which should be attached to this form.

REFERENCE   Page 1 of 1

A1: REGULATORY GUIDANCE

The afore mentioned employer is the sponsoring employer of the following occupational pension scheme

Name of Pension Scheme

Pension Scheme registration number

I understand that the occupational pension scheme referred to is a

Defined benefit scheme ⬚ Hybrid scheme ⬚ Money purchase scheme ⬚

The following address is the last known address of the Trustees or the Managers of the scheme according to the employers records.

Name

Firm name (where applicable)

Address

Postcode

Telephone   Fax

Email

If the address of the scheme is different please provide details below

Address

Postcode

Telephone   Fax

Please tick to confirm that notification of this insolvency event has been sent today to

The Pension Protection Fund ⬚ The Pensions Regulator ⬚

The Trustees or managers of the Pension Scheme ⬚

Is any of the information in this notice commercially sensitive? yes ⬚ no ⬚

The information provided above is correct to the best of my knowledge and belief and complies with the notification requirement set out in Section 120 of the Pensions Act 2004.

Signed

Dated

Please send this form to: The Pension Protection Fund, Knollys House, 17 Addiscombe Road, Croydon, Surrey CR0 6SR T 0845 600 2541 F 020 8633 4900

Also to: Pensions Regulator, Diagnostic and Monitoring Team, Invicta House, Trafalgar Place, Brighton BN1 4DW.

Section 120 Insolvency Event Notice   Page 2 of 2

Appendix 3

Multi-employer pension schemes

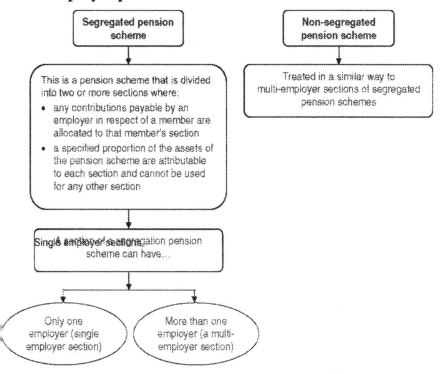

Segregated pension scheme

This is a pension scheme that is divided into two or more sections where:

- any contributions payable by an employer in respect of a member are allocated to that member's section
- a specified proportion of the assets of the pension scheme are attributable to each section and cannot be used for any other section

A single employer segregation pension scheme can have...

Only one employer (single employer section)

More than one employer (a multi-employer section)

Non-segregated pension scheme

Treated in a similar way to multi-employer sections of segregated pension schemes

Single employer sections

Each section is treated similarly to a separate single employer pension scheme in the Pension Protection Fund process.

An insolvency event relating to the sponsoring employer of that section triggers the assessment period.

The assets/liabilities of that section are only relevant for the Pension Protection Fund purposes.

The Pension Protection Fund will only assume responsibility for that section.

Segregated pension schemes

Multi-employer sections

May have 3 different structures on the withdrawal (insolvency) of a sponsoring employer

---

Requirement for partial wind-up	No requirement for partial wind-up	Options for partial wind-up
Case 1 On the insolvency of an employer or an application under section 129 in that section – a new 'segregated' part is created: • an insolvency event of any participating employer triggers an assessment period for the newly created part; • the assets/liabilities of the segregated part determine entry into the Pension Protection Fund. A valuation of the whole section is necessary, in order to arrive at a valuation of the segregated part.	**Case 2** Last man standing approach: • the assessment period is not triggered until the **last** employer in that section becomes insolvent or there is an application under section 129 in respect of that last employer; • the Pension Protection Fund must only approve a pension scheme status notice in respect of the **last** participating employer; • the valuation should be carried out in respect of the entire section.	**Case 3** The Pension Protection Fund will assume that trustees will opt for partial wind-up and the section will be treated as in **Case 1**: • if trustees decide not to do so, they must notify the Pension Protection Fund and insolvency practitioner; • the insolvency practitioner must then issue a 'withdrawal notice' confirming that the pension scheme has been rescued.

Appendix 4

Information to be included in the notification of the status of the scheme

Regulation 9(3) of the Pension Protection Fund (Entry Rules) Regulations 2005

A notice issued by an insolvency practitioner under section 122(2)(a) or (b) or by a former insolvency practitioner under section 122(4) shall be in writing and shall contain the following information –

a   the name or type of notice issued;

b   the date on which the notice is issued;

c   the name, address and pension scheme registration number of the scheme in respect of which the notice is issued;

d   the name of the employer in relation to the scheme in respect of which the notice is issued;

e   the name of the insolvency practitioner or former insolvency practitioner and the address at which that insolvency practitioner may be contacted by the Board in connection with the issue of the notice;

f   a statement by the insolvency practitioner or former insolvency practitioner that, as the case may be, a scheme rescue has occurred or a scheme rescue is not possible or that he has been unable to confirm that a scheme rescue has occurred or that a scheme rescue is not possible;

g   if a scheme rescue has occurred, the date or the approximate date of the scheme rescue and, if there is a new employer in relation to the scheme, the name and address of that employer in relation to the scheme;

h   if a scheme rescue is not possible, a statement from the insolvency practitioner or former insolvency practitioner as to why, in their opinion, this is not possible;

i   if section 122(4) applies and the former insolvency practitioner has not been able to confirm in relation to the scheme that a scheme rescue is not possible, a statement from that insolvency practitioner as to why, in their opinion, this is the case;

j   a statement that the notice issued will not become binding until it has been approved by the Board; **and**

k   whether, in the opinion of the insolvency practitioner or former insolvency practitioner, the notice issued contains any commercially sensitive information.

Appendix 5

Events triggering obligation to file a 'scheme rescue uncertain' notice under section 122(3)

Companies

a Where the procedure for a voluntary arrangement has commenced but for whatever reason no voluntary arrangement has effect.

b Where a company has entered a moratorium with a view to the proposal of a voluntary arrangement and the moratorium has terminated without a voluntary arrangement taking effect.

c Where the company enters administration, the appointment of an administrator in respect of the company ceases to have effect, except where:

    i the company moves from administration into winding up pursuant to paragraph 83 (moving from administration to creditor's voluntary liquidation) of Schedule B1 to the 1986 Act or pursuant to an order of the court under Rule 2.132 of the Insolvency Rules or

    ii a winding up order is made by the court immediately upon the appointment of the administrator ceasing to have effect.

d Where an administrative receiver vacates office under section 45.

e Where the winding up proceedings are stayed or the winding up order is rescinded or discharged, except where the court has made an administration order.

Partnerships

References are to provisions of the Rules and of the Act as applied by an order under section 420

a Where the procedure for a voluntary arrangement has commenced under section 2 of the 1986 Act but for whatever reason no voluntary arrangement has effect or a moratorium with a view to a voluntary arrangement has terminated without the voluntary arrangement taking effect, whichever is applicable.

b Where an administration order has been made in relation to the partnership under Part 2, the order is discharged, except where:

    i a winding up order is made by the court immediately upon the discharge of the administration order; **or**

    ii the discharge is pursuant to an order of the court for the administration to be converted into winding up under rule 2.61(1) of the Insolvency Rules 1986 without the amendments made by the Insolvency (Amendment) Rules 2003.

(These events will be amended when the Insolvency Partnerships Order 1994 is amended to apply to partnerships the administration regime introduced by the Enterprise Act 2002.)

c Where an order for the winding up of the partnership has been made by the court, the winding up proceedings are stayed or the winding up order is rescinded or discharged.

Individuals

a Where the procedure for a voluntary arrangement has commenced but for whatever reason no voluntary arrangement has effect.

b Where an individual has been adjudged bankrupt, the bankruptcy order is annulled or rescinded.

c Where an insolvency administration order is annulled or rescinded.

Other situations triggering a 'scheme rescue uncertain' notice

Deeds of arrangement

Where a deed of arrangement made by or in respect of the individual has been registered under the Deeds of Arrangement Act 1914, but the deed is void in accordance with the provisions of section 3(1) of that Act.

For full details, please see Regulation 6 of the Pension Protection Fund (Entry Rules) Regulations 2005.

A1.7: Guidance from the PPF for undertaking entry valuation Part 1 – Overview

1.1 Introduction

1.1.1   The Pensions Act 2004 (the Act) sets out the conditions that must be met for the Pension Protection Fund to assume responsibility for a scheme.

1.1.2   In high-level terms, in order for the Pension Protection Fund to assume responsibility for a scheme, the scheme must satisfy the following key criteria:

- the scheme must be a scheme which is eligible for the Pension Protection Fund;
- the scheme must not have commenced wind up before 6 April 2005;
- an insolvency event must have occurred in relation to the scheme's employer which is a qualifying insolvency event;
- there must be no chance that the scheme can be rescued; and
- there must be insufficient assets in the scheme to secure benefits on wind up that are at least equal to the compensation that the Pension Protection Fund would pay if it assumed responsibility for the scheme.

1.1.3   If a qualifying insolvency event occurs in relation to an employer of an eligible scheme, this will trigger the beginning of an assessment period. During this period the Pension Protection Fund will assess whether or not it must assume responsibility for the scheme.

1.1.4   Part of this process involves looking at the scheme's assets and liabilities to determine whether the scheme can afford to secure benefits that are at least equal to the compensation that the Pension Protection Fund would pay if it assumed responsibility for the scheme.

1.1.5   If the scheme can secure benefits at least equal to the compensation payable by the Pension Protection Fund, it will be ordered to wind up outside of the Pension Protection Fund by securing benefits in the market or run on as a closed scheme if it qualifies under section 153 of the Act.

1.1.6   If it cannot and the relevant process and procedures have been completed, then the Pension Protection Fund will assume responsibility for the scheme and compensation will then become payable.

1.1.7   A Pension Protection Fund assessment period is likely to last a minimum of one year and could be longer, depending on the complexity of the financial situation of both the employer and the scheme, and the possibility of a scheme rescue.

1.1.8   The valuation under section 143 will determine whether the scheme has sufficient funds to pay at least the Pension Protection Fund levels of compensation as set out above.

1.2 Purpose of this guidance

1.2.1   This guidance is intended for actuaries undertaking valuations to determine the level of funding in accordance with section 143 of the Act.

1.2.2   The Act and associated regulations set out the high level principles relating to the valuation with this guidance setting out the detailed assumptions and discount rates to be applied.

1.2.3   The legislation and associated regulations relating to these valuations came into force on 6 April 2005.

1.3 Purpose of the section 143 valuation

1.3.1   The purpose of the valuation is to determine whether the Board of the Pension Protection Fund should assume responsibility for a scheme. This valuation is only required within a Pension Protection Fund assessment period and the Board of the Pension Protection Fund will instruct an actuary to carry out the valuation.

1.3.2   Once the valuation has been completed the Board of the Pension Protection Fund must approve it in accordance with section 144. The valuation becomes legally binding once it has been approved and the period within which the approval may be reviewed has expired.

1.3.3   Where the valuation establishes that the assets are not sufficient to meet the protected liabilities, the Board of the Pension Protection Fund will assume responsibility for the scheme and pay compensation to scheme members in accordance with Schedule 7 to the Act. Where the assets are sufficient to meet the protected liabilities the scheme will be ordered to wind up outside of the Pension Protection Fund by securing benefits in the market.

1.4 Legislative requirements

1.4.1   The Act sets out the requirement for the Board of the Pension Protection Fund to obtain an actuarial valuation of an eligible scheme where either:

- a qualifying insolvency event has occurred in relation to the employer (section 127(1));
- the trustees of the scheme make an application to the Board of the Pension Protection Fund (section 128(1)) under section 129.

1.4.2   An eligible scheme is defined by section 126 and associated regulations.

1.5 Who completes the valuation?

1.5.1   The actuarial valuation must be prepared and signed by a person appointed by the Board of the Pension Protection Fund who must meet the criteria specified in section 143(11)(a)(ii) and the valuation regulations.

1.6 Where to send valuation information

1.6.1   Details relating to the section 143 valuation (the entry valuation) should be provided to the Pension Protection Fund by the notified date.

1.6.2   For further details about the Pension Protection Fund please visit the Pension Protection Fund website at:
www.pensionprotectionfund.org.uk

1.6.3   The contact address for the Pension Protection Fund is:
Pension Protection Fund
Knollys House
Levels 8 & 9
17 Addiscombe Road
CROYDON
CR0 6SR
Tel: 0845 600 2541

1.7 Legislation or authority for actuarial valuations

The Pensions Act 2004 (the Act)

The Pension Protection Fund (Valuation Regulations) 2005
SI 2005/672 ('the valuation regulations')

The Pension Protection Fund (Partially Guaranteed Schemes) (Modification) Regulations 2005

SI 2005/277

The Pension Protection Fund (Pension Compensation Cap) Order 2005 SI2005/825 ('the Cap regulations')

The Occupational Pension Schemes (Modification of Pension Protection Provisions) Regulations 2005

SI 2005/705

The Occupational Pension Schemes (Levies) Regulations 2005
SI 2005/842

The Pension Protection Fund (Compensation) Regulations 2005
SI 2005/670

The Pension Protection Fund (Multi-employer Schemes)(Modification) Regulations 2005
SI2005/441

The Pension Protection Fund (Hybrid Schemes)(Modification) Regulations 2005
SI2005/449

Part 2 – Introduction

2.1   Under section 143 of the Act the Board of the Pension Protection Fund must obtain an actuarial valuation of an eligible scheme (an 'entry valuation') where either:
- a qualifying insolvency event has occurred in relation to the employer (section 127(1) of the Act): or
- the trustees of the scheme make an application to the Pension Protection Fund (section 128(1)) under section 129 of the Act.

2.2   An eligible scheme is defined by section 126 of the Act and the Pension Protection Fund (Entry Rules) Regulations 2005.

2.3   The Board of the Pension Protection Fund will issue a notice to the trustees or managers of the scheme setting out the requirement for the section 143 valuation and the time when it must be submitted.

2.4   When the Pension Protection Fund decide to obtain the valuation, in most cases the trustees will be approached to ask the pension scheme actuary to complete the valuation.

2.5   Once obtained, the Pension Protection Fund should consider whether to approve the valuation. Following approval, trustees will be required to notify members of their entitlements under the approved valuation. Members have the opportunity to dispute these entitlements and can request a review (Schedule 9)

2.6   The valuation becomes legally binding once any rights of review have been exhausted.

2.7   In this guidance note 'relevant time' has the meaning given in either sections 127(4)(b) or 128(3)(b) of the Act and the valuation regulations as appropriate.

2.8   The actuarial valuation must be prepared and signed by a person meeting the criteria specified in section 143(11)(a)(ii) of the Act and the valuation regulations.

Part 3 – Protected liabilities

3.1   The scheme's protected liabilities are defined in section 131 of the Act. The amount of the protected liabilities relating to benefits for or in respect of members and to wind-up expenses shall be determined in accordance with section 143 of the Act, the valuation regulations and this guidance note.

3.2   The amount of protected liabilities relating to liabilities that are not liabilities to or in respect of members shall be determined in accordance with section 143 of the Act, the valuation regulations and this guidance. The liabilities to members are taken to be the estimated cost of securing scheme benefits (applying the provisions of Schedule 7) to members by purchasing an annuity at the market rate.

Part 4 – Benefits for and in respect of members

4.1   The benefits for and in respect of members of the scheme should be valued as at the relevant time and should be determined as at that date in accordance with Schedule 7 to the Act and associated regulations – paras 4(4), 6(4), 9(4), 12(4), 13(4), 16(3)(b), 17(4), 18(4), 20(4), 20(7), 20(8), 23(1), 23(2), 24(1), 24(2), 24(6), 25(1), 25(2), 26(9), 26(10), 28(6), 28(7), 30, 31(2), 31(3), 33, 35(6), 36(5), 37(4), and the scheme's admissible rules (as defined in paragraph 35 of Schedule 7). The benefits to be valued for any reviewable ill health pensions should be as determined and notified by the Board of the Pension Protection Fund in accordance with section 141(2) of the Act.

4.2   In accordance with section 143(7) of the Act the value of liabilities should not be limited to the value of the assets, even where the scheme rules may so provide.

4.3   For the purpose of determining and valuing the benefits, the compensation cap should be assumed to increase by 1.5 % a year relative to limited price index increases during any period of deferment after the relevant time.

4.4   Normal pension age for a member or applicable to different parts of a member's benefit should be determined as provided within Schedule 7 to the Act, paragraph 34. Benefits for non-pensioners must be valued as payable at the normal pension age applicable to each part of the benefit.

4.5   The Act provides that in certain circumstances where the Board of the Pension Protection Fund is satisfied that it is not possible to identify one or more elements of the benefit formulae as defined in Schedule 7 to the Act, they may direct how the benefit should be calculated. Where this is the case the scheme actuary must apply to the Board of the Pension Protection Fund for a determination to be made.

4.6   Where a scheme with more than one employer operates a sectionalised scheme separate valuations will be required for each separate section of the scheme setting out the assets and benefits attributable to each section.

4.7   For schemes with a partial crown guarantee the valuation should only be of the part of the scheme that is not covered by the crown guarantee.

4.8   For a hybrid 'better off' scheme the assets and benefits will relate to only those members where the defined benefits exceed the defined contribution benefits at the relevant time.

4.9   The liability in respect of money purchase benefits shall be disregarded for the purposes of determining the protected liabilities. Money purchase benefits which have been converted into defined benefit rights on retirement before the relevant date must be valued in the same way as other benefits for pensioners.

Part 5 – Assets

5.1   Assets must be taken into account as specified in the valuation regulations. The actuary may also consider a section 75 debt, contribution notices, financial services directions and restoration orders that falls due to the scheme before the valuation is approved even if it falls due after the relevant time of the valuation as an asset of the scheme. Furthermore he can assign assets a different value from that shown in the relevant accounts if he thinks it appropriate, and take into account any other amounts that might fall due to the scheme after the relevant time if in his opinion it is appropriate that it should be counted as an asset.

5.2.   Where there is a section 75 (of the Pensions Act 1995) debt, contribution notice, financial support direction or restoration order the actuary should obtain advice from the Board of the Pension Protection Fund as to how much of that debt should be taken into account when establishing the assets.

5.3   Advice should also be sought from the Board of the Pension Protection Fund where the valuation of any asset not included in the relevant accounts is to be used to determine assets for this valuation, for example:

- assets acquired after the relevant time;
- proceeds from any relevant insurance policy.

5.4   The assets in respect of money purchase benefits shall be disregarded in accordance with section 143(11)(d) of the Act.

Part 6 – Data

In assessing the scheme's protected liabilities to and in respect of its members the trustees or managers of the scheme must take appropriate action to ensure that as far as practical all potential scheme beneficiaries have been identified. The actuarial valuation must include a description of the action taken and detail any residual concerns.

Part 7 – Valuation method

7.1   Any reasonable age definition may be used for the purpose of the calculation provided consistency with the revaluation and increase periods can be demonstrated.

7.2   For each scheme member the protected liability must be calculated as the present value of the accrued benefits using the assumptions specified in Appendix 1.

Part 8 – Expenses

Expenses must be determined as specified in Appendix 1.

Part 9 – Reporting

9.1   The results of the valuation must be provided to the Board of the Pension Protection Fund in accordance with regulation 9 of the valuation regulations.

9.2   A certificate in the form set out in Appendix 2 of this guidance note must also be provided to the Board of the Pension Protection Fund.

.3   Both documents must be provided to the Board of the Pension Protection Fund once the valuation has been completed and certified by the actuary. This must be done as soon as practicably possible following completion of the valuation but must be within 28 days of completion.

Part 10 – Review

10.1   This guidance note will be reviewed at least annually. It may be reviewed and revised at more frequent intervals, as the Board of the Pension Protection Fund deem appropriate.

Appendix 1: Basis for use when undertaking valuations

1 Yield in deferment

For each non-pensioner the liability for the period of deferment must be obtained by discounting the benefit at normal pension age at the adjusted net index-linked gilt yield shown below. As this yield implicitly allows for increases to normal pension age no allowance should be made for increases to benefits between the relevant date and normal pension age.

Adjusted net index-linked gilt yield = Yield A (i) – 0.5%

(i)   Yield A should be determined daily as 50% of the sum of the FTSE Actuaries' Government Securities Index-Linked annualised Real Yields over 15 years assuming:
        a. 5% inflation; and
        b. 0% inflation.

For any dates where yields are not available the yields for the nearest preceding date should be used.

2 Yield in payment

For each pensioner and each non-pensioner for the period from which payments are assumed to commence the liability must be obtained by reference to the following (adjusted) yields:

Pensions with no increases in payment
        Yield = Yield B (ii)

(ii)   Yield B should be determined daily as the annualised yield on the FTSE Actuaries' Government 10 year Fixed Interest Index.

For any dates where the yield is not available the yield for the nearest preceding date should be used.

Pensions increasing in payment
        Adjusted yield = Yield C (iii) – 0.5%

(iii)   Yield C should be determined daily as 50% of the sum of the FTSE Actuaries' Government Securities Index-Linked annualised Real Yields over five years assuming:
        a. 5% inflation; and
        b. 0% inflation.

For any dates where yields are not available the yields for the nearest preceding date should be used.

3 Mortality

The mortality tables to be used in respect of a member and the member's dependant shall be PMA92 (for males) and PFA92 (for females), as appropriate, in each case with the medium cohort mortality improvement rates. These mortality tables are published by the actuarial profession. For each individual, the set of mortality rates used shall be those applicable to that individual's year of birth.

The derived rates shall be subject to an age rating based on an individual's benefit size as follows:

Pension size*	Age rating
< 25% x compensation cap	+ 2
25% - 50% x compensation cap	0
> 50% x compensation cap	-2

* For non-pensioners to include revaluation to calculation date only, and to include the pension equivalent (calculated on the basis of actuarial equivalence) of any lump sum entitlement.

4 Assumptions for contingent benefits

a) Proportions married

Where the scheme provides for survivor pensions:

For pensioners:

Where the scheme makes provision for survivor pensions for 'relevant partners' an assumption consistent with 90% (males) or 80% (females) at normal pension age.

Where the scheme does not make provision for survivor pensions for 'relevant partners' other than legal spouses an assumption consistent with 80% (males) or 70% (females) at normal pension age.

For non-pensioners:

Where the scheme makes provision for survivor pensions for 'relevant partners' the assumption must be, at the assumed date of retirement or earlier death, 90% (males) or 80% (females).

Where the scheme does not make provision for survivor pensions for 'relevant partners' other than legal spouses the assumption must be, at the assumed date of retirement or earlier death, 80% (males) or 70% (females).

b) Age difference between member and dependant

Female assumed to be 3 years younger than male.

c) Children's pensions

No specific additional allowance to be included for prospective children's pensions. Children's pensions already in payment should be assumed to cease at age 18, or age 23 if currently aged over 17.

5 Expenses

a) Estimated wind-up expenses

3% of any liability value up to £50million plus:

- 2% of any liabilities between £50million and £100million;
- 1% of any liabilities in excess of £100million.

b) Benefit installation/payment expenses

For the purposes of the certificate these should be included as part of the liabilities for or in respect of members.

A1: REGULATORY GUIDANCE

Pensioners - Age related scale

Age	Expense allowance per member £
< 60	450
60 – 70	400
70 – 80	300
80 +	250

Non-pensioners

An allowance of £500 per member should be made.

Appendix 2: Certificate for the purposes of section 143 of the Pensions Act 2004

Scheme name:

Relevant date:

End of period covered by relevant accounts:

Protected liabilities £'000

a. Liabilities for and in respect of members, including expenses of payment

b. Liabilities other than for and in respect of members

c. Estimated cost of winding-up

Total

Assets

Funding level in accordance with section 143 of the %
Pensions Act 2004

I certify the protected liabilities (a) and (c) have been determined in accordance with the provisions of the Pensions Act 2004 and its relevant regulations and the Pension Protection Fund guidance for professionals #1, version _____

The value of the assets and protected liabilities (b) have been provided by

_____

In my opinion appropriate action/insufficient action* has been taken to ensure that as far as practical all potential scheme beneficiaries have been identified. The formal report on the actuarial valuation includes a description of the action taken and details my residual concerns where appropriate.

*delete as appropriate

A copy of the formal report on the actuarial valuation for the purposes of section 143 of the Pensions Act 2004 is attached.

Signature .... Date ....

Name ....

Qualification ....

Employer...

A1.8: Guidance from the PPF for undertaking the risk-based levy valuation

Part 1 – Overview

1.1 Introduction

1.1.1 To calculate the risk based pension protection levy the Pension Protection Fund Board must take account of scheme underfunding. To obtain a consistent basis for determining underfunding schemes will be required to complete a Pension Protection Fund valuation. This valuation will be based on the level of assets and liabilities for the scheme. The liabilities will be based on the scheme benefits taking into account key features of the levels of compensation paid by the Board of the Pension Protection Fund as set out in Schedule 7 of the Act.

1.1.2 All schemes will be charged an initial levy based on scheme factors only for the levy year commencing April 2005.

1.1.3 The risk based pension protection levy will apply from April 2006. Schemes submitting a Pension Protection Fund valuation prior to 31 March 2006 will be charged a levy based on risk using the information provided in the valuation. The purpose of the risk based levy is to reflect the differing levels of risk pension schemes pose to the fund.

1.2 Purpose of this guidance

1.2.1 This guidance is intended for actuaries undertaking valuations to determine the level of underfunding in accordance with section 179 of the Act. Such guidance was envisaged in paragraph (4) of section 179. The valuation results will be used to set and calculate the risk based pension protection levy in accordance with section 175.

1.2.2 The legislation and associated regulations relating to these valuations came into force on 6 April 2005.

1.3 Legislative requirements

1.3.1 Section 179 of the Act requires schemes to undertake a Pension Protection Fund valuation to establish the level of the scheme's assets and liabilities in order to set the risk based levy.

1.3.2 The associated regulations set out the high level principles concerning the way in which the valuation should be conducted with this guidance setting out the detailed assumptions and discount rates.

1.4 Why is this valuation necessary and when is it needed by?

1.4.1 The valuation will provide the Board of the Pension Protection Fund with information on the level of underfunding within a scheme. This will inform the calculation of the risk based pension protection levy.

1.4.2 Schemes have considerable discretion in choosing when to provide their first Pension Protection Fund valuation, but the:

- relevant time ('relevant time' for the purposes of section 179 of the Act, means the date in relation to which the assets and liabilities of the eligible scheme are calculated) of the valuation must be no earlier than 1 November 2004 and no later than 5 April 2008, but see paragraph 3.2 below; and
- valuation must be sent to the Pensions Regulator within a year of the relevant time.

.4.3   After the initial valuation, schemes must provide the Pensions Regulator with further valuations at regular intervals. The relevant time of each subsequent valuation must be no later than three years after the relevant time of the previous valuation and, again, the valuation must be sent to the Pensions Regulator within a year of the relevant time.

.4.4   This time scale allows for the valuation to be undertaken in line with a scheme's normal valuation cycle, however, any scheme may complete a Pension Protection Fund valuation at any time after April 2005. Once a Pension Protection Fund valuation is completed, the levies imposed on that scheme will reflect the risk factors – the level of risk that the scheme poses to the Pension Protection Fund.

.4.5   To pay a risk based levy based on the level of Pension Protection Fund liabilities for the levy year commencing 1 April 2006 schemes must complete and provide the relevant information relating to a section 179 valuation to the Board of the Pension Protection Fund by 31 March 2006.

.5 Frequency of valuations

.5.1   Schemes must undertake levy valuations in accordance with section 179 of the Act and associated regulations at least once every three years.

.5.2   Schemes wanting to provide a valuation on a more regular basis may do so. The most recent valuation information provided by 31 March each year will be used to calculate the risk based levy.

.6 Where to send valuation information

.6.1   Details relating to the levy valuation should be provided to the Pensions Regulator as part of the normal annual scheme return form process. Where the scheme return form has already been completed and returned to the Pensions Regulator, the valuation details should be provided on the form contained at Appendix 2, and forwarded to the Pension Protection Fund.

.6.2   For further details about the valuation process please go to the Pension Protection Fund website at:

www.pensionprotectionfund.org.uk

1.6.3   The contact address for the Pension Protection Fund is:

Pension Protection Fund
Knollys House Levels 8 & 9
17 Addiscombe Road
CROYDON CR0 6SR

Tel: 0845 600 2541

1.7 Legislation or authority for actuarial valuations

The Pensions Act 2004 (the Act) The Pension Protection Fund (Valuation Regulations) 2005

SI 2005/672 ('the valuation regulations')

The Pension Protection Fund (Partially Guaranteed Schemes)(Modification) Regulations 2005

SI 2005/277

The Pension Protection Fund (Pension Compensation Cap) Order 2005

SI2005/825 ('the Cap regulations')

The Occupational Pension Schemes (Modification of Pension Protection Provisions) Regulations 2005

SI 2005/705

The Occupational Pension Schemes (Levies) Regulations 2005

SI 2005/842

The Pension Protection Fund (Compensation) Regulations 2005

SI 2005/670

The Pension Protection Fund (Multi-employer Schemes)(Modification) Regulations 2005

SI2005/441

The Pension Protection Fund (Hybrid Schemes)(Modification) Regulations 2005

SI2005/449

Part 2 – Introduction

2.1   Under section 179 of the Act the trustees or managers of eligible schemes are required to provide the Board of the Pension Protection Fund with an actuarial valuation of the scheme at prescribed intervals and containing prescribed information.

2.2   An eligible scheme is defined by section 126 of the Act and associated regulations.

2.3   In this guidance, 'relevant time' has the meaning given in the valuation regulations as appropriate.

2.4   The actuarial valuation must be prepared and signed by a person meeting the criteria specified in section 179(2) of the Act and the valuation regulations.

2.5   The section 179 valuation is a simplified valuation based on the scheme's liabilities but taking into account certain key elements of the Pension Protection Fund compensation as set out in Schedule 7.

Part 3 – Protected liabilities

3.1   The scheme's protected liabilities are defined in section 131 of the Act. The amount of the protected liabilities relating to benefits for or in respect of members and to wind-up expenses shall be determined in accordance with section 179 of the Act, the valuation regulations and this guidance note.

3.2   The scheme actuary may use prudent approximations in calculating the protected liabilities. Such approximations may include using liability data from a previous valuation, including one carried out prior to 1 November 2004, and rolling forward those liabilities on a prudent basis to the relevant time.

3.3   The scheme actuary is required to certify in his report that, in his opinion, the calculated value of the protected liabilities is unlikely to have been understated.

Part 4 – Benefits for and in respect of members

4.1   The benefits for and in respect of members of the scheme should be valued as at the relevant time. For the purposes of this valuation the amount of the protected liabilities relating to benefits for or in respect of members and to wind-up expenses shall be determined as being the scheme benefits (reflecting the provisions of the

PPF Valuation Regulations which require scheme benefits, not PPF compensation, to be valued for a s179 valuation) but taking account of the following:

- applying the cap of the amount published in Pension Protection Fund guidance as currently appropriate at the normal pension age for the scheme to the benefits for those members under normal pension age and not in receipt of pension;
- applying the cap of the amount published in Pension Protection Fund guidance as currently appropriate for their age at the valuation date to the benefits for those members under normal pension age for the scheme and in receipt of pension (there is no requirement, for a section 179 valuation, to take account of the pension equivalent of any lump sum paid at retirement) ;
- reducing the benefits by 10% in respect of those members under normal pension age on a pro-rata basis, excluding ill health, survivors benefits, etc;
- disregarding any indexation applicable to pre 6 April 1997 service on a pro-rata basis;
- allowing for indexation up to RPI but capped at 2.5% on service from 6 April 1997.

4.2   In accordance with section 179(5) of the Act the value of liabilities should not be limited to the value of the assets, even where the scheme rules may so provide.

4.3   For section 179 valuation purposes, benefits for an active member should be calculated as though he had become a deferred pensioner immediately before the valuation date. In practice PPF compensation may be calculated slightly differently.

4.4   The pre-retirement decrements to be used to value benefits for non-pensioners are retirement at Normal Pension Age and death before Normal Pension Age.

4.5   For section 179 valuation purposes, Normal Pension Age for a scheme member should be assumed to be the same as MFR Pension Age. This is the age at which the member will first become entitled under the provisions of the scheme to receive a full pension on retirement of an amount determined without a reduction to take account of its payment before a later age (but disregarding any entitlement to pension on retirement in the event of illness, incapacity or redundancy). See Regulation 7(10) of the Occupational Pension Schemes (Minimum Funding Requirement and Actuarial Valuations) Regulations 1996.

Paragraphs 34(1) and 34(2) of Schedule 7 to the Pensions Act 2004 should not be applied.

There will therefore be one Normal Pension Age for each scheme member for section 179 valuation purposes. In practice PPF compensation may, of course, be payable in two or more tranches beginning at different ages, but this should be ignored for the purpose of a section 179 valuation.

4.6   It should be assumed that there is no commutation of pension at retirement for non-pensioners.

4.7   Where a scheme with more than one employer operates a sectionalised scheme, separate valuations will be required for each separate section of the scheme setting out the assets and benefits attributable to each section.

4.8   For schemes with a partial crown guarantee the valuation must only be of that part of the scheme that is not covered by a Crown guarantee.

4.9   For a hybrid "better of" scheme the assets and benefits will relate to only those members where the defined benefits exceed the defined contribution benefits at the relevant time.

4.10   The liability in respect of money-purchase benefits shall be disregarded for the purposes of determining the protected liabilities.

Part 5 – Assets

5.1   Assets must be taken into account as specified in the valuation regulations. The valuation regulations specify that for the purposes of determining a section 179 valuation the appropriate person shall adopt the value given of the assets of the scheme stated in the relevant accounts, less the amount of the external liabilities, and that value shall be taken to be the value of those assets at the relevant time.

5.2   The assets in respect of money-purchase benefits should not be included in the assets in accordance with section 179 (6) of the Act.

Part 6 – Data

6.1   The Pension Protection Fund regards it as best practice for trustees or managers to take appropriate action to ensure that, as far as is practicable, all potential scheme beneficiaries have been identified and that the associated membership data is correct. To the extent that there are residual uncertainties about the membership data, prudent approximations by the scheme actuary will be acceptable. This is an aspect of the prudent estimation of protected liabilities described in Part 3.

Part 7 – Valuation method

7.1   Any reasonable age definition may be used for the purpose of the calculation provided consistency with the revaluation and increase periods can be demonstrated.

7.2   For each scheme member the protected liability must be calculated as the present value of the accrued benefits using the assumptions specified in Appendix 1.

Part 8 – Expenses

8.1   Expenses must be determined as specified in Appendix 1.

Part 9 – Reporting

9.1   The scheme actuary's report on the section 179 valuation should be addressed and sent to the trustees. The certificate in Appendix 2 should form part of the scheme actuary's report. The results of the section 179 valuation should be included on the next annual scheme return form issued by the Pensions Regulator.

9.2   If the levy calculation in respect of a levy year commencing on 1 April in year (x) is to be based on the latest section 179 valuation results, then:
   • either these latest results must be incorporated into the annual scheme return sent to the Pensions Regulator in year (x-1)
   • or the certificate attached at Appendix 2 must be completed electronically on the Pension Protection Fund website (from the homepage go to the Guidance Section and follow the link to Valuation Guidance) and provided to the Board of the Pension Protection Fund by 31 March in year (x).

Part 10 – Review

10.1   This guidance note will be reviewed at least annually. It may also be reviewed and revised at more frequent intervals as the Board of the Pension Protection Fund deems appropriate.

Appendix 1: Basis for use when undertaking valuations

Version 2: effective in respect of valuation reports signed on or after 1 November 2005:

1 Yield in deferment

For each non-pensioner the liability for the period of deferment must be obtained by discounting the benefit at normal pension age at the adjusted net index-linked gilt yield shown below. As this yield implicitly allows for increases to normal pension age no allowance should be made for increases to benefits between the relevant date and normal pension age.

Adjusted net index-linked gilt yield = Yield A (i)– 0.5%

(i) Yield A should be determined daily as 50% of the sum of the FTSE Actuaries Government Securities Index-Linked annualised Real Yields over 15 years assuming:

a 5% inflation; and

b 0% inflation

For any dates where yields are not available the yields for the nearest preceding date should be used. Yields should be calculated to two places of decimals (e.g. 2.04% p.a.)

2 Yield in payment

For each pensioner and each non-pensioner for the period from which payments are assumed to commence the liability must be obtained by reference to the following (adjusted) yields:

Pensions with no increases in payment

Yield = Yield B (ii)

(ii) Yield B should be determined daily as the annualised yield on the FTSE Actuaries Government 10 year Fixed Interest Index.

For any dates where the yield is not available the yield for the nearest preceding date should be used. Yields should be calculated to two places of decimals (e.g. 4.76% p.a.)

Pensions increasing in payment

Adjusted yield = Yield C (iii) – 0.5%

(iii) Yield C should be determined daily as 50% of the sum of the FTSE Actuaries Government Securities Index-Linked annualised Real Yields over 5 years assuming

a 5% inflation; and

b 0% inflation

For any dates where yields are not available the yields for the nearest preceding date should be used. Yields should be calculated to two places of decimals (e.g.1.93% p.a.)

3 Mortality

The mortality tables to be used in respect of a member and the member's dependant shall be PMA92 (for males) and PFA92 (for females), as appropriate, in each case with the medium cohort mortality improvement rates. These mortality tables are published by the actuarial profession. For each individual, the set of mortality rates used shall be those applicable to that individual's year of birth.

4 Assumptions for contingent benefits

a) Proportions married

Where the scheme provides for survivor pensions:

For pensioners:

Where the scheme makes provision for survivor pensions for 'relevant partners' an assumption consistent with 90% (males) or 80% (females) at normal pension age. Where the scheme does not make provision for survivor pensions for 'relevant partners' other than legal spouses an assumption consistent with 80% (males) or 70% (females) at normal pension age.

For non-pensioners:

Where the scheme makes provision for survivor pensions for 'relevant partners' the assumption must be, at the assumed date of retirement or earlier death, 90% (males) or 80% (females).

Where the scheme does not make provision for survivor pensions for 'relevant partners' other than legal spouses the assumption must be, at the assumed date of retirement or earlier death, 80% (males) or 70% (females).

b) Age difference between member and dependant

Female assumed to be 3 years younger than male.

c) Children's pensions

No specific additional allowance to be included for prospective children's pensions. Children's pensions already in payment should be assumed to cease at age 18, or age 23 if currently aged over 17.

5 Expenses

a) Estimated wind-up expenses

3% of liabilities (excluding benefit installation / payment expenses) up to £50 million; plus
2% of liabilities (excluding benefit installation / payment expenses) between £50 million and £100 million; plus
1% of liabilities (excluding benefit installation / payment expenses) in excess of £100 million.

b) Benefit installation/payment expenses

Non-pensioners

An allowance of £500 per member should be made.

Pensioners

An age-related allowance per member should be made, according to the table below:

Age	Expense allowance per member (£)
< 60	450
60 – 70	400
70 – 80	300
80 +	250

Appendix 2: Section 179 Valuation Certificate

Section 179 Valuation Certificate

Pension
Protection
Fund

Scheme / Section Details

Full name of scheme

Pension Scheme Registration number

Does this scheme have sections or segregated parts? (see note below)   Yes ○   No ●

Name of section or segregated part of scheme

Section number (XXX)   of (XXX)

Address of scheme (or section, where appropriate)

Post code

Valuation Details (all figures in pounds, not thousands or millions)

Total assets .... £

Amount of external liabilities deducted to reach this figure .... £

Date of relevant accounts ....

Total protected liabilities, excluding external liabilities .... £

Liabilities for pensioners, excluding expenses .... £

Liabilities for all deferred pensioners, excluding expenses .... £

Liabilities for active members, excluding expenses .... £

Estimated costs of winding up (excluding the estimated expenses of benefit installation/payment) .... £

Estimated expenses of benefit installation/payment .... £

Effective date of this valuation

Version number of section 179 guidance used for this valuation   1

Certification

☐ I certify that this valuation has been carried out in accordance with the Pension Protection Fund (Valuation) Regulations 2005 and with the latest section 179 guidance issued by the Board of the Pension Protection Fund. I also certify that the calculated value of the protected liabilities (excluding the external liabilities) is, in my opinion, unlikely to have been understated.

Name   Qualification

Date   Employer

Note
As per regulation 8 of the Pension Protection Fund (Valuation) Regulations 2005, a separate valuation
and certificate should be prepared for each section or segregated part of a multi employer scheme.

A2   Legislation

A2.1:   Pensions Act 2004 ss.22-58; 120-181; 221-233

Powers in relation to winding up of occupational pension schemes

22   Powers to wind up occupational pension schemes

In section 11 of the Pensions Act 1995 (powers to wind up occupational pension schemes)-

(a) omit subsection (3),

(b) before subsection (4) insert-

"(3A) The Authority may, during an assessment period (within the meaning of section 132 of the Pensions Act 2004 (meaning of "assessment period" for the purposes of Part 2 of that Act)) in relation to an occupational pension scheme, by order direct the scheme to be wound up if they are satisfied that it is necessary to do so in order-

(a) to ensure that the scheme's protected liabilities do not exceed its assets, or

(b) if those liabilities do exceed its assets, to keep the excess to a minimum.

(3B) In subsection (3A)-

(a) "protected liabilities" has the meaning given by section 131 of the Pensions Act 2004, and

(b) references to the assets of the scheme are references to those assets excluding any assets representing the value of any rights in respect of money purchase benefits (within the meaning of that Act) under the scheme.",

(c) at the end of subsection (4) insert-

"This subsection is subject to sections 28, 135 and 219 of the Pensions Act 2004 (winding up order made when freezing order has effect in relation to scheme, during assessment period under Part 2 of that Act etc).", and

(d) after subsection (6) insert-

"(6A) Subsection (6) does not have effect to authorise the Authority to make an order as mentioned in paragraph (a) or (b) of that subsection, if their doing so would be unlawful as a result of section 6(1) of the Human Rights Act 1998 (unlawful for public authority to act in contravention of a Convention right)."

23   Freezing orders

(1) This section applies to an occupational pension scheme which is not a money purchase scheme.

(2) The Regulator may make a freezing order in relation to such a scheme if and only if-

(a) the order is made pending consideration being given to the making of an order in relation to the scheme under section 11(1)(c) of the Pensions Act 1995 (c. 26) (power to wind up schemes where necessary to protect the generality of members), and

(b) the Regulator is satisfied that-

(i) there is, or is likely to be if the order is not made, an immediate risk to the interests of members under the scheme or the assets of the scheme, and

(ii) it is necessary to make the freezing order to protect the interests of the generality of the members of the scheme.

But no freezing order may be made in relation to a scheme during an assessment period (within the meaning of section 132) in relation to the scheme (see section 135(11)).

(3) A freezing order is an order directing that during the period for which it has effect-

(a) no benefits are to accrue under the scheme rules to, or in respect of, members of the scheme, and

(b) winding up of the scheme may not begin.

(4) A freezing order may also contain one or more of the following directions which have effect during the period for which the order has effect-

(a) a direction that no new members, or no specified classes of new member, are to be admitted to the scheme;

(b) a direction that-

(i) no further contributions or payments, or

(ii) no further specified contributions or payments,

are to be paid towards the scheme by or on behalf of the employer, any members or any specified members of the scheme;

(c) a direction that any amount or any specified amount which-

(i) corresponds to any contribution which would be due to be paid towards the scheme on behalf of a member but for a direction under paragraph (b), and

(ii) has been deducted from a payment of any earnings in respect of an employment,

is to be repaid to the member in question by the employer;

(d) a direction that no benefits, or no specified benefits, are to be paid to or in respect of any members or any specified members under the scheme rules;

(e) a direction that payments of all benefits or specified benefits under the scheme rules to or in respect of all the members or specified members may only be made from the scheme if they are reduced in a specified manner or by a specified amount;

(f) a direction that-

(i) no transfers or no specified transfers of, or no transfer payments or no specified transfer payments in respect of, any member's rights under the scheme rules are to be made from the scheme, or

(ii) no other steps or no specified other steps are to be taken to discharge any liability of the scheme to or in respect of a member of the scheme in respect of pensions or other benefits;

(g) a direction that no statements of entitlement are to be provided to members of the scheme under section 93A of the Pension Schemes Act 1993 (c. 48) (salary related schemes: right to statement of entitlement);

(h) a direction that-

(i) no refunds of, or no specified refunds of, or in respect of, contributions paid by or in respect of a member towards the scheme are to be made from the scheme, or

(ii) refunds or specified refunds of, or in respect of, contributions paid by or in respect of a member towards the scheme may only be made from the scheme if they are determined in a specified manner and satisfy such other conditions as may be specified.

(5) In subsection (4)(b)-

(a) the references to contributions do not include contributions due to be paid before the order takes effect, and

(b) the references to payments towards a scheme include payments in respect of pension credits where the person entitled to the credit is a member of the scheme.

(6) A freezing order may not contain a direction under subsection (4)(d) or (e) which reduces the benefits payable to or in respect of a member, for the period during which the order has effect, below the level to which the trustees or managers of the scheme would have power to reduce them if a winding up of the scheme had begun at the time when the freezing order

ook effect.

7) A direction under subsection (4)(f) may, in particular, provide that transfers or specified transfers of, or transfer payments or specified transfer payments in respect of, any member's rights under the scheme rules may not be made from the scheme unless the amounts paid out from the scheme in respect of the transfers or transfer payments are determined in a specified manner and the transfer or transfer payments satisfy such other conditions as may be specified.

8) A freezing order may also require the trustees or managers of the scheme to obtain an actuarial valuation within a specified period.

9) A freezing order containing such a requirement must specify-

    (a) the date by reference to which the assets and liabilities are to be valued,

    (b) the assets and liabilities which are to be taken into account,

    (c) the manner in which the valuation must be prepared,

    (d) the information and statements which it must contain, and

    (e) any other requirements that the valuation must satisfy.

10) For the purposes of subsection (8)-

"an actuarial valuation" means a written valuation of the scheme's assets and liabilities prepared and signed by the actuary;

"the actuary" means-

    (a) the actuary appointed under section 47(1)(b) of the Pensions Act 1995 (c. 26) (professional advisers) in relation to the scheme, or

    (b) if no such actuary has been appointed-

        (i) a person with prescribed qualifications or experience, or

        (ii) a person approved by the Secretary of State.

11) In this section "specified" means specified in the freezing order.

24 Consequences of freezing order

1) If a freezing order is made in relation to a scheme any action taken in contravention of the order is void except to the extent that the action is validated by an order under section 26.

2) A freezing order in relation to a scheme does not prevent any increase in a benefit which is an increase which would otherwise accrue in accordance with the scheme or any enactment during the period for which the order has effect, unless the order contains a direction to the contrary.

3) A freezing order in relation to a scheme does not prevent the scheme being wound up in pursuance of an order under section 11 of the Pensions Act 1995 (power to wind up occupational pension schemes).

4) If a freezing order contains a direction under section 23(4)(b) that no further contributions, or no further specified contributions, are to be paid towards a scheme during the period for which the order has effect-

    (a) any contributions which are the subject of the direction and which would otherwise be due to be paid towards the scheme during that period are to be treated as if they do not fall due, and

    (b) any obligation to pay those contributions (including any obligation under section 49(8) of the Pensions Act 1995 to pay amounts deducted corresponding to such contributions) is to be treated as if it does not arise.

(5) If a freezing order contains a direction under section 23(4)(f) (no transfers or discharge of member's rights) it does not prevent-

(a) giving effect to a pension sharing order or provision, or

(b) giving effect to a pension earmarking order in a case where-

(i) the order requires a payment to be made if a payment in respect of any benefits under the scheme becomes due to a person, and

(ii) a direction under section 23(4)(d) or (e) does not prevent the payment becoming due.

(6) For the purposes of subsection (5)-

"pension sharing order or provision" means an order or provision falling within section 28(1) of the Welfare Reform and Pensions Act 1999 (c. 30) (activation of pension sharing);

"pension earmarking order" means-

(a) an order under section 23 of the Matrimonial Causes Act 1973 (c. 18) (financial provision orders in connection with divorce etc) so far as it includes provision made by virtue of section 25B or 25C of that Act (powers to include provision about pensions),

(b) an order under section 12A(2) or (3) of the Family Law (Scotland) Act 1985 (c. 37) (powers in relation to pension lump sums when making a capital sum order), or

(c) an order under Article 25 of the Matrimonial Causes (Northern Ireland) Order 1978 (S.I. 1978/1045 (N.I.15)) so far as it includes provision made by virtue of Article 27B or 27C of that Order (Northern Ireland powers corresponding to those mentioned in paragraph (a)).

(7) Regulations may modify any provisions of-

(a) Chapter 4 of Part 4 of the Pension Schemes Act 1993 (c. 48) (protection for early leavers: transfer values), or

(b) Chapter 5 of that Part (protection for early leavers: cash transfer sums and contribution refunds),

in their application to an occupational pension scheme in relation to which a freezing order is made containing a direction under section 23(4)(f), (g) or (h) (no transfers etc in respect of member's rights or refunds of contributions etc from the scheme).

(8) Disregarding subsection (1), if a freezing order made in relation to a scheme is not complied with, section 10 of the Pensions Act 1995 (c. 26) (civil penalties) applies to any trustee or manager of the scheme who has failed to take all reasonable steps to secure compliance.

(9) Subsection (8) does not apply in the case of non-compliance with a direction under section 23(4)(c) (direction that certain deducted contributions are to be repaid by the employer).

(10) In such a case, section 10 of the Pensions Act 1995 (civil penalties) applies to an employer who, without reasonable excuse, fails to repay an amount as required by the direction.

25 Period of effect etc of freezing order

(1) A freezing order must specify the period for which it has effect.

(2) The period specified must not exceed three months.

(3) The Regulator may on one or more occasions by order extend the period for which the order has effect.

(4) But the total period for which the order has effect must not exceed six months.

5) This section is subject to sections 27, 28 and 29 (effect of winding up and assessment period on freezing orders).

6 Validation of action in contravention of freezing order

1) If a freezing order is made in relation to a scheme, the Regulator may by order validate action taken in contravention of the order.

2) Any of the following persons may apply to the Regulator for an order under this section validating particular action-

(a) the trustees or managers of the scheme;

(b) any person directly affected by the action.

7 Effect of determination to wind up scheme on freezing order

1) This section applies where-

(a) the Regulator determines to make an order under section 11 of the Pensions Act 1995 (c. 26) (power to wind up occupational pension schemes) in relation to a scheme ("a winding up order"),

(b) that determination is made during the period for which a freezing order has effect in relation to the scheme,

(c) the case is not one to which the special procedure in section 98 applies (immediate exercise of powers where immediate risk to assets etc), and

(d) the winding up order accordingly cannot be made until the expiry of the period specified in section 96(5) (no exercise during period of referral to the Tribunal etc).

2) In such a case the freezing order is to continue to have effect until-

(a) where the winding up order is made, it ceases to have effect under section 28 from the time when that order is made, or

(b) the determination to make the winding up order is revoked.

3) Subsection (2) is subject to the Regulator's power under section 101 to revoke the freezing order at any time.

8 Effect of winding up order on freezing order

1) This section applies where-

(a) an order is made under section 11 of the Pensions Act 1995 ("the 1995 Act") (power to wind up occupational pension schemes) in relation to a scheme, and

(b) the order is made during the period for which a freezing order has effect in relation to the scheme.

(2) In such a case-

(a) the winding up of the scheme in pursuance of the order under section 11 of the 1995 Act is to be taken as beginning at the time when the freezing order took effect, and

(b) the freezing order ceases to have effect from the time when the order under section 11 of the 1995 Act is made.

(3) The Regulator may by order direct any specified person-

(a) to take such specified steps as it considers are necessary as a result of the winding up of the scheme being deemed under subsection (2)(a) to have begun at the time when the freezing order took effect, and

(b) to take those steps within a specified period.

4) If the trustees or managers of a scheme fail to comply with a direction to them contained in an order under this section, section 10 of the 1995 Act (civil penalties) applies to any trustee or manager who has failed to take all reasonable steps to secure compliance.

(5) That section also applies to any other person who, without reasonable excuse, fails to comply with a direction to him contained in an order under this section.

(6) In this section "specified" means specified in an order under this section.

29 Effect of assessment period under Part 2 on freezing order

Where an assessment period (within the meaning of section 132) begins in relation to a scheme, any freezing order in relation to the scheme ceases to have effect when the assessment period begins.

30 Power to give a direction where freezing order ceases to have effect

(1) This section applies where-

(a) the Regulator revokes a freezing order in relation to a scheme or it otherwise ceases to have effect, and

(b) at the time when the freezing order ceases to have effect, the Regulator has not made an order under section 11 of the Pensions Act 1995 (c. 26) ("the 1995 Act") in relation to the scheme.

(2) In such a case the Regulator may make an order under this section in relation to the scheme containing a direction that, if specified conditions are met, specified benefits are to accrue under the scheme rules to, or in respect of, specified members of the scheme in respect of specified periods of service being service in employment which but for the freezing order would have qualified the member in question for those benefits under the scheme rules.

(3) The conditions mentioned in subsection (2) may include-

(a) a requirement that specified benefits do not accrue to, or in respect of, a member or a specified member unless a contribution of a specified amount is paid by or on behalf of the member towards the scheme within a specified period;

(b) a requirement that a contribution of a specified amount must be paid by or on behalf of the employer within a specified period;

(c) a requirement that such contributions as are specified under paragraph (a) or (b) are to be accepted for the period for which the freezing order had effect or any part of that period.

(4) Where the freezing order contained a direction under section 23(4)(d) or (e) and any amount of any benefit under the scheme rules was not paid as a result of the direction-

(a) the direction does not affect any entitlement to that benefit, and

(b) any benefit to which a member, or a person in respect of a member, remains entitled at the end of the period for which the freezing order had effect is an amount which falls due to the member or, as the case may be, the person at the end of that period.

(5) If an order made under this section in relation to a scheme is not complied with, section 10 of the 1995 Act (civil penalties) applies to a trustee or a manager of the scheme who has failed to take all reasonable steps to secure compliance.

(6) Subsection (7) applies if-

(a) an order is made under this section in relation to a scheme,

(b) the order contains a requirement as described in subsection (3)(b) that a contribution of a specified amount must be paid by or on behalf of the employer within a specified period, and

(c) the contribution is not paid within that period.

(7) In such a case-

(a) section 10 of the 1995 Act applies to the employer if he has failed, without reasonable excuse, to secure compliance,

(b) the amount which for the time being remains unpaid after the end of the specified period is to be treated as a debt due from the employer to the trustees or managers of the scheme, and

(c) except in prescribed circumstances, the trustees or managers must, within a prescribed period, give notice of the failure to pay to the Regulator and to the member.

(8) If in any case subsection (7)(c) is not complied with, section 10 of the 1995 Act applies to any trustee or manager who has failed to take all reasonable steps to secure compliance.

(9) In this section "specified" means specified in an order under this section.

31 Notification of trustees, managers, employers and members

(1) This section applies where-

(a) a freezing order is made in relation to a scheme,

(b) an order is made under section 26 validating action taken in contravention of a freezing order made in relation to a scheme,

(c) an order is made under section 28 directing specified steps to be taken following the winding up of a scheme, or

(d) an order is made under section 30 in relation to a scheme where a freezing order ceases to have effect.

(2) The Regulator must, as soon as reasonably practicable after the order has been made, notify-

(a) the trustees or managers of the scheme, and

(b) the employer in relation to the scheme,

of the fact that the order has been made and of its effect.

(3) The Regulator may by order direct the trustees or managers of the scheme to notify-

(a) all the members of the scheme, or

(b) the members of the scheme specified in the order,

of the fact that the order mentioned in subsection (1) has been made and of its effect.

(4) Notification is to be within the period and in the manner specified in the order under subsection (3).

(5) If the trustees or managers of a scheme fail to comply with a direction to them contained in an order made under subsection (3), section 10 of the Pensions Act 1995 (c. 26) (civil penalties) applies to any trustee or manager who has failed to take all reasonable steps to secure compliance.

32 Sections 23 to 31: supplementary

(1) An order may be made in relation to a scheme under any of sections 23, 25, 26, 28, 30 and 31-

(a) in spite of any enactment or rule of law, or any rule of the scheme, which would otherwise operate to prevent the order being made, and

(b) without regard to any such enactment, rule of law or rule of the scheme as would otherwise require, or might otherwise be taken to require, the implementation of any procedure or the obtaining of any consent, with a view to the making of the order.

(2) Subsection (1) does not have effect to authorise the Regulator to make an order as mentioned in that subsection if its doing so would be unlawful as a result of section 6(1) of the Human Rights Act 1998 (c. 42) (unlawful for public authority to act in contravention of a

Convention right).

Trustees of occupational pension schemes

33   Prohibition orders

For section 3 of the Pensions Act 1995 (c. 26) (prohibition orders) substitute-

"3   Prohibition orders

(1) The Authority may by order prohibit a person from being a trustee of-

(a) a particular trust scheme,

(b) a particular description of trust schemes, or

(c) trust schemes in general,

if they are satisfied that he is not a fit and proper person to be a trustee of the scheme or schemes to which the order relates.

(2) Where a prohibition order is made under subsection (1) against a person in respect of one or more schemes of which he is a trustee, the order has the effect of removing him.

(3) The Authority may, on the application of any person prohibited under this section, by order revoke the order either generally or in relation to a particular scheme or description of schemes.

(4) An application under subsection (3) may not be made-

(a) during the period within which the determination to exercise the power to make the prohibition order may be referred to the Tribunal under section 96(3) or 99(7) of the Pensions Act 2004, and

(b) if the determination is so referred, until the reference, and any appeal against the Tribunal's determination, has been finally disposed of.

(5) A revocation made at any time under this section cannot affect anything done before that time.

(6) The Authority must prepare and publish a statement of the policies they intend to adopt in relation to the exercise of their powers under this section.

(7) The Authority may revise any statement published under subsection (6) and must publish any revised statement.

(8) In this section "the Tribunal" means the Pensions Regulator Tribunal established under section 102 of the Pensions Act 2004."

34 Suspension orders

In section 4 of the Pensions Act 1995 (c. 26) (suspension orders)-

(a) after subsection (1)(a) insert-

"(aa) pending consideration being given to the institution of proceedings against him for an offence involving dishonesty or deception,",

(b) in subsection (2)-

(i) in paragraph (a) after "paragraph (a)" insert "or (aa)",

(ii) after "have effect" insert "in relation to a trust scheme", and

(iii) after "section 3(1)" insert "in relation to that scheme",

(c) after subsection (5) insert-

"(5A) An application under subsection (5) may not be made-

(a) during the period within which the determination to exercise the power to make an order under subsection (1) may be referred to the Tribunal under section 96(3) or 99(7) of the Pensions Act 2004, and

(b) if the determination is so referred, until the reference, and any appeal against the Tribunal's determination, has been finally disposed of.", and

(d) after subsection (6) insert-

"(7) In this section "the Tribunal" means the Pensions Regulator Tribunal established under section 102 of the Pensions Act 2004."

35 Appointments of trustees by the Regulator

(1) In section 7 of the Pensions Act 1995 (appointment of trustees)-

(a) omit subsection (4), and

(b) after subsection (5) insert-

"(5A) An application may be made to the Authority in relation to a trust scheme by-

(a) the trustees of the scheme,

(b) the employer, or

(c) any member of the scheme,

for the appointment of a trustee of the scheme under subsection (3)(a) or (c)."

(2) In section 8 of that Act (consequences of appointment of trustees under section 7), for subsections (1) and (2) substitute-

"(1) An order under section 7 appointing a trustee may provide for any fees and expenses of trustees appointed under the order to be paid-

(a) by the employer,

(b) out of the resources of the scheme, or

(c) partly by the employer and partly out of those resources.

(2) Such an order may also provide that an amount equal to the amount (if any) paid out of the resources of the scheme by virtue of subsection (1)(b) or (c) is to be treated for all purposes as a debt due from the employer to the trustees of the scheme."

36 Independent trustees

(1) Part 1 of the Pensions Act 1995 (c. 26) (occupational pension schemes) is amended as follows.

(2) In section 22 (circumstances in which provisions relating to independent trustees apply)-

(a) in subsection (1)(b) omit "or" at the end of sub-paragraph (i) and after that sub-paragraph insert-

"(ia) the interim receiver of the property of a person who is the employer in relation to the scheme, or",

(b) in subsection (2), after "a scheme" insert "by virtue of subsection (1)",

(c) after subsection (2) insert-

"(2A) To the extent that it does not already apply by virtue of subsection (1), this section also applies in relation to a trust scheme-

(a) at any time during an assessment period (within the meaning of section 132 of the Pensions Act 2004) in relation to the scheme, and

(b) at any time, not within paragraph (a), when the scheme is authorised under section 153 of that Act (closed schemes) to continue as a closed scheme.", and

(d) after subsection (2A) (inserted by paragraph (c) above) insert-

"(2B) The responsible person must, as soon as reasonably practicable, give notice of an event within subsection (2C) to-

(a) the Authority,

(b) the Board of the Pension Protection Fund, and

(c) the trustees of the scheme.

(2C) The events are-

(a) the practitioner beginning to act as mentioned in subsection (1)(a), if immediately before he does so this section does not apply in relation to the scheme;

(b) the practitioner ceasing to so act, if immediately after he does so this section does not apply in relation to the scheme;

(c) the official receiver beginning to act in a capacity mentioned in subsection (1)(b)(i), (ia) or (ii), if immediately before he does so this section does not apply in relation to the scheme;

(d) the official receiver ceasing to act in such a capacity, if immediately after he does so this section does not apply in relation to the scheme.

(2D) For the purposes of subsection (2B) "the responsible person" means-

(a) in the case of an event within subsection (2C)(a) or (b) the practitioner, and

(b) in the case of an event within subsection (2C)(c) or (d), the official receiver.

(2E) Regulations may require prescribed persons in prescribed circumstances where this section begins or ceases to apply in relation to a trust scheme by virtue of subsection (2A) to give a notice to that effect to-

(a) the Authority,

(b) the Board of the Pension Protection Fund, and

(c) the trustees of the scheme.

(2F) A notice under subsection (2B), or regulations under subsection (2E), must be in writing and contain such information as may be prescribed."

(3) For sections 23 and 24 (appointment of independent trustees) substitute-

"23 Power to appoint independent trustees

(1) While section 22 applies in relation to a trust scheme, the Authority may by order appoint as a trustee of the scheme a person who-

(a) is an independent person in relation to the scheme, and

(b) is registered in the register maintained by the Authority in accordance with regulations under subsection (4).

(2) In relation to a particular trust scheme, no more than one trustee may at any time be an independent trustee appointed under subsection (1).

(3) For the purposes of this section a person is independent in relation to a trust scheme only if-

(a) he has no interest in the assets of the employer or of the scheme otherwise than as trustee of the scheme,

(b) he is neither connected with, nor an associate of-

(i) the employer,

(ii) any person for the time being acting as an insolvency practitioner in relation to the employer, or

(iii) the official receiver acting in any of the capacities mentioned in section 22(1)(b) in relation to the employer, and

(c) he satisfies any prescribed requirements;

and any reference in this Part to an independent trustee is to be construed accordingly.

(4) Regulations must provide for the Authority to compile and maintain a register of persons who satisfy the prescribed conditions for registration.

(5) Regulations under subsection (4) may provide-

(a) for copies of the register or of extracts from it to be provided to prescribed persons in prescribed circumstances;

(b) for the inspection of the register by prescribed persons in prescribed circumstances.

(6) The circumstances which may be prescribed under subsection (5)(a) or (b) include the payment by the person to whom the copy is to be provided, or by whom the register is to be inspected, of such reasonable fee as may be determined by the Authority.

(7) This section is without prejudice to the powers conferred by section 7."

(4) In section 25 (appointment and powers of independent trustees: further provisions)-

(a) for subsection (4)(a) substitute-

"(a) he must as soon as reasonably practicable give written notice of that fact to the Authority, and",

(b) after subsection (5) insert-

"(5A) Section 10 applies to any person who, without reasonable excuse, fails to comply with subsection (4)(a).", and

(c) for subsection (6) substitute-

"(6) An order under section 23(1) may provide for any fees and expenses of the trustee appointed under the order to be paid-

(a) by the employer,

(b) out of the resources of the scheme, or

(c) partly by the employer and partly out of those resources.

(7) Such an order may also provide that an amount equal to the amount (if any) paid out of the resources of the scheme by virtue of subsection (6)(b) or (c) is to be treated for all purposes as a debt due from the employer to the trustees of the scheme.

(8) Where, by virtue of subsection (6)(b) or (c), an order makes provision for any fees or expenses of the trustee appointed under the order to be paid out of the resources of the scheme, the trustee is entitled to be so paid in priority to all other claims falling to be met out of the scheme's resources."

37 Disqualification

In section 30 of the Pensions Act 1995 (c. 26) (consequences of disqualification under section 29), for subsection (1) substitute-

"(1) Where a person who is a trustee of a trust scheme becomes disqualified under section 29 in relation to the scheme, his becoming so disqualified has the effect of removing him as a trustee."

Contribution notices where avoidance of employer debt

38 Contribution notices where avoidance of employer debt

(1) This section applies in relation to an occupational pension scheme other than-

(a) a money purchase scheme, or

(b) a prescribed scheme or a scheme of a prescribed description.

(2) The Regulator may issue a notice to a person stating that the person is under a liability to pay the sum specified in the notice (a "contribution notice")-

(a) to the trustees or managers of the scheme, or

(b) where the Board of the Pension Protection Fund has assumed responsibility for the scheme in accordance with Chapter 3 of Part 2 (pension protection), to the Board.

(3) The Regulator may issue a contribution notice to a person only if-

(a) the Regulator is of the opinion that the person was a party to an act or a deliberate failure to act which falls within subsection (5),

(b) the person was at any time in the relevant period-

(i) the employer in relation to the scheme, or

(ii) a person connected with, or an associate of, the employer,

(c) the Regulator is of the opinion that the person, in being a party to the act or failure, was not acting in accordance with his functions as an insolvency practitioner in relation to another person, and

(d) the Regulator is of the opinion that it is reasonable to impose liability on the person to pay the sum specified in the notice.

(4) But the Regulator may not issue a contribution notice, in such circumstances as may be prescribed, to a person of a prescribed description.

(5) An act or a failure to act falls within this subsection if-

(a) the Regulator is of the opinion that the main purpose or one of the main purposes of the act or failure was-

(i) to prevent the recovery of the whole or any part of a debt which was, or might become, due from the employer in relation to the scheme under section 75 of the Pensions Act 1995 (c. 26) (deficiencies in the scheme assets), or

(ii) otherwise than in good faith, to prevent such a debt becoming due, to compromise or otherwise settle such a debt, or to reduce the amount of such a debt which would otherwise become due,

(b) it is an act which occurred, or a failure to act which first occurred-

(i) on or after 27th April 2004, and

(ii) before any assumption of responsibility for the scheme by the Board in accordance with Chapter 3 of Part 2, and

(c) it is either-

(i) an act which occurred during the period of six years ending with the determination by the Regulator to exercise the power to issue the contribution notice in question, or

(ii) a failure which first occurred during, or continued for the whole or part of, that period.

(6) For the purposes of subsection (3)-

(a) the parties to an act or a deliberate failure include those persons who knowingly assist in the act or failure, and

(b) "the relevant period" means the period which-

(i) begins with the time when the act falling within subsection (5) occurs or the failure to act falling within that subsection first occurs, and

(ii) ends with the determination by the Regulator to exercise the power to issue the contribution notice in question.

(7) The Regulator, when deciding for the purposes of subsection (3)(d) whether it is reasonable to impose liability on a particular person to pay the sum specified in the notice, must have regard to such matters as the Regulator considers relevant including, where relevant, the following matters-

(a) the degree of involvement of the person in the act or failure to act which falls within subsection (5),

(b) the relationship which the person has or has had with the employer (including, where the employer is a company within the meaning of subsection (11) of section 435 of the Insolvency Act 1986 (c. 45), whether the person has or has had control of the employer within the meaning of subsection (10) of that section),

(c) any connection or involvement which the person has or has had with the scheme,

(d) if the act or failure to act was a notifiable event for the purposes of section 69 (duty to notify the Regulator of certain events), any failure by the person to comply with any obligation imposed on the person by subsection (1) of that section to give the Regulator notice of the event,

(e) all the purposes of the act or failure to act (including whether a purpose of the act or failure was to prevent or limit loss of employment),

(f) the financial circumstances of the person, and

(g) such other matters as may be prescribed.

(8) For the purposes of this section references to a debt due under section 75 of the Pensions Act 1995 (c. 26) include a contingent debt under that section.

(9) Accordingly, in the case of such a contingent debt, the reference in subsection (5)(a)(ii) to preventing a debt becoming due is to be read as including a reference to preventing the occurrence of any of the events specified in section 75(4C)(a) or (b) of that Act upon which the debt is contingent.

(10) For the purposes of this section-

(a) section 249 of the Insolvency Act 1986 (connected persons) applies as it applies for the purposes of any provision of the first Group of Parts of that Act,

(b) section 435 of that Act (associated persons) applies as it applies for the purposes of that Act, and

(c) section 74 of the Bankruptcy (Scotland) Act 1985 (c. 66) (associated persons) applies as it applies for the purposes of that Act.

(11) For the purposes of this section "insolvency practitioner", in relation to a person, means-

(a) a person acting as an insolvency practitioner, in relation to that person, in accordance with section 388 of the Insolvency Act 1986, or

(b) an insolvency practitioner within the meaning of section 121(9)(b) (persons of a prescribed description).

39   The sum specified in a section 38 contribution notice

(1) The sum specified by the Regulator in a contribution notice under section 38 may be either the whole or a specified part of the shortfall sum in relation to the scheme.

(2) Subject to subsection (3), the shortfall sum in relation to a scheme is-

(a) in a case where, at the relevant time, a debt was due from the employer to the trustees or managers of the scheme under section 75 of the Pensions Act 1995 (c. 26) ("the 1995 Act") (deficiencies in the scheme assets), the amount which the Regulator estimates to be the amount of that debt at that time, and

b) in a case where, at the relevant time, no such debt was due, the amount which the Regulator estimates to be the amount of the debt under section 75 of the 1995 Act which would become due if-

(i) subsection (2) of that section applied, and

(ii) the time designated by the trustees or managers of the scheme for the purposes of that subsection were the relevant time.

(3) Where the Regulator is satisfied that the act or failure to act falling within section 38(5) resulted-

(a) in a case falling within paragraph (a) of subsection (2), in the amount of the debt which became due under section 75 of the 1995 Act being less than it would otherwise have been, or

(b) in a case falling within paragraph (b) of subsection (2), in the amount of any such debt calculated for the purposes of that paragraph being less than it would otherwise have been,

the Regulator may increase the amounts calculated under subsection (2)(a) or (b) by such amount as the Regulator considers appropriate.

(4) For the purposes of this section "the relevant time" means-

(a) in the case of an act falling within subsection (5) of section 38, the time of the act, or

(b) in the case of a failure to act falling within that subsection-

(i) the time when the failure occurred, or

(ii) where the failure continued for a period of time, the time which the Regulator determines and which falls within that period.

(5) For the purposes of this section-

(a) references to a debt due under section 75 of the 1995 Act include a contingent debt under that section, and

(b) references to the amount of such a debt include the amount of such a contingent debt.

40   Content and effect of a section 38 contribution notice

(1) This section applies where a contribution notice is issued to a person under section 38.

(2) The contribution notice must-

(a) contain a statement of the matters which it is asserted constitute the act or failure to act which falls within subsection (5) of section 38,

(b) specify the sum which the person is stated to be under a liability to pay, and

(c) identify any other persons to whom contribution notices have been or are issued as a result of the act or failure to act in question and the sums specified in each of those notices.

(3) Where the contribution notice states that the person is under a liability to pay the sum specified in the notice to the trustees or managers of the scheme, the sum is to be treated as a debt due from the person to the trustees or managers of the scheme.

(4) In such a case, the Regulator may, on behalf of the trustees or managers of the scheme, exercise such powers as the trustees or managers have to recover the debt.

(5) But during any assessment period (within the meaning of section 132) in relation to the scheme, the rights and powers of the trustees or managers of the scheme in relation to any debt due to them by virtue of a contribution notice are exercisable by the Board of the Pension Protection Fund to the exclusion of the trustees or managers and the Regulator.

(6) Where, by virtue of subsection (5), any amount is paid to the Board in respect of a debt due by virtue of a contribution notice, the Board must pay the amount to the trustees or managers of the scheme.

(7) Where the contribution notice states that the person is under a liability to pay the sum specified in the notice to the Board, the sum is to be treated as a debt due from the person to the Board.

(8) Where the contribution notice so specifies, the person to whom the notice is issued ("P")

is to be treated as jointly and severally liable for the debt with any persons specified in the notice who are persons to whom corresponding contribution notices are issued.

(9) For the purposes of subsection (8), a corresponding contribution notice is a notice which-

(a) is issued as a result of the same act or failure to act falling within subsection (5) of section 38 as the act or failure as a result of which P's contribution notice is issued,

(b) specifies the same sum as is specified in P's contribution notice, and

(c) specifies that the person to whom the contribution notice is issued is jointly and severally liable with P, or with P and other persons, for the debt in respect of that sum.

(10) A debt due by virtue of a contribution notice is not to be taken into account for the purposes of section 75(2) and (4) of the Pensions Act 1995 (c. 26) (deficiencies in the scheme assets) when ascertaining the amount or value of the assets or liabilities of a scheme.

41 Section 38 contribution notice: relationship with employer debt

(1) This section applies where a contribution notice is issued to a person ("P") under section 38 and condition A or B is met.

(2) Condition A is met if, at the time at which the contribution notice is issued, there is a debt due under section 75 of the Pensions Act 1995 ("the 1995 Act") (deficiencies in the scheme assets) from the employer-

(a) to the trustees or managers of the scheme, or

(b) where the Board of the Pension Protection Fund has assumed responsibility for the scheme in accordance with Chapter 3 of Part 2 (pension protection), to the Board.

(3) Condition B is met if, after the contribution notice is issued but before the whole of the debt due by virtue of the notice is recovered, a debt becomes due from the employer to the trustees or managers of the scheme under section 75 of the 1995 Act.

(4) The Regulator may issue a direction to the trustees or managers of the scheme not to take any or any further steps to recover the debt due to them under section 75 of the 1995 Act pending the recovery of all or a specified part of the debt due to them by virtue of the contribution notice.

(5) If the trustees or managers fail to comply with a direction issued to them under subsection (4), section 10 of the 1995 Act (civil penalties) applies to any trustee or manager who has failed to take all reasonable steps to secure compliance.

(6) Any sums paid-

(a) to the trustees or managers of the scheme in respect of any debt due to them by virtue of the contribution notice, or

(b) to the Board in respect of any debt due to it by virtue of the contribution notice, are to be treated as reducing the amount of the debt due to the trustees or managers or, as the case may be, to the Board under section 75 of the 1995 Act.

(7) Where a sum is paid to the trustees or managers of the scheme or, as the case may be, to the Board in respect of the debt due under section 75 of the 1995 Act, P may make an application under this subsection to the Regulator for a reduction in the amount of the sum specified in P's contribution notice.

(8) An application under subsection (7) must be made as soon as reasonably practicable after the sum is paid to the trustees or managers or, as the case may be, to the Board in respect of the debt due under section 75 of the 1995 Act.

(9) Where such an application is made to the Regulator, the Regulator may, if it is of the opinion that it is appropriate to do so-

(a) reduce the amount of the sum specified in P's contribution notice by an amount which it considers reasonable, and

(b) issue a revised contribution notice specifying the revised sum.

(10) For the purposes of subsection (9), the Regulator must have regard to such matters as the Regulator considers relevant including, where relevant, the following matters-

(a) the amount paid in respect of the debt due under section 75 of the 1995 Act since the contribution notice was issued,

(b) any amounts paid in respect of the debt due by virtue of that contribution notice,

(c) whether contribution notices have been issued to other persons as a result of the same act or failure to act falling within subsection (5) of section 38 as the act or failure as a result of which P's contribution notice was issued,

(d) where such contribution notices have been issued, the sums specified in each of those notices and any amounts paid in respect of the debt due by virtue of those notices,

(e) whether P's contribution notice specifies that P is jointly and severally liable for the debt with other persons, and

(f) such other matters as may be prescribed.

(11) Where-

(a) P's contribution notice specifies that P is jointly and severally liable for the debt with other persons, and

(b) a revised contribution notice is issued to P under subsection (9) specifying a revised sum,

the Regulator must also issue revised contribution notices to those other persons specifying the revised sum and their joint and several liability with P for the debt in respect of that sum.

(12) For the purposes of this section-

(a) references to a debt due under section 75 of the 1995 Act include a contingent debt under that section, and

(b) references to the amount of such a debt include the amount of such a contingent debt.

42 Section 38 contribution notice: clearance statements

(1) An application may be made to the Regulator under this section for the issue of a clearance statement within paragraph (a), (b) or (c) of subsection (2) in relation to circumstances described in the application.

(2) A clearance statement is a statement, made by the Regulator, that in its opinion in the circumstances described in the application-

(a) the applicant would not be, for the purposes of subsection (3)(a) of section 38, a party to an act or a deliberate failure to act falling within subsection (5)(a) of that section,

(b) it would not be reasonable to impose any liability on the applicant under a contribution notice issued under section 38, or

(c) such requirements of that section as may be prescribed would not be satisfied in relation to the applicant.

(3) Where an application is made under this section, the Regulator-

(a) may request further information from the applicant;

(b) may invite the applicant to amend the application to modify the circumstances described.

(4) Where an application is made under this section, the Regulator must as soon as reasonably practicable-

(a) determine whether to issue the clearance statement, and

(b) where it determines to do so, issue the statement.

(5) A clearance statement issued under this section binds the Regulator in relation to the exercise of the power to issue a contribution notice under section 38 to the applicant unless-

(a) the circumstances in relation to which the exercise of the power under that section arises are not the same as the circumstances described in the application, and

(b) the difference in those circumstances is material to the exercise of the power.

Financial support directions

43 Financial support directions

(1) This section applies in relation to an occupational pension scheme other than-

(a) a money purchase scheme, or

(b) a prescribed scheme or a scheme of a prescribed description.

(2) The Regulator may issue a financial support direction under this section in relation to such a scheme if the Regulator is of the opinion that the employer in relation to the scheme-

(a) is a service company, or

(b) is insufficiently resourced,

at a time determined by the Regulator which falls within subsection (9) ("the relevant time").

(3) A financial support direction in relation to a scheme is a direction which requires the person or persons to whom it is issued to secure-

(a) that financial support for the scheme is put in place within the period specified in the direction,

(b) that thereafter that financial support or other financial support remains in place while the scheme is in existence, and

(c) that the Regulator is notified in writing of prescribed events in respect of the financial support as soon as reasonably practicable after the event occurs.

(4) A financial support direction in relation to a scheme may be issued to one or more persons.

(5) But the Regulator may issue such a direction to a person only if-

(a) the person is at the relevant time a person falling within subsection (6), and

(b) the Regulator is of the opinion that it is reasonable to impose the requirements of the direction on that person.

(6) A person falls within this subsection if the person is-

(a) the employer in relation to the scheme,

(b) an individual who-

(i) is an associate of an individual who is the employer, but

(ii) is not an associate of that individual by reason only of being employed by him, or

(c) a person, other than an individual, who is connected with or an associate of the employer.

(7) The Regulator, when deciding for the purposes of subsection (5)(b) whether it is reasonable to impose the requirements of a financial support direction on a particular

person, must have regard to such matters as the Regulator considers relevant including, where relevant, the following matters-

(a) the relationship which the person has or has had with the employer (including, where the employer is a company within the meaning of subsection (11) of section 435 of the Insolvency Act 1986 (c. 45), whether the person has or has had control of the employer within the meaning of subsection (10) of that section),

(b) in the case of a person falling within subsection (6)(b) or (c), the value of any benefits received directly or indirectly by that person from the employer,

(c) any connection or involvement which the person has or has had with the scheme,

(d) the financial circumstances of the person, and

(e) such other matters as may be prescribed.

(8) A financial support direction must identify all the persons to whom the direction is issued.

(9) A time falls within this subsection if it is a time which falls within a prescribed period which ends with the determination by the Regulator to exercise the power to issue the financial support direction in question.

(10) For the purposes of subsection (3), a scheme is in existence until it is wound up.

(11) No duty to which a person is subject is to be regarded as contravened merely because of any information or opinion contained in a notice given by virtue of subsection (3)(c). This is subject to section 311 (protected items).

44 Meaning of "service company" and "insufficiently resourced"

(1) This section applies for the purposes of section 43 (financial support directions).

(2) An employer ("E") is a "service company" at the relevant time if-

(a) E is a company within the meaning given by section 735(1) of the Companies Act 1985 (c. 6),

(b) E is a member of a group of companies, and

(c) E's turnover, as shown in the latest available accounts for E prepared in accordance with section 226 of that Act, is solely or principally derived from amounts charged for the provision of the services of employees of E to other members of that group.

(3) The employer in relation to a scheme is insufficiently resourced at the relevant time if-

(a) at that time the value of the resources of the employer is less than the amount which is a prescribed percentage of the estimated section 75 debt in relation to the scheme, and

(b) there is at that time a person who falls within subsection (6)(b) or (c) of section 43 and the value at that time of that person's resources is not less than the amount which is the difference between-

(i) the value of the resources of the employer, and

(ii) the amount which is the prescribed percentage of the estimated section 75 debt.

(4) For the purposes of subsection (3)-

(a) what constitutes the resources of a person is to be determined in accordance with regulations, and

(b) the value of a person's resources is to be determined, calculated and verified in a prescribed manner.

(5) In this section the "estimated section 75 debt", in relation to a scheme, means the amount which the Regulator estimates to be the amount of the debt which would become due from

the employer to the trustees or managers of the scheme under section 75 of the Pensions Act 1995 (c. 26) (deficiencies in the scheme assets) if-

(a) subsection (2) of that section applied, and

(b) the time designated by the trustees or managers of the scheme for the purposes of that subsection were the relevant time.

(6) When calculating the estimated section 75 debt in relation to a scheme under subsection (5), the amount of any debt due at the relevant time from the employer under section 75 of the Pensions Act 1995 (c. 26) is to be disregarded.

(7) In this section "the relevant time" has the same meaning as in section 43.

45 Meaning of "financial support"

(1) For the purposes of section 43 (financial support directions), "financial support" for a scheme means one or more of the arrangements falling within subsection (2) the details of which are approved in a notice issued by the Regulator.

(2) The arrangements falling within this subsection are-

(a) an arrangement whereby, at any time when the employer is a member of a group of companies, all the members of the group are jointly and severally liable for the whole or part of the employer's pension liabilities in relation to the scheme;

(b) an arrangement whereby, at any time when the employer is a member of a group of companies, a company (within the meaning given in section 736 of the Companies Act 1985 (c. 6)) which meets prescribed requirements and is the holding company of the group is liable for the whole or part of the employer's pension liabilities in relation to the scheme;

(c) an arrangement which meets prescribed requirements and whereby additional financial resources are provided to the scheme;

(d) such other arrangements as may be prescribed.

(3) The Regulator may not issue a notice under subsection (1) approving the details of one or more arrangements falling within subsection (2) unless it is satisfied that the arrangement is, or the arrangements are, reasonable in the circumstances.

(4) In subsection (2), "the employer's pension liabilities" in relation to a scheme means-

(a) the liabilities for any amounts payable by or on behalf of the employer towards the scheme (whether on his own account or otherwise) in accordance with a schedule of contributions under section 227, and

(b) the liabilities for any debt which is or may become due to the trustees or managers of the scheme from the employer whether by virtue of section 75 of the Pensions Act 1995 (deficiencies in the scheme assets) or otherwise.

46 Financial support directions: clearance statements

(1) An application may be made to the Regulator under this section for the issue of a clearance statement within paragraph (a), (b) or (c) of subsection (2) in relation to circumstances described in the application and relating to an occupational pension scheme.

(2) A clearance statement is a statement, made by the Regulator, that in its opinion in the circumstances described in the application-

(a) the employer in relation to the scheme would not be a service company for the purposes of section 43,

(b) the employer in relation to the scheme would not be insufficiently resourced for the purposes of that section, or

(c) it would not be reasonable to impose the requirements of a financial support direction, in relation to the scheme, on the applicant.

(3) Where an application is made under this section, the Regulator-

(a) may request further information from the applicant;

(b) may invite the applicant to amend the application to modify the circumstances described.

(4) Where an application is made under this section, the Regulator must as soon as reasonably practicable-

(a) determine whether to issue the clearance statement, and

(b) where it determines to do so, issue the statement.

(5) A clearance statement issued under this section binds the Regulator in relation to the exercise of the power to issue a financial support direction under section 43 in relation to the scheme to the applicant unless-

(a) the circumstances in relation to which the exercise of the power under that section arises are not the same as the circumstances described in the application, and

(b) the difference in those circumstances is material to the exercise of the power.

47 Contribution notices where non-compliance with financial support direction

(1) This section applies where there is non-compliance with a financial support direction issued in relation to a scheme under section 43.

(2) The Regulator may issue a notice to any one or more of the persons to whom the direction was issued stating that the person is under a liability to pay to the trustees or managers of the scheme the sum specified in the notice (a "contribution notice").

(3) The Regulator may issue a contribution notice to a person only if the Regulator is of the opinion that it is reasonable to impose liability on the person to pay the sum specified in the notice.

(4) The Regulator, when deciding for the purposes of subsection (3) whether it is reasonable to impose liability on a particular person to pay the sum specified in the notice, must have regard to such matters as the Regulator considers relevant including, where relevant, the following matters-

(a) whether the person has taken reasonable steps to secure compliance with the financial support direction,

(b) the relationship which the person has or has had with the employer (including, where the employer is a company within the meaning of subsection (11) of section 435 of the Insolvency Act 1986 (c. 45), whether the person has or has had control of the employer within the meaning of subsection (10) of that section),

(c) in the case of a person to whom the financial support direction was issued as a person falling within section 43(6)(b) or (c), the value of any benefits received directly or indirectly by that person from the employer,

(d) the relationship which the person has or has had with the parties to any arrangements put in place in accordance with the direction (including, where any of those parties is a company within the meaning of subsection (11) of section 435 of the Insolvency Act 1986, whether the person has or has had control of that company within the meaning of subsection (10) of that section),

(e) any connection or involvement which the person has or has had with the scheme,

(f) the financial circumstances of the person, and

(g) such other matters as may be prescribed.

5) A contribution notice may not be issued under this section in respect of non-compliance with a financial support direction in relation to a scheme where the Board of the Pension Protection Fund has assumed responsibility for the scheme in accordance with Chapter 3 of Part 2 (pension protection).

8 The sum specified in a section 47 contribution notice

1) The sum specified by the Regulator in a contribution notice under section 47 may be either the whole or a specified part of the shortfall sum in relation to the scheme.

2) The shortfall sum in relation to a scheme is-

(a) in a case where, at the time of non-compliance, a debt was due from the employer to the trustees or managers of the scheme under section 75 of the Pensions Act 1995 (c. 26) ("the 1995 Act") (deficiencies in the scheme assets), the amount which the Regulator estimates to be the amount of that debt at that time, and

(b) in a case where, at the time of non-compliance, no such debt was due, the amount which the Regulator estimates to be the amount of the debt under section 75 of the 1995 Act which would become due if-

(i) subsection (2) of that section applied, and

(ii) the time designated by the trustees or managers of the scheme for the purposes of that subsection were the time of non-compliance.

3) For the purposes of this section "the time of non-compliance" means-

(a) in the case of non-compliance with paragraph (a) of subsection (3) of section 43 (financial support directions), the time immediately after the expiry of the period specified in the financial support direction for putting in place the financial support,

(b) in the case of non-compliance with paragraph (b) of that subsection, the time when financial support for the scheme ceased to be in place,

(c) in the case of non-compliance with paragraph (c) of that subsection, the time when the prescribed event occurred in relation to which there was the failure to notify the Regulator, or

(d) where more than one of paragraphs (a) to (c) above apply, whichever of the times specified in the applicable paragraphs the Regulator determines.

9 Content and effect of a section 47 contribution notice

1) This section applies where a contribution notice is issued to a person under section 47.

2) The contribution notice must-

(a) contain a statement of the matters which it is asserted constitute the non-compliance with the financial support direction in respect of which the notice is issued, and

(b) specify the sum which the person is stated to be under a liability to pay.

3) The sum specified in the notice is to be treated as a debt due from the person to the trustees or managers of the scheme.

4) The Regulator may, on behalf of the trustees or managers of the scheme, exercise such powers as the trustees or managers have to recover the debt.

5) But during any assessment period (within the meaning of section 132) in relation to the scheme, the rights and powers of the trustees or managers of the scheme in relation to any debt due to them by virtue of a contribution notice, are exercisable by the Board of the Pension Protection Fund to the exclusion of the trustees or managers and the Regulator.

6) Where, by virtue of subsection (5), any amount is paid to the Board in respect of a debt

due by virtue of a contribution notice, the Board must pay the amount to the trustees or managers of the scheme.

(7) The contribution notice must identify any other persons to whom contribution notices have been or are issued in respect of the non-compliance in question and the sums specified in each of those notices.

(8) Where the contribution notice so specifies, the person to whom the notice is issued ("P") is to be treated as jointly and severally liable for the debt with any persons specified in the notice who are persons to whom corresponding contribution notices are issued.

(9) For the purposes of subsection (8), a corresponding contribution notice is a notice which-

(a) is issued in respect of the same non-compliance with the financial support direction as the non-compliance in respect of which P's contribution notice is issued,

(b) specifies the same sum as is specified in P's contribution notice, and

(c) specifies that the person to whom the contribution notice is issued is jointly and severally liable with P, or with P and other persons, for the debt in respect of that sum.

(10) A debt due by virtue of a contribution notice is not to be taken into account for the purposes of section 75(2) and (4) of the Pensions Act 1995 (c. 26) (deficiencies in the scheme assets) when ascertaining the amount or value of the assets or liabilities of a scheme.

50 Section 47 contribution notice: relationship with employer debt

(1) This section applies where a contribution notice is issued to a person ("P") under section 47 and condition A or B is met.

(2) Condition A is met if, at the time at which the contribution notice is issued, there is a debt due from the employer to the trustees or managers of the scheme under section 75 of the Pensions Act 1995 ("the 1995 Act") (deficiencies in the scheme assets).

(3) Condition B is met if, after the contribution notice is issued but before the whole of the debt due by virtue of the notice is recovered, a debt becomes due from the employer to the trustees or managers of the scheme under section 75 of the 1995 Act.

(4) The Regulator may issue a direction to the trustees or managers of the scheme not to take any or any further steps to recover the debt due to them under section 75 of the 1995 Act pending the recovery of all or a specified part of the debt due to them by virtue of the contribution notice.

(5) If the trustees or managers fail to comply with a direction issued to them under subsection (4), section 10 of the 1995 Act (civil penalties) applies to any trustee or manager who has failed to take all reasonable steps to secure compliance.

(6) Any sums paid-

(a) to the trustees or managers of the scheme in respect of any debt due to them by virtue of the contribution notice, or

(b) to the Board of the Pension Protection Fund in respect of any debt due to it by virtue of the contribution notice (where it has assumed responsibility for the scheme in accordance with Chapter 3 of Part 2 (pension protection)),

are to be treated as reducing the amount of the debt due to the trustees or managers or, as the case may be, to the Board under section 75 of the 1995 Act.

(7) Where a sum is paid to the trustees or managers of the scheme or, as the case may be, to the Board in respect of the debt due under section 75 of the 1995 Act, P may make an application under this subsection to the Regulator for a reduction in the amount of the sum specified in P's contribution notice.

(8) An application under subsection (7) must be made as soon as reasonably practicable after

the sum is paid to the trustees or managers or, as the case may be, to the Board in respect of the debt due under section 75 of the 1995 Act.

(9) Where such an application is made to the Regulator, the Regulator may, if it is of the opinion that it is appropriate to do so-

(a) reduce the amount of the sum specified in P's contribution notice by an amount which it considers reasonable, and

(b) issue a revised contribution notice specifying the revised sum.

(10) For the purposes of subsection (9), the Regulator must have regard to such matters as the Regulator considers relevant including, where relevant, the following matters-

(a) the amount paid in respect of the debt due under section 75 of the 1995 Act since the contribution notice was issued,

(b) any amounts paid in respect of the debt due by virtue of that contribution notice,

(c) whether contribution notices have been issued to other persons in respect of the same non-compliance with the financial support direction in question as the non-compliance in respect of which P's contribution notice was issued,

(d) where such contribution notices have been issued, the sums specified in each of those notices and any amounts paid in respect of the debt due by virtue of those notices,

(e) whether P's contribution notice specifies that P is jointly and severally liable for the debt with other persons, and

(f) such other matters as may be prescribed.

(11) Where-

(a) P's contribution notice specifies that P is jointly and severally liable for the debt with other persons, and

(b) a revised contribution notice is issued to P under subsection (9) specifying a revised sum,

the Regulator must also issue revised contribution notices to those other persons specifying the revised sum and their joint and several liability with P for the debt in respect of that sum.

51   Sections 43 to 50: interpretation

(1) In sections 43 to 50-

"group of companies" means a holding company and its subsidiaries within the meaning given by section 736(1) of the Companies Act 1985 (c. 6) and "member" in relation to such a group is to be construed accordingly;

"holding company" has the meaning given by section 736(1) of that Act.

(2) For the purposes of those sections-

(a) references to a debt due under section 75 of the Pensions Act 1995 (c. 26) include a contingent debt under that section, and

(b) references to the amount of such a debt include the amount of such a contingent debt.

(3) For the purposes of those sections-

(a) section 249 of the Insolvency Act 1986 (c. 45) (connected persons) applies as it applies for the purposes of any provision of the first Group of Parts of that Act,

(b) section 435 of that Act (associated persons) applies as it applies for the purposes of that Act, and

(c) section 74 of the Bankruptcy (Scotland) Act 1985 (c. 66) (associated persons) applies as it applies for the purposes of that Act.

Transactions at an undervalue

52   Restoration orders where transactions at an undervalue

(1) This section applies in relation to an occupational pension scheme other than-

(a) a money purchase scheme, or

(b) a prescribed scheme or a scheme of a prescribed description.

(2) The Regulator may make a restoration order in respect of a transaction involving assets of the scheme if-

(a) a relevant event has occurred in relation to the employer in relation to the scheme, and

(b) the transaction is a transaction at an undervalue entered into with a person at a time which-

(i) is on or after 27th April 2004, but

(ii) is not more than two years before the occurrence of the relevant event in relation to the employer.

(3) A restoration order in respect of a transaction involving assets of a scheme is such an order as the Regulator thinks fit for restoring the position to what it would have been if the transaction had not been entered into.

(4) For the purposes of this section a relevant event occurs in relation to the employer in relation to a scheme if and when on or after the appointed day-

(a) an insolvency event occurs in relation to the employer, or

(b) the trustees or managers of the scheme make an application under subsection (1) of section 129 or receive a notice from the Board of the Pension Protection Fund under subsection (5)(a) of that section (applications and notifications prior to the Board assuming responsibility for a scheme).

(5) For the purposes of subsection (4)-

(a) the "appointed day" means the day appointed under section 126(2) (no pension protection under Chapter 3 of Part 2 if the scheme begins winding up before the day appointed by the Secretary of State),

(b) section 121 (meaning of "insolvency event") applies for the purposes of determining if and when an insolvency event has occurred in relation to the employer, and

(c) the reference to an insolvency event in relation to the employer does not include an insolvency event which occurred in relation to him before he became the employer in relation to the scheme.

(6) For the purposes of this section and section 53, a transaction involving assets of a scheme is a transaction at an undervalue entered into with a person ("P") if the trustees or managers of the scheme or appropriate persons in relation to the scheme-

(a) make a gift to P or otherwise enter into a transaction with P on terms that provide for no consideration to be provided towards the scheme, or

(b) enter into a transaction with P for a consideration the value of which, in money or money's worth, is significantly less than the value, in money or money's worth, of the consideration provided by or on behalf of the trustees or managers of the scheme.

(7) In subsection (6) "appropriate persons" in relation to a scheme means a person who, or several persons each of whom is a person who, at the time at which the transaction in question is entered into, is-

(a) a person of a prescribed description, and

(b) entitled to exercise powers in relation to the scheme.

8) For the purposes of this section and section 53-

"assets" includes future assets;

"transaction" includes a gift, agreement or arrangement and references to entering into a transaction are to be construed accordingly.

9) The provisions of this section apply without prejudice to the availability of any other remedy, even in relation to a transaction where the trustees or managers of the scheme or appropriate persons in question had no power to enter into the transaction.

53   Restoration orders: supplementary

1) This section applies in relation to a restoration order under section 52 in respect of a transaction involving assets of a scheme ("the transaction").

2) The restoration order may in particular-

(a) require any assets of the scheme (whether money or other property) which were transferred as part of the transaction to be transferred back-

(i) to the trustees or managers of the scheme, or

(ii) where the Board of the Pension Protection Fund has assumed responsibility for the scheme, to the Board;

(b) require any property to be transferred to the trustees or managers of the scheme or, where the Board has assumed responsibility for the scheme, to the Board if it represents in any person's hands-

(i) any of the assets of the scheme which were transferred as part of the transaction, or

(ii) property derived from any such assets so transferred;

(c) require such property as the Regulator may specify in the order, in respect of any consideration for the transaction received by the trustees or managers of the scheme, to be transferred-

(i) by the trustees or managers of the scheme, or

(ii) where the Board has assumed responsibility for the scheme, by the Board,

to such persons as the Regulator may specify in the order;

(d) require any person to pay, in respect of benefits received by him as a result of the transaction, such sums (not exceeding the value of the benefits received by him) as the Regulator may specify in the order-

(i) to the trustees or managers of the scheme, or

(ii) where the Board has assumed responsibility for the scheme, to the Board.

3) A restoration order is of no effect to the extent that it prejudices any interest in property which was acquired in good faith and for value or any interest deriving from such an interest.

4) Nothing in subsection (3) prevents a restoration order requiring a person to pay a sum of money if the person received a benefit as a result of the transaction otherwise than in good faith and for value.

5) Where a person has acquired an interest in property from a person or has received a benefit as a result of the transaction and-

(a) he is one of the trustees or managers or appropriate persons who entered into the transaction as mentioned in subsection (6) of section 52, or

(b) at the time of the acquisition or receipt-

(i) he has notice of the fact that the transaction was a transaction at an undervalue,

(ii) he is a trustee or manager, or the employer, in relation to the scheme, or

(iii) he is connected with, or an associate of, any of the persons mentioned in paragraph (a) or (b)(ii),

then, unless the contrary is shown, it is to be presumed for the purposes of subsections (3) and (4) that the interest was acquired or the benefit was received otherwise than in good faith.

(6) For the purposes of this section-

(a) section 249 of the Insolvency Act 1986 (c. 45) (connected persons) applies as it applies for the purposes of any provision of the first Group of Parts of that Act,

(b) section 435 of that Act (associated persons) applies as it applies for the purposes of that Act, and

(c) section 74 of the Bankruptcy (Scotland) Act 1985 (c. 66) (associated persons) applies as it applies for the purposes of that Act.

(7) For the purposes of this section "property" includes-

(a) money, goods, things in action, land and every description of property wherever situated, and

(b) obligations and every description of interest, whether present or future or vested or contingent, arising out of, or incidental to, property.

(8) References in this section to where the Board has assumed responsibility for a scheme are to where the Board has assumed responsibility for the scheme in accordance with Chapter 3 of Part 2 (pension protection).

54 Content and effect of a restoration order

(1) This section applies where a restoration order is made under section 52 in respect of a transaction involving assets of a scheme.

(2) Where the restoration order imposes an obligation on a person to do something, the order must specify the period within which the obligation must be complied with.

(3) Where the restoration order imposes an obligation on a person ("A") to transfer or pay a sum of money to a person specified in the order ("B"), the sum is to be treated as a debt due from A to B.

(4) Where the trustees or managers of the scheme are the persons to whom the debt is due, the Regulator may on their behalf, exercise such powers as the trustees or managers have to recover the debt.

(5) But during any assessment period (within the meaning of section 132) in relation to the scheme, the rights and powers of the trustees or managers of the scheme in relation to any debt due to them by virtue of a restoration order are exercisable by the Board of the Pension Protection Fund to the exclusion of the trustees or managers and the Regulator.

(6) Where, by virtue of subsection (5), any amount is transferred or paid to the Board in respect of a debt due by virtue of a restoration order, the Board must pay the amount to the trustees or managers of the scheme.

55 Contribution notice where failure to comply with restoration order

(1) This section applies where-

(a) a restoration order is made under section 52 in respect of a transaction involving assets of a scheme ("the transaction"), and

(b) a person fails to comply with an obligation imposed on him by the order which is not an obligation to transfer or pay a sum of money.

(2) The Regulator may issue a notice to the person stating that the person is under a liability to pay the sum specified in the notice (a "contribution notice")-

(a) to the trustees or managers of the scheme, or

(b) where the Board of the Pension Protection Fund has assumed responsibility for the scheme in accordance with Chapter 3 of Part 2 (pension protection), to the Board.

(3) The sum specified by the Regulator in a contribution notice may be either the whole or a specified part of the shortfall sum in relation to the scheme.

(4) The shortfall sum in relation to the scheme is the amount which the Regulator estimates to be the amount of the decrease in the value of the assets of the scheme as a result of the transaction having been entered into.

56 Content and effect of a section 55 contribution notice

(1) This section applies where a contribution notice is issued to a person under section 55.

(2) The contribution notice must-

(a) contain a statement of the matters which it is asserted constitute the failure to comply with the restoration order under section 52 in respect of which the notice is issued, and

(b) specify the sum which the person is stated to be under a liability to pay.

(3) Where the contribution notice states that the person is under a liability to pay the sum specified in the notice to the trustees or managers of the scheme, the sum is to be treated as a debt due from the person to the trustees or managers of the scheme.

(4) In such a case, the Regulator may, on behalf of the trustees or managers of the scheme, exercise such powers as the trustees or managers have to recover the debt.

(5) But during any assessment period (within the meaning of section 132) in relation to the scheme, the rights and powers of the trustees or managers of the scheme in relation to any debt due to them by virtue of a contribution notice, are exercisable by the Board of the Pension Protection Fund to the exclusion of the trustees or managers and the Regulator.

(6) Where, by virtue of subsection (5), any amount is paid to the Board in respect of a debt due by virtue of a contribution notice, the Board must pay the amount to the trustees or managers of the scheme.

(7) Where the contribution notice states that the person is under a liability to pay the sum specified in the notice to the Board, the sum is to be treated as a debt due from the person to the Board.

Sections 38 to 56: partnerships and limited liability partnerships
57 Sections 38 to 56: partnerships and limited liability partnerships

(1) For the purposes of any of sections 38 to 56, regulations may modify any of the definitions mentioned in subsection (2) (as applied by any of those sections) in relation to-

(a) a partnership or a partner in a partnership;

(b) a limited liability partnership or a member of such a partnership.

(2) The definitions mentioned in subsection (1) are-

(a) section 249 of the Insolvency Act 1986 (c. 45) (connected persons),

(b) section 435 of that Act (associated persons),

(c) section 74 of the Bankruptcy (Scotland) Act 1985 (c. 66) (associated persons), and

(d) section 736 of the Companies Act 1985 (c. 6) (meaning of "subsidiary" and "holding company" etc).

(3) Regulations may also provide that any provision of sections 38 to 51 applies with such modifications as may be prescribed in relation to-

(a) any case where a partnership is or was-

(i) the employer in relation to an occupational pension scheme, or

(ii) for the purposes of any of those sections, connected with or an associate of the employer;

(b) any case where a limited liability partnership is-

(i) the employer in relation to an occupational pension scheme, or

(ii) for the purposes of any of those sections, connected with or an associate of the employer.

(4) Regulations may also provide that any provision of sections 52 to 56 applies with such modifications as may be prescribed in relation to a partnership or a limited liability partnership.

(5) For the purposes of this section-

(a) "partnership" includes a firm or entity of a similar character formed under the law of a country or territory outside the United Kingdom, and

(b) references to a partner are to be construed accordingly.

(6) For the purposes of this section, "limited liability partnership" means-

(a) a limited liability partnership formed under the Limited Liability Partnerships Act 2000 (c. 12) or the Limited Liability Partnerships Act (Northern Ireland) 2002 (c. 12 (N.I.)), or

(b) an entity which is of a similar character to such a limited liability partnership and which is formed under the law of a country or territory outside the United Kingdom,

and references to a member of a limited liability partnership are to be construed accordingly.

(7) This section is without prejudice to-

(a) section 307 (power to modify this Act in relation to certain categories of scheme), and

(b) section 318(4) (power to extend the meaning of "employer").

Applications under the Insolvency Act 1986

58 Regulator's right to apply under section 423 of Insolvency Act 1986

(1) In this section "section 423" means section 423 of the Insolvency Act 1986 (transactions defrauding creditors).

(2) The Regulator may apply for an order under section 423 in relation to a debtor if-

(a) the debtor is the employer in relation to an occupational pension scheme, and

(b) condition A or condition B is met in relation to the scheme.

(3) Condition A is that an actuarial valuation under section 143 obtained by the Board of the Pension Protection Fund in respect of the scheme indicates that the value of the assets of the scheme at the relevant time, as defined by that section, was less than the amount of the protected liabilities, as defined by section 131, at that time.

(4) Condition B is that an actuarial valuation, as defined by section 224(2), obtained by the trustees or managers of the scheme indicates that the statutory funding objective in section 222 is not met.

(5) In a case where the debtor-

(a) has been adjudged bankrupt,

(b) is a body corporate which is being wound up or is in administration, or

(c) is a partnership which is being wound up or is in administration, subsection (2) does not enable an application to be made under section 423 except with the permission of the court.

(6) An application made under this section is to be treated as made on behalf of every victim of the transaction who is-

(a) a trustee or member of the scheme, or

(b) the Board.

(7) This section does not apply where the valuation mentioned in subsection (3) or (4) is made by reference to a date that falls before the commencement of this section.

(8) Expressions which are defined by section 423 for the purposes of that section have the same meaning when used in this section.

CHAPTER 2
INFORMATION RELATING TO EMPLOYER'S INSOLVENCY ETC
Insolvency events

120   Duty to notify insolvency events in respect of employers

(1) This section applies where, in the case of an occupational pension scheme, an insolvency event occurs in relation to the employer.

(2) The insolvency practitioner in relation to the employer must give a notice to that effect within the notification period to-

(a) the Board,

(b) the Regulator, and

(c) the trustees or managers of the scheme.

(3) For the purposes of subsection (2) the "notification period" is the prescribed period beginning with the later of-

(a) the insolvency date, and

(b) the date the insolvency practitioner becomes aware of the existence of the scheme.

(4) A notice under this section must be in such form and contain such information as may be prescribed.

121   Insolvency event, insolvency date and insolvency practitioner

(1) In this Part each of the following expressions has the meaning given to it by this section-

"insolvency event"

"insolvency date"

"insolvency practitioner".

(2) An insolvency event occurs in relation to an individual where-

(a) he is adjudged bankrupt or sequestration of his estate has been awarded;

(b) the nominee in relation to a proposal for a voluntary arrangement under Part 8 of the Insolvency Act 1986 (c. 45) submits a report to the court under section 256(1) or 256A(3) of that Act which states that in his opinion a meeting of the individual's creditors should be summoned to consider the debtor's proposal;

(c) a deed of arrangement made by or in respect of the affairs of the individual is registered in accordance with the Deeds of Arrangement Act 1914 (c. 47);

(d) he executes a trust deed for his creditors or enters into a composition contract;

(e) he has died and-

(i) an insolvency administration order is made in respect of his estate in accordance with an order under section 421 of the Insolvency Act 1986, or

  (ii) a judicial factor appointed under section 11A of the Judicial Factors (Scotland) Act 1889 (c. 39) is required by that section to divide the individual's estate among his creditors.

(3) An insolvency event occurs in relation to a company where-

  (a) the nominee in relation to a proposal for a voluntary arrangement under Part 1 of the Insolvency Act 1986 submits a report to the court under section 2 of that Act (procedure where nominee is not the liquidator or administrator) which states that in his opinion meetings of the company and its creditors should be summoned to consider the proposal;

  (b) the directors of the company file (or in Scotland lodge) with the court documents and statements in accordance with paragraph 7(1) of Schedule A1 to that Act (moratorium where directors propose voluntary arrangement);

  (c) an administrative receiver within the meaning of section 251 of that Act is appointed in relation to the company;

  (d) the company enters administration within the meaning of paragraph 1(2)(b) of Schedule B1 to that Act;

  (e) a resolution is passed for a voluntary winding up of the company without a declaration of solvency under section 89 of that Act;

  (f) a meeting of creditors is held in relation to the company under section 95 of that Act (creditors' meeting which has the effect of converting a members' voluntary winding up into a creditors' voluntary winding up);

  (g) an order for the winding up of the company is made by the court under Part 4 or 5 of that Act.

(4) An insolvency event occurs in relation to a partnership where-

  (a) an order for the winding up of the partnership is made by the court under any provision of the Insolvency Act 1986 (c. 45) (as applied by an order under section 420 of that Act (insolvent partnerships));

  (b) sequestration is awarded on the estate of the partnership under section 12 of the Bankruptcy (Scotland) Act 1985 (c. 66) or the partnership grants a trust deed for its creditors;

  (c) the nominee in relation to a proposal for a voluntary arrangement under Part 1 of the Insolvency Act 1986 (as applied by an order under section 420 of that Act) submits a report to the court under section 2 of that Act (procedure where nominee is not the liquidator or administrator) which states that in his opinion meetings of the members of the partnership and the partnership's creditors should be summoned to consider the proposal;

  (d) the members of the partnership file with the court documents and statements in accordance with paragraph 7(1) of Schedule A1 to that Act (moratorium where directors propose voluntary arrangement) (as applied by an order under section 420 of that Act);

  (e) an administration order under Part 2 of that Act (as applied by section 420 of that Act) is made in relation to the partnership.

(5) An insolvency event also occurs in relation to a person where an event occurs which is a prescribed event in relation to such a person.

(6) Except as provided by subsections (2) to (5), for the purposes of this Part an event is not to be regarded as an insolvency event in relation to a person.

(7) The Secretary of State may by order amend subsection (4)(e) to make provision

consequential upon any order under section 420 of the Insolvency Act 1986 (insolvent partnerships) applying the provisions of Part 2 of that Act (administration) as amended by the Enterprise Act 2002 (c. 40).

(8) "Insolvency date", in relation to an insolvency event, means the date on which the event occurs.

(9) "Insolvency practitioner", in relation to a person, means-

(a) a person acting as an insolvency practitioner, in relation to that person, in accordance with section 388 of the Insolvency Act 1986;

(b) in such circumstances as may be prescribed, a person of a prescribed description.

(10) In this section-

"company" means a company within the meaning given by section 735(1) of the Companies Act 1985 (c. 6) or a company which may be wound up under Part 5 of the Insolvency Act 1986 (c. 45) (unregistered companies);

"person acting as an insolvency practitioner", in relation to a person, includes the official receiver acting as receiver or manager of any property of that person.

(11) In applying section 388 of the Insolvency Act 1986 under subsection (9) above-

(a) the reference in section 388(2)(a) to a permanent or interim trustee in sequestration must be taken to include a reference to a trustee in sequestration, and

(b) section 388(5) (which includes provision that nothing in the section applies to anything done by the official receiver or the Accountant in Bankruptcy) must be ignored.

Status of scheme

122 Insolvency practitioner's duty to issue notices confirming status of scheme

(1) This section applies where an insolvency event has occurred in relation to the employer in relation to an occupational pension scheme.

(2) An insolvency practitioner in relation to the employer must-

(a) if he is able to confirm that a scheme rescue is not possible, issue a notice to that effect (a "scheme failure notice"), or

(b) if he is able to confirm that a scheme rescue has occurred, issue a notice to that effect (a "withdrawal notice").

(3) Subsection (4) applies where-

(a) in prescribed circumstances, insolvency proceedings in relation to the employer are stayed or come to an end, or

(b) a prescribed event occurs.

(4) If a person who was acting as an insolvency practitioner in relation to the employer immediately before this subsection applies has not been able to confirm in relation to the scheme-

(a) that a scheme rescue is not possible, or

(b) that a scheme rescue has occurred,

he must issue a notice to that effect.

(5) For the purposes of this section-

(a) a person is able to confirm that a scheme rescue has occurred in relation to an occupational pension scheme if, and only if, he is able to confirm such matters as are prescribed for the purposes of this paragraph, and

(b) a person is able to confirm that a scheme rescue is not possible, in relation to such a scheme if, and only if, he is able to confirm such matters as are prescribed for the purposes of this paragraph.

(6) Where an insolvency practitioner or former insolvency practitioner in relation to the employer issues a notice under this section, he must give a copy of that notice to-

(a) the Board,

(b) the Regulator, and

(c) the trustees or managers of the scheme.

(7) A person must comply with an obligation imposed on him by subsection (2), (4) or (6) as soon as reasonably practicable.

(8) Regulations may require notices issued under this section-

(a) to be in a prescribed form;

(b) to contain prescribed information.

123 Approval of notices issued under section 122

(1) This section applies where the Board receives a notice under section 122(6) ("the section 122 notice").

(2) The Board must determine whether to approve the section 122 notice.

(3) The Board must approve the section 122 notice if, and only if, it is satisfied-

(a) that the insolvency practitioner or former insolvency practitioner who issued the notice was required to issue it under that section, and

(b) that the notice complies with any requirements imposed by virtue of subsection (8) of that section.

(4) Where the Board makes a determination for the purposes of subsection (2), it must issue a determination notice and give a copy of that notice to-

(a) the Regulator,

(b) the trustees or managers of the scheme,

(c) the insolvency practitioner or the former insolvency practitioner who issued the section 122 notice,

(d) any insolvency practitioner in relation to the employer (who does not fall within paragraph (c)), and

(e) if there is no insolvency practitioner in relation to the employer, the employer.

(5) In subsection (4) "determination notice" means a notice which is in the prescribed form and contains such information about the determination as may be prescribed.

Board's duties

124 Board's duty where there is a failure to comply with section 122

(1) This section applies where in relation to an occupational pension scheme-

(a) the Board determines under section 123 not to approve a notice issued under section 122 by an insolvency practitioner or former insolvency practitioner in relation to the employer, or

(b) an insolvency practitioner or former insolvency practitioner in relation to the employer fails to issue a notice under section 122 and the Board is satisfied that such a notice ought to have been issued under that section.

(2) The obligations on the insolvency practitioner or former insolvency practitioner imposed by subsections (2) and (4) of section 122 are to be treated as obligations imposed on the Board and the Board must accordingly issue a notice as required under that section.

(3) Subject to subsections (4) and (5), where a notice is issued under section 122 by the Board

by virtue of this section, it has effect as if it were a notice issued under section 122 by an insolvency practitioner or, as the case may be, former insolvency practitioner in relation to the employer.

(4) Where a notice is issued under section 122 by virtue of this section, section 122(6) does not apply and the Board must, as soon as reasonably practicable, give a copy of the notice to-

(a) the Regulator,

(b) the trustees or managers of the scheme,

(c) the insolvency practitioner or former insolvency practitioner mentioned in subsection (1),

(d) any insolvency practitioner in relation to the employer (who does not fall within paragraph (c)), and

(e) if there is no insolvency practitioner in relation to the employer, the employer.

(5) Where the Board-

(a) is required to issue a notice under section 122 by virtue of this section, and

(b) is satisfied that the notice ought to have been issued at an earlier time,

it must specify that time in the notice and the notice is to have effect as if it had been issued at that time.

125   Binding notices confirming status of scheme

(1) Subject to subsection (2), for the purposes of this Part, a notice issued under section 122 is not binding until-

(a) the Board issues a determination notice under section 123 approving the notice,

(b) the period within which the issue of the determination notice under that section may be reviewed by virtue of Chapter 6 has expired, and

(c) if the issue of the determination notice is so reviewed-

(i) the review and any reconsideration,

(ii) any reference to the PPF Ombudsman in respect of the issue of the notice, and

(iii) any appeal against his determination or directions,

has been finally disposed of and the determination notice has not been revoked, varied or substituted.

(2) Where a notice is issued under section 122 by the Board by virtue of section 124, the notice is not binding until-

(a) the period within which the issue of the notice may be reviewed by virtue of Chapter 6 has expired, and

(b) if the issue of the notice is so reviewed-

(i) the review and any reconsideration,

(ii) any reference to the PPF Ombudsman in respect of the issue of the notice, and

(iii) any appeal against his determination or directions,

has been finally disposed of and the notice has not been revoked, varied or substituted.

(3) Where a notice issued under section 122 becomes binding, the Board must as soon as reasonably practicable give a notice to that effect together with a copy of the binding notice to-

(a) the Regulator,

(b) the trustees or managers of the scheme,

(c) the insolvency practitioner or former insolvency practitioner who issued the notice under section 122 or, where that notice was issued by the Board by virtue of section

124, the insolvency practitioner or former insolvency practitioner mentioned in subsection (1) of that section,

(d) any insolvency practitioner in relation to the employer (who does not fall within paragraph (c)), and

(e) if there is no insolvency practitioner in relation to the employer, the employer.

(4) A notice under subsection (3)-

(a) must be in the prescribed form and contain such information as may be prescribed, and

(b) where it is given in relation to a withdrawal notice issued under section 122(2)(b) which has become binding, must state the time from which the Board ceases to be involved with the scheme (see section 149).

CHAPTER 3

PENSION PROTECTION

Eligible schemes

126   Eligible schemes

(1) Subject to the following provisions of this section, in this Part references to an "eligible scheme" are to an occupational pension scheme which-

(a) is not a money purchase scheme, and

(b) is not a prescribed scheme or a scheme of a prescribed description.

(2) A scheme is not an eligible scheme if it is being wound up immediately before the day appointed by the Secretary of State by order for the purposes of this subsection.

(3) Regulations may provide that where-

(a) an assessment period begins in relation to an eligible scheme (see section 132), and

(b) after the beginning of that period, the scheme ceases to be an eligible scheme,

the scheme is, in such circumstances as may be prescribed, to be treated as remaining an eligible scheme for the purposes of such of the provisions mentioned in subsection (4) as may be prescribed.

(4) Those provisions are-

(a) any provision of this Part, and

(b) any other provision of this Act in which "eligible scheme" has the meaning given by this section.

(5) Regulations may also provide that a scheme which would be an eligible scheme in the absence of this subsection is not an eligible scheme in such circumstances as may be prescribed.

Circumstances in which Board assumes responsibility for eligible schemes

127   Duty to assume responsibility for schemes following insolvency event

(1) This section applies where a qualifying insolvency event has occurred in relation to the employer in relation to an eligible scheme.

(2) The Board must assume responsibility for the scheme in accordance with this Chapter if-

(a) the value of the assets of the scheme at the relevant time was less than the amount of the protected liabilities at that time (see sections 131 and 143),

(b) after the relevant time a scheme failure notice is issued under section 122(2)(a) in relation to the scheme and that notice becomes binding, and

(c) a withdrawal event has not occurred in relation to the scheme in respect of a withdrawal notice which has been issued during the period-

(i) beginning with the occurrence of the qualifying insolvency event, and

(ii) ending immediately before the issuing of the scheme failure notice under section 122(2)(a),

nd the occurrence of such a withdrawal event in respect of a withdrawal notice issued luring that period is not a possibility (see section 149).

3) For the purposes of this section, in relation to an eligible scheme an insolvency event "the current event") in relation to the employer is a qualifying insolvency event if-

(a) it occurs on or after the day appointed under section 126(2), and

(b) it-

(i) is the first insolvency event to occur in relation to the employer on or after that day, or

(ii) does not occur within an assessment period (see section 132) in relation to the scheme which began before the occurrence of the current event.

4) For the purposes of this section-

(a) the reference in subsection (2)(a) to the assets of the scheme is a reference to those assets excluding any assets representing the value of any rights in respect of money purchase benefits under the scheme rules, and

(b) "the relevant time" means the time immediately before the qualifying insolvency event occurs.

5) This section is subject to sections 146 and 147 (cases where Board must refuse to assume responsibility for a scheme).

128 Duty to assume responsibility for schemes following application or notification

1) This section applies where, in relation to an eligible scheme, the trustees or managers of the scheme-

(a) make an application under subsection (1) of section 129 (a "section 129 application"), or

(b) receive a notice from the Board under subsection (5)(a) of that section (a "section 129 notification").

(2) The Board must assume responsibility for the scheme in accordance with this Chapter if-

(a) the value of the assets of the scheme at the relevant time was less than the amount of the protected liabilities at that time (see sections 131 and 143),

(b) after the relevant time the Board issues a scheme failure notice under section 130(2) in relation to the scheme and that notice becomes binding, and

(c) a withdrawal event has not occurred in relation to the scheme in respect of a withdrawal notice which has been issued during the period-

(i) beginning with the making of the section 129 application or, as the case may be, the receipt of the section 129 notification, and

(ii) ending immediately before the issuing of the scheme failure notice under section 130(2),

and the occurrence of such a withdrawal event in respect of a withdrawal notice issued during that period is not a possibility (see section 149).

(3) In subsection (2)-

(a) the reference in paragraph (a) to the assets of the scheme is a reference to those assets excluding any assets representing the value of any rights in respect of money purchase benefits under the scheme rules, and

(b) "the relevant time" means the time immediately before the section 129 application was made or, as the case may be, the section 129 notification was received.

(4) An application under section 129(1) or notification under section 129(5)(a) is to be disregarded for the purposes of subsection (1) if it is made or given during an assessment period (see section 132) in relation to the scheme which began before the application was made or notification was given.

(5) This section is subject to sections 146 and 147 (cases where Board must refuse to assume responsibility for a scheme).

129 Applications and notifications for the purposes of section 128

(1) Where the trustees or managers of an eligible scheme become aware that-

(a) the employer in relation to the scheme is unlikely to continue as a going concern, and

(b) the prescribed requirements are met in relation to the employer,

they must make an application to the Board for it to assume responsibility for the scheme under section 128.

(2) Where the Board receives an application under subsection (1), it must give a copy of the application to-

(a) the Regulator, and

(b) the employer.

(3) An application under subsection (1) must-

(a) be in the prescribed form and contain the prescribed information, and

(b) be made within the prescribed period.

(4) Where the Regulator becomes aware that-

(a) the employer in relation to an eligible scheme is unlikely to continue as a going concern, and

(b) the requirements mentioned in subsection (1)(b) are met in relation to the employer,

it must give the Board a notice to that effect.

(5) Where the Board receives a notice under subsection (4), it must-

(a) give the trustees or managers of the scheme a notice to that effect, and

(b) give the employer a copy of that notice.

(6) The duty imposed by subsection (1) does not apply where the trustees or managers of an eligible scheme become aware as mentioned in that subsection by reason of a notice given to them under subsection (5).

(7) The duty imposed by subsection (4) does not apply where the Regulator becomes aware as mentioned in that subsection by reason of a copy of an application made by the trustees or managers of the eligible scheme in question given to the Regulator under subsection (2).

(8) Regulations may require notices under this section to be in the prescribed form and contain the prescribed information.

130 Board's duty where application or notification received under section 129

(1) This section applies where the Board-

(a) receives an application under subsection (1) of section 129 and is satisfied that paragraphs (a) and (b) of that subsection are satisfied in relation to the application, or

(b) is notified by the Regulator under section 129(4).

(2) If the Board is able to confirm that a scheme rescue is not possible, it must as soon as reasonably practicable issue a notice to that effect (a "scheme failure notice").

3) If the Board is able to confirm that a scheme rescue has occurred, it must as soon as reasonably practicable issue a notice to that effect (a "withdrawal notice").

4) The Board must, as soon as reasonably practicable, give a copy of any notice issued under subsection (2) or (3) to-

(a) the Regulator,

(b) the trustees or managers of the scheme, and

(c) the employer.

5) For the purposes of this section-

(a) the Board is able to confirm that a scheme rescue has occurred in relation to an occupational pension scheme if, and only if, it is able to confirm such matters as are prescribed for the purposes of this paragraph, and

(b) the Board is able to confirm that a scheme rescue is not possible in relation to such a scheme if, and only if, it is able to confirm such matters as are prescribed for the purposes of this paragraph.

6) For the purposes of this Part a notice issued under subsection (2) or (3) is not binding until-

(a) the period within which the issue of the notice may be reviewed by virtue of Chapter 6 has expired, and

(b) if the issue of the notice is so reviewed-

(i) the review and any reconsideration,

(ii) any reference to the PPF Ombudsman in respect of the issue of the notice, and

(iii) any appeal against his determination or directions,

has been finally disposed of and the notice has not been revoked, varied or substituted.

7) Where a notice issued under subsection (2) or (3) becomes binding, the Board must as soon as reasonably practicable give a notice to that effect together with a copy of the binding notice to-

(a) the Regulator,

(b) the trustees or managers of the scheme, and

(c) the employer.

8) Notices under this section must be in the prescribed form and contain such information as may be prescribed.

9) A notice given under subsection (7) in relation to a withdrawal notice under subsection (3) which has become binding must state the time from which the Board ceases to be involved with the scheme (see section 149).

131   Protected liabilities

(1) For the purposes of this Chapter the protected liabilities, in relation to an eligible scheme, at a particular time ("the relevant time") are-

(a) the cost of securing benefits for and in respect of members of the scheme which correspond to the compensation which would be payable, in relation to the scheme, in accordance with the pension compensation provisions (see section 162) if the Board assumed responsibility for the scheme in accordance with this Chapter,

(b) liabilities of the scheme which are not liabilities to, or in respect of, its members, and

(c) the estimated cost of winding up the scheme.

(2) For the purposes of determining the cost of securing benefits within subsection (1)(a), references in sections 140 to 142 and Schedule 7 (pension compensation provisions) to the

assessment date are to be read as references to the date on which the time immediately after the relevant time falls.

Restrictions on schemes during the assessment period

132 Assessment periods

(1) In this Part references to an assessment period are to be construed in accordance with this section.

(2) Where, in relation to an eligible scheme, a qualifying insolvency event occurs in relation to the employer, an assessment period-

    (a) begins with the occurrence of that event, and

    (b) ends when-

        (i) the Board ceases to be involved with the scheme (see section 149),

        (ii) the trustees or managers of the scheme receive a transfer notice under section 160, or

        (iii) the conditions in section 154(2) (no scheme rescue but sufficient assets to meet protected liabilities etc) are satisfied in relation to the scheme,

whichever first occurs.

(3) In subsection (2) "qualifying insolvency event" has the meaning given by section 127(3).

(4) Where, in relation to an eligible scheme, an application is made under section 129(1) or a notification is received under section 129(5)(a), an assessment period-

    (a) begins when the application is made or the notification is received, and

    (b) ends when-

        (i) the Board ceases to be involved with the scheme (see section 149),

        (ii) the trustees or managers of the scheme receive a transfer notice under section 160, or

        (iii) the conditions in section 154(2) (no scheme rescue but sufficient assets to meet protected liabilities etc) are satisfied in relation to the scheme,

        whichever first occurs.

(5) For the purposes of subsection (4) an application under section 129(1) or notification under section 129(5)(a) is to be disregarded if it is made or given during an assessment period in relation to the scheme which began before the application was made or notification was given.

(6) This section is subject to section 159 (which provides for further assessment periods to begin in certain circumstances where schemes are required to wind up or continue winding up under section 154).

133 Admission of new members, payment of contributions etc

(1) This section applies where there is an assessment period in relation to an eligible scheme.

(2) No new members of any class may be admitted to the scheme during the assessment period.

(3) Except in prescribed circumstances and subject to prescribed conditions, no further contributions (other than those due to be paid before the beginning of the assessment period) may be paid towards the scheme during the assessment period.

(4) Any obligation to pay contributions towards the scheme during the assessment period (including any obligation under section 49(8) of the Pensions Act 1995 (c. 26) to pay amounts deducted corresponding to such contributions) is to be read subject to subsection (3) and section 150 (obligation to pay contributions when assessment period ends).

(5) No benefits may accrue under the scheme rules to, or in respect of, members of the scheme during the assessment period.

(6) Subsection (5) does not prevent any increase, in a benefit, which would otherwise accrue in accordance with the scheme or any enactment.

This subsection is subject to section 138 (which limits the scheme benefits payable during an assessment period).

(7) Subsection (5) does not prevent the accrual of money purchase benefits to the extent that they are derived from income or capital gains arising from the investment of payments which are made by, or in respect of, a member of the scheme.

(8) Where a person is entitled to a pension credit derived from another person's shareable rights under the scheme, nothing in this section prevents the trustees or managers of the scheme discharging their liability in respect of the credit under Chapter 1 of Part 4 of the Welfare Reform and Pensions Act 1999 (c. 30) (sharing of rights under pension arrangements) by conferring appropriate rights under the scheme on that person.

(9) In subsection (8)-

"appropriate rights" has the same meaning as in paragraph 5 of Schedule 5 to that Act (pension credits: mode of discharge);

"shareable rights" has the same meaning as in Chapter 1 of Part 4 of that Act (sharing of rights under pension arrangements).

(10) Any action taken in contravention of this section is void.

(11) Disregarding subsection (10), section 10 of the Pensions Act 1995 (civil penalties) applies to any trustee or manager of a scheme who fails to take all reasonable steps to secure compliance with this section.

134 Directions

(1) This section applies where there is an assessment period in relation to an eligible scheme.

(2) With a view to ensuring that the scheme's protected liabilities do not exceed its assets or, if they do exceed its assets, that the excess is kept to a minimum, the Board may give a relevant person in relation to the scheme directions regarding the exercise during that period of his powers in respect of-

(a) the investment of the scheme's assets,
(b) the incurring of expenditure,
(c) the instigation or conduct of legal proceedings, and
(d) such other matters as may be prescribed.

(3) In subsection (2)-

(a) "relevant person" in relation to a scheme means-

(i) the trustees or managers of the scheme,
(ii) the employer in relation to the scheme, or
(iii) such other persons as may be prescribed, and

(b) the reference to the assets of the scheme is a reference to those assets excluding any assets representing the value of any rights in respect of money purchase benefits under the scheme rules.

(4) The Board may revoke or vary any direction under this section.

(5) Where a direction under this section given to the trustees or managers of a scheme is not complied with, section 10 of the Pensions Act 1995 (c. 26) (civil penalties) applies to any such trustee or manager who has failed to take all reasonable steps to secure compliance with the direction.

(6) That section also applies to any other person who, without reasonable excuse, fails to comply with a direction given to him under this section.

135 Restrictions on winding up, discharge of liabilities etc

(1) This section applies where there is an assessment period in relation to an eligible scheme.

(2) Subject to subsection (3), the winding up of the scheme must not begin during the assessment period.

(3) Subsection (2) does not apply to the winding up of the scheme in pursuance of an order by the Regulator under section 11(3A) of the Pensions Act 1995 (Regulator's powers to wind up occupational pension schemes to protect Pension Protection Fund) directing the scheme to be wound up (and section 219 makes provision for the backdating of the winding up).

(4) During the assessment period, except in prescribed circumstances and subject to prescribed conditions-

(a) no transfers of, or transfer payments in respect of, any member's rights under the scheme rules are to be made from the scheme, and

(b) no other steps may be taken to discharge any liability of the scheme to or in respect of a member of the scheme in respect of-

(i) pensions or other benefits, or

(ii) such other liabilities as may be prescribed.

(5) Subsection (4)-

(a) is subject to section 138, and

(b) applies whether or not the scheme was being wound up immediately before the assessment period or began winding up by virtue of subsection (3).

(6) Subsection (7) applies where, on the commencement of the assessment period-

(a) a member's pensionable service terminates, and

(b) he becomes a person to whom Chapter 5 of Part 4 of the Pension Schemes Act 1993 (c. 48) (early leavers: cash transfer sums and contribution refunds) applies.

Section 150(5) (retrospective accrual of benefits in certain circumstances) is to be disregarded for the purposes of determining whether a member falls within paragraph (a) or (b).

(7) Where this subsection applies, during the assessment period-

(a) no right or power conferred by that Chapter may be exercised, and

(b) no duty imposed by that Chapter may be discharged.

(8) Where a person is entitled to a pension credit derived from another person's shareable rights (within the meaning of Chapter 1 of Part 4 under of the Welfare Reform and Pensions Act 1999 (c. 30) (sharing of rights under pension arrangements)) under the scheme, nothing in subsection (4) prevents the trustees or managers of the scheme discharging their liability in respect of the credit in accordance with that Chapter.

(9) Any action taken in contravention of this section is void, except to the extent that the Board validates the action (see section 136).

(10) Disregarding subsection (9), where there is a contravention of this section, section 10 of the Pensions Act 1995 (c. 26) (civil penalties) applies to any trustee or manager who has failed to take all reasonable steps to secure compliance with this section.

(11) The Regulator may not make a freezing order (see section 23) in relation to the scheme during the assessment period.

136 Power to validate contraventions of section 135

(1) The Board may validate an action for the purposes of section 135(9) only if it is satisfied that to do so is consistent with the objective of ensuring that the scheme's protected

liabilities do not exceed its assets or, if they do exceed its assets, that the excess is kept to a minimum.

(2) Where the Board determines to validate, or not to validate, any action of the trustees or managers for those purposes, it must issue a notice to that effect and give a copy of that notice to-

(a) the Regulator,

(b) the trustees or managers of the scheme,

(c) any insolvency practitioner in relation to the employer or, if there is no such insolvency practitioner, the employer, and

(d) any other person who appears to the Board to be directly affected by the determination.

(3) A notice under subsection (2) must contain a statement of the Board's reasons for the determination.

(4) The validation of an action does not take effect-

(a) until-

(i) the Board has issued a notice under subsection (2) relating to the determination, and

(ii) the period within which the issue of that notice may be reviewed by virtue of Chapter 6 has expired, and

(b) if the issue of the notice is so reviewed, until-

(i) the review and any reconsideration,

(ii) any reference to the PPF Ombudsman in respect of the issue of the notice, and

(iii) any appeal against his determination or directions,

has been finally disposed of.

(5) In subsection (1) the reference to the assets of the scheme is a reference to those assets excluding any assets representing the value of any rights in respect of money purchase benefits under the scheme rules.

137   Board to act as creditor of the employer

(1) Subsection (2) applies where there is an assessment period in relation to an eligible scheme.

(2) During the assessment period, the rights and powers of the trustees or managers of the scheme in relation to any debt (including any contingent debt) due to them by the employer, whether by virtue of section 75 of the Pensions Act 1995 (c. 26) (deficiencies in the scheme assets) or otherwise, are exercisable by the Board to the exclusion of the trustees or managers.

(3) Where, by virtue of subsection (2), any amount is paid to the Board in respect of such a debt, the Board must pay that amount to the trustees or managers of the scheme.

138   Payment of scheme benefits

(1) Subsections (2) and (3) apply where there is an assessment period in relation to an eligible scheme.

(2) The benefits payable to or in respect of any member under the scheme rules during the assessment period must be reduced to the extent necessary to ensure that they do not exceed the compensation which would be payable to or in respect of the member in accordance with this Chapter if-

(a) the Board assumed responsibility for the scheme in accordance with this Chapter, and

(b) the assessment date referred to in Schedule 7 were the date on which the assessment period began.

(3) But where, on the commencement of the assessment period-

(a) a member's pensionable service terminates, and

(b) he becomes a person to whom Chapter 5 of Part 4 of the Pension Schemes Act 1993 (c. 48) (early leavers: cash transfer sums and contribution refunds) applies,

no benefits are payable to or in respect of him under the scheme during the assessment period.

(4) Section 150(5) (retrospective accrual of benefits in certain circumstances) is to be disregarded for the purposes of determining whether a member falls within paragraph (a) or (b) of subsection (3).

(5) Nothing in subsection (3) prevents the payment of benefits attributable (directly or indirectly) to a pension credit, during the assessment period, in accordance with subsection (2).

(6) Where at any time during the assessment period the scheme is being wound up, subject to any reduction required under subsection (2) and to subsection (3), the benefits payable to or in respect of any member under the scheme rules during that period are the benefits that would have been so payable in the absence of the winding up of the scheme.

(7) Subsections (2), (3) and (6) are subject to sections 150(1) to (3) and 154(13) (which provide for the adjustment of amounts paid during an assessment period when that period ends other than as a result of the Board assuming responsibility for the scheme).

(8) For the purposes of subsections (2) and (3) the trustees or managers of the scheme may take such steps as they consider appropriate (including steps adjusting future payments under the scheme rules) to recover any overpayment or pay any shortfall.

(9) Section 10 of the Pensions Act 1995 (c. 26) (civil penalties) applies to a trustee or manager of a scheme who fails to take all reasonable steps to secure compliance with subsections (2) and (3).

(10) Regulations may provide that, where there is an assessment period in relation to an eligible scheme-

(a) in such circumstances as may be prescribed subsection (2) does not operate to require the reduction of benefits payable to or in respect of any member;

(b) the commencement of a member's pension or payment of a member's lump sum or other benefits is, in such circumstances and on such terms and conditions as may be prescribed, to be postponed for the whole or any part of the assessment period for which he continues in employment after attaining normal pension age.

(11) For the purposes of subsection (10)-

(a) "normal pension age", in relation to an eligible scheme and any pension or other benefit under it, means the age specified in the scheme rules as the earliest age at which the pension or other benefit becomes payable without actuarial adjustment (disregarding any scheme rule making special provision as to early payment on the grounds of ill health), and

(b) where different ages are so specified in relation to different parts of a pension or other benefit-

(i) subsection (10) has effect as if those parts were separate pensions or, as the case may be, benefits, and

(ii) in relation to a part of a pension or other benefit, the reference in that subsection to normal pension age is to be read as a reference to the age specified in the scheme rules as the earliest age at which that part becomes so payable.

(12) Regulations may provide that, in prescribed circumstances, where-

(a) a member of the scheme died before the commencement of the assessment period, and

(b) during the assessment period, a person becomes entitled under the scheme rules to a benefit of a prescribed description in respect of the member,

the benefit, or any part of it, is, for the purposes of subsection (2), to be treated as having become payable before the commencement of the assessment period.

(13) Nothing in subsection (2) or (3) applies to money purchase benefits.

139   Loans to pay scheme benefits

(1) Subsection (2) applies where section 138(2) applies in relation to an eligible scheme.

(2) Where the Board is satisfied that the trustees or managers of the scheme are not able to pay benefits under the scheme rules (reduced in accordance with section 138(2)) as they fall due, it may, on an application by the trustees or managers, lend to them such amounts as the Board considers appropriate for the purpose of enabling them to pay those benefits.

(3) Where an amount lent to the trustees or managers of a scheme under subsection (2) is outstanding at-

(a) the time the Board ceases to be involved with the scheme, or

(b) if earlier-

(i) the time during the assessment period when an order is made under section 11(3A) of the Pensions Act 1995 (c. 26) directing the winding up of the scheme, or

(ii) where no such order is made during that period, the time when the assessment period ends because the conditions in section 154(2) or (5) are satisfied,

that amount, together with the appropriate interest on it, falls to be repaid by the trustees or managers of the scheme to the Board at that time.

(4) No loan may be made under subsection (2) after the time mentioned in subsection (3)(b)(i).

(5) In subsection (2) the reference to "benefits" does not include money purchase benefits.

(6) In subsection (3) "the appropriate interest" on an amount lent under subsection (2) means interest at the prescribed rate from the time the amount was so lent until repayment.

(7) Subject to this section, the Board may make a loan under subsection (2) on such terms as it thinks fit.

Ill health pensions

140   Reviewable ill health pensions

(1) This section applies where there is an assessment period in relation to an eligible scheme.

(2) The Board may review a reviewable ill health pension in respect of a member if-

(a) disregarding section 141, the member would be entitled to compensation under paragraph 3 of Schedule 7 in respect of the pension if the Board assumed responsibility for the scheme,

(b) the member did not attain normal pension age in respect of the pension before the assessment date, and

(c) the pension is attributable to the member's pensionable service.

(3) An ill health pension in respect of a member is reviewable for the purposes of subsection (2) if the member is entitled to the pension by reason of an award under the scheme rules ("the award") which was made-

(a) in the period of three years ending immediately before the assessment date, or

(b) before the end of the prescribed period beginning with the assessment date, in response to an application made before that date.

(4) Where-

(a) before the assessment date, an application was made under the scheme for the award of a pension before normal pension age by virtue of any provision of the scheme rules making special provision as to early payment of pension on grounds of ill health, and

(b) the trustees or managers of the scheme failed to decide the application before the end of the period mentioned in subsection (3)(b),

section 10 of the Pensions Act 1995 (c. 26) (civil penalties) applies to any trustee or manager who has failed to take all reasonable steps to secure that the application was decided before the end of that period.

(5) Where-

(a) the award was made in response to an application which-

(i) was made on or after the assessment date, or

(ii) was made before that date but not decided by the trustees or managers of the scheme before the end of the period mentioned in subsection (3)(b), and

(b) in the absence of this subsection, the award would take effect before the assessment date,

the award is, for the purposes of determining the compensation payable under this Chapter in a case where the Board assumes responsibility for the scheme, to be treated as taking effect after the date on which the decision to make the award was made.

(6) Regulations must prescribe the procedure to be followed in relation to the review of a pension under this section and any subsequent decision under section 141.

141   Effect of a review

(1) This section applies where, during an assessment period in relation to an eligible scheme, the Board reviews an ill health pension by virtue of section 140.

(2) Where the conditions of subsection (3) are satisfied, the Board may determine that the compensation payable in respect of the pension, in a case where the Board assumes responsibility for the scheme, is to be determined in the prescribed manner on and after the relevant date.

(3) The conditions are-

(a) that the annual rate of compensation which would be payable under this Part in respect of the pension at the assessment date, if the Board assumed responsibility for the scheme, exceeds the notional reviewed rate of compensation in respect of the pension,

(b) that the Board is satisfied-

(i) that the decision to make the award was made in ignorance of, or was based upon a mistake as to, a material fact relevant to the decision,

(ii) that, at the time that decision was made, the member knew or could reasonably have been expected to know of that fact and that it was relevant to the decision, and

(iii) that, had the trustees or managers known about, or not been mistaken as to, that fact, they could not reasonably have decided to make the award, and

(c) that the Board is not satisfied that the criteria in the admissible rules governing entitlement to early payment of pension on grounds of ill health were satisfied in respect of the member at any time after that decision but before the assessment date.

(4) For the purposes of subsection (2) "the relevant date" means the date during the assessment period on which a scheme valuation in relation to the scheme becomes binding.

(5) The power to make a decision in respect of the pension under subsection (2) may only be exercised at a time which falls-

(a) during the assessment period but before the time the Board first approves a scheme valuation under section 144 in relation to the scheme, and

(b) within a reasonable period beginning with the assessment date or, where the decision to make the award was made at a later date, that date.

(6) Regulations made for the purposes of subsection (2) may, in particular, include provision applying any provision of Schedule 7 with such modifications as may be prescribed.

142   Sections 140 and 141: interpretation

(1) For the purposes of sections 140 and 141-

"admissible rules" is to be construed in accordance with Schedule 7;

"assessment date" means the date on which the assessment period begins;

"ill health pension", in relation to a scheme, means a pension which, immediately before the assessment date, is a pension to which a person is entitled under the admissible rules in circumstances where that entitlement arose before normal pension age by virtue of any provision of the admissible rules making special provision as to early payment of pension on grounds of ill health;

"normal pension age", in relation to a scheme and any pension under it, means the age specified in the admissible rules as the earliest age at which the pension becomes payable without actuarial adjustment (disregarding any admissible rule making special provision as to early payment on the grounds of ill health) and sub-paragraphs (2) and (3) of paragraph 34 of Schedule 7 apply in relation to this section as they apply in relation to that Schedule;

"notional reviewed rate of compensation", in respect of an ill health pension, means-

(a) the annual rate of compensation which would be payable in respect of the pension at the assessment date, if the Board assumed responsibility for the scheme and the compensation so payable at that date was determined in accordance with regulations under section 141(2), or

(b) if no such compensation would have been so payable at that date, nil;

"pensionable service" is to be construed in accordance with Schedule 7;

"scheme valuation", in relation to a scheme, means a valuation under section 143 of the assets and protected liabilities of the scheme as at the time immediately before the assessment period begins.

(2) For the purposes of section 140(4)-

(a) the definition of "normal pension age" in subsection (1), and

(b) sub-paragraphs (2) and (3) of paragraph 34 of Schedule 7 as they apply by virtue of that definition, have effect as if the references in those provisions to the admissible rules were references to the scheme rules.

(3) Paragraph 37(4) of Schedule 7 (references to "ill health" to be construed in accordance with regulations) applies in relation to sections 140 and 141 and this section as if, in that provision, the reference to that Schedule included a reference to those sections and this section.

(4) In those sections references to the Board assuming responsibility for the scheme are to the Board assuming responsibility for the scheme in accordance with this Chapter at the time the assessment period in question comes to an end.

Valuation of assets and liabilities

143 Board's obligation to obtain valuation of assets and protected liabilities

(1) This section applies in a case within subsection (1) of section 127 or 128.

(2) For the purposes of determining whether the condition in subsection (2)(a) of the section in question is satisfied, the Board must, as soon as reasonably practicable, obtain an actuarial valuation of the scheme as at the relevant time.

(3) For those purposes, regulations may provide that any of the following are to be regarded as assets or protected liabilities of the scheme at the relevant time if prescribed requirements are met-

(a) a debt due to the trustees or managers of the scheme by virtue of a contribution notice issued under section 38, 47 or 55 during the pre-approval period;

(b) an obligation arising under financial support for the scheme (within the meaning of section 45) put in place during the pre-approval period in accordance with a financial support direction issued under section 43;

(c) an obligation imposed by a restoration order made under section 52 during the pre-approval period in respect of a transaction involving assets of the scheme.

(4) For the purposes of this section, regulations may prescribe how-

(a) the assets and the protected liabilities of eligible schemes, and

(b) their amount or value,

are to be determined, calculated and verified.

(5) Regulations under subsection (4) may provide, in particular, that when calculating the amount or value of assets or protected liabilities of an eligible scheme at the relevant time which consist of any of the following-

(a) a debt (including any contingent debt) due to the trustees or managers of the scheme from the employer under section 75 of the Pensions Act 1995 (c. 26) (deficiencies in the scheme assets),

(b) a debt due to the trustees or managers of the scheme by virtue of a contribution notice issued under section 38, 47 or 55,

(c) an obligation arising under financial support for the scheme (within the meaning of section 45) put in place in accordance with a financial support direction issued under section 43, or

(d) an obligation imposed by a restoration order made under section 52 in respect of a transaction involving assets of the scheme,

account must be taken in the prescribed manner of prescribed events which occur during the pre-approval period.

(6) Subject to any provision made under subsection (4), the matters mentioned in paragraphs (a) and (b) of that subsection are to be determined, calculated and verified in accordance with guidance issued by the Board.

(7) In calculating the amount of any liabilities for the purposes of this section, a provision of the scheme rules which limits the amount of the scheme's liabilities by reference to the value of its assets is to be disregarded.

(8) The duty imposed by subsection (2) ceases to apply if and when the Board ceases to be involved with the scheme.

(9) Nothing in subsection (2) requires the actuarial valuation to be obtained during any period when the Board considers that an event may occur which, by virtue of regulations under subsection (3) or (4), may affect the value of the assets or the amount of the protected liabilities of the scheme for the purposes of the valuation.

(10) In a case where there are one or more reviewable ill health pensions (within the meaning of section 140), nothing in subsection (2) requires the actuarial valuation to be obtained during the period mentioned in section 141(5)(b) (period during which Board may exercise its power to make a decision following a review) relating to any such pension.

(11) For the purposes of this section-

    (a) "actuarial valuation", in relation to the scheme, means a written valuation of the assets and protected liabilities of the scheme which-

        (i) is in the prescribed form and contains the prescribed information, and

        (ii) is prepared and signed by-

        (a) a person with prescribed qualifications or experience, or

        (b) a person approved by the Secretary of State,

    (b) "the pre-approval period", in relation to the scheme, means the period which-

        (i) begins immediately after the relevant time, and

        (ii) ends immediately before the time the Board first approves a valuation of the scheme under section 144 after the relevant time,

    (c) "the relevant time"-

        (i) in a case within subsection (1) of section 127, has the meaning given in subsection (4)(b) of that section, and

        (ii) in a case within subsection (1) of section 128, has the meaning given in subsection (3)(b) of that section, and

    (d) references to "assets" do not include assets representing the value of any rights in respect of money purchase benefits under the scheme rules.

144   Approval of valuation

(1) This section applies where the Board obtains a valuation in respect of a scheme under section 143.

(2) Where the Board is satisfied that the valuation has been prepared in accordance with that section, it must-

    (a) approve the valuation, and

    (b) give a copy of the valuation to-

        (i) the Regulator,

        (ii) the trustees or managers of the scheme, and

        (iii) any insolvency practitioner in relation to the employer or, if there is no such insolvency practitioner, the employer.

(3) Where the Board is not so satisfied, it must obtain another valuation under that section.

145   Binding valuations

(1) For the purposes of this Chapter a valuation obtained under section 143 is not binding until-

(a) it is approved under section 144,

(b) the period within which the approval may be reviewed by virtue of Chapter 6 has expired, and

(c) if the approval is so reviewed-

(i) the review and any reconsideration,

(ii) any reference to the PPF Ombudsman in respect of the approval, and

(iii) any appeal against his determination or directions,

has been finally disposed of.

(2) For the purposes of determining whether or not the condition in section 127(2)(a) or, as the case may be, section 128(2)(a) (condition that scheme assets are less than protected liabilities) is satisfied in relation to a scheme, a binding valuation is conclusive.

This subsection is subject to section 172(3) and (4) (treatment of fraud compensation payments).

(3) Where a valuation becomes binding under this section the Board must as soon as reasonably practicable give a notice to that effect together with a copy of the binding valuation to-

(a) the Regulator,

(b) the trustees or managers of the scheme, and

(c) any insolvency practitioner in relation to the employer or, if there is no such insolvency practitioner, the employer.

(4) A notice under subsection (3) must be in the prescribed form and contain the prescribed information.

Refusal to assume responsibility

146   Schemes which become eligible schemes

(1) Regulations may provide that where the Board is satisfied that an eligible scheme was not such a scheme throughout such period as may be prescribed, the Board must refuse to assume responsibility for the scheme under this Chapter.

(2) Where, by virtue of subsection (1), the Board is required to refuse to assume responsibility for a scheme, it-

(a) must issue a notice to that effect (a "withdrawal notice"), and

(b) give a copy of that notice to-

(i) the Regulator,

(ii) the trustees or managers of the scheme, and

(iii) any insolvency practitioner in relation to the employer or, if there is no such insolvency practitioner, the employer.

(3) For the purposes of this Part a withdrawal notice issued by virtue of this section is not binding until-

(a) the period within which the issue of the notice may be reviewed by virtue of Chapter 6 has expired, and

(b) if the issue of the notice is so reviewed-

(i) the review and any reconsideration,

(ii) any reference to the PPF Ombudsman in respect of the issue of the notice, and

(iii) any appeal against his determination or directions,

has been finally disposed of and the notice has not been revoked, varied or substituted.

(4) Where a withdrawal notice issued by virtue of this section becomes binding, the Board must as soon as reasonably practicable give a notice to that effect together with a copy of the binding notice to-

(a) the Regulator,

(b) the trustees or managers of the scheme, and

(c) any insolvency practitioner in relation to the employer or, if there is no such insolvency practitioner, the employer.

(5) Notices under this section must be in the prescribed form and contain such information as may be prescribed.

(6) A notice given under subsection (4) must state the time from which the Board ceases to be involved with the scheme (see section 149).

147   New schemes created to replace existing schemes

(1) The Board must refuse to assume responsibility for a scheme ("the new scheme") under this Chapter where it is satisfied that-

(a) the new scheme was established during such period as may be prescribed,

(b) the employer in relation to the new scheme was, at the date of establishment of that scheme, also the employer in relation to a scheme established before the new scheme (the "old scheme"),

(c) a transfer or transfers of, or a transfer payment or transfer payments in respect of, any rights of members under the old scheme has or have been made to the new scheme, and

(d) the main purpose or one of the main purposes of establishing the new scheme and making the transfer or transfers, or transfer payment or transfer payments, was to enable those members to receive compensation under the pension compensation provisions in respect of their rights under the new scheme in circumstances where, in the absence of the transfer or transfers, regulations under section 146 would have operated to prevent such payments in respect of their rights under the old scheme.

(2) Where, under subsection (1), the Board is required to refuse to assume responsibility for a scheme, it-

(a) must issue a notice to that effect (a "withdrawal notice"), and

(b) give a copy of that notice to-

(i) the Regulator,

(ii) the trustees or managers of the scheme, and

(iii) any insolvency practitioner in relation to the employer or, if there is no such insolvency practitioner, the employer.

(3) For the purposes of this Part a withdrawal notice issued under this section is not binding until-

(a) the period within which the issue of the notice may be reviewed by virtue of Chapter 6 has expired, and

(b) if the issue of the notice is so reviewed-

(i) the review and any reconsideration,

(ii) any reference to the PPF Ombudsman in respect of the issue of the notice, and

(iii) any appeal against his determination or directions,

has been finally disposed of and the notice has not been revoked, varied or substituted.

(4) Where a withdrawal notice issued under this section becomes binding, the Board must as soon as reasonably practicable give a notice to that effect together with a copy of the binding notice to-

(a) the Regulator,

(b) the trustees or managers of the scheme, and

(c) any insolvency practitioner in relation to the employer or, if there is no such insolvency practitioner, the employer.

(5) Notices under this section must be in the prescribed form and contain such information as may be prescribed.

(6) A notice given under subsection (4) must state the time from which the Board ceases to be involved with the scheme (see section 149).

148   Withdrawal following issue of section 122(4) notice

(1) This section applies where-

(a) a notice under section 122(4) (inability to confirm status of scheme) is issued in relation to an eligible scheme and becomes binding, and

(b) a withdrawal event has not occurred in relation to the scheme in respect of a withdrawal notice which has been issued during the period-

(i) beginning with the occurrence of the last insolvency event in relation to the employer, and

(ii) ending immediately before the notice under section 122(4) becomes binding, and the occurrence of such a withdrawal event in respect of a withdrawal notice issued during that period is not a possibility (see section 149).

(2) The Board must determine whether any insolvency event-

(a) has occurred in relation to the employer since the issue of the notice under section 122(4), or

(b) is likely to so occur before the end of the period of six months beginning with the date on which this section applies.

(3) If the Board determines under subsection (2) that no insolvency event has occurred or is likely to occur as mentioned in that subsection, it must issue a notice to that effect (a "withdrawal notice").

(4) Where-

(a) no withdrawal notice is issued under subsection (3) before the end of the period mentioned in subsection (2)(b), and

(b) no further insolvency event occurs in relation to the employer during that period, the Board must issue a notice to that effect (a "withdrawal notice").

(5) Where the Board is required to issue a withdrawal notice under this section, it must give a copy of the notice to-

(a) the Regulator,

(b) the trustees or managers of the scheme, and

(c) the employer.

(6) For the purposes of this Part, a withdrawal notice issued under this section is not binding until-

(a) the period within which the issue of the notice may be reviewed by virtue of Chapter 6 has expired, and

(b) if the issue of the notice is so reviewed-

(i) the review and any reconsideration,

(ii) any reference to the PPF Ombudsman in respect of the issue of the notice, and

(iii) any appeal against his determination or directions,

has been finally disposed of and the notice has not been revoked, varied or substituted.

(7) Where a withdrawal notice issued under this section becomes binding, the Board must as soon as reasonably practicable give a notice to that effect together with a copy of the binding notice to-

(a) the Regulator,

(b) the trustees or managers of the scheme, and

(c) the employer.

(8) Notices under this section must be in the prescribed form and contain such information as may be prescribed.

(9) A notice given under subsection (7) must state the time from which the Board ceases to be involved with the scheme (see section 149).

Cessation of involvement with a scheme

149 Circumstances in which Board ceases to be involved with an eligible scheme

(1) Where an assessment period begins in relation to an eligible scheme, the Board ceases to be involved with the scheme, for the purposes of this Part, on the occurrence of the first withdrawal event after the beginning of that period.

(2) For this purpose the following are withdrawal events in relation to a scheme-

(a) a withdrawal notice issued under section 122(2)(b) (scheme rescue has occurred) becoming binding;

(b) a withdrawal notice issued under section 130(3) (scheme rescue has occurred) becoming binding;

(c) a withdrawal notice issued under or by virtue of section 146 or 147 (refusal to assume responsibility) becoming binding;

(d) a withdrawal notice issued under section 148 (no insolvency event has occurred or is likely to occur) becoming binding;

and references in this Chapter to a "withdrawal event" are to be construed accordingly.

(3) Subsection (4) applies where a withdrawal notice mentioned in subsection (2) is issued in relation to a scheme and becomes binding and-

(a) an insolvency event in relation to the employer occurs during the interim period and, if subsection (4) did not apply, the event would not be a qualifying insolvency event within the meaning given by subsection (3) of section 127 solely because the condition in sub-paragraph (ii) of paragraph (b) of that subsection would not be satisfied, or

(b) an application under section 129(1) is made, or a notification under section 129(5)(a) is given, in relation to the scheme during the interim period and, if subsection (4) did not apply, the application or notification would be disregarded for the purposes of-

(i) subsection (1) of section 128 by virtue of subsection (4) of that section, and

(ii) subsection (4) of section 132 by virtue of subsection (5) of that section.

(4) In such a case, the withdrawal notice is to be treated for the purposes of subsections (1) and (2), as if the time when it became binding was the time immediately before-

(a) in a case falling within subsection (3)(a), the occurrence of the insolvency event, and

(b) in a case falling within subsection (3)(b), the making of the application under section 129(1) or, as the case may be, the giving of the notification under section 129(5)(a).

(5) For the purposes of subsection (3), the "interim period" in relation to a scheme means the period beginning with the issuing of the withdrawal notice in relation to the scheme and ending with that notice becoming binding.

(6) For the purposes of this Chapter-

(a) the occurrence of a withdrawal event in relation to a scheme in respect of a withdrawal notice issued during a particular period ("the specified period") is a possibility until each of the following are no longer reviewable-

(i) any withdrawal notice which has been issued in relation to the scheme during the specified period,

(ii) any failure to issue such a withdrawal notice during the specified period,

(iii) any notice which has been issued by the Board under Chapter 2 or this Chapter which is relevant to the issue of a withdrawal notice in relation to the scheme during the specified period or to such a withdrawal notice which has been issued during that period becoming binding,

(iv) any failure to issue such a notice as is mentioned in sub-paragraph (iii), and

(b) the issue of, or failure to issue, a notice is to be regarded as reviewable-

(i) during the period within which it may be reviewed by virtue of Chapter 6, and

(ii) if the matter is so reviewed, until-

(a) the review and any reconsideration,

(b) any reference to the PPF Ombudsman in respect of the matter, and

(c) any appeal against his determination or directions,

has been finally disposed of.

150 Consequences of the Board ceasing to be involved with a scheme

(1) Where-

(a) an assessment period comes to an end by virtue of the Board ceasing to be involved with an eligible scheme, and

(b) during the assessment period any amount of any benefit payable to a member, or to a person in respect of a member, under the scheme rules was not paid by reason of section 138 (requirement to pay benefits in accordance with the pension compensation provisions),

that amount falls due to the member, or as the case may be, person at the end of that period.

(2) Where the winding up of the scheme began before the end of the assessment period (whether by virtue of section 219 (backdating the winding up of eligible schemes) or otherwise), the reference in subsection (1)(b) to the amount of any benefit payable to a member, or to a person in respect of a member, under the scheme rules is a reference to the amount so payable taking account of any reduction required by virtue of sections 73 to 73B of the Pensions Act 1995 (c. 26) (provisions relating to the winding up of certain schemes).

(3) Where-

(a) an assessment period comes to an end by virtue of the Board ceasing to be involved with an eligible scheme, and

(b) during the assessment period the amount of benefit paid to a member, or to a person in respect of a member, under the scheme rules exceeded the amount that would have been payable in the absence of section 138(6) (requirement to disregard winding up when paying benefits during assessment period),

the trustees or managers of the scheme must, at the end of that period, take such steps as they consider appropriate (including steps to adjust future payments under the scheme rules) to recover an amount equal to the excess from the person to whom it was paid.

(4) Subsections (1) to (3) are without prejudice to section 73A(2)(b) of the Pensions Act 1995 (c. 26) (requirement to adjust benefits paid to reflect liabilities which can be met on winding up).

(5) Regulations may provide that, in cases within paragraph (a) of subsection (1), benefits are to accrue under the scheme rules, in such circumstances as may be prescribed, to or in respect of members of the scheme in respect of any specified period of service being service in employment which, but for section 133(5), would have qualified the member in question for those benefits under the scheme rules.

(6) Regulations under subsection (5) may in particular make provision-

(a) for benefits not to accrue to, or in respect of, a member unless contributions are paid by or on behalf of the member towards the scheme within a prescribed period;

(b) for contributions towards the scheme which, but for section 133, would have been payable by or on behalf of the employer (otherwise than on behalf of an employee) during the assessment period, to fall due;

(c) requiring that such contributions as are mentioned in paragraph (a) or (b) are accepted for the assessment period or any part of that period;

(d) modifying section 31 of the Welfare Reform and Pensions Act 1999 (c. 30) (reduction of benefit where a person's shareable rights are subject to a pension debit), in its application in relation to cases where benefits accrue under the scheme by virtue of regulations under subsection (5).

(7) In this section "contributions" means, in relation to an eligible scheme, contributions payable towards the scheme by or on behalf of the employer or the active members of the scheme in accordance with the schedule of contributions maintained under section 227 in respect of the scheme.

Reconsideration

151 Application for reconsideration

(1) Where subsection (2) or (3) applies in relation to an eligible scheme, the trustees or managers of the scheme may make an application to the Board under this section for it to assume responsibility for the scheme in accordance with this Chapter.

(2) This subsection applies where-

(a) a scheme failure notice has been issued under section 122(2)(a) in relation to the scheme, that notice has become binding and the trustees or managers have received a copy of the binding notice under section 125(3),

(b) the valuation obtained by the Board under section 143 in respect of the scheme has become binding, and

(c) the Board would have been required to assume responsibility for the scheme under section 127 but for the fact that the condition in subsection (2)(a) of that section was no satisfied.

(3) This subsection applies where-

(a) the Board has issued a scheme failure notice under subsection (2) of section 130 in relation to the scheme, that notice has become binding and the trustees or managers have received a copy of the binding notice under subsection (7) of that section,

(b) the valuation obtained by the Board under section 143 in respect of the scheme has become binding, and

(c) the Board would have been required to assume responsibility for the scheme under section 128 but for the fact that the condition in subsection (2)(a) of that section was no satisfied.

(4) An application under this section must be in the prescribed form, contain the prescribed information and be accompanied by-

(a) a protected benefits quotation in the prescribed form, and

(b) audited scheme accounts for a period which-

(i) begins with such date as may be determined in accordance with regulations, and

(ii) ends with a date which falls within the prescribed period ending with the day on which the application is made.

(5) An application under this section must be made within the authorised period.

(6) In this section "the authorised period" means the prescribed period which begins-

(a) where subsection (2) applies, with the later of-

(i) the day on which the trustees or managers received the copy of the binding notice mentioned in paragraph (a) of that subsection, and

(ii) the day on which they received a copy of the binding valuation mentioned in paragraph (b) of that section, and

(b) where subsection (3) applies, with the later of-

(i) the day on which the trustees or managers received the copy of the binding notice mentioned in paragraph (a) of that subsection, and

(ii) the day on which they received a copy of the binding valuation mentioned in paragraph (b) of that subsection.

(7) Where the Board receives an application under subsection (1), it must give a copy of the application to the Regulator.

(8) For the purposes of this section-

"audited scheme accounts", in relation to a scheme, means-

(a) accounts obtained by the trustees or managers of the scheme ("the scheme accounts") which are prepared in accordance with subsections (9) to (11) and audited by the auditor in relation to the scheme, and

(b) a report by the auditor, in the prescribed form, as to whether or not such requirements as may be prescribed are satisfied in relation to the scheme accounts;

"auditor", in relation to a scheme, has the meaning given by section 47 of the Pensions Act 1995 (c. 26);

"protected benefits quotation", in relation to a scheme, means a quotation for one or more annuities from one or more insurers, being companies willing to accept payment in respect of the members from the trustees or managers of the scheme, which would provide in respect of each member of the scheme from the reconsideration time-

(a) benefits for or in respect of the member corresponding to the compensation which would be payable to or in respect of the member in accordance with the pension compensation provisions if the Board assumed responsibility for the scheme by virtue of this section, or

(b) benefits in accordance with the member's entitlement or accrued rights (including pension credit rights within the meaning of section 124(1) of the Pensions Act 1995 (c. 26)) under the scheme rules (other than his entitlement or rights in respect of money purchase benefits),

whichever benefits can, in the case of that member, be secured at the lower cost;

"the reconsideration time", in relation to an application under this section, means the time immediately before the end of the period to which the audited scheme accounts mentioned in subsection (4)(b) relate.

(9) The scheme accounts are prepared in accordance with this subsection if, subject to subsections (10) and (11), they-

(a) include a statement of the assets of the scheme (excluding any assets representing the value of any rights in respect of money purchase benefits under the scheme rules) as at the reconsideration time, and

(b) are prepared in accordance with such other requirements as may be prescribed.

(10) Subject to subsection (11), regulations under subsection (4) of section 143 (other than regulations made by virtue of subsection (5) of that section), and guidance under subsection (6) of that section, apply to the scheme accounts as they apply for the purposes of a valuation under that section.

(11) Regulations may provide that, where an asset of a prescribed description has been acquired during the assessment period, the value assigned to the asset as at the reconsideration time is to be determined, for the purposes of the scheme accounts, in the prescribed manner.

(12) For the purposes of this section-

(a) regulations may prescribe how the cost of securing the benefits mentioned in paragraph (a) of the definition of "protected benefits quotation" in subsection (8) is to be determined, calculated and verified, and

(b) subject to any provision made under paragraph (a), that cost is to be determined, calculated and verified in accordance with guidance issued by the Board.

(13) Where the scheme is being wound up, for the purposes of determining the benefits which fall within paragraph (b) of the definition of "protected benefits quotation" in subsection (8) no account is to be taken of the winding up of the scheme.

152 Duty to assume responsibility following reconsideration

(1) This section applies where an application is made in respect of a scheme in accordance with section 151.

(2) The Board must assume responsibility for the scheme in accordance with this Chapter if it is satisfied that the value of the assets of the scheme at the reconsideration time is less than the aggregate of-

(a) the amount quoted in the protected benefits quotation accompanying the application,

(b) the amount at that time of the liabilities of the scheme which are not liabilities to, or in respect of, members of the scheme, and

(c) the estimated costs of winding up the scheme at that time.

(3) Where the Board makes a determination for the purposes of subsection (2), it must issue a determination notice and give a copy of that notice to-

(a) the trustees or managers of the scheme, and

(b) the Regulator.

(4) In subsection (3) "determination notice" means a notice which is in the prescribed form and contains such information about the determination as may be prescribed.

(5) But where the Board is satisfied of the matters mentioned in subsection (2), it is not required to assume responsibility for the scheme under subsection (2) until the determination notice issued under subsection (3) becomes binding.

(6) For the purposes of subsection (5) a determination notice is not binding until-

(a) the period within which the issue of the notice may be reviewed by virtue of Chapter 6 has expired, and

(b) if the issue of the notice is so reviewed-

(i) the review and any reconsideration,

(ii) any reference to the PPF Ombudsman in respect of the issue of the notice, and

(iii) any appeal against his determination or directions,

has been finally disposed of and the notice has not been revoked, varied or substituted.

(7) Where a determination notice issued under subsection (3) becomes binding, the Board must as soon as reasonably practicable give a notice to that effect together with a copy of the binding notice to-

(a) the trustees or managers of the scheme, and

(b) the Regulator.

(8) A notice under subsection (7) must be in the prescribed form and contain such information as may be prescribed.

(9) The Board may-

(a) for the purposes of subsection (2), obtain its own valuation of the assets of the scheme as at the reconsideration time (within the meaning of section 151), and

(b) for the purposes of subsection (2)(b), obtain its own valuation of the liabilities of the scheme as at that time;

and where it does so, subsections (9)(b), (10) and (11) of section 151 apply in relation to the valuation as they apply in relation to the scheme accounts (within the meaning of that section).

(10) Regulations under subsection (4) of section 143, and guidance under subsection (6) of that section, apply for the purposes of this section in relation to the estimated costs within subsection (2)(c) as they apply for the purposes of section 143 in relation to protected liabilities within section 131(1)(c).

(11) In this section references to the assets of the scheme do not include assets representing the value of any rights in respect of money purchase benefits under the scheme rules.

(12) This section is subject to sections 146 and 147 (refusal to assume responsibility for a scheme).

Closed schemes

153   Closed schemes

(1) This section applies where section 151(2) or (3) (scheme rescue not possible but scheme has sufficient assets to meet the protected liabilities) applies in relation to an eligible scheme.

2) If the trustees or managers of the scheme are unable to obtain a full buy-out quotation, they must, within the authorised period, apply to the Board for authority to continue as a closed scheme.

3) For the purposes of determining whether they must make an application under subsection (2), the trustees or managers of the scheme must take all reasonable steps to obtain a full buy-out quotation in respect of the scheme.

4) An application under subsection (2) must-

(a) be in the prescribed form and contain the prescribed information, and

(b) be accompanied by evidence in the prescribed form which shows that the trustees or managers of the scheme have complied with the obligation under subsection (3) but were unable to obtain a full buy-out quotation.

5) Where the Board receives an application under subsection (2), if it is satisfied that the trustees or managers have complied with the obligation under subsection (3) but were unable to obtain a full buy-out quotation, it must authorise the scheme to continue as a closed scheme.

6) Where the Board determines an application in respect of a scheme under this section, it must issue a determination notice and give a copy of that notice to-

(a) the trustees or managers of the scheme, and

(b) the Regulator.

7) In this section-

authorised period" has the same meaning as in section 151;

determination notice" means a notice which is in the prescribed form and contains such information about the determination as may be prescribed;

full buy-out quotation", in relation to a scheme, means a quotation for one or more annuities from one or more insurers (being companies willing to accept payment in respect of the members from the trustees or managers of the scheme) which would provide in respect of each member of the scheme, from a relevant date, benefits in accordance with the member's entitlement or accrued rights, including pension credit rights, under the scheme rules (other than his entitlement or rights in respect of money purchase benefits);

pension credit rights" has the meaning given by section 124(1) of the Pensions Act 1995 (c. 26);

relevant date" means a date within the authorised period.

8) If the trustees or managers of the scheme fail to comply with subsection (2) or (3), section 10 of the Pensions Act 1995 (civil penalties) applies to any trustee or manager who has failed to take all reasonable steps to secure compliance.

Winding up

154 Requirement to wind up schemes with sufficient assets to meet protected liabilities

1) Where, in relation to an eligible scheme, an assessment period within section 132(2) or (4) comes to an end because the conditions in subsection (2) of this section are satisfied, the trustees or managers of the scheme must-

(a) wind up the scheme, or

(b) where the winding up of the scheme began before the assessment period (whether by virtue of section 219 or otherwise), continue the winding up of the scheme.

2) The conditions are-

(a) that subsection (2) or (3) of section 151 (scheme rescue not possible but scheme has sufficient assets to meet the protected liabilities) applies in relation to the scheme,

(b) that-

(i) the trustees or managers did not make an application under that section or section 153(2) within the authorised period (within the meaning of section 151(6)) (or any such application has been withdrawn), or

(ii) if such an application was made, it has been finally determined, and

(c) that, if an application was made under section 151, the Board is not required to assume responsibility for the scheme by virtue of section 152(2).

(3) For the purposes of subsection (2)(b)(ii) an application is not finally determined until-

(a) the Board has issued a determination notice in respect of the application under section 152 or, as the case may be, section 153,

(b) the period within which the issue of the notice may be reviewed by virtue of Chapter 6 has expired, and

(c) if the issue of the notice is so reviewed-

(i) the review and any reconsideration,

(ii) any reference to the PPF Ombudsman in respect of the issue of the notice, and

(iii) any appeal against his determination or directions,

has been finally disposed of.

(4) Where, in relation to an eligible scheme, an assessment period within section 159(3) comes to an end because the conditions in subsection (5) of this section are satisfied, the trustees or managers of the scheme must continue the winding up of the scheme begun (whether in accordance with this section or otherwise) before that assessment period.

(5) The conditions are-

(a) that an application is made by, or notice is given to, the trustees or managers of the scheme under section 157 (applications and notifications where closed schemes have insufficient assets),

(b) that the valuation obtained by the Board in respect of the scheme under section 158(3) has become binding, and

(c) that the Board is not required to assume responsibility for the scheme by virtue of section 158(1) (duty to assume responsibility for closed scheme).

(6) Where a scheme is wound up in accordance with subsection (1)(a), the winding up is to be taken as beginning immediately before the assessment period.

(7) Without prejudice to the power to give directions under section 134, but subject to any order made under subsection (8), the Board may give the trustees or managers of the scheme directions relating to the manner of the winding up of the scheme under this section (and may vary or revoke any such direction given by it).

(8) The Regulator may by order direct any person specified in the order-

(a) to take such steps as are so specified as it considers are necessary as a result of-

(i) the winding up of the scheme beginning, by virtue of subsection (6), immediately before the assessment period, or

(ii) the winding up of the scheme being continued under subsection (1)(b), and

(b) to take those steps within a period specified in the order.

(9) If the trustees or managers of a scheme fail to comply with a direction to them under subsection (7), or contained in an order under subsection (8), section 10 of the Pensions Act 1995 (c. 26) (civil penalties) applies to any trustee or manager who has failed to take all reasonable steps to secure compliance.

(10) That section also applies to any other person who, without reasonable excuse, fails to comply with a direction to him contained in an order under subsection (8).

(11) The winding up of a scheme under this section is as effective in law as if it had been made under powers conferred by or under the scheme.

(12) This section must be complied with in relation to a scheme-

(a) in spite of any enactment or rule of law, or any rule of the scheme, which would otherwise operate to prevent the winding up, and

(b) without regard to any such enactment, rule of law or rule of the scheme as would otherwise require or might otherwise be taken to require the implementation of any procedure or the obtaining of any consent with a view to the winding up.

(13) Where an assessment period in relation to an eligible scheme comes to an end by virtue of the conditions in subsection (2) or (5) being satisfied, subsections (1) to (4) of section 150 apply as they apply where an assessment period comes to an end by virtue of the Board ceasing to be involved with the scheme, except that in subsection (2) of that section the reference to section 219 is to be read as a reference to subsection (6) of this section.

(14) Where a public service pension scheme is required to be wound up under this section, the appropriate authority may by order make provision modifying any enactment in which the scheme is contained or under which it is made.

(15) In subsection (14) "the appropriate authority", in relation to a scheme, means such Minister of the Crown or government department as may be designated by the Treasury as having responsibility for the particular scheme.

Provisions applying to closed schemes

155 Treatment of closed schemes

(1) In this section "closed scheme" means an eligible scheme which is authorised under section 153 to continue as a closed scheme.

(2) The provisions mentioned in subsection (3) apply in relation to a closed scheme at any time when the trustees or managers of the scheme are required to wind up or continue winding up the scheme under section 154 as if that time fell within an assessment period in relation to the scheme.

(3) The provisions are-

(a) section 40(5) and (6) (Board to act as creditor for debt due by virtue of a contribution notice under section 38);

(b) section 49(5) and (6) (Board to act as creditor for debt due by virtue of a contribution notice under section 47);

(c) section 54(5) and (6) (Board to act as creditor for debt due by virtue of a restoration order under section 52);

(d) section 56(5) and (6) (Board to act as creditor for debt due by virtue of a contribution notice under section 55);

(e) section 133 (admission of new members, payment of contributions etc);

(f) section 134 (directions);

(g) section 137 (Board to act as creditor of the employer).

(4) Regulations may require the trustees or managers of a closed scheme in relation to which the provisions mentioned in subsection (3) apply to comply with such requirements as may be prescribed when providing for the discharge of any liability to, or in respect of, a member of the scheme for pensions or other benefits.

156 Valuations of closed schemes

(1) Regulations may make provision requiring the trustees or managers of closed schemes to obtain actuarial valuations of the scheme at such intervals as may be prescribed for the purposes of enabling them to determine-

(a) the benefits payable under the scheme rules;

(b) whether to make an application under section 157.

(2) Regulations under this section may prescribe how-

(a) the assets, the full scheme liabilities and the protected liabilities in relation to closed schemes, and

(b) their amount or value,

are to be determined, calculated and verified.

(3) Subject to any provision made under subsection (2), those matters are to be determined, calculated and verified in accordance with guidance issued by the Board.

(4) In calculating the amount of any liabilities for the purposes of a valuation required by virtue of this section, a provision of the scheme rules which limits the amount of the scheme's liabilities by reference to the value of its assets is to be disregarded.

(5) Nothing in regulations under this section may require the trustees or managers of a closed scheme to obtain an actuarial valuation of the scheme until-

(a) the period within which the issue of the determination notice, under section 153(6), in respect of the Board's determination to authorise the scheme to continue as a closed scheme, may be reviewed by virtue of Chapter 6 has expired, and

(b) if the issue of the notice is so reviewed-

(i) the review and any reconsideration,

(ii) any reference to the PPF Ombudsman in respect of the issue of the notice, and

(iii) any appeal against his determination or directions,

has been finally disposed of and the notice has not been revoked, varied or substituted.

(6) In this section, in relation to a scheme-

"actuarial valuation" means a written valuation of-

(a) the scheme's assets,

(b) the full scheme liabilities, and

(c) the protected liabilities in relation to the scheme,

prepared and signed by the actuary;

"the actuary" means-

(a) the actuary appointed under section 47(1)(b) of the Pensions Act 1995 (c. 26) (professional advisers) in relation to the scheme, or

(b) if no such actuary has been appointed-

(i) a person with prescribed qualifications or experience, or

(ii) a person approved by the Secretary of State;

"assets" do not include assets representing the value of any rights in respect of money purchase benefits under the scheme rules;

"closed scheme" has the same meaning as in section 155;

"full scheme liabilities" means-

(a) the liabilities under the scheme rules to or in respect of members of the scheme,

(b) other liabilities of the scheme, and

(c) the estimated cost of winding up the scheme;

"liabilities" does not include liabilities in respect of money purchase benefits under the scheme rules.

Reconsideration of closed schemes

157 Applications and notifications where closed schemes have insufficient assets

(1) If at any time the trustees or managers of a closed scheme become aware that the value of the assets of the scheme is less than the amount of the protected liabilities in relation to the scheme, they must, before the end of the prescribed period beginning with that time, make an application to the Board for it to assume responsibility for the scheme.

(2) Where the Board receives an application under subsection (1), it must give a copy of the application to the Regulator.

(3) If at any time the Regulator becomes aware that the value of the assets of the scheme is less than the amount of the protected liabilities in relation to the scheme, it must give the Board a notice to that effect.

(4) Where the Board receives a notice under subsection (3), it must give the trustees or managers of the scheme a notice to that effect.

(5) The duty imposed by subsection (1) does not apply where the trustees or managers of a closed scheme become aware as mentioned in that subsection by reason of a notice given to them under subsection (4).

(6) The duty imposed by subsection (3) does not apply where the Regulator becomes aware as mentioned in that subsection by reason of a copy of an application made by the trustees or managers of the closed scheme being given to it under subsection (2).

(7) Regulations may require notices and applications under this section to be in the prescribed form and contain the prescribed information.

(8) If the trustees or managers of a closed scheme fail to comply with subsection (1), section 10 of the Pensions Act 1995 (c. 26) (civil penalties) applies to any trustee or manager who has failed to take all reasonable steps to secure compliance.

(9) In this section-

"assets", in relation to a scheme, do not include assets representing the value of any rights in respect of money purchase benefits under the scheme rules;

"closed scheme" has the same meaning as in section 155.

158 Duty to assume responsibility for closed schemes

(1) Where the trustees or managers of a closed scheme-

(a) make an application under subsection (1) of section 157, or

(b) receive a notice from the Board under subsection (4) of that section,

the Board must assume responsibility for the scheme in accordance with this Chapter if the value of the assets of the scheme at the relevant time was less than the amount of the protected liabilities at that time.

(2) In subsection (1) the reference to the assets of the scheme is a reference to those assets excluding any assets representing the value of any rights in respect of money purchase benefits under the scheme rules.

(3) For the purposes of determining whether the condition in subsection (1) is satisfied, the Board must, as soon as reasonably practicable, obtain an actuarial valuation (within the meaning of section 143) of the scheme as at the relevant time.

(4) Subject to subsection (6), subsection (3) of section 143 applies for those purposes as it applies for the purposes mentioned in subsection (2) of that section (and the definitions contained in paragraphs (b) and (d) of subsection (11) of that section apply accordingly).

(5) Subject to subsection (6), the following provisions apply in relation to a valuation obtained under subsection (3) as they apply in relation to a valuation obtained under section 143-

(a) subsections (4) to (7) and (11)(b) and (d) of that section;

(b) section 144 (approval of valuation), other than subsection (2)(b)(iii) (duty to give copy of approved valuation to employer's insolvency practitioner);

(c) section 145 (binding valuations), other than subsection (3)(c) (duty to give copy of binding valuation to employer's insolvency practitioner).

(6) In the application of sections 143 and 145 by virtue of subsection (4) or (5)-

(a) subsections (3), (5) and (11)(b) and (d) of section 143 apply as if the references to "the relevant time" were references to that term as defined in subsection (8) below, and

(b) subsection (2) of section 145 applies as if the reference to section 128(2)(a) included a reference to subsection (1) of this section.

(7) An application under subsection (1) of section 157, or notification under subsection (4) of that section, is to be disregarded for the purposes of subsection (1) if it is made or given during an assessment period (see sections 132 and 159) in relation to the scheme which began before the application was made or notification was given.

(8) In this section-

"closed scheme" has the same meaning as in section 155;

"the relevant time" means the time immediately before the application mentioned in subsection (1)(a) was made, or (as the case may be) the notice mentioned in subsection (1)(b) was received, by the trustees or managers of the scheme.

159   Closed schemes: further assessment periods

(1) Subsection (3) applies where-

(a) an application is made under subsection (1) of section 157 in relation to a closed scheme, or

(b) the trustees or managers of the scheme receive a notice under subsection (4) of that section.

(2) For the purposes of subsection (1) an application under subsection (1) of section 157, or notification under subsection (4) of that section, is to be disregarded if it is made or given during an assessment period (see section 132 and this section) in relation to the scheme which began before the application was made or notification was given.

(3) An assessment period-

(a) begins when the application is made or the notice is received by the trustees or managers of the scheme, and

(b) ends when-

(i) the trustees or managers receive a transfer notice under section 160, or

(ii) the conditions in section 154(5) (closed scheme with sufficient assets to meet protected liabilities etc) are satisfied in relation to the scheme,

whichever first occurs.

(4) In this section "closed scheme" has the same meaning as in section 155.

Assumption of responsibility for a scheme

160   Transfer notice

(1) This section applies where the Board is required to assume responsibility for a scheme under section 127, 128, 152 or 158.

(2) The Board must give the trustees or managers a notice (a "transfer notice").

(3) In a case to which section 127 or 128 applies, a transfer notice may not be given until the valuation obtained under section 143 is binding.

(4) In a case to which section 158 applies, a transfer notice may not be given until the valuation obtained under subsection (3) of that section is binding.

(5) A transfer notice may not be given in relation to a scheme during any period when the issue of, or failure to issue, a withdrawal notice under or by virtue of section 146 or 147 (refusal to assume responsibility) is reviewable (see section 149(6)(b)).

(6) The Board must give a copy of any notice given under subsection (2) to-

(a) the Regulator, and

(b) any insolvency practitioner in relation to the employer or, if there is no such insolvency practitioner, the employer.

(7) This section is subject to section 172(1) and (2) (no transfer notice within first 12 months of assessment period or when fraud compensation application is pending).

161   Effect of Board assuming responsibility for a scheme

(1) Where a transfer notice is given to the trustees or managers of an eligible scheme, the Board assumes responsibility for the scheme in accordance with this Chapter.

(2) The effect of the Board assuming responsibility for a scheme is that-

(a) the property, rights and liabilities of the scheme are transferred to the Board, without further assurance, with effect from the time the trustees or managers receive the transfer notice,

(b) the trustees or managers of the scheme are discharged from their pension obligations from that time, and

(c) from that time the Board is responsible for securing that compensation is (and has been) paid in accordance with the pension compensation provisions,

and, accordingly, the scheme is to be treated as having been wound up immediately after that time.

(3) In subsection (2)(a) the reference to liabilities of the scheme does not include any liability to, or in respect of, any member of the scheme, other than-

(a) liabilities in respect of money purchase benefits, and

(b) such other liabilities as may be prescribed.

(4) In subsection (2)(b) "pension obligations" in relation to the trustees or managers of the scheme means-

(a) their obligations to provide pensions or other benefits to or in respect of persons (including any obligation to provide guaranteed minimum pensions within the meaning of the Pension Schemes Act 1993 (c. 48)), and

(b) their obligations to administer the scheme in accordance with the scheme rules and this or any other enactment.

(5) Schedule 6 makes provision in respect of the transfer of the property, rights and liabilities of a scheme under subsection (2)(a).

(6) Regulations may make further provision regarding such transfers.

(7) Without prejudice to the generality of subsection (6), regulations may authorise the Board to modify a term of a relevant contract of insurance if-

(a) any rights or liabilities under the contract are transferred to the Board by virtue of subsection (2)(a), and

(b) as a result of the transfer, the Board is required, by reason of that term, to pay a specified amount or specified amounts to a specified person who, immediately before the time mentioned in subsection (2)(a), was a member of the scheme or a person entitled to benefits in respect of such a member.

(8) In subsection (7)-

"relevant contract of insurance" means a contract of insurance which-

(a) is entered with a view to securing the whole or part of the scheme's liability for-

(i) any pension or other benefit payable to or in respect of one particular person whose entitlement to payment of a pension or other benefit has arisen, and

(ii) any benefit which will be payable in respect of that person on his death, and

(b) is a contract-

(i) which may not be surrendered, or

(ii) in respect of which the amount payable on surrender does not exceed the liability secured;

"specified" means specified in, or determined in accordance with, the contract of insurance.

162   The pension compensation provisions

(1) Schedule 7 makes provision for compensation to be paid in relation to a scheme for which the Board assumes responsibility in accordance with this Chapter, including provision for-

(a) periodic compensation to be paid to or in respect of members,

(b) lump sum compensation to be paid to members,

(c) a cap to be imposed on the periodic compensation and lump sum compensation payable, and

(d) annual increases to be made to periodic compensation.

(2) In this Part references to the pension compensation provisions are to the provisions of, and the provisions made by virtue of, this section, sections 140 to 142, 161(2)(c), 164 and 168 and Schedule 7.

(Those references do not include any provision of, or made by virtue of, section 170 (discharge of liabilities in respect of money purchase benefits).)

163   Adjustments to be made where the Board assumes responsibility for a scheme

(1) This section applies where the Board assumes responsibility for an eligible scheme in accordance with this Chapter.

(2) Any benefits (other than money purchase benefits) which-

(a) were payable under the scheme rules to any member, or to any person in respect of any member, during the period beginning with the assessment date and ending with the receipt by the trustees or managers of the transfer notice, and

(b) have been paid before the trustees or managers receive the transfer notice,

are to be regarded as going towards discharging any liability of the Board to pay compensation to the member or, as the case may be, person in accordance with the pension compensation provisions.

(3) Regulations may provide that, in prescribed circumstances, where-

(a) a member of the scheme died before the commencement of the assessment period, and

(b) during the period mentioned in subsection (2)(a), a person became entitled under the scheme rules to a benefit of a prescribed description in respect of the member,

the benefit, or any part of it, is, for the purposes of subsection (2), to be treated as having become payable before the assessment date.

4) The Board must-

(a) if any amount paid, during the period mentioned in subsection (2)(a), by the trustees or managers of the scheme to a member, or to a person in respect of a member, exceeded the entitlement of that member or person under the pension compensation provisions, take such steps as it considers appropriate (including adjusting future compensation payments made in accordance with those provisions) to recover an amount equal to the aggregate of-

(i) the amount of the excess, and

(ii) interest on that amount, at the prescribed rate, for the period which begins when the excess was paid by the trustees or managers and ends with the recovery of the excess, and

(b) if any amount so paid was less than that entitlement (or no amount was paid in respect of that entitlement), pay an amount to the member or person concerned equal to the aggregate of-

(i) the amount of the shortfall, and

(ii) interest on that amount, at the prescribed rate, for the period which begins when the shortfall ought to have been paid by the trustees or managers and ends with the payment of the shortfall by the Board.

(5) In subsection (4) references to an amount paid do not include-

(a) an amount paid in respect of any money purchase benefit, or

(b) any other amount of a prescribed description.

(6) Nothing in subsection (4) requires the Board-

(a) to recover any amount from a person in such circumstances as may be prescribed, or

(b) to recover from any person any amount which it considers to be trivial.

(7) In this section "assessment date" is to be construed in accordance with Schedule 7.

164 Postponement of compensation entitlement for the assessment period

(1) Regulations may provide that, where the Board assumes responsibility for an eligible scheme, the entitlement of any member of the scheme to compensation under this Chapter is, in such circumstances as may be prescribed, postponed for the whole or any part of the assessment period for which he continued in employment after attaining normal pension age.

(2) Regulations under subsection (1) may provide that the postponement is on such terms and conditions (including those relating to increments) as may be prescribed.

(3) In subsection (1) the reference to "normal pension age" is to normal pension age, within the meaning of paragraph 34 of Schedule 7, in relation to the pension or lump sum in respect of which the entitlement to compensation arises.

165 Guaranteed minimum pensions

(1) The Board must notify the Commissioners of Inland Revenue where, by reason of it assuming responsibility for an eligible scheme in accordance with this Chapter, the trustees or managers of the scheme are discharged from their liability to provide a guaranteed minimum pension (within the meaning of the Pension Schemes Act 1993 (c. 48)) to or in respect of a member of the scheme.

(2) Notification under subsection (1) must be given as soon as reasonably practicable.

(3) In section 47 of the Pension Schemes Act 1993 (further provision concerning entitlement to a guaranteed minimum pension for the purposes of section 46), after subsection (7) insert-

"(8) For the purposes of section 46, a person shall be treated as entitled to a guaranteed minimum pension to which he would have been entitled but for the fact that the trustees or managers were discharged from their liability to provide that pension on the Board of the Pension Protection Fund assuming responsibility for the scheme."

166 Duty to pay scheme benefits unpaid at assessment date etc

(1) This section applies where the Board assumes responsibility for a scheme in accordance with this Chapter.

(2) Subject to subsection (4), the Board must pay any amount by way of pensions or other benefits which a person had become entitled to payment of under the scheme rules before the assessment date but which remained unpaid at the time the transfer notice was received by the trustees or managers of the scheme.

(3) If, immediately before the assessment date, the person is entitled to the amount but has postponed payment of it, subsection (2) does not apply.

(4) Subsection (2) does not apply in relation to the amount of-

    (a) any transfer payment, or

    (b) any payment in respect of a refund of contributions.

(5) Regulations may provide that, in prescribed circumstances, where-

    (a) a member of the scheme died before the commencement of the assessment period, and

    (b) during the period beginning with the assessment date and ending with the receipt by the trustees or managers of the transfer notice, a person became entitled under the scheme rules to a benefit of a prescribed description in respect of the member,

that person's entitlement to the benefit, or to any part of it, is, for the purposes of subsection (2), to be treated as having arisen before the assessment date.

(6) Regulations may make provision requiring the Board, in such circumstances as may be prescribed, to take such steps (including making payments) as may be prescribed in respect of rights of prescribed descriptions to which members of the scheme were entitled immediately before the commencement of the assessment period.

(7) For the purposes of regulations made under subsection (6)-

    (a) this Chapter (other than this subsection), and

    (b) the scheme rules (including any relevant legislative provision within the meaning of section 318(3)),

are to have effect subject to such modifications as may be prescribed.

(8) In this section "assessment date" is to be construed in accordance with Schedule 7.

167 Modification of Chapter where liabilities discharged during assessment period

(1) Regulations may modify any of the provisions of this Chapter as it applies to cases-

    (a) where any liability to provide pensions or other benefits to or in respect of any member or members under a scheme is discharged during an assessment period in relation to the scheme by virtue of-

        (i) regulations under section 135(4), or

        (ii) the Board validating any action mentioned in section 135(9), or

    (b) where, in prescribed circumstances, any such liability of a prescribed description is discharged on the assessment date but before the commencement of the assessment period.

(2) In this section "assessment date" is to be construed in accordance with Schedule 7.

168   Administration of compensation

1) Regulations may make further provision regarding the operation and administration of his Chapter.

2) Regulations under subsection (1) may, in particular, make provision-

(a) prescribing the manner in which and time when compensation is to be paid (including provision requiring periodic compensation to be paid by instalments);

(b) for calculating the amounts of compensation according to a prescribed scale or otherwise adjusting them to avoid fractional amounts or facilitate computation;

(c) prescribing the circumstances and manner in which compensation to which a person ("the beneficiary") is entitled may be made to another person on behalf of the beneficiary for any purpose (including the discharge in whole or in part of an obligation of the beneficiary or any other person);

(d) for the payment or distribution of compensation to or among persons claiming to be entitled on the death of any person and for dispensing with strict proof of their title;

(e) for the recovery of amounts of compensation paid by the Board in excess of entitlement (together with interest on such amounts for the period from payment until recovery);

(f) specifying the circumstances in which payment of compensation can be suspended.

3) In this section "compensation" means compensation payable under Schedule 7 or under section 141(2).

Discharge of Board's liabilities

169   Discharge of liabilities in respect of compensation

(1) This section applies where the Board assumes responsibility for an eligible scheme in accordance with this Chapter.

(2) The Board may provide for the discharge of any liability imposed by this Chapter to provide compensation-

(a) by the taking out of a policy of insurance or a number of such policies;

(b) by the entry into an annuity contract or a number of such contracts;

(c) by the transfer of the benefit of such a policy or policies or such a contract or contracts;

(d) in prescribed circumstances, by the payment of a cash sum calculated in the prescribed manner.

170   Discharge of liabilities in respect of money purchase benefits

(1) This subsection applies where-

(a) the Board assumes responsibility for an eligible scheme in accordance with this Chapter, and

(b) one or more members are entitled, or have accrued rights, under the scheme rules to money purchase benefits.

(2) Regulations must make provision in respect of cases to which subsection (1) applies requiring the Board to secure that liabilities in respect of such benefits transferred to the Board under section 161 are discharged by it in the prescribed manner.

(3) The provision made under subsection (2) must include provision prescribing the manner in which protected rights are to be given effect to.

(4) In this section-

"accrued rights", under the scheme rules of a scheme, include pension credit rights within the meaning of section 124(1) of the Pensions Act 1995 (c. 26);

"protected rights" has the meaning given by section 10 of the Pension Schemes Act 1993 (c. 48) (protected rights and money purchase benefits).

Equal treatment

171   Equal treatment

(1) This section applies where-

(a) a woman has been employed on like work with a man in the same employment,

(b) a woman has been employed on work rated as equivalent with that of a man in the same employment, or

(c) a woman has been employed on work which, not being work in relation to which paragraph (a) or (b) applies, was, in terms of the demands made on her (for instance under such headings as effort, skill and decision), of equal value to that of a man in the same employment,

and service in that employment was pensionable service under an occupational pension scheme.

(2) If, apart from this subsection, any of the payment functions so far as it relates (directly or indirectly) to that pensionable service-

(a) is or becomes less favourable to the woman than it is to the man, or

(b) is or becomes less favourable to the man than it is to the woman,

that function has effect with such modifications as are necessary to ensure that the provision is not less favourable.

(3) Subsection (2) does not operate in relation to any difference as between a woman and a man in the operation of any of the payment functions if the Board proves that the difference is genuinely due to a material factor which-

(a) is not the difference of sex, but

(b) is a material difference between the woman's case and the man's case.

(4) Subsection (2) does not apply in such circumstances as may be prescribed.

(5) This section has effect in relation to the exercise of any payment function in so far as it relates (directly or indirectly) to any pensionable service on or after 17th May 1990.

(6) In this section-

"payment function" means any function conferred on the Board by or by virtue of this Chapter which relates to a person's entitlement to or the payment of any amount under or by virtue of-

(a) the pension compensation provisions,

(b) section 166 (duty to pay scheme benefits unpaid at assessment date etc),

(c) section 169 (discharge of liabilities in respect of compensation), or

(d) section 170 (discharge of liabilities in respect of money purchase benefits);

"pensionable service" has the meaning given by section 124(1) of the Pensions Act 1995 (c. 26).

Relationship with fraud compensation regime

172   Relationship with fraud compensation regime

(1) No transfer notice may be given in respect of a scheme within the first 12 months of an assessment period in relation to the scheme.

) Where an application has been made under section 182 (application for fraud
mpensation payment), no transfer notice may be given until-

(a) the Board has determined the application,

(b) the period within which the Board's determination may be reviewed by virtue of
Chapter 6 has expired, and

(c) if the determination is so reviewed-

(i) the review and any reconsideration,

(ii) any reference to the PPF Ombudsman in respect of the determination, and

(iii) any appeal against his determination or directions,

as been finally disposed of.

) Subsection (4) applies where during an assessment period in relation to a scheme the
oard determines to make one or more fraud compensation payments ("the fraud
ompensation") to the trustees or managers of the scheme under Chapter 4 of this Part.

) For the purposes of determining whether the condition in section 127(2)(a), 128(2)(a),
52(2) or 158(1) is satisfied, any fraud compensation payment which becomes payable after
he relevant time is, to the extent that it relates to a loss incurred by the scheme before that
me, to be regarded as an asset of the scheme at that time.

) For the purposes of subsection (4) "the relevant time"-

(a) in the case of section 127(2)(a), has the same meaning as in that provision,

(b) in the case of section 128(2)(a), has the same meaning as in that provision,

(c) in the case of section 152(2) means the reconsideration time (within the meaning of
section 151), and

(d) in the case of section 158(1), has the same meaning as in that provision.

) Subsection (4) does not apply to the extent that the fraud compensation is payable in
espect of a reduction in the value of money purchase assets of the scheme.

or this purpose "money purchase assets" means assets representing the value of any rights
respect of money purchase benefits under the scheme rules.

he fund

73   Pension Protection Fund

) The Pension Protection Fund shall consist of-

(a) property and rights transferred to the Board under section 161(2)(a),

(b) contributions levied under section 174 or 175 (initial and pension protection levies),

(c) money borrowed by the Board under section 115 for the purposes of this Chapter,

(d) any income or capital gain credited under subsection (2),

(e) any amount paid to the Board by virtue of section 139 (repayment of loans to
trustees or managers and payment of interest),

(f) amounts recovered under section 163(4)(a) or by virtue of section 168(2)(e)
(overpayments),

(g) any amount paid to the Board in respect of a debt due to the Board under section
40(7) by virtue of a contribution notice under section 38,

(h) any property transferred or amounts paid to the Board as required by a restoration
order under section 52,

(i) any amount paid to the Board in respect of a debt due to the Board under section
56(7) by virtue of a contribution notice under section 55,

(j) amounts transferred from the Fraud Compensation Fund under section 187 (fraud
compensation transfer payments), and

(k) amounts of a prescribed description (other than amounts paid, directly or indirectly, to the Board by the Crown).

(2) The Board must credit to the Pension Protection Fund any income or capital gain arising from the assets in the Fund.

(3) The following are to be paid or transferred out of the Pension Protection Fund-

(a) any sums required to meet liabilities transferred to the Board under section 161(2)(a),

(b) any sums required to make payments in accordance with the pension compensation provisions,

(c) any sums required for the repayment of, and the payment of interest on, money within subsection (1)(c),

(d) any sums required to make loans under section 139 (loans to trustees or managers),

(e) any sums required to make payments under section 163(4)(b) (underpayments during the assessment period),

(f) any sums required to make payments under section 166 (payment of unpaid scheme benefits etc),

(g) any sums required to discharge liabilities under section 169 or 170 (discharge of liabilities in respect of compensation or money purchase benefits),

(h) any sums required to meet any liabilities arising from obligations imposed on the Board by a restoration order under section 52,

(i) any property (other than sums) required to meet any liabilities-

(i) transferred to the Board as mentioned in paragraph (a) and arising from obligations imposed by a restoration order under section 52, or

(ii) arising from obligations imposed on the Board by such an order,

(j) any sums required to meet expenditure incurred by virtue of section 161(5) and paragraph 7 of Schedule 6 (expenditure associated with transfer of property, rights and liabilities to the Board), and

(k) sums required for prescribed purposes.

(4) No other amounts are to be paid or transferred out of the Pension Protection Fund.

(5) In subsection (1) (other than paragraph (d)) and subsection (3) (other than paragraph (c)) any reference to a provision of this Act is to be read as including a reference to any provision in force in Northern Ireland corresponding to that provision.

The levies

174   Initial levy

(1) Regulations must make provision for imposing a levy ("the initial levy") in respect of eligible schemes for the period ("the initial period") which-

(a) begins with the day appointed for this purpose by the regulations, and

(b) ends on the following 31st March or, if the regulations so provide, 12 months after the day referred to in paragraph (a).

(2) The regulations must prescribe-

(a) the factors by reference to which the initial levy is to be assessed,

(b) the rate of the levy, and

(c) the time or times during the initial period when the levy, or any instalment of the levy, becomes payable.

(3) Regulations under this section may only be made with the approval of the Treasury.

175 Pension protection levies

1) For each financial year falling after the initial period, the Board must impose both of the following-

(a) a risk-based pension protection levy in respect of all eligible schemes;

(b) a scheme-based pension protection levy in respect of eligible schemes.

In this Chapter "pension protection levy" means a levy imposed in accordance with this section.

2) For the purposes of this section-

(a) a risk-based pension protection levy is a levy assessed by reference to-

(i) the difference between the value of a scheme's assets (disregarding any assets representing the value of any rights in respect of money purchase benefits under the scheme rules) and the amount of its protected liabilities,

(ii) except in relation to any prescribed scheme or scheme of a prescribed description, the likelihood of an insolvency event occurring in relation to the employer in relation to a scheme, and

(iii) if the Board considers it appropriate, one or more other risk factors mentioned in subsection (3), and

(b) a scheme-based pension protection levy is a levy assessed by reference to-

(i) the amount of a scheme's liabilities to or in respect of members (other than liabilities in respect of money purchase benefits), and

(ii) if the Board considers it appropriate, one or more other scheme factors mentioned in subsection (4).

(3) The other risk factors referred to in subsection (2)(a)(iii) are factors which the Board considers indicate one or more of the following-

(a) the risks associated with the nature of a scheme's investments when compared with the nature of its liabilities;

(b) such other matters as may be prescribed.

(4) The other scheme factors referred to in subsection (2)(b)(ii) are-

(a) the number of persons who are members, or fall within any description of member, of a scheme;

(b) the total annual amount of pensionable earnings of active members of a scheme;

(c) such other factors as may be prescribed.

(5) The Board must, before the beginning of each financial year, determine in respect of that year-

(a) the factors by reference to which the pension protection levies are to be assessed,

(b) the time or times by reference to which those factors are to be assessed,

(c) the rate of the levies, and

(d) the time or times during the year when the levies, or any instalment of levy, becomes payable.

(6) Different risk factors, scheme factors or rates may be determined in respect of different descriptions of scheme.

(7) The rate determined in respect of a description of scheme may be nil.

(8) In this section-

"initial period" is to be construed in accordance with section 174;

"pensionable earnings", in relation to an active member under a scheme, means the earnings by reference to which a member's entitlement to benefits would be calculated under the scheme rules if he ceased to be an active member at the time by reference to which the factor within subsection (4)(b) is to be assessed.

(9) In this section and sections 176 to 181 "financial year" means a period of 12 months ending with 31st March.

(10) The Board's duty to impose pension protection levies in respect of any financial year is subject to-

    (a) section 177 (amounts to be raised by the pension protection levies), and

    (b) section 180 (transitional provision).

176   Supplementary provisions about pension protection levies

(1) The Board must consult such persons as it considers appropriate in the prescribed manner before making a determination under section 175(5) in respect of a financial year if-

    (a) that year is the first financial year for which the Board is required to impose levies under section 175,

    (b) any of the proposed levy factors or levy rates is different, or applies to a different description of scheme, from the levy factors and levy rates in respect of the pension protection levies imposed in the previous financial year, or

    (c) no consultation has been required under this subsection in relation to the pension protection levies imposed for either of the previous two financial years.

(2) The Board must publish details of any determination under section 175(5) in the prescribed manner.

177   Amounts to be raised by the pension protection levies

(1) Before determining the pension protection levies to be imposed for a financial year, the Board must estimate the amount which will be raised by the levies it proposes to impose.

(2) The Board must impose levies for a financial year in a form which it estimates will raise an amount not exceeding the levy ceiling for the financial year.

(3) The pension protection levies imposed for a financial year must be in a form which the Board estimates will result in at least 80% of the amount raised by the levies for that year being raised by the risk-based pension protection levy.

(4) For the first financial year after the transitional period, regulations may modify subsection (2) so as to provide that the reference to the levy ceiling for the financial year is to be read as a reference to such lower amount as is prescribed.

(5) For the second financial year after the transitional period and for any subsequent financial year, the Board must impose pension protection levies in a form which it estimates will raise an amount which does not exceed by more than 25% the amount estimated under subsection (1) in respect of the pension protection levies imposed for the previous financial year.

(6) The Secretary of State may by order substitute a different percentage for the percentage for the time being specified in subsection (5).

(7) Before making an order under subsection (6), the Secretary of State must consult such persons as he considers appropriate.

(8) Regulations under subsection (4), or an order under subsection (6), may be made only with the approval of the Treasury.

(9) In this section-

    (a) "risk-based pension protection levy" and "scheme-based pension protection levy" are to be construed in accordance with section 175, and

    (b) "transitional period" has the meaning given by section 180(3).

178   The levy ceiling

1) The Secretary of State must, before the beginning of each financial year for which levies are required to be imposed under section 175, specify by order the amount which is to be the levy ceiling for that year for the purposes of section 177.

2) An order under subsection (1) in respect of the first financial year for which levies are imposed under section 175 may be made only with the approval of the Treasury.

3) Subject to subsection (8), the amount specified under subsection (1) for a financial year ("the current year") after the first year for which levies are imposed under section 175 must be-

(a) where it appears to the Secretary of State that the level of earnings in the review period has increased, the amount specified under subsection (1) for the previous financial year increased by the earnings percentage for that review period specified under subsection (6), and

(b) in any other case, the amount specified under subsection (1) for the previous financial year.

4) In subsection (3)-

"level of earnings" means the general level of earnings obtaining in Great Britain;

"review period" in relation to the current year means the period of 12 months ending with the prescribed date in the previous financial year.

5) For the purposes of subsection (3), the Secretary of State must, in respect of each review period, review the general level of earnings obtaining in Great Britain and any changes in that level; and for the purposes of such a review the Secretary of State may estimate the general level of earnings in such manner as he thinks appropriate.

6) Where it appears to the Secretary of State that the general level of earnings has increased during the review period, he must by order specify the percentage by which that level has so increased ("the earnings percentage").

7) The Secretary of State must discharge the duties imposed by subsections (5) and (6) in respect of a review period before the beginning of the prescribed period which ends at the time the first financial year after the review period begins.

8) The Secretary of State may, on the recommendation of the Board and with the approval of the Treasury, make an order under subsection (1) in respect of a financial year which specifies an amount exceeding the amount required to be specified under subsection (3).

9) Before making a recommendation for the purposes of subsection (8), the Board must consult such persons as it considers appropriate in the prescribed manner.

179   Valuations to determine scheme underfunding

1) For the purposes of enabling risk-based pension protection levies (within the meaning of section 175) to be calculated in respect of eligible schemes, regulations may make provision requiring the trustees or managers of each such scheme to provide the Board or the Regulator on the Board's behalf-

(a) with an actuarial valuation of the scheme at such intervals as may be prescribed, and

(b) with such other information as the Board may require in respect of the assets and protected liabilities of the scheme at such times as may be prescribed.

2) For the purposes of this section, in relation to a scheme-

"an actuarial valuation" means a written valuation of the scheme's assets and protected liabilities prepared and signed by the actuary;

"the actuary" means-

    (a) the actuary appointed under section 47(1)(b) of the Pensions Act 1995 (c. 26) (professional advisers) in relation to the scheme, or

    (b) if no such actuary has been appointed-

        (i) a person with prescribed qualifications or experience, or

        (ii) a person approved by the Secretary of State.

(3) Regulations under this section may prescribe how-

    (a) the assets and the protected liabilities of schemes, and

    (b) their amount or value,

are to be determined, calculated and verified.

(4) Subject to any provision made under subsection (3), those matters are to be determined, calculated and verified in accordance with guidance issued by the Board.

(5) In calculating the amount of any liabilities for the purposes of a valuation required by virtue of this section, a provision of the scheme rules which limits the amount of the scheme's liabilities by reference to the value of its assets is to be disregarded.

(6) In this section references to "assets" do not include assets representing the value of any rights in respect of money purchase benefits under the scheme rules.

180   Pension protection levies during the transitional period

(1) Regulations may provide that in respect of any financial year during the transitional period-

    (a) sections 175 and 177(3) are to apply with such modifications as may be prescribed;

    (b) section 177(2) is to apply as if the reference to the levy ceiling for the financial year were a reference to such lower amount as is specified in the regulations.

(2) Regulations which contain provision made by virtue of subsection (1)(b) may only be made with the approval of the Treasury.

(3) For the purposes of this section "the transitional period" means the prescribed period beginning immediately after the initial period (within the meaning of section 174).

(4) If the transitional period begins with a date other than 1st April, regulations may provide that any provision of this section or of sections 175 to 179 applies, with such modifications as may be prescribed, in relation to-

    (a) the period beginning at the same time as the transitional period and ending with the following 31st March, and

    (b) the financial year which begins immediately after that period.

181   Calculation, collection and recovery of levies

(1) This section applies in relation to-

    (a) the initial levy imposed under section 174 in respect of a scheme, and

    (b) any pension protection levy imposed under section 175 in respect of a scheme.

(2) The levy is payable to the Board by or on behalf of-

    (a) the trustees or managers of the scheme, or

    (b) any other prescribed person.

(3) The Board must in respect of the levy-

    (a) determine the schemes in respect of which it is imposed,

    (b) calculate the amount of the levy in respect of each of those schemes, and

    (c) notify any person liable to pay the levy in respect of the scheme of the amount of the levy in respect of the scheme and the date or dates on which it becomes payable.

(4) The Board may require the Regulator to discharge, on the Board's behalf, its functions under subsection (3) in respect of the levy.

(5) Where a scheme is an eligible scheme for only part of the period for which the levy is imposed, except in prescribed circumstances, the amount of the levy payable in respect of the scheme for that period is such proportion of the full amount as that part bears to that period.

(6) An amount payable by a person on account of the levy is a debt due from him to the Board.

(7) An amount so payable may be recovered-

(a) by the Board, or

(b) if the Board so determines, by the Regulator on its behalf.

(8) Regulations may make provision relating to-

(a) the collection and recovery of amounts payable by way of any levy in relation to which this section applies;

(b) the circumstances in which any such amount may be waived.

PART 3
SCHEME FUNDING

Introductory

221 Pension schemes to which this Part applies

(1) The provisions of this Part apply to every occupational pension scheme other than-

(a) a money purchase scheme, or

(b) a prescribed scheme or a scheme of a prescribed description.

(2) Regulations under subsection (1)(b) may provide for exemptions from all or any of the provisions of this Part.

Scheme funding

222 The statutory funding objective

(1) Every scheme is subject to a requirement ("the statutory funding objective") that it must have sufficient and appropriate assets to cover its technical provisions.

(2) A scheme's "technical provisions" means the amount required, on an actuarial calculation, to make provision for the scheme's liabilities.

(3) For the purposes of this Part-

(a) the assets to be taken into account and their value shall be determined, calculated and verified in a prescribed manner, and

(b) the liabilities to be taken into account shall be determined in a prescribed manner and the scheme's technical provisions shall be calculated in accordance with any prescribed methods and assumptions.

(4) Regulations may-

(a) provide for alternative prescribed methods and assumptions,

(b) provide that it is for the trustees or managers to determine which methods and assumptions are to be used in calculating a scheme's technical provisions, and

(c) require the trustees or managers, in making their determination, to take into account prescribed matters and follow prescribed principles.

(5) Any provision of the scheme rules that limits the amount of the scheme's liabilities by reference to the value of its assets shall be disregarded.

223   Statement of funding principles

(1) The trustees or managers must prepare, and from time to time review and if necessary revise, a written statement of-

(a) their policy for securing that the statutory funding objective is met, and

(b) such other matters as may be prescribed.

This is referred to in this Part as a "statement of funding principles".

(2) The statement must, in particular, record any decisions by the trustees or managers as to-

(a) the methods and assumptions to be used in calculating the scheme's technical provisions, and

(b) the period within which, and manner in which, any failure to meet the statutory funding objective is to be remedied.

(3) Provision may be made by regulations-

(a) as to the period within which a statement of funding principles must be prepared, and

(b) requiring it to be reviewed, and if necessary revised, at such intervals, and on such occasions, as may be prescribed.

(4) Where any requirement of this section is not complied with, section 10 of the Pensions Act 1995 (c. 26) (civil penalties) applies to a trustee or manager who has failed to take all reasonable steps to secure compliance.

224   Actuarial valuations and reports

(1) The trustees or managers must obtain actuarial valuations-

(a) at intervals of not more than one year or, if they obtain actuarial reports for the intervening years, at intervals of not more than three years, and

(b) in such circumstances and on such other occasions as may be prescribed.

(2) In this Part-

(a) an "actuarial valuation" means a written report, prepared and signed by the actuary, valuing the scheme's assets and calculating its technical provisions,

(b) the effective date of an actuarial valuation is the date by reference to which the assets are valued and the technical provisions calculated,

(c) an "actuarial report" means a written report, prepared and signed by the actuary, on developments affecting the scheme's technical provisions since the last actuarial valuation was prepared, and

(d) the effective date of an actuarial report is the date by reference to which the information in the report is stated.

(3) The intervals referred to in subsection (1)(a) are between effective dates of the valuations, and-

(a) the effective date of the first actuarial valuation must be not more than one year after the establishment of the scheme, and

(b) the effective date of any actuarial report must be not more than one year after the effective date of the last actuarial valuation, or, if more recent, the last actuarial report.

(4) The trustees or managers must ensure that a valuation or report obtained by them is received by them within the prescribed period after its effective date.

(5) Nothing in this section affects any power or duty of the trustees or managers to obtain actuarial valuations or reports at more frequent intervals or in other circumstances or on other occasions.

(6) An actuarial valuation or report (whether obtained under this section or in pursuance of any other power or duty) must be prepared in such a manner, give such information, contain such statements and satisfy such other requirements as may be prescribed.

(7) The trustees or managers must secure that any actuarial valuation or report obtained by them (whether obtained under this section or in pursuance of any other power or duty) is made available to the employer within seven days of their receiving it.

(8) Where subsection (1), (4) or (7) is not complied with, section 10 of the Pensions Act 1995 (c. 26) (civil penalties) applies to a trustee or manager who has failed to take all reasonable steps to secure compliance.

225 Certification of technical provisions

(1) When an actuarial valuation is carried out, the calculation of the technical provisions must be certified by the actuary.

(2) The certificate must state that in the opinion of the actuary the calculation is made in accordance with regulations under section 222.

(3) If the actuary cannot give the certificate required by subsection (2) he must report the matter in writing to the Regulator within a reasonable period after the end of the period within which the valuation must be received by the trustees or managers.

Section 10 of the Pensions Act 1995 (civil penalties) applies to the actuary if he fails without reasonable excuse to comply with this subsection.

226 Recovery plan

(1) If having obtained an actuarial valuation it appears to the trustees or managers of a scheme that the statutory funding objective was not met on the effective date of the valuation, they must, within the prescribed time-

　　(a) if there is no existing recovery plan in force, prepare a recovery plan;

　　(b) if there is an existing recovery plan in force, review and if necessary revise it.

(2) A recovery plan must set out-

　　(a) the steps to be taken to meet the statutory funding objective, and

　　(b) the period within which that is to be achieved.

(3) A recovery plan must comply with any prescribed requirements and must be appropriate having regard to the nature and circumstances of the scheme.

(4) In preparing or revising a recovery plan the trustees or managers must take account of prescribed matters.

(5) Provision may be made by regulations as to other circumstances in which a recovery plan may or must be reviewed and if necessary revised.

(6) The trustees or managers must, except in prescribed circumstances, send a copy of any recovery plan to the Regulator within a reasonable period after it is prepared or, as the case may be, revised.

The copy of any recovery plan sent to the Regulator must be accompanied by the prescribed information.

(7) Where any requirement of this section is not complied with, section 10 of the Pensions Act 1995 (c. 26) (civil penalties) applies to a trustee or manager who has failed to take all reasonable steps to secure compliance.

227 Schedule of contributions

(1) The trustees or managers must prepare, and from time to time review and if necessary revise, a schedule of contributions.

(2) A "schedule of contributions" means a statement showing-

    (a) the rates of contributions payable towards the scheme by or on behalf of the employer and the active members of the scheme, and

    (b) the dates on or before which such contributions are to be paid.

(3) Provision may be made by regulations-

    (a) as to the period within which, after the establishment of a scheme, a schedule of contributions must be prepared,

    (b) requiring the schedule of contributions to be reviewed, and if necessary revised, at such intervals, and on such occasions, as may be prescribed, and

    (c) as to the period for which a schedule of contributions is to be in force.

(4) The schedule of contributions must satisfy prescribed requirements.

(5) The schedule of contributions must be certified by the actuary and-

    (a) the duty to prepare or revise the schedule is not fulfilled, and

    (b) the schedule shall not come into force,

    until it has been so certified.

(6) The certificate must state that, in the opinion of the actuary-

    (a) the schedule of contributions is consistent with the statement of funding principles, and

    (b) the rates shown in the schedule are such that-

        (i) where the statutory funding objective was not met on the effective date of the last actuarial valuation, the statutory funding objective can be expected to be met by the end of the period specified in the recovery plan, or

        (ii) where the statutory funding objective was met on the effective date of the last actuarial valuation, the statutory funding objective can be expected to continue to be met for the period for which the schedule is to be in force.

(7) Where the statutory funding objective was not met on the effective date of the last actuarial valuation, the trustees or managers must send a copy of the schedule of contributions to the Regulator within a reasonable period after it is prepared or, as the case may be, revised.

(8) Where any requirement of the preceding provisions of this section is not complied with, section 10 of the Pensions Act 1995 (civil penalties) applies to a trustee or manager who has failed to take all reasonable steps to secure compliance.

(9) If the actuary is unable to give the certificate required by subsection (6), he must report the matter in writing to the Regulator within a reasonable period after the end of the period within which the schedule is required to be prepared or, as the case may be, revised.

Section 10 of the Pensions Act 1995 (c. 26) (civil penalties) applies to the actuary if he fails without reasonable excuse to comply with this subsection.

(10) The provisions of subsections (1), (3) and (5) to (9) above do not apply in relation to a schedule of contributions imposed by the Regulator under section 231 or, as the case may be, where such a schedule of contributions is in force.

228   Failure to make payments

(1) This section applies where an amount payable in accordance with the schedule of contributions by or on behalf of the employer or an active member of a scheme is not paid on or before the due date.

(2) If the trustees or managers have reasonable cause to believe that the failure is likely to be of material significance in the exercise by the Regulator of any of its functions, they must,

except in prescribed circumstances, give notice of the failure to the Regulator and to the members within a reasonable period.

(3) The amount unpaid (whether payable by the employer or not), if not a debt due from the employer to the trustees or managers apart from this subsection, shall be treated as such a debt.

(4) Section 10 of the Pensions Act 1995 (civil penalties) applies-

(a) where subsection (2) above is not complied with, to a trustee or manager who has failed to take all reasonable steps to secure compliance with that subsection;

(b) to the employer if he fails without reasonable excuse to make a payment required of him-

(i) in accordance with the schedule of contributions, or

(ii) by virtue of subsection (3) above.

(5) This section applies in relation to a schedule of contributions imposed by the Regulator under section 231 as in relation to one agreed between the trustees or managers and the employer.

229   Matters requiring agreement of the employer

(1) The trustees or managers must obtain the agreement of the employer to-

(a) any decision as to the methods and assumptions to be used in calculating the scheme's technical provisions (see section 222(4));

(b) any matter to be included in the statement of funding principles (see section 223);

(c) any provisions of a recovery plan (see section 226);

(d) any matter to be included in the schedule of contributions (see section 227).

(2) If it appears to the trustees or managers that it is not otherwise possible to obtain the employer's agreement within the prescribed time to any such matter, they may (if the employer agrees) by resolution modify the scheme as regards the future accrual of benefits.

(3) No modification may be made under subsection (2) that on taking effect would or might adversely affect any subsisting right of-

(a) any member of the scheme, or

(b) any survivor of a member of the scheme.

For this purpose "subsisting right" and "survivor" have the meanings given by section 67A of the Pensions Act 1995 (c. 26).

(4) Any such modification must be-

(a) recorded in writing by the trustees or managers, and

(b) notified to the active members within one month of the modification taking effect.

(5) If the trustees or managers are unable to reach agreement with the employer within the prescribed time on any such matter as is mentioned in subsection (1), they must report the failure in writing to the Regulator within a reasonable period.

(6) Where subsection (1), (4) or (5) is not complied with, section 10 of the Pensions Act 1995 (civil penalties) applies to a trustee or manager who has failed to take all reasonable steps to secure compliance.

230   Matters on which advice of actuary must be obtained

(1) The trustees or managers must obtain the advice of the actuary before doing any of the following-

(a) making any decision as to the methods and assumptions to be used in calculating the scheme's technical provisions (see section 222(4));

(b) preparing or revising the statement of funding principles (see section 223);

(c) preparing or revising a recovery plan (see section 226);

(d) preparing or revising the schedule of contributions (see section 227);

(e) modifying the scheme as regards the future accrual of benefits under section 229(2).

(2) Regulations may require the actuary to comply with any prescribed requirements when advising the trustees or managers of a scheme on any such matter.

(3) The regulations may require the actuary to have regard to prescribed guidance.

"Prescribed guidance" means guidance that is prepared and from time to time revised by a prescribed body and, if the regulations so provide, is approved by the Secretary of State.

(4) Where subsection (1) is not complied with, section 10 of the Pensions Act 1995 (civil penalties) applies to a trustee or manager who has failed to take all reasonable steps to secure compliance.

231   Powers of the Regulator

(1) The powers conferred by this section are exercisable where it appears to the Regulator with respect to a scheme (as a result of a report made to it or otherwise)-

(a) that the trustees or managers have failed to comply with the requirements of section 223 with respect to the preparation or revision of a statement of funding principles;

(b) that the trustees or managers have failed to obtain an actuarial valuation as required by section 224(1);

(c) that the actuary is unable, on an actuarial valuation required by section 224(1), to certify the calculation of the scheme's technical provisions;

(d) that the trustees or managers have failed to comply with the requirements of section 226 with respect to the preparation or revision of a recovery plan;

(e) that the trustees or managers have failed to comply with the requirements of section 227 with respect to the preparation or revision of a schedule of contributions;

(f) that the actuary is unable to certify a schedule of contributions (see section 227(6));

(g) that the employer has failed to make payments in accordance with the schedule of contributions, or that are required of him by virtue of section 228(3), and the failure is of material significance;

(h) that the trustees or managers have been unable to reach agreement with the employer within the prescribed time as to a matter in relation to which such agreement is required (see section 229(5)).

(2) In any of those circumstances the Regulator may by order exercise all or any of the following powers-

(a) it may modify the scheme as regards the future accrual of benefits;

(b) it may give directions as to-

(i) the manner in which the scheme's technical provisions are to be calculated, including the methods and assumptions to be used in calculating the scheme's technical provisions, or

(ii) the period within which, and manner in which, any failure to meet the statutory funding objective is to be remedied;

(c) it may impose a schedule of contributions specifying-

(i) the rates of contributions payable towards the scheme by or on behalf of the employer and the active members of the scheme, and

(ii) the dates on or before which such contributions are to be paid.

3) No modification may be made under subsection (2)(a) that on taking effect would or might adversely affect any subsisting right of-

(a) any member of the scheme, or

(b) any survivor of a member of the scheme.

For this purpose "subsisting right" and "survivor" have the meanings given by section 67A of the Pensions Act 1995.

(4) In exercising any of the powers conferred by this section the Regulator must comply with any prescribed requirements.

(5) The powers conferred by this section are in addition to any other powers exercisable by the Regulator under this Act or the Pensions Act 1995 (c. 26).

Supplementary provisions

232 Power to modify provisions of this Part

Regulations may modify the provisions of this Part as they apply in prescribed circumstances.

233 Construction as one with the Pensions Act 1995

This Part shall be construed as one with Part 1 of the Pensions Act 1995 (c. 26).

A2.2: The Occupational Pension Schemes (Winding Up and Deficiency on Winding Up etc)(Amendment) Regulations 2004 (SI 2004/403)

Made	*18th February 2004*
Laid before Parliament	*23rd February 2004*
Coming into force	*15th March 2004*

The Secretary of State for Work and Pensions, in exercise of the powers conferred upon him by sections 73(3), 75(5), 124(1) and 174(2) and (3) of the Pensions Act 1995 and of all other powers enabling him in that behalf, after consultation with such persons as he considered appropriate, hereby makes the following Regulations:

Citation, commencement, interpretation and application

1. - (1) These Regulations may be cited as the Occupational Pension Schemes (Winding Up and Deficiency on Winding Up etc.) (Amendment) Regulations 2004 and shall come into force on 15th March 2004.

(2) In these Regulations -

"the Act" means the Pensions Act 1995;

"the Winding Up Regulations" means the Occupational Pension Schemes (Winding Up) Regulations 1996; and

"the Deficiency on Winding Up Regulations" means the Occupational Pension Schemes (Deficiency on Winding Up etc.) Regulations 1996.

(3) For the purposes of these Regulations, the time when a scheme begins to be wound up shall be determined in accordance with subsections (3A) to (3E) of section 124 of the Act.

(4) These Regulations shall apply to any occupational pension scheme to which section 75 of the Act (deficiencies in the assets) applies in any case where the scheme begins, or has begun, to wind up and the date by reference to which the assets and liabilities of the scheme are determined, calculated and verified for the purposes of that section is a date falling on or after the date on which these Regulations come into force.

Amendment of the Winding Up Regulations

2. - (1) The Winding Up Regulations shall be amended as provided for by the following paragraphs of this regulation.

(2) In paragraph (1) of regulation 4 (calculation of amounts of liabilities), for the words "regulation 4A and" there shall be substituted the words "regulations 4A and 4B and".

(3) At the end of the heading to regulation 4A (calculation of liabilities where employer not insolvent) there shall be added the words "and where winding up commences before 11th June 2003".

(4) At the beginning of paragraph (1) of regulation 4A, after the words "In the case of a scheme" there shall be inserted the words "which has begun to wind up before 11th June 2003 and".

(5) After regulation 4A, there shall be inserted the following regulation -

Calculation of liabilities where employer not insolvent and where winding up commences on or after 11th June 2003

4B. - (1) This regulation shall apply in the case of a scheme which begins to wind up on or after 11th June 2003 in circumstances where the employer was not insolvent at the time the winding up of the scheme commenced.

(2) In the case of a scheme to which this regulation applies, regulation 4 shall have effect as if -

(a) for the words "paragraph (3)" in paragraph (1)(c), there were substituted the words "paragraphs (2A) and (3)";

(b) after paragraph (2) there were inserted the following paragraph -

" (2A) For the purpose of calculating the amount of the liabilities for the accrued rights to any pensions or other benefits of members of the scheme (including any increase to a pension) and for any future pensions, or other future benefits, attributable (directly or indirectly) to pension credits (including any increase to a pension) that have arisen on or before the crystallisation date or, as the case may be, the amount of the liabilities for any entitlement of members of the scheme to the payment of any pension or other benefit (including any increase to a pension) that has arisen on or before that date -

(a) it shall be assumed that all such liabilities will be discharged by the purchase of annuities of a kind described in section 74(3)(c); and

(b) paragraph (1)(b) above shall not have effect; and

(c) for paragraph (5) there were substituted the following paragraph -

"(5) If, when the assets of the scheme are applied in accordance with section 73(2) towards satisfying the liabilities mentioned in section 73(3), those liabilities, as calculated in accordance with the rules of the scheme (without any reduction by reason of them falling within a class of liability which is to be satisfied after another class), cannot in the opinion of the actuary be fully satisfied by applying assets of a value equal to the amount of those liabilities calculated in accordance with paragraph (1), then the amount to be taken as the amount of those liabilities for the purposes of section 73(2) shall be increased accordingly.".

(3) For the purposes of paragraph (1) above, an employer is insolvent if a relevant insolvency event within the meaning given by section 75(4) has occurred in relation to that employer.".

Amendment of the Deficiency on Winding Up Regulations

3. - (1) The Deficiency on Winding Up Regulations shall be amended as provided for by the following paragraphs of this regulation.

(2) At the beginning of regulation 3 (calculation of the value of scheme liabilities and assets), for the words "Subject to regulation 3A" there shall be substituted the words "Subject to regulations 3A and 3B".

(3) At the end of the heading to regulation 3A (valuation of liabilities where employer not insolvent) there shall be added the words "and where winding up commences before 11th June 2003".

(4) After regulation 3A, there shall be inserted the following regulation -

" Valuation of liabilities where employer not insolvent and where winding up commences on or after 11th June 2003

3B. - (1) This regulation shall apply in the case of a scheme to which regulation 4B of the Occupational Pension Schemes (Winding Up) Regulations 1996 (calculation of liabilities where employer not insolvent and where winding up commences on or after 11th June 2003) applies.

(2) In the case of a scheme to which this regulation applies, paragraph (1)(b) of regulation 3A (valuation of the liabilities where employer not insolvent) shall have effect as if for paragraph (1B) in quotation marks there were substituted the following paragraph -

" (1B) When calculating the liabilities of the scheme for any -

(a) accrued rights that exist on or before the applicable time to the payment of any pension or other benefit under the scheme (including any increase to a pension);

(b) future pensions, or other future benefits, attributable (directly or indirectly) to pension credits (including any increase to a pension) which have arisen on or before the applicable time; and

(c) entitlement to the payment of a pension or other benefit (including any increase in a pension) that has arisen on or before the applicable time,

it shall be assumed that all such liabilities will be discharged by the purchase of annuities of the type described in section 74(3)(c) (discharge of liabilities by insurance - annuity purchase) and, for the purposes of the calculation, the actuary shall estimate the costs of purchasing any such annuities.".".

Signed by authority of the Secretary of State for Work and Pensions.
Malcolm Wicks, Minister of State, Department for Work and Pensions
18th February 2004

The Occupational Pension Schemes (Winding Up) (Amendment) Regulations 2004

Made	*15th April 2004*
Laid before Parliament	*19th April 2004*
Coming into force	*10th May 2004*

The Secretary of State for Work and Pensions, in exercise of the powers conferred upon him by sections 97(1), 181(1) and 182(2) of the Pension Schemes Act 1993, and sections 73(7), 124(1), and (3E) and 174(2) of the Pensions Act 1995, and all other powers enabling him in that behalf, having consulted with such persons as he considered appropriate, hereby makes the following Regulations:

Citation, commencement, interpretation and application

1. - (1) These Regulations may be cited as the Occupational Pension Schemes (Winding Up) (Amendment) Regulations 2004 and shall come into force on 10th May 2004.

(2) In these Regulations -

(a) "the 1996 Regulations" means the Occupational Pension Schemes (Winding Up) Regulations 1996;

(b) "the transitional period" has the meaning given in regulation 3(2) of the 1996 Regulations;

(c) the time when a scheme begins to be wound up shall be determined in accordance with regulation 2 of the 1996 Regulations.

(3) The revocations made by regulation 2 and the amendments of the 1996 Regulations made by regulation 3 of these Regulations have effect only in relation to occupational pension schemes which begin to be wound up on or after the date on which these Regulations come into force and before the end of the transitional period.

evocations

In relation to such schemes as are mentioned in regulation 1(3) -

) regulation 3(5) of the 1996 Regulations is hereby revoked;

) regulation 3(3) of the Pension Sharing (Consequential and Miscellaneous) Amendments egulations 2000 is hereby revoked;

nd accordingly section 73(3)(c) of the Pensions Act 1995 has effect as amended only by ection 38(1) of the Welfare Reform and Pensions Act 1999.

mendment of the 1996 Regulations

In relation to such schemes as are mentioned in regulation 1(3), regulation 3 of the 1996 egulations (modifications of section 73(3) of the Pensions Act 1995) is amended as follows -

) by substituting for paragraph (1)(b) -

b) in the case of a scheme which begins to be wound up on or after 10 May 2004 and before e expiry of the transitional period, subject to the modifications in paragraphs (5A) to (6).";

) by inserting the following paragraphs after paragraph (4) -

5A) In paragraph (d) of section 73(3), for "(b) and (c)" there shall be substituted "(aa) and)."

5B) After that paragraph there is inserted -

e) any liability for increases to pensions referred to in paragraph (c).".";

) by substituting for paragraph (6) -

(6) In the words following paragraph (e) of section 73(3) as inserted by paragraph (5B) for e words "paragraphs (b) to (d)" there shall be substituted the words "paragraphs (aa) to)".";

d) by substituting for paragraph (8) -

(8) In the case of any scheme to which section 73(3) applies with the modifications entioned in paragraphs (5A) to (6), regulation 7(3)(b)(iv) of the Occupational Pension chemes (Transfer Values) Regulations 1996, has effect with the substitution for "(d)" of e)".".

igned by authority of the Secretary of State for Work and Pensions.

Malcolm Wicks, Minister of State, Department for Work and Pensions

5th April 2004

A2.3: The Occupational Pension Schemes (Winding Up, Deficiency on Winding Up and Transfer Values)(Amendment) Regulations 2005 (SI 2005/72)

Made	*19 January 2005*
Laid before Parliament	*25 January 2005*
Coming into force	*15 February 2005*

The Secretary of State for Work and Pensions, in exercise of the powers conferred upon him by sections 113, 181(1) and 182(2) of the Pension Schemes Act 1993 and sections 73(3), 75(5) 124(1) and 174(2) and (3) of the Pensions Act 1995 and of all other powers enabling him in that behalf, after consultation with such persons as he considered appropriate, hereby makes the following Regulations:

Citation, commencement and interpretation

1. - (1) These Regulations may be cited as the Occupational Pension Schemes (Winding Up Deficiency on Winding Up and Transfer Values) (Amendment) Regulations 2005 and shall come into force on 15 February 2005.

(2) In these Regulations -

"the Deficiency on Winding Up Regulations" means the Occupational Pension Schemes (Deficiency on Winding Up etc.) Regulations 1996;

"the Transfer Values Regulations" means the Occupational Pension Schemes (Transfer Values) Regulations 1996; and

"the Winding Up Regulations" means the Occupational Pension Schemes (Winding Up Regulations 1996.

Amendment of the Winding Up Regulations

2. - (1) The Winding Up Regulations shall be amended as provided for by the following paragraphs of this regulation.

(2) In regulation 4(1) (calculation of amounts of liabilities) for "regulations 4A and 4B" there shall be substituted "regulations 4A to 4C".

(3) At the beginning of regulation 4B(1) (calculation of liabilities where employer not insolvent and where winding up commences on or after 11th June 2003) there shall be inserted "Subject to regulation 4C,".

(4) After regulation 4B there shall be inserted the following regulation -

"Calculation of liabilities where winding up commences, and date of calculation falls, on or after 15 February 2005

4C. - (1) This regulation shall apply in the case of a scheme which begins to wind up on or after 15 February 2005 ("the commencement date"), and the date by reference to which the liabilities and assets of the scheme are determined, calculated and verified for the purposes of section 75 is a date falling on or after the commencement date.

(2) In the case of a scheme to which this regulation applies, regulation 4 shall have effect as if -

(a) for the words "paragraph (3)" in paragraph (1)(c), there were substituted the words "paragraphs (2A) and (3)";

(b) after paragraph (2) there were inserted the following paragraph -

" (2A) For the purpose of calculating the amount of the liabilities for the accrued rights to any pensions or other benefits of members of the scheme (including any increase to a pension) and for any future pensions, or other future benefits, attributable (directly or indirectly) to pension credits (including any increase to a pension) that have arisen on or before the crystallisation date or, as the case may be, the amount of the liabilities for any entitlement of members of the scheme to the payment of any pension or other benefit (including any increase to a pension) that has arisen on or before that date -

a) it shall be assumed that all such liabilities will be discharged by the purchase of annuities of a kind described in section 74(3)(c); and

b) paragraph (1)(b) above shall not have effect."; and

c) in paragraph (5) there were substituted the words "section 73(3)" for the words "section 73(3)(aa) or (b)"."

Amendment of the Deficiency on Winding Up Regulations

8. - (1) The Deficiency on Winding Up Regulations shall be amended as provided for by the following paragraphs of this regulation.

(2) In regulation 3(1) (calculation of the value of scheme liabilities and assets) for "regulations 3A and 3B" there shall be substituted "regulations 3A to 3D".

(3) At the beginning of regulation 3B(1) (valuation of liabilities where employer not insolvent and where winding up commences on or after 11th June 2003) there shall be inserted "Subject to regulation 3C,".

(4) After regulation 3B, there shall be inserted the following regulations -

" Valuation of liabilities where winding up commences, and date of calculation falls, on or after 15 February 2005

3C. - (1) This regulation shall apply in the case of a scheme which begins to wind up on or after 15 February 2005 ("the commencement date"), and the date by reference to which the liabilities and assets of the scheme are determined, calculated and verified for the purposes of section 75 is a date falling on or after the commencement date.

(2) In the case of a scheme to which this regulation applies, regulation 3 shall have effect as if -

    (a) in paragraph (1) -

        (i) at the beginning of sub-paragraph (a), there were inserted the words "except to the extent that the liabilities are in respect of any entitlement to a pension or other benefit that has arisen under the scheme and in respect of which paragraph (1B) applies,";

        (ii) for the words "paragraphs (2) and (3)" in sub-paragraph (a), there were substituted the words "paragraphs (2)(a) to (c) and (3)";

        (iii) for the words "paragraphs (3) and (4)" in sub-paragraph (b), there were substituted the words "paragraphs (1B), (3) and (4)";

        (iv) for the words "regulations 3(2) and (3)" in sub-paragraph (c), there were substituted the words "regulations 3(2)(a) to (c) and (3)"; and

        (v) after the words "and 4 to 8 of the MFR Regulations" in sub-paragraph (c), there were inserted the words "or as respects paragraphs (1A) and (1B)"; and

    (b) after paragraph (1) there were inserted the following paragraphs:

" (1A) The liabilities of a scheme which are to be taken into account under paragraph (1) above shall include all expenses (except the cost of annuities taken into account by virtue of paragraph (1B)) which, in the opinion of the trustees or managers of the scheme, are likely to be incurred in connection with the winding up of the scheme.

(1B) When calculating the liabilities of the scheme for any -

(a) accrued rights that exist on or before the applicable time to the payment of an pension or other benefit under the scheme (including any increase to a pension);

(b) future pensions, or other future benefits, attributable (directly or indirectly) t pension credits (including any increase to a pension) which have arisen on or before th applicable time; and

(c) entitlement to the payment of a pension or other benefit (including any increase in pension) that has arisen on or before the applicable time,

it shall be assumed that all such liabilities will be discharged by the purchase c annuities of the type described in section 74(3)(c) and, for the purposes of the calculation the actuary shall estimate the costs of purchasing any such annuities.

Valuation of liabilities where there is more than one employer

3D. - (1) This regulation shall apply where there is a scheme to which regulation 4 (multi employer schemes) applies (including a section of a scheme in relation to which there i more than one employer which is treated as a separate scheme for the purposes of section 7. and the circumstances described in paragraph (2) apply.

(2) The circumstances are that -

(a) the scheme is not being wound up;

(b) a relevant insolvency event occurs in relation to an employer in relation to the scheme; and

(c) the applicable time is on or after 15 February 2005.

(3) In the case of a scheme to which this regulation applies, regulation 3 shall have effec with the modifications set out in regulation 3C(2)(a) and (b).".".

(5) In the Note at the end of the form of certificate set out in Schedule 1 (form of actuary's certificate), for "does not reflect the cost" there shall be substituted "may not reflect the actual cost".

Amendment of the Transfer Values Regulations

4. In regulation 11 of the Transfer Values Regulations (disclosure) -

(a) in paragraph (4) -

(i) after sub-paragraph (b)(iv) the word "and" shall be omitted, and;

(ii) after sub-paragraph (b)(v) there shall be inserted -

" and

(vi) where the scheme has begun to wind up, explaining that -

(aa) the value of the member's guaranteed cash equivalent may be affected by the scheme's winding up;

(bb) a decision to take a guaranteed cash equivalent should be given carefu consideration; and

(cc) the member should consider taking independent financial advice before deciding whether to take the guaranteed cash equivalent."; and

(b) after that paragraph there shall be inserted -

" (4A) For the purposes of paragraph (4)(b)(vi), the question whether a scheme has begun to wind up shall be determined in accordance with section 124(3A) to (3D) of the 1995 Act.".

Signed by authority of the Secretary of State for Work and Pensions.
Malcolm Wicks, Minister of State, Department for Work and Pensions
19 January 2005

A2.4: Pensions Regulator (Notifiable Events) Regulations 2005 (SI 2005/900)

Made	*23rd March 2005*
Laid before Parliament	*31st March 2005*
Coming into force	*6th April 2005*

The Secretary of State for Work and Pensions, in exercise of the powers conferred upon him by sections 69(2), 315(2) and 318(1) of the Pensions Act 2004, and of all other powers enabling him in that behalf, by this instrument, which contains regulations made before the end of the period of six months beginning with the coming into force of the provisions of that Act by virtue of which they are made, makes the following Regulations:

Citation, commencement and interpretation

1. - (1) These Regulations may be cited as the Pensions Regulator (Notifiable Events) Regulations 2005, and shall come into force on 6th April 2005.

(2) In these Regulations -

"the Act" means the Pensions Act 2004;

"business" includes trade or profession;

"control" has the meaning given to it in section 435(10) of the Insolvency Act 1986 (meaning of "associate" - meaning of "control"), and "controlling company" is to be construed accordingly;

"debt" includes a contingent debt;

"director" has the meaning given to it in section 741(1) ("director" and "shadow director") of the Companies Act 1985;

"key employer posts" means the Chief Executive and any director or partner responsible in whole or in part for the financial affairs of the employer;

"key scheme posts" means the auditor and the actuary appointed to a scheme under section 47(1) of the Pensions Act 1995 (professional advisers);

"scheme assets" means the value of the assets according to the most recent actuarial valuation carried out under section 224 of the Act (actuarial valuations and reports), or if no such valuation has been carried out, the most recent valuation carried out under section 56 of the Pensions Act 1995 (minimum funding requirement) and regulations made thereunder.

Notifiable events

2. - (1) The events prescribed for the purposes of section 69(2)(a) of the Act (duty to notify the Regulator of certain events - prescribed events in respect of an eligible scheme) are -

(a) any decision by the trustees or managers to take action which will, or is intended to, result in any debt which is or may become due to the scheme not being paid in full;

(b) two or more changes in the holders of any key scheme post within the previous 12 months;

(c) a decision by the trustees or managers of a scheme ("the relevant scheme") to make a transfer payment to, or accept a transfer payment from, another scheme the value of which is more than the lower of -

(i) 5 per cent of the value of the scheme assets of the relevant scheme, and

(ii) £1,500,000 (one million five hundred thousand pounds);

(d) a decision by the trustees or managers to grant benefits, or a right to benefits, or more favourable terms than those provided for by the scheme rules, without either seeking advice from the actuary (appointed under section 47(1) of the Pensions Act 1995) or securing additional funding where such funding was advised by the actuary;

(e) a decision by the trustees or managers to grant benefits, or a right to benefits, to a member the cost of which is more than the lower of -

(i) 5 per cent of the scheme assets, and

(ii) £1,500,000 (one million five hundred thousand pounds).

(2) The events prescribed for the purposes of section 69(2)(b) of the Act (duty to notify the Regulator of certain events - prescribed events in respect of the employer in relation to an eligible scheme) are -

(a) any decision by the employer to take action which will, or is intended to, result in a debt which is or may become due to the scheme not being paid in full;

(b) a decision by the employer to cease to carry on business in the United Kingdom;

(c) where applicable, receipt by the employer of advice that it is trading wrongfully within the meaning of section 214 of the Insolvency Act 1986 (wrongful trading), or circumstances being reached in which a director or former director of the company knows that there is no reasonable prospect that the company will avoid going into insolvent liquidation within the meaning of that section, and for this purpose section 214(4) of that Act applies;

(d) any breach by the employer of a covenant in an agreement between the employer and a bank or other institution providing banking services, other than where the bank or other institution agrees with the employer not to enforce the covenant;

(e) any change in the employer's credit rating, or the employer ceasing to have a credit rating;

(f) where the employer is a company, a decision by a controlling company to relinquish control of the employer company;

(g) two or more changes in the holders of any key employer posts within the previous 12 months;

(h) the conviction of an individual, in any jurisdiction, for an offence involving dishonesty, if the offence was committed while the individual was a director or partner of the employer.

Signed by authority of the Secretary of State for Work and Pensions
Malcolm Wicks, Minister of State, Department for Work and Pensions
23 March 2005

A2.5: Occupational Pension Schemes (Early Leavers: Cash Transfer Sums and Contribution Refunds) Regulations 2006 (SI 2006/33)

Made	*9th January 2006*
Laid before Parliament	*12th January 2006*
Coming into force	*6th April 2006*

The Secretary of State for Work and Pensions makes the following regulations in exercise of the powers conferred by sections 101AC(2)(a), 101AE(2), 101AF, 113A, 181(1), 182(2) and 183 of the Pension Schemes Act 1993[1].

This instrument contains regulations which are made before the end of the period of six months beginning with the coming into force of the provisions of the Pensions Act 2004 by virtue of which the regulations are made[2]:

Citation, commencement, interpretation and application

1. —(1) These Regulations may be cited as the Occupational Pension Schemes (Early Leavers: Cash Transfer Sums and Contribution Refunds) Regulations 2006 and shall come into force on 6th April 2006.

(2) In these Regulations—

"the Act" means the Pension Schemes Act 1993;

"the 1995 Act" means the Pensions Act 1995[3];

"the 2004 Act" means the Pensions Act 2004.

(3) These Regulations apply only where the member's pensionable service under the occupational pension scheme terminates on or after 6th April 2006.

Calculation and verification of cash transfer sum

2. —(1) Except in a case to which, or to the extent to which, paragraph (2) or (4) applies, cash transfer sums are to be calculated and verified in such manner as may be approved in particular cases by the scheme actuary or in relation to a scheme to which section 47(1)(b) of the 1995 Act (professional advisers) does not apply, by—

(a) a Fellow of the Institute of Actuaries[4];

(b) a Fellow of the Faculty of Actuaries[5]; or

(c) a person with other actuarial qualifications who is approved by the Secretary of State, at the request of the trustees of the scheme in question, as being a proper person to act for the purposes of these Regulations in connection with that scheme,

and, subject to paragraph (2), in this regulation and in regulation 4 "actuary" means the scheme actuary or, in relation to a scheme to which section 47(1)(b) of the 1995 Act does not apply, the actuary referred to in sub-paragraph (a), (b) or (c) of this paragraph.

(2) Where the member in respect of whom a cash transfer sum is to be calculated and verified is a member of a scheme having particulars from time to time set out in regulations made under section 7 of the Superannuation Act 1972[6] (superannuation of persons employed in local government service, etc.), that cash transfer sum shall be calculated and verified in such manner as may be approved by the Government Actuary or by an actuary authorised by the Government Actuary to act on his behalf for that purpose and in such a case "actuary" in this regulation and in regulation 4 means the Government Actuary or the actuary so authorised.

(3) Except in a case to which paragraph (4) applies, cash transfer sums are to be calculated and verified by adopting methods and making assumptions which—

(a) if not determined by the trustees of the scheme in question, are notified to them by the actuary; and

(b) are certified by the actuary to the trustees of the scheme—

(i) as being consistent with the calculation of cash equivalents under the requirements of Chapter 4 of Part 4 of the Act (transfer values),

(ii) as being consistent with "Retirement Benefit Schemes – Transfer Values (GN11)" published by the Institute of Actuaries and the Faculty of Actuaries and current at the date on which the cash transfer sum is calculated,

(iii) as being consistent with the methods adopted and assumptions made, at the time when the certificate is issued, in calculating the benefits to which entitlement arises under the rules of the scheme in question for a person who is acquiring transfer credits under those rules.

(4) Where a cash transfer sum or any portion of a cash transfer sum relates to money purchase benefits which do not fall to be valued in a manner which involves making estimates of the value of benefits, then that cash transfer sum or that portion shall be calculated and verified in such manner as may be approved in particular cases by the trustees of the scheme and in accordance with methods consistent with the requirements of Chapter 4 of Part 4 of the Act.

Contribution refund; investments etc.

3. For the purposes of these Regulations, where under the rules of the scheme—

(a) interest is payable on a member's employee contributions to the scheme, the amount of the contribution refund shall be increased by the interest so payable; or

(b) a member's employee contributions to the scheme fall to be invested and the member is entitled to the surrender value of the investments derived from those contributions, the amount of the contribution refund shall be increased or, as the case may be, reduced to the amount of that surrender value,

and in the following provisions of these Regulations references to a contribution refund are, where applicable, to the contribution refund as so increased or, as the case may be, reduced.

Reduction of cash transfer sums and contribution refunds

4. —(1) In the case of a scheme to which Part 3 of the 2004 Act applies (scheme funding), the cash transfer sum in respect of a member may be reduced by the trustees or managers of the scheme if the GN11 insufficiency conditions are met.

(2) The GN11 insufficiency conditions are that the actuary's last relevant GN11 report shows that at the effective date of the report—

(a) the scheme had assets that were insufficient to pay the full amount of cash equivalents under Chapter 4 of Part 4 of the Act in respect of all the members, and

(b) the assets were insufficient to pay in full any category of liabilities that is a category of liabilities for the benefits in respect of which the member's cash equivalent is being calculated.

(3) If the GN11 insufficiency conditions are met the trustees may reduce any part of the member's cash transfer sum that is payable in respect of such a category of liabilities as are

mentioned in paragraph (2)(b) by a percentage not exceeding the GN11 deficiency percentage.

(4) The GN11 deficiency percentage is the same as the percentage by which a member's cash equivalent for such a category of liabilities is being reduced.

(5) The references in this regulation to the actuary's last relevant GN11 report is to his last report, in accordance with "Retirement Benefit Schemes – Transfer Values (GN11)" published by the Institute of Actuaries and the Faculty of Actuaries, before the cash transfer sum is calculated.

(6) If by virtue of regulations made under section 232 of the 2004 Act (power to modify provisions of Part 3), Part 3 of that Act applies to a section of a scheme as if that section were a separate scheme, paragraphs (1) and (2) shall apply to a section as if that section were a separate scheme, and as if the reference to a scheme were accordingly a reference to that section.

(7) Where a scheme begins to wind up after the member's pensionable service terminates but before the trustees or managers have used the cash transfer sum or paid the contribution refund to the member, the cash transfer sum or contribution refund may be reduced to the extent necessary for the scheme to comply with the winding up provisions (as defined in section 73B(10)(a) of the 1995 Act[Z]) and regulations made under those provisions.

(8) If, by virtue of regulations made under section 73B(4)(b)(i) of the 1995 Act by virtue of section 73B(5) of that Act, the winding up provisions (as so defined) apply to a section of a scheme as if that section were a separate scheme, paragraph (7) shall apply as if that section were a separate scheme and as if the references therein to a scheme were accordingly references to that section.

(9) A member's cash transfer sum or contribution refund under the scheme may be reduced if the member has incurred some monetary obligation due to the employer or to the scheme and arising out of a criminal, negligent or fraudulent act or omission by that member.

(10) A member's cash transfer sum or contribution refund under the scheme may be reduced by reason of paragraph (9) to the extent only that the reduction does not exceed the amount of the monetary obligation in question.

(11) A reduction under paragraph (9) must not take effect where there is a dispute as to the amount of the monetary obligation in question, unless the obligation has become enforceable under an order of a competent court or in consequence of an award of an arbitrator, or in Scotland, an arbiter to be appointed (failing agreement between the parties) by the sheriff.

(12) In a case where two or more paragraphs of this regulation fall to be applied to a cash transfer sum or paragraphs (7) and (9) fall to be applied to a contribution refund, they shall be applied in the order in which they occur in this regulation.

Increases of cash transfer sum and contribution refund
5. —(1) Subject to paragraph (2), if there is a failure by the trustees or managers of the scheme to comply with section 101AG(2) of the Act (duty to act within a reasonable period) in relation to the cash transfer sum, the cash transfer sum shall be increased by the amount, if any, by which the cash transfer sum as calculated in accordance with regulations 2 and 4 falls short of what it would have been had the cash transfer sum been calculated on the date

on which the trustees or managers should have done what was needed to carry out the member's requirement.

(2) If there is a failure by the trustees or managers of the scheme to comply with section 101AG(2) of the Act without reasonable excuse the cash transfer sum shall be increased by—

(a) interest on that sum calculated on a daily basis over the period from the date on which they received the member's notice under section 101AD(2) of the Act (exercise of right under section 101AB) to the date on which they do what is needed to carry out that requirement, at an annual rate of one per cent above the Bank of England base rate; or

(b) the amount, if any, by which the cash transfer sum as calculated in accordance with regulations 2 and 4 falls short of what it would have been had the cash transfer sum been calculated on the date on which the trustees or managers should have done what was needed to carry out the member's requirement,

whichever is the greater.

(3) If there is a failure by the trustees or managers of the scheme to comply with section 101AG(4) of the Act without reasonable excuse the contribution refund shall be increased by interest on that sum calculated on a daily basis over the period from the date on which they received the member's notice under section 101AD(2) of the Act to the date on which they do what is needed to carry out the member's requirement at an annual rate of one per cent above the Bank of England base rate.

(4) In this regulation "Bank of England base rate" means—

(a) the rate announced from time to time by the Monetary Policy Committee of the Bank of England as the official dealing rate, being the rate at which the Bank is willing to enter into transactions for providing short term liquidity in the money markets; or

(b) where an order under section 19 of the Bank of England Act 1998[8] (Treasury's reserve powers) is in force, any equivalent rate determined by the Treasury under that section.

Cash transfer sums: requirements to be met by receiving schemes

6. The prescribed requirements referred to in section 101AE(2)(a)(ii) and (b)(ii) of the Act (cash transfer sum to be used for acquiring transfer credits or rights under another occupational pension scheme or a personal pension scheme) are that—

(a) if the member's cash transfer sum (or any portion of it to be used under section 101AE(2)(a) or (b) of the Act) comprises, or includes, section 9(2B) rights, then the occupational pension scheme or personal pension scheme under whose rules transfer credits or rights are to be acquired is one to which, had those rights been accrued rights, a transfer of liability in respect of those accrued rights could have been made in accordance with regulation 7 of the Contracting-out (Transfer and Transfer Payment) Regulations 1996[9] (transfer of liability in respect of section 9(2B) rights: general), and in this paragraph "section 9(2B) rights" has the meaning given to that expression in regulation 1(2) of those Regulations; and

(b) if the scheme in respect of which the member acquires a right under section 101AB(1)(a) of the Act (right to cash transfer sum and contribution refund) is a scheme which is registered by the Her Majesty's Revenue and Customs under section 153 of the Finance Act 2004[10] (registration of pension schemes) (but not a scheme which was immediately before 6th April 2006 approved under Chapter III of Part XIV of the Income and Corporation Taxes Act 1988[11] (pension scheme etc: retirement annuities)), then the scheme or personal pension scheme in respect of which the cash transfer sum is to be used is a scheme so registered or is a qualifying recognised overseas pension scheme within the meaning of section 169(2) of the Finance Act 2004[12] (recognised transfers).

Information

7. —(1) The statement given under subsection (2)(a) of section 101AC of the Act (notification of right to cash transfer sum or contribution refund) must in addition to the matters specified in subsections (2) and (3) of that section also specify—

(a) if the amount of the cash transfer sum or contribution refund has been reduced in accordance with regulation 4, the reason for the reduction;

(b) details of any reduction required from the cash transfer sum or contribution refund in accordance with regulation 4;

(c) details of any set off of the contribution refund against the refund payment made in accordance with section 101AG(5)(b) or 101AH(3)(b) of the Act (powers of trustees or managers where right not exercised);

(d) details of any tax liability in respect of the contribution refund;

(e) if an amount is to be deducted from a refund under section 61(2) of the Act[13] (deduction of contributions equivalent premium from refund of scheme contributions), details of the amount certified under section 63 of the Act[14] (further provisions concerning calculations relating to premiums);

(f) how the exercise of the member's right mentioned in subsection (2)(a)(i) of section 101AC of the Act will affect his other rights, if any, under the scheme;

(g) that if on a winding up of a scheme the cash transfer sum or contribution refund may be reduced in accordance with regulation 4(7), that the member will be informed that there may be reductions and that if the scheme does begin to be wound up that he will be informed if the cash transfer sum or contribution refund is to be reduced; and

(h) that if the member does not exercise his right on or before the reply date or such later date as the trustees or managers may allow in his case under section 101AI(2) of the Act (rights under section 101AB: further provisions), the trustees or managers will be entitled to pay the contribution refund to him.

(2) Where in relation to a member—

(a) a payment is made out of an occupational pension scheme (A) to the trustees or managers of another occupational pension scheme (B); and

(b) transfer credits have been allowed to the member under scheme (B),

the trustees or managers of scheme (A) shall on the written request of the trustees or managers of scheme (B) provide the trustees or managers of scheme (B) within a period of one month beginning with the date of the request, information in writing as to the amount of the employee contributions made to scheme (A) by or on behalf of the member so far as they relate to the transfer payment.

Signed by authority of the Secretary of State for Work and Pensions.

Stephen Timms
Minister of State, Department for Work and Pensions
9th January 2006

A2: LEGISLATION

Notes:

[1] 1993 c.48, sections 101AA to 101AF are inserted by section 264 of the Pensions Act 2004 (c.35); section 113A is inserted by paragraph 18 of Schedule 12 to the Pensions Act 2004; section 181(1) of the Act is cited because of the meanings given to "prescribe" and "regulations"; and section 183(3) is amended by paragraph 32 of Schedule 12 to the Pensions Act 2004.

[2] *See* section 317 of the Pensions Act 2004 under which the requirement to consult such persons as the Secretary of State considers appropriate does not apply to regulations made before the end of the period of six months beginning with the coming into force of the provisions of that Act by virtue of which the regulations are made.

[3] 1995 c.26.

[4] The Institute of Actuaries is located at Staple Inn Hall, High Holborn, London WC1V 7QJ.

[5] The Faculty of Actuaries is located at Maclaurin House, 18 Dublin Street, Edinburgh EH1 3PP.

[6] 1972 c.11.

[7] Section 73B is inserted by section 270 of the Pensions Act 2004.

[8] 1998 c.11.

[9] S.I.1996/1462; the relevant amending instrument is S.I. 1997/786; S.I.1996/1462 is modified by S.I. 1996/1977.

[10] 2004 c.12. Section 153 is amended by paragraphs 2 and 3 of Schedule 10 to the Finance Act 2005 (c.7).

[11] 1988 c.1.

[12] Section 169 is amended by paragraph 36 of Schedule 10 to the Finance Act 2005.

[13] Section 61 is amended by paragraph 55 of Schedule 5 to the Pensions Act 1995, paragraph 5(2) of Schedule 5 to the Child Support, Pensions and Social Security Act 2000 (c.19) and paragraph 12 of Schedule 12 to the Pensions Act 2004.

[14] Section 63 is amended by paragraph 57 of Schedule 5 and Part 3 of Schedule 7 to the Pensions Act 1995, paragraph 56 of Schedule 1 to the Social Security Contributions (Transfer of Functions, etc) Act 1999 (c.2) and paragraph 5 of Schedule 5 to the Child Support, Pensions and Social Security Act 2000.

A2.6: Occupational Pension Schemes (Scheme Funding) Regulations 2005 (SI 2005/3377)

Made	*8th December 2005*
Laid before Parliament	*9th December 2005*
Coming into force	*30th December 2005*

ARRANGEMENT OF REGULATIONS

The Secretary of State for Work and Pensions makes the following Regulations in exercise of the powers conferred by paragraph 5(3C) and (4A) of Schedule 1 to the Pension Schemes (Northern Ireland) Act 1993[1] and now vested in him[2], sections 68(2)(e) and 124(1) and 174(2)(a) of the Pensions Act 1995[3], and sections 69(2)(a), 221(1)(b) and (2), 222(3) and (4)(b) and (c), 223(1)(b) and (3), 224(1)(b), (4) and (6), 226(1) and (3) to (6), 227(3)(a) and (b) and (4), 228(2), 229(2) and (5), 230(2) and (3), 231(4), 232, 315(2), (4), (5) and (6) and 318(1) of the Pensions Act 2004[4].

In accordance with section 120(1) of the Pensions Act 1995 and section 317(1) of the Pensions Act 2004, the Secretary of State has consulted such persons as he considers appropriate before making these Regulations[5].

This instrument is made before the end of the period of six months beginning with the coming into force of the provisions of Part 3 of the Pensions Act 2004 by virtue of which it is made.

Citation and commencement

1. These Regulations may be cited as the Occupational Pension Schemes (Scheme Funding) Regulations 2005 and shall come into force on 30th December 2005.

Interpretation

2. —(1) In these Regulations—

"the 1993 Act" means the Pension Schemes Act 1993[6];

"the 1995 Act" means the Pensions Act 1995;

"the 2004 Act" means the Pensions Act 2004;

"the actuary", in relation to a scheme, means the actuary appointed under section 47(1)(b) of the 1995 Act (professional advisers) in relation to that scheme;

"the commencement date" means 30th December 2005;

"insurance policy" means an insurance policy which is a contract on human life or a contract of annuity on human life, but excluding a contract which is linked to investment funds;

"pension credit rights" has the meaning given by section 124(1) of the 1995 Act[7];

"the relevant accounts", for the purposes of identifying and valuing the assets of a scheme, are audited accounts for the scheme—

    (a) which comply with the requirements imposed under section 41 of the 1995 Act[8] (provision of documents for members), and

    (b) which are prepared in respect of a period ending with the effective date of the valuation.

(2) In these Regulations "scheme" must be read in appropriate cases in accordance with the modifications of Part 3 of the 2004 Act made by paragraphs 1, 4, 5 and 7 of Schedule 2 (multi-employer sectionalised schemes, partly foreign schemes and schemes with a partial public authority guarantee), and "employer" and "member" must be construed accordingly.

Determination of assets and liabilities

3. —(1) The assets of a scheme to be taken into account for the purposes of Part 3 of the 2004 Act are the assets attributed to the scheme in the relevant accounts, excluding—

    (a) any resources invested (or treated as invested by or under section 40 of the 1995 Act) in contravention of section 40(1) of the 1995 Act (employer-related investments);

    (b) any amounts treated as a debt due to the trustees or managers under section 75(2) or (4) of the 1995 Act[9] (deficiencies in the assets) or section 228(3) of the 2004 Act (amounts due in accordance with a schedule of contributions) which are unlikely to be recovered without disproportionate cost or within a reasonable time, and

    (c) where it appears to the actuary that the circumstances are such that it is appropriate to exclude them, any rights under an insurance policy.

(2) The liabilities of a scheme to be taken into account for the purposes of Part 3 of the 2004 Act are any liabilities—

    (a) in relation to a member of the scheme by virtue of—

        (i) any right that has accrued to or in respect of him to future benefits under the scheme rules, or

(ii) any entitlement to the present payment of a pension or other benefit which he has under the scheme rules, and

(b) in relation to the survivor of a member of the scheme, by virtue of any entitlement to benefits, or right to future benefits which he has under the scheme rules in respect of the member.

3) For the purposes of paragraph (2)—

"right" includes a pension credit right, and

"the survivor" of a member is a person who—

(a) is the widow, widower or surviving civil partner of the member, or

(b) has survived the member and has any entitlement to benefit, or right to future benefits, under the scheme in respect of the member.

4) Where rights under an insurance policy are excluded under paragraph (1)(c), the liabilities secured by the policy shall be disregarded for the purposes of paragraph (2).

5) Where arrangements are being made by the scheme for the transfer to or from it of accrued rights and any pension credit rights, until such time as the trustees or managers of the scheme to which the transfer is being made ("the receiving scheme") have received assets of the full amount agreed by them as consideration for the transfer, it shall be assumed—

(a) that the rights have not been transferred, and

(b) that any assets transferred in respect of the transfer of those rights are assets of the scheme making the transfer and not of the receiving scheme.

Valuation of assets and determination of the amount of liabilities

4. —(1) Subject to paragraph (2), the value to be given to the assets of a scheme for the purposes of Part 3 of the 2004 Act is the value given to those assets in the relevant accounts, less the amount of the external liabilities.

(2) The value to be given to any rights under an insurance policy taken into account under regulation 3(1) is the value the actuary considers appropriate in the circumstances of the case.

(3) In paragraph (1), "the external liabilities" of a scheme are such liabilities of the scheme (other than liabilities within regulation 3(2)) as are shown in the net assets statement in the relevant accounts, and their amount shall be taken to be the amount shown in that statement in respect of them.

(4) The assets of the scheme shall be valued, and the amount of the liabilities determined, by reference to the same date.

Calculation of technical provisions

5. —(1) Subject to paragraphs (2) and (3), it is for the trustees or managers of a scheme to determine which method and assumptions are to be used in calculating the scheme's technical provisions.

(2) The method used in calculating a scheme's technical provisions must be an accrued benefits funding method.

(3) In determining which accrued benefits funding method and which assumptions are to be used, the trustees or managers must—

(a) follow the principles set out in paragraph (4), and

(b) in the case of a scheme under which the rates of contributions payable by the employer are determined—

    (i) by or in accordance with the advice of a person other than the trustees or managers, and

    (ii) without the employer's agreement,

take account of the recommendations of that person.

(4) The principles to be followed under paragraph (3) are—

(a) the economic and actuarial assumptions must be chosen prudently, taking account, if applicable, of an appropriate margin for adverse deviation;

(b) the rates of interest used to discount future payments of benefits must be chosen prudently, taking into account either or both—

    (i) the yield on assets held by the scheme to fund future benefits and the anticipated future investment returns, and

    (ii) the market redemption yields on government or other high-quality bonds;

(c) the mortality tables used and the demographic assumptions made must be based on prudent principles, having regard to the main characteristics of the members as a group and expected changes in the risks to the scheme, and

(d) any change from the method or assumptions used on the last occasion on which the scheme's technical provisions were calculated must be justified by a change of legal, demographic or economic circumstances.

Statement of funding principles

6. —(1) A statement under section 223 of the 2004 Act must include the following matters, in addition to those specified in that section—

(a) any funding objectives provided for in the rules of the scheme, or which the trustees or managers have adopted, in addition to the statutory funding objective;

(b) whether there are arrangements for a person other than the employer or a member of the scheme to contribute to the funds held by the scheme, and, if there are such arrangements, the circumstances in which they apply;

(c) whether there is a power to make payments to the employer out of funds held for the purposes of the scheme and, if there is such a power, the circumstances in which it may be exercised;

(d) whether there are discretionary powers to provide or increase benefits for, or in respect of, all or any of the members and, if there are such powers, the extent to which they are taken into account in the funding of the scheme;

(e) the policy of the trustees or managers regarding the reduction of the cash equivalent of benefits which have accrued to or in respect of members on account of the state of the funding of the scheme, and

(f) the intervals at which the trustees or managers will obtain actuarial valuations in accordance with section 224(1)(a) of the 2004 Act, and the circumstances in which and occasions on which they will, or will consider whether to, obtain actuarial valuations in addition to those obtained at such intervals.

(2) The first statement under section 223 of the 2004 Act in respect of a scheme must be prepared by the trustees or managers within 15 months after the effective date of the first actuarial valuation obtained by them under section 224 of that Act.

3) A statement under section 223 must be reviewed, and if necessary revised—

(a) within 15 months after the effective date of each subsequent actuarial valuation, and

(b) within a reasonable period after any occasion on which the Regulator has exercised any of the powers conferred by section 231(2) of the 2004 Act in relation to the scheme.

4) A statement under section 223 must specify the date on which it was prepared, or, if it has been revised, the date on which it was last revised.

Actuarial valuations and reports

7. —(1) In addition to the regular valuations provided for in section 224(1)(a) of the 2004 Act, the trustees or managers of a scheme must obtain an actuarial valuation where the Regulator has given directions under section 231(2)(b)(i) of that Act as to the manner in which the scheme's technical provisions are to be calculated.

2) Where the trustees or managers have obtained an actuarial valuation or an actuarial report, they must ensure that it is received by them—

(a) in the case of a valuation under section 224(1)(a), within 15 months after its effective date;

(b) in the case of a valuation where the Regulator has given directions under section 231(2)(b)(i)—

(i) within three months after the date of the directions if the effective date of the valuation is before the date of the directions, and

(ii) within six months after the effective date of the valuation if that date is the same as or later than the date of the directions;

(c) in the case of a report, within 12 months after its effective date.

3) Where the assets taken into account in an actuarial valuation include rights under an insurance policy, the valuation must state the reason why the value given to such rights is considered appropriate in the circumstances of the case.

4) An actuarial valuation must include—

(a) the actuary's certification of the calculation of the technical provisions, in the relevant form set out in Schedule 1, and

(b) the actuary's estimate of the solvency of the scheme.

5) An actuarial report must include an assessment by the actuary of changes in the value of the scheme's assets since the last actuarial valuation was prepared.

6) In paragraph (4), "the actuary's estimate of the solvency of the scheme" means—

(a) except in the case referred to in sub-paragraph (b), an estimate by the actuary of whether, on the effective date of a valuation, the value of assets of the scheme to be taken into account under paragraph (1) of regulation 3 exceeded or fell short of the sum of—

(i) the cost of purchasing annuities, of the type described in section 74(3)(c) of the 1995 Act[10] (discharge of liabilities by purchase of annuities satisfying prescribed requirements) and on terms consistent with those in the available market, which would be sufficient to satisfy the liabilities taken into account under paragraph (2) of regulation 3, and

(ii) the other expenses which, in the opinion of the actuary, would be likely to be incurred in connection with a winding up of the scheme, and the amount of the excess or, as the case may be, the shortfall;

(b) where the actuary considers that it is not practicable to make an estimate in accordance with sub-paragraph (a), an estimate of the solvency of the scheme on the effective date of the valuation made in such manner as the actuary considers appropriate in the circumstances of the case.

(7) Where the actuary's estimate of solvency is made under paragraph (6)(b), the valuation must include a brief account of the principles adopted in making the estimate.

Recovery plan

8. —(1) Where section 226(1) of the 2004 Act applies, and the trustees or managers of a scheme are required, following an actuarial valuation, either to prepare a recovery plan or to review and if necessary revise an existing recovery plan, they must do so—

(a) in the case of the first actuarial valuation obtained by them under section 224 of the Act and each subsequent valuation under section 224(1)(a), within 15 months after the effective date of the valuation;

(b) in the case of a valuation under section 224(1)(b) and regulation 7(1), within whichever period is applicable under regulation 7(2)(b).

(2) In preparing or revising a recovery plan, the trustees or managers must take account of the following matters—

(a) the asset and liability structure of the scheme;

(b) its risk profile;

(c) its liquidity requirements;

(d) the age profile of the members, and

(e) in the case of a scheme under which the rates of contributions payable by the employer are determined—

(i) by or in accordance with the advice of a person other than the trustees or managers, and

(ii) without the agreement of the employer,

the recommendations of that person.

(3) A recovery plan must be reviewed, and if necessary revised, where the Regulator has given directions under section 231(2)(b)(ii) of the 2004 Act as to the period within which, and manner in which, a failure to meet the statutory funding objective is to be remedied.

(4) Where paragraph (3) applies, the review and any necessary revision must be completed within a reasonable period after the date of the Regulator's directions.

(5) A recovery plan may be reviewed, and if necessary revised, where the trustees or managers consider that there are reasons that may justify a variation to it.

(6) A recovery plan must specify the date on which it was prepared, or, if it has been revised, the date on which it was last revised.

(7) A copy of any recovery plan sent to the Regulator by the trustees or managers of a scheme must be accompanied—

(a) in a case where the plan has been prepared or revised following an actuarial valuation, by a summary of the information contained in the valuation, and

(b) in a case where the plan has been revised in the circumstances described in paragraph (5), by an explanation of the reasons for the revision.

(8) The commencement of the winding up of an eligible scheme, as defined in section 126 of the 2004 Act (eligible schemes), during the recovery period specified in the scheme's recovery plan is a notifiable event for the purposes of section 69(2)(a) of that Act (duty to notify the Regulator of prescribed events in respect of eligible schemes).

Schedule of contributions

9. —(1) A schedule of contributions for a scheme must be prepared within 15 months after the effective date of the first actuarial valuation following the establishment of the scheme.

(2) Where a schedule of contributions has been prepared, it must be reviewed, and if necessary revised —

(a) within 15 months after the effective date of each subsequent actuarial valuation under section 224(1)(a) of the 2004 Act;

(b) within whichever period is applicable under regulation 7(2)(b) after any valuation under section 224(1)(b) and regulation 7(1), and

(c) within a reasonable period after any revision of a recovery plan under regulation 8(3) or (5).

Content and certification of schedules of contributions

10. —(1) A schedule of contributions must show the rates and due dates of all contributions (other than voluntary contributions) payable towards the scheme by or on behalf of the employer and the active members during the relevant period.

(2) In this regulation, "the relevant period" means the period of five years after the date on which the schedule is certified, or, in a case where —

(a) a recovery plan is in force, and

(b) the period set out in the recovery plan as the period within which the statutory funding objective is to be met is longer than five years after the date on which the schedule is certified,

that longer period.

(3) The schedule must show separately —

(a) the rates and due dates of contributions payable by or on behalf of active members of the scheme;

(b) the rates and due dates of the contributions payable by or on behalf of the employer, and

(c) if separate contributions to satisfy liabilities other than those referred to in regulation 3(2) which are likely to fall due for payment by the trustees or managers during the relevant period are made to the scheme, the rates and due dates of those contributions.

(4) Where additional contributions are required in order to give effect to a recovery plan, the rates and dates of those contributions must be shown separately from the rates and dates of contributions otherwise payable.

(5) The schedule must be signed by the trustees or managers of the scheme, and make provision for signature by the employer in order to signify his agreement to the matters included in it.

(6) The schedule must incorporate the actuary's certification, in the relevant form set out in Schedule 1.

Records

11. −(1) The trustees or managers of a scheme to which Part 3 of the 2004 Act applies must keep records of all contributions made to the scheme by any person, showing separately—

(a) the aggregate amounts of contributions paid by or on behalf of active members of the scheme (whether by deductions from their earnings or otherwise) and the dates on which they are paid, distinguishing voluntary contributions from other contributions, and showing the amounts of voluntary contributions paid by each member, and

(b) the aggregate amounts of contributions paid by or on behalf of each person who is an employer in relation to the scheme and the dates on which they are paid.

(2) The trustees or managers must also keep records of any action taken by them to recover—

(a) the amount of any contributions which are not paid on the date on which they are due, and

(b) the amount of any debt which has arisen under section 75(2) or (4) of the 1995 Act (deficiencies in the assets).

Failure to make payments

12. The trustees or managers of a scheme are not required to give notice, under section 228(2 of the 2004 Act (requirement to notify Regulator of failure likely to be of material significance), of a failure to make a payment in accordance with the schedule of contributions where they have given the Regulator notice of the failure under—

(a) section 49(9)(b) of the 1995 Act[11] (failure to remit deductions from members' earnings), or

(b) section 30(7)(c) of the 2004 Act (failure to pay employer's contributions in accordance with Regulator's order).

Period for obtaining employer's agreement

13. Where, following an actuarial valuation, the trustees or managers of a scheme are required under section 229(1) of the 2004 Act to obtain the agreement of the employer to any of the matters mentioned in paragraphs (a) to (d) of that provision, they must do so within 15 months after the effective date of the valuation.

Powers of the Regulator

14. −(1) In exercising any of the powers conferred by section 231 of the 2004 Act in the case of a scheme of the kind referred to in regulations 5(3)(b) and 8(2)(e), the Regulator must take into account any relevant recommendations made to the trustees or managers under those regulations.

(2) In exercising the power in section 231(2)(b)(i) to give directions as to the manner in which a scheme's technical provisions are to be calculated, the Regulator must include a direction specifying the effective date by reference to which assets are valued and the amount of liabilities is determined.

Guidance relating to actuarial advice

15. When advising the trustees or managers of a scheme on any of the matters specified in section 230(1) of the 2004 Act, the actuary shall have regard to the guidance note "Occupational Pension Schemes – scheme funding matters on which advice of actuary must be obtained" (GN49) prepared and published by the Institute of Actuaries and the Faculty of

Actuaries and approved for the purposes of these Regulations by the Secretary of State, with such revisions as have been so approved[12].

Modification of shared cost schemes

16. —(1) The trustees of a shared cost scheme to which Part 3 of the 2004 Act applies may by resolution modify the scheme with a view to making such provision that, where any additional contributions are required to give effect to a recovery plan, those contributions are payable by the employer and the members in the appropriate proportions, unless the employer and the trustees or managers agree—

(a) that the additional contributions should be payable by the employer alone, or

(b) that he should pay a greater proportion than would otherwise fall to be paid by him.

(2) In paragraph (1)—

"shared cost scheme" means a scheme under the provisions of which—

(a) the level of benefits expected to be provided is defined;

(b) contributions are payable by the employer and the active members in specified proportions, and

(c) if—

(i) it appears to the trustees or managers, or

(ii) an actuarial valuation shows,

that otherwise the assets of the scheme will (or are likely to) fall short of its technical provisions, the rates of contributions payable by both the active members and the employer may be increased in specified proportions, and

"the appropriate proportions" means those specified proportions.

(3) For the purposes of paragraph (2) there shall be disregarded—

(a) voluntary contributions by members and any associated contributions by the employer, and

(b) any temporary suspension of the liability to make contributions, or alteration in the proportions in which the contributions are payable, under any provision of the scheme allowing such a suspension or alteration in any circumstances.

Exemptions – general

17. —(1) Part 3 of the 2004 Act does not apply to—

(a) a scheme which—

(i) is established by or under an enactment (including a local Act), and

(ii) is guaranteed by a public authority;

(b) a pay-as-you-go scheme;

(c) a scheme which is made under section 2 of the Parliamentary and other Pensions Act 1987[13] (power to provide for pensions for Members of the House of Commons etc.);

(d) a scheme which is treated as such by virtue of paragraph 4 or 5 of Schedule 2 to these Regulations and—

(i) in the cases described in paragraphs 4(2) and 5(2)(a) of that Schedule, applies to members in employment outside the member States, and

(ii) in the cases described in paragraphs 4(3) and 5(2)(b) of that Schedule, applies to members in employment outside the United Kingdom;

(e) a scheme which—

(i) provides relevant benefits;

(ii) is neither a relevant statutory scheme nor a tax approved scheme, or, from 6th April 2006, is not a tax registered scheme, and

(iii) has fewer than 100 members;

(f) a section 615(6) scheme which has fewer than 100 members;

(g) a scheme which has fewer than two members;

(h) a scheme which has fewer than 12 members, where all the members are trustees of the scheme and either —

> (i) the provisions of the scheme provide that all decisions which fall to be made by the trustees are made by the unanimous agreement of the trustees who are members of the scheme, or

> (ii) the scheme has a trustee who is an independent trustee in relation to the scheme for the purposes of section 23 of the 1995 Act[14] (power to appoint independent trustees) and is registered in the register maintained by the Authority in accordance with regulations made under subsection (4) of that section;

(i) a scheme which has fewer than 12 members, where a company is a trustee of the scheme and all the members of the scheme are directors of the company and either —

> (i) the provisions of the scheme provide that any decision made by the company in its capacity as trustee is made only by the unanimous agreement of the directors who are members of the scheme, or

> (ii) one of the directors is a trustee who is independent in relation to the scheme for the purposes of section 23 of the 1995 Act and is registered in the register maintained by the Authority in accordance with regulations made under subsection (4) of that section;

(j) a scheme under which the only benefits provided for (other than money purchase benefits) are death benefits, if the death benefits are secured by insurance policies or annuity contracts;

(k) a scheme which is the subject of a scheme failure notice under section 122 or 130 of the 2004 Act;

(l) subject to regulation 18, a scheme which is being wound up, or

(m) the Chatsworth Settlement Estate Pension Scheme.

(2) In paragraph (1) —

"enactment" includes an enactment comprised in, or in an instrument under, an Act of the Scottish Parliament;

"pay-as-you-go scheme" means an occupational pension scheme under which there is no requirement for assets to be set aside in advance for the purpose of providing benefits under the scheme (disregarding any requirements relating to additional voluntary contributions);

"public authority" means —

(a) a Minister of the Crown (within the meaning of the Ministers of the Crown Act 1975)[15];

(b) a government department (including any body or authority exercising statutory functions on behalf of the Crown);

(c) the Scottish Ministers;

(d) the National Assembly for Wales, or

(e) a local authority;

"relevant benefits" has the meaning given in section 612(1) of the Income and Corporation Taxes Act 1988[16] (interpretation) or, from 6th April 2006, section 393B of the Income Tax (Earnings and Pensions) Act 2003[17] (relevant benefits);

"relevant statutory scheme" has the meaning given in section 611A(1) of the Income and Corporation Taxes Act 1988[18] (definition of relevant statutory scheme);

"section 615(6) scheme" means a scheme with such a superannuation fund as is mentioned in section 615(6) of the Income and Corporation Taxes Act 1988[19] (funds for the provision of benefits in respect of employment outside the United Kingdom);

"a tax approved scheme" means a scheme which is approved or was formerly approved under section 590 or 591 of the Income and Corporation Taxes Act 1988[20] (approval of retirement benefit schemes) or in respect of which an application for such approval has been duly made but has not been determined;

"a tax registered scheme" means a scheme which is, or is treated as, registered under Chapter 2 of Part 4 of the Finance Act 2004 (registration of pension schemes).

(3) In paragraph (2), "local authority" means—
    (a) in relation to England, a county council, a district council, a London borough council, the Greater London Authority, the Common Council of the City of London in its capacity as a local authority or the Council of the Isles of Scilly;
    (b) in relation to Wales, a county council or county borough council;
    (c) in relation to Scotland, a council constituted under section 2 of the Local Government etc. (Scotland) Act 1994[21] (constitution of councils);
    (d) an administering authority as defined in Schedule 1 to the Local Government Pension Scheme Regulations 1997[22].

(4) Where Part 3 of the 2004 Act ceases to apply to a scheme to which it previously applied, because the scheme satisfies any of the criteria for exemption in paragraph (1), that does not affect any rights or obligations arising before Part 3 ceased to apply.

Exemption connected with winding up

18. —(1) Where the winding up of a scheme begins on or after the commencement date, the exemption provided for in regulation 17(1)(l) is subject to the condition set out in paragraph (2).

(2) The condition referred to in paragraph (1) is that the trustees or managers of the scheme ensure that they receive, before the end of each scheme year following the scheme year in which the winding up of the scheme begins, the actuary's estimate of the solvency of the scheme as at the end of the preceding scheme year.

(3) In paragraph (2)—

"the actuary's estimate of the solvency of the scheme" means—
    (a) except in the case referred to in sub-paragraph (b), an estimate by the actuary of whether, at the end of the relevant scheme year, the value of assets of the scheme to be taken into account under paragraph (1) of regulation 3 exceeded or fell short of the sum of—
        (i) the cost of purchasing annuities, of the type described in section 74(3)(c) of the 1995 Act[23] and on terms consistent with those in the available market, which would be sufficient to satisfy the liabilities to be taken into account under paragraph (2) of regulation 3, and

(ii) the other expenses which, in the opinion of the actuary, would be likely to be incurred in connection with the winding up of the scheme,

and the amount of the excess or, as the case may be, the shortfall;

(b) where the actuary considers that it is not practicable to make an estimate in accordance with sub-paragraph (a), an estimate of the solvency of the scheme at the end of the relevant scheme year made in such manner as the actuary considers appropriate in the circumstances of the case;

"scheme year" means—

(a) either—

(i) a year specified for the purposes of the scheme rules in any document which contains those rules, or

(ii) if no such year is specified, the period of 12 months commencing on 1st April or on such date as the trustees or managers select, or

(b) such other period (if any) exceeding six months but not exceeding 18 months as is selected by the trustees or managers in connection with—

(i) the commencement or termination of the scheme, or

(ii) a variation of the date on which the year or period referred to in paragraph (a) is to commence.

Modification of provisions of the 2004 Act

19. Schedule 2 has effect for the purpose of modifying Part 3 of the 2004 Act and these Regulations as they apply in the circumstances specified there.

Supplementary and consequential provisions, transitional provisions and savings

20. —(1) Schedule 3 has effect for the purpose of making supplementary provisions and consequential amendments connected with the commencement of Part 3 of the 2004 Act and Part IV of the Pensions (Northern Ireland) Order 2005[24] and the coming into force of these Regulations.

(2) Schedule 4 has effect for the purpose of making transitional modifications of the 2004 Act and these Regulations, and saving the effect of repealed provisions of the 1995 Act and provisions revoked by these Regulations.

Revocations

21. The enactments mentioned in Schedule 5 are revoked to the extent specified, subject to the savings in Schedule 4.

Signed by authority of the Secretary of State for Work and Pensions.

Stephen C. Timms
Minister of State, Department for Work and Pensions
8th December 2005

SCHEDULE 1
Regulations 7(4)(a) and 10(6)
ACTUARY'S CERTIFICATES

Form of actuary's certification of the calculation of technical provisions

Name of scheme

Calculation of technical provisions

I certify that, in my opinion, the calculation of the scheme's technical provisions as at *[insert effective date of valuation on which the calculation is based]* is made in accordance with regulations under section 222 of the Pensions Act 2004. The calculation uses a method and assumptions determined by the *[trustees][managers][delete whichever does not apply]* of the scheme and set out in the Statement of Funding Principles dated *[dd mm yyyy]*.

Signature: Date:

Name: Qualification

Address: Name of employer (if applicable)

Form of actuary's certification of schedule of contributions

Name of scheme

Adequacy of rates of contributions

1.   I certify that, in my opinion, the rates of contributions shown in this schedule of contributions are such that—

      the statutory funding objective can be expected to be met by the end of the period specified in the recovery plan dated *[dd mm yyyy]*(a).

      the statutory funding objective can be expected to continue to be met for the period for which the schedule is to be in force(b).

      [delete whichever alternative does not apply]

Adherence to statement of funding principles

2.   I hereby certify that, in my opinion, this schedule of contributions is consistent with the Statement of Funding Principles dated *[dd mm yyyy]*.

The certification of the adequacy of the rates of contributions for the purpose of securing that the statutory funding objective can be expected to be met is not a certification of their adequacy for the purpose of securing the scheme's liabilities by the purchase of annuities, if the scheme were to be wound up.

Signature: Date

Name   Qualification

Address   Name of employer (if applicable)

(a) This applies where the statutory funding objective was not met on the effective date of the last actuarial valuation.

(b) This applies where the statutory funding objective was met on the effective date of the last actuarial valuation.

SCHEDULE 2

Regulation 19

MODIFICATIONS OF THE ACT AND REGULATIONS

Multi-employer schemes

1. —(1) Where—

(a) a scheme in relation to which there is more than one employer is divided into two or more sections, and

(b) the provisions of the scheme are such that they meet conditions A and B,

Part 3 of the 2004 Act and these Regulations shall apply as if each section of the scheme were a separate scheme.

(2) Condition A is that contributions payable to the scheme by an employer, or by a member in employment under that employer, are allocated to that employer's section (or, if more than one section applies to the employer, to the section which is appropriate in respect of the employment in question).

(3) Condition B is that a specified part or proportion of the assets of the scheme is attributable to each section and cannot be used for the purposes of any other section.

(4) In their application to a scheme—

(a) which has been such a scheme as is mentioned in sub-paragraph (1);

(b) which is divided into two or more sections, at least one of which applies only to members who are not in pensionable service under the section;

(c) the provisions of which have not been amended so as to prevent conditions A and B being met in relation to two or more sections, and

(d) in relation to one or more sections of which those conditions have ceased to be met at any time by reason only of there being no members in pensionable service under the section and no contributions which are to be allocated to it,

Part 3 of the 2004 Act and these Regulations apply as if the section in relation to which those conditions have ceased to be satisfied were a separate scheme.

(5) For the purposes of sub-paragraphs (1) to (4), any provisions of the scheme by virtue of which contributions or transfers of assets may be made to make provision for death benefits are disregarded.

(6) But if sub-paragraph (1) or (4) applies and, by virtue of any provisions of the scheme, contributions or transfers of assets to make provision for death benefits are made to a section ("the death benefits section") the assets of which may only be applied for the provision of death benefits, the death benefits section is also to be treated as if it were a seperate scheme for the purpose of Part 3 of the 2004 Act and these Regulations.

(7) For the purpose of this paragraph, any provisions of a scheme by virtue of which assets attributable to one section may on the winding up of the scheme or a section be used for the purposes of another section are disregarded.

(8) In their application in a case of the kind described in sub-paragraph (1) or (4), the forms set out in Schedule 1 are modified as follows—

(a) after "*Name of scheme*", there is inserted "*and name of section*", and

(b) for "scheme" and "scheme's", wherever else they occur, there is substituted "section" and "section's".

2. In the application of section 229 of the 2004 Act to a scheme in relation to which there is more than one employer, references to the employer have effect as if they were references to a person nominated by the employers, or by the rules of the scheme, to act as the employers' representative for the purposes of the section or, if no such nomination is made—

(a) for the purposes of agreement to any of the matters mentioned in subsection (1) of that section, to all of the employers other than any employer who has waived his rights under that sub-section, and

(b) for the purposes of agreement to a modification of the scheme under subsection (2) of that section, to all of the employers.

Frozen or paid-up schemes

3. In the application of Part 3 of the 2004 Act and these Regulations to a scheme which has no active members, references to the employer have effect as if they were references to the person who was the employer immediately before the occurrence of the event after which the scheme ceased to have any such members.

Schemes covering United Kingdom and foreign employment

4. —(1) This paragraph applies in the cases described in sub-paragraphs (2) and (3).

(2) The first case referred to in sub-paragraph (1) is where a scheme—

(a) has its main administration in the United Kingdom;

(b) applies to members in employment in the member States and members in employment outside the member States;

(c) is divided into two or more sections, and

(d) makes provision whereby—

(i) different sections of the scheme apply to members in employment in the member States and to members in employment outside the member States;

(ii) contributions payable to the scheme in respect of a member are allocated to the section applying to that member's employment, and

(iii) a specified part or proportion of the assets of the scheme is attributable to each section and cannot be used for the purposes of any other section.

(3) The second case referred to in sub-paragraph (1) is where a scheme—

(a) has its main administration outside the member States;

(b) applies to members in employment in the United Kingdom and members in employment outside the United Kingdom;

(c) is divided into two or more sections, and

(d) makes provision whereby—

(i) different sections of the scheme apply to members in employment in the United Kingdom and to members in employment outside the United Kingdom;

(ii) contributions payable to the scheme in respect of a member are allocated to the section applying to that member's employment, and

(iii) a specified part or proportion of the assets of the scheme is attributable to each section and cannot be used for the purposes of any other section.

(4) Where this paragraph applies, Part 3 of the 2004 Act and these Regulations shall apply as if each section of the scheme were a separate scheme.

5. —(1) This paragraph applies in the case described in sub-paragraph (2).

(2) The case referred to in sub-paragraph (1) is where a scheme either—
> (a) satisfies the criteria in sub-paragraphs (a) and (b) of paragraph 4(2), but is not divided into sections in the manner described in sub-paragraphs (c) and (d) of that paragraph, or
> (b) satisfies the criteria in sub-paragraphs (a) and (b) of paragraph 4(3), but is not divided into sections in the manner described in sub-paragraphs (c) and (d) of that paragraph,

and part of the scheme is or was treated as a separate scheme under section 611(3) of the Income and Corporation Taxes Act 1988[25].

(3) Where this paragraph applies, Part 3 of the 2004 Act and these Regulations shall apply as if the separated parts of the scheme were separate schemes.

Schemes undertaking cross-border activities
6. —(1) This paragraph applies where the trustees or managers of a scheme are authorised under section 288 of the 2004 Act to accept contributions from European employers or approved under section 289 of that Act to accept contributions from a particular European employer.

(2) Where this paragraph applies, and subject to sub-paragraphs (3) and (4), Part 3 of the 2004 Act and these Regulations shall apply as if they were subject to the following modifications—
> (a) in section 224 of the Act—
>> (i) in subsection (1)(a), the words from "or," to the end of the subsection are omitted;
>> (ii) paragraphs (c) and (d) of subsection (2) are omitted;
>> (iii) the word "and" at the end of paragraph (a) of subsection (3) and paragraph (b) of that subsection are omitted;
>> (iv) the words "or report" in subsections (4), (6) and (7) and the words "or reports" in subsection (5) are omitted;
> (b) in section 226—
>> (i) in subsection (1), for the words from "within the prescribed time" to the end of the subsection there is substituted—
>> " (a) send a summary of the valuation to the Regulator within a reasonable period, and
>> (b) take such steps as are necessary to ensure that the statutory funding objective is met within two years after that date.", and
>> (ii) subsections (2) to (6) are omitted;
> (c) in section 227, for the words "by the end of the period specified in the recovery plan" in subsection (6)(b)(i) there is substituted "within two years after that date";
> (d) in section 231, the words from "with respect to" in paragraph (d) of subsection (1) to the end of that paragraph are omitted;
> (e) in regulations 6(2) and (3)(a), 7(2)(a), 9(1) and (2)(a) and 13 of these Regulations, for "15 months" there is substituted "12 months";

(f) in regulation 7(2), the words "or an actuarial report" are omitted;

(g) regulations 7(2)(c) and (5), 8, 9(2)(c) and 17(1)(a) and (e) to (i) are omitted;

(h) in regulation 10—

(i) in paragraph (2), for "five years", where those words first appear, there is substituted "two years", and the words from "or, in a case where" to the end of that paragraph are omitted;

(ii) in paragraph (4), for "give effect to a recovery plan", there is substituted "comply with section 226", and

(i) in Schedule 1, in the first of the alternative statements in the form of certification of the adequacy of the rates of contributions, for "by the end of the period specified in the recovery plan dated [*dd/mm/yyyy*]" there is substituted "within two years after the effective date of the last actuarial valuation".

3) In the case of a pre-23rd September 2005 scheme—

(a) section 226 of the 2004 Act applies as if it were subject to the following modifications in place of the modifications in sub-paragraph (2)(b)—

(i) for the words from "they must, within the prescribed time" in subsection (1) to the end of that subsection there is substituted—

" they must—

(a) send a summary of the valuation to the Regulator within a reasonable period, and

(b) take such steps as are necessary to ensure that the statutory funding objective is met—

(i) if the valuation is the first valuation the trustees or managers have obtained under section 224, by 22nd September 2008, and

(ii) in any other case, within two years after that date.", and

(ii) subsections (2) to (6) are omitted;

(b) these Regulations apply as if, in addition to the modifications in sub-paragraph (2)(e) to (i), paragraph 2(a)(i) of Schedule 4 is modified so that, after "this Schedule" there is inserted "and, without prejudice to any of those requirements, by reference to an effective date which is no later than 22nd September 2006".

(4) In sub-paragraph (3), "pre-23rd September 2005 scheme" has the meaning given by article 3 of the Pensions Act 2004 (Commencement No. 8) Order 2005[26].

Schemes with a partial guarantee by a public authority

7. Where such a guarantee has been given as is mentioned in regulation 17(1)(a)(ii) in respect of only part of a scheme, Part 3 of the 2004 Act and these Regulations shall apply as if that part and the other part of the scheme were separate schemes.

Schemes relating to certain defence contractors

8. —(1) This paragraph applies in the case of a scheme under which variations to the rate of contributions payable towards the scheme by the employer are subject, either in particular cases or generally, to the consent of—

(a) the Secretary of State for Defence;

(b) a person duly authorised by him, or

(c) a company of which the Secretary of State for Defence or a nominee of his is a shareholder, or a subsidiary (within the meaning of section 736 of the Companies Act 1985[27]) of such a company.

(2) Where this paragraph applies, sections 224(7) and 229 of the 2004 Act shall apply as if references to the employer were both to the employer and the Secretary of State for Defence or, in a case where the consent of a company is required, both to the employer and that company.

Schemes under which the rates of contributions are determined by the trustees or managers or by the actuary

9. —(1) In the case of a scheme under which—

(a) the rates of contributions payable by the employer are determined by the trustees or managers without the agreement of the employer, and

(b) no person other than the trustees or managers is permitted to reduce those rates or to suspend payment of contributions,

section 229 of the 2004 Act and regulation 13 shall apply as if they were subject to the modifications set out in sub-paragraphs (2) and (3), and the reference to section 229 in paragraph 8(2) above shall be read as a reference to that section as modified by sub-paragraph (2).

(2) The modifications of section 229 of the 2004 Act are as follows—

(a) in the heading, for "**agreement of the employer**" there is substituted "**consultation or agreement**";

(b) in subsection (1), for "obtain the agreement of the employer to" there is substituted "consult the employer regarding";

(c) in subsection (2), for the words before "(if the employer agrees)" there is substituted "After consulting the employer regarding any such matter, the trustees or managers may";

(d) subsection (5) is omitted, and

(e) in subsection (6), for "(1), (4) or (5)" there is substituted "(1) or (4)".

(3) The modifications of regulation 13 are as follows—

(a) in the heading, for "**obtaining employer's agreement**" there is substituted "**consulting employer**", and

(b) in the text, for "obtain the agreement of the employer to" there is substituted "consult the employer regarding".

(4) Where the power of the trustees or managers to determine the rates of contributions payable by the employer without the employer's agreement is subject to conditions, the modifications provided for in sub-paragraphs (2) and (3) have effect only in circumstances where the conditions are satisfied.

(5) In the case of a scheme under which the rates of contributions payable by the employer are determined by the actuary without the agreement of the employer, section 227(6) of the 2004 Act shall apply as if it required that, in addition to the matters specified there, the actuary's certificate must state that the rates shown in the schedule of contributions are not lower than the rates he would have provided for if he, rather than the trustees or managers of the scheme, had the responsibility of preparing or revising the schedule, the statement of funding principles and any recovery plan.

(6) In the case to which sub-paragraph (5) applies, regulation 10(6) and Schedule 1 apply as if the form of certification of the adequacy of the rates of contributions shown in the schedule of contributions included an additional statement that—

I also certify that the rates of contributions shown in this schedule are not lower than I would have provided for had I had responsibility for preparing or revising the schedule, the statement of funding principles and any recovery plan".

(7) Where the power of the actuary to determine the rates of contributions payable by the employer without the employer's agreement is subject to conditions, the modifications provided for in sub-paragraphs (5) and (6) have effect only in circumstances where the conditions are satisfied.

(8) In the case of a scheme to which paragraph 8 applies, the references to the employer's agreement in sub-paragraphs (4), (5) and (7) of this paragraph shall be read as if the extended meaning of "employer" given by paragraph 8(2) applied.

Schemes which are not required to appoint an actuary

10. Where a scheme is exempt from the application of section 47(1)(b) of the 1995 Act (requirement to appoint a scheme actuary) by virtue of regulations made under subsection (5) of that section, Part 3 of the 2004 Act and these Regulations shall apply as if references to the actuary were to an actuary authorised by the trustees or managers to provide such valuations and certifications as may be required under that Part and these Regulations.

Schemes with fewer than 100 members

11. —(1) This paragraph applies in the case of a scheme which—
(a) had fewer than 100 members on the effective date of its last actuarial valuation;
(b) is not exempted from the application of Part 3 of the 2004 Act by regulation 17(1), and
(c) is not a scheme in relation to which the application of that Part of the Act is modified by paragraph 6 of this Schedule.

(2) Where this paragraph applies—
(a) section 224(1)(a) of the 2004 Act shall apply as if it required the trustees or managers of the scheme to obtain an actuarial valuation the effective date of which is not more than three years after that of the last such valuation, and an actuarial report for any intervening year at any time in which the scheme had 100 or more members, and
(b) section 224(3) of that Act shall apply as if—
(i) all but paragraph (b) were omitted, and
(ii) that paragraph required that the effective date of any actuarial report must be an anniversary of the effective date of the last actuarial valuation.

Schemes subject to a change of circumstances affecting the certification of the schedule of contributions

12. —(1) In circumstances where the actuary considers that, because of the possibility of significant changes in the value of the assets of the scheme or in the scheme's technical provisions since the effective date of the last actuarial valuation, he is unable to certify the schedule of contributions in the terms set out in paragraph (b) of section 227(6) of the 2004

Act, that paragraph applies as if it provided for a statement that the rates shown in tha schedule are such that—

(a) where the statutory funding objective was not met on the effective date of the las actuarial valuation, the statutory funding objective could have been expected on tha date to be met by the end of the period specified in the recovery plan, or

(b) where the statutory funding objective was met on the effective date of the las actuarial valuation, the statutory funding objective could have been expected on tha date to continue to be met for the period for which the schedule is to be in force.

(2) In circumstances where the statutory funding objective was met on the effective date o the last actuarial valuation but the actuary considers that, having regard to—

(a) the rates of contributions payable towards the scheme since that date, or

(b) the rates of contributions payable since that date taken together with the possibility of significant changes in the value of the assets of the scheme or in the scheme': technical provisions,

he is unable to certify the schedule of contributions in the terms set out in paragraph (b)(ii, of section 227(6) of the 2004 Act, that paragraph applies as if it provided for a statement tha¹ the rates shown in that schedule are such that the statutory funding objective could have been expected on that date to be met by the end of the period for which the schedule is to be in force.

(3) In the case to which sub-paragraph (1) applies, regulation 10(6) and Schedule 1 apply as if the alternative statements in the form of certification of the adequacy of the rates o¹ contributions shown in the schedule of contributions were as follows—

"the statutory funding objective could have been expected on [*effective date of valuationon which the schedule is based*] to be met by the end of the period specified in the recovery plan.

the statutory funding objective could have been expected on [*effective date of valuationon which the schedule is based*] to continue to be met for the period for which the schedule is to be in force."

(4) In the case to which sub-paragraph (2) applies, regulation 10(6) and Schedule 1 apply as if the alternative statements in the form of certification of the adequacy of the rates of contributions shown in the schedule of contributions were replaced by the following statement—

" "the statutory funding objective could have been expected on [*effective date of valuationon which the schedule is based*] to be met by the end of the period for which the schedule is to be in force.".

(5) Where paragraph 6 of this Schedule applies, sub-paragraphs (1) and (3) of this paragraph apply as if the references to the period specified in the recovery plan were to the period of two years from the effective date of the last actuarial valuation.

SCHEDULE 3

Regulation 20(1)

SUPPLEMENTARY AND CONSEQUENTIAL PROVISIONS

Occupational Pension Schemes (Contracting-out) Regulations 1996

. —(1) The Occupational Pension Schemes (Contracting-out) Regulations 1996[28] are amended as follows.

2) In regulation 1(2) (interpretation)—
  (a) after the definition of "the 1995 Act" insert—
  " "the 2004 Act" means the Pensions Act 2004;";
  (b) omit the definition of "minimum funding requirement".

3) In regulation 6(2) (information to be confirmed by an employer in writing), for sub-paragraph (g) substitute—

 (g) in the case of a scheme to which Part 3 of the 2004 Act (scheme funding) applies, that the requirements of sections 224, 225, 226 (if applicable) and 227 of that Act and any regulations under those provisions are complied with.".

4) In regulation 18 (requirement as to the resources of a salary-related contracted-out scheme)—
  (a) in paragraph (1), for the words from "the amount of the resources of the scheme must be" to the end substitute "either the resources of the scheme must be sufficient to enable the scheme to meet the statutory funding objective provided for in section 222(1) of the 2004 Act, or the actuary to the scheme must have certified under section 227(6)(b)(i) of that Act that in his opinion the rates shown in the schedule of contributions are such that the statutory funding objective can be expected to be met by the end of the period specified in the recovery plan.";
  (b) in paragraph (2), for "section 56 of the 1995 Act" substitute "Part 3 of the 2004 Act";
  (c) after paragraph (2) add the following paragraph—

(3) In a case where the trustees of a scheme are authorised under section 288 of the 2004 Act to accept contributions from European employers or approved under section 289 of that Act to accept contributions from a particular European employer, paragraph (1) has effect with the substitution for the words "by the end of the period specified in the recovery plan" of "within two years after the date of the last actuarial valuation under section 224 of the 2004 Act".".

5) In regulation 49(4)(a)(i) (determination of cash equivalent of rights under a scheme which is not a money purchase scheme)—
  (a) for "section 56 of the 1995 Act applies (minimum funding requirement)" substitute "Part 3 of the 2004 Act applies (scheme funding)";
  (b) for "subsection (1) of that section" substitute "section 222(1) of that Act".

6) In regulation 72 (transitional requirements as to sufficiency of resources of salary-related schemes)—
  (a) in paragraph (1A), for "section 58 of the 1995 Act" substitute "section 227 of the 2004 Act";

(b) in paragraph (3), for "section 56(3) of the 1995 Act (minimum funding requirement)" substitute "section 222(3) of the 2004 Act (statutory funding objective)";

(c) in paragraph (6), for "section 56 of the 1995 Act" substitute "Part 3 of the 2004 Act".

(7) The amendments in this paragraph have effect subject to paragraph 17 of Schedule 4.

Occupational Pension Schemes (Disclosure of Information) Regulations 1996

2. —(1) Subject to paragraph 3, the Occupational Pension Schemes (Disclosure of Information) Regulations 1996[29] ("the Disclosure Regulations") are amended as follows.

(2) In regulation 1(2) (interpretation)—

(a) after the definition of "the 1995 Act" insert—

" "the 2004 Act" means the Pensions Act 2004;";

(b) after the definition of "public service pension scheme" insert—

" "the Regulator" means the Pensions Regulator established under section 1 of the 2004 Act;".

(3) In regulation 5 (information to be made available to individuals)—

(a) in paragraph (1), for "paragraphs (2) to (12)" substitute "paragraphs (2) to (12ZA)";

(b) after paragraph (12) insert the following paragraph—

" (12ZA) Where the trustees of a scheme to which Part 3 of the 2004 Act applies have obtained an actuarial valuation or report under section 224 of that Act, they shall furnish the information mentioned in paragraphs 17 to 22 of Schedule 2, in the form of a summary funding statement, as of course to all members and beneficiaries (except excluded persons), within a reasonable period after the date by which they are required by that section to ensure that the valuation or report is received by them.";

(c) after paragraph (12AA) insert the following paragraph—

"(12AB) If a scheme has been modified by the Regulator under section 231(2)(a) of the 2004 Act (modifications as regards the future accrual of benefits), the trustees must inform all active members of the fact within one month of the modification taking effect.";

(d) in paragraph (12A) (sectionalised multi-employer schemes)—

(i) for "Schedule 5 to the Occupational Pension Schemes (Minimum Funding Requirement and Actuarial Valuations) Regulations 1996" substitute "Schedule 2 to the Occupational Pension Schemes (Scheme Funding) Regulations 2005";

(ii) for "section 56 of the 1995 Act" substitute "Part 3 of the 2004 Act", and

(iii) for "section 56 does not apply" substitute "Part 3 does not apply".

(4) In regulation 6(1)(c) (annual report to contain actuary's certificate)—

(a) for "section 56 of the 1995 Act" substitute "Part 3 of the 2004 Act", and

(b) before "that Act" insert "section 227 of".

(5) For the heading to regulation 7, substitute "**Availability of other documents**".

(6) For sub-paragraphs (a) to (c) in regulation 7(1), substitute the following sub-paragraphs—

" (a) the statement of funding principles where required under section 223 of the 2004 Act;

(b) where Part 3 of the 2004 Act applies to the scheme, the last actuarial valuation under section 224 of that Act received by the trustees, or, if an actuarial report under that section was received by them more recently than the last actuarial valuation, both that valuation and any report received subsequently;

(c) any recovery plan prepared under section 226 of the 2004 Act which is currently in force;

(ca) the payment schedule where required under section 87 of the 1995 Act or schedule of contributions where required under section 227 of the 2004 Act, and".

7) In Schedule 2 (information to be made available to individuals), after paragraph 16 add—

17. A summary, based on the last actuarial valuation under section 224 of the 2004 Act received by the trustees and any actuarial report received subsequently, of the extent to which the assets of the scheme are adequate to cover its technical provisions.

18. An explanation of any change in the funding position of the scheme—

(a) in the case of the first summary funding statement issued in respect of the scheme, since the last actuarial valuation in respect of the scheme under regulation 30 of the Occupational Pension Schemes (Minimum Funding Requirement and Actuarial Valuations) Regulations 1996[30] (ongoing actuarial valuations), or, if no such valuation was obtained, since the last actuarial valuation under the rules of the scheme, and

(b) in the case of any subsequent summary funding statement, since the date of the last summary funding statement.

19. The actuary's estimate of solvency contained in the last actuarial valuation under section 224 of the 2004 Act received by the trustees.

20. A summary of any recovery plan prepared under section 226 of the 2004 Act which is currently in force.

21. Whether the scheme has been modified under section 231(2)(a) of the 2004 Act, is subject to directions under section 231(2)(b) of that Act or bound by a schedule of contributions imposed under section 231(2)(c) of that Act, and if so an account of the circumstances in which the modification was made, the direction given or the schedule of conditions imposed.

22. Whether any payment has been made to the employer under section 37 of the 1995 Act [31](payment of surplus to employer)—

(a) in the case of the first summary funding statement issued in respect of the scheme, in the 12 months preceding the date on which it is prepared, and

(b) in the case of any subsequent summary funding statement, since the date of the last such statement,

and, if so, the amount of the payment.".

3. —(1) Until the trustees or managers of a scheme have prepared a schedule of contributions under section 227 of the 2004 Act (in accordance with regulation 9(1) of, or paragraph 5 of Schedule 4 to, these Regulations), the Disclosure Regulations have effect in relation to a scheme to which Part 3 of the 2004 Act applies as if—

(a) the amendments in paragraph 2 of this Schedule had not been made;

(b) those Regulations included the requirement in sub-paragraph (2) of this paragraph, and

(c) regulations 1(2) (so far as material), 10 and 11 of those Regulations applied in respect of that requirement.

(2) The requirement referred to in paragraph (1)(b) is that, before 22nd September in 2006 and each subsequent year the trustees or managers of the scheme furnish all members and beneficiaries (except excluded persons) with the following information, in the form of a summary funding statement—

(a) a summary, based on the last actuarial valuation under regulation 30 of the Occupational Pension Schemes (Minimum Funding Requirement and Actuarial Valuations) Regulations 1996 ("the MFR Regulations") received by the trustees or managers or, if no such valuation was obtained, the last actuarial valuation under the rules of the scheme, of the extent to which the assets of the scheme are adequate to meet its liabilities as they fall due;

(b) an explanation of any change in the funding position of the scheme—

(i) in the case of the first summary statement issued in respect of the scheme since the last actuarial valuation in respect of the scheme under regulation 30 of the MFR Regulations, or, if no such valuation was obtained, since the last actuarial valuation under the rules of the scheme, and

(ii) in the case of any subsequent summary funding statement, since the date of the last summary funding statement;

(c) any estimate by the actuary of the solvency of the scheme, or, if the actuary has made more than one estimate of solvency, the latest such estimate;

(i) whether any payment has been made to the employer under section 37 of the 1995 Act—in the case of the first summary funding statement issued in respect of the scheme, in the 12 months preceding the date on which it is prepared, and

(ii) in the case of any subsequent summary funding statement, since the date of the last such statement,

and, if so, the amount of the payment.

(3) The trustees or managers of a scheme are not required to comply with the requirement in sub-paragraph (2) in any year if the scheme had fewer than 100 members during the 12 months ending on 31st August in that year.

(4) A summary funding statement furnished under sub-paragraph (2) must be accompanied by a written statement that further information about the scheme is available, giving the address to which enquiries about it should be sent.

Occupational Pension Schemes (Scheme Administration) Regulations 1996

4. —(1) The Occupational Pension Schemes (Scheme Administration) Regulations 1996[32] are amended as follows.

(2) In regulation 1(2) (interpretation), after the definition of "the 1995 Act" insert—

" "the 2004 Act" means the Pensions Act 2004;".

(3) In regulation 16A(2)[33] (circumstances in which notice of an employer's failure to make payments to trustees or managers need not be given), for sub-paragraph (b) substitute the following—

"(b) where the scheme is exempt from the requirement to prepare, review and if necessary revise a schedule of contributions under section 227 of the 2004 Act, by virtue of any of sub-paragraphs (a) to (i) and (k) to (m) of regulation 17(1) of the Occupational Pension Schemes (Scheme Funding) Regulations 2005; or".

Occupational Pension Schemes (Transfer Values) Regulations 1996
5. —(1) The Occupational Pension Schemes (Transfer Values) Regulations 1996[34] are amended as follows.

(2) In regulation 1(2) (interpretation), after the definition of "the 1995 Act" insert—

"the 2004 Act" means the Pensions Act 2004;".

(3) In regulation 7 (manner of calculation and verification of cash equivalents)—
    (a) insert the word "and" at the end of paragraph (3)(b)(ii);
    (b) omit the word "and" at the end of paragraph (3)(b)(iii), and
    (c) omit paragraphs (3)(b)(iv) and (4).

(4) In regulation 8 (further provisions as to calculation of cash equivalents)—
    (a) in paragraph (4), for "section 56 of the 1995 Act (minimum funding requirement)" substitute "Part 3 of the 2004 Act (scheme funding)";
    (b) in paragraph (4B), omit "then, subject to paragraph (4D)";
    (c) omit paragraphs (4D) to (4I), (4K) and (4L);
    (d) in paragraph (5)—
        (i) for "section 61 of the 1995 Act" substitute "section 232 of the 2004 Act";
        (ii) for "section 56" substitute "Part 3", and
        (iii) for "paragraphs (4), (4A) and (4G)" substitute "paragraphs (4) and (4A)", and
    (e) omit paragraph (6).

Personal and Occupational Pension Schemes (Pensions Ombudsman) Regulations 1996
6. —(1) The Personal and Occupational Pension Schemes (Pensions Ombudsman) Regulations 1996[35] are amended as follows.

(2) In regulation 4(2) (compliance with particular requirements excluded from ombudsman's jurisdiction), after sub-paragraph (g) add—

' "or the requirements under Part 3 of the Pensions Act 2004.".

Occupational Pension Schemes (Winding Up) Regulations 1996
7. —(1) The Occupational Pension Schemes (Winding Up) Regulations 1996[36] are amended as follows.

(2) In regulation 12(3) (winding up of sectionalised schemes etc.)—
(a) for "Schedule 5 to the MFR Regulations" substitute "Schedule 2 to the Occupational Pension Schemes (Scheme Funding) Regulations 2005", and
(b) for "section 56" substitute "Part 3 of the Pensions Act 2004".

(3) In regulation 13 (hybrid schemes), omit paragraphs (6) and (7).

Occupational Pension Schemes (Contracting-out) Regulations (Northern Ireland) 1996
8. —(1) The Occupational Pension Schemes (Contracting-out) Regulations (Northern Ireland) 1996[37] are amended as follows.

(2) In regulation 49(4)(a)(i) (determination of cash equivalent of rights under a scheme which is not a money purchase scheme)—

(a) for "Article 56 of the Order applies (minimum funding requirement)" substitute "Part IV of the 2005 Order[38] applies (scheme funding)", and

(b) for "Article 56(1)" substitute "Article 201(1) of that Order".

Pension Sharing (Valuation) Regulations 2000

9. —(1) The Pension Sharing (Valuation) Regulations 2000[39] are amended as follows.

(2) In regulation 1(2) (interpretation), after the definition of "the 1999 Act" insert—

" "the 2004 Act" means the Pensions Act 2004;".

(3) In regulation 4 (calculation and verification of cash equivalents)—

(a) insert the word "and" at the end of paragraph (3)(b)(i);

(b) omit the word "and" at the end of paragraph (3)(b)(ii), and

(c) omit paragraphs (3)(b)(iii) and (4).

(4) In regulation 5 (further provisions as to calculation of cash equivalents)—

(a) in paragraph (3), for "section 56 of the 1995 Act" substitute "Part 3 of the 2004 Act";

(b) in paragraph (3B), omit "then, subject to paragraph (3D)";

(c) omit paragraphs (3D) to (3I), (3K) and (3L);

(d) in paragraph (4)—

(i) for "Schedule 5 to the Occupational Pension Schemes (Minimum Funding Requirement and Actuarial Valuations) Regulations 1996" substitute "Schedule 2 to the Occupational Pension Schemes (Scheme Funding) Regulations 2005";

(ii) for "section 56 of the 1995 Act" substitute "Part 3 of the 2004 Act", and

(iii) for "paragraphs (3), (3A) and (3G)" substitute "paragraphs (3) and (3A)", and

(e) in paragraph (5), for "paragraphs (3) and (3F)" substitute "paragraph (3)".

Pension Sharing (Implementation and Discharge of Liability) Regulations 2000

10. —(1) The Pension Sharing (Implementation and Discharge of Liability) Regulations 2000[40] are amended as follows.

(2) In regulation 1(2) (interpretation), after the definition of "the 1999 Act" insert—

" "the 2004 Act" means the Pensions Act 2004;".

(3) In regulation 16 (adjustments to the amount of pension credit)—

(a) in paragraph (2), for "section 56 of the 1995 Act" substitute "Part 3 of the 2004 Act (scheme funding)";

(b) in paragraph (2B), omit "then, subject to paragraph (2D)";

(c) omit paragraphs (2D) to (2I), (2K) and (2L), and

(d) in paragraph (3)—

(i) for "Schedule 5 to the Occupational Pension Schemes (Minimum Funding Requirement and Actuarial Valuations) Regulations 1996" substitute "Schedule 2 to the Occupational Pension Schemes (Scheme Funding) Regulations 2005";

(ii) for "section 56 of the 1995 Act (minimum funding requirement)" substitute "Part 3 of the 2004 Act", and

(iii) for "paragraphs (2), (2A) and (2G)" substitute "paragraphs (2) and (2A)".

Pension Sharing (Pension Credit Benefit) Regulations 2000

11. —(1) The Pension Sharing (Pension Credit Benefit) Regulations 2000[41] are amended as follows.

(2) In regulation 1(2) (interpretation), after the definition of "the 1999 Act" insert—

" "the 2004 Act" means the Pensions Act 2004;".

(3) In regulation 24 (calculation and verification of cash equivalents)—
(a) insert the word "and" at the end of paragraph (3)(b)(ii);
(b) omit the word "and" at the end of paragraph (3)(b)(iii), and
(c) omit paragraphs (3)(b)(iv) and (4).

(4) In regulation 27 (increases and reductions of cash equivalents)—
(a) in paragraph (4), for "section 56 of the 1995 Act" substitute "Part 3 of the 2004 Act";
(b) in paragraph (4B), omit "then, subject to paragraph (4D)";
(c) omit paragraphs (4D) to (4I), (4K) and (4L);
(d) in paragraph (4M), for "paragraphs (4J) and (4K)" substitute "paragraph (4J)", and
(e) in paragraph (5)—
(i) for "Schedule 5 to the Occupational Pension Schemes (Minimum Funding Requirement and Actuarial Valuations) Regulations 1996" substitute "Schedule 2 to the Occupational Pension Schemes (Scheme Funding) Regulations 2005";
(ii) for "section 56 of the 1995 Act" substitute "Part 3 of the 2004 Act", and
(iii) for "paragraphs (4), (4A) and (4G)" substitute "paragraphs (4) and (4A)".

Stakeholder Pension Schemes Regulations 2000
12. —(1) The Stakeholder Pension Schemes Regulations 2000[42] are amended as follows.

(2) In regulation 19 (requirement for trustees of a stakeholder pension scheme established under a trust), omit "except the reference to section 56 in section 35(2) and 35(5)(b) of that Act".

Occupational Pension Schemes (Republic of Ireland Schemes Exemption) Regulations 2000

13. —(1) The Occupational Pension Schemes (Republic of Ireland Schemes Exemption) Regulations 2000[43] are amended as follows.

(2) In regulation 1(3) (interpretation), after the definition of "the 1995 Act" insert—

" "the 2004 Act" means the Pensions Act 2004;".

(3) In regulation 2 (exemption of Republic of Ireland schemes – general provision), after "the 1995 Act" insert "or the 2004 Act".

(4) In the Schedule, at the end insert—

Provision of the 2004 Act	*Purpose of provision*
Part 3	Scheme funding

Occupational Pension Schemes (Administration and Audited Accounts) (Amendment) Regulations 2005
14. —(1) The Occupational Pension Schemes (Administration and Audited Accounts) (Amendment) Regulations 2005[44] are amended as follows.

(2) In the substituted regulation 16A of the Occupational Pension Schemes (Scheme Administration) Regulations 1996 set out in regulation 4(5) (circumstances in which trustees or managers do not need to notify failure to pay contributions), for paragraph (d) substitute the following—

" (d) the scheme is exempt from the requirement to prepare, review and if necessary revise a schedule of contributions under section 227 of the 2004 Act, by virtue of any of sub-paragraphs (a) to (i) and (k) to (m) of regulation 17(1) of the Occupational Pension Schemes (Scheme Funding) Regulations 2005.".

SCHEDULE 4

Regulation 20(2)

TRANSITIONAL PROVISIONS AND SAVINGS

PART 1

Transitional provisions

1. Paragraphs 2 to 7 of this Schedule apply to a scheme which—
    (a) is either—
        (i) subject to section 56 of the 1995 Act (minimum funding requirement), or
        (ii) exempted from the application of that section by regulation 28 of the Occupational Pension Schemes (Minimum Funding Requirement and Actuarial Valuations) Regulations 1996[45] ("the 1996 Regulations"),
        immediately before the commencement date, and
    (b) becomes subject to Part 3 of the 2004 Act (scheme funding) on that date.

    2. Section 224 of the 2004 Act (actuarial valuations and reports) applies to the scheme as if—
    (a) it included a requirement for the trustees or managers of the scheme—
        (i) to obtain an actuarial valuation ("the first valuation under the 2004 Act"), in accordance with the requirements specified in paragraph 3 of this Schedule, and
        (ii) to ensure that the first valuation under the 2004 Act is received by them within the relevant period specified in paragraph 4 of this Schedule;
    (b) neither paragraph (a) of subsection (1) nor subsection (4) applied in relation to the first valuation under the 2004 Act, and
    (c) paragraph (a) of subsection (3) were omitted.

3. —(1) Except where sub-paragraph (3), (5) or (7) applies, the trustees or managers of the scheme must obtain the first valuation under the 2004 Act by reference to an effective date not more than one year after the commencement date.

(2) Sub-paragraph (3) applies where—
    (a) the trustees or managers received, before the commencement date, in accordance with any provisions of section 57 of the 1995 Act (valuation and certification of assets and liabilities) and the 1996 Regulations, or receive—
        (i) on or after the commencement date, and
        (ii) within one year of its effective date,
        in accordance with any such provisions which continue in force under Part 2 of this Schedule, an actuarial valuation by reference to an effective date on or after 21st September 2002, and
    (b) neither sub-paragraph (5) nor sub-paragraph (7) applies.

(3) Where this sub-paragraph applies, the trustees or managers must obtain the first actuarial valuation under the 2004 Act by reference to an effective date which is—

(a) no earlier than 22nd September 2005, and

(b) not more than three years after the effective date of the last valuation they received under the 1995 Act.

(4) Subject to sub-paragraph (8), sub-paragraph (5) applies where —

(a) immediately before the commencement date, the trustees or managers were required under section 57(2)(a) of the 1995 Act to obtain an actuarial valuation by virtue of a certificate in the terms set out in that provision, or

(b) on or after the commencement date, the trustees or managers receive a certificate in the terms set out in section 57(2)(a) of the 1995 Act in consequence of the requirements saved by paragraph 15 of this Schedule,

and the trustees or managers have determined before that date, or determine subsequently, that the valuation should be obtained by reference to an effective date which is no earlier than 22nd September 2005 and not more than three years after the effective date of the last valuation they received under the 1995 Act.

(5) Where this sub-paragraph applies, the trustees or managers must obtain the first valuation under the 2004 Act by reference to the effective date they have determined.

(6) Subject to sub-paragraph (8), sub-paragraph (7) applies where —

(a) immediately before the commencement date, the trustees or managers were required under section 57(2)(b) of the 1995 Act to obtain an actuarial valuation by virtue of the occurrence of an event of the kind described in regulation 13 of the 1996 Regulations (section 75 debts in multi-employer schemes), and

(b) they have determined before that date, or determine subsequently, that the valuation should be obtained by reference to an effective date which is no earlier than 22nd September 2005 and not more than three years after the effective date of the last valuation they received under the 1995 Act.

(7) Where this sub-paragraph applies, the trustees or managers must obtain the first valuation under the 2004 Act by reference to the effective date they have determined.

(8) In a case where, but for this provision, sub-paragraph (5) would apply, by virtue of the receipt by the trustees or managers of a certificate in the terms set out in section 57(2)(a) of the 1995 Act, and sub-paragraph (7) would also apply, by virtue of the occurrence of an event of the kind described in regulation 13 of the 1996 Regulations, sub-paragraph (5) applies only if the certificate was received before the event occurred and sub-paragraph (7) applies only if the event occurred before the certificate was received.

4. The trustees or managers must ensure that the first valuation under the 2004 Act is received by them —

(a) where paragraph 3(1) applies, or where paragraph 3(3) applies and the trustees or managers obtained that valuation by reference to an effective date which is after 29th December 2005, within 15 months after its effective date;

(b) where paragraph 3(3) applies and the trustees or managers obtained that valuation by reference to an effective date between 22nd September and 29th December 2005, within 18 months after its effective date;

(c) where paragraph 3(5) applies, within 18 months after the date on which the certificate referred to in paragraph 3(4) is signed, and

(d) where paragraph 3(7) applies, within 18 months after the date on which the even‌ referred to in paragraph 3(6) occurred.

5. Section 227 of the 2004 Act (schedule of contributions) applies to the scheme as if i‌ included a requirement for the trustees or managers of the scheme to prepare a schedule o‌ contributions ("the first schedule of contributions under the 2004 Act") within the same‌ period as that within which they are required by paragraph 4 to ensure that they receive th‌ first valuation under the 2004 Act.

6. In the circumstances described in paragraph 4(b), (c), and (d), regulation 6(2) of thes‌ Regulations (first statement of funding principles) applies to the scheme, and regulation‌ 8(1)(a) and 13 apply in relation to the first valuation under the 2004 Act, as if the perio‌ there referred to were the same period as that within which the trustees or managers ar‌ required by paragraph 4 to ensure that they receive the first valuation under the 2004 Act.

7. References in sections 224 to 231 of the 2004 Act to actuarial valuations or schedules o‌ contributions shall be taken to exclude any such valuation or schedule of contribution‌ under the 1995 Act as in force before the commencement date or as continued in force b‌ paragraphs 9 to 16 of this Schedule.

PART 2

Savings

8. Paragraphs 9 to 19 of this Schedule apply to a scheme which —
(a) is subject to section 56 of the 1995 Act immediately before the commencement date‌ and
(b) becomes subject to Part 3 of the 2004 Act on that date.

9. Sections 56 and 58 to 60 of the 1995 Act, regulations 15 to 17 and 19 to 27 of the 199‌ Regulations and Schedules 2 and 4 to those Regulations continue to apply to the scheme‌ from the commencement date until the date on which the first schedule of contribution‌ under the 2004 Act comes into force.

10. Where —
(a) immediately before the commencement date, the trustees or managers of the‌ scheme were required under section 57(1)(a) of the 1995 Act and regulation 10 of the‌ 1996 Regulations (time limits for minimum funding valuations) to obtain an actuaria‌ valuation within a period ending on or after the commencement date, and
(b) they have determined before that date, or determine subsequently, that the‌ valuation should be obtained by reference to an effective date before 22nd September‌ 2005,
those provisions apply to the scheme on and after the commencement date in respect of that valuation.

11. Where —
(a) immediately before the commencement date, the trustees or managers of the‌ scheme were required under section 57(2)(a) of the 1995 Act to obtain an actuarial‌ valuation within the period specified in section 57(4)(a) of that Act, and

(b) they have determined before that date, or determine subsequently, that the valuation should be obtained by reference to an effective date before 22nd September 2005,

those provisions apply to the scheme on and after the commencement date in respect of that valuation.

12. Where—

(a) immediately before the commencement date, the trustees or managers of the scheme were required under section 57(2)(b) of the 1995 Act to obtain an actuarial valuation by virtue of the occurrence of an event of the kind described in regulation 13 of the 1996 Regulations, and

(b) they have determined before that date, or determine subsequently, that the valuation should be obtained by reference to an effective date before 22nd September 2005,

those provisions apply to the scheme on and after the commencement date in respect of that valuation, subject to the modification that the valuation must be obtained within the period of six months beginning with the date on which the relevant event occurred.

13. Where—

(a) immediately before the commencement date, the trustees or managers of the scheme were required under section 41(1)(a) and (2)(c) of the 1995 Act and regulation 30 of the 1996 Regulations (ongoing actuarial valuations and statements) to obtain an actuarial valuation within a period ending on or after the commencement date, and an accompanying statement in the form set out in Schedule 6 to those Regulations, and

(b) they have determined before that date, or determine subsequently, that the valuation should be obtained by reference to an effective date before 22nd September 2005,

those provisions apply to the scheme on and after the commencement date in respect of that valuation and statement.

14. Where a requirement to obtain a valuation is preserved by any of paragraphs 10 to 13 of this Schedule, section 57(5) to (7) of the 1995 Act, regulations 3 to 9 of the 1996 Regulations and (except in the case to which paragraph 13 applies) regulation 14 of and Schedule 1 to those Regulations apply in respect of that valuation.

15. Where, immediately before the commencement date, the trustees or managers of the scheme were required under section 57(1)(b) of the 1995 Act and regulation 18 of the 1996 Regulations (occasional and periodic certification of adequacy of contributions) to obtain annual certificates as to the adequacy of contributions payable towards the scheme, those provisions, sections 57(5) to (7) of that Act and Schedule 3 to the 1996 Regulations apply to the scheme until the effective date of the first valuation under the 2004 Act relating to the scheme.

16. Section 61 of the 1995 Act (supplementary), regulation 2 of the 1996 Regulations (interpretation) and regulation 29 of, and Schedule 5 to, those Regulations (modifications) apply, so far as material, on and after the commencement date in relation to the provisions of the Act and Regulations saved by paragraphs 9 to 15 of this Schedule.

17. Where any provision of the 1995 Act or the 1996 Regulations applies to the scheme on or after the commencement date by virtue of this Schedule, any reference to that provision in the Occupational Pension Schemes (Contracting-out) Regulations 1996[46] ("the Contracting-out Regulations") applies in relation to the scheme on and after the commencement date as if—

(a) in the case of a provision of the 1995 Act, the repeal of that provision by the 2004 Act had not come into force on that date in accordance with the Pensions Act 2004 (Commencement No. 8) Order 2005[47] ("the Commencement Order");

(b) in the case of a provision in the 1996 Regulations, those Regulations had not been revoked by regulation 21, and

(c) the amendments of the Contracting-out Regulations in paragraph 1 of Schedule 3 to these Regulations had not come into force.

18. Where any provision of the 1995 Act or the 1996 Regulations applies to the scheme on or after the commencement date by virtue of this Schedule, regulation 4(2) of the Personal and Occupational Pension Schemes (Pensions Ombudsman) Regulations 1996[48] shall be taken to include a reference to that provision notwithstanding its repeal by the 2004 Act in accordance with the Commencement Order or the revocation of the 1996 Regulations by regulation 21.

19. Any reference to the 1995 Act or the 1996 Regulations in—

(a) the Occupational Pension Schemes (Winding Up) Regulations 1996[49];

(b) the Occupational Pension Schemes (Deficiency on Winding Up etc.) Regulations 1996[50], or

(c) the Occupational Pension Schemes (Employer Debt) Regulations 2005[51],

applies to the scheme on and after the commencement date as if, where the reference is to a provision of the Act, the repeal of that provision by the 2004 Act had not come into force on that date in accordance with the Commencement Order, and, where the reference is to a provision in the 1996 Regulations, those Regulations had not been revoked by regulation 21.

SCHEDULE 5

Regulation 21
REVOCATIONS

(1)	(2)	(3)
Regulations revoked	References	Extent of revocation
The Occupational Pension Schemes (Minimum Funding Requirement and Actuarial Valuations) Regulations 1996	S.I. 1996/1536	The whole Regulations
The Occupational Pension Schemes (Investment) Regulations 1996	S.I. 1996/3127	Regulation 12
The Personal and Occupational Pension Schemes (Miscellaneous Amendments) Regulations 1997	S.I. 1997/786	Paragraph 8 of Schedule 1 and the entry

		relating to SI 1996/1536 in Schedule 2
The Personal and Occupational Pension Schemes (Miscellaneous Amendments) (No. 2) Regulations 1997	S.I. 1997/3038	Regulation 4
The Personal and Occupational Pension Schemes (Miscellaneous Amendments) Regulations 1999	S.I. 1999/3198	Regulation 8
The Occupational Pension Schemes (Miscellaneous Amendments) Regulations 2000	SI 2000/679	Regulation 3
The Pension Sharing (Consequential and Miscellaneous Amendments) Regulations 2000	S.I. 2000/2691	Regulation 4
The Occupational Pension Schemes (Minimum Funding Requirement and Miscellaneous Amendments) Regulations 2002	S.I. 2002/380	Regulation 2
The Occupational Pension Schemes (Minimum Funding Requirement and Actuarial Valuations) Amendment Regulations 2004	S.I. 2004/3031	The whole Regulations
The Occupational Pension Schemes (Employer Debt) Regulations 2005	S.I. 2005/678	Paragraph 1 of Schedule 2
The Occupational Pension Schemes (Winding up etc.) Regulations 2005	S.I. 2005/706	Paragraph 9 of the Schedule
The Occupational Pension Schemes (Employer Debt etc.) (Amendment) Regulations 2005	SI 2005/2224	Regulation 6

Notes:

[1] 1993 c.49; paragraph 5(3C) of Schedule 1 was inserted by Article 138(2) of the Pensions (Northern Ireland) Order 1995 (S.I. 1995/3213 (N.I. 22)); paragraph 5(4A) of Schedule 1 was added by paragraph 77(5)(d) of Schedule 1 to the Social Security Contributions (Transfer of Functions, etc.) (Northern Ireland) Order 1999 (S.I.1999/671), and is cited for the definition of "regulations".

[2] See paragraph 5(4A) of Schedule 1 to the Pension Schemes (Northern Ireland) Act 1993.

[3] 1995 c.26; section 124(1) is cited for the definitions of "prescribed" and "regulations".

[4] 2004 c.35; section 318(1) is cited for the definitions of "modifications", "prescribed" and "regulations".

[5] Section 120(1) of the Pensions Act 1995 provides that the Secretary of State must consult such persons as he considers appropriate before making regulations by virtue of Part 1 of that Act. Section 317(1) of the Pensions Act 2004 makes similar provision with respect to regulations under that Act. The duty under the 2004 Act does not apply where regulations

are made within six months of the coming into force of the provisions under which they are made.

[6] 1993 c.48.

[7] The definition of "pension credit rights" was inserted into section 124(1) of the 1995 Act by paragraph 61(3) of Schedule 12 to the Welfare Reform and Pensions Act 1999 (c.30).

[8] Section 41 was amended by paragraph 12 of Schedule 5 to the Child Support, Pension and Social Security Act 2000 (c.19) and paragraph 52 of Schedule 12 to the Pensions Act 2004.

[9] Section 75 was amended by section 271 of the Pensions Act 2004.

[10] Section 74(3)(c) was amended by S.I. 2001/3649. [11] Section 49(9)(b) of the 1995 Act was inserted by section 10(1) of the Welfare Reform and Pensions Act 1999.

[12] Copies of GN49 may be obtained from the Institute of Actuaries, Staple Inn Hall, High Holborn, London WC1V 7QJ and from the Faculty of Actuaries, Maclaurin House, 18 Dublin Street, Edinburgh EH1 3PP.

[13] 1987 c.45.

[14] Section 23 was substituted by the Pensions Act 2004, section 36(3).

[15] 1975 c.26.

[16] 1988 c.1; the definition of "relevant benefits" was amended by paragraph 10(1) of Schedule 10 to the Finance Act 1999 (c.16). Section 612(1) is repealed by Part 3 of Schedule 42 to the Finance Act 2004 (c.12) with effect from 6th April 2006.

[17] 2003 c.1; section 393B is inserted by section 249(3) of the Finance Act 2004 with effect from 6th April 2006..

[18] Section 611A was inserted by paragraph 15 of Schedule 6 to the Finance Act 1989 (c.26) and amended by paragraph 5 of Schedule 5 to the Finance Act 1999. The section is repealed by Part 3 of Schedule 42 to the Finance Act 2004 with effect from 6th April 2006.

[19] Section 615(6) was amended by paragraph 11 of Schedule 10 to the Finance Act 1999.

[20] Section 590 is amended by paragraph 3 of Schedule 6 to the Finance Act 1989.

[21] 1994 c.39.

[22] S.I. 1997/1612.

[23] Section 74(3)(c) was amended by S.I. 2001/3649.

[24] S.I. 2005/255 (N.I. 1).

[25] 1988 c.1; section 611 is repealed by Part 3 of Schedule 42 to the Finance Act 2004 with effect from 6th April 2006.

[26] S.I. 2005/3331 (C.141).

[27] 1985 c.6; section 736 was substituted by section 144(1) of the Companies Act 1989 (c.40).

[28] S.I. 1996/1172; relevant amending instruments are S.I. 1997/786 and 2002/681.

[29] S.I. 1996/1655; relevant amending instruments are S.I. 1997/786 and 2002/459.

[30] S.I. 1996/1536. Regulation 30 was amended by S.I. 1997/786.

[31] Section 37 is substituted by section 250 of the Pensions Act 2004.

[32] S.I. 1996/1715; relevant amending instruments are S.I. 2000/679 and 2005/2426.

[33] Regulation 16A was inserted by S.I. 2000/679 and amended by S.I. 2005/2426.

[34] S.I. 1996/1847; relevant amending instruments are S.I. 1997/786, 2003/1727 and 2005/706.

[35] S.I. 1996/2475, to which there are amendments not relevant to these Regulations.

[36] S.I. 1996/3126, to which there are amendments not relevant to these Regulations.

[37] S.R. (NI) 1996 No. 493; to which there are amendments not relevant to these Regulations.

[38] For the purposes of these Regulations "2005 Order" refers to S.I. 2005/255 (N.I. 1).

[39] S.I. 2000/1052; relevant amending instruments are S.I. 2000/2691 and 2005/706.

40] S.I. 2000/1053, amended by S.I. 2005/706; there are other amending instruments but one is relevant.

41] S.I. 2000/1054, amended by S.I. 2005/706; there are other amending instruments but one is relevant.

42] S.I. 2000/1403, to which there are amendments not relevant to these Regulations.

43] S.I. 2000/3198, to which there are amendments not relevant to these Regulations.

44] S.I. 2005/2426.

45] S.I. 1996/1536; relevant amending instruments are S.I. 1997/786 and 1997/3038.

46] S.I. 1996/1172; relevant amending instruments are S.I. 1997/786 and 2002/681.

47] S.I. 2005/3331.

48] S.I. 1996/2475, to which there are amendments not relevant to these Regulations.

49] S.I. 1996/3126, to which there are amendments not relevant to these Regulations.

50] S.I. 1996/3128, amended by S.I. 1997/786 and 3038, 1999/3198, 2002/380, 2004/403, 2005/72 and 678.

51] S.I. 2005/678, amended by S.I. 2005/2224.

A2.7: Occupational Pension Schemes (Employer Debt) Regulations 2005 SI (2005/678)

Made 11th March 2005
Laid before Parliament 16th March 2005
Coming into force 6th April 2005

ARRANGEMENT OF REGULATIONS

The MFR Regulations
The Occupational Pension Schemes (Winding Up) Regulations 1996
The Occupational Pension Schemes (Investment) Regulations 1996

The Secretary of State for Work and Pensions, in exercise of the powers conferred upon him by sections 40(1) and (2), 49(2) and (3), 57(2) and (4), 60(2), 68(2)(e), 75(1)(b), (5), (6D)(b)(i) and (10), 75A(1) to (4), 89(2), 118(1), 119, 124(1), 125(3) and 174(2) and (3) of the Pensions Act 1995[1] and of all other powers enabling him in that behalf, by this instrument, which is consequential on section 271 of the Pensions Act 2004[2], and is made before the end of the

eriod of six months beginning with the coming into force of that section, hereby makes the
ollowing Regulations:

reliminary

itation, commencement, application and extent

- (1) These Regulations may be cited as the Occupational Pension Schemes (Employer
ebt) Regulations 2005.

!) These Regulations come into force on 6th April 2005.

3) These Regulations do not apply to -

(a) any scheme other than a money purchase scheme if a debt to the trustees or managers
of the scheme has been treated as arising under section 75(1) of the 1995 Act before that
date;

(b) any scheme which immediately before that date was regarded by virtue of regulation
2 of the Occupational Pension Schemes (Winding Up) Regulations 1996[3] as having
begun to be wound up before that date for the purposes of those Regulations; or

(c) any scheme which according to the rules in section 124(3A) to (3E) of the 1995 Act[4]
began to wind up before that date.

4) These Regulations extend to England and Wales and Scotland.

nterpretation

.. - (1) In these Regulations--

the 1993 Act" means the Pension Schemes Act 1993[5];

the 1995 Act" means the Pensions Act 1995;

the 2004 Act" means the Pensions Act 2004;

the 1996 Regulations" means the Occupational Pension Schemes (Deficiency on Winding
Jp etc.) Regulations 1996[6];

the actuary" means the actuary appointed for the scheme in pursuance of subsection (1)(b)
f section 47 of the 1995 Act or, in the case of a scheme to which that provision does not
apply by virtue of regulations made under subsection (5) of that section, an actuary
otherwise authorised by the trustees or managers to provide such valuations or
ertifications as may be required under these Regulations;

the applicable time" means the time as at which the value of the assets of a scheme and the
amount of its liabilities are to be determined, calculated and verified for the purposes of
section 75 of the 1995 Act;

employer" has the same meaning as in section 75 of the 1995 Act (but see paragraph (2) and
egulations 9 and 13);

employment-cessation event" has the meaning given in regulation 6(4);

the MFR Regulations" means the Occupational Pension Schemes (Minimum Funding
Requirement and Actuarial Valuations) Regulations 1996[7];

money purchase scheme" means an occupational pension scheme under which all the
benefits that may be provided other than death benefits are money purchase benefits;

multi-employer scheme" means a scheme in relation to which there is more than one
employer (including, except in regulation 8, any section of a scheme treated under that
egulation as a scheme if there is more than one employer in relation to that section);

the tax condition", in relation to a scheme, means-

(a) that the scheme has been approved by the Commissioners of the Board of Inland Revenue for the purposes of section 590 or 591 of the Taxes Act at any time before 6th April 2006; or

(b) that the scheme is registered under section 153 of the Finance Act 2004[8];

"the Taxes Act" means the Income and Corporation Taxes Act 1988[9].

(2) In these Regulations "scheme" must be read in appropriate cases in accordance with the modifications of section 75 of the 1995 Act made by regulation 8, 14 or 15, as the case may be; and "employer" and "member" must be read accordingly.

(3) References in these Regulations to the guidance in GN19 are to the guidelines on winding up and scheme asset deficiency (GN19), prepared and published by the Institute of Actuaries and the Faculty of Actuaries[10] and approved for the purposes of these Regulations by the Secretary of State, with such revisions as have been so approved at the applicable time.

(4) References in these Regulations to the guidance in GN 27 are to the guidelines on minimum funding requirement (GN 27), prepared and published by the Institute of Actuaries and the Faculty of Actuaries and approved for the purposes of the MFR Regulations by the Secretary of State, with such revisions as have been so approved at the applicable time.

(5) Subject to the previous provisions of this regulation, expressions used in these Regulations have the same meaning as in Part 1 of the 1995 Act (see section 124).

Disapplication of the 1996 Regulations

3. The 1996 Regulations do not apply in any case where these Regulations apply (and accordingly they only apply to a scheme as respects which regulation 1(3)(a), (b) or (c) applies).

Schemes to which section 75 of the 1995 Act does not apply

4. - (1) Section 75 of the 1995 Act does not apply to any scheme which is -

(a) a public service pension scheme under the provisions of which there is no requirement for assets related to the intended rate or amount of benefit under the scheme to be set aside in advance (disregarding requirements relating to additional voluntary contributions);

(b) a scheme which is made under section 7 of the Superannuation Act 1972[11] (superannuation of persons employed in local government etc.) and provides pensions to local government employees;

(c) a scheme which is made under section 2 of the Parliamentary and Other Pensions Act 1987[12] (power to provide for pensions for Members of the House of Commons etc.);

(d) a scheme in respect of which a relevant public authority, as defined in section 307(4) of the 2004 Act, has given a guarantee or made any other arrangements for the purposes of securing that the assets of the scheme are sufficient to meet its liabilities;

(e) a scheme which does not meet the tax condition;

(f) a scheme which -

(i) has been categorised by the Commissioners of the Board of Inland Revenue for the purposes of its approval as a centralised scheme for non-associated employers;

(ii) which is not contracted-out; and

(iii) under the provisions of which the only benefits that may be provided on or after retirement (other than money purchase benefits derived from the payment of voluntary contributions by any person) are lump sum benefits which are not calculated by reference to a member's salary;

(g) a scheme with such a superannuation fund as is mentioned in section 615(6) of the Taxes Act (fund established to provide superannuation benefits in respect of persons' employment in a trade or undertaking wholly outside the United Kingdom);

(h) a scheme with fewer than two members;

(i) a scheme with fewer than twelve members where all the members are trustees of the scheme and either -

(i) the rules of the scheme provide that all decisions are made only by the trustees who are members of the scheme by unanimous agreement; or

(ii) the scheme has a trustee who is independent in relation to the scheme for the purposes of section 23 of the 1995 Act[13] (power to appoint independent trustees) (see subsection (3) of that section) and is registered in the register maintained by the Authority in accordance with regulations made under subsection (4) of that section;

(j) a scheme with fewer than twelve members where all the members are directors of a company which is the sole trustee of the scheme and either –

(i) the rules of the scheme provide that all decisions are made only by the members of the scheme by unanimous agreement, or

(ii) one of the directors of the company is independent in relation to the scheme for the purposes of section 23 of the 1995 Act and is registered in the register maintained by the Authority in accordance with regulations made under subsection (4) of that section;

(k) the Chatsworth Settlement Estate Pension Scheme; or

(l) the scheme established by the Salvation Army Act 1963[14].

(2) Before 6th April 2006 paragraph (1)(e) applies with the addition at the end of the words "and is not a relevant statutory scheme providing relevant benefits"; and for the purposes of that paragraph "relevant statutory scheme" and "relevant benefits" have the same meaning as in Chapter 1 of Part 14 of the Taxes Act (see sections 611A and 612(1) of that Act).

Valuations
Calculation of the value of scheme liabilities and assets: defined benefit schemes
5. - (1) The liabilities and assets of a scheme which are to be taken into account for the purposes of section 75(2) and (4) of the 1995 Act and their amount or value must be determined, calculated and verified by the actuary as at the applicable time -

(a) in the case of liabilities in respect of pensions or other benefits, on the assumption that the liabilities will be discharged by the purchase of annuities of the kind described in section 74(3)(c) of the 1995 Act (discharge of liabilities: annuity purchase);

(b) subject to sub-paragraph (a), on the general assumptions specified in regulation 3(2)(a) to (c) and (3) of the MFR Regulations (determination, valuation and verification of assets and liabilities: general);

(c) subject to sub-paragraph (a) and paragraphs (2), (3), (5) and (6), in accordance with regulations 4 to 8 of the MFR Regulations (determination and valuation of assets and liabilities);

(d) subject to sub-paragraph (e), so far as the guidance given in GN 27 applies as respects regulations 3(2)(a) to (c) and (3) and 4 to 8 of the MFR Regulations or as respects sub-paragraph (a) and paragraphs (2) and (3) of this regulation, in accordance with that guidance; and

(e) in accordance with the guidance given in GN 19 so far as that guidance applies for the purposes of these Regulations.

(2) For the purposes of paragraph (1)(a) the actuary must estimate the cost of purchasing the annuities.

(3) The liabilities of a scheme which are to be taken into account under paragraph (1) include all expenses (except the cost of the annuities referred to in paragraph (1)(a)) which, in the opinion of the trustees or managers of the scheme, are likely to be incurred in connection with the winding up of the scheme.

(4) Where in these Regulations (or in the MFR Regulations as applied by this regulation) there is a reference to the value of any asset or the amount of any liability being calculated or verified in accordance with the opinion of the actuary or as he thinks appropriate, he must comply with any relevant provision in the guidance given in GN 27 or, as the case may be, GN 19 in making that calculation or verification.

(5) The value of the assets and the amount of the liabilities of a scheme which are to be taken into account for the purposes of section 75(2) and (4) of the 1995 Act must be certified by the actuary in the form set out in Schedule 1 to these Regulations, but if the scheme is being wound up on the date as at which the valuation is made, the actuary must modify the note at the end of the certificate by omitting the words from "if the scheme" onwards.

(6) For the purposes of this regulation -

(a) references in regulations 3(2), 4, 5, 7 and 8 of the MFR Regulations to the relevant date are to be taken as references to the applicable time;

(b) regulations 4(1), 7(1) and 8(2) of the MFR Regulations have effect with the substitution for the words "the minimum funding requirement is met" of the words "the value of the assets of the scheme is less than the amount of the liabilities of the scheme";

(c) regulation 6(1)(b) of the MFR Regulations has effect with the addition at the end of the words "(and any amount treated as a debt due to the trustees or managers of the scheme under section 75(2) or (4) by virtue of the valuation in question)".

(7) In its application for the purposes of this regulation in a case where the applicable time falls after the scheme has begun to be wound up, regulation 6(1) of the MFR Regulations[15] has effect with the addition after sub-paragraph (c) of the words -

" ; and for the purposes of sub-paragraph (a), regulation 5(1)(a) of the Occupational Pension Schemes (Investment) Regulations 1996 (exclusion of employer-related investments over 5 per cent. of current market value) shall be disregarded.".

(8) This regulation has effect subject to regulation 7 (multi-employer schemes: valuations for employment cessation events).

Multi-employer schemes
Multi-employer schemes: general
6. - (1) In its application to a multi-employer scheme, section 75 of the 1995 Act has effect in relation to each employer as if -

(a) the reference in section 75(2)(a) to a time which falls before any relevant event in relation to the employer which occurs while the scheme is being wound up were a reference to a time which falls before relevant events have occurred in relation to all the employers;

(b) the reference in section 75(2) to an amount equal to the difference being treated as a debt due from the employer were a reference to an amount equal to that employer's share of the difference being treated as a debt due from that employer;

(c) the references in section 75(3)(a)(i) and (b) to no relevant event of the kind there mentioned occurring in relation to the employer were references to no event of that kind occurring in relation to all the employers;

(d) the reference in section 75(4)(a) to a relevant event ("the current event") occurring in relation to the employer were a reference to a relevant event or an employment-cessation event occurring only in relation to that employer;

(e) the reference in section 75(4) to an amount equal to the difference being treated as a debt due from the employer were--

    (i) in a case where the difference is ascertained immediately before a relevant event occurs in relation to the employer, a reference to an amount equal to the employer's share of the difference being treated as a debt due from the employer; and

    (ii) in a case where the difference is ascertained immediately before an employment cessation event occurs in relation to the employer, a reference to an amount equal to the sum of the cessation expenses attributable to the employer and the employer's share of the difference being treated as a debt due from the employer; and

(f) section 75(4)(d) and (e) were omitted.

2) For the purposes of paragraph (1), an employer's share of the difference is -

(a) such proportion of the total difference as, in the opinion of the actuary after consultation with the trustees or managers, the amount of the scheme's liabilities attributable to employment with that employer bears to the total amount of the scheme's liabilities attributable to employment with the employers; or

(b) if the scheme provides for the total amount of that debt to be otherwise apportioned amongst the employers, the amount due from that employer under that provision.

3) For the purposes of paragraph (2) -

(a) the total amount of the scheme's liabilities which are attributable to employment with the employers; and

(b) the amount of the liabilities attributable to employment with any one employer,

are such amounts as are determined, calculated and verified by the actuary in accordance with the guidance given in GN 19; and a determination under this paragraph must be certified by the actuary as being in accordance with that guidance.

4) For the purposes of these Regulations an employment-cessation event occurs in relation to an employer if he ceases to be an employer employing persons in the description of employment to which the scheme relates at a time when at least one other person continues to employ such persons.

5) For the purposes of paragraph (1), the cessation expenses attributable to an employer are all expenses which, in the opinion of the trustees or managers of the scheme, are likely to be incurred in connection with the employment-cessation event occurring in relation to the employer.

Multi-employer schemes: valuations for employment cessation events

7. - (1) This regulation applies where -

(a) section 75 applies with the modifications referred to in regulation 6; and

(b) the amount of the liabilities of a scheme immediately before an employment cessation event is being determined in order to determine whether a debt is to be treated as due from the employer under section 75(4) of the 1995 Act.

(2) Regulation 5 applies -

(a) with the omission of paragraphs (1)(a) and (2) and the references to those provisions in paragraph (1)(b), (c) and (d) (by virtue of which liabilities for pensions and other benefits are to be valued on the assumption that they will be discharged by the purchase of annuities); and

(b) with the omission of paragraph (3).

Multi-employer schemes: sectionalised schemes

8. - (1) In its application to a multi-employer scheme--

(a) which is divided into two or more sections; and

(b) the provisions of which are such that the sections meet conditions A and B,

section 75 of the 1995 Act and the provisions of these Regulations (apart from this regulation) apply as if each section of the scheme were a separate scheme.

(2) Condition A is that contributions payable to the scheme by an employer, or by a member in employment under that employer, are allocated to that employer's section (or, if more than one section applies to that employer, to the section which is appropriate in respect of the employment in question).

(3) Condition B is that a specified part or proportion of the assets of the scheme is attributable to each section and cannot be used for the purposes of any other section.

(4) In their application to a scheme -

(a) which has been such a scheme as is mentioned in paragraph (1);

(b) which is divided into two or more sections, one or more of which apply only to members who are not in pensionable service under the section;

(c) the provisions of which have not been amended so as to prevent conditions A and B being met in relation to two or more sections; and

(d) in relation to one or more sections of which those conditions have ceased to be met at any time by reason only of there being no members in pensionable service under the section and no contributions which are to be allocated to it,

section 75 of the 1995 Act and the provisions of these Regulations (apart from this paragraph) apply as if any section in relation to which those conditions have ceased to be met were a separate scheme.

(5) For the purposes of paragraphs (1) to (4), any provisions of the scheme by virtue of which contributions or transfers of assets may be made to make provision for death benefits are disregarded.

(6) But if paragraph (1) or (4) applies and, by virtue of any provisions of the scheme, contributions or transfers of assets to make such provision are made to a section ("the death benefits section") the assets of which may only be applied for the provision of death benefits, the death benefits section is also to be treated as a separate scheme.

7) For the purpose of this regulation, any provisions of the scheme by virtue of which assets attributable to one section may on the winding up of the scheme or a section be used for the purposes of another section are disregarded.

Former employers
Former employers
9. - (1) In the application of section 75 of the 1995 Act and these Regulations to a scheme which has no active members, references to employers include every person who employed persons in the description of employment to which the scheme relates immediately before the occurrence of the event after which the scheme ceased to have any active members.

(2) In the application of section 75 of the 1995 Act and these Regulations to a scheme, references to employers include-

(a) any pre-April 1997 participator (see paragraph (7)); and

(b) any person who has ceased on or after 6th April 1997 and before the applicable time to be a person employing persons in the description of employment to which the scheme relates, unless -

(i) when he so ceased the scheme was not being wound up and continued to have active members; and

(ii) condition A, B, C or D is met.

(3) Condition A is that no debt was treated as becoming due from him under section 75(2) or (4) of the 1995 Act (or, if he so ceased before 6th April 2005, under section 75(1) of that Act) by virtue of his so ceasing.

(4) Condition B is that such a debt was treated as becoming due from him and has been paid before the applicable time.

(5) Condition C is that such a debt was treated as becoming due from him and has not been so paid solely because he was not notified of the debt, and of the amount of it, sufficiently in advance of the applicable time for it to be paid before that time.

(6) Condition D is that such a debt was treated as becoming due from him but at the applicable time it is excluded from the value of the assets of the scheme because it is unlikely to be recovered without disproportionate cost or within a reasonable time.

(7) In this regulation "pre-April 1997 participator" means a person who immediately before 6th April 2005 was regarded as an employer for the purposes of the 1996 Regulations by virtue of regulation 6 of those Regulations (ceasing to participate: transitional provision).

Money purchase schemes
Money purchase schemes: fraud and levy deficiencies etc.
10. - (1) Notwithstanding subsection (1)(a) of section 75 of the 1995 Act, that section applies to money purchase schemes as if -

(a) subsection (2) -

(i) provided that if the levy deficit condition is met the levy deficit is to be treated as a debt due from the employer to the trustees or managers of the scheme; and

(ii) was not subject to subsection (3) of that section;

(b) subsection (4) provided that where the criminal reduction conditions are met the criminal deficit is to be treated as a debt due from the employer to the trustees or managers of the scheme; and

(c) subsections (4A) to (4C) and (6) were omitted.

(2) The levy deficit condition is that an amount payable by way of general levy in respect of any money purchase scheme exceeds the value of the unallocated assets of the scheme either -

(a) at the time when the amount first becomes payable to the Secretary of State; or

(b) at a later time designated by the trustees or managers of the scheme for the purposes of this paragraph.

(3) The criminal reduction conditions are that -

(a) a reduction in the aggregate value of the allocated assets of the scheme occurs;

(b) the reduction is attributable to an act or omission which -

(i) constitutes an offence prescribed for the purposes of section 81(1)(c) of the 1995 Act; or

(ii) in the case of an act or omission which occurred outside England and Wales or Scotland, would constitute such an offence if it occurred in England and Wales or in Scotland; and

(c) immediately after the act or omission or, if that time cannot be determined, at the earliest time when the auditor of the scheme knows that the reduction has occurred, the amount of that reduction exceeds the value of the unallocated assets of the scheme.

(4) In this section -

"allocated assets", in relation to a scheme, means assets which have been specifically allocated for the provision of benefits to or in respect of members (whether generally or individually) or for the payment of the scheme's expenses (and "unallocated" is to be read accordingly);

"the criminal deficit" means the amount of the excess mentioned in paragraph (3)(c);

"the levy deficit" means the amount of the excess mentioned in paragraph (2);

"the general levy" means the levy imposed under section 175 of the 1993 Act by regulation 3(1) or (2) of the Occupational and Personal Pension Schemes (General Levy) Regulations 2005[16].

Money purchase schemes: valuations etc.

11. - (1) For the purposes of section 75 of the 1995 Act as applied by regulation 10, this regulation applies instead of regulation 5 and 7.

(2) In the case of a scheme other than an ear-marked scheme -

(a) the value at any time of the unallocated assets of the scheme is to be taken to be the value of those assets as certified in a statement by the scheme's auditor; and

(b) the amount of the criminal reduction in the aggregate value of the allocated assets of the scheme at any time is to be calculated by subtracting the actual aggregate value of those assets at that time from the notional aggregate value of those assets.

(3) The notional aggregate value mentioned in paragraph (2)(b) is to be taken to be the sum of the values of the assets -

(a) as stated in the audited accounts which most immediately precede the relevant act or omission; or

(b) if there are none, as certified in a statement by the scheme's auditor,

adjusted appropriately to take account of any alteration in their values (other than any alteration attributable to that act or omission) between the date as at which those accounts are prepared or, as the case may be, as at which that statement is given and the time in question.

(4) The actual aggregate value mentioned in paragraph (2)(b) is to be calculated in the same manner as it was calculated for the purposes of the accounts mentioned in paragraph (3)(a) or, as the case may be, the statement mentioned in paragraph (3)(b).

(5) In the case of an ear-marked scheme -
(a) the value at any time of the unallocated assets of the scheme; and
(b) the amount of the criminal reduction in the aggregate value of the allocated assets of the scheme,
are the amounts certified in a statement by the relevant insurer.

(6) In this regulation -

"ear-marked scheme" means a scheme under which all the benefits are secured by one or more policies of insurance or annuity contracts, being policies or contracts specifically allocated to the provision of benefits for individual members or any other person who has a right to benefits under the scheme; and

"the relevant insurer", in relation to such a scheme, is the insurer with whom the insurance contract or annuity contract is made.

Multi-employer money purchase schemes

12. - (1) In its application to a money purchase scheme that is a multi-employer scheme regulation 10 applies with the substitution for paragraph (1) of the following paragraphs -
"(1) Notwithstanding subsection (1)(a) of section 75 of the 1995 Act, that section applies to money purchase schemes as if -
(a) subsection (2) -
(i) provided that if the levy deficit condition is met each employer's share of the levy deficit is to be treated as a debt due from that employer to the trustees or managers of the scheme; and
(ii) was not subject to subsection (3) of that section;
(b) subsection (4) provided that where the criminal reduction conditions are met each employer's share of the criminal deficit is to be treated as a debt due from the employer to the trustees or managers of the scheme; and
(c) subsections (4A) to (4C) and (6) were omitted.

(1A) For the purposes of paragraph (1), an employer's share of the levy deficit or the criminal deficit is -
(a) such proportion of that total deficit as, in the opinion of the actuary, the amount of the scheme's liabilities attributable to employment with that employer bears to the total amount of the scheme's liabilities attributable to employment with the employers; or
(b) if the scheme provides for the total amount of that debt to be otherwise apportioned amongst the employers, the amount due from that employer under that provision.

(1B) For the purposes of paragraph (1A) -
(a) the total amount of the scheme's liabilities which are attributable to employment with the employers; and
(b) the amount of the liabilities attributable to employment with any one employer,

are such amounts as are determined, calculated and verified by the actuary in accordance with the guidance given in GN 19; and a determination under this paragraph must be certified by the actuary as being in accordance with that guidance.".

(2) Regulation 6 does not apply to a money purchase scheme that is a multi-employer scheme.

Former employers of money purchase schemes

13. Regulation 9 does not apply to a money purchase scheme, but in the application of section 75 of the 1995 Act and these Regulations to such a scheme which has no active members references to employers include every person who employed persons in the description of employment to which the scheme relates immediately before the occurrence of the event after which the scheme ceased to have any active members.

Other schemes treated as more than one scheme

Schemes covering United Kingdom and foreign employment

14. - (1) Paragraph (2) applies where a scheme which applies to members in employment in the United Kingdom and members in employment outside the United Kingdom is divided into two or more sections and the provisions of the scheme are such that--

(a) different sections of the scheme apply to members in employment in the United Kingdom and to members in employment outside the United Kingdom ("the United Kingdom section" and "the foreign section");

(b) contributions payable to the scheme in respect of a member are allocated to the section applying to that member's employment;

(c) a specified part or proportion of the assets of the scheme is attributable to each section and cannot be used for the purposes of any other section; and

(d) the United Kingdom section meets the tax condition and the foreign section does not do so.

(2) If this paragraph applies -

(a) section 75 of the 1995 Act and these Regulations (apart from this regulation) apply as if each section of the scheme were a separate scheme; and

(b) the reference to the scheme in the form set out in Schedule 1 may be modified appropriately.

(3) Paragraph (4) applies where -

(a) a scheme applies to members in employment in the United Kingdom and members in employment outside the United Kingdom;

(b) paragraph (2) does not apply to the scheme; and

(c) part of the scheme meets paragraph (b) of the tax condition by virtue of that part having been treated as a separate scheme under section 611(3) of the Taxes Act that is treated as becoming a registered pension scheme under paragraph 1(1) of Schedule 36 to the Finance Act 2004 by virtue of paragraph 1(2) of that Schedule.

(4) If this paragraph applies -

(a) section 75 of the 1995 Act and these Regulations (apart from this regulation) apply as if the approved and unapproved parts of the scheme were separate schemes; and

(b) the reference to the scheme in the form set out in Schedule 1 may be modified appropriately.

5) Paragraph (6) applies where -

(a) a scheme has been such a scheme as is mentioned in paragraph (1) or (3),

(b) the scheme is divided into two or more sections, some or all of which apply only to members who are not in pensionable service under the section;

(c) the provisions of the scheme have not been amended so as to prevent the conditions in paragraph (1) or, as the case may be, paragraph (3) being met in relation to two or more sections; and

(d) in relation to one or more sections of the scheme those conditions have ceased to be met at any time by reason only of there being no members in pensionable service under the section and, in the case of paragraph (1), no contributions which are to be allocated to it.

6) If this paragraph applies -

(a) section 75 of the 1995 Act and these Regulations (apart from this regulation) apply as if any section in relation to which those conditions have ceased to be met were a separate scheme; and

(b) the reference to the scheme in the form set out in Schedule 1 may be modified appropriately.

7) Before 6th April 2006 paragraph (3) applies with the substitution for sub-paragraph (c) of the following paragraph -

"(c) part of the scheme meets paragraph (a) of the tax condition by virtue of section 611(3) of the Taxes Act."

Schemes with partial government guarantee

15. - (1) This regulation applies if a relevant public authority has -

(a) given a guarantee in relation to any part of a scheme, any benefits payable under the scheme or any member of the scheme; or

(b) made any other arrangements for the purposes of securing that the assets of the scheme are sufficient to meet any part of its liabilities.

(2) Where this regulation applies -

(a) section 75 of the 1995 Act and these Regulations (apart from this regulation) apply as if the guaranteed part of the scheme and the other part of the scheme were separate schemes; and

(b) the reference to the scheme in the form set out in Schedule 1 may be modified appropriately.

(3) In this regulation -

"the guaranteed part of the scheme" means the part of the scheme -

(a) in relation to which the guarantee has been given;

(b) which relates to benefits payable under the scheme in relation to which the guarantee has been given; or

(c) which relates to benefits payable under the scheme in relation to the liabilities for which those other arrangements have been made; and

"relevant public authority" has the meaning given in section 307(4) of the 2004 Act.

Supplementary
Modification of schemes: apportionment of section 75 debts
16. - (1) This regulation applies for the purposes of section 68(2)(e) of the 1995 (power of trustees to modify schemes by resolution for prescribed purposes).

(2) In the case of a trust scheme (whether or not a money purchase scheme) which apart from this regulation could not be modified for the purpose of making provision for the total amount of a debt due under section 75(2) or (4) of the 1995 Act to be apportioned amongst the employers in different proportions from those which would otherwise apply by virtue of regulation 6(2)(a) or, as the case may be, regulation 10(1A) (as it has effect by virtue of regulation 12), for the purposes of section 68(2)(e), such a modification of the scheme is a modification for a prescribed purpose.

Disregard of staying of voluntary winding up of employer for purposes of section 75 of the 1995 Act
17. - (1) This regulation applies for the purposes of section 75(6D)(i) of the 1995 Act (by virtue of which where a members' voluntary winding up of an employer is stayed section 75 of the 1995 Act has effect as if the resolution for the winding up had never been passed and any debt which arose under that section by virtue of the passing of the resolution had never arisen, except where the winding up is stayed in prescribed circumstances).

(2) The circumstances that are prescribed are where the stay is granted for a limited period.

Consequential amendments
18. The Regulations specified in Schedule 2 are amended as specified in that Schedule.

Signed by authority of the Secretary of State for Work and Pensions.

Malcolm Wicks

Minister of State, Department for Work and Pensions

11th March 2005

SCHEDULE 1
Regulation 5
Form of Actuary's Certificate
Actuarial Certificate Given for the Purposes of Regulation 5 of the Occupational Pension Schemes (Employer Debt) Regulations 2005

Name of scheme

Date as at which valuation is made

1 Comparison of value of scheme assets with amount of scheme liabilities

In my opinion, at the above date the value of the assets of the scheme was less than the amount of the liabilities of the scheme.

The value of the assets of the scheme was

The amount of the liabilities was

The amount of the difference was

Valuation principles

The scheme's assets and liabilities are valued in accordance with section 75(5) of the Pensions Act 1995, the Occupational Pension Schemes (Employer Debt) Regulations 2005 and the guidelines on winding up and scheme asset deficiency (GN19) and on minimum funding requirement (GN27) prepared and published by the Institute of Actuaries and the Faculty of Actuaries (so far as those guidelines are applicable).

Signature   Date

Name   Qualification

Address   Name of employer (if applicable)

Note:

The valuation of the amount of the liabilities of the scheme may not reflect the actual cost of securing those liabilities by the purchase of annuities if the scheme were to have been wound up on the date as at which the valuation is made.

SCHEDULE 2
Regulation 18
Consequential Amendments
The MFR Regulations
1. - (1) The MFR Regulations are amended as follows.

(2) In regulation 2(2)-
(a) for "relevant insolvency event" substitute "relevant event"; and
(b) for "same meaning as in section 75" substitute "meaning given in section 75(6A)".

(3) In regulation 13 (duty to obtain minimum funding valuations: section 75 debts in multi-employer schemes) -
(a) in paragraph (1) for "section 75(1)" substitute "section 75(2) or (4)"; and
(b) in paragraph (3) for "has the same meaning as in section 75(3)" substitute "means the time as at which the value of the assets of a scheme and the amount of its liabilities are to be determined, calculated and verified for the purposes of section 75".

(4) In regulation 19 (records) in paragraph (3)(c) for "section 75(1)" substitute "section 75(2) or (4)".

(5) In Schedule 4 (methods of securing shortfall in cases of serious underprovision) –
(a) in paragraph 1(1) for the definition of "section 75(1) shortfall" substitute -
" "section 75 shortfall", in relation to a scheme, means so much of the amount treated by section 75(2) or (4) as a debt due from the employer to the trustees or managers at the applicable time (as defined in regulation 2(1) of the Occupational Pension Schemes (Employer Debt) Regulations 2005), as is attributable to the value of the scheme assets falling short of the amount of the scheme liabilities by more than 10 per cent;"
(b) for "section 75(1) shortfall", wherever else it occurs, substitute "section 75 shortfall";
(c) in paragraphs 1(2), 2(2)(a), 3(3)(a), 4(2)(b) and (4) for "relevant insolvency event" substitute "relevant event".

The Occupational Pension Schemes (Winding Up) Regulations 1996
2. In regulation 10(2) of the Occupational Pension Schemes Winding Up Regulations 1996 for "relevant insolvency event" and "subsection (4) of section 75 (definition of relevant insolvency events)" substitute "relevant event" and "subsection (6A) of section 75 (definition of relevant events)" respectively.

The Occupational Pension Schemes (Investment) Regulations 1996
3. In regulation 6 of the Occupational Pension Schemes (Investment) Regulations 1996[17] (investments to which restrictions do not apply) in paragraph (7)(c) for "section 75(1)" substitute "section 75(2) or (4)".

Notes
[1] 1995 c. 26. Section 75 is amended by s.271 of the Pensions Act 2004 (c. 35). Section 75A is inserted by s.272 of the Pensions Act 2004. Section 89(2) is amended by paragraph 66 of Schedule 12 to the Pensions Act 2004. Section 124(1) is cited for the meaning it gives to "prescribed" and "regulations".
[2] 2004 c. 35. *See* section 120 of the Pensions Act 1995 which provides that the Secretary of State must consult such persons as he may consider appropriate before making regulations for the purposes of the provisions for the purposes of which these Regulations are made. This duty does not apply where regulations are made before the end of the period of six months beginning with the coming into force of any enactment on which the regulations are consequential.
[3] S.I. 1996/3126.
[4] Subsections (3) to (3E) were inserted in section 124 by section 49(2) of the Child Support, Pensions and Social Security Act 2000 (c. 19).
[5] 1993 c. 48.
[6] S.I. 1996/3128.
[7] S.I. 1996/1536.
[8] 2004 c. 12.
[9] 1988 c. 1.
[10] The publications GN19 and GN27 may be obtained from the Institute of Actuaries, Staple Inn Hall, High Holborn, London WC1V 7QJ and from the Faculty of Actuaries, Maclaurin House, 18 Dublin Street, Edinburgh EH1 3PP.
[11] 1972 c. 11.
[12] 1987 c. 45.
[13] Section 23 is substituted by section 36(3) of the Pensions Act 2004.
[14] 1963 c.xxxii.
[15] Regulation 6(1)(c) is substituted by regulation 8(2) of S.I. 1997/786.
[16] S.I. 2005/626.
[17] S.I. 1996/3127.

2.8: Occupational Pension Schemes (Employer Debt etc) (Amendment) Regulations 2005 (SI 2005/2224)

Made	9th August 2005
Laid before Parliament	12th August 2005
Coming into force	2nd September 2005

ARRANGEMENT OF REGULATIONS

The Secretary of State for Work and Pensions, in exercise of the powers conferred upon him by sections 10(3), 56(3), 75(1)(b), (5) and (10), 75A(1) to (7), 89(2), 118(1)(a) and (b), 119, 124(1), 125(3) and 174(2) and (3) of the Pensions Act 1995[1] and sections 93(2)(q), 135(4), 315(2) and 318(1) and (4)(a) of, and paragraph 21(e) of Schedule 1 to, the Pensions Act 2004[2] and of all other powers enabling him in that behalf, by this instrument, which is consequential on sections 271 and 272 of the Pensions Act 2004[3], and is made before the end of the period of six months beginning with the coming into force of those sections, hereby makes the following Regulations:

Citation, commencement and interpretation

1. —(1) These Regulations may be cited as the Occupational Pension Schemes (Employer Debt etc.) (Amendment) Regulations 2005.

(2) These Regulations come into force on 2nd September 2005.

(3) Regulation 2(1), (2)(c), (3) and (5) does not apply if the employment-cessation event occurs before that date.

(4) Regulation 4(2) does not apply if the applicable time is before that date.

(5) In these Regulations—

"the 2004 Act" means the Pensions Act 2004;

"the 2005 Regulations" means the Occupational Pension Schemes (Employer Debt) Regulations 2005[4];

"the applicable time" has the meaning given in regulation 2(1) of the 2005 Regulations (interpretation);

"employment-cessation event" has the meaning given in regulation 6(4) of the 2005 Regulations (multi-employer schemes: general).

Multi-employer schemes: employment-cessation events and withdrawal arrangements e
2. —(1) At the end of regulation 2(1) of the 2005 Regulations (interpretation) add—

" "withdrawal arrangement" and "approved withdrawal arrangement" are to be read i accordance with paragraph 1(1) of Schedule 1A to these Regulations.".

(2) In regulation 5 of the 2005 Regulations (calculation of the value of scheme liabilities an assets: defined benefit schemes)—

(a) in paragraph (1)(c) after "paragraphs (2), (3)," insert "(3A),";

(b) after paragraph (3) insert—

" (3A) If the modification specified in regulation 7(3) has applied in the case of a employment-cessation event that occurred in relation to an employer before the applicabl time—

(a) the liabilities of the scheme that are attributable to employment with that employe and

(b) the debts treated as due under section 75(4) of the 1995 Act in accordance with tha modification,

are not to be taken into account under paragraph (1).";

(c) in paragraph (8) for "valuations for employment cessation events" substitut "employment-cessation events and withdrawal arrangements".

(3) For regulation 7 of the 2005 Regulations (multi-employer schemes: valuations fo employment cessation events) substitute—

"Multi-employer schemes: employment-cessation events and withdrawal arrangement
7. —(1) This regulation applies where—

(a) section 75 of the 1995 Act applies to a trust scheme with the modifications referred t in regulation 6 (multi-employer schemes: general); and

(b) as a result of the occurrence of an employment-cessation event in relation to a employer, a debt ("the cessation debt") calculated on the basis of assets and liabilitie valued in accordance with regulation 5 is treated as due from the employer ("the cessation employer") under section 75(4) of that Act.

(2) If the cessation employer notifies the Authority in writing that he proposes to enter into a withdrawal arrangement—

(a) the Authority may issue a direction that the cessation debt is to be unenforceable fo such period as the Authority may specify in the direction, and where such a direction has been issued the debt is unenforceable for that period; and

(b) the Authority may issue a direction that if an approved withdrawal arrangement ha come into force within that period, section 75 of the 1995 Act is to apply in the case of the employment-cessation event with the modification specified in paragraph (3) instead o the modification referred to in regulation 6(1)(e)(ii), and where such a direction has been issued and such an arrangement has so come into force, that modification so applies.

(3) The modification is that section 75 of the 1995 Act has effect as if the reference in section 75(4) to an amount equal to the difference being treated as a debt due from the employer were a reference to—

(a) amount A being treated as a debt due from the employer; and

(b) unless and until the Authority issue a direction that it is not to be so treated, amount B being treated as a debt due from the guarantors at the guarantee time for which (if there is more than one guarantor) they are jointly or, if the approved withdrawal arrangement so provides, jointly and severally liable,

here amount A is calculated in accordance with regulation 7A and amount B is calculated accordance with regulation 7B.

) In this regulation—

he guarantee time" means the earliest time when an event specified in paragraph 1(3) of chedule 1A to these Regulations occurs; and

he guarantors" means such one or more of the parties to the approved withdrawal rrangement as are specified in the arrangement as the persons who are the guarantors for e purposes of this regulation.

) The Authority may issue a direction extending the period mentioned in paragraph (2)(a) y such further period as they may specify (so that the debt is unenforceable for the xtended period).

) The Authority may only issue a direction under paragraph (3)(b)—
(a) before the guarantee time, and
(b) if the Authority consider that the approved withdrawal arrangement is no longer required.

) Schedule 1A to these Regulations applies for the purpose of making further provision in ases where this regulation applies; and in that Schedule and regulations 7A and 7B "the essation employer" has the same meaning as in this regulation.

alculation of amounts due from cessation employer by virtue of regulation 7

A. —(1) For the purposes of regulation 7(3), amount A depends on whether or not a debt (a scheme funding basis debt") would have been treated as due from the cessation employer nder section 75(4) of the 1995 Act if—
(a) regulation 5 had applied with the modifications specified in paragraph (4); and
(b) section 75(4) had applied in accordance with regulation 6(1)(d) and (e) but subject to the modifications of regulation 6 specified in paragraph (5) (instead of in accordance with the modification specified in regulation 7(3)).
(2) If a debt would have been so treated, amount A is the sum of the scheme funding basis debt and the cessation expenses attributable to the employer.

) If a debt would not have been so treated, amount A is equal to the amount of the essation expenses attributable to the employer.

) The modifications of regulation 5 are that—
(a) paragraphs (1)(a) and (2) and the references to those provisions in paragraph (1)(b), (c) and (d) (by virtue of which liabilities for pensions and other benefits are to be valued on the assumption that they will be discharged by the purchase of annuities) are omitted;
(b) paragraph (3) and the references to that paragraph in paragraph (1)(c) and (d) (by virtue of which winding up expenses are to be taken into account) are omitted; and
(c) in paragraph (5) for the words "for the purposes of section 75(2) and (4) of the 1995 Act" there are substituted the words "for the purposes of section 75(2) of the 1995 Act and for the purposes of section 75(4) of the 1995 Act where no approved withdrawal arrangement has been entered into by the employer".

) The modifications of regulation 6 are that—

(a) for paragraph (ii) of paragraph (1)(e) there is substituted —

"(ii) in a case where the difference is ascertained immediately before an employmen cessation event occurs in relation to the employer, a reference to an amount equal to th employer's share of the difference, less the relevant transferred liabilities deductior being treated as a debt due from the employer;";

(b) after paragraph (5) there is added —

"(6) In this regulation "the relevant transferred liabilities deduction" means the amount c any relevant transferred liabilities, less the value of the corresponding assets.

(7) For the purposes of paragraph (6) —

(a) "corresponding assets", in relation to relevant transferred liabilities, means the asset transferred from the scheme in connection with the transfer from the scheme of thos liabilities; and

(b) the value of the corresponding assets is to be determined —

(i) in the case of corresponding assets that are assets of the scheme at the applicabl time, as at that time; and

(ii) in the case of corresponding assets that are not assets of the scheme at that time as at the date of the transfer of the assets.

(8) For the purposes of paragraph (6) —

(a) "relevant transferred liabilities" means liabilities in respect of members —

(i) which are transferred from the scheme in circumstances where the conditions se out in paragraphs (2)(a) or (b) and (3)[a] of regulation 12 of the Occupational Pensior Schemes (Preservation of Benefit) Regulations 1991[5] (transfer without consent) ar met;

(ii) which are so transferred during the period beginning with the applicable tim and ending with the date on which the approved withdrawal arrangement i approved ("the relevant period");

(iii) the transfer of which reduces the amount of the scheme's liabilities attributable t employment with the employer in relation to whom the employment-cessation even has occurred; and

(iv) in connection with the transfer of which there is a transfer of correspondin assets during the relevant period; and

(b) the amount of the relevant transferred liabilities is to be calculated in accordance with regulation 5 as modified by regulation 7A(4).".

(6) The value of the assets and the amount of the liabilities of a scheme which are to be taker into account for the purposes of determining whether a scheme funding basis debt woulc have been treated as due as mentioned in paragraph (1) must be certified by the actuary ir the form set out in Schedule 1B to these Regulations, but —

(a) if the actuary is of the opinion that the value of the assets of the scheme was not less than the amount of the liabilities of the scheme —

(i) substituting in the first sentence of the comparison of value of scheme assets witl amount of scheme liabilities for the words "was less" the words "was not less"; and

(ii) omitting the last sentence of that comparison; and

(b) if the scheme is being wound up on the date as at which the valuation is made omitting from the Note the words from "if the scheme" onwards.

7) In this regulation "the cessation expenses attributable to the employer" has the meaning given by regulation 6(5).

Calculation of amounts due from guarantors by virtue of regulation 7

8. —(1) For the purposes of regulation 7(3), amount B depends on whether the approved withdrawal arrangement provides for amount B to be the amount provided for under paragraph (2).

2) If the approved withdrawal arrangement so provides, amount B is equal to the amount (if any) that would be the amount of the debt due from the cessation employer under section 75(4) of the 1995 Act if—

(a) the employment-cessation event had occurred at the guarantee time;

(b) the cessation employer had not entered into an approved withdrawal arrangement; and

(c) there were no cessation expenses attributable to the employer.

3) If the approved withdrawal arrangement does not provide for amount B to be the amount provided for under paragraph (2), amount B is equal to the amount that would be the amount treated as due from the cessation employer under section 75(4) of the 1995 Act if the cessation employer had not entered into an approved withdrawal arrangement, less the sum of—

(a) the amount that is amount A for the purposes of regulation 7(3);

(b) if the amount that the approved withdrawal arrangement provides for the cessation employer to pay exceeds that amount, an amount equal to the excess; and

(c) the relevant transferred liabilities deduction.

4) The value of the assets and the amount of the liabilities of a scheme which are to be taken into account for the purposes of determining the amount (if any) that would be the amount of the debt due from the cessation employer under section 75(4) of the 1995 Act in the case mentioned in paragraph (2) must be certified by the actuary in the form set out in Schedule 1 to these Regulations, but—

(a) substituting for the reference to regulation 5 a reference to paragraph (2) of this regulation;

(b) if the actuary is of the opinion that the value of the assets of the scheme was not less than the amount of the liabilities of the scheme—

(i) substituting in the first sentence of the comparison of value of scheme assets with amount of scheme liabilities for the words "was less" the words "was not less"; and

(ii) omitting the last sentence of that comparison; and

(c) if the scheme is being wound up on the date as at which the valuation is made, omitting from the Note the words from "if the scheme" onwards.

5) In this regulation—

"the cessation expenses attributable to the employer" has the meaning given by regulation 6(5); and

"the relevant transferred liabilities deduction" has the meaning given by regulation 6(6), as inserted by the modification of regulation 6 made by regulation 7A(5)(b), except that for the purposes of this regulation the amount of the relevant transferred liabilities is to be calculated in accordance with regulation 5 without the modifications made by regulatio 7A(4).".

(4) In regulation 9 of the 2005 Regulations (former employers)—

(a) in paragraph (2)(b)(ii) for "condition A, B" substitute "condition A, B, BB";

(b) after paragraph (4) insert—

" (4A) Condition BB is that such a debt was treated as becoming due from him, th modification in regulation 7(3) applied, and the amount treated as becoming due fron him under regulation 7(3)(a) has been paid before the applicable time.".

(5) The Schedules set out in the Schedule to these Regulations are inserted after Schedule to the 2005 Regulations.

The Pensions Regulator's functions under the 2005 Regulations

3. —(1) The following functions under the 2005 Regulations are regulatory functions for th purposes of Part 1 of the 2004 Act—

(a) the power to issue directions under regulation 7;

(b) the power to issue a notice under paragraph 1(3)(c) of Schedule 1A; and

(c) the power to issue a notice under paragraph 2 of Schedule 1A.

(2) The Pensions Regulator may, if it thinks fit, delegate the functions specified in paragrapl (1) to the Determinations Panel established under section 9 of the 2004 Act (th Determinations Panel).

Minor amendments of the 2005 Regulations

4. —(1) In regulation 4(1) of the 2005 Regulations (schemes to which section 75 of the 199! Act does not apply) omit sub-paragraph (l) (the scheme established by the Salvation Army Act 1963[6]).

(2) In regulation 10 of the 2005 Regulations (money purchase schemes: fraud and levy deficiencies etc.), as it applies by virtue of regulation 12 of those Regulations (multi employer money purchase schemes), in paragraph (1A)(a) (under which, unless the scheme makes contrary provision, an employer's share of the levy deficit or the criminal deficit is such proportion of the total deficit as, in the opinion of the actuary, the amount of the scheme's liabilities attributable to employment with that employer bears to the total amoun of the scheme's liabilities attributable to employment with the employers) for "the actuary substitute "the trustees or managers".

(3) In paragraph 2 of Schedule 2 to the 2005 Regulations (consequential amendment of the Occupational Pension Schemes (Winding Up) Regulations 1996[7]) for "the Occupationa Pension Schemes Winding Up Regulations 1996" substitute "the Occupational Pensior Schemes (Winding Up) Regulations 1996".

Consequential amendments of the Pensions Regulator (Financial Support Directions etc. Regulations 2005

5. In regulation 15(2) of the Pensions Regulator (Financial Support Directions etc. Regulations 2005[8] (former employers)—

(a) for "condition A, B" substitute "condition A, AA, B"; and

(b) after sub-paragraph (a) insert—

" (aa) condition AA is that—

(i) such a debt became due;

(ii) the modification in regulation 7(3) of the Occupational Pension Schemes (Employer Debt) Regulations 2005 (multi-employer schemes: employment-cessation events and withdrawal arrangements) applied, and

(iii) the amount treated as becoming due from him under regulation 7(3)(a) of those Regulations has been paid;".

Amendment of the Occupational Pension Schemes (Minimum Funding Requirement and Actuarial Valuations) Regulations 1996

. In regulation 6(1)(b) of the Occupational Pension Schemes (Minimum Funding Requirement and Actuarial Valuations) Regulations 1996[9] (excluded assets) for "60(5) or 5(1)" substitute "or 60(5) or under section 75(1), as it has effect before 6th April 2005, or under section 75(2) or (4), as it has effect on or after that date".

Amendment of the Pension Protection Fund (Entry Rules) Regulations 2005

. In regulation 16(1)(a)(ii) of the Pension Protection Fund (Entry Rules) Regulations 2005[10] restrictions on winding up, discharge of liabilities etc.) for "section 94(1)(a)" substitute section 94(1)(aa)"[11].

David Blunkett
Secretary of State for Work and Pensions
th August 2005

SCHEDULE

Regulation 2(5)
Schedules inserted in the 2005 Regulations

SCHEDULE 1A
Multi-employer schemes: employer-cessation events and approved withdrawal arrangements

Withdrawal arrangements
. —(1) For the purposes of these Regulations—
a) a withdrawal arrangement is an arrangement that meets the conditions specified in sub-paragraph (2), and
b) a withdrawal arrangement is approved if the details—
i) of the arrangement, and
ii) if the arrangement is amended, of any amendments of the arrangement,
are approved by the Authority.

2) The conditions are that—
(a) the arrangement consists of an agreement to which the trustees of the scheme and the cessation employer are parties;
(b) the agreement is enforceable under the law of England and Wales, and the parties to the agreement have agreed that—
(i) that law applies to the agreement; and
(ii) they are subject to the jurisdiction of the court in England and Wales as respects the agreement;
(c) the agreement provides that at or before a time specified in the agreement the cessation employer will pay an amount equal to or greater than the amount that is amount A for the purposes of regulation 7(3)(a);

(d) the agreement—

(i) provides that if an event specified in sub-paragraph (3) occurs whilst th
agreement is in force the parties to the agreement who are specified in the agreemen
as the persons who are the guarantors for the purposes of regulation 7 (th
"guarantors") (who may be or include the cessation employer) will pay an amoun
equal to the amount that is amount B for the purposes of regulation 7(3)(b) (bu
without prejudice to their powers to make a payment on account of that amount a
any earlier time);

(ii) if there are two or more guarantors, provides whether or not the guarantors are t
be jointly and severally liable for that amount for those purposes; and

(iii) provides whether or not that amount is to be the amount provided for unde
regulation 7B(2);

(e) the agreement provides that an amount payable under paragraph (c) or (d) i
payable—

(i) to the trustees of the scheme; or

(ii) if the Board of the Pension Protection Fund has assumed responsibility for th
scheme in accordance with Chapter 3 of Part 2 of the 2004 Act (pension protection'
to the Board on behalf of the trustees of the scheme;

(f) the agreement provides that one or more of the parties to the agreement other tha
the trustees of the scheme are to bear any expenses incurred by the parties in connectio
with—

(i) the making of the agreement; or

(ii) the making of any calculations by the actuary for the purposes of the agreement;

(g) the agreement will continue in force until—

(i) the winding up of the scheme is completed;

(ii) the Authority issue a notice to the parties to the agreement stating that th
Authority consider that the agreement is no longer required; or

(iii) the agreement is replaced by another agreement that is approved by th
Authority as an approved withdrawal arrangement,

whichever occurs first.

(3) The events are that—

(a) the scheme begins to be wound up;

(b) an event occurs as a result of which there is no person who is an employer in relatio
to the scheme for the purposes of these Regulations in relation to whom a relevant even
has not occurred for the purposes of section 75 of the 1995 Act (see section 75(6A) of tha
Act[12]);

(c) the Authority issue a notice to the parties to the agreement stating that they conside
that the amount referred to in sub-paragraph (2)(d)(i) should be paid.

(4) The Authority may not issue such a notice at any time unless the Authority consider tha
it is reasonable for the guarantors to be required to pay that amount at that time.

(5) In forming an opinion for the purposes of sub-paragraph (4), the Authority must hav
regard to such matters as the Authority consider relevant including—

(a) whether the guarantors have taken reasonable steps to comply with the approve
withdrawal arrangement;

(b) whether the guarantors have complied with their obligations under paragraph 5; and

(c) the guarantors' financial circumstances.

Approval of withdrawal arrangements

2. —(1) Approval by the Authority of an agreement as a withdrawal arrangement is to be given in a notice issued by the Authority.

(2) Such an approval may be given subject to such conditions as the Authority consider appropriate.

(3) The Authority may not approve an agreement as a withdrawal arrangement unless they are satisfied that—

(a) the agreement meets the conditions in paragraph 1(2); and

(b) the guarantors have or will have such resources that the debt becoming due under section 75 of the 1995 Act is more likely to be met if the agreement is approved.

3.—(1) Nothing in this Schedule prevents the Authority from approving as a withdrawal arrangement an agreement that will take effect only if an employment-cessation event occurs in relation to an employer.

(2) And in the case of such an approval, references in paragraphs 1 and 2 to that event and debt must be read accordingly.

(3) But, subject to that, references in these Regulations to an approved withdrawal arrangement only include references to an arrangement approved under this paragraph if the agreement has taken effect.

4.—(1) Paragraphs 1, 2 and 5 of this Schedule apply to any arrangement replacing an approved withdrawal arrangement as they applied to the replaced arrangement.

(2) No directions may be issued under regulation 7(2) as a result of a notification about an arrangement that is to replace another arrangement if—

(a) directions have been issued under that regulation as a result of a notification about the replaced arrangement; and

(b) the replaced arrangement is an approved withdrawal arrangement that has come into force.

(3) But if an approved withdrawal arrangement replaces another such arrangement—

(a) any directions issued under regulation 7(2) as a result of a notification about the replaced arrangement continue to apply, and

(b) after the replacing arrangement comes into force the references to the approved withdrawal arrangement in regulations 7(3)(b), (4) and (6) and 7B(1) to (3) and in regulation 6(6)(b), as inserted by regulation 7A(5)(b), are to be taken as references to the replacing arrangement.

(4) Once sub-paragraph (2) has applied to an arrangement ("the second arrangement") that is to replace another arrangement—

(a) no further directions may be issued under regulation 7(2) as a result of a notification about any arrangement that is to replace the second arrangement or any subsequent replacing arrangement;

(b) sub-paragraph (3)(a) continues to apply to any directions about the arrangement replaced by the second arrangement notwithstanding the replacement of the second arrangement, or any subsequent replacement, by an approved withdrawal arrangement, and

(c) if such a replacement of the second arrangement or subsequent replacement occurs, references in sub-paragraph (3)(b) to the replacing arrangement are references to the latest replacing arrangement.

Notifiable events

5. —(1) Where an approved withdrawal arrangement is in force in relation to a scheme, each relevant person must give notice to the Authority if such an event as is mentioned in sub-paragraph (3) occurs in relation to that person.

(2) For the purposes of this paragraph each of the guarantors is a relevant person.

(3) The following are the events referred to in sub-paragraph (1)—
(a) any decision by the relevant person to take action which will, or is intended to, result in a debt which is or may become due—
(i) to the trustees of the scheme, or
(ii) if the Board of the Pension Protection Fund has assumed responsibility for the scheme in accordance with Chapter 3 of Part 2 of the 2004 Act, to the Board,
not being paid in full;
(b) a decision by the relevant person to cease to carry on business (including any trade or profession) in the United Kingdom or, if the relevant person ceases to carry on such business without taking such a decision, his doing so;
(c) where applicable, receipt by the relevant person of advice that the person is trading wrongfully within the meaning of section 214 of the Insolvency Act 1986[13] (wrongful trading), or circumstances occurring in which a director or former director of the company knows that there is no reasonable prospect that the company will avoid going into insolvent liquidation within the meaning of that section, and for this purpose section 214(4) of that Act applies;
(d) any breach by the relevant person of a covenant in an agreement between the relevant person and a bank or other institution providing banking services, other than where the bank or other institution agrees with the relevant person not to enforce the covenant;
(e) any change in the relevant person's credit rating, or the relevant person ceasing to have a credit rating;
(f) where the relevant person is a company, a decision by a controlling company to relinquish control of the relevant person or, if the controlling company relinquishes such control without taking such a decision, its doing so;
(g) two or more changes in the holders of any key relevant person posts within a period of 12 months;
(h) where the relevant person is a company or partnership, the conviction of an individual, in any jurisdiction, for an offence involving dishonesty, if the offence was committed while the individual was a director or partner of the relevant person;
(i) an insolvency event occurring in relation to the relevant person for the purposes of Part 2 of the 2004 Act (see section 121 of that Act: insolvency event, insolvency date and insolvency practitioner).

(4) A notice under sub-paragraph (1) must be given in writing as soon as reasonably practicable after the relevant person becomes aware of the event.

(5) No duty to which a relevant person is subject is to be regarded as contravened merely because of any information or opinion contained in a notice under this paragraph.

(6) But sub-paragraph (5) does not require any person to disclose protected items within the meaning of section 311 of the 2004 Act (protected items).

(7) Section 10 of the 1995 Act (civil penalties) applies to any relevant person who without reasonable excuse fails to comply with an obligation imposed on him under this paragraph.

(8) In this paragraph—

"control" has the meaning given in section 435(10) of the Insolvency Act 1986 (meaning of "associate"- meaning of "control") and "controlling company" is to be read accordingly;

"director" has the meaning given in section 741(1) of the Companies Act 1985[14] (meaning of "director" and "shadow director");

"key relevant person posts" means the Chief Executive and any director or partner responsible in whole or in part for the financial affairs of the relevant person.

SCHEDULE 1B

Form of Actuary's certificate: scheme funding basis debts in approved withdrawal arrangement cases

Actuarial Certificate Given for the Purposes of Regulation 7A(6) of the Occupational Pension Schemes (Employer Debt) Regulations 2005

Name of scheme[b]

Date as at which valuation is made[c]

1 Comparison of value of scheme assets with amount of scheme liabilities

In my opinion, at the above date the value of the assets of the scheme was less than the amount of the liabilities of the scheme.

The value of the assets of the scheme was

The amount of the liabilities was

The amount of the difference was

2 Valuation principles[d]

[e]The scheme's assets and liabilities are valued in accordance with regulation 5 of the Occupational Pension Schemes (Employer Debt) Regulations 2005, subject to the modifications specified in regulation 7A(4) of those Regulations, and the guidelines on winding up and scheme asset deficiency (GN19) and on minimum funding requirement (GN27) prepared and published by the Institute of Actuaries and the Faculty of Actuaries (so far as those guidelines are applicable).

Signature   Date

Name   Qualification

Address   Name of employer (if applicable)

Note

The valuation of the amount of the liabilities of the scheme may not reflect the actual cost of securing those liabilities by the purchase of annuities if the scheme were to have been wound up on the date as at which the valuation is made.".[f]

Notes:

[1] 1995 c.26. Section 75 was amended by section 271 of the Pensions Act 2004 (c.35) and modified by regulations 6, 8 to 10 and 13 to 15 of S.I. 2005/678. Section 89(2) was amended by paragraph 66 of Schedule 12 to the Pensions Act 2004. Section 75A was inserted by section 272 of the Pensions Act 2004. Section 124(1) is cited for the meaning it gives to "prescribed" and "regulations".

[2] 2004 c.35. Section 93(2)(q) and paragraph 21(e) of Schedule 1 refer to functions of the Regulator, which by virtue of section 7(1)(b) and (2)(b) include functions expressed to be conferred on "the Authority" by or by virtue of the Pensions Act 1995. Section 318(1) is cited for the meaning it gives to "prescribed" and "regulations".

[3] *See* section 120 of the Pensions Act 1995 and section 317 of the Pensions Act 2004 which provide that the Secretary of State must consult such persons as he may consider appropriate before making regulations for the purposes of the provisions for the purposes of which these Regulations are made. This duty does not apply where regulations are made before the end of the period of six months beginning with the coming into force of any enactment on which the regulations are consequential (in the case of section 120) or by virtue of which the regulations are made (in the case of section 317).

[4] S.I. 2005/678.

[5] S.I. 1991/167. Relevant amendments of regulation 12 were made by regulation 35 of S.I. 1992/1531, regulation 2(a) of S.I. 1993/1822, paragraph 30(15) of Schedule 2 to S.I. 1994/1062, regulation 2(4) of S.I. 1995/3067, regulation 2(7) of S.I. 1996/2131, paragraph 3(3) of Schedule 1 to S.I. 1997/786, regulation 2 of S.I. 1999/2543 and regulation 27 of S.I. 2000/1403.

[6] 1963 c.xxxii.

[7] S.I. 1996/3126.

[8] S.I. 2005/2188.

[9] S.I. 1996/1536. Regulation 6(1)(b) was amended by regulation 12(1) of S.I. 1996/3127.

[10] S.I. 2005/590.

[11] Section 94(1)(aa) of the Pension Schemes Act 1993 (c.48) was inserted by section 154(2) of the Pensions Act 1995 (c.26).

[12] Subsection (6A) was inserted in section 75 by section 271(5) of the Pensions Act 2004.

[13] 1986 c.45. Section 214 was modified by section 90 of, and Schedule 15 to, the Building Societies Act 1986 (c.53) and by section 23 of, and Schedule 10 to, the Friendly Societies Act 1992 (c.40). Regulation 5 of the Limited Liability Partnerships Regulations 2001 (S.I. 2001/1090) applies section 214 to limited liability partnerships with modifications including that references to a company include references to such partnerships and references to a director include references to a member (see regulation 5(2)(a) and (b)).

[14] 1985 c.6. Under regulation 4 of, and Part 1 of Schedule 2 to, S.I. 2001/1090 section 741 (except subsection (3)) applies to limited liability partnerships with the modifications set out in regulation 4(1).

[a] Amended by Correction Slip. Page 4, regulation 2(3), inserted regulation 7A(5)(b), in the inserted regulation 6(8)(a)(i), line two; "...paragraphs (2)(a) or (b) and 93)..." should read "...paragraphs (2)(a) or (b) and (3)...";

[b] Amended by Correction Slip. Page 12, Schedule, in the inserted Schedule 1B, line three; insert a line spacing immediately below "Name of scheme";

[c] Amended by Correction Slip. Page 12, Schedule, in the inserted Schedule 1B, line four; "Date as at which valuation is made" should be inserted on a new line followed by a line spacing immediately below;

[d] Amended by Correction Slip. Page 12, Schedule, in the inserted Schedule 1B, line ten; "Valuation principles" should be inserted immediately after the number "2" followed by a line spacing immediately below;

[e] Amended by Correction Slip. Page 12, Schedule, in the inserted Schedule 1B, line ten; the paragraph beginning, "The scheme's assets...", should begin on line 12 below the line spacing following "2 Valuation principles"; and

[f] Amended by Correction Slip. Page 12, Schedule, in the inserted Schedule 1B, last line; "up on the date as at which the valuation is made. " should read "up on the date as at which the valuation is made.".".

A2.9: Occupational Pension Schemes (Winding up etc) Regulations 2005 SI (2005/706)

Made	*22nd March 2005*
Laid before Parliament	*23rd March 2005*
Coming into force, except for	
paragraph 4 of the Schedule,	*6th April 2005*
paragraph 4 of the Schedule	*6th April 2006*

ARRANGEMENT OF REGULATIONS

The Secretary of State for Work and Pensions, in exercise of the powers conferred upon him by sections 9, 25(2), 97(1), (2)(b) and (3), 101I, 101L, 113, 181(1) and 183(3) of the Pension Schemes Act 1993[1], sections 49(2)(b), 56(3), 57(1) and (5), 68(2)(e), 73(2)(b), (6), (7) and (9), 73A(7), (8)(a) and (b) and (10), 73B(4), (5) and (8), 74(2) and (3)(e), 76(2), 91(5)(c), 118(1)(a) and (b), 119, 124(1) and (3E), 174(2)(a) and (3) of the Pensions Act 1995[2] and sections 30(1) and (2) and 83(4) and (6) of, and paragraph 8(1) of Schedule 5 to, the Welfare Reform and

Pensions Act 1999[3], and of all other powers enabling him in that behalf, by this instrument which is consequential on section 270 of the Pensions Act 2004[4] and section 326 of and Part 3 of Schedule 42 to the Finance Act 2004[5] and is made before the end of the period of six months beginning with the coming into force of those provisions[6], and having consulted such persons as the Secretary of State considers appropriate with respect to regulations 16 and 17[7], hereby makes the following Regulations:

Citation, commencement and application

1. - (1) These Regulations may be cited as the Occupational Pension Schemes (Winding up etc.) Regulations 2005.

(2) These Regulations, apart from paragraph 4 of the Schedule, come into force on 6th April 2005 and that paragraph comes into force on 6th April 2006.

(3) Regulations 3 to 13 do not apply in the case of any scheme which -

(a) was regarded by virtue of regulation 2 of the Occupational Pension Schemes (Winding Up) Regulations 1996[8] (commencement of winding up) as having begun to be wound up before 6th April 2005 for the purposes of those Regulations; or

(b) in accordance with section 124(3A) to (3E) of the 1995 Act began to wind up before that date.

Interpretation

2. - (1) In these Regulations--

"the 1995 Act" means the Pensions Act 1995;

"the 1999 Act" means the Welfare Reform and Pensions Act 1999;

"the 2004 Act" means the Pensions Act 2004;

"assessment period" has the meaning given by section 132 of the 2004 Act (assessment periods);

"the tax condition", in relation to a scheme, means -

(a) that the scheme has been approved by the Commissioners of the Board of Inland Revenue for the purposes of section 590 or 591 of the Income and Corporation Taxes Act 1988[9] (conditions for approval of retirement benefit schemes or discretionary approval) at any time before 6th April 2006; or

(b) that the scheme is registered under section 153 of the Finance Act 2004 (registration of pension schemes).

(2) In these Regulations "scheme" must be read in appropriate cases in accordance with the modifications of sections 73 to 74 of the 1995 Act made by regulation 13 (multi-employer sectionalised schemes, schemes with partial government guarantee and partly foreign schemes); and "employer" and "member" must be read accordingly.

(3) Subject to paragraphs (1) and (2) and regulation 12 (commencement of winding up), expressions used in these Regulations have the same meaning as in Part 1 of the 1995 Act (see section 124 of that Act).

Winding up
Schemes to which section 73 of the 1995 Act does not apply

3. - (1) Section 73 of the 1995 Act does not apply to any scheme which is -

(a) a public service pension scheme under the provisions of which there is no requirement for assets related to the intended rate or amount of benefit under the scheme to be set aside in advance (disregarding requirements relating to voluntary contributions);

(b) a scheme which is made under section 7 of the Superannuation Act 1972[10] (superannuation of persons employed in local government etc.) and provides pensions to local government employees;

(c) a scheme which is made under section 2 of the Parliamentary and Other Pensions Act 1987[11] (power to provide for pensions for Members of the House of Commons etc.);

(d) a scheme in respect of which a relevant public authority, as defined in subsection (4) of section 307 of the 2004 Act (modification of that Act in relation to certain categories of schemes), has given a guarantee or made any other arrangements for the purposes of securing that the assets of the scheme are sufficient to meet its liabilities;

(e) a scheme which does not meet the tax condition;

(f) a scheme which -

(i) has been categorised by the Commissioners of the Board of Inland Revenue for the purposes of its approval as a centralised scheme for non-associated employers,

(ii) which is not contracted-out; and

(iii) under the provisions of which the only benefits that may be provided on or after retirement (other than money purchase benefits derived from the payment of voluntary contributions by any person) are lump sum benefits which are not calculated by reference to a member's salary;

(g) a scheme –

(i) the only benefits provided by which (other than money purchase benefits) are death benefits; and

(ii) under the provisions of which no member has accrued rights (other than rights to money purchase benefits);

(h) a scheme with such a superannuation fund as is mentioned in section 615(6) of the Income and Corporation Taxes Act 1988[12] (fund established to provide superannuation benefits in respect of persons' employment in a trade or undertaking wholly outside the United Kingdom);

(i) a scheme with fewer than two members;

(j) a scheme with fewer than 12 members where all the members are trustees of the scheme and either -

(i) the rules of the scheme provide that all decisions are made only by the trustees who are members of the scheme by unanimous agreement; or

(ii) the scheme has a trustee who is independent in relation to the scheme for the purposes of section 23 of the 1995 Act[13] (power to appoint independent trustees) (see subsection (3) of that section) and is registered in the register maintained by the Authority in accordance with regulations made under subsection (4) of that section;

(k) a scheme with fewer than 12 members where all the members are directors of a company which is the sole trustee of the scheme and either -

(i) the rules of the scheme provide that all decisions are made only by the members of the scheme by unanimous agreement; or

(ii) one of the directors of the company is independent in relation to the scheme for the purposes of section 23 of the 1995 Act and is registered in the register maintained by the Authority in accordance with regulations made under subsection (4) of that section;

(l) the Chatsworth Settlement Estate Pension Scheme; or

(m) the scheme established by the Salvation Army Act 1963[14].

(2) Before 6th April 2006 paragraph (1)(e) applies with the addition at the end of the words "and is not a relevant statutory scheme providing relevant benefits"; and for the purposes of that paragraph "relevant statutory scheme" and "relevant benefits" have the same meaning as in Chapter 1 of Part 14 of the Income and Corporation Taxes Act 1988[15] (see sections 611A and 612(1) of that Act).

Corresponding PPF liability: modifications of the pension compensation provisions etc.
4. - (1) For the purposes of section 73 of the 1995 Act, when determining the corresponding PPF liability in relation to any liability of a scheme to or in respect of a member for pensions or other benefits, the pension compensation provisions apply as if -

(a) those provisions applied to all schemes to which section 73 of the 1995 Act applies and any reference in the pension compensation provisions to members, employers or any other expression the construction of which is dependent on the meaning of "scheme" were to be read accordingly (but subject to the following provisions of this regulation);

(b) sections 140 to 142, 164 and 168(2)(a) and (c) to (f) of the 2004 Act were omitted;

(c) Schedule 7 to that Act (pension compensation provisions) applied -

(i) with the substitution for the references in paragraphs 5(4A), 15(5A) and 19(5A)[16] to the Board of references to the trustees or managers of the scheme;

(ii) with the substitution for the references in paragraphs 20(1)(a) and 32(1)(a) to the commencement of the assessment period of references to the commencement of the winding up period;

(iii) with the substitution for the reference in paragraph 35(4) to the time immediately before the assessment period which begins on the assessment date of a reference to the time immediately before the winding up period begins;

(iv) with the addition at the end of paragraph 35(5) of the words--

" and in this sub-paragraph as it applies for the purposes of section 73(4)(b) of the Pensions Act 1995, "the employer" includes both any person included by virtue of regulation 4(1)(a) of the Occupational Pension Schemes (Winding up etc.) Regulations 2005 and any person who is the employer apart from by virtue of that regulation.";

(v) with the substitution for other references to the assessment date of references to the winding up date; and

(vi) with the omissions specified in paragraph (2);

(d) no determination might be made under paragraph 29 of Schedule 7 (Board's powers to alter rates of revaluation and indexation) after the time as at which the corresponding PPF liability is determined for the purposes of section 73 of the 1995 Act;

(e) no order might be made under paragraph 30 of that Schedule (Secretary of State's powers to vary any percentage paid as compensation) after that time;

(f) the Pension Protection Fund (Compensation) Regulations 2005 applied with the modifications specified in paragraph (3); and

(g) (so far as they are included in the pension compensation provisions) the Pension Protection Fund (Hybrid Schemes) (Modification) Regulations 2005[17] applied with the substitution for the reference in regulation 3(2) of those Regulations to the assessment date of a reference to the winding up date.

(2) The omissions are -

(a) paragraphs 2, 20(4), 23A[18], 24, 25, 27 and 31A[19] and all references to those paragraphs;

(b) in paragraph 26 -

(i) in sub-paragraphs (2)(b)(i), (6B)(a)[20] and (9)(a) and (b), the words "or a connected occupational pension scheme";

(ii) in sub-paragraph (6B)(b) the words "or a relevant connected occupational pension scheme"; and

(iii) the words following sub-paragraph (6B)(b).

(3) The modifications are--

(a) in regulation 4 (compensation for surviving dependants) -

(i) in paragraph (2) omit the words following "otherwise)"; and

(ii) for regulation 4(3) substitute--

"(3) In the case of a surviving dependant the circumstances are where the admissible rules of the scheme provide for the payment of pension or other benefits to that person.";

(b) for references in regulations 5, 6, 9, 10(1), 11(1), 12(1), 13, 14 and 15 to the assessment date, wherever they occur, substitute references to the winding up date; and

(c) omit regulation 16 (modification of admissible rules).

(4) In this regulation -

(a) "corresponding PPF liability" has the meaning given in section 73(5) of the 1995 Act;

(b) "the pension compensation provisions" has the same meaning as in Part 2 of the 2004 Act (see section 162 of that Act); and

(c) "the winding up date" means the date on which the winding up period began or, if the crystallisation date for the scheme for the purposes of regulation 4 of the Occupational Pension Schemes (Winding Up) Regulations 1996 (calculation of amounts of liabilities) is an earlier date, that date.

(5) In the case of any scheme in relation to which there is no assessment period during the winding up period, section 73(4)(b) applies as if the words from "to the extent" to "the corresponding PPF liability" were omitted.

Early leaver's rights: deemed election for contribution refund

5. Where, on the commencement of the winding up period, a member becomes a person to whom Chapter 5 of Part 4 of the 1993 Act[21] applies (early leavers: cash transfer sums and contribution refunds), that Chapter applies as if -

(a) he had elected on the day on which that period begins for a contribution refund;

(b) he had accordingly acquired a right to such a refund (and not a right to a cash transfer sum) under section 101AB of that Act; and

(c) all steps required to be taken under that Chapter preliminary to that election had been taken.

Adjustments to discretionary awards

6. - (1) For the purposes of section 73A of the 1995 Act[22] (operation of scheme during winding up period) and this regulation, "discretionary award", in relation to an occupational pension scheme, means an award of a pension or other benefit under the scheme where either -

(a) entitlement to the award arises as a result of the exercise of a discretion conferred by the scheme rules that may be exercised in circumstances specified in those rules; or

(b) the amount awarded depends on the exercise of such a discretion.

(2) Where section 73A of the 1995 Act applies, the circumstances in which trustees or managers of the scheme are required to adjust any such entitlement as is referred to in section 73A(7)(a) are where -

(a) the entitlement to a pension or other benefit is -

(i) the entitlement of a member; or

(ii) the entitlement to a pension or other benefit in respect of a member other than a member who dies during the winding up period; and

(b) it appears to the trustees or managers that as a result of -

(i) the discretionary award in question;

(ii) that award and any other awards under the scheme rules to which section 73A(7)(a) applies; or

(iii) all the awards under the scheme rules to which that section applies and any entitlements in respect of the member to which section 73A(7)(b) applies ("survivor entitlements"),

the total amount of the liability for pensions and other benefits in respect of the member is greater than it was immediately before the commencement of the winding up period.

(3) In those circumstances, the trustees or managers are required to adjust the entitlement -

(a) to the discretionary award;

(b) to that award and the other awards mentioned in paragraph (2)(b)(ii); or

(c) to the awards and entitlements mentioned in paragraph (2)(b)(iii),

in such manner as they think fit so that the total amount of that liability does not exceed its amount immediately before the commencement of the winding up period.

(4) If -

(a) the commencement of the winding up of the scheme is backdated (whether in accordance with section 154 of the 2004 Act or otherwise); and

(b) the requirement under paragraph (3) to adjust any entitlement arises as a result of that backdating,

the adjustment must be made with effect from the time the award takes effect.

(5) Where a discretionary award takes effect during a period that is a winding up period or an assessment period in relation to a scheme, the trustees or managers of the scheme must give the person to whom the award is made notice in writing not later than one month after the date on which the award is made -

(a) that the award may be adjusted by virtue of this regulation; or

(b) where the award takes effect before the scheme has begun to be wound up, that it may be so adjusted if the scheme begins to be wound up and the commencement of the winding up is backdated.

(6) Such a notice may be given by post and, if the person to whom it is given is not in employment to which the scheme relates, is to be treated as having been given if it is sent to him by post to his last address known to the trustees or managers.

Adjustments to survivors' benefits

7. - (1) Where section 73A of the 1995 Act applies, the circumstances in which trustees or managers of the scheme are required to adjust any such entitlement as is referred to in section 73A(7)(b) are where -

    (a) it appears to the trustees or managers that as a result of –

        (i) the entitlement in question having arisen; or

        (ii) that entitlement and any other entitlements under the scheme rules to which section 73A(7)(b) applies having arisen;

        the amount of the total liability for pensions and other benefits in respect of the member is greater than it was immediately before the commencement of the winding up period, or

    (b) regulation 6(3) requires the trustees or managers to adjust the entitlement.

(2) In the circumstances mentioned in paragraph (1)(a), the trustees or managers are required to adjust the entitlement or entitlements in such manner as they think fit so that the total amount of the liability for pensions and other benefits in respect of the member does not exceed its amount immediately before the commencement of the winding up period.

(3) See regulation 6(3) for the manner in which the trustees or managers are required to adjust the entitlement or entitlements where that regulation applies.

(4) If -

    (a) the commencement of the winding up of the scheme is backdated (whether in accordance with section 154 of the 2004 Act or otherwise); and

    (b) the requirement under paragraph (2) to adjust any entitlement arises as a result of that backdating,

    the adjustment must be made with effect from the time the award takes effect.

(5) Where any such entitlement of a person as is referred to in section 73A(7)(b) of the 1995 Act arises during a period that is a winding up period or an assessment period in relation to a scheme, the trustees or managers of the scheme must give the person notice in writing not later than one month after the date on which it arises -

    (a) that it may be adjusted by virtue of this regulation; or

    (b) where the entitlement arises before the scheme has begun to be wound up, that it may be so adjusted if the scheme begins to be wound up and the commencement of the winding up is backdated.

(6) Such a notice may be given by post and is to be treated as having been given to the person if it is sent to him by post to his last address known to the trustees or managers.

Entitlement to death benefits treated as arising before commencement of winding up period

8. - (1) This regulation applies where -

    (a) an occupational pension scheme to which section 73 of the 1995 Act applies is being wound up;

    (b) a member of the scheme died before the winding up began;

    (c) during the winding up period a person ("the beneficiary") becomes entitled under the scheme rules to one or more benefits within paragraph (2) in respect of the member; and

    (d) the beneficiary could have become so entitled before the winding up period began had the trustees or managers of the scheme taken any action earlier.

(2) The benefits are -

(a) a pension of a kind permitted by the pension death benefit rules set out in section 167 of the Finance Act 2004 (pension death benefit rules); and

(b) a lump sum of a kind permitted by the lump sum death benefit rule set out in section 168 of that Act (lump sum death benefit rule).

(3) For the purposes of section 73B(6)(a)[23] (liabilities to which the winding up provisions do not apply) -

(a) the beneficiary's entitlement to payment of so much of the pension (if any) as is attributable to the period between the member's death and the commencement of the winding up period; and

(b) the beneficiary's entitlement to payment of the lump sum,

are to be treated as having arisen immediately before the commencement of the winding up period.

(4) In the case of a scheme which begins to be wound up before 6th April 2006, this regulation has effect as if the benefits referred to in paragraph (2) were -

(a) a pension payable to the deceased member's former spouse or dependant; and

(b) a lump sum calculated by reference to the member's remuneration.

Calculation of the value or amount of scheme assets and liabilities

9. For regulation 4 of the Occupational Pension Schemes (Winding Up) Regulations 1996[24] (calculation of amounts of liabilities) substitute -

'Calculation of the value or amount of scheme assets and liabilities

4. - (1) The liabilities of a scheme to which section 73 applies and their amount or value must be determined, calculated and verified by the actuary of the scheme -

(a) on the assumption that any questions relating to any person's entitlement to a pension or other benefit are to be determined as at the crystallisation date;

(b) on the assumption that liabilities in respect of pensions or other benefits will be discharged by the purchase of annuities of the kind described in section 74(3)(c)[25] (discharge of liabilities: annuity purchase) and include the expenses involved in discharging them;

(c) subject to sub-paragraph (b) and paragraph (4), on the general assumptions specified in regulations 7(2), (3) and (7) to (10) and 8(2) of the MFR Regulations[26] (determination and valuation of liabilities and further provisions as to valuation: methodology, assumptions, etc.) so far as they relate to the calculation and verification of liabilities; and

(d) otherwise in accordance with the guidance given in GN 19[27], so far as that guidance applies for the purposes of these Regulations.

(2) For the purpose of paragraph (1)(b) the actuary must estimate the cost of purchasing the annuities.

(3) A calculation of the value or amount of the liabilities of a scheme for the purposes of section 73 must be accompanied by a statement that it is in accordance with the guidance mentioned in paragraph (1)(d).

(4) For the purposes of this regulation, regulations 7 and 8 of the MFR Regulations are modified as follows -

(a) references in regulations 7(3), (7) and (8) and 8(2) of the MFR Regulations to the relevant date are to be taken as references to the date as at which the calculation is made (being a date not earlier than the crystallisation date or the commencement of winding up, if later);

(b) in regulation 7(3) the words "subject to paragraphs (4) and (5)" are omitted; and

(c) paragraph (i) of regulation 8(2)(a) is omitted.

(5) Paragraph (6) applies if, when the assets of the scheme are applied in accordance with section 73(3) towards satisfying any liability of the scheme mentioned in section 73(4), that liability, as calculated in accordance with the rules of the scheme (without any reduction by reason of its falling within a class of liability which is to be satisfied after another class), is in the opinion of the actuary fully satisfied by applying assets of a value less than the amount of that liability calculated in accordance with paragraph (1).

(6) If this paragraph applies the amount to be taken as the amount of that liability for the purposes of section 73(3) is to be reduced accordingly.

(7) Paragraph (8) applies if, when the assets of the scheme are so applied, the liabilities mentioned in section 73(3), as calculated in accordance with the rules of the scheme (without any reduction by reason of their falling within a class of liability which is to be satisfied after another class), cannot in the opinion of the actuary be fully satisfied by applying assets of a value equal to the amount of those liabilities calculated in accordance with paragraph (1).

(8) If this paragraph applies the amount to be taken as the amount of those liabilities for the purposes of section 73(3) is to be increased accordingly.

(9) If section 73 does not apply to any liability by virtue of -

(a) section 73B(6)(d) (which provides that the winding up provisions do not apply to liabilities the discharge of which is validated under section 136 of the Pensions Act 2004) or

(b) regulation 10(2) of the Occupational Pension Schemes (Winding up etc.) Regulations 2005 (which makes similar provision as respects liabilities discharged by virtue of regulations under section 135(4) of that Act),

the value of any corresponding assets is to be deducted from the value of the assets of the scheme for the purposes of section 73.

(10) For the purposes of paragraph (9), "the value of any corresponding assets" means -

(a) in a case where assets of the scheme at the crystallisation date are transferred from the scheme in consideration for the discharge, the value of those assets at that date; and

(b) in a case where assets that are not assets of the scheme at that date are so transferred, the value of those assets at the date of the discharge.

(11) Subject to paragraph (12), in this regulation "the crystallisation date" means--

(a) in the case of a scheme where--

(i) the trustees or managers determined (whether in pursuance of section 38 (power to defer winding up) or otherwise) that the scheme was not for the time being to be wound up, despite rules otherwise requiring it to be so;

(ii) the time when the paragraph of section 73(4) into which the liability in respect of any person falls is determined is fixed under the provisions of the scheme; and

(iii) that time falls on or after the date of the determination mentioned in paragraph (i) and before the date on which the scheme begins to be wound up,

the date when that time occurs; and

(b) otherwise, the date on which the scheme begins to be wound up.

(12) Where the trustees or managers of a scheme--

(a) determined before 6th April 1997 that the scheme was not for the time being to be wound up, despite rules otherwise requiring it to be so; and

(b) before that date determined a time (being a time before 6th April 1997) when the amounts or descriptions of liabilities of the scheme were to be determined for the purposes of any rule of the scheme requiring the assets of the scheme to be applied on winding up in satisfying the amounts of certain liabilities to or in respect of members before other such liabilities,

the date when that time occurs is the crystallisation date.".

Discharge of liabilities during assessment period

10. - (1) This regulation applies in any case where any liability of a scheme in respect of a member has been discharged by virtue of regulations under section 135(4) of the 2004 Act (power to make regulations permitting discharge of scheme's liabilities during an assessment period).

(2) Sections 73 to 73B of the 1995 Act (except section 73B(4)(b)(iii)) apply as if references to liabilities did not include the discharged liability.

(3) Section 74(2) and (4) of the 1995 Act[28] applies as if the trustees or managers of the scheme had -

(a) in accordance with arrangements prescribed under section 74(2) of that Act, provided for the discharge of the discharged liability in one or more of the ways mentioned in section 74(3) of that Act; and

(b) applied any amount available to them in accordance with section 73 of that Act in one or more of those ways.

Requirements to be met where liabilities discharged on winding up

11. In regulation 8 of the Occupational Pension Schemes (Winding Up) Regulations 1996 (requirements to be satisfied by transferee schemes, annuities etc.) after paragraph (5) add -

"(6) For the purposes of section 74(3)(e)[29] (liabilities treated as discharged where the trustees have provided for them to be discharged by the payment of a cash sum in circumstances where prescribed requirements are met), the circumstances which are prescribed are -

(a) where the payment is a contribution refund under Chapter 5 of Part 4 of the 1993 Act; or

(b) where the payment -

(i) is made to a member who has a right under the scheme rules to the payment of a lump sum that is a trivial commutation lump sum or a winding up lump sum for the purposes of Part 1 of Schedule 29 to the Finance Act 2004 (see paragraphs 7 to 10 of that Schedule (registered pension schemes: authorised lump sums: trivial commutation lump sum and winding up lump sum)); and

(ii) does not contravene any trivial commutation restriction that applies in the circumstances in question.

(7) In this regulation "trivial commutation restriction" means a restriction imposed by -

(a) regulation 19, 20 or 60 of the Occupational Pension Schemes (Contracting-out Regulations 1996[30] (lump sum benefits and salary related contracted-out schemes trivial commutation of benefits derived from section 9(2B) rights and trivial commutation of guaranteed minimum pensions);

(b) regulation 2 of the Occupational Pension Scheme (Assignment, Forfeiture Bankruptcy etc.) Regulations 1997[31] (commutation of a pension under an occupational pension scheme); or

(c) regulation 3(2)(b) of the Pension Sharing (Pension Credit Benefit) Regulations 2000[32] (commutation of the whole of pension credit benefit).

(8) Before 6th April 2006 this regulation applies with the modification in paragraph (9).

(9) For paragraph (6)(b)(i) substitute -

"(i) extinguishes the whole or part of the person's entitlement to benefits under the scheme;

(ia) does not contravene Revenue restrictions; and".

(10) For the purposes of this regulation a payment does not contravene Revenue restrictions if -

(a) in the case of a scheme that is an approved scheme for the purposes of Chapter 1 of Part 14 of the Income and Corporation Taxes Act 1988 (see section 612(1) of that Act), it is permitted under the scheme rules in accordance with its approval for those purposes and

(b) in the case of a scheme that is a relevant statutory scheme for those purposes (see section 611A of that Act), it is permitted under the regulations or rules governing the scheme as such a scheme.".

Commencement of winding up

12. - (1) Regulation 12 of the Occupational Pension Schemes (Winding Up Notices and Reports etc.) Regulations 2002[33] (time when winding up taken to begin) does not apply in any case where in accordance with section 124(3A) to (3E) of the 1995 Act a scheme begins to wind up on or after 6th April 2005.

(2) Accordingly, in such a case -

(a) that section applies for the purpose of determining the time when that scheme winds up for the purposes of -

(i) sections 73 to 74 of the 1995 Act;

(ii) these Regulations; and

(iii) the Occupational Pension Schemes (Winding Up) Regulations 1996; and

(b) regulation 2 of those Regulations does not apply.

(3) If immediately before 6th April 2005 a scheme was regarded as having begun to be wound up for any purpose by virtue of regulation 2 of the Occupational Pension Schemes (Winding Up) Regulations 1996, paragraphs (1) and (2) do not affect the time when it is to be taken as having begun to be wound up for that purpose.

Multi-employer sectionalised schemes, schemes with partial government guarantee and partly foreign schemes

13. In any case where, by virtue of regulation 12, 12A or 12B of the Occupational Pension Schemes (Winding Up) Regulations 1996[34] (winding up of sectionalised schemes, schemes with partial government guarantee and partly foreign schemes), sections 73 to 74 of the 1995 Act apply to a scheme as if different parts of the scheme were separate schemes, these Regulations (apart from this regulation) also so apply.

Consequential amendments

14. The Occupational Pension Schemes (Winding Up) Regulations 1996 have effect with the amendments in Part 1 of the Schedule and the Regulations specified in Part 2 of the Schedule have effect with the amendments in that Part.

Transfer values

Amendments of the Occupational Pension Schemes (Transfer Values) Regulations 1996

15. - (1) The Occupational Pension Schemes (Transfer Values) Regulations 1996[35] are amended as follows.

(2) In regulation 7(3)(b)(iv)[36] (manner of calculation and verification of cash equivalents) for the words from "the liabilities" to "winding-up)" substitute "the liabilities for the benefits in respect of which the cash equivalents are being calculated".

(3) In regulation 8[37] (further provisions as to calculation of cash equivalents and increases and reductions of cash equivalents (other than guaranteed cash equivalents)) for paragraphs (4) and (4A) substitute -

"(4) In the case of a scheme to which section 56 of the 1995 Act (minimum funding requirement) applies, the cash equivalent in respect of a member may be reduced by the trustees of the scheme if the GN11 insufficiency conditions are met.

(4A) The GN11 insufficiency conditions are that the actuary's last relevant GN11 report (see paragraph (4J)) shows that at the effective date of the report -

    (a) the scheme had assets that were insufficient to pay the full amount of the cash equivalent in respect of all the members, and

    (b) the assets were insufficient to pay in full any category of liabilities that is a category of liabilities for benefits in respect of which the member's cash equivalent is being calculated.

(4B) If the GN11 insufficiency conditions are met then, subject to paragraph (4D), the trustees may reduce any part of the member's cash equivalent that is payable in respect of such a category of liabilities as are mentioned in paragraph (4A)(b) by a percentage not exceeding the GN11 deficiency percentage.

(4C) The GN11 deficiency percentage for any such part of a member's cash equivalent is the percentage by which the actuary's last relevant GN11 report shows that the assets were insufficient to pay that category of liabilities.

(4D) The total reduction made in a member's cash equivalent under paragraph (4) must not reduce the member's cash equivalent below the MFR basis minimum for the member.

(4E) For the purposes of this regulation, the MFR basis minimum for the member is the minimum amount required in accordance with regulation 7(3)(b)(iv) to pay in full the liabilities for the benefits in respect of which the member's cash equivalent is being calculated, but this is subject to paragraph (4F).

(4F) If the GN11 insufficiency conditions and the MFR insufficiency conditions are both met the MFR basis minimum for the member for the purposes of paragraph (4D) may be reduced by the trustees of the scheme in accordance with paragraph (4H).

(4G) The MFR insufficiency conditions are that the last relevant MFR valuation statement (see paragraph (4K)) shows that at the effective date of the valuation -

(a) the scheme had assets that were insufficient to pay in full the liabilities of the scheme in respect of pensions and other benefits towards which the assets would be required by section 73 of the 1995 Act to be applied in the order determined under that section, and

(b) the assets were insufficient to pay in full any category of liabilities to which that order applies that are liabilities for benefits in respect of which the member's cash equivalent is being calculated.

(4H) The reduction that may be made under paragraph (4F) is that any part of the MFR basis minimum for the member that relates to that category of liabilities may be reduced by a percentage not exceeding the MFR deficiency percentage.

(4I) The MFR deficiency percentage for any such part of the MFR basis minimum for the member is the percentage by which the last relevant MFR valuation statement shows that the assets were insufficient to pay that category of liabilities.

(4J) The references in this regulation to the actuary's last relevant GN11 report are to his last report before the guarantee date in accordance with "Retirement Benefit Schemes - Transfer Values (GN11)" published by the Faculty of Actuaries and the Institute of Actuaries and current at the guarantee date[38].

(4K) The references in this regulation to the last relevant MFR valuation statement are to the statement made by the actuary in accordance with Schedule 1 to the Occupational Pension Schemes (Minimum Funding Requirement and Actuarial Valuations) Regulations 1996 (minimum funding valuation statements) and contained in the last actuarial valuation under section 57 of the 1995 Act (valuation and certification of assets and liabilities) before the guarantee date.

(4L) If the last relevant MFR valuation statement refers to an order for applying assets determined under section 73 that is an order modified by regulations made under that section, then the reduction under paragraph (4F) is to be made by reference to the order as so modified.".

(4) In regulation 8(5) for "paragraph (4)" and "the reference" substitute "paragraphs (4), (4A) and (4G)" and "the references" respectively.

(5) In regulation 8(12) for "section 73 of the 1995 Act and regulations made under that section" substitute "the winding up provisions (as defined in section 73B(10)(a) of the 1995 Act) and regulations made under those provisions".

(6) In regulation 8(13) for "under section 73 of the 1995 Act, section 73 of that Act applies" substitute "under section 73B(4)(b)(i) of the 1995 Act by virtue of section 73B(5) of that Act, the winding up provisions (as so defined) apply".

(7) In regulation 9(3) (increases and reductions of guaranteed cash equivalents) for "section 73 of the 1995 Act and regulations made under that section" substitute "the winding up provisions (as defined in section 73B(10)(a) of the 1995 Act) and regulations made under those provisions".

(8) In regulation 9(4) for "under section 73 of the 1995 Act, section 73 of that Act applies" substitute "under section 73B(4)(b)(i) of the 1995 Act by virtue of section 73B(5) of that Act, the winding up provisions (as so defined) apply".

(9) Paragraphs (2) to (4) only apply to the calculation of cash equivalents where the guarantee date is on or after 6th April 2005 and the scheme has not begun to be wound up before that date.

(10) In paragraph (9) "the guarantee date" has the meaning given by subsection (2) of section 93A of the 1993 Act[39] (salary-related schemes: right to statement of entitlement).

(11) Paragraphs (5) to (8) only apply where the scheme begins to be wound up on or after 6th April 2005.

Pension sharing
Amendments of the Pension Sharing (Valuation) Regulations 2000
16. - (1) The Pension Sharing (Valuation) Regulations 2000[40] are amended as follows.

(2) In regulation 4(3)(b)(iii) (occupational pension schemes: manner of calculation and verification of cash equivalents) for the words from "the liabilities" to "up)" substitute "liabilities for the benefits in respect of which the cash equivalent is being calculated".
(3) In regulation 5 (occupational pension schemes: further provisions as to calculation of cash equivalents and increases and reductions of cash equivalents) for paragraphs (3) and (3A) substitute -

"(3) In the case of a scheme to which section 56 of the 1995 Act applies, the cash equivalent may be reduced by the trustees or managers if the GN11 insufficiency conditions are met.

(3A) The GN11 insufficiency conditions are that the actuary's last relevant GN11 report (see paragraph (3J)) shows that at the effective date of the report -
    (a) the scheme had assets that were insufficient to pay the full amount of the cash equivalent in respect of all the members, and
    (b) the assets were insufficient to pay in full any category of liabilities that is a category of liabilities for the benefits in respect of which the cash equivalent is being calculated.

(3B) If the GN11 insufficiency conditions are met then, subject to paragraph (3D), the trustees or managers may reduce any part of the cash equivalent that relates to such a category of liabilities as are mentioned in paragraph (3A)(b) by a percentage not exceeding the GN11 deficiency percentage.

(3C) The GN11 deficiency percentage for any such part of the cash equivalent is the percentage by which the actuary's last relevant GN11 report shows that the assets were insufficient to pay that category of liabilities.

(3D) The total reduction made in the cash equivalent under paragraph (3) must not reduce the cash equivalent below the MFR basis minimum for the transferor.

(3E) For the purposes of this regulation, the MFR basis minimum for the transferor is the minimum amount required in accordance with regulation 4(3)(b)(iii) to pay in full the liabilities for the benefits in respect of which the cash equivalent is being calculated, but this is subject to paragraph (3F).

(3F) If the GN11 insufficiency conditions and the MFR insufficiency conditions are both met, the MFR basis minimum for the transferor for the purposes of paragraph (3D) may be reduced by the trustees or managers in accordance with paragraph (3H).

(3G) The MFR insufficiency conditions are that the last relevant MFR valuation statement (see paragraph (3K)) shows that at the effective date of the valuation -
(a) the scheme had assets that were insufficient to pay in full the liabilities of the scheme in respect of pensions and other benefits towards which the assets would be required by section 73 of the 1995 Act to be applied in the order determined under that section, and
(b) the assets were insufficient to pay in full any category of liabilities to which that order applies that are liabilities for benefits in respect of which the cash equivalent is being calculated.

(3H) The reduction that may be made under paragraph (3F) is that any part of the MFR basis minimum for the transferor that relates to that category of liabilities may be reduced by a percentage not exceeding the MFR deficiency percentage.

(3I) The MFR deficiency percentage for any such part of the MFR basis minimum for the transferor is the percentage by which the last relevant MFR valuation statement shows that the assets were insufficient to pay that category of liabilities.

(3J) The references in this regulation to the actuary's last relevant GN11 report are to his last report before the valuation day in accordance with "Retirement Benefit Schemes - Transfer Values (GN11)" published by the Faculty of Actuaries and the Institute of Actuaries and current at the valuation day.

(3K) The references in this regulation to the last relevant MFR valuation statement are to the statement made by the actuary in accordance with Schedule 1 to the Occupational Pension Schemes (Minimum Funding Requirement and Actuarial Valuations) Regulations 1996 and contained in the last actuarial valuation under section 57 of the 1995 Act before the valuation day.

(3L) If the last relevant MFR valuation statement refers to an order for applying assets determined under section 73 of the 1995 Act that is an order modified by regulations made under that section, then the reduction under paragraph (3F) is to be made by reference to the order as so modified.".

(4) In regulation 5(4) for "paragraph (3)", "the reference" and "a reference" substitute "paragraphs (3), (3A) and (3G)", "the references" and "references" respectively.

(5) In regulation 5(5) for "paragraph (3)" substitute "paragraphs (3) and (3F)".

(6) In regulation 5(6) for the words from "sections 73" onwards substitute "the winding up provisions (as defined in section 73B(10)(a) of the 1995 Act) and regulations made under those provisions".

(7) In regulation 5(7) for the words from "the Occupational" to "applies" substitute "regulations made under section 73B(4)(b)(i) of the 1995 Act by virtue of section 73B(5) of that Act, the winding up provisions (as so defined) apply".

(8) Paragraphs (2) to (5) only apply if the relevant proceedings commenced on or after 6th April 2005 and the scheme has not begun to be wound up before that date.

(9) In paragraph (8) "the relevant proceedings" means the proceedings for the dissolution or annulment of marriage in connection with which the relevant order or provision was made; and in this paragraph "the relevant order or provision" means the order or provision mentioned in section 28(1) of the 1999 Act (activation of pension sharing) for the purposes of which the valuation is made.

(10) Paragraphs (6) and (7) only apply where the scheme begins to be wound up on or after 6th April 2005.

Amendments of the Pension Sharing (Implementation and Discharge of Liability) Regulations 2000

17. - (1) The Pension Sharing (Implementation and Discharge of Liability) Regulations 2000[41] are amended as follows.

(2) In regulation 16 (adjustments to the amount of the pension credit: occupational pension schemes which are underfunded on the valuation day) for paragraphs (2) and (2A) substitute -

"(2) In the case of a scheme to which section 56 of the 1995 Act applies, the lesser amount referred to in paragraph 8(1) of Schedule 5 to the 1999 Act (adjustments to amount of pension credit) may be determined for the purposes of that paragraph by reducing the pension credit if the GN11 insufficiency conditions are met.

(2A) The GN11 insufficiency conditions are that the actuary's last relevant GN11 report (see paragraph (2J)) shows that at the effective date of the report -
(a) the scheme had assets that were insufficient to pay the full amount of the cash equivalent in respect of all the members, and
(b) the assets were insufficient to pay in full any category of liabilities for benefits to which the pension credit relates.

(2B) If the GN11 insufficiency conditions are met then, subject to paragraph (2D), the trustees or managers may reduce any part of the pension credit that relates to benefits the liabilities for which fall within such a category as is mentioned in paragraph (2A)(b) by a percentage not exceeding the GN11 deficiency percentage.

(2C) The GN11 deficiency percentage for any such part of the pension credit is the percentage by which the actuary's last relevant GN11 report shows that the assets were insufficient to pay the category of liabilities into which the liabilities for those benefits falls.

(2D) The total reduction made in a pension credit under paragraph (2) must not reduce the cash equivalent in respect of the pension credit below the MFR basis minimum for the person entitled to the credit.

(2E) For the purposes of this regulation, the MFR basis minimum for such a person is the minimum amount required in accordance with regulation 4(3)(b)(iii) of the Pension Sharing (Valuation) Regulations 2000 to pay in full the liabilities for the benefits in respect of which the cash equivalent is being calculated, but this is subject to paragraph (2F).

(2F) If the GN11 insufficiency conditions and the MFR insufficiency conditions are both met, the MFR basis minimum for the person for the purposes of paragraph (2D) may be reduced in accordance with paragraph (2H).

(2G) The MFR insufficiency conditions are that the last relevant MFR valuation statement (see paragraph (2K)) shows that at the effective date of the valuation -
  (a) the scheme had assets that were insufficient to pay in full the liabilities of the scheme in respect of pensions and other benefits towards which the assets would be required by section 73 of the 1995 Act to be applied in the order determined under that section, and
  (b) the assets were insufficient to pay in full any category of liabilities to which that order applies that are liabilities for benefits to which the pension credit relates.

(2H) The reduction that may be made under paragraph (2F) is that any part of the MFR basis minimum for the person that relates to that category of liabilities may be reduced by a percentage not exceeding the MFR deficiency percentage.

(2I) The MFR deficiency percentage for any such part of the MFR basis minimum for the person is the percentage by which the last relevant MFR valuation statement shows that the assets were insufficient to pay that category of liabilities.

(2J) The references in this regulation to the actuary's last relevant GN11 report are to his last report before the valuation day in accordance with "Retirement Benefit Schemes - Transfer Values (GN11)" published by the Faculty of Actuaries and the Institute of Actuaries and current at the valuation day.

(2K) The references in this regulation to the last relevant MFR valuation statement are to the statement made by the actuary in accordance with Schedule 1 to the Occupational Pension Schemes (Minimum Funding Requirement and Actuarial Valuations) Regulations 1996 and contained in the last actuarial valuation under section 57 of the 1995 Act before the valuation day.

(2L) If the last relevant MFR valuation statement refers to an order for applying assets determined under section 73 of the 1995 Act that is an order modified by regulations made under that section, then the reduction under paragraph (2F) is to be made by reference to the order as so modified.".

(3) In regulation 16(3) for "paragraph (2)", "the reference" and "a reference" substitute "paragraphs (2), (2A) and (2G)", "the references" and "references" respectively.

(4) This regulation only applies if the relevant proceedings commenced on or after 6th April 2005 and the scheme has not begun to be wound up before that date.

(5) In paragraph (4) "the relevant proceedings" means the proceedings for the dissolution or annulment of marriage in connection with which the order or provision mentioned in section 28(1) of the 1999 Act that resulted in entitlement to the pension credit in question was made.

Amendments of the Pension Sharing (Pension Credit Benefit) Regulations 2000
18. - (1) The Pension Sharing (Pension Credit Benefit) Regulations 2000[42] are amended as follows.

(2) In regulation 15(4) (further conditions on which liability for pension credit benefit may be discharged) for sub-paragraph (b) substitute -
    " (b) the winding up provisions (as defined in section 73B(10)(a) of the 1995 Act) and regulations made under those provisions do not apply;".

(3) In regulation 24(3)(b)(iv) (manner of calculation and verification of cash equivalents) for the words from "the liabilities" to "that Act" substitute "liabilities for the benefits in respect of which the cash equivalent is being calculated".

(4) In regulation 27 (increases and reductions of cash equivalents before a statement of entitlement has been sent to the eligible member) for paragraphs (4) and (4A) substitute -

"(4) In the case of a scheme to which section 56 of the 1995 Act applies, the cash equivalent in respect of an eligible member may be reduced by the trustees or managers of the scheme if the GN11 insufficiency conditions are met.

(4A) The GN11 insufficiency conditions are that the actuary's last relevant GN11 report (see paragraph (4J)) shows that at the effective date of the report -
    (a) the scheme had assets that were insufficient to pay the full amount of the cash equivalent in respect of all the members, and
    (b) the assets were insufficient to pay in full any category of liabilities that is a category of liabilities for benefits in respect of which the eligible member's cash equivalent is being calculated.

(4B) If the GN11 insufficiency conditions are met then, subject to paragraph (4D), the trustees or managers may reduce any part of the eligible member's cash equivalent that is payable in respect of such a category of liabilities as are mentioned in paragraph (4A)(b) by a percentage not exceeding the GN11 deficiency percentage.

(4C) The GN11 deficiency percentage for any such part of an eligible member's cash equivalent is the percentage by which the actuary's last relevant GN11 report shows that the assets were insufficient to pay that category of liabilities.

(4D) The total reduction made in an eligible member's cash equivalent under paragraph (4) must not reduce the member's cash equivalent below the MFR basis minimum for the member.

(4E) For the purposes of this regulation, the MFR basis minimum for the eligible member is the minimum amount required in accordance with regulation 24(3)(b)(iv) to pay in full the liabilities for the benefits in respect of which the member's cash equivalent is being calculated, but this is subject to paragraph (4F).

(4F) If the GN11 insufficiency conditions and the MFR insufficiency conditions are both met, the MFR basis minimum for the eligible member for the purposes of paragraph (4D) may be reduced by the trustees or managers in accordance with paragraph (4H).

(4G) The MFR insufficiency conditions are that the last relevant MFR valuation statement (see paragraph (4K)) shows that at the effective date of the valuation -

(a) the scheme had assets that were insufficient to pay in full the liabilities of the scheme in respect of pensions and other benefits towards which the assets would be required by section 73 of the 1995 Act to be applied in the order determined under that section, and

(b) the assets were insufficient to pay in full any category of liabilities to which that order applies that are liabilities for benefits in respect of which the eligible member's cash equivalent is being calculated.

(4H) The reduction that may be made under paragraph (4F) is that any part of the MFR basis minimum for the eligible member that relates to that category of liabilities may be reduced by a percentage not exceeding the MFR deficiency percentage.

(4I) The MFR deficiency percentage for any such part of the MFR basis minimum for the eligible member is the percentage by which the last relevant MFR valuation statement shows that the assets were insufficient to pay that category of liabilities.

(4J) The references in this regulation to the actuary's last relevant GN11 report are to his last report before the reference date in accordance with "Retirement Benefit Schemes - Transfer Values (GN11)" published by the Faculty of Actuaries and the Institute of Actuaries and current at the reference date.

(4K) The references in this regulation to the last relevant MFR valuation statement are to the statement made by the actuary in accordance with Schedule 1 to the Occupational Pension Schemes (Minimum Funding Requirement and Actuarial Valuations) Regulations 1996 and contained in the last actuarial valuation under section 57 of the 1995 Act before the reference date.

(4L) If the last relevant MFR valuation statement refers to an order for applying assets determined under section 73 of the 1995 Act that is an order modified by regulations made under that section, then the reduction under paragraph (4F) is to be made by reference to the order as so modified.

(4M) In paragraphs (4J) and (4K) "the reference date" means the date by reference to which the cash equivalent is determined.".

(5) In regulation 27(5) for "paragraph (4)", "the reference" and "a reference" substitute "paragraphs (4), (4A) and (4G)", "the references" and "references" respectively.

(6) In regulation 27(9) for "section 73 of the 1995 Act and the Occupational Pension Schemes (Winding Up) Regulations 1996" substitute "the winding up provisions and regulations made under those provisions".

(7) In regulation 27(10) for "under section 73 of the 1995 Act, section 73 of that Act applies" substitute "under section 73B(4)(b)(i) of the 1995 Act by virtue of section 73B(5) of that Act, the winding up provisions apply".

(8) In regulation 27(13) at the end insert –

" ; and

"the winding up provisions" means sections 73 to 74 of the 1995 Act.".

(9) In regulation 28(3) (increases and reductions of cash equivalents once the statement of entitlement has been sent to the eligible member) for "sections 73 and 74 of the 1995 Act and the Occupational Pension Schemes (Winding Up) Regulations 1996" substitute "the winding up provisions (as defined in regulation 27(13)) and regulations made under those provisions".

(10) In regulation 28(4) for "the Occupational Pension Schemes (Winding Up) Regulations 1996, section 73 of the 1995 Act applies" substitute "regulations made under section 73B(4)(b)(i) of the 1995 Act by virtue of section 73B(5) of that Act, the winding up provisions (as so defined) apply".

(11) This regulation only applies if the relevant proceedings commenced on or after 6th April 2005 and the scheme has not begun to be wound up before that date.

(12) In paragraph (11) "the relevant proceedings" means the proceedings for the dissolution or annulment of marriage in connection with which the order or provision mentioned in section 28(1) of the 1999 Act that resulted in entitlement to the pension credit in question was made.

Signed by authority of the Secretary of State for Work and Pensions.

Malcolm Wicks
Minister of State, Department for Work and Pensions
22nd March 2005

SCHEDULE

Regulation 14
Consequential amendments

PART 1
THE OCCUPATIONAL PENSION SCHEMES (WINDING UP) REGULATIONS 1996

1. In regulation 2 for paragraph (1) substitute -
" (1) The time when a scheme begins to be wound up shall be determined for the purposes of these Regulations in accordance with this regulation -
(a) if in accordance with section 124(3A) to (3E) the scheme began to wind up before 6th April 2005; or
(b) if immediately before that date the scheme was treated by virtue of this regulation as having begun to be wound up for those purposes.

(1A) See section 124(3A) to (3E) for the time when a scheme begins to wind up in any other case.".

2. In regulation 3[43] (modifications of s.73(3) etc.) -
(a) in the heading, at the end add "for schemes beginning to be wound up before 6th April 2005";
(b) in paragraph (1) after "Section 73(3) applies" insert "if the scheme begins to be wound up before 6th April 2005";
(c) in paragraph (1)(b) omit "and before the expiry of the transitional period";

(d) omit paragraphs (1)(c), (2) and (7);

(e) in paragraph (8), as it applies where regulation 3(d) of the Occupational Pension Schemes (Winding Up) (Amendment) Regulations 2004[44] (which substitutes a new paragraph (8) in regulation 3) does not apply, omit "and 8(4)"; and

(f) after paragraph (8) add -

"(9) Paragraph (8) does not apply where regulation 7(3)(b)(iv) of the Occupational Pension Schemes (Transfer Values) Regulations 1996 applies with the amendments in regulation 15 of the Occupational Pension Schemes (Winding up etc.) Regulations 2005.".

3. In regulation 5 (modification of schemes to fix time for settling priority of liabilities on winding up), as it applies to schemes beginning to be wound up on or after 6th April 2005 -

(a) for "section 73(3)" substitute "section 73(4)"; and

(b) for "section 73(2) and (3)" substitute "section 73(3) and (4)".

4. In regulation 7 (requirements applicable to notices of discharge under regulation 6) in the definition of "scheme administrator" in paragraph (8), for "section 630(1) of the Income and Corporation Taxes Act 1988" substitute "section 270 of the Finance Act 2004".

5. In regulation 11(1)(b) (records and information), as it applies to schemes beginning to be wound up on or after 6th April 2005, for "section 73(3)" substitute "section 73(4)".

6. For paragraph (1) of regulation 12[45] (winding up of sectionalised schemes), as it applies to schemes beginning to be wound up on or after 6th April 2005, substitute –

"(1) If -

(a) a scheme in relation to which there is more than one employer is divided into two or more sections; and

(b) the provisions of the scheme are such that they meet conditions A and B,

sections 73 to 74 apply as if each section of the scheme were a separate scheme.

(1A) Condition A is that contributions payable to the scheme by an employer, or by a member in employment under that employer, are allocated to that employer's section (or, if more than one section applies to the employer, to the section which is appropriate in respect of the employment in question).

(1B) Condition B is that a specified part or proportion of the assets of the scheme is attributable to each section and cannot be used for the purposes of any other section.

(1C) In their application to a scheme -

(a) which has been such a scheme as is mentioned in paragraph (1);

(b) which is divided into two or more sections, some or all of which apply only to members who are not in pensionable service under the section;

(c) the provisions of which have not been amended so as to prevent conditions A and B being met in relation to two or more sections; and

(d) in relation to one or more sections of which those conditions have ceased to be met at any time by reason only of there being no members in pensionable service under the section and no contributions which are to be allocated to it,

sections 73 to 74 apply as if the section in relation to which those conditions have ceased to be met were a separate scheme.

(1D) For the purposes of paragraphs (1) to (1C), any provisions of the scheme by virtue of which contributions or transfers of assets may be made to make provision for death benefits are disregarded.

(1E) But if paragraph (1) or (1C) applies and, by virtue of any provisions of the scheme, contributions or transfers of assets to make provision for death benefits are made to a section ("the death benefits section") the assets of which may only be applied for the provision of death benefits, the death benefits section is also to be treated as a separate scheme.

(1F) For the purpose of this regulation, any provisions of a scheme by virtue of which assets attributable to one section may on the winding up of the scheme or a section be used for the purposes of another section are disregarded.".

7. After regulation 12 insert -

"Schemes with partial government guarantee
12A. - (1) This regulation applies if a relevant public authority has -
(a) given a guarantee in relation to any part of a scheme, any benefits payable under the scheme or any member of the scheme; or
(b) made any other arrangements for the purposes of securing that the assets of the scheme are sufficient to meet any part of its liabilities.

(2) Where this regulation applies, sections 73 to 74 and the provisions of these Regulations (apart from this regulation) apply as if the guaranteed part of the scheme and the other part of the scheme were separate schemes.

(3) In this regulation -
"the guaranteed part of the scheme" means the part of the scheme -
(a) in relation to which the guarantee has been given;
(b) which relates to benefits payable under the scheme in relation to which the guarantee has been given; or
(c) which relates to benefits payable under the scheme in relation to the liabilities for which those other arrangements have been made; and
"relevant public authority" has the meaning given in subsection (4) of section 307 of the Pensions Act 2004 (modification of that Act in relation to certain categories of schemes).

Schemes covering United Kingdom and foreign employment
12B. - (1) --(1) Paragraph (2) applies where a scheme which applies to members in employment in the United Kingdom and members in employment outside the United Kingdom is divided into two or more sections and the provisions of the scheme are such that--
(a) different sections of the scheme apply to members in employment in the United Kingdom and to members in employment outside the United Kingdom ("the United Kingdom section" and "the foreign section");
(b) contributions payable to the scheme in respect of a member are allocated to the section applying to that member's employment;
(c) a specified part or proportion of the assets of the scheme is attributable to each section and cannot be used for the purposes of any other section; and

(d) the United Kingdom section meets the tax condition (as defined in regulation 2(1) of the Occupational Pension Schemes (Winding up etc.) Regulations 2005) and the foreign section does not do so.

(2) If this paragraph applies sections 73 to 74 and the provisions of these Regulations (apart from this regulation) apply as if each section of the scheme were a separate scheme.

(3) Paragraph (4) applies where -
(a) a scheme applies to members in employment in the United Kingdom and members in employment outside the United Kingdom;
(b) paragraph (2) does not apply to the scheme; and
(c) part of the scheme is registered under section 153 of the Finance Act 2004 (registration of pension schemes) by virtue of that part having been treated as a separate scheme under section 611(3) of the Income and Corporation Taxes Act 1988 that is treated as becoming a registered pension scheme under paragraph 1(1) of Schedule 36 to the Finance Act 2004 by virtue of paragraph 1(2) of that Schedule.

(4) If this paragraph applies, sections 73 to 74 and the provisions of these Regulations (apart from this regulation) apply as if the approved and unapproved parts of the scheme were separate schemes.

(5) In their application to a scheme -
(a) which has been such a scheme as is mentioned in paragraph (1) or (3);
(b) which is divided into two or more sections, some or all of which apply only to members who are not in pensionable service under the section;
(c) the provisions of which have not been amended so as to prevent the conditions in paragraph (1) or, as the case may be, paragraph (3) being met in relation to two or more sections; and
(d) in relation to one or more sections of which those conditions have ceased to be met at any time by reason only of there being no members in pensionable service under the section and, in the case of paragraph (1), no contributions which are to be allocated to it,
sections 73 to 74 apply and the provisions of these Regulations (apart from this regulation) apply as if any section in relation to which those conditions have ceased to be met were a separate scheme.

(6) Before 6th April 2006 paragraph (3) applies with the substitution for sub-paragraph (c) of the following paragraph -
" (c) part of the scheme has been approved by the Commissioners of the Board of Inland Revenue for the purposes of section 590 or 591 of the Income and Corporation Taxes Act 1988 by virtue of section 611(3) of that Act;".".

PART 2
OTHER REGULATIONS

Occupational Pension Schemes (Contracting-out) Regulations 1996
8. - (1) The Occupational Pension Schemes (Contracting-out) Regulations 1996[46] are amended as follows.

(2) In regulation 48 (special provision for overseas schemes) -
(a) in paragraph (5)(c) for "paragraphs (a) to (e) of section 73(3)" substitute "section 73(4)"
(b) in paragraph (5)(ca) -

(i) for "in those paragraphs" substitute "in section 73(4)"; and

(ii) after "earlier paragraphs" insert "of that section";

(c) paragraph (5A) is omitted.

) In regulation 72(2) (transitional requirements as to sufficiency of resources of salary-related schemes) for the words from "paragraphs (a) to (e)" to the end substitute "section 3(4) of the 1995 Act (liabilities towards which scheme assets must be applied first on inding up).".

ccupational Pension Schemes (Minimum Funding Requirement and Actuarial Valuations) egulations 1996

. - (1) The Occupational Pension Schemes (Minimum Funding Requirement and Actuarial aluations) Regulations 1996[47] are amended as follows.

:) In regulation 7(1)(a) (determination and valuation of liabilities) for "section 73(3)" ubstitute "section 73(4)".

3) In Schedule 1 (minimum funding valuation statements) for "section 73(3)", in each place here it occurs, substitute "section 73(4)".

)ccupational Pension Schemes (Disclosure of Information) Regulations 1996

0. In regulation 5(15) of the Occupational Pension Schemes (Disclosure of Information) .egulations 1996[48] (time when a scheme begins to be wound up for the purposes of egulation 5 of those Regulations) for the words "in accordance" onwards substitute -

(a) in a case where regulation 2 of the Occupational Pension Schemes (Winding Up) .egulations 1996 applies, in accordance with that regulation, and

o) in any other case, in accordance with section 124(3A) and (3B) of the 1995 Act (but subject ɔ section 124(3C) and (3E)).".

)ccupational Pension Schemes (Payments to Employers) Regulations 1996

1. In regulation 15(3) of the Occupational Pension Schemes (Payments to Employers) legulations 1996[49] (which makes provision about when a scheme begins to be wound up or the purposes of the saving in regulation 15(2) relating to the revocation of regulations nentioned in regulation 15(1)) for "any regulations made under section 73 of the 1995 Act" ubstitute "the Occupational Pension Schemes (Winding Up) Regulations 1996 (see both egulation 2 of those Regulations, as amended by paragraph 1 of the Schedule to the)ccupational Pension Schemes (Winding Up) Regulations 2005, and also regulation 12 of hose Regulations of 2005)".

)ccupational Pension Schemes (Assignment, Forfeiture, Bankruptcy etc.) Regulations 1997

2. In regulation 2(3) of the Occupational Pension Schemes (Assignment, Forfeiture, 3ankruptcy etc.) Regulations 1997[50] (circumstances when a scheme is being wound up for he purposes of regulation 2(1)) for "regulation 2 of the Occupational Pension Schemes Winding Up) Regulations 1996 apply" substitute "section 124(3A) and (3B) of the 1995 Act ipply (but subject to section 124(3C) and (3E))".

Jotes:

1] 1993 c.48. Section 9 is amended by sections 136(3) and (4), 151 and 177 of, and paragraphs ⒈1 and 24 of Schedule 5 and Part 3 of Schedule 7 to, the Pensions Act 1995 (c.26) and section (1) of, and paragraph 35(1) to (4) of Schedule 1 to, the Social Security Contributions Transfer of Functions, etc.) Act 1999 (c.2). Section 25(2) is substituted by paragraph 33(b) of

Schedule 5 to the Pensions Act 1995 and amended by paragraph 40(a) of Schedule 1 to t**
Social Security Contributions (Transfer of Functions, etc.) Act 1999. Section 97 is amende
by paragraph 4 of Schedule 6 to the Pensions Act 1995 and by section 56 of, and paragrap
8(1) of Schedule 5 to, the Child Support, Pensions and Social Security Act 2000 (c.1*
Sections 101I and 101L are inserted by section 37 of the Welfare Reform and Pensions A
1999 (c.30). Section 113 was amended by section 1(2)(a) of the Employment Rights (Dispu
Resolution) Act 1998 (c.8) and by section 52 of the Child Support, Pensions and Soci
Security Act 2000. Section 181(1) is cited for the meaning it gives to "prescribe" ar
"regulations". Section 183(3) was amended by sections 122, 173 and 177 of, and paragraph ∘
of Schedule 3, paragraph 15(b) of Schedule 6 and Part 1 of Schedule 7 to, the Pensions A
1995, and by section 84(1) of, and paragraphs 28 and 42 of Schedule 12 to, the Welfa
Reform and Pensions Act 1999.

[2] 1995 c.26. Section 73 is substituted and sections 73A and 73B are inserted by section 270*
of the Pensions Act 2004 (c.35). Section 74(2) is amended by sections 270(2)(b) and 320 c
and Part 1 of Schedule 13 to, that Act. Section 74(3)(e) is inserted by section 270(2)(c) of th
Act. Section 118(2) was amended by section 47(3) of the Child Support, Pensions and Soci
Security Act 2000. Section 124(1) is cited for the meaning it gives to "prescribed" an
"regulations". Subsections (3A) to (3E) are inserted into section 124 by section 49(2) of th
Child Support, Pensions and Social Security Act 2000.

[3] 1999 c.30.

[4] 2004 c.35.

[5] 2004 c.12.

[6] *See* section 185 of the Pension Schemes Act 1993 and section 120 of the Pensions Act 199
which provide that the Secretary of State must consult such persons as he may conside
appropriate before making regulations for the purposes of the provisions for the purposes ∘
which these Regulations are made. This duty does not apply where regulations are mad
before the end of the period of six months beginning with the coming into force of an
enactment upon which the regulations are consequential.

[7] *See* section 83(11) of the Welfare Reform and Pensions Act 1999.

[8] S.I. 1996/3126.

[9] 1988 c.1.

[10] 1972 c.11.

[11] 1987 c.45.

[12] Section 615(6) was amended by section 79 of, and paragraph 11 of Schedule 10 to, th
Finance Act 1999 (c.16).

[13] Section 23 is substituted by section 36(3) of the Pensions Act 2004.

[14] 1963 c.xxxii.

[15] Section 611A was inserted by section 75 of, and paragraph 15 of Schedule 6 to, th
Finance Act 1989 (c.26) and amended by section 52(1) of, and paragraph 5 of Schedule 5 t∘
the Finance Act 1999. The definition of "relevant benefits" was amended by section 79 o
and paragraph 10(1) of Schedule 10 to, the Finance Act 1999.

[16] Paragraphs 5, 15 and 19 are modified in their application to cash balance schemes b
regulation 25 of the Pension Protection Fund (Compensation) Regulations 2005 (S.
2005/670).

[17] S.I. 2005/449.

[18] Paragraph 23A is inserted by regulation 3 of the Occupational Pension Scheme
(Modification of Pension Protection Provisions) Regulations 2005 (S.I 2005/705).

[19] Regulation 3(4) of the Pension Protection Fund (Hybrid Schemes) (Modification) Regulations 2005 modifies Schedule 7 in its application to hybrid schemes so that it reads as if it contained paragraph 31A.

[20] Sub-paragraph (6B) is inserted by regulation 22 of the Pension Protection Fund (Compensation) Regulations 2005.

[21] Chapter 5 of Part 4 of the Pension Schemes Act 1993 is inserted by section 264 of the Pensions Act 2004.

[22] Section 73A is inserted by section 270 of the Pensions Act 2004.

[23] Section 73B is inserted by section 270 of the Pensions Act 2004.

[24] Regulation 4(1) is amended by regulation 2 of S.I. 2004/403 and regulation 2(2) of S.I. 2005/72. (See also regulations 4A and 4B which are inserted respectively by regulation 3(3) of S.I. 2002/380 and regulation 2(5) of S.I. 2004/403). Regulation 4C is inserted by regulation 2(4) of S.I. 2005/72.

[25] Section 74(3)(c) was amended by S.I. 2001/3649.

[26] S.I. 1996/1536; relevant amending instruments are S.I. 1997/786 and 2000/2691.

[27] The publication GN19 may be obtained from the Institute of Actuaries, Staple Inn Hall, High Holborn, London WC1V 7QJ and from the Faculty of Actuaries, Maclaurin House, 18 Dublin Street, Edinburgh EH1 3PP.

[28] Section 74(2) and (4) is amended by sections 270(2)(b) and (d) and 320 of, and Part 1 of Schedule 13 to, the Pensions Act 2004.

[29] Paragraph (e) is inserted by section 270(2)(c) of the Pensions Act 2004.

[30] S.I. 1996/1172; relevant amending instruments are S.I. 1997/786, 2000/2975 and 2002/681.

[31] S.I. 1997/785; the relevant amending instrument is S.I. 2002/681.

[32] S.I. 2000/1054.

[33] S.I. 2002/459.

[34] Regulation 12 is amended by S.I. 1997/786 and the Schedule to these Regulations. Regulations 12A and 12B are inserted by the Schedule to these Regulations.

[35] S.I. 1996/1847.

[36] Regulation 7(3)(b)(iv) is amended by S.I. 1997/786.

[37] Regulation 8 is amended by S.I. 2003/1727.

[38] The publication GN11 may be obtained from the Institute of Actuaries, Staple Inn Hall, High Holborn, London WC1V 7QJ and from the Faculty of Actuaries, Maclaurin House, 18 Dublin Street, Edinburgh EH1 3PP.

[39] Section 93A is inserted by section 153 of the Pensions Act 1995 and amended by section 84(1) of, and paragraph 34 of Schedule 12 to, the Welfare Reform and Pensions Act 1999.

[40] S.I. 2000/1052 as amended by S.I. 2000/2691 and 2003/1727.

[41] S.I. 2000/1053; the relevant amending instrument is S.I. 2003/1727.

[42] S.I. 2000/1054; the relevant amending instruments are S.I. 2000/2691 and 2003/1727.

[43] Regulation 3 was amended by S.I. 1999/3198 and 2004/1140.

[44] S.I. 2004/1140.

[45] Regulation 12 was amended by S.I. 1997/786.

[46] S.I. 1996/1172; the relevant amending instrument is S.I. 1997/786.

[47] S.I. 1996/1536; the relevant amending instrument is S.I. 2004/3031.

[48] S.I. 1996/1655; the relevant amending instrument is S.I. 1997/786.

[49] S.I. 1996/2156, to which there are amendments not relevant to these Regulations.

[50] S.I. 1997/785, to which there are amendments not relevant to these Regulations.

A2.10: Occupational Pension Schemes (Winding up Procedure) regulations 2006 [in draft]

Made ----[ ]
Laid before Parliament [ ]
Coming into force --2006

The Secretary of State, being a Minister designated[1]for the purposes of section 2(2) of the European Communities Act 1972[2], in relation to matters relating to personal and occupational pensions makes the following Regulations in exercise of the powers conferred by section 2(2) of that Act and sections 113(1), 181(1) and 182(2) and (3) of the Pension Schemes Act 1993[3] and sections 60(2)(h), 69(2)(a) and 318(1) of the Pensions Act 2004[4].

In accordance with section 185(1) of the Pensions Schemes Act 1993[5] and section 317(1) of the Pensions Act 2004, the Secretary of State has consulted such persons as he considers appropriate before making these Regulations.

Citation and commencement

1. These Regulations may be cited as the Occupational Pension Schemes (Winding up Procedure Requirement) Regulations 2006 and shall come into force on [2006].

Application

2.—(1) These Regulations apply to an occupational pension scheme in respect of which a recovery plan has been prepared under section 226 of the Pensions Act 2004 (recovery plan) and the scheme begins to wind up during the recovery period.

(2) In this regulation, the "recovery period" means the period specified in the scheme's recovery plan in accordance with section 226(2)(b) of that Act.

Amendment of the Pensions Act 2004 [section 2(2) of the European Communities Act 1972]

3.—(1) After section 231 of the Pensions Act 2004 (powers of the Regulator) insert—

"Requirements for winding up procedure

231A.—(1) Where an occupational pension scheme in respect of which a recovery plan has been prepared under section 226 begins to wind up during the recovery period, the trustees or managers of the scheme must as soon as reasonably practicable—

    (a) prepare a winding up procedure, if there is no existing winding up procedure in force;

    (b) if there is an existing winding up procedure in force, review and if necessary revise it.

(2) A winding up procedure must—

    (a) set out the steps to be taken to discharge the liabilities to or in respect of the members of the scheme, in respect of pensions or other benefits, in accordance with section 74 of the Pensions Act 1995 (discharge of liabilities by insurance etc.), and

    (b) be appropriate having regard to the nature and circumstances of the scheme.

(3) A winding up procedure must—

    (a) set out the action to be taken to establish the liabilities to or in respect of the members of the scheme, in respect of pensions or other benefits, and to recover any assets of the scheme;

(b) give an estimate of the amount of time it will take to establish those liabilities and to recover any such assets;

(c) give an indication of which of the accrued rights or benefits (if any), to which a person is entitled under the scheme, are likely to be affected by a reduction in actuarial value;

(d) specify the manner in which the liabilities to or in respect of the members of the scheme, in respect of pensions or other benefits, will be discharged in accordance with section 74(3) of the Pensions Act 1995;

(e) give an estimate of the amount of time it will take to discharge those liabilities.

(4) The requirement imposed by subsection (3)(c) applies only to the extent that the trustees or managers have sufficient information to give such an indication.

(5) The trustees or managers must send a copy of any winding up procedure to the Regulator as soon as reasonably practicable after it has been prepared or, as the case may be, revised.

(6) Where any requirement of this section is not complied with, section 10 of the Pensions Act 1995 (civil penalties) applies to a trustee or manager who has failed to take all reasonable steps to secure compliance.

(7) In this section "recovery period", in relation to an occupational pension scheme, means the period specified in the scheme's recovery plan in accordance with section 226(2)(b).".

Amendment of the Occupational Pension Schemes (Disclosure of Information) Regulations 1996

[sections 113 and 182(2) and (3) of the Pension Schemes Act 1993]

4.—(1) Amend the Occupational Pension Schemes (Disclosure of Information) Regulations 1996[6] as follows.

(2) In regulation 7(1) (availability of other documents), after sub-paragraph (d) insert—

"(e) an outline of the winding up procedure prepared or revised under section 231A of the 2004 Act,".

Amendment of the Register of Occupational and Personal Pension Schemes Regulations 2005

[sections 60(2)(h) and 318(1) of the Pensions Act 2004]

5.—(1) Amend the Register of Occupational and Personal Pension Schemes Regulations 2005[7] as follows.

(2) In regulation 3 (registrable information)—

(a) after paragraph (1)(f) add—

"(g) in the case where an occupational pension scheme in respect of which a recovery plan has been prepared under section 226 of the Act begins to wind up during the recovery period, the date on which the winding up commenced;".

(b) after paragraph (5) add—

"(6) In paragraph (1)(g), "recovery period" means the period specified in the scheme's recovery plan in accordance with section 226(2)(b) of the Act.".

Amendment of the Occupational Pension Schemes (Scheme Funding) Regulations 2005

[sections 69(2)(a) and 318(1) of the Pensions Act 2004]

6.—(1) Amend the Occupational Pension Schemes (Scheme Funding) Regulations 2005[8] as follows.

(2) In regulation 8 (recovery plan), omit paragraph (8).

(3) In regulation 17 (exemptions – general)—

(a) in paragraph (1)(l), for "subject to regulation 18" substitute "subject to paragraph (1A) and regulation 18";

(b) after paragraph (1) insert—

(1A) Section 231A of the 2004 Act applies to a scheme in respect of which a recovery plan has been prepared under section 226 of the 2004 Act and the scheme begins to wind up during the recovery period.

(4) In paragraph (2), in the appropriate alphabetical place insert—

""recovery period" means the period specified in the scheme's recovery plan in accordance with section 226(2)(b) of the 2004 Act.".

Signed by authority of the Secretary of State for Work and Pensions.

[Name]

Minister of State,

[2006] Department for Work and Pensions

Notes:

[1] See S.I. 2004/3328.

[2] 1972 c.68.

[3] 1993 c.48; section 113(1) was amended by section 52(1) of the Child Support, Pensions and Social Security Act 2000 (c.19). Section 181(1) is cited because of the meaning there given to "prescribed" and "regulations".

[4] 2004 c.35; section 318(1) is cited because of the meaning there given to "prescribed" and "regulations".

[5] Section 185(1) is amended by paragraph 80(a) of Schedule 5 to the Pensions Act 1995 (c.26).

[6] S.I. 1996/1655; the relevant amending instrument is S.I. 2005/3377.

[7] S.I. 2005/597.

[8] S.I. 2005/3377.

A3   Case law

A3.1:   Bradstock Group Pension Scheme [2002] 69 PBLR

UK: England and Wales: High Court: Chancery Division, 2002 June 17

Headnote

Minimum funding requirement – MFR – Scheme in deficit – Claim against the employer – Pensions Act 1995 s75 – Debt on the employer – Whether recoverable – Whether trustees can make compromise where there is a statutory debt – Scheme in wind-up

Facts

A pension scheme was in deficit according to the minimum funding requirements of the Pensions Act 1995 ss55-61. Under the Pensions Act 1975 s75 the trustees were required to make good some of the deficit by reclaiming the debt from the employer.

The employer had no realistic prospect of settling the debt within the statutory time scale; the trustees negotiated a compromise with the company under which the scheme was to be wound-up resulting in less than they were entitled to but more than they would have received had the company been put into liquidation.

The trustees applied to the court for ratification of the compromise, in particular seeking a declaration that the trustees had a power to compromise a statutory debt.

Law

There is no reason why as a matter of construction or public policy trustees are not able to compromise or otherwise deal with a statutory debt arising under Pensions Act 1995 s75 in the exercise of their powers under Trustee Act 1925.

It is contrary to the purpose of the minimum funding requirement (MFR) legislation if trustees are prevented from compromising any debt due under the legislation and being forced to take steps which would produce less for a scheme.

Decision

The trustees were permitted to make a compromise.

Cases referred to

Johnson v Moreton [1980] AC 37
Public Trustees v Paul Cooper (unrep) 20 December 1999

Also reported at

Bradstock Group Pension Scheme Trustees Ltd v Bradstock Group plc and others [2002] (10 July) The Times Law Reports; [2002] Law Society's Gazette 99/36 19 September p40

Legislation referred to

Trustee Act 1925 s15

Pensions Act 1995 ss55 to 61, 75

Insolvency Act 1986 s247(2)

Statutory instruments

Occupational Pension Schemes (Deficiency on Winding Up etc) Regulations 1996 SI No 3128

Judgment

In the High Court of Justice, Chancery Division

Between

Bradstock Group Pension Scheme Trustees Limited
Claimant

and

Bradstock Group Plc
Bradstock Group Services Ltd
Gordon Douglas
Defendants

CHARLES ALDOUS QC

sitting as Deputy High Court judge

The Claimant, Bradstock Group Pension Scheme Trustees Ltd, is the Trustee of the Bradstock Group Pension Scheme ('the Scheme'), an exempt approved occupational pension scheme governed by a definitive deed and rules dated 23 March 1983, as subsequently amended. Bradstock Group Services Ltd is the principal employer under the Scheme, with the holding company, Bradstock Group PLC being the other employer. The main business of the Bradstock Group is reinsurance broking. As at 1 April 2001 there were 46 active members of the Scheme, 454 deferred members and 36 pensioners.

The Scheme, which is a final salary scheme, is subject to the statutory minimum funding requirements ('MFR') imposed by Sections 55 to 61 Pensions Act 1995 and associated regulations. In short these require periodic actuarial valuations of the Scheme. If funding a deficiency is disclosed, the actuary has to certify a schedule of contributions designed to ensure that the Scheme is fully funded by a pre-ordained date. Where, as in this case, the MFR valuation disclosed a serious under-provision (that is where the assets are less than 90% of the liabilities) the employer is to be required to bring the Scheme up to at least 90% of the MFR by 5 April 2003 by stepped interim payments. The MFR regime continues to operate so long as the Scheme is on going. If the Scheme is wound up or the employer goes into liquidation, Section 75 comes into operation; which in broad terms creates an unsecured non-preferential debt owed by the employer for the whole shortfall. Where, as here, there is more than one employer (and in the absence of any modifications of the Scheme by the Trustee) the Section 75 debt is to be apportioned between the employers in proportion to the amounts of the Scheme's liabilities attributable to each employee's employment.

The Scheme is in very substantial deficit. An actuarial valuation as at 1 October 2000 reported a deficit in the Scheme's funding of over £26 million, representing a funding level of only 59%. A MFR valuation as at 1 April 2001, signed off in December, reported a MFR deficit of over £14.5 million, representing a funding level of 74%. The Scheme actuary reported recently that if the MFR valuation was projected to March 2002 the deficit would be [approximately] £15.5 million. As a result of the MFR valuation, the Trustee served a MFR schedule on the two employer companies ('the Employers') setting out the necessary payments to bring the Scheme up to the 90% level by 5 April 2003, in accordance with Section 60. This schedule required a payment of £1.7 million by 30 June 2002.

The Employers have no realistic prospect of being able to pay the June instalment and the remaining funds required to be paid by April 2003. Unless the deficit can be compromised, the Group will be forced into liquidation. Although the Employers will be liable for the deficit under Section 75, because of the Group's financial position if it is forced into liquidation, the Trustee will only receive a small proportion of this deficit. The Trustee, with experienced professional legal and accountancy advice, has negotiated a compromise sought by the Employers under which the Scheme will receive significantly more than it would recover in a liquidation, but still considerably less than the full amount of the MFR deficit; with the result that pension benefits will have to be scaled back substantially.

Under the proposed compromise, which was subject to Court approval, the Scheme is to be wound up following notice by the Employers to discontinue contributions and simultaneously the Section 75 debt is to be compromised by an immediate cash payment plus deferred consideration, suitably secured and guaranteed.

The application brought by the Trustees for directions as to whether to enter into the compromise is in accordance with the circumstances in which trustees customarily apply to the Court for guidance, as set out by Hart J in Public Trustees v Paul Cooper (unrep) 20 December 1999. The Third Defendant was joined as a representative beneficiary of the Scheme, being a deferred member. All three parties were represented by leading counsel; Mr Furness QC for the Trustee, Mr Inglis-Jones QC for the representative beneficiary and Mr Ham QC for the Employers.

The application raised two issues. First, whether it is possible as a matter of law to compromise a statutory debt arising under Section 75 Pensions Act 1995, and second whether, if so, the Court regards the proposed compromise as one which in the circumstances a reasonable and properly advised trustee could enter into in the exercise of its powers. In making the application the Trustee was not surrendering its discretion to the Court.

Because of the urgency, I made an Order at the hearing to enable the Deed of Compromise to be entered into without delay. This judgment deals only with the first issue, namely whether it is possible as a matter of law to compromise a Section 75 debt in the way proposed. The issue as to whether, if so, it was reasonable for the Trustee to do so was heard in private and in the absence of the Employers. I was taken through the evidence filed by both the Trustee and the representative beneficiary, including accountants' reports and legal advice. It is sufficient for the purpose of this judgment to say that I was entirely satisfied that it was a reasonable compromise for the Trustee to enter into. The terms of the compromise had been reached after extensive negotiations between the parties and their advisers. No better terms could be secured. The financial position of the Group had been examined by the Trustee's accountants, Baker Tilly, who had provided a series of reports assessing the worth of the compromise against likely recoveries in a liquidation. This had in turn been scrutinised by PKF, accountants, appointed by the Third Defendant.

The Trustee and the Third Defendant and their respective advisers were unanimous in the view that the compromise was in the best interest of the general body of members, in that, if no compromise was agreed, the Group would be forced into insolvency proceedings within a very short time, resulting, as I say, in the Scheme receiving significantly less. This would be so even if the Group did not survive in the long term and subsequently went into liquidation before the Scheme was finally wound up and the full deferred consideration received. The Trustees did not therefore have the option of rejecting the compromise, of the Scheme continuing and the Employers meeting their MFR payments.

Returning to the first issue; although Mr Inglis-Jones QC said that he thought the Trustees could compromise a Section 75 debt, he very properly put forward possible contrary arguments. One of which was that the effect, if this were permitted, would be to allow Trustees and Employers to contract out of the statutory MFR regime, which is impermissible. I should refer to Section 75; subsection (1) reads as follows:

'If, in the case of an occupational pension scheme, the value at the applicable time of the assets of the scheme is less than the amount at that time of the liabilities of the scheme, an amount equal to the difference shall be treated as a debt due from the employer to the trustees or managers of the scheme.'

Liabilities and assets are to be valued in accordance with regulations (section 75(5)), which are currently the Occupational Pension Schemes (Deficiency on Winding Up etc) Regulations 1996 SI No 3128 ('the Deficiency Regulations') as amended, with effect from 19 March 2002 by the 2002 Regulations. 'The application time' is defined (section 75(3)) as:
'(a) if the scheme is being wound up before a relevant insolvency event occurs in relation to the employer at any time when it is being wound up before such an event occurs and
(b) otherwise, immediately before the relevant insolvency event occurs.'

'Relevant insolvency event' for a company means going into liquidation as defined in section 247(2) of the Insolvency Act 1986.

I was referred to the well known authority of *Johnson v Moreton [1980] AC* p. 37 in which the House of Lords held that a tenant of an agricultural holding could not contract out of his statutory right to security of tenure. Two general principles are to be deduced from this decision. First, that one cannot contract out of a statutory right or obligation if it is implicit from the whole statutory code that it does not merely provide for private rights and obligations but that there is also a public interest underlying it which will be undermined by any right to contract out. Second, that even where contracting out is not expressly prohibited, it will not be permitted if by necessary implication it can be seen that to be able to contract out would defeat the very object of the statutory provision and reinstate the mischief which the statutory provision was designed to remedy (see in particular Ld Salmon at p52; Ld Hailsham at pp58-61, and Ld Simon at pp67-68).

It was rightly accepted that it was not possible to contract out of the trustees' and employer's obligations to comply with the MFR regulations nor in advance to contract out of the provisions of Section 75. If it were permissible, employers would be able to insert appropriate exclusionary provisions in the Scheme document which would defeat the whole purpose of the legislation. Many of the provisions are mandatory. Statutory obligations are imposed on trustees to ensure compliance. Underlying the provisions is the need not only to protect members and pensioners but to maintain public confidence in occupational pension schemes generally. Whilst the Scheme is ongoing trustees cannot waive the need for compliance nor negotiate a more lenient schedule of contributions than the regulations prescribed; nor equally can they, in my judgment, contract out of the effect of Section 75 in advance of the Section coming into play. However, there is a clear distinction between this and trustees compromising or setting a debt which has arisen under Section 75 in the best way they reasonably can for the benefit of their Scheme members. Allowing trustees to compromise Section 75 liabilities does not offend the mischief of the Act. Section 75 characterises the shortfall as a debt. I can see no reason why as a matter of construction or public policy trustees should not be able to compromise or otherwise deal with such a debt in the exercise of their powers under Section 15 Trustees Act 1925. To do so is not a case of contracting out of the provision but rather of enforcing it by means which the trustees honestly and reasonably believe secures the largest amount towards the shortfall. In other words it is giving effect to the legislation in the best practical way, consistent with the exercise of the trustees' general powers. This is the very opposite of contracting out. Here the Trustee has agreed to the compromise in the knowledge of the funding deficit and the Employers' financial position, seeking to obtain payment of as much of the shortfall as it believes it can reasonably recover. Trustees can compromise a claim under Section 75 just as they could decide not to enforce it if in doing so they would incur costs which were disproportionate to any reasonably expected recovery. There is no overriding statutory purpose or public interest to require trustees to enforce the claim to a Section 75 debt to the point of forcing the employer into liquidation, regardless of the recovery. Indeed it would be contrary to the purpose of the MFR legislation if trustees were to be prevented from compromising the debt and forced to take steps which would produce less for the Scheme when this would be a conflict with their ordinary duties as trustees towards their members. The position is no different where, as here, the Scheme is to be put into winding up as part of the compromise, when this would have happened in any event and where it is appropriate to compromise the debt once it has arisen.

A question arose as to whether by reason of the reference to 'any time' in Section 75(3) a trustee could serve more than one deficit notice whilst the Scheme was in the course of winding up and before the employer went into liquidation. If so, the issue was whether it could be said that more than one debt could arise in the future which trustees could not fetter their right to enforce by compromising it in advance. It may take a considerable time to complete the winding up. Even if not strictly a separate debt, could it be said that trustees cannot compromise a Section 75 debt as the amount might vary during the course of the winding up because of changed financial circumstances affecting the size of the deficit? Could it be said that trustees cannot deprive themselves of the right to serve a further notice?

I am inclined to the view that the reference to 'any time' merely enables the amount of the shortfall to be determined by the actuary at any time within the course of the winding up, but once determined and certified it is no longer open to issue a second certificate at a later date. If it had been open to serve further certificates one would expect to see a mechanism providing for recalculation of the deficit, both upwards and downwards, from time to time during the winding up to take account of changed conditions. However, I am aware that some specialists take a different view. The point was not argued out before me. It is unnecessary for me to decide this as the answer here lies in the terms of Section 15 Trustee Act, which permits trustees to compromise both accrued and prospective liabilities, at least where one of those liabilities has arisen or is about to arise in the circumstances set out above.

Accordingly there is in my judgment no obstacle as a matter of law or principle to the proposed compromise of the Employer's Section 75 liability.

Representation

Michael Furness QC (instructed by Pinsent Curtis Biddle) appeared on behalf of the claimant.

Nigel Inglis-Jones QC and Nicolas Stallworthy (instructed by Nabarro Nathanson) appeared on behalf of the representative beneficiary.

Robert Ham QC (instructed by Ashurst Morris Crisp) appeared on behalf of the employers.

Comment

There is an increasing understanding by the courts of the difficulties facing pension schemes, especially in wind-up and especially where the assets are less than they might have been. This decision, together with the Owens Corning decision ([2000] 68 PBLR) reflect the new pragmatism and commercialism of the courts in helping trustees make difficult and unpalatable decisions in difficult cases. The issue which has yet to be settled, and where there are contrasting approaches in this and the Corning case, is in the representation of the members or other parties affected. The courts are as yet uncomfortable with ex-parte applications, but until there is a reformed OPRA with a power to make such decisions on behalf of trustees it will be a brave (though sensible) trustee who would make such applications without arranging for separate representation. However Lord Woolf has mentioned from time to time that separate representation should be kept to a minimum, and certainly the cost to a pension scheme already in deficit to have separate counsel and solicitors can be disproportionate. Maybe it is time for a short protocol to be devised by the Association of Pension Lawyers and the courts to allow for ex-parte applications in suitable cases.

Importance φφφφ

3.2: Phoenix Venture Holdings Ltd [2005] 38 PBLR, [2005] EWHC 1379 (Ch)

UK: England and Wales: High Court: Chancery Division: Companies Court, 2005 May 20

Headnote

Insolvency of employer – Pension Protection Fund – Multi-employer pension scheme – Winding up – Company's application for injunction to restrain trustee from presenting winding up petition – Size of debt – Whether debt arises before completion of actuary's calculations

Facts

Phoenix was one of a scheme's six participating employers; in April 2005 the principal employer was placed into administration. The scheme was then put into winding-up in accordance with its own rules by the trustee a week or so later.

At that time the amount of the deficit attributable to the company as an employer under the Pensions Act 1995 ss75 was £200,000. The trustee immediately executed a deed of amendment purporting to amend the scheme so as to confer on itself power to apportion the deficit amongst all employers in such shares as the trustee might in its absolute discretion think fit.

The trustee indicated that it would then be seeking from the company payment of about 15m, and then resolved that all the scheme's participating employers were jointly and severally liable for the whole of the deficit estimated to be in excess of £400m. The company disputed the validity of that resolution.

Later, in May, the trustee further resolved to apportion £25m as the share of the deficit as at the end of April attributable to the company and reserved the right to apportion to the company a further part of the deficit. Accordingly the prospective liability of the company was increased from £200,000 to £15m, £25m or £400m by the exercise of certain powers conferred by the scheme or by statute.

The company contended that such powers did not authorise what was done nor were they validly exercised; it applied for an injunction to restrain the trustee from presenting a petition to wind up the company or applying for an administration order in respect of the company on the ground that the debts of £400m or £25m alleged to be due by the company to the trustee were bona fide disputed on substantial grounds.

The company complained that in the space of a little over three weeks the prospective liability of the Company was increased from £200,000 (being the default position under the Regulations) to £15m to £400m and then back to £25m by the exercise of certain powers conferred by the Scheme or by statute. It contended that such powers did not authorise what was done nor were they validly exercised on a number of grounds each of which gives rise to a bona fide dispute on substantial grounds.

Law

There cannot be a debt until a sum certain has been ascertained. The designation of the time is so that the Actuary may know as of what date his calculations should be made. But until those calculations have been made in the prescribed manner the difference between the value of the assets and the amount of the liabilities cannot be ascertained and an amoun equal to that difference remains uncertain.

A debt can only arise after the commencement of the winding up of a scheme when th actuary has made the prescribed calculations and a deficit emerges. Accordingly it wa necessary to substitute the word 'after' for the word 'when'. A debt arises when th calculations are made and its amount quantified.

Pension Protection Fund (Multi-Employer Schemes) Regulations 2005 (SI 2005/441) are unusual complexity even in the field of pensions legislation.

Decision

The resolutions of the trustees requiring payment of the buy-out deficit were void. Th company accepted that the sums of £200,000 and a further sum of about £1.5m in anoth scheme were contingent or prospective liabilities such as the trustee would be entitled present a petition for the winding up of the company. The court enjoined the trustee fro presenting any petition to wind up the company for a period to be specified. If security f £1.7m were provided in that period then the injunction would continue so as to preclud reliance on either resolution. If such security were not provided within that period then th injunction would be discharged so as to permit the trustee to rely on its status as contingent or prospective creditor in the sums of £200,000 and £1.5m.

Cases referred to

Re Hastings-Bass [1975] Ch 25
Mann v Goldstein [1968] 1 WLR 1091
Stonegate Securities Ltd v Gregory [1980] 1 Ch 576
Vatcher v Paull [1915] AC 372

Legislation referred to

Pensions Act 1995 ss 23(1), 68, 75, 75A
Pensions Act 2004 s121
Companies Act 1985 s425
Insolvency Act 1986 s124(1)

Statutory instruments

The Occupational Pension Schemes (Employer Debt) Regulations 2005 *SI 2005 No 678 r* *6(2)(a)*
Pension Protection Fund (Multi-Employer Schemes) Regulations 2005 *SI 2005 No 441*

Judgment

Re Phoenix Venture Holdings Ltd (Company No 2692 of 2005)
[2005] EWHC 1379 (Ch)
Chancery Division
Sir Andrew Morritt V-C
20 May 2005

[2005] All ER (D) 325 (May)
[2005] EWHC 1379 (Ch)
Chancery Division (Companies Court)
20 May 2005

SIR ANDREW MORRITT VC

This is the application of Phoenix Venture Holdings Ltd ('the Company') for an injunction to restrain Independent Trustee Services Ltd ('the Trustee') as the sole trustee of the MG Rover Group Pension Scheme ('the Scheme') from:

(1) presenting a petition to wind up the Company, or

(2) applying for an administration order in respect of the Company, on the ground that the debt alleged to be due by the Company to the Trustee of:

(a) £400m as claimed in a letter dated 5 May 2005 from the Trustee to the Company to have been apportioned to it by a resolution of the Trustee made on 28 April 2005, or

(b) £25m allegedly apportioned to the Company by a resolution of the Trustee made on 12 May 2005,

is in each case bona fide disputed on substantial grounds.

In summary, the Scheme was put into winding-up in accordance with its own rules by the Trustee on 19 April 2005. At that time the amount of the deficit attributable to the Company as an employer under ss75 and 75A Pensions Act 1995 and Reg.6(2)(a) The Occupational Pension Schemes (Employer Debt) Regulations 2005 (SI 2005/678) was approximately £200,000. On the same day, that is 19 April 2005, the Trustee executed a Deed of Amendment ('the Deed of Amendment') purporting to amend the scheme pursuant to Rule 5 thereof or under s68(2) Pensions Act 1995 so as to confer on itself power to apportion the deficit amongst all employers in such shares as the Trustee might in its absolute discretion think fit. In a telephone conversation between representatives of the Trustee and the Company on 28 April 2005, the representatives of the Trustee indicated that the Trustee would be seeking from the Company, through the exercise of that power, payment of about £15m. Yet on the same day, in response to the Company's indication that a sum of £15m would be beyond its means, those representatives resolved on behalf of the Trustee that all the Scheme's participating employers should be jointly and severally liable for the whole of the deficit estimated to be in excess of £400m. The Company disputed the validity of that resolution. On 12 May 2005, the Trustee further resolved to apportion £25m as the share of the deficit as at 28 April 2005 attributable to the Company, and reserved the right to apportion to the Company a further part of the deficit. Thus, in the space of a little over three weeks the prospective liability of the Company was increased from £200,000 (being the default position under the Regulations) to £15m to £400m and then back to £25m by the exercise of certain powers conferred by the Scheme or by statute. The Company contends that such powers did not authorise what was done nor were they validly exercised on a number of grounds each of which gives rise to a bona fide dispute on substantial grounds. But before considering those grounds it is necessary to set out the facts in greater detail and to describe the statutory background.

Facts

In May 2001 Techtronic (2000) Ltd acquired the MG Rover Group from BMW.

A new MG Rover Group Pension scheme was set up by a Deed and Rules dated 2 May 2001 to commence with effect from 9 May 2001. There were six participating employers namely:

a) MG Rover Group Ltd with about 4,700 employees,

b) Powertrain Ltd with about 1,200 employees,

c) the Company with 8 current employees and 2 deferred or pensioner members,

d) Phoenix Venture Resourcing Ltd, with 59 employees,

(e) Phoenix Venture Distribution Ltd, with 7 employees

(f) MG Sport and Racing Ltd, with about 41 employees.

The Scheme contains the following relevant rules:

(a) Rule 5 confers a power to modify the provisions of the Scheme in the following terms:

'5.1Subject to Rules 5.2 and 5.3, the Principal Employer and the Trustees may together by deed change all or any of the provisions of this deed or other provisions of the Scheme including this Rule 5 in any way. Any change shall take effect from the date specified in the deed making the change, which date may be earlier or later than the date of that deed.'

(b) Rule 28 deals with the situation of the withdrawal of an employer and provides:

'28.1 An Employer shall cease to participate in the Scheme forthwith upon the happening of any of the following [events]: ...

(b) an Insolvency Event in relation to that Employer. ...

28.3   With effect from the date on which an Employer becomes a Former Employer, it is not liable to make contributions to the Scheme apart from those due to be made on or before that date, and its liability to observe and perform the provisions of the Scheme shall cease.'

(c) Rule 31 provides for the closure of the Scheme in these terms:

'31 Closing the Scheme

31.1 On and with effect from the first of the dates specified in Rule 31.2:

(a) all the Members shall cease to accrue benefits and shall cease to be Members; and

(b) no Employee shall be admitted to Membership; and

(c) the Scheme will be continued as a closed fund.

31.2   The dates are:

(a) the date on which the Principal Employer ceases to participate in the Scheme in consequence of the Rule 28.1(b) or (c) {withdrawal of employer};'

Such a closure enables the scheme to be wound up in accordance with Rule 35.

(d) Rule 34 deals with what is described as the transfer of powers. So far as relevant it provides:

'34.1 If the Principal Employer either:

(a) ceases to participate in the Scheme following an Insolvency Event in relation to the Principal Employer; or

(b) has its name struck off the register by the Registrar of Companies

then all the powers of the Principal Employer (including the Old Principal Employer) in relation to the Scheme shall be exercisable by the Trustees in the place of the Principal Employer. In that event Rule 2.4 shall apply to those powers in the place of Rule 2.3.'

In that connection it is necessary to note Rules 2.3 and 2.4 which are in the following terms:

'2.3Subject to Rule 2.2, each of the Principal Employer and the Employers in making any decision or in giving or withholding its agreement or consent or in exercising or not exercising any power in relation to the Scheme shall do so at its absolute and uncontrolled discretion and for its own benefit and shall owe no duty to any Employer, Employee Beneficiary or any other person.

2.4 Subject to the performance of their duties and Rule 2.2, the Trustees in making any decision or in giving or withholding their agreement or consent or in exercising or no' exercising any power in relation to the Scheme shall do so at their absolute and uncontrolled discretion.'

On 6 April 2005 the Pensions Act 2004 came into force and the Pension Protection Fund ('PPF') came into existence. I shall have to consider in due course the conditions under which the liabilities of the Scheme may be taken over by the PPF.

On 8 April 2005 MG Rover Group Ltd, the Principal Employer under the Scheme was placed in administration (Powertrain Ltd was also placed into administration on that day). The effects of MG Rover Group Ltd as Principal Employer going into administration included the following:

(i) Scheme members ceased to accrue benefits,

(ii) the Scheme continued as a closed fund,

(iii)the powers in relation to the Scheme of the MG Rover Group Ltd as Principal Employer became exercisable by the Trustee under Rule 34.1.

On 12 April 2005 MG Sport and Racing Ltd was put into administration, and the Trustee was appointed to be trustee of the Scheme by The Pensions Regulator under s23(1) of Pensions Act 1995.

On 18 April 2005 the previously existing trustees were removed.

On 19 April 2005 the Trustee put the Scheme into winding-up in accordance with Rule 35. One consequence was that ss75 and 75A Pensions Act 1995, as amended by Pensions Act 2004, together with associated regulations, came into operation. These provisions created a liability on employers to fund any deficit in the scheme as certified by the Actuary. At that time the prospective liability of the Company pro rata to the service of those of its employees who had accrued benefits under the Scheme was approximately £200,000. On the same day, the Trustee executed a Deed of Amendment. It recited the Scheme, the administration of MG Group Rover Ltd, the fact that it was the Principal Employer, and the relevant provisions of the Rules, s68 Pensions Act 1995 and Reg.16 of the Employer Debt Regulations. It continued:

'This deed provides as follows:

1   In exercise of the power contained in Rule 5 of the Deed and Rules, its power to exercise all the powers of the principal employer under Rule 34.1 of the Deed and Rules and its power to exercise all trustee discretions pursuant to section 25(2) of the 1995 Act the Trustee hereby AMENDS the Deed and Rules with effect from the date of this deed as follows:

1.1 The following is added as a new Rule 35.1 and the existing Rules 35.1 to 35.5 are renumbered as Rules 35-36 accordingly:

'If a debt arises under section 75A of the 1995 Act when the Scheme commences winding-up, the debt shall be apportioned amongst the Employers in such shares as the Trustee in its absolute discretion determines.'

1.2 All references in the Deed and Rules to Rules 35.1 to 35.5 are replaced with references to Rules 35.2 to 35.6 respectively.

2   If and to the extent that the amendment described in clause 1 of this deed is deemed to be ineffective or invalid, the Trustee hereby RESOLVES to amend the Deed and Rules as described in Clause 1 of this deed pursuant to the power vested in it under section 68(2) of the 1995 Act.'

On 22 April 2005 the Trustee notified the Company of the Deed of Amendment and asked for information as to the current financial position of the Company in order to ascertain whether it was possible to negotiate an apportionment of the s75 liability in a way which would not make the Company insolvent.

Phoenix Distribution Ltd was put into administration on 26 April 2005.

On 27 April 2005 the Company responded to the Trustee's request seeking further information as to the basis on which the Trustee proposed to allocate the s.75 debt, i.e. whether or not it would be more than that prospectively payable in default of any such apportionment.

On 28 April 2005 there was a telephone conversation between Mr Martin and Mr Kotecha of the Trustee, and Mr Towers and Mr Beale, directors of the Company, in which the Trustee required the Company, within five working days, to accept liability for £15m or undergo an insolvency event so that the Scheme might enter the PPF. The reason for fixing on that figure is apparent from a note of the telephone conversation which records the following:
'[Mr Beale] said he was confused that even if we had £15 million available how could we as directors with responsibilities to creditors and shareholders get comfortable with paying £15 million when a fair allocation of the debt was only £1.7 million which he did not feel anyone was disputing.

[Mr Martin] said he did not want to get into legal points but as pointed out they had complete discretion over allocation of the debt. [Mr Martin] said it was a matter for the [the Company] to take advice on.

[Mr Beale] then asked if [Mr Martin] felt the 15 million was a fair allocation.

[Mr Kotecha] replied that £15 million was not an allocation of [the Company's] proportion of the debt it was just the minimum amount the trustees would need to justify putting the members through the uncertainty of waiting 12 to 18 months and the scheme incurring additional costs and the risk of not getting into the PPF.'

The reason why the Trustee considered that there might be such a delay in getting the Scheme into PPF appears further from paragraphs 37 and 38 below.

On the same day the Trustee passed the first apportionment resolution. It recites the power of the directors of the Trustee to pass resolutions, the appointment of the Trustee as trustee of the Scheme and the commencement of the winding-up of the Scheme on 19 April 2005. It continues:

IT IS HEREBY RESOLVED that:

1   in relation to the Scheme the Company designates 28 April 2005 as the time for the purposes of section 75(2)(a) of the Pensions 1995 Act (the '1995 Act') (as modified by the Occupational Pension Schemes (Employer Debt) Regulations 2005); and

2   in exercise of its powers, in particular of the power conferred on it as the Scheme's trustee under Rule 35.1 of the Scheme's Definitive Deed and Rules dated 2 May 2001 (as amended by a Deed of Amendment dated 19 April 2004), the Company apportions the deb* arising under section 75A of the 1995 Act jointly and severally to all the Scheme's participating employers, which are listed below...'

Then the names of the six participating employers are set out.

On 29 April 2005 the Trustee wrote to the Company giving notice that it had certified 28 April 2005 to be the applicable time for the purposes of s75(2)(b) Pensions Act 1995, indicating that it estimated the s75 debt to be some £400m, and also indicating that it had or would apportion such deficit to all six participating employers jointly and severally.

On 4 May 2005 Phoenix Venture Resourcing Ltd went into creditors voluntary winding up. This was an event of some significance as that company was the fifth of the six participating employers to undergo an insolvency event. It has been one of the Trustee's contentions that until the Company also undergoes some such event, PPF could not accept the Scheme. I shall have to consider that point later.

On 5 May 2005 the solicitors for the Company received a letter from the solicitors for the Trustee demanding payment of £400m from the Company by 4.30 pm on that day 'on account' of the s75 debt, failing which insolvency proceedings would be commenced without further notice. Later the same day the solicitors for the Company faxed the solicitors for the Trustee claiming that the apportionment was invalid and seeking an undertaking by 3.45 pm that no insolvency proceedings would be issued otherwise than on seven days' prior written notice.

The following day, no such undertaking having been given, this application was issued. It is supported by the witness statement of Mr Beale, a director of the Company, made on 9 May 2005.

On 11 May 2005 the Actuary to the Scheme wrote to the Trustee indicating that he estimated the Scheme deficiency as at 28 April 2005 as 'highly unlikely to be less than £410m'. The Actuary also calculated the additional amount needed to provide benefits at the level of those available from PPF as £210m to £215m.

On 12 May 2005 the Trustee obtained a written opinion of counsel as to the exercise of the power of apportionment. In paragraphs 13 and 14 he advised them of the factors they should bear in mind when exercising the power to apportion the deficit. He said:

'13 I now turn to the factors the trustee ought to bear in mind in reaching its decision, which I would summarise as follows:
(1) The desirability of maximising the return to the Scheme.
(2) The fact (if they consider it the case) that [the Company] may be able to pay more than its allocated share of the debt on the statutory basis.
(3) The fact (if they consider it to be the case) that it is unlikely that the other employer companies will pay a significant proportion of their own statutory share of the debt.
(4) The adverse effect which this allocation will have on the shareholders and creditors of [the Company] (because it may be rendered insolvent).
(5) The fact that in making such an allocation they are allocating a greater share of the debt than is attributable to the service of members with [the Company], and on a basis which is unrelated to that service. They must consider whether it is fair, in the circumstances, to do that.
(6) The implications for the scheme so far as the PPF is concerned of increasing [the Company's] share of the debt.

14 The trustee should bear in mind, for the purpose of the present exercise, that although it may regard the power as being available for the purpose of increasing the amount of the section 75 debt which can be recovered, it must not use the power for the purpose of rendering [the Company] insolvent so as to get into the PPF. It is however permissible for the trustee to be motivated when considering whether to use the power to recover greater amount of the section 75 debt, by a desire to qualify for the PPF.'

The Trustee further exercised the power of apportionment, allocating £25m as part of the liability under s75A of the 1995 Act, to the Company on that day. The resolution of the Directors of the Trustee contained the same recitals as before. It recited the designation of 28 April 2005 as the time for the purpose of s75(2) Pensions Act 1995 and the previous exercise of the power of apportionment on that day. It continues:

'7 One employer company, Phoenix Venture Holdings Ltd ('PVH') has challenged the said resolution on the basis (inter alia) that a joint and several apportionment is outside the scope of the power. The Company disputes this challenge but now wishes to re-exercise the said power with the second exercise of the power to apply if, and only if, the apportionment that the Company made on 28 April 2005 is held to be void.

8 Before making the resolution set out below the Company has considered and taken account of the matters set out in the Opinion of Mr Michael Furness QC dated 12 May 2005 (a copy of which is annexed to this resolution). It has also considered the financial information to be derived from the documents which are to be exhibited to the witness statement of Mr Christopher Martin in the current proceedings against PVH.

9 The Company wishes to allocate the sum of £25m out of the section 75 debt to PVH. The Company accepts the advice of the Scheme actuary that the total section 75 debt is likely to be between £420 and £430 million and very unlikely to be less than £410 million.

IT IS HEREBY resolved that:

1 In the exercise of the power conferred by rule 35.1 of the Definitive Deed and Rules of the Scheme dated 2 May 2001 (as amended by a Deed of Amendment dated 19 April 2005) and any other relevant power the Company apportions £25m as the share of difference between assets and liabilities in the Scheme as at 28 April 2005 attributable to PVH.

2 The Company reserves the right to make further exercises of the said power in future in respect of that part of the said difference not hereby apportioned to PVH, including the right to allocate a further part of the difference to PVH.'

It is now necessary to consider the legislative background. It falls into two parts. The first part deals with the ascertainment of the Scheme deficit and apportionment of any such liability amongst participating employers. The second part deals with the conditions to be satisfied if the Scheme and its liabilities are to be taken over by PPF.

The deficit

S75 of the Pensions Act 1995 provides for the deficit as certified by the Actuary to be recovered from the employer. The relevant provisions are in the following terms:

'75 Deficiencies in the assets

(1) This section applies in relation to an occupational pension scheme other than a scheme which is –

(a)   a money purchase scheme, or

(b)   a prescribed scheme or a scheme of a prescribed description.

(2) If –

(a)   at any time which falls –

(i) when a scheme is being wound up, but

(ii) before any relevant event in relation to the employer which occurs while the scheme is being wound up,

the value of the assets of the scheme is less than the amount at that time of the liabilities of the scheme, and

(b)   the trustees or managers of the scheme designate that time for the purposes of this subsection (before the occurrence of an event within paragraph (a)(ii)),

an amount equal to the difference shall be treated as a debt due from the employer to the trustees or managers of the scheme. ...

(5) For the purposes of subsections (2) and (4), the liabilities and assets to be taken into account, and their amount or value, must be determined, calculated and verified by a prescribed person and in the prescribed manner. ...

(6A)   For the purposes of this section, a relevant event occurs in relation to the employer in relation to an occupational pension scheme if and when –

(a)   an insolvency event occurs in relation to the employer, ...

(6C) For the purposes of this section –

(a)   section 121 of the 2004 Act applies for the purposes of determining if and when an insolvency event has occurred in relation to the employer,'

The definition of Insolvency Event in s121 Pensions Act 2004 is contained in s121(3) and includes entry into administration, passing a resolution for winding up and an order to wind up. In the light of the arguments to which I shall refer later it is necessary to identify the time when 'the debt from the employer' referred to in s75(2) first arises.

Counsel for the Trustee submitted that the debt arose on the designation of the time provided for in s75(2). Counsel for the Company contended that it was the first moment when the deficit had been ascertained by the Actuary in accordance with s75(5). I prefer the latter submission. There cannot be a debt until a sum certain has been ascertained. The designation of the time is so that the Actuary may know as of what date his calculations should be made. But until those calculations have been made in the prescribed manner the difference between the value of the assets and the amount of the liabilities cannot be ascertained and an amount equal to that difference remains uncertain.

In the case of schemes with more than one employer, s75A authorises regulations to make appropriate modifications to s75. Such regulations may provide for the circumstances in which a debt is to be treated as due under s75 from an employer in relation to a multi-employer scheme. Such regulations are contained in the Employer Debt Regulations to which I have referred. The relevant regulations are in the following form:

'6 Multi-employer schemes: general

(1) In its application to a multi-employer scheme, section 75 of the 1995 Act has effect in relation to each employer as if -

(a)   the reference in section 75(2)(a) to a time which falls before any relevant event in relation to the employer which occurs while the scheme is being wound up were a reference to a time which falls before relevant events have occurred in relation to all the employers;

(b)   the reference in section 75(2) to an amount equal to the difference being treated as a debt due from the employer were a reference to an amount equal to that employer's share of the difference being treated as a debt due from that employer; ...

(2) For the purposes of paragraph (1), an employer's share of the difference is -

(a)   such proportion of the total difference as, in the opinion of the actuary after consultation with the trustees or managers, the amount of the scheme's liabilities attributable to employment with that employer bears to the total amount of the scheme's liabilities attributable to employment with the employers; or

(b)   if the scheme provides for the total amount of that debt to be otherwise apportioned amongst the employers, the amount due from that employer under that provision.'

Thus in the case of a multi-employer scheme the debt is 'the share of the difference'. The share of the difference is either that which the Actuary considers to be attributable to the employment with that employer when compared with the employment by all employers or the amount due under any provision in the Scheme for apportionment of 'that debt' amongst the employers. The sum of £200,000 is the amount which is estimated to be the share of the difference attributable to the Company under Reg.6(2)(a).

I should also note in passing the provisions for modification of schemes to make provision for such an apportionment contained in Reg.16 of the Employer Debt Regulations. That provides as follows:

'16 Modification of schemes: apportionment of section 75 debts

(1) This regulation applies for the purposes of section 68(2)(e) of the 1995 (power of trustees to modify schemes by resolution for prescribed purposes).

(2) In the case of a trust scheme (whether or not a money purchase scheme) which apart from this regulation could not be modified for the purpose of making provision for the total amount of a debt due under section 75(2) or (4) of the 1995 Act to be apportioned amongst the employers in different proportions from those which would otherwise apply by virtue of regulation 6(2)(a) or, as the case may be, regulation 10(1A) (as it has effect by virtue of regulation 12), for the purposes of section 68(2)(e), such a modification of the scheme is a modification for a prescribed purpose.'

Qualification for PPF

I turn then to the qualification for entry into PPF. PPF was set up under the Pensions Act 2004. In the case of schemes it takes over, it provides benefits at various levels. Thus it continues to pay 100% of pensions in payment but subsequent increases are restricted by limited price indexation. In the case of other members the PPF pays 90% of the pension entitlement but subject to a cap of £25,000 per annum. Under the Pensions Act 2004, if an employer suffers an insolvency act as defined in s121, notice of that fact must be given to the board of PPF, The Pensions Regulator and the trustees of the scheme.

If the scheme is an eligible scheme as defined in s126, and it is common ground that this Scheme is, then PPF is under a duty to assume responsibility for it if the conditions specified in s127 are satisfied. One of those conditions is that the insolvency event is a qualifying insolvency event, see s.127(1). It will be such an event if it occurs after the commencement of the Act and is the first in relation to that employer, see s127(3). In that case an assessment period commences on the occurrence of the qualifying insolvency event and will continue until, in effect, the Scheme is taken over by PPF under s160, or the PPF ceases to be involved either because the Scheme has sufficient assets to meet certain prescribed liabilities or specified events or conditions occur or are satisfied, see ss154 and 149. Another condition is the issue of a failure notice in accordance with s127(2)(b) but none has been issued in this case.

In a multi-employer scheme the Pension Protection Fund (Multi-Employer Schemes) Regulations 2005 (SI 2005/441) apply. The relevant regulations are Regulation 1(3), 61, 62 and 64. These are of unusual complexity even in the field of pensions legislation. Reg.1(3), so far as relevant, provides;

'(3) In the application of Part 2 of the Act and of these Regulations to a multi-employer scheme, or a section of a multi-employer scheme, 'employer' includes -

(a) in the case of a scheme which has no active members, every person who was the employer of persons in the description of employment to which the scheme, or section, relates immediately before the time at which the scheme, or section, ceased to have any active members in relation to it unless, after that time -

(i) a debt under section 75 of the Pensions Act 1995 (deficiencies in the assets) becomes due from that person to the scheme, or section; and
(ii) either -

(aa) the full amount of the debt has been paid by that person to the trustees or managers of the scheme, or section, or

(bb) in circumstances where a legally enforceable agreement has been entered into between that person and the trustees or managers of the scheme, or section, the effect of which is to reduce the amount which is payable in respect of the debt, the reduced amount of the debt has been paid in full by that person to those trustees or managers; and'

Thus each of the six participating employers in the Scheme is within the definition, including the Company, but might cease to be an employer if, but only if, it paid the whole of the debt due by it to the Scheme under s75 or an amount reduced under a legally enforceable agreement. The latter provision is amplified in Reg.2(3) so as to require the legally enforceable reduction to be effected by a scheme of arrangement under s425 Companies Act 1985.

Reg.61 provides in paragraph (1) for how the legislation is to be applied where an insolvency event occurs in relation to all employers. Paragraph (2) provides:

'(2) This paragraph applies to a non-segregated scheme the rules of which do not provide for the partial winding up of the scheme when an employer in relation to the scheme ceases to participate in the scheme in circumstances where -

(a) an insolvency event occurs in relation to one or more of the employers in relation to the scheme at a time when an insolvency event has occurred in relation to all other employers in relation to the scheme and, where applicable, an insolvency practitioner is still required by law to be appointed to act in relation to each of those employers; or'

Reg.62 provides that the duty to notify of an insolvency event in relation to an employer under s.120 applies in the case of a multi-employer scheme when 'an insolvency event occurs in relation to any employer'.

Reg 64 imposes the duty to assume responsibility for a multi-employer scheme by modifying s127. Reg 64(1)(b) provides that:
'(b)In its application to a non-segregated scheme to which paragraph (2) of regulation 61 applies -

    (i)   for subsection (1) there were substituted the following subsection -

    (1)   'This section applies where a qualifying insolvency event has occurred in relation to one or more of the employers in relation to the non-segregated scheme which is, for the purposes of this Part, an eligible scheme at a time when an insolvency event has occurred in relation to all other employers in relation to the scheme and, where applicable, an insolvency practitioner is still required by law to be appointed to act in relation to each of those employers'; and

    (ii)   for subsection (3), there were substituted the following subsection -

(3) 'For the purposes of this section, an insolvency event ('the current event') in relation to an employer in relation to an eligible scheme is a qualifying insolvency event if -

    (a)   it occurs -

        (i) simultaneously in relation to one or more of the employers at a time when that or those employers are the only employers in relation to the scheme, or

        (ii) in relation to an employer at a time when an insolvency event has occurred in relation to all other employers in relation to the scheme and, where applicable, an insolvency practitioner is still required by law to be appointed to act in relation to each of those employers,'

The Trustee originally contended (prior to receipt of Counsel's opinion on 12 May 2005, and in particular at the time of its discussion with the Company on 28 April 2005 referred to above, and apparently having discussed the matter with someone at PPF) that if the Company ceases to be an employer within the meaning of the definition contained in Reg 1(3) without such an insolvency event occurring in relation to it, then under the regulations there must be further insolvency events in relation to all of the other employers if PPF is to be obliged to assume responsibility for the Scheme.

In reaching that conclusion the Trustee laid stress on the use of the word 'all' in Regs 61(2)(a) and 64(1)(b)(i)(1). As at 28 April 2005, the Trustee was concerned, if its construction of the Regulations was correct, at the time it might take to ensure a second insolvency event in relation to all the other five employers.

This is disputed by the Company. It points out that the insolvency events do not have to be contemporaneous or simultaneous for all employers, and points to the provisions of s121(3) and Multi-Employer Regulations Reg 61(2)(a). The Company contends that the Company may cease to be an employer within Reg 1(3) without an insolvency event having occurred in relation to it, in which eventuality it will be the case that all employers will have sustained an insolvency event, and any previous impediment to the Scheme being considered for admission to PPF will have disappeared.

Thus, on the Company's interpretation, acceptance of the Scheme by PPF does not necessitate the winding-up of the Company.

Further, the Company contends that even on the Trustee's interpretation of the requirements of the Regulations before this Court, the cesser of its status as an employer pursuant to Reg 1.3 without an insolvency event having occurred in relation to it would not give rise to any delay because a further insolvency event would only be needed in relation to one of the five employers, and the compulsory winding-up of Phoenix Venture Resourcing Ltd (which is already in creditors' voluntary liquidation) could be obtained simply and quickly.

The parties have invited me to determine this point of construction which lies at the heart of the conditions to be satisfied if a scheme is to be accepted by PPF. I am reluctant to do so in these proceedings unless it is essential. The Pensions Regulator may well have a view it would wish the court to consider but it is not a party and has been given no opportunity to do so. Further, the point is, I believe, susceptible to more argument than I have heard. For example, it is necessary to consider the amendments made by Reg.64 in the context of the Act and the other amendments as a whole and the policy behind it. It may well be that there have been a number of relevant reports and other policy statements, none of which I have seen.

The issues
The issues before me arise in relation to the successive steps taken by the Trustee on and after 19 April 2005. They are, in summary:

1   Was the Deed of Amendment authorised by either power on which the Trustee relied, namely Rule 5 or the Scheme or s68 Pensions Act 1995 and Reg16 of the Employer Debt Regulations? And, if so

2   Was the Resolution made by the Trustee on 28 April 2005, purporting to apportion the debt arising under s75A jointly and severally to all the Scheme's participating employers, authorised by Rule 35.1 as introduced on 19th April 2005 and, if so, was it properly exercised? And, if not

3   Was the resolution made by the Trustee on 12 May 2005 purporting to apportion £25m as the share of the difference as at 28 April 2005 attributable to the Company authorised by Rule 35.1 as so introduced and, if so, was it properly exercised?

4   In the light of my conclusions on those issues, does the Trustee have locus standi to petition to wind up the Company? If so in respect of what debt and on what terms?

I will deal with those issues in that order.

The deed of amendment
I have already quoted the material provisions. The Trustee relied on Rule 5 and s68 Pensions Act 1995 and Reg.16 of the Employer Debt Regulations. That Regulation makes it clear that s68 can only be relied on if the Scheme cannot otherwise be modified for the purpose of making provision for apportionment of a debt arising from s75 Pensions Act 1995. Accordingly, it is necessary to consider the scope of Rule 5 first.

It is common ground that by 19 April 2005 that power was exercisable by the Trustee alone because of the provisions of Rule 34.1. It is not suggested that the limitations imported by Rules 5.2 or 5.3, to which the rule is subject, have any application. The power extends to changing 'all or any of the provisions of this Deed or other provisions of the Scheme...in any way'.

Counsel for the Company contended that there was a limitation as to the apportionment which might be made under Reg.16 for the purpose of

'making provision for the total amount of a debt due under section 75(2) or (4) of the 1995 Act to be apportioned amongst the employers in different proportions from those which would otherwise apply by virtue of regulation 6(2)(a)'

and that limitation is to be imported into apportionments made pursuant to amendments made under Rule 5.

I do not accept that submission. There is no such limitation in Rule 5 and I can see no reason to limit the words of that rule by reference to Reg.16 which only applies if Rule 5 does not extend at least to that limitation. Given that Rule 5 does authorise the amendment made under it, there is no reason for any further reference to Reg.16.

Counsel for the Company also contended that in exercising the power to amend the scheme contained in Rule 5, the Trustee was bound to have regard to the interests of the Company. I agree, but there is no indication that it did not.

Accordingly, the succeeding issues must be approached on the footing that the Scheme conferred on the Trustee a power in these terms:

'If a debt arises under s.75A of the 1995 Act when the Scheme commences winding up, the debt shall be apportioned amongst the Employers in such shares as the Trustee in its absolute discretion determines.'

The resolution dated 28 April 2005
By this document the Trustee purported to apportion:

'the debt arising under s.75A of the 1995 Act jointly and severally to all the Scheme's participating employers...'

Counsel for the Company raised a number of objections to this document, namely (1) no debt under s75A had by then arisen so that there was nothing to apportion; (2) the imposition of a joint and several liability in respect of the whole is not an apportionment at all, and (3) if otherwise valid the exercise of the power was made for a collateral purpose or without adequate consideration of the interests of the Company.

The phrase 'debt arising under s75A of the 1995 Act' also appears in the condition attached to the power conferred by the amendment by the words 'If a debt arises under s75A of the 1995 Act when the Scheme commences winding up'. It seems to have been intended to have the same meaning. In the context of the power the meaning is to be ascertained from the evident understanding that a debt arose on the commencement of the winding up of the Scheme; but it does not. The debt can only arise after the commencement of the winding up of the Scheme when the Actuary has made the prescribed calculations and a deficit emerges and is certified by him in accordance with Reg.5 and Schedule 1 of the Employer Debt Regulations. Accordingly, it appears to me that it is necessary to substitute the word 'after' for the word 'when'. So read, the debt arises when the calculations have been made and its amount has been certified. It follows that the condition precedent to the exercise of the power to apportion is not satisfied before the completion of the Actuary's calculations and their certification by him as prescribed, nor is there any subject-matter on which the resolution can operate.

Accordingly, in my judgment, the resolution of 28 April 2005 is of no effect for those two reasons.

I would also uphold the second objection. Even if it is assumed that the power had arisen and there was subject-matter on which it could operate, the creation of a joint and several liability for the whole is not an 'apportionment' in 'shares' amongst a class of six employers. The fact that the power is exercisable by the Trustee in its absolute discretion cannot extend the meaning of the words 'apportion' or 'shares'.

In these circumstances I conclude that the resolution of 28 April 2005 was not a valid exercise of the power introduced by amendment on 19 April 2005 with the consequence that the third objection of the Company does not arise.

The resolution of 12 May 2005

This resolution provides that the Trustee:

'apportions £25m as the share of difference between assets and liabilities in the Scheme as at 28th April 2005 attributable to [the Company]'.

That is to apply if, but only if, the Resolution made on 28 April 2005 is held to be void. As I have concluded that that resolution is void, the validity of the later resolution must now be considered.

The Company contends that it is void too. Its submissions, in summary, are (1) the power of apportionment is exercisable once only and was exhausted by the Resolution made on 28 April 2005; (2) the power of apportionment does not permit the reservation of a right to exercise the power to apportion a second time; (3) as no debt had arisen under s75A, the power was not exercisable nor was there any subject-matter on which the apportionment could operate; (4) if otherwise valid, the exercise of the power was made for a collateral purpose or without adequate consideration of the interests of the Company.

I can deal with the first two of these objections quite shortly. Given my decision in relation to the Resolution made on 28 April 2005, there has been no exercise of the power to apportion. Accordingly, there is no question of any re-exercise of the power or of the power being spent. Nor can I see any reason why the power should not be exercised again in respect of a further part of the debt. But even if the reservation by clause 2 was impermissible, that could only invalidate any further exercise because clause 2 is plainly severable from clause 1. This would leave the provisions of clause 1 unaffected.

The third objection is similar to that which I have upheld in relation to the Resolution of 28 April 2005. The power is exercisable 'if a debt arises under s75A of the 1995 Act' after 'the scheme commences winding up'. As no debt arises until the Actuary completes his calculations and certifies its amount as prescribed, the power was not exercisable on 12 May 2005. In the case of this resolution the subject-matter is 'the share of difference between assets and liabilities in the Scheme as at 28 April 2005 attributable to [the Company]'. This follows the wording of the Employer Debt Regs.6.1(b) and 6.2(a) in which 'share of the difference' is substituted for 'the amount of the difference' in s.75(2) Pensions Act 1995.

Accordingly, the share of the difference is what is to be treated as a debt due from that employer. It does not seem to me that this change in wording leads to any change in outcome. The position remains that as the difference has not been ascertained as prescribed by s.75(5), so the share of the difference cannot be apportioned under the power. In my judgment the Resolution dated 12 May 2005 is also invalid because the event on the happening of which the power was exercisable had not occurred and there was no subject matter on which its exercise could operate.

In these circumstances the fourth objection arising in relation to this Resolution does not arise.

The locus standi of the trustee

In the light of my conclusions in relation to both the Resolutions relied on, there has been no apportionment within Employer Debt Regulations Reg.6.2(b). Accordingly, at present, the position is governed by Reg.6.2(a) so that the share of any deficit attributable to the Company is

'such proportion of the total difference as, in the opinion of the actuary after consultation with the trustees or managers, the amount of the scheme's liabilities attributable to employment with that employer bears to the total amount of the scheme's liabilities attributable to employment with the employers.'

The Company accepts that in relation to this scheme the likely outcome of the actuary's deliberations will be to ascertain that about £200,000 is due from it. I should also mention that there is another scheme, with which I am not directly concerned, in which the share of the deficit attributable to the Company on the same basis is about £1.5m. The Company accepts that those amounts are contingent or prospective liabilities such that the Trustee would be entitled under s.124(1) Insolvency Act 1986 to present a petition for the winding-up of the Company under s122(1)(f) as amplified by s123(2).

It follows that in relation to those amounts the Trustee does now have locus standi to present a petition founded on the contingent or prospective liabilities to which I have referred, see *Mann v Goldstein [1968] 1 WLR 1091* and *Stonegate Securities Ltd v Gregory [1980] 1 Ch 576, 589*. The Company contends that it is ready, willing and able to secure payment of those sums but has not done so because it has never been asked to do so, the Trustee having been insistent on payment of the much larger liabilities for which the Trustee contends.

Counsel for the Trustee accepts that the Company should have the opportunity to secure such sums before it presents a petition to wind it up based on those liabilities alone. I am sure that that is the right course to take. Failure to have secured the several sums of £200,000 and £1.5m hitherto cannot, in the circumstances, be evidence of insolvency. Thus, the Company must be given the option to do so. I will consider with counsel later how long it should have for that purpose.

These conclusions are sufficient to dispose of this application. However, I should record a number of other submissions made by the Company on which it has not been necessary hitherto to express a view. The first relates to the purpose of either resolution. The Company submits that the purpose was to drive it into insolvency so that the Scheme might qualify for acceptance by PPF. It submits that such a purpose is collateral to the true purpose for which the power may be exercised and invalidates it. It relies on the speech of Lord Parker of Waddington in *Vatcher v Paull [1915] AC 372*. At page 378 he said:

'The term fraud in connection with frauds on a power does not necessarily denote any conduct on the part of the appointor amounting to fraud in the common law meaning of the term or any conduct which could be properly termed dishonest or immoral. It merely means that the power has been exercised for a purpose, or with an intention, beyond the scope of or not justified by the instrument creating the power. Perhaps the most common instance of this is where the exercise is due to some bargain between the appointor and appointee, whereby the appointor, or some other person not an object of the power, is to derive a benefit. But such a bargain is not essential. It is enough that the appointor's purpose and intention is to secure a benefit for himself, or some other person not an object of the power. In such a case the appointment is invalid, unless the Court can clearly distinguish between the quantum of the benefit bona fide intended to be conferred on the appointee and the quantum of the benefit intended to be derived by the appointor or to be conferred on a stranger...'

That was stated in relation to the conferment of benefit. I know of no authority in relation to the apportionment of liabilities but such a principle must, mutatis mutandis, apply with even greater force to such a case.

There is an issue between the parties whether the desire of the Trustee to ensure that the Scheme is accepted by PPF and its opinion that to do so the Company must be wound up vitiates both resolutions because its desire was not merely the motive behind but was the intention and purpose of the exercise of the power by the two resolutions I have considered. Had I reached different conclusions on the prior points, I would have concluded that this is a serious issue which merits cross-examination at a trial.

Arising out of that point is another. If it be the case that the Trustee's belief, to which I have previously referred, that PPF is under no obligation to accept the Scheme unless the Company is wound up is wrong in law, then the exercise of the power to apportion may be liable to be set aside for mistake, see *Re: Hastings-Bass [1975] Ch. 25, 41F-H*. This too would require a trial, first to establish the point of law and then to investigate the issue of mistake.

Then there is the point to which counsel for the Company referred, whether the discretion of the Trustee was exercised at all when passing the Resolution of 12 May 2005. The period between the transmission of Counsel's opinion to the Trustee and the making of the Resolution does give rise to speculation as to whether the Trustee by its officers ever gave proper consideration to the factors which Counsel advised them to bear in mind, in particular the legitimate interests of the Company, its creditors and contributories and whether the basis for the apportionment, being wholly unrelated to service with the Company, is, in the circumstances, fair. In this respect also I would have concluded, had it been material to do so, that there is a serious issue which can only be determined at a trial after cross-examination.

All three of these issues would have demonstrated a bona fide dispute on substantial grounds sufficient to justify the relief sought.

For all these reasons, but subject to any further argument on the form of my order, I shall enjoin the Trustee from presenting any petition to wind-up the Company for a period to be specified. If security for £1.7m is provided in that period, then the injunction will continue so as to preclude reliance on either resolution for the purpose of presenting, pursuing or supporting a petition to wind up the Company. If such security is not provided within that period, then the injunction will be discharged so as to permit the Trustee to rely on its status as a contingent or prospective creditor in the sums of £200,000 and £1.5m to which I have referred.

Is it going to be Mr Newman or Mr Tamlyn then?

MR TAMLYN: I am sorry, my Lord. It is going to be me. First of all, can I apologise for Mr Green not being here at the moment. As to terms of the order, my Lord, as I understand it, your Lordship is willing to grant the injunction subject to payment into court of security in the sum of ...

THE VICE-CHANCELLOR: You will have to speak up.

MR TAMLYN: I am sorry, my Lord. As I understand it from your Lordship's judgment, you are willing to grant the injunction . . .

THE VICE-CHANCELLOR: Well, how long do you want for securing £1.7 million?

MR TAMLYN: We would like a period of 14 days.

THE VICE-CHANCELLOR: Yes. (After a pause): Yes, Mr. Furness, what do you say to that?

MR. FURNESS: My Lord, we have no problem with 14 days. In terms of what constitutes security, we imagine that will be either a payment into court or some other cash payment.

THE VICE-CHANCELLOR: Well, I was going to say provision of security to the satisfaction of the trustee or as may be appointed by the court.

MR. FURNESS: My Lord, yes.

THE VICE-CHANCELLOR: Then you can agree between you what you think is the most satisfactory form but, if you cannot agree, then it will have to come back to me to decide.

MR. FURNESS: Certainly, my Lord.

THE VICE-CHANCELLOR: So I would invite the respective juniors to agree a minute which gives a period of 14 days for providing security for £1.7 million to the satisfaction of the trustee or as may be appointed by the court, and I will then grant an injunction to restrain any form of reliance on either of the resolutions for winding up a company. That injunction will continue after the period of 14 days. In the meantime, for the 14 days, I grant an injunction to restrain any petition based on any debt.

MR FURNESS: My Lord, thank you. That is very clear.

THE VICE-CHANCELLOR: If you would agree a minute to that effect.

MR FURNESS: My Lord, yes.

THE VICE-CHANCELLOR: Now, what about costs?

MR TAMLYN: I make my application for the costs of the application and I also make application that they be paid on the indemnity basis.

THE VICE-CHANCELLOR: On what ground?

MR TAMLYN: On the following grounds, my Lord. First of all, as your Lordship has found, with the exception of the relatively small sum of £200,000, the threat of the presentation of the petition was an abuse of process because the trustee lacked standing to present a petition.

The second point, and more general, my Lord, is this: our position had been, as it were, from the arguments expressed in correspondence on 6 May, so the day after the demand letter – our position has always been that this matter raised a number of issues which should be determined by Part 8 proceedings, we said at the time. We subsequently obviously changed our view to Part 7 proceedings with the coming of the second resolution and the need for cross-examination. But our position was always that it should be determined by ordinary court process. As we will see from the correspondence in a moment, that was refused by the trustee who wanted to press on with having the issues raised in the present context.

Now, in my submission, that was always quite plainly inappropriate and has led to a very considerable incurring of costs really to no good end whatsoever. In particular, for example, one thinks of this issue which has been raised and debated by counsel in this case as to whether there could be a determination as a matter of statutory interpretation of the final employer point, and had the parties dealt through their lawyers in the context of normal litigation with that kind of issue, the parties could have been well on the way to reaching, hopefully, some sort of final determination on that issue before the courts. And the same applies quite generally to other issues. But, instead, the trustee took the view that he wanted to pursue his threat of winding up – a matter of considerable concern obviously to my clients given the background to issues of this sort – and to. . .what are undoubtedly complex pension points in the context of a winding up petition.

So, in my submission, it was an abuse of process not merely in terms of lack of standing but also in terms of the way that this matter was brought before the court with the incorrect apparatus behind it, as it were.

Could I just hand up a very short bundle of correspondence and just make one or two points on the basis of that, my Lord. I think your Lordship has read most of it but there are just one or two points that I would like to . . .

THE VICE-CHANCELLOR: Well, if you wish, but it is really necessary? Can you not describe it?

MR TAMLYN: Well, certainly.

THE VICE-CHANCELLOR: I mean, you have made your points. What does the correspondence add to that?

MR TAMLYN: Well, my Lord, let me just say this. Obviously with the 5 May letter there was the demand for payment of £400 million on account within a few hours. At that stage, reading the letter, it seems that the trustee was relying on the debt which he claimed was actually due. As is set out in our evidence, we on the same day sought an undertaking not to present within seven days. Any sort of undertaking was not forthcoming until about nine o'clock in the evening, by which time a hearing had been settled for nine o'clock in the morning. Preparation had been put into applying ex parte for an injunction before Mr Justice Pumfrey on Friday 6 May.

A3: CASE LAW

Throughout this period, as I say, we were saying that this matter was appropriate to be determined by normal court process, which the trustee refused. Then we had a letter the following Tuesday from the trustee's solicitors asking us to outline what our case was in greater detail, so what we agreed to do was to give our skeleton and we received a skeleton in response. So we put in our skeleton on the basis that the threat to wind up was based on the 5 May letter, but the skeleton argument that came back late afternoon on the Thursday of course changed tack, the contingent debt point being raised for the first time and, furthermore, with the further resolution which was in fact referred to as the £25 million resolution.

So there has been rather a number of change in tacks, and the way that this matter has been brought before the court with the refusal to give even an undertaking at first so that we could do without the ex parte hearing, and so on and so forth, and with the change of tacks in the trustee's case, has resulted in the wasting of costs, my Lord. So those are the various points I make as to why we should be awarded our costs on the indemnity basis.

THE VICE-CHANCELLOR: Yes. Yes, Mr. Furness?

MR FURNESS: My Lord, on the question of costs, clearly we fought and lost this application on the basis of £25 million or £400 million, and we cannot really have any objection to paying the costs on the standard basis because we substantially lost the application, and I do not say anything on the general principle about the fact that we did end up obviously with an undisputed debt of £200,000.

However, we do resist paying costs on the indemnity as opposed to the standard basis. The first basis that my learned friend refers to for indemnity costs is the abuse of process point. Now, in fact we are not in a position of a creditor who, it turns out, is attempting to present a petition when he does not have locus standi to do so. There are authorities which say it is an abuse of process for someone who is not a creditor to present a petition, but the point is that we are a creditor, albeit for a much smaller amount than we hoped to establish and, in my submission, there is evidence before your Lordship of the insolvency of the company for winding up purposes. So in principle the presentation of a petition is not an abuse of process here. Of course the company must be given the chance to give security for the debt because it is only a prospective debt but we are not, in my submission, here in the territory of an abuse of process in the sense that we have been found to be a creditor who was not a creditor. We have always been entitled, subject to the provision of security, to present this petition.

The other basis on which my learned friend seeks indemnity costs is really on the basis of the way the proceedings have been conducted by the trustee. Well, of course we have taken points and we have lost those points, and it is, as I accepted, to that extent, right that we should pay costs. But the normal basis for paying those costs, if you take litigation which is ultimately unsuccessful or you oppose an application unsuccessfully, is that you pay on the standard basis. Yes, it is the case that, as it turns out from your Lordship's judgment, we were wrong, with the benefit of hindsight, to resist this application. That merits an order on standard basis but not of itself on an indemnity basis.

We do not accept that the way that matters have developed over the last week has necessarily increased the costs. For example, the second resolution raises substantially the same issues as the first resolution. We were, in any event, in my submission, right to consider making the second resolution because if, as turned out to be the case, there were well warranted concerns about the first resolution, it was sensible to us to attempt the second resolution and at least to have both of them before your Lordship rather than do one and then try another one later and find that we are back here in these or similar proceedings for a second time round.

Yes, the trustee's position and the trustee's thinking on the way that this application should be conducted or resisted has changed over a short period of time, essentially over a period of seven days between the proceedings having commenced and the hearing coming on for trial, but that is not, in my submission, of itself a reason for awarding indemnity costs. The trustees have clarified their position in the face of opposition and, I agree, to some extent changed their position, but in the end, when the matter came before your Lordship, the trustees had formulated their case really in the way that it needed to be formulated to be conducted. Now, it is unfortunate perhaps that it was not formulated on that basis on day one, as opposed to on day three of four (i.e. the Thursday) working days after the proceedings began. But it was formulated by that stage and the other side had ample opportunity to respond in the context of the timescale of these proceedings overall.

So, in my submission, this is not a case where the way in which the litigation has been conducted warrants indemnity costs.

THE VICE CHANCELLOR: Yes, Mr Tamlyn.

MR TAMLYN: Very briefly, my Lord, on the abuse of process point, of course I acknowledge that there was a standing in respect of the £200,000. That was not the threat that was made in the 5 May letter, that was on the basis of a £400 million debt immediately due. The fact of the matter is that this case has never been about the £200,000 at all, it has always been about whether there has been any dispute as to the larger liability, whether it be £400 million, £25 million or £15 million, or whatever.

The essential point, my Lord, is this. The trustee took the decision to try and bring these issues before the court in the context which threatened my client with winding up. He made that choice rather than going down the usual route, and he did so in circumstances where he must have been aware that there were numerous issues which were bona fide disputed by the company, and yet he started on that route and he persisted in that route. As a result, costs have been wasted to an incredible degree, my Lord. So those are my submissions.

THE VICE-CHANCELLOR: The question arises now as to the costs of these proceedings. It is accepted that the trustee should pay the company its costs. The question is on what basis they should be assessed.

On behalf of the company, counsel has pointed out that the threats were, on my judgment, an abuse of the process; that the company had always suggested proceedings for the establishment of the debt but the trustees rushed on in conduct which he described as inappropriate. He suggested that this precluded sensible settlement talks, and described as inappropriate a demand for payment of £400 million within a few hours. He relied on the fact that when asked for an undertaking not to present the winding up petition except on seven days' notice, even that was refused.

On behalf of the trustee Mr Furness responds that, all right, his clients have lost but this was perfectly ordinary litigation and there is no conduct which has been established which justifies the more penal level of an indemnity assessment over and above the standard assessment. He suggests that the second resolution did not add anything to the costs incurred also in relation to the first. He pointed out, rightly, that even on my judgment they have locus standi ultimately to pursue a winding up petition based on a contingent debt of £200,000 if it is not paid within the next 14 days.

I think this is one of those cases where I should order the assessment of costs on an indemnity basis. It appears to me that the trustee made three quick, consecutive, exorbitant demands of £15 million, £400 million and £25 million in the knowledge that at least the second two could not possibly be satisfied by the company. Instead of initiating proceedings to establish the liability or, alternatively, to enter into meaningful discussions about what it might be, it refused to give any undertaking in relation to insolvency proceedings which were plainly threatened, and forced the company to take these proceedings which have been successful. I think both the pre-action conduct and the post-action conduct merit an order for assessment on an indemnity basis, and I will so order.

MR TAMLYN: I am very grateful for that, my Lord. There is one further point which is that we would also apply for an interim order in respect of our costs.

THE VICE-CHANCELLOR: Yes. You mean an interim payment.

MR TAMLYN: An interim payment, yes, just for part of our costs, not a summary assessment, I should make clear. (After a pause): My Lord, I should make clear that this is not all of our costs. This was prepared on 17 May. That matter has taken longer than was envisaged at the time of preparation of this statement, but your Lordship will see that our total bill at that time was in the order of £101,000. I therefore make application that the sum of £50,000 be paid by way of interim costs.

THE VICE-CHANCELLOR: What do you say, Mr Furness? Have you seen this bill before?

MR FURNESS: I saw it immediately before I walked into court, my Lord. Parts of it are, I am afraid, illegible on my copy and possibly also on your Lordship's, but the bottom line is clear. I do not think I can resist an interim payment. I think it is probably a fairly usual order in these circumstances. And £50,000, which is about half of the total bill here, I would have thought – but if I can just take instruction. (After a pause): I am sorry, my Lord. (After a pause): There is no problem with paying that sum, my Lord. It will require some investments to be disinvested and I am instructed to ask for 28 days to pay it. I think the usual order . . .

THE VICE-CHANCELLOR: So you agree £50,000?

MR FURNESS: £50,000 in 28 days, my Lord, yes.

THE VICE-CHANCELLOR: What do you say about 28 days?

MR TAMLYN: Well, my Lord, we do object to that. We say that the sum should be coming from the trustee company personally, and the position then as to any indemnity that he might have under the estate is a matter for him. We object to that and say the usual 14 days.

THE VICE-CHANCELLOR: What harm will it do you if it is paid with interest?

MR TAMLYN: If it is paid with interest then . . .

THE VICE-CHANCELLOR: Why is it not set off by way of security against what you are going to have to put in the other way?

MR TAMLYN: Well, my Lord, if we could include a provision to that effect, then . . . .

MR FURNESS: I do not think I could really resist that my Lord, no.

THE VICE-CHANCELLOR: No. If you set it off, that can be done immediately.

MR TAMLYN: We would accept that, my Lord.

THE VICE-CHANCELLOR: Then the order for costs will be trustee to pay the company's costs to be subject to a detailed assessment on an indemnity basis; an interim payment of £50,000 on account of those costs to be set off against the liability of the company to provide security for the sum of £200,000 as required by my order. Again, if you could put all that in a minute.

MR FURNESS: My Lord, just for the sake of completeness, and I am not suggesting that there is any question of an appeal, but obviously nobody had had a chance to consider your Lordship's judgment, I am instructed to ask for leave to appeal. I can imagine what your Lordship's response to that is going to be, but I will ask anyway.

MR NEWMAN: My Lord, I was going to deal with the costs of appeal. In our submission, your Lordship's threshold for dealing with this case as regards the fraud on the power issue was merely an arguable case, and it is, in our respectful submission, virtually impossible to see how that order is going to be set aside on an appeal.

With regard to the first issue, we submit it is a plain matter of construction and therefore the permission should be refused on that basis.

MR FURNESS: I am sorry, my Lord, one other point. Would your Lordship anyway extend the time for appealing to 28 days because it would be sensible to have 14 days after the payment in date.

THE VICE-CHANCELLOR: Yes. I will refuse permission to appeal on the basis I do not think there is a real prospect of success, and I will extend the time for applying for permission to the Court of Appeal to 28 days.

I would like to consider with both of you the question of getting a transcript of my judgment. One of the disadvantages of dealing with it on an oral basis is the length of time it takes to get a transcript and the amount of work involved in putting it into the correct form. I have got a very full note, and indeed most of it is verbatim. If and when your solicitor bespeaks a transcript, would you require the transcriber to apply to my clerk for a copy of my notes, which includes all the inserts and then, as and when that has been provided, I would invite you and Mr Green to go through it as you would if it had been a draft which I was about to hand down.

MR FURNESS: My Lord, yes.

THE VICE-CHANCELLOR: And then submit it to me for final approval. That, I think, is the best way of getting it to you quickly.

MR. FURNESS: Thank you, my Lord, yes. We will do that.

Representation

Mr Brian Green QC, Mr Paul Newman and Mr Lloyd Tamlyn (instructed by Herbert Smith LLP) appeared on behalf of the applicant.

Mr Michael Furness QC and Mr David Allison (instructed by Wragge & Co) appeared on behalf of the trustee.

Comment

This is the first decision on both the procedure to obtain cover under the Pension Protection Fund, and under the way the operati9on of the multi-employer regulations work. Because of this, there is now doubt it will discussed for several years to come.

Its main interest is in the way it overtly and tacitly criticises the drafting of the regulations – and by implication the system of pensions protection we have built. Simplification is still a war to be won, and the immense complexity of the current regulations (understandable in the light of the policy objective, but which merely goes to the unworkability of the objective) is testament to the ultimate lack of sustainability of the system.

The trustees were of course placed in an unenviable situation. They were having to protect the interests of their members who were contingently faced with a very substantial deficit, not knowing whether the PPF would pick up the tab if they had not taken sufficient steps to protect their interests and trying to apply law which was new, untested and incomprehensible. So it must be to their credit that they managed to mount an action, produce credible arguments and even think f an appeal when they lost. It was an action in which the Regulator should also have appeared, and where the costs should have been underwritten by the Regulator who stood most to gain and lose by this action, and where public policy issues were critical.

One lesson for the trustees and the Regulator lies in the debate about costs following the decision; the trustees had to pay full indemnity costs o0n the grounds that the matter could better have been dealt with in a less confrontational manner than a full blooded trial. Time was clearly pressing, but one possible solution, not discussed, was whether the Pensions Regulator could have given an opinion. Whatever the proper procedure, trustees will need considerable support from the Regulator and the PPF that pursuing proper remedies does not mean aggression at all costs (rather contrary to some of the impression given in some of the guidance notes) and this shot across the bows by the court is very welcome and will no doubt be taken notice of by those who draft the guidance notes. Confrontation, even where big sums are involved, is not always the best way in which to resolve issues of procedure or interpretation.

Importance φφφφφ

DEALING WITH PENSIONS

A4 Miscellaneous

A4.1: FSD Flowchart

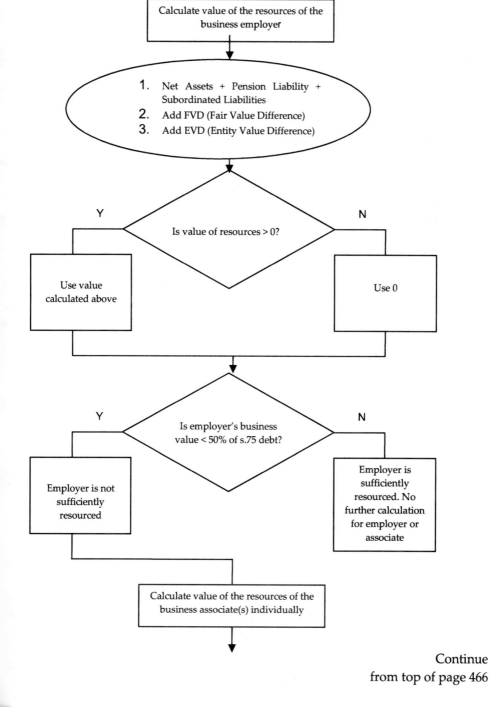

Continue
from top of page 466

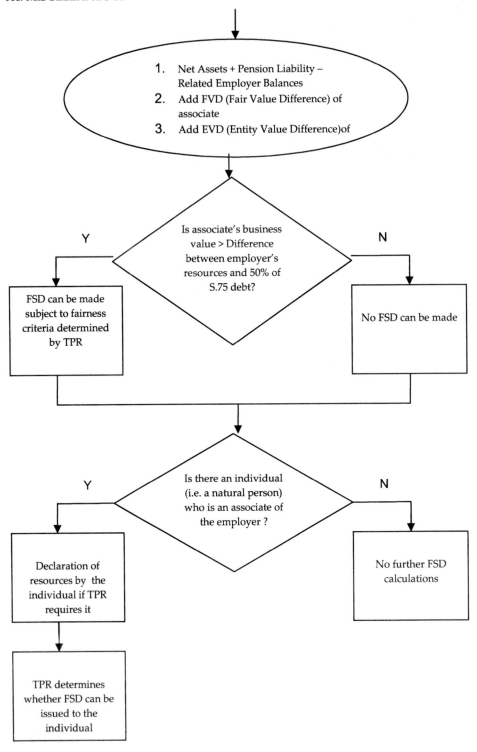

Index

TUPE: Law & Practice

Dr. Stephen Hardy, senior lecturer, University of Manchester,
Dr. Wyn Derbyshire, Pensions Partner, SJ Berwin LLP and Stephen Maffey,
Insolvency Partner, SJ Berwin LLP

Price £75.00   ISBN: 1 904905 18 8

For UK employers and their advisers, the new TUPE Regulations (introduced on 6 April 2006), have been eagerly awaited. They have taken the government five years to finalise, following extensive consultation and they usher in a new regime to govern the rights of employees on a takeover or merger of the business which employs them.

The new TUPE regulations replace regulations introduced 25 years ago and introduce a number of reforms:

extending the scope to "service provision changes" (i.e. contracting-out);
clarification of the overall definition of 'a relevant transfer';
determining key issues relating to transfer dismissals and changes to terms and conditions;
clearer pensions obligations;
strengthened consultation rights; and
the widening of the application of TUPE where the transferor is insolvent.

This book provides a guide to the changes, first setting them in the context of the existing TUPE protections. It explores the practical issues to which these have given rise and some of the controversies they have created, particularly in relation to the key areas of insolvency and pensions. The book examines the impact of European law on this area as well as looking at trade union action in the UK in this context. It is an ideal guide for employers and their advisers, and an invaluable reference work for economists, policy-makers, and academics and students.

Contents

Chapter 1: TUPE in Context
Chapter 2: Employment Rights in TUPE
Chapter 3: Pensions and TUPE
Chapter 4: TUPE and Insolvency
Chapter 5: Outsourcing and TUPE
Chapter 6: New TUPE in Practice 2006

To order a copy, please contact:
Turpin Distribution Services, Pegasus Drive, Stratton Business Park, Biggleswade, Bedfordshire SG18 8TQ. Tel: 01767 604951. Fax 01767 601640